"This book provides a clear, readable, and in-depth treatment of data binding, with detailed discussions of best practices in the presentation and use of data. Brian communicates his knowledge on the mechanics of data binding to give the low-level understanding that makes all the difference when building sophisticated applications and troubleshooting difficult problems. Effective data binding can enormously reduce the amount of code in your applications and will allow new levels of sophistication in your development. Read this book."

—Jonathan Cogley, chief executive officer, Thycotic,
ASPInsider, and C# MVP

"The .NET Framework 2.0, Visual Studio .NET 2005, and Windows Forms 2.0 incorporate the most powerful data-binding platform yet, and absolutely need a book like this to expose it. Brian's extensive data-binding knowledge and experience shine through as he comprehensively explores its many facets, starting with the fundamentals before tackling a wide variety of real-world scenarios. I've always thought a data-binding book was necessary, and I'm glad Brian found the time to write his."

—Michael Weinhardt, freelance author and application developer

"*Data Binding with Windows Forms 2.0* earns a gold star and a prized place in my development book library. Brian is an exceptional teacher of technology, best practices, and technique. He continues to educate at every presentation I attend; his book carries that quality to paper. I found this book to be highly informative and full of all the important steps and examples necessary to learn this technology. In this book, Brian demonstrates a firm grasp on the concepts and I really enjoy his efforts to promote best practices at every chance. Definitively a cover-to-cover read."

—Randy Hayes, president, Expert Network Solutions, Inc.

"Brian's direct and well-organized presentation makes this much misunderstood topic finally understandable."

—Sahil Malik, author of Pro ADO.NET 2.0 and C# MVP

Data Binding with Windows Forms 2.0

- Coding standards at Idesign.net.
- Sample code at softinsight.com / data binding book
- programming Windows Presentation Foundation by Chris Sells
- Data Sources Window

oaresteve@edu.msu   3/25/06   Smart Music Studio
~~Smartstudio~~

Microsoft .NET Development Series

John Montgomery, *Series Advisor*
Don Box, *Series Advisor*
Martin Heller, *Series Editor*

The **Microsoft .NET Development Series** is supported and developed by the leaders and experts of Microsoft development technologies including Microsoft architects and DevelopMentor instructors. The books in this series provide a core resource of information and understanding every developer needs in order to write effective applications and managed code. Learn from the leaders how to maximize your use of the .NET Framework and its programming languages.

Titles in the Series

For more information go to www.awprofessional.com/msdotnetseries/

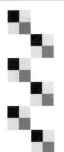

Data Binding with Windows Forms 2.0

Programming Smart Client Data Applications with .NET

■ Brian Noyes

Joe,

Thanks for having me out to speak at the group. Hope the book helps accelerate your forms development!

♦♦Addison-Wesley

Upper Saddle River, NJ • Boston • Indianapolis • San Francisco
New York • Toronto • Montreal • London • Munich • Paris • Madrid
Capetown • Sydney • Tokyo • Singapore • Mexico City

This Book Is Safari Enabled

The Safari® Enabled icon on the cover of your favorite technology book means the book is available through Safari Bookshelf. When you buy this book, you get free access to the online edition for 45 days.

Safari Bookshelf is an electronic reference library that lets you easily search thousands of technical books, find code samples, download chapters, and access technical information whenever and wherever you need it.

To gain 45-day Safari Enabled access to this book:

- Go to http://www.awprofessional.com/safarienabled
- Complete the brief registration form
- Enter the coupon code MHFN-2WYE-INB8-TVE5-8C28

If you have difficulty registering on Safari Bookshelf or accessing the online edition, please e-mail customer-service@safaribooksonline.com.

Visit us on the Web: www.awprofessional.com

Library of Congress Cataloging-in-Publication Data:

Noyes, Brian.
　Data binding with Windows Forms 2.0 : programming smart client data
applications with .NET / Brian Noyes.
　　p. cm.
　Includes index.
　ISBN 0-321-26892-X (pbk. : alk. paper)
　1. Computer software—Development. 2. User interfaces (Computer systems) 3. Microsoft Windows
(Computer file) 4. Microsoft .NET. I. Title.

　QA76.76.D47N685 2006
　005.1—dc22

2005027499

ISBN 0-321-26892-X
Text printed in the United States on recycled paper at Courier in Stoughton, Massachusetts.
First printing, January 2006

To my son, Nathan. You have added a wonderful new dimension to my life that I didn't even know I was missing. And to my beautiful wife, Robin. Sharing my life with you brings me happiness every day.

Contents

Foreword

WOULD JAMES BOND be just as effective an agent without all the tools and gadgets that Q provides? Would he be able to get out of those tight spots without them or would it simply just take him longer? Would he still have his license to kill? Would anyone else be a superagent just by having access to the tools? What makes *Bond, James Bond* effective—is it the tools, or is it his training, knowledge, and skills that transcend tools and technologies?

I think that the same set of questions is applicable to building modern applications using Visual Studio: What makes a developer productive and effective—is it the tools, the wizards, and the .NET Framework classes, or is it the knowledge of how to best design and build applications? Can you really build maintainable, robust, reusable, extensible, secure, and consistent applications simply by doing drag-and-drop in Visual Studio? What does it take to train a developer to be productive and have that developer figure out the correct ways of using new tools and the associated techniques as time goes by? Will that developer be able to extend and improve on the basic offering of the tools and the Framework classes when needed, customize and specialize the generated code, and when appropriate, use those tools in a different scenario than what Microsoft had in mind?

Nowhere are these questions more apt than when it comes to data binding and data access. The Data Sources window in Visual Studio 2005 generates tons of specialized code, and the designers hook up that code to the visual controls, all in a seamless, automated manner. But is that all there is to it? I am convinced that the key for achieving goals such as maintainability, quality, and extensibility is the understanding of what exactly the tools generate and why and understanding and appreciating the overall design approach and the implicit best practices involved. Only once you have that do you stand a fighting chance. The reason is simple—the machine-generated code as well as the Framework classes (such as the DataGridView) are designed for the broadest possible set of applications and use cases. The moment you deviate from the garden path (as you inevitably will), you are on your own, and only your skills and knowledge can carry you forward at that point. I believe that the purpose of wizards is not to allow anyone to develop applications. Rather, the aim is to off-shoulder from the skilled developers the time-consuming, detailed, mundane, and repetitive tasks, allowing them to be more productive and to focus on the application's logic and the required use cases. I think that to use these tools, you need a "license to wizard"—and only after understanding what and why the designers generate are you allowed to take advantage of it.

This book is all about the *what* and the *why* of binding to data sources in a Windows Forms application built using Visual Studio 2005. The book goes into great detail in explaining the rationale behind the designer-generated code, recommends best practices, gives tips and tricks, demystifies the machine-generated code and how to extend it, and shows how to compensate for its limitations. Not only that, but this book also prepares you to unleash the power and user-friendliness of the smart client today and tomorrow. This book is your license to wizard, designed to make you the James Bond of data binding, and I think that says it all.

—*Juval Löwy*
  August 2005

Preface

WHEN I FIRST started discussing this book with the editors at Addison-Wesley, I was a little skeptical. My gut reaction was, "Will anyone need a whole book focused on data binding?" I mean, Windows Forms is just GUI stuff, right? You drag this, you drop that, you hook up a few event handlers, and you move on to build the rest of your enterprise application—all the middle-tier goo that ties your head in knots.

As I thought more about it, I realized that a significant percentage of the work that people do in Windows Forms applications is centered around data binding, and most of the problems developers encounter are related to getting data-binding scenarios to work correctly. Add to that the multitude of new capabilities in Windows Forms 2.0 and Visual Studio 2005 related to data binding, and I quickly became convinced that this book would be a good idea. Hopefully you will agree after you have finished reading it.

Data binding is a powerful capability that has finally matured in Windows Forms 2.0 through the capabilities in the .NET Framework classes, combined with the rich designer support provided by Visual Studio 2005. By using data binding properly, you can save yourself from writing a lot of unnecessary code, provide your users a rich interactive experience for working with data that functions well, and produce code that is easy to maintain. To get it working correctly across a variety of use cases, you need to know more than how to set a few properties on controls—you need to understand what is going on under the hood, especially if you want to support complex scenarios that require going beyond the basic capabilities of the data-binding components in the .NET Framework.

Due to the growth of smart client architecture, Windows Forms applications are becoming more prominent in business systems. Web browser-based applications leave a lot to be desired; they cannot support many of today's common scenarios. They don't harness the capabilities of the client machine, and they are constrained by the request-response model of browser-based applications and the connectivity issues that surround them. So the importance of being able to code complex data application scenarios in Windows Forms is growing, and luckily the capabilities in .NET services are rapidly maturing to keep pace.

Who Should Read This Book?

The primary audience for this book is intermediate to advanced Windows Forms developers who want to learn about the new data-binding features in Windows Forms 2.0 and refine their coding practices for data-bound applications. This book dives deep into advanced features of the data-binding mechanisms in Windows Forms, data-bound controls, working with data sources, and creating custom data-bound objects and collections. If you spend a significant amount of time working with data in Windows Forms applications, then this book is for you.

If you are a beginner Windows Forms developer, this book will help you quickly learn how to support data binding. Many of the features in Windows Forms 2.0 take developers through wizards and designer features that are helpful for beginning programmers, and you will learn about those features in this book. In addition, Appendixes C and D are geared for beginner programmers to get up to speed on the basics of Windows Forms and data access.

Conventions

Developing applications is more about tools and less about code. However, there is a lot of code in this book, and I have adopted some common conventions to help make things easier. References to classes, variables, namespaces, and other artifacts that manifest themselves in code are in a `monospace` font; this helps you distinguish an instance of the `DataSet` class from a conceptual discussion of data sets. Short code listings are presented inline within the text using a different monospace font:

```
private void Form1_Load(object sender, EventArgs e)
{
    m_EmployeesTableAdapter.Fill(northwindDataSet.Employees);
}
```

Longer listings use a similar font, but are identified with listing numbers, for example, Listing 4.1. Within code listings, **bold** highlights particularly relevant portions of the code, especially "evolving code." When I remove details that aren't relevant to a discussion, you'll see a comment with an ellipsis (// . . .). This means that more code is needed to complete the example or more code generated by the designer exists, but you don't need it to understand the concept. On occasion, explanatory comments show context:

```
public partial class CustomersDataSet : System.Data.DataSet {
    // ...

    // Nested typed DataTable definition
    public partial class CustomersDataTable : System.Data.DataTable,
        System.Collections.IEnumerable {
        // Strongly typed indexer for accessing rows
        public CustomersRow this[int index] { ... }

        // ...
    }
}
```

I use a conversational tone to discuss the kinds of objects you deal with in data-binding scenarios, for example, when describing the `DataSet` class in this book. However, much of the time when discussing *data sets* I am not talking about an instance of a `DataSet` class, but of an instance of a derived typed `DataSet` class. Although it would still be technically correct to refer to that class as a `DataSet` because it "is a" `DataSet` through inheritance, I find it annoying when too many words are called out as a code artifacts. So, when something really is a code artifact and can only be discussed correctly in that context, it's set in the `monospace` font. I favor the terms *data set*, *data table*, and *table adapter* when discussing concepts surrounding those types of objects, and reserve `DataSet`, `DataTable`, and `CustomersTableAdapter` for citing a specific class type or instance, and the capabilities defined by that code artifact.

Discussing components and controls can also be confusing, depending on how precise you want to be with your language. Technically, all controls in Windows Forms are *components*, because the `Control` class derives from the `Component` class. Many of the concepts surrounding data binding apply to both components, such as the `BindingSource` component discussed in depth in this book, and controls, such as a `DataGridView` control. Unfortunately, many people think of *components* as nonvisual objects that are used by your form and *controls* as objects that have a visual rendering on your forms. To avoid having to say controls and components ad nauseam, when I discuss a concept that applies to both nonvisual components and controls, I simply say *components*. So when you see *components*, think "this applies to controls as well, because they inherit from components."

System Requirements

This book was written with the code base of .NET 2.0 and Visual Studio 2005 over the course of Beta 1, several Community Technical Previews, and ultimately Beta 2. The code presented in this book runs with Beta 2. I worked closely with the Windows Client product team at Microsoft, and there are no feature changes planned between Beta 2 and product release. However, some minor syntax may change between production and the release of .NET 2.0. If they do affect the code or concepts, I will provide corrections through the Web site for the book (www.softinsight.com/databindingbook), as well as updated code that will run on Visual Studio 2005 once it is released.

If you plan to run the samples available on the book's Web site, or the walkthroughs and code listings in the book, you will need Visual Studio 2005 installed on your machine, and you will need access to a SQL Server 2000 or 2005 database server on which the Northwind sample database has been installed. Additionally, you will need to have permissions on that database to create new databases for some of the samples.

There are multiple versions of Visual Studio 2005 to choose from. All of the features discussed in this book even work in the Express versions of Visual Studio 2005, which are free. You can develop all of the samples in this book in Visual C# 2005 Express or Visual Basic 2005 Express with SQL Server 2005 Express, but because Express versions of Visual Studio don't support data connections using server paths (they only support file path-based connections to SQL Express databases), you will have to create the sample databases and data in SQL Express, and then alter the connection strings and the way you set up connections based in Express.

The samples and scripts included in the book assume you are working on a machine with a standard, professional, or enterprise version of Visual Studio 2005 installed, along with a default instance of either SQL Server 2000 or 2005 on your local machine. To run the samples without that configuration will require modifying the connection string settings for all of the samples that run against a database. The modifications needed are discussed on the book's Web site, and the differences in connection strings are highlighted in many places in the sample code.

Additionally, Northwind doesn't ship with SQL Server 2005, but is available as a separate installable download that will work with SQL Server 2005 from MSDN Downloads at www.microsoft.com/downloads/details.aspx?FamilyID=06616212-0356-46A0-8DA2-EEBC53A68034&displaylang=en. The download provides scripts and MDF files that can be attached to SQL Server 2005 or used with SQL Server 2005 Express.

Choice of Language

I chose to write this book in C#. The download code is available in both C# and Visual Basic code. It is a fact of life that there will continue to be a mix of C# and Visual Basic available in articles, books, and samples for a long time to come. Even though I prefer C# myself, I am not a language bigot and feel Visual Basic is a solid choice for developers who have a strong background in earlier versions of Visual Basic.

I firmly believe that to be an effective .NET developer, you need to be able to read code from either language, even if you spend most of your time with one. If you aren't already comfortable reading C# code, I encourage you to use this opportunity to get comfortable reading it. It will expand your horizons in terms of the amount of reference material that is available to you, it may help you in your job, and it will give you bragging rights over the many silly and close-minded C# developers who cannot read Visual Basic.

Coding Standards

Yes, I have coding standards, and you should too. It is as simple as that, but unfortunately not done nearly enough by development organizations. Coding standards are an important tool in making sure that code is bug free, but they are even more essential for making sure that your code base is maintainable. Code written by one developer on your team should look like the code written by all the other developers so that it can be maintained and extended if necessary. Code reviews go hand-in-hand with your coding standard and are also something that should be a regular part of your development process.

We have an excellent coding standard at IDesign, which can be downloaded from our site at www.idesign.net. You can use as is, or you can use it to develop your own coding standard. Our standard includes a lot of information that goes beyond simple syntax; it has a lot of best practices for .NET development and design.

For the code presented in this book, I used the IDesign coding standard for naming member variables, properties, methods, and event handlers. Any member of a class, whether just a variable or a control on a form, is given a prefix of m_ and PascalCasing is used for the rest of the name. This is different from the Microsoft standard (which varies somewhat across different product teams), and that is okay. You can use whatever standard you want, as long as you are consistent. I won't go into the arguments and justifications of coding standard here, but I want to short-circuit any complaints or e-mails that might result.

You will see code snippets where this convention isn't followed (when I am discussing designer-generated code), because the naming conventions generated by the designer differ from our coding standard. So when discussing the raw code generated by the designer, I will demonstrate the way they generate the code; when I am writing code or focusing on other aspects of the code, I will rename the things generated by the designer to comply with IDesign coding standard.

Code First Versus Design Features First

One of the hardest decisions I had to make when writing this book was the order in which to present the concepts: Should I start by discussing code that you can write by hand to get things working in an application, or should I start by walking through all the different combinations of design features in Visual Studio that will write the code for you?

You can get a lot of data binding done through a combination of drag-and-drop interactions in the Visual Studio designer and by setting properties for objects on a form in the Properties window and other windows. When coding production applications, the Visual Studio designer is where you will start 90 percent of the time. Ultimately, those interactions are just having the designer write the code so that you don't have to. This allows applications to be written much faster and helps figure out how to get data-binding scenarios working even if you don't really understand the code that is being generated.

If this book's goal were to cover more introductory level concepts across a wider scope of topics, then sticking to the designer with a little bit of code explanation would be sufficient. However, my goal is to provide a deep technical tutorial on all aspects of Windows Forms data binding for developers who want to tackle complex scenarios that go beyond the designers. Whenever you thoroughly want to understand what is going on, you need to really think about things at the code level, not at the level where the designer, wizards, and windows in Visual Studio are doing magic things for you.

As a result, I chose to tackle things from a code-first perspective. As you progress through the book, for most common scenarios there are ways to get the Visual Studio designers to write most or all of the code for you. But to maintain that code and to go beyond those common scenarios, you also need to be able to write that code by hand (if need be), and know what all the right pieces and parts are to hook together. The chapters are arranged to first introduce a concept and to show you the raw code that enables you to get that concept working. Then, if there's a corresponding designer way of getting that code written, that's covered next.

For example, Chapters 3 and 4 describe data-binding mechanisms in Windows Forms and how to write the code to hook up controls to data sources. Then Chapter 5 shows how to use the Data Sources window to write a lot of that code for you. If you find it easier to learn by seeing things through the designer first and then unraveling the code, you might want to read the chapters and sections focused on the designer features first, and then return to previous sections to understand the code that was written on your behalf.

Northwind—The Database That Will Never Die

To show examples of data binding, you need some data to work with. One approach is to create new databases with new data in them to use in examples. While that may provide more interesting data for the samples, it has the downside of requiring you to learn a new schema and to set up those data sources on your machine to try out the demos. Because most interesting data usually belongs to someone, to avoid having to worry about copyrights and permissions to use the data, I created some sample databases for a few simple examples, but most of the examples use the tried-and-true Northwind database that is installed as part of the samples for SQL Server 2000 with a typical install. Also, through some downloadable scripts from Microsoft, you can get a Northwind instance installed on SQL Server 2005 or SQL Express 2005 as well. See the book's Web site for detailed instructions on how to do that.

Although many people are bored with Northwind (I count myself in that crowd), it does have the advantage of familiarity, and it is ubiquitously available and can be added easily as long as you have SQL Server. If you are already familiar with Northwind, you know about the Customers, Orders, and Order Details tables; if you aren't, you can learn this fairly simple schema easily.

Overview of the Book

This book starts with some background in peripheral concepts surrounding data binding: how data-bound Windows Forms applications fit into the bigger picture of distributed application architecture, particularly smart clients. It then delves into the new data-binding features in Windows Forms 2.0 and more advanced topics. The following is an overview of each chapter.

Chapter 1, Building Data-Bound Applications with Windows Forms, introduces the concepts of data binding, along with a quick walkthrough sample using the designer to generate a data-binding application. The data application architecture lays the groundwork for the other pieces to create a rich and robust data application.

Chapter 2, Working with Typed Data Sets and Table Adapters, shows how to use the new Visual Studio 2005 typed data set designer to generate most of the data access code needed in applications through simple drag-and-drop and wizard operations in the designer. It discusses the benefits of typed data sets, how to create and use them, and how to create and use typed table adapters to fill and update those data sets. It also covers how to use table adapters to perform ad hoc and custom queries.

Chapter 3, Introducing Data Binding in Windows Forms, starts delving into coding mechanisms in Windows Forms for data binding. It demonstrates how to perform simple and complex binding of data to controls, and introduces BindingSource, one of the most important data-binding tools available in .NET 2.0.

Chapter 4, Binding Controls to Data Sources, builds on Chapter 3, further peeling back the layers on the use of the BindingSource component, and includes detailed coverage of using the Binding object for simple binding with automatic formatting and for handling binding events.

Chapter 5, Generating Bound Controls with the Visual Studio Designer, introduces the designer features for generating data-binding code: drag-and-drop operations, wizards, and property grid interactions. It covers the Data Sources window in detail and the associated wizards.

Chapter 6, Presenting Data with the DataGridView Control, provides in-depth coverage of the DataGridView control, a rich tabular control for Windows Forms that is new in .NET 2.0. The chapter steps through basic usage as well as advanced scenarios and describes customizing the content of cells, implementing cell-oriented grids, handling grid events, as well as many other features of the grid.

Chapter 7, Understanding Data-Binding Interfaces, discusses the many interfaces involved in making the data-binding process work, and shows you which interfaces you need to implement when and what is involved. This chapter will help cement your understanding of the real mechanisms that drive data binding.

Chapter 8, Implementing Custom Data-Bound Controls, shows how to implement custom controls in Windows Forms for rendering data and what is required at the control level to use the data-binding interfaces exposed by data collections and objects. It also discusses additional things to consider when creating data-bound controls.

Chapter 9, Implementing Custom Data-Bound Business Objects and Collections, covers how to create custom business objects and collections that you can use in data binding. It discusses implementing appropriate interfaces, and shows samples and how they get used. It provides detailed coverage of the BindingList<T> generic class, which makes creating custom collections of data objects a snap.

Chapter 10, Validating Data Input and Handling Errors, describes validation mechanisms in Windows Forms and how to properly harness those mechanisms. It discusses error handling at the form and data-binding levels, along with strategies for managing concurrency violations.

Appendix A, Binding to Data in ASP.NET, gives a quick introduction to ASP.NET data binding for developers who will have to write both Windows and Web applications.

Appendix B, Binding Data in WinFx Applications, looks at the data-binding mechanisms in WinFx, the next generation presentation subsystem for Windows, so you can compare it to Windows Forms data binding.

Appendix C, Programming Windows Forms Applications, introduces the fundamentals of building Windows Forms applications. Written for beginning Windows Forms programmers, it will make the rest of the applications in the book understandable. It isn't intended to be a comprehensive lesson on all aspects of Windows Forms programming, just the essentials.

Appendix D, Accessing Data with ADO.NET, is a comprehensive overview of performing data access with ADO.NET. It covers many concepts, including retrieving and updating data with data sets and data readers, working with stored procedures, and managing transactions, as well as how to work with XML as a data source in .NET.

Sample Download Code and Updates

You can download all of the sample code used in this book at www.softin-sight.com/databindingbook. I will also post any changes, corrections, and updates relevant to the book at that location, and will post instructions on how to modify the sample code to run on the Express versions of Visual Studio and SQL Server 2005.

You can also find links to all of the above at the book's page on Addison-Wesley's site at www.awprofessional.com/title/032126892X.

Acknowledgments

THIS BOOK, LIKE most books, took a great deal of effort and time to write. I could not have written it without the help and support of a number of key individuals, who are as much a part of this book as I am.

In terms of emotional support, my wife, Robin, was the model of a patient and supporting spouse while watching me pass on far too many opportunities to spend time with her and with friends because I had to work on this book. My son, Nathan, born a few months before I finished the book, was probably too young to realize how much I was neglecting him. But that didn't stop me from realizing it and promising myself that would be different in the future.

On the technical side, Joe Stegman, Steve Lasker, and Mark Rideout from the Windows Client team at Microsoft were invaluable and always available for me to ask questions, get great answers, and make sure that this book was technically correct and teaching best practices with the latest capabilities in .NET 2.0. In addition, Greg Robinson, David Mack, Norman Headlam, Martin Heller, Charles Parker, and Rajesh Patel all helped out considerably in making sure the manuscript was correct, readable, and flowed well.

Without the outstanding folks at Addison-Wesley, this book never would have happened, and their unflagging support throughout the writing and editorial process has been greatly appreciated. Thanks to Karen Gettman and Stephane Thomas for getting the project going; Elizabeth Zdunich and Ebony Haight for keeping me on track in the middle; most of all, Joan Murray and Jessica D'Amico for getting me to the finish line; and Julie Nahil and Rebeca Greenberg for providing all the (considerable) production support. After working with them on this book, I can't image wanting to work with any other publisher. Any time I had a question or concern, it was answered within days if not hours, and they kept the pressure on to stay on schedule while still being very understanding of outside conflicts and pressures.

Last but not least, special thanks to my colleagues and friends Juval Löwy and Michele Leroux Bustamante at IDesign. Working with you both has been the pinnacle of my career, and I feel lucky to have the opportunity to work with and learn from you. I was especially pleased to have Juval write the foreword for this book, his clever analogies capturing the value of this book better than I could ever have summarized myself.

About the Author

BRIAN NOYES IS a software architect, trainer, writer, and speaker with IDesign, Inc. (www.idesign.net), a premier .NET architecture and design consulting and training company. He has been developing software systems for more than fifteen years, speaks at many major software conferences around the world, and writes for a variety of software journals and magazines. He is based in Alexandria, Virginia, but is a Southern California surf bum at heart, having grown up there. Prior to becoming a full time software developer, Brian flew F-14 Tomcats in the U.S. Navy and graduated from Navy Fighter Weapons School (TopGun) and the U.S. Naval Test Pilot School. Brian has a master's degree in computer science from the University of Colorado, Boulder, a master's degree in aerospace engineering from the Naval Postgraduate School, and a bachelor's degree in aerospace engineering from the U.S. Naval Academy.

■ 1 ■
Building Data-Bound Applications with Windows Forms

I T IS ALMOST impossible to design a significant application without dealing with data in some form. If the application is a simple arcade game, the data may be a log of past scores or configuration data that lets a user customize the way the application behaves. If the application is a graphical design tool, the data may be a complex graph of objects that need to be manipulated by the application and by the user and saved when the application or document is closed. If the application is a high-end enterprise business application, the data might be an aggregation of complex relational data residing in multiple distributed databases, objects, and files used in the processing that the application performs.

To build any of these kinds of applications, you need a good way to store the data, load it, and manipulate it. If the data will be exposed directly to the user through a presentation tier application, you need intuitive ways to present the data and let the user interact with it. Most of this book is focused on just that—providing rich data presentation and interaction for users of your Windows Forms applications. However, there is a lot more to building a good data-bound application than just the presentation aspects. This chapter not only introduces the key concepts of data binding, it also tries to paint the picture of the bigger context in which your Windows Forms application lives.

What Is Data Binding?

Data binding is a solution to a problem that developers used to solve over and over in user-interface applications. In the past, if you wanted to present data to a user, you had to retrieve the data from where it was stored and get it into your application. You then had to write custom code to render the data with graphics, or you could manually populate properties on controls with the data to display it. The way that you approached this would be different for each situation, each type of data, and each type of presentation that you provided. If the user was allowed to interact with the data and make modifications or additions to it through the user interface, you had to write custom code to collect the modified values from the user interface and push them back into the underlying data objects or collections in memory. You also needed code that persisted the changed values to the data store from which it came. This required a lot of repetitive and error-prone code, which always cries out for a better solution. Figure 1.1 depicts this process.

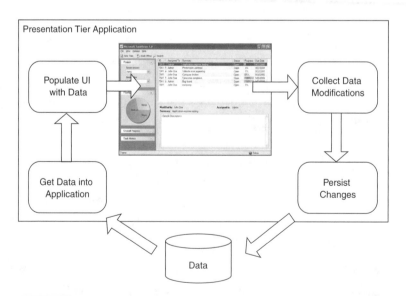

FIGURE 1.1: Data-Binding Process

Data binding encapsulates all of these steps into components that help present the data, which reduces the amount of code that you need to write. Some of that code goes into the data-bound controls that present the data, and some of it goes into nonvisual components that make data binding easier (this is described in detail in Chapters 7–9).

Data binding also involves providing easy-to-understand patterns for how you write code to hook up data to controls for presentation and editing. Finally, it involves developer tools that help write the code for you, using intuitive design-time interactions provided by Visual Studio 2005. The overall process of presenting and editing data is still basically the same as when no data binding is involved, but using data binding significantly reduces the amount and complexity of the code you have to write.

Data binding has been around in various forms in different environments since early versions of tools like Visual Basic, FoxPro, and Delphi. Many early attempts at data binding left a lot to be desired—they either exposed too many details to the programmer, provided inconsistent or unreliable behavior to the user, or were just too complicated to use and understand. Data-binding capabilities have been part of the .NET Framework for both Windows Forms and ASP.NET Web forms since version 1.0 of each. The data-binding capabilities of Windows Forms controls in .NET 1.0 and 1.1 were a big improvement over previous environments, but they still fell short in many situations. Significant improvements have been made in Windows Forms 2.0, making it both quicker and easier to get data-bound applications up and running.

Your First Data-Bound Windows Forms 2.0 Application

To get your hands dirty early with Windows Forms 2.0 and Visual Studio 2005, the following procedures give a quick demonstration of their easy and powerful new capabilities. You can either follow along if you have a machine with Visual Studio 2005 handy or just use the figures to visualize the process. You will:

1. Create a Windows application project

2. Add a new data source and a data connection

3. Select data objects

4. Customize data sources control mappings

5. Generate data-bound controls

6. Run an application

Don't worry about understanding all of the steps at this point; they will be described in detail in later chapters.

Creating a Windows Application Project

1. Start Visual Studio 2005. You'll see the Start Page (shown in Figure 1.2). Click Create to display the New Project dialog. If you don't see the Start Page, select File > New > Project from the menu.

2. In the New Project dialog (see Figure 1.3), expand the *Visual C#* option under *Project types*, and select the *Windows Application* template.

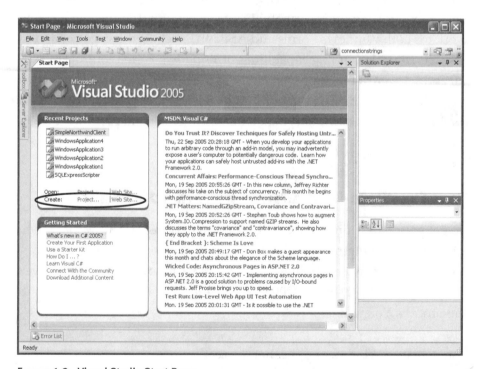

FIGURE 1.2: Visual Studio Start Page

3. Name the project **FirstDataApp**, select a working directory for the application in the Location field, and click *OK*.

At this point, you will have an open Windows Forms project with the default `Form1` class displayed in the designer (see Figure 1.4).

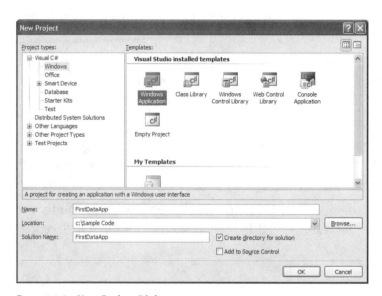

FIGURE 1.3: New Project Dialog

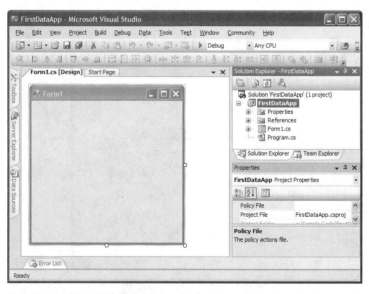

FIGURE 1.4: Empty Windows Forms Project

Adding a New Data Source and a Data Connection

1. From the *Data* menu, select *Add New Data Source*. This displays the Data Source Configuration wizard (see Figure 1.5).

2. Select *Database* as the data source type and click *Next*. This displays a page to set your data connection (see Figure 1.6).

   Select the data connection that you want to use. The options available depend on whether you have previously configured data connections in Visual Studio 2005. Assuming that you haven't configured a connection to the Northwind database yet, you will need to add a new connection. If you have already set up data connections in Visual Studio 2005, continue with step 7.

3. Click the *New Connection* button. The first time you do this in Visual Studio 2005, the dialog shown in Figure 1.7 is displayed so you can select a data source provider.

4. Under *Data source*, select Microsoft SQL Server. The option under *Data provider* defaults to .NET Framework Provider for SQL Server. Click *OK*.

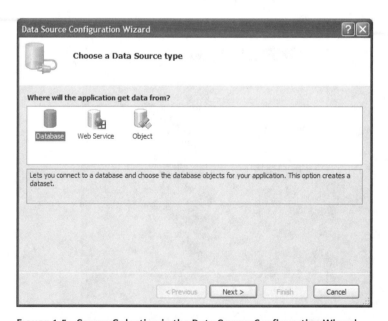

FIGURE 1.5: Source Selection in the Data Source Configuration Wizard

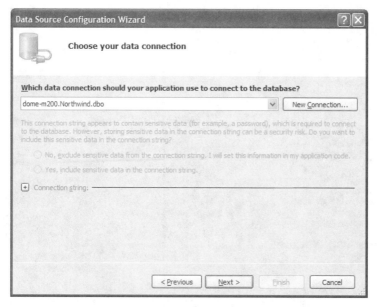

FIGURE 1.6: Data Source Configuration Wizard Connection Selection

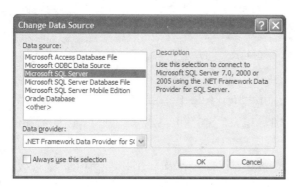

FIGURE 1.7: Data Source Provider Selection

5. In the Add Connection dialog (see Figure 1.8), enter **localhost** as the server name (if you are working with a local default instance of SQL Server 2000 or 2005 with Northwind on it). If you need help getting a database set up, are working with a nondefault instance, or need to work with SQL Server 2005 Express instead, see the book's Web site for instructions.

6. Select *Use Windows Authentication*, enter **Northwind** as the database, and click *OK*.

FIGURE 1.8: Add Connection Dialog

7. This redisplays the connection selection step of the Data Source Configuration wizard (Figure 1.6). Click *Next*. The page in Figure 1.9 is displayed.

8. To save the connection string information to the application configuration file, accept the default and click *Next*.

Selecting Data Objects

The last page of the Data Source Configuration wizard (Figure 1.10) displays a tree of the database objects contained in the database (in this case, the Northwind database) you selected in the connection step. This includes tables, views, stored procedures, and functions for a SQL Server database.

1. Expand the Tables node and select the *Employees* table.

2. Leave the data set name at the bottom as NorthwindDataSet and click *Finish*.

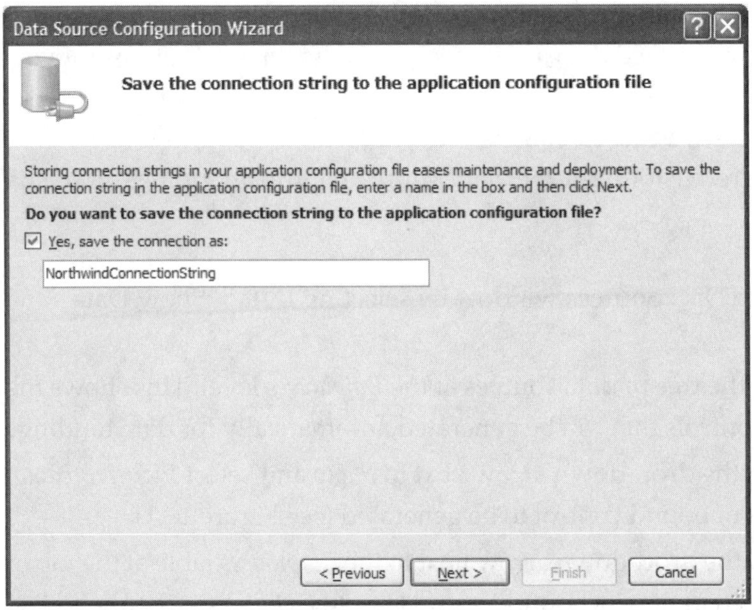

FIGURE 1.9: Saving the Connection String

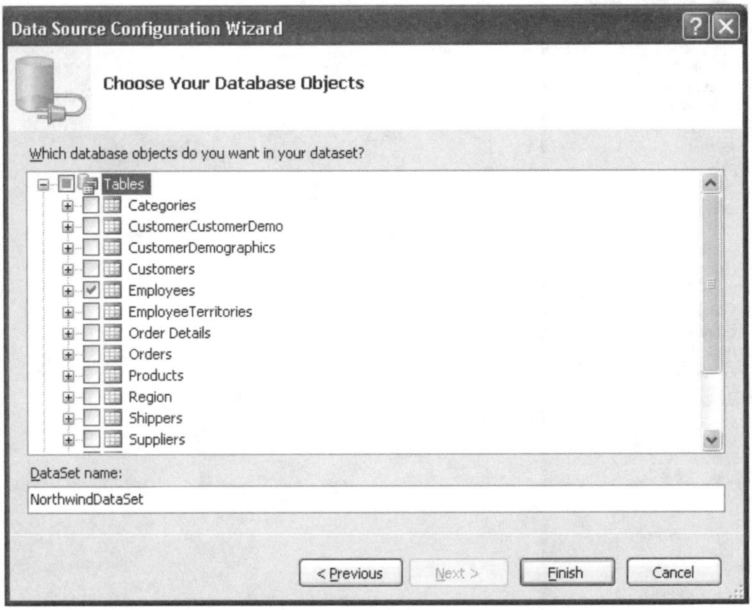

FIGURE 1.10: Database Object Selection

By completing this simple wizard, the designer generates approximately 2,000 lines of well-tuned data access code and data type definitions for you.

Customizing Data Sources Control Mappings

This procedure customizes the data source control mappings in Visual Studio.

1. Open the Data Sources window by selecting Data > Show Data Sources.

2. Expand the tree of data sources at the *Employees* level. This shows the tree of controls that can be generated automatically for data binding.

3. Click on the drop-down arrow next to *Photo* and select *PictureBox* as the kind of bound control to be generated (see Figure 1.11).

4. Click on the drop-down arrow next to the *Employees* table at the top of the tree, changing its bound control type to *Details* (see Figure 1.12).

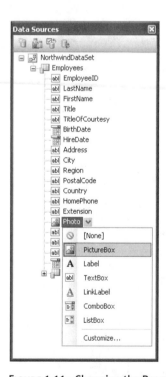

FIGURE 1.11: Changing the Bound Control Type for the Photo Field

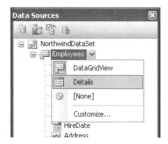

FIGURE 1.12: Changing the Bound Control Type for the Employees Table

Generating Data-Bound Controls

Now you are ready to generate some data-bound controls on the form.

1. Left-click and hold on the *Employees* node in the Data Sources tree, drag it onto the upper left part of the form, about a half-inch down from the title bar, and release the mouse button.

   – The Visual Studio designer generates an entire form with appropriate bound controls for each column in the Employees table. It also generates a `Label` control next to each data-bound control based on the name of the column, and even does intelligent things with the label such as breaking up the `EmployeeID` column name into a label whose `Text` property is set to Employee ID:. The designer also names each of the controls, so instead of getting controls named `TextBox1`, `TextBox2`, and so on like you do when you drag controls out from the Toolbox, the designer identifies them with names like `employeeIDTextBox` and `lastNameTextBox`.

   – An instance of the `NorthwindDataSet` class is added to the form as a member, along with a table adapter, which is an instance of the `EmployeesTableAdapter` that was generated in the section Selecting Data Objects. The table adapter fills the data set and persists changes from it back into the database.

   – A `BindingSource` component, which is used to tie the data source to the bound controls, is added.

   – A `BindingNavigator` is also added. This provides navigation controls at the top of the form. These let you page through the records in the table one at a time, add new records, save changes to the records, or delete records.

– All the code is written behind the scenes to hook up the data-binding properties of the components generated, as well as code to retrieve the contents of the Employees table from the database into the data set instance used by the form, and to save changes back to the database after it has been edited through the bound controls.

After doing this simple drag-and-drop operation, the designer writes about 600 lines of code (for you!) to lay out all those controls and hook them up to the data source.

2. Let's do one last thing in the designer to make the result a little prettier. Select the PictureBox control that was added for the *Photo* field, to the right of the *Photo:* label in the form.

3. In the Properties window in the bottom right of the Visual Studio IDE, scroll through the list of properties and right-click on *SizeMode*.

4. Select *Zoom* in the drop-down list (see Figure 1.13).

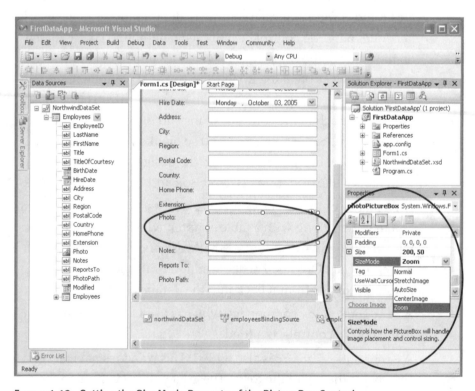

FIGURE 1.13: Setting the SizeMode Property of the PictureBox Control

Running the Application

1. To run the application, press F5 or select Debug > Start Debugging from the menu.

You should see the application running, as shown in Figure 1.14. Without writing a single line of code by hand, you have a reasonably complex data access form which lets you view a set of records that has data types including text, dates, and images. You can use the navigation controls at the top of the form to page through the records, edit records, create new records, delete records, and save the changes made to records from memory back to the database.

If you aren't saying "Wow!", then you are either really hard to impress or you haven't spent much time trying to write applications like this before

FIGURE 1.14: Running FirstDataApp

using Visual Studio 2005. With past technologies it took writing a lot of code—on par with the thousands of lines of code the designer just wrote for you—to get something like this form hooked up and working correctly. And you had to write that same code over and over for every form like this you needed. It is likely that you made some mistakes along the way and had bugs in your forms that were (hopefully) caught in testing. This probably led to digging around in that code to find the problem and get it working correctly. With the designer writing the code, not only do you get it done in a miniscule fraction of the time, but the code is much more likely to be correct the first time for basic scenarios.

At this point you may be wondering, "If it's this simple, why do I need this big book to figure out data binding in Windows Forms 2.0?" Well, the real world is never simple. Although the designer simplifies coding common scenarios like the form we just generated, there will always be complex scenarios that your users or your marketing folks will want your application to support and that the designer isn't capable of coding for you. To address those scenarios, and to better understand all the simpler scenarios where the designer does help you, you need to dig a little deeper and spend a little more time. Also, anytime code is generated for you, it's risky to proceed with development if you don't understand the code that was generated. You will have to maintain that code, and you may have to make direct modifications to it or write similar code by hand to support more advanced scenarios. For all these reasons, you need to understand the material covered in the rest of this book.

Data-Binding Landscape

A number of things come into play to make data binding happen. First, you need the data. From the perspective of a presentation layer client application, this comes in the form of in-memory data sources. You need controls or components that are designed to work with that data to automatically present it and push changes back to the data source. This functionality may be encapsulated in the top-level controls that the user sees on the screen, reside in some intermediary component the acts as a middleman between a control type and a data type, or involve a combination of both the control and an intermediary component. If you will have multiple controls on a form that are all bound to the same data source and want those controls to behave as a unit, staying synchronized with changes to the underlying data source, you're going to need some support from the container of those controls to keep them all in sync. These mechanisms are all present in Windows Forms data binding.

You can use a variety of data sources to accomplish data binding in Windows Forms, such as data sets, custom collections, or individual business objects. You can bind those data sources directly to Windows Forms controls that are part of the .NET Framework, purchase third-party control libraries that support data binding, or write your own data-bound controls. Windows Forms 2.0 introduces a `BindingSource` component that lets you code complex data-binding scenarios with a lot less—and more maintainable—code. And the `Form` class itself also has built-in support to manage the synchronization of multiple controls on a form that are all bound to a single data source.

Data Sources

One thing you will need to keep straight as you read this book is the kind of data sources you are working with. You need to deal with several categories of data sources in a data-bound Windows Forms application, such as data sources that exist

- At the data persistence layer or data tier, including relational databases, XML files, object storage mechanisms, and simple data files of some sort.

- In the layers in your application, between the data persistence layer (e.g., database) and the data presentation layer (e.g., Windows Forms application), including objects and data structures in the services, and business and data access layers that your Windows Forms application works with. Layered application architecture is discussed later in this chapter and will be mentioned throughout the book; it is an important concept to make a part of your application development strategy.

- In the Windows Forms application itself. This is the most important kind of data source that we will be focusing on in this book. The application may retrieve those data sources through other layers in your architecture, or it may obtain them directly from the database, through a service, or from files on disk.

Ultimately, **data sources** in the context of this book are objects in memory within the process of the Windows Forms application. These data sources present data to the user and are the sources users interact with through data-bound controls.

Data Objects and Collections

Data sources in a Windows Forms application are composed of object instances. A data source may be a single instance of a single object, or it may be a collection of object instances, where the collection itself is an instance of a container object. Those instances may be of almost any type, including types in the .NET Framework or types that you create as class or structure definitions. As a result, discussing data binding can get a little confusing, because you have to talk in generalized terms about the things that you are binding to. They may be a `DataSet`, an `ArrayList`, a `BindingList<Customer>`, a `Customer`, a `Foo`, or some unknown type that you program against through an interface reference without knowing the actual object type. Additionally, even once you get down to the individual object level, you need to describe the parts of that object that you are using for data binding, and those may be properties, fields, variables, or columns.

Throughout this book, I refer to an object as a **data item** if it's contained within some sort of collection that is being used for data binding. That may be an instance of a `Customer` class within a `BindingList<Customer>` collection, or it may be a `DataRow` within a `DataTable` within a `DataSet`. I refer to collections of objects as a **collection** or a **list**. However, to be used for many data-binding scenarios, a collection has to implement the `IList` interface to be properly described as a list.

The part of a data item being bound to could be a public property on an object instance, or it could be a column within a data row (also sometimes referred to as a **field**). For these situations, I use the term **property**, and if the collection is a data table, you can translate this to mean "the column within the data row that is the current data item."

You can think of a **data member** as a relative path to some piece of information within an object that contains data. If the object is a single instance of a data item, then the data member may just be the name of the property on the object that you want to use for data binding. For example, when you set up data binding to a `TextBox` control (covered in detail in Chapters 3 and 4), you create an instance of the `Binding` class. The second parameter to the constructor is the data source, and the third parameter is the data member. The following example shows how to pass a reference to an instance of a Customer object as the data source and pass "CompanyName" as the data member:

```
Customer cust = new Customer();
cust.CompanyName = "Northwind Traders";
Binding bind = new Binding("Text", cust, "CompanyName", true);
m_TextBox.DataBindings.Add(bind);
```

If the object itself is a container of multiple collections of objects, such as a `DataSet` that contains more than one `DataTable`, or is a custom object that has a property that exposes a child collection of objects, then the data member is the name of the property exposed from that container object. For example, when you set up data binding for a `BindingSource` component, (covered in detail in Chapters 3 and 4) to a complex object hierarchy, you can set the `DataSource` property to the top-level data container object, and use the `DataMember` property to resolve the part of that container that holds the list of data you are binding to. For example:

```
public class Order
{
    public int OrderId { ... }
    public DateTime OrderDate { ... }
    public BindingList<OrderDetail> Details { ... }
}

public class Customer
{
```

```
    public BindingList<T> Orders { ... }
}

public class MyForm : Form
{
    private BindingSource m_BindingSource = new BindingSource();
    Customer m_Customer = new Customer();
    private void OnFormLoad(object sender, EventArgs args)
    {
        m_BindingSource.DataSource = m_Customer;
      m_BindingSource.DataMember = "Orders";
        Binding textBoxBinding =
            new Binding("Text",m_BindingSource, "OrderDate",true);
    }
}
```

In this example, Orders is the relative path within the Customer object to the list that the BindingSource component is bound to. The data source and data member for that binding source represents a list collection itself. That binding source is then used as the data source for a Binding object, specifying the data member as OrderDate—a path within the current item in the data source list.

DataSets or Not, That Is the Question...

I refer to data sets (specifically, typed data set classes) extensively throughout the book. Chapter 2 covers how data sets work in more detail, but I want to briefly touch on them here to give an overview of how they will be used in this book. The use of data sets in Windows Forms applications is a topic that seems to incite heated debates throughout the .NET development community. Some people object to using data sets within the presentation layer because they assert that this couples your presentation tier to the data tier through the schema contained in the data set. They argue that you need to use custom business objects and collections in the presentation layer to make sure those objects are decoupled from the data tier schema. And depending on how you approach the use of data sets, they may be correct. But if you are smart about when, where, and how you use data sets, they can be a big time saver, help your application perform better, and make it easier to maintain.

You can completely decouple the data sets in your presentation layer from the actual schema in your data tier by defining the data sets that sit in between your presentation and data layers in the layers themselves. You can populate those data sets in your business layer or data access layer by iterating over the data retrieved from your data tier. You would have to do almost the same thing to populate a custom business object collection. By using data sets, you get

- A highly functional container for data that can be strongly typed
- Automatic change tracking for contained data
- Seamless data-binding support

This doesn't mean that all of the examples in this book use data sets; numerous examples use custom business objects and collections for data binding as well. The mechanisms of Windows Forms support data sets and other kinds of objects equally. If you choose to use custom objects, you will be responsible for writing all of the code yourself to create those objects with the proper patterns and interface implementations to make them work correctly in data-binding scenarios. You will see in Chapter 9 that creating a rich container class for data items that approaches the functionality provided by data sets involves a great deal of work.

If you have a bias against data sets, you should take a look at .NET 2.0. A lot of the shortcomings of data sets in .NET 1.1, particularly with typed data sets, have been overcome in .NET 2.0. As demonstrated in the walk-through earlier in this chapter, typed data sets give you a lot of power and let Visual Studio write thousands of lines of highly functional data access code for you with just a few simple drag-and-drop operations in the designer. With .NET 2.0, you can also work with data tables on their own without needing to create a data set to contain them.

If you aren't working with data sets, then the collections you work with will be instances of other types. You can and will most often use one of the rich container classes that are included in the .NET Framework. These include the types defined in the `System.Collections` namespace, which let you store any kind of object in a type-unsafe way and, even better, the generic collections defined in the `System.Collections.Generic` and

`System.ComponentModel` namespaces, which allow you to define type-safe collections. In almost all cases in .NET 2.0, you should favor the generic collections over the type-unsafe versions in the `System.Collections` namespace. Chapter 9 goes into more detail about this, including a discussion about working with custom business objects and collections, but you will see many simple examples before then that use the `BindingList<T>` generic collection class. You can also use the `List<T>` class for many data-binding scenarios, but `BindingList<T>` is a better choice in most cases for Windows Forms data-binding usage. As described in Chapter 9, if you need to, you can define your own collection classes and use them in data-binding scenarios. The interfaces you need to implement for that collection class are described in Chapters 7 and 9.

Data-Bound Controls

Most of the controls that ship with.NET Framework support data binding to some degree, because they all inherit from the `Control` base class, which implements the `IBindableComponent` interface. That interface defines the contract for supporting a collection of simple binding objects (instances of the `Binding` class) through a `DataBindings` collection on the component that implements the interface. The interface also allows the implementing component to be associated with a `BindingContext`, which helps keep components that are bound to the same data source synchronized with changes in that data source. More complex controls can also add their own support for more advanced forms of data binding by exposing additional data-binding properties at the control level, such as a `DataSource`, `DataMember`, `DisplayMember`, or `ValueMember` property.

If the controls that ship with.NET Framework don't meet your needs, you have a number of options that let you still take advantage of data binding. You could

- Design your own controls, derived from the `Control` base class directly or indirectly. At a minimum, your control will inherit these simple data-binding capabilities because it will inherit the implementation of `IBindableComponent`.

- Add your own complex data-binding properties to support whatever additional forms of data binding you want.

- Derive a control from the built-in controls, such as a `DataGridView`, and inherit all the rich data-binding features already present in that control, while specializing or modifying its behavior to your needs.

- Get more low level and implement `IBindableComponent` yourself on any component on which you want to be able to data bind the properties.

- Turn to the rich market of third-party components available for .NET. These provide specialized behaviors that are intended to save you significant development time for more advanced, but common, data-binding and presentation scenarios.

Chapters 3–6 cover `DataGridView` and other data-bound controls, and Chapter 8 discusses how to implement your own data-bound controls.

Layered Application Architecture

I have already mentioned layers in your application several times in this chapter, and I will continue to do so throughout the book. Layered application architecture is a very important concept and something you should consider adopting in any nontrivial application. In layered application architecture, you divide the functions of your application into separate layers. The number of layers you choose is up to you, but the most common approach is to separate your application into presentation, business logic, and data access layers (see Figure 1.15). These represent a stack of layers with the presentation at the top, business logic in the middle, and data access at the bottom. The classes created within each of those layers should be focused on the purpose of that layer, and you should try to keep the concerns of one layer from leaking into the other, especially details from higher layers leaking into lower layers. Because lower layers are also intended to provide isolation, or decoupling, from the details that lie below them, you should also try to avoid leaking too many details up through a layer as well.

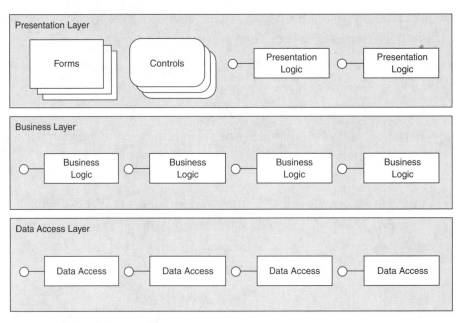

FIGURE 1.15: Application Layers

For example, things like controls and drawing are the concerns of the presentation layer, so classes defined in your business logic layer shouldn't contain direct references to controls if at all possible. If there is complex logic associated with the presentation of controls, you may want to break out a separate presentation logic layer, especially if you are developing a framework for presentation that will be reused across many forms or across multiple applications. The data access layer is intended to hide the intricate details of the data storage tier from the rest of the application. You want to be able to make minor redesign decisions at the data storage tier without having to change details throughout the rest of your application; the extent to which this is possible depends on what you do with the data in your application, as well as the scope of what is changed.

"What is the point?" you might ask. It sounds like a lot of extra complexity. If all your application does is retrieve data from a database, present it on the screen, allow the user to interact with the data, and then store the results back on the database, why can't you just embed all that data access logic right in the Windows Forms classes that use the data? The answer is that you can, but if you have ever built large complex applications

Layers vs. Tiers

It is worthwhile to differentiate between a layer and a tier. People talk about n-tier applications all the time, but the term is often used incorrectly.

A *layer* is a logical separation of a module of code from the rest of the application. Usually there is some physical packaging that provides physical separation, such as putting the data access and business layer components into separate .NET class library assemblies from the rest of the application. However, a multi-layer application may often run on a single machine, often within a single process.

A *tier* usually means physical separation at the machine level or, at a minimum, at the process level. A typical three-tier application architecture has the presentation layer code running on a client machine, the business logic and data access layers running on a middle-tier application server, and the database running on its own server as the third tier.

that do those things, you will know that embedding the data access code into the forms themselves leads to maintainability nightmares.

For example, if a query accesses the Customers table in 20 different forms, and then you change the schema of the Customers table, possibly removing or renaming a column, you would now have to track down everywhere in your forms that you were directly accessing the database to get Customer data and fix the queries. If instead you had centralized all the data access against the database into a data access layer, and there is only one class that ever touches the Customers table directly, then you only have to modify one class for the query.

This doesn't mean that the effects of that change can't be felt downstream in multiple forms, but it does mean that the frontline damage of a schema change is confined to the data access layer class that touches the table. You will have to analyze how the resulting data is being used to see if you will need to modify the classes that use that data access class.

This also lets you reuse that data access class in multiple places in your application without having to rewrite the query code over and over again, which can be a big time savings. Finally, there is a benefit from the perspective of understanding and maintaining the application. In a large application, it is not uncommon to have different developers who focus on presentation, business logic, and data access. By having all of the data access code separated from the Windows Forms application code, the people coding the Windows Forms stuff don't have to know a thing about SQL if they don't want to.

You may also wonder why you should bother with a business layer if you don't have any complicated business logic in your application that needs to be separated into its own layer. Won't you end up creating a whole layer with a bunch of classes that do nothing except pass data through from the data access layer to the presentation layer and vice versa? That is a lot of work and code to maintain if it's not doing any real processing currently.

If you can guarantee that your application will never grow beyond its current complexity, maybe you don't need to bother with a business layer. However, most applications grow in complexity beyond what they were originally envisioned to do, and they usually involve things like data validation logic, workflow, and processing rules. All these things logically belong in the business layer, and if you didn't include one in your original architecture, you would need to choose between embedding that code in the presentation layer or data access layer, with all the maintainability downsides described earlier for embedding data access code, or you would need to modify your application architecture to add the code where it belongs. While it is usually perfectly acceptable to add components and code to existing parts of your application architecture as your application evolves, it isn't usually a good idea to be modifying your application architecture midstream. You will usually end up with an inconsistent mess that may have unexpected side effects, and it will certainly be more difficult to maintain.

A typical configuration for a three-tier smart client application is shown in Figure 1.16. The presentation tier runs the presentation layer code and, possibly, any number of support libraries that could be considered separate layers within the presentation tier as well. Smart client applications will also often have their own local data cache to support offline operations. The business logic and data access layers typically run on a middle-tier application server, and the data storage is done on a separate back-end server as the data tier. For smaller-scale smart client applications that use Web services for communications between the client (presentation tier) and the middle tier, the middle-tier server may also host the Web service that provides the façade into the middle tier that the client communicates through. In larger-scale applications, things may be separated into more tiers, with a presentation (client) tier, Web server tier, business logic and data access middle tier, and a data tier. With the advent of automatic deployment and update mechanisms like ClickOnce, you can also choose to deploy business logic and data access layers to the client machine to harness its processing power, eliminating the need for a middle-tier server, or at least reducing the processing load on it.

The primary advantage of dividing applications into separate tiers is scalability—being able to leverage the processing power of multiple machines to handle a single application operation. Other benefits include security and fault tolerance. The trade-off is usually performance (any time you cross a process boundary, there is usually a fairly large performance penalty for doing so) and complexity. These are all things that a good architect takes into consideration when deciding how to factor application

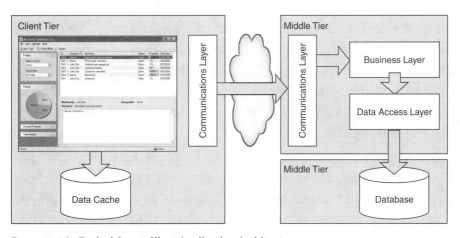

FIGURE 1.16: Typical Smart Client Application Architecture

functionality into layers, processes, and tiers. However, a prerequisite for separating an application into multiple tiers is to first break it up into multiple layers. Each layer provides a decoupling point where you can break the application into multiple tiers if it makes sense to do so.

So, remember that layers represent a logical separation of different portions of the code that implement different portions of the application's functionality, and the tiers are the physical layers at a machine level that the application is broken up into. You should always strive to divide your application into layers to achieve better decoupling and maintainability, more opportunities for reuse, and more flexibility in determining the application architecture.

In terms of building Windows Forms data applications with .NET, this means that for any serious application, you will always have multiple Visual Studio projects that contain the application code. You will have the Windows Forms project that contains your forms and the event handling logic that sits behind them. You may have some additional class library projects that contain custom controls that are used in the Windows Forms—so those controls can be used across multiple projects—but those controls would still be considered part of the presentation layer. You will then have at least one other class library project that contains the data access layer classes; these get the data from the data tier into your application and pass modified data from your Windows Forms application back to the data tier for storage. If the data layer itself is fairly complex, you may want to divide the data layer into multiple Visual Studio class library projects, one for each category of data that the application works with. For example, the `CustomersDataAccess` class library could contain all the data access code for customers, orders, and order details, and the `Supply-DataAccess` class library could contain all the code for the products, suppliers, and shippers.

"What," you may be asking yourself, "does all this have to do with data binding?" The thing you need to realize is that Visual Studio capabilities have the potential to encourage you to employ bad design practices. As you saw in the walkthrough example earlier in this chapter, there is a rich data-binding experience in Visual Studio within a Windows Forms application if you pull the database information directly into your Windows Forms project, create a typed data set and its associated data adapters in the project, and then set up the data binding based on the data sources that result. However, if you follow that pattern, you are putting data access code directly in your Windows Forms project, which is exactly what you shouldn't do for the reasons just discussed. So even though you will see a lot of demos that do this—and I even do it in some places in the book to simplify the samples and keep them focused on data binding and not the overall application architecture—you shouldn't plan on doing this in production applications.

What Is a Smart Client?

The subtitle of this book includes the term *smart client*, and it's that kind of application that I had in mind for most of the scenarios used in the examples throughout the book. As such, I think it is worthwhile to quickly define what constitutes a smart client application.

A **smart client application** is first and foremost a rich client application, or fat client, that runs on the user's desktop. This most often means a Windows Forms application in a .NET world, but it could also be a Visual Studio Tools for Office application, or it could be a smart device user interface. Smart client applications typically aren't standalone applications that run exclusively on the user's desktop; they are most often distributed applications, and the Windows Forms application is just the presentation tier portion of the application that communicates over the network to middle-tier application servers, Web services, or back-end databases.

Smart client applications often support offline use, allowing the application to still be useful when not connected to the network, or when the back-end servers of the application are unreachable, such as when using a laptop computer on an airline or in a customer's offsite location. Smart client applications can be most effectively operated if they support automatic deployment and update over the network, such as using the ClickOnce technology that is part of .NET 2.0 (and which is the topic of my forthcoming book in this series, written with Duncan Mackenzie). Finally, a smart client ideally runs under a constrained security context on the user's machine, and it prevents the smart client application from doing anything it wasn't designed to do, or anything that the user isn't willing to let it do based on who created the application or where it came from.

This book focuses on presenting data in a Windows Forms application and lets you interact with that data in a rich way. This is only a small slice of the architectural and technological considerations you need to master in order to develop a large-scale smart client application. To design and develop smart client applications, you will also need to become acquainted with distributed communications, data caching and synchronization, automatic deployment and update, and code access security. However, having a rich user interface is one of the most critical factors for moving to a smart client architecture successfully instead of just building Web applications. Learning how to build good data-bound interfaces will help you along the path to being able to build successful smart client applications.

Where Are We?

Well, you are at the beginning, really. This chapter was just intended to get the ball rolling, both to give you a quick sense of what data binding in Windows Forms is all about and what its capabilities are, and more importantly to help you understand where data binding fits into the bigger picture of building real-world, enterprise-scale, smart client data-driven applications in .NET.

Some key takeaways from this chapter are

- In the context of this book, a data source is a collection of objects or an individual object in memory in the client application that will be used for data binding.

- You can use data sets or custom collections with equal ease for data binding in Windows Forms 2.0.

- The terms data sources, data items, properties, and data members should be understood, because the rest of this book assumes that you do.

- Smart client applications should be designed with separate layers for business logic and data access, and those layers will often be deployed to a separate middle-tier server for large-scale applications.

The next chapter dives into using the new typed data set and table adapter features in .NET 2.0 to get data into your Windows Forms applications to be used as the data source for data-binding scenarios.

2

Working with Typed Data Sets and Table Adapters

To set up data binding in a Windows Forms application, you need a data source. A **data source** is an in-memory object that is typically a container for a collection of other objects, or it may be a single instance of an object itself. One of the most common and easiest ways to set up data binding is to use **data sets** (instances of the DataSet class or a derived typed data set class). This chapter briefly introduces what data sets are and how they work as a review for those who have not worked with them. It then dives right into the new features for creating and working with typed data sets in .NET Framework 2.0 to create a data access layer for your application using mostly designer features.

A Quick Review of DataSets

The DataSet type is a complex in-memory container for data. The DataSet class contains a collection of DataTable instances that contain the relational data stored in a data set. Each DataTable instance contains a collection of DataColumn instances that define the schema of the data within the table, and a collection of DataRow instances that provide access to the contained data as rows. To work with an instance of a data set, you typically create a data adapter for the data provider you are working with and use the data adapter to fill the data set based on a database query. Filling the data set creates the tables, columns, and rows within the data set to contain the data returned by the query, as shown in the following example:

```
string connString =
 "server=localhost;database=Northwind;trusted_connection=true";
// SQL Server 2005 Express connection string:
// string connString =
// @"server=.\SQLEXPRESS;AttachDbFileName=
// C:\temp\Northwind.mdf;trusted_connection=true";
SqlConnection conn = new SqlConnection(connString);
string query =
 "SELECT CustomerID, CompanyName, ContactName, Phone FROM Customers";
SqlDataAdapter adapter = new SqlDataAdapter(query, conn);
DataSet data = new DataSet();
adapter.Fill(data,"Customers");
```

When working with untyped data sets (instances of the DataSet class), the pattern illustrated in this example is common. You first create an instance of a connection and pass the connection string to the constructor for the SqlConnection object. If you are working with SQL Server 2005 Express, the connection string is a little different: you use the AttachDbFilename property instead of the database or Initial Catalog property. Once you have a connection object, you create an instance of a SqlDataAdapter and pass in the SELECT query and the connection object. The query that you pass to the constructor of the data adapter sets that object's SelectCommand property, which will be used whenever the Fill method is called.

When the Fill method is called, a number of things happen:

- The connection is opened if it isn't already open.
- The SqlCommand object referenced by the SelectCommand property on the adapter is executed.
- The data set is inspected to see if it already contains a table with the appropriate name and schema to place the returned rows into. The name depends on whether a table name was specified in the call to the Fill method, as was "Customers" in the code sample.
- If there is an existing table, the results are added to that table or overwrite existing rows in the table, depending on the constraints on that table and the current value of the FillCommandBehavior property.

- If there isn't an existing table, a new table is added to the data set and the results are placed in that table.

- The connection is closed if it was opened by the `Fill` method.

Data sets also let you update the database using optimistic concurrency. To support this, each data table keeps track of a `RowState` flag for each row that says whether it is unmodified, modified, added, or deleted. The table also maintains an additional copy of each modified row so that it can preserve the values originally retrieved from the database as well as the current values. It uses these to detect whether the row in the database has been modified by someone else between when the data set was filled and when you go back to perform an update to the database using that data.

To perform updates to the database using a `DataSet`, you use the `Update` method on a data adapter. The `Update` method functions similarly to the `Fill` method described earlier in this chapter, except that it executes a separate command for each row in each table in the data set that it finds with a row state of modified, added, or deleted. The data adapter uses the `SqlCommand` objects referenced by the `UpdateCommand`, `InsertCommand`, and `DeleteCommand` properties to execute these commands. ADO.NET 2.0 has an option to batch the queries to avoid unnecessary round-trips to the database; it uses the `UpdateBatchSize` property on the data adapter.

In addition to these capabilities, the `DataSet` type also supports defining constraints on the tables contained within it to enforce primary key constraints, unique key constraints, and foreign key constraints. You can also define data relations so you can navigate easily from a parent row in one table to related child rows in another table, or vice versa, and you can define `DataView` instances to wrap a `DataTable`. Those views can be used to sort or filter the data contained within the table without modifying the actual contents in the table, much like a view in a database works against the tables in the database.

The bottom line is that the `DataSet` class is a highly capable data container designed to work seamlessly with the data-binding features of Windows Forms. If you need to learn more about the basics of the `DataSet` class and how to work with it, as well as other data access topics in general, see Appendix D.

Given all that capability in the `DataSet` class itself, why would you need anything else? Well, using the `DataSet` class directly and data adapters have two significant downsides in their basic form: type safety and the coding practices they generate. The problem with type safety is that the columns within a `DataTable` need to be able to contain any type of column contents to satisfy the schema of whatever data source they are mapped to. This is implemented by making the column simply hold an `Object` reference. Because all types derive from `Object` in .NET, the column can therefore hold a reference to any type; hence, the data set can be used with any underlying storage mechanism as long as the types of the store can be mapped into a .NET type. This approach makes the data set very flexible in containing data. But you usually have to give something up for flexibility, and in this case type safety is the first thing you give up.

The Quest for Type Safety

When you create a `DataTable` by loading a data set programmatically, from XML, or from a database query, the types of the columns are automatically specified, and the data set can use these column types for runtime type checking. However, the indexer on the `DataRow` class that lets you access the columns in a row is simply exposed as an `Object` reference. This means that your code can attempt to assign any type value to a column and there isn't any way the compiler can tell whether it will succeed or fail. You'll want to avoid this when you're developing code for a strongly typed platform like .NET. What you really want is for the compiler to be able to detect as many type incompatibilities as possible at design time, so that you don't ship a product that can blow up for improper casts or assignments.

To make a data set type safe, you basically have to wrap it in an API that is specific to each schema that you plan to put in it. This means writing a new class with strongly typed properties for all the tables and rows (the schema elements) for every data set you want to implement. Yuck! Who is going to bother to do that?

Well, the good news is that the code you need to write is a direct conversion of the data's schema, so it is a perfect candidate for code generation. The ability to generate a typed data set for any schema you want is part of Visual Studio—it simply involves running either a command line tool or using some of the built-in designers in the Visual Studio environment.

Using Visual Studio 2005 to create a typed data set from a database generates more than just the typed data set; it also generates something new called a **table adapter**, which provides a type-safe way of populating the data set from the database. You will learn how to work with both typed data sets and table adapters in this chapter, and then you'll use these mechanisms for the bulk of the data retrieval and update used throughout the rest of the book.

The other problem that typed data sets address is tied into the type safety aspect and resolves certain unsavory coding practices that untyped data sets induce. Take a look at the code in Listing 2.1.

LISTING 2.1: **Working with Data in a DataSet**

```
private void UpdateCustomer(DataSet ds, string custID,
    string compName, string contactName, string title, string phone)
{
    DataRow[] rows = ds.Tables["Customers"].Select(
        "CustomerID = 'ALFKI'");
    DataRow row = rows[0];
    row["CompanyName"] = compName;
    row["ContactName"] = contactName;
    row["ContactTitle"] = title;
    row[10] = phone;
}
```

If you believe in writing maintainable code, seeing hard-coded column and table names and/or indices like in this code example should make you nervous—if the underlying schema changes, you have to hunt down all the places where the table and column names are used. If you use indices to get at the columns in a row, as the last line of code in this snippet does, the problem is even worse. At best, you can use find and replace, which is error prone and time consuming; often you will miss something, and you won't know about the problem until runtime. Hopefully your regression tests are comprehensive enough that any problems will be caught during test, but often differences between the actual schema and the hard-coded column names or indices aren't found until after the product has shipped.

Using typed data sets solves these problems. When you create a typed data set, code is generated that wraps the data set in a type-safe way by exposing tables and columns as strongly typed properties. If you program against those properties, the compiler will prevent you from assigning a value to a column that has the incorrect type. These properties also make sure you won't be trying to access a schema element that doesn't exist. If your schema changes, you simply regenerate the typed data set. If any of your code is trying to access parts of the schema that have been renamed or have gone away, you will get compilation errors instead of runtime errors. Tracking down disconnects with specific line information about what is broken will let you solve the problem much faster and reliably than with untyped data sets.

Another implicit benefit is that typed data sets expose the data set's schema through strongly typed properties and methods, and that enhances productivity. When you have a lot of different database entities, it gets difficult to remember the exact schema of the data you are dealing with. When you work with typed data sets, IntelliSense tells you exactly what the table names and column names are when you drill down to a row, and IntelliSense autocompletes those names when you're typing, so you don't even have to type them out yourself. These benefits of typed data sets help you develop code that works against the data set more quickly, which translates to cost savings.

The type information contained in a typed data set is also an enabler for design tools to make you even more productive. When you add a typed data set to a Windows Form, for example, the designer can reflect on that type to determine what tables are available, what the columns are within those tables, what their names and types are, what relationships exist between tables in the data set, and so on. Using that information, the designer and Properties window can provide you the ability to hook up common data-binding scenarios using only drag-and-drop and property grid interactions, and the designer will generate all the corresponding code. That translates to major productivity gains. As a result, you should always favor using typed data sets over untyped data sets, unless there is no way for you to have the schema information about what a data set will contain at design time.

Keep in mind that typed data sets have no effect on runtime data binding. The data-binding mechanisms of Windows Forms have to be type agnostic to work with any kind of data set or any object collection. You should still use typed data sets for the programmatic code type safety they provide, as well as the ability to use those data sets with the design-time features of Visual Studio, but ultimately they have no significant effect on what happens at runtime with data binding.

Typed Data Set Internals

Before discussing how to create the typed data sets, let's look at what is generated when you do create them. Lots of examples in this book use them, and knowing what will be in a given typed data set based on some knowledge of the schema from whence it came will help you unravel the mysteries of typed data sets.

A typed data set is implemented as a set of classes derived from the basic classes that compose a data set. You get a class derived from the `DataSet` itself, and a class derived from the `DataTable` and `DataRow` classes, for each table in the data set. For example, creating a typed data set that contains the Customers table from Northwind would result in the set of classes shown in Figure 2.1 (using UML notation).

After generating the typed data set to contain the Customers table, you end up with a class derived from `DataSet` named `CustomersDataSet` (you can name it whatever you like). Within the `CustomersDataSet` class definition are two nested class definitions: `CustomersDataTable` derived from `DataTable`, and `CustomersRow` derived from `DataRow`. Each of these classes defines a number of additional properties and methods that provide type-safe access to the underlying data. At the data set level, the main property of interest is the `Customers` property, which gives you type-safe access to the `CustomersDataTable` instance held by the data set.

The `CustomersDataTable` class exposes a type-safe indexer that lets you iterate through the rows within the table as instances of the type-safe

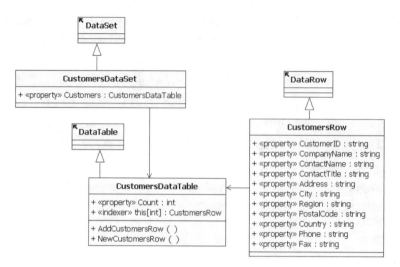

FIGURE 2.1: Typed Customers Data Set Class Hierarchy

`CustomersRow` class. A `Count` property is exposed that allows you to find out how many rows there are for iteration purposes, or if you are just accessing the rows in a read-only way, you can use a `foreach` loop in C#. There are named properties for each of the columns in the table, such as `CustomerIDColumn`, `CompanyNameColumn`, and so on, each of type `DataColumn`, from which you can obtain type information about the columns by name, as you will see shortly in some sample code. The `CustomersDataTable` class also exposes a type-safe method named `NewCustomerRow` for creating a new row of type `CustomersRow`, and then you can call the `AddCustomerRow` method after populating the row to add it to the table as an inserted row.

New in .NET 2.0 is that the typed data table class exposes a set of strongly typed events that can notify you each time a row in the table is updated, inserted, or deleted. These events are exposed in pairs, named `Customers-RowChanging`, `CustomersRowChanged`, `CustomersRowDeleting`, and `CustomersRowDeleted`. The `CustomersRowChanging` event fires before the change is committed to the table, allowing you to perform data validation, and the `CustomersRowChanged` event fires after the change has been made to the table; the same applies to the deletion-related events. The change events cover insertions into the table as well as modifications to existing rows. The event arguments passed to event handlers for those events include a reference to the affected row, along with an enumerated value that indicates the specific action that was performed on the row.

The CustomersRow class then exposes each of the columns of the row through typed properties that match the specific type of data held by that column. This lets you get or set the value of that column within the row as a strongly typed value. By default, the names of those properties will match the names of the columns in the schema that was used to generate the typed data set. However, you can override this default naming to create a different property name than the underlying column name, which is useful if you have a different naming convention for columns in a database than you use for properties in your code. You can also use this to avoid needing to update all the code that consumes the data set if you have a simple column name change at the database level without the type or semantics of the column changing. To use this feature, set the column's Name property to what you want it to look like in consuming code, and set the Source property to the name of the column in the database.

Using typed data sets lets you write code like that shown in Listing 2.2 instead of what you saw in Listing 2.1 with untyped data sets.

LISTING 2.2: Strongly Typed Access to Data in a Typed Data Set

```
public void UpdateCustomer(CustomersDataSet custData, string custID,
   string compName, string contactName, string title, string phone)
{
   string custIDColumnName =
      custData.Customers.CustomerIDColumn.ColumnName;
   CustomersDataSet.CustomersRow[] rows =
      (CustomersDataSet.CustomersRow[])ds.Customers.Select(
      custIDColumnName + "='" + custID + "'");
   CustomersDataSet.CustomerRow row = rows[0];
   row.CompanyName = compName;
   row.ContactName = contactName;
   row.ContactTitle = title;
   row.Phone = phone;
}
```

Although this code may look slightly more verbose due to the nested type definitions for the CustomersRow under the CustomersDataSet, the beauty of the code in Listing 2.2 is that there aren't any hard-coded schema references. There aren't any string literals for table or column names, and you don't have to index any column positions because you can more easily and clearly get to them through the typed properties exposed on the typed row object. The `CustomerIDColumn` public property on the table class and the `ColumnName` property on the `DataColumn` instance it represents gets to the column name without having to be hard coded. By doing this, even if the schema changes, the code won't necessarily have to.

The other part that isn't apparent from a block of code like this is actually one of the best benefits of typed data sets from a productivity standpoint: IntelliSense! Because of the type definitions that underlie this code, you get full IntelliSense on the properties and methods that the typed classes add. So if you haven't memorized all the column names exactly, you can just scroll through the member names after typing the "." next to the typed data row variable to locate a column.

So what happens if the database schema changes and the DBA decides to rename the `Phone` column to `PhoneNo`? Well, as long as the DBA at least tells you of the change, you can quickly regenerate the `CustomersDataSet` class and its contained classes, and recompile. If you do this, anywhere in your code that you referenced the `CustomersRow.Phone` property, you would get a compiler error like the following:

```
D:\Code\Chapter 2\TypedDataSets\Form1.cs(25,17): error CS0117:
'TypedDataSets.CustomersDataSet.CustomersRow' does not contain a
definition for 'Phone'
```

You could simply click through the compiler errors in the Task pane in Visual Studio, change the column names to `PhoneNo` instead of `Phone`, and try to compile again. You could also resolve this by changing the `Name` property of the `PhoneNo` column back to `Phone` after regenerating the data set, and leave the `Source` property set to `PhoneNo`.

If the DBA had changed the type of the column instead of the name, you would get the following errors for each of those references:

```
D:\Code\Chapter 2\TypedDataSets\Form1.cs(25,25): error CS0029: Cannot
implicitly convert type 'string' to 'int'
```

This is a huge benefit. Granted that you would still have to click through all the compiler errors and decide how to resolve them. Of course, maybe you would decide to do a global find-and-replace operation or use some of the refactoring tools that are new in Visual Studio 2005. But the big difference between using the typed data set classes and when you were coding against the tables and columns using strings for their names is that you are pretty much guaranteed by the compiler that you will find all the affected lines of code—as long as you only program against the type-safe properties of the typed data set, table, and row.

It may be tempting at times to use some of the properties and methods of the `DataSet` base class, such as the `Rows` or `Columns` collection. These are still exposed on your typed data set class because they derive from `DataSet`. However, you should try to get any untyped reference back into a typed variable reference as quickly as possible so that you can maintain the benefit of using typed data sets throughout your code. When you do need to use one of the base class methods that returns an untyped row, such as the `Select` method shown in Listing 2.2, make sure to cast the result to the typed version of the row before you use it so that you can take full advantage of the type safety provided by the typed data sets.

To fill a typed data set or update a data source using a typed data set, you use code almost exactly like what you saw at the beginning of the chapter for filling an untyped data set. Because the typed data set is a derived class from `DataSet`, the data adapter uses methods of the base `DataSet` class to populate the typed data set instance during a `Fill` operation and to extract and propagate changes during an `Update` operation. This was how you had to work with typed data sets in .NET 1.X, and the problem was that you had to throw away some type safety at the point you interacted with the data source. How do you know whether the data adapter is configured properly to work with that strongly typed data set? You don't, and so you won't find out about errors again until runtime.

In .NET 2.0, a new construct brings type safety to the adapter between a data source and a type-safe data set. That construct, called a table adapter, will be discussed in detail later in this chapter.

Creating Typed Data Sets

There are several paths within Visual Studio 2005 for creating typed data sets. You can use the Data Sources window to create a typed data set and tie it to a database through a wizard, or you can use the data set designer and have more direct control over what gets created. You already saw one quick example of creating a typed data set with the Data Sources window in Chapter 1, and Chapter 5 describes how to use that window in more detail. This chapter focuses on creating typed data sets with the data set designer.

Under the covers, the starting point for a typed data set is actually just an XML Schema Definition (XSD) file. The schema defines a root document element that will represent the data set itself. It needs at least one child element, which will represent a table within the data set. That table element can represent its columns as either attributes or child elements. The schema definition can contain any number of elements defined as the first child of the root element, and those each become additional tables within the data set.

When you are working in Visual Studio, its designers and wizards "hide" that you're actually working with XSD files. After creating a typed data set as part of your project, you will see an XSD file in Solution Explorer, but whenever you open the file, it opens in the data set designer, which lets you deal with the data set's type definition at an abstract level—you don't need to know anything about XSD itself.

Creating Typed Data Sets with the Data Set Designer

To help you become familiar with the Visual Studio features for creating typed data sets, the following sections step you through the process of creating a data access layer for parts of the Northwind database. You need to:

1. Create a data access layer class library project and add a typed data set definition to it, and set up a data connection in Server Explorer for the database you will work with.

2. Add tables to the data set by dragging them from Server Explorer into the data set designer.

Creating a Typed Data Set and Setting Up a Data Connection

1. Create a new C# Class Library project in Visual Studio 2005 and name it **NorthwindDataAccess** (see Figure 2.2). Click *OK*.

   Note: You're creating a class library here, not a Windows application. Too many demos and samples have you generate your data access code in the client application. That is just bad practice from an architectural perspective; I recommend always placing your data access code in a separate class library that you can manage separately from your client application, and potentially reuse it across more than one client application.

2. Solution Explorer should be visible in the IDE. If it is not, display it by selecting Solution Explorer from the View menu. Delete the Class1.cs file that is added to the class library by default by right-clicking on it in Solution Explorer and selecting Delete from the context menu.

3. Right-click on the NorthwindDataAccess project in Solution Explorer and select Add > New Item from the pop-up menu. Select the *DataSet* item in the Add New Item dialog as shown in Figure 2.3.

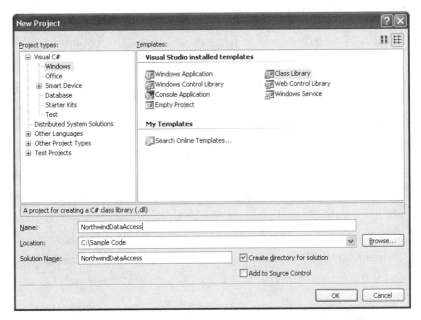

FIGURE 2.2: Creating a Data Access Class Library Project in Visual Studio 2005

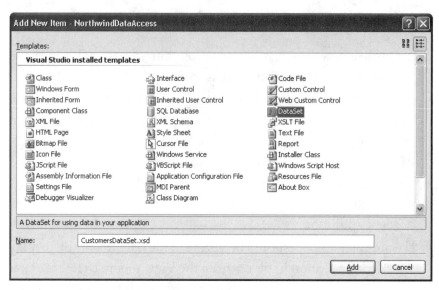

FIGURE 2.3: Adding a Typed Dataset Definition to a Project

4. Name the data set `CustomersDataSet` and click the *Add* button. This adds a CustomersDataSet.xsd file to your project and opens the data set designer with a blank canvas.

5. You can manually add items to a data set definition by dragging and dropping components from the Toolbox to the design surface, in the same way you design Windows Forms using the Toolbox and the design surface for a form. But one of the more powerful aspects of the data set designer is its ability to create data set table definitions by dragging items from a database onto the design surface from the Server Explorer window.

   To see this in action, open the Server Explorer window (View > Server Explorer), and create a new data connection to the Northwind database if you don't already have one. If you stepped through the example in Chapter 1, you already have a data connection for Northwind and you can skip to step 9 below. If you still need to add the data connection, right-click on the Data Connections node in the Server Explorer tree and select Add Connection from the context menu.

   The first time you do this, the Change Data Source dialog displays (see Figure 2.4). You can select the data source that you want to use for this connection in this dialog. The entries in the list are self-explanatory, and the combo box at the bottom lets you select from the available providers for that kind of data source. For SQL Server, the .NET Framework Data Provider for SQL Server should be selected by default, which is what you want. If you are working with SQL Server 2005 Express, select the *Microsoft SQL Server Database File* option at the top.

6. After selecting the data source (or if you have added other data connections before), the Add Connection dialog displays if you are using SQL Server 2000 or 2005 (see Figure 2.5), or the dialog shown in Figure 2.6 displays for SQL Server 2005 Express.

7. Do one of the following:

   – For SQL Server 2000 or 2005, enter **localhost** for the server name to use the local machine's default instance of SQL Server (or whatever server name makes sense for your development environment), and enter **Northwind** as the database name at the bottom.

   – For SQL Server 2005 Express, enter the file path to the MDF file containing the Northwind database.

8. Select *Use Windows Authentication* for the logon information. Click *OK*.

9. Now that you have set up the data connection, expand the Northwind node that you added under *Data Connections* and expand the Tables node to see all the tables that are defined in the Northwind database.

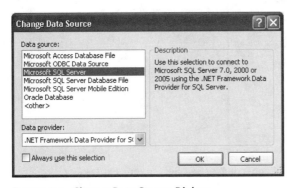

FIGURE 2.4: Change Data Source Dialog

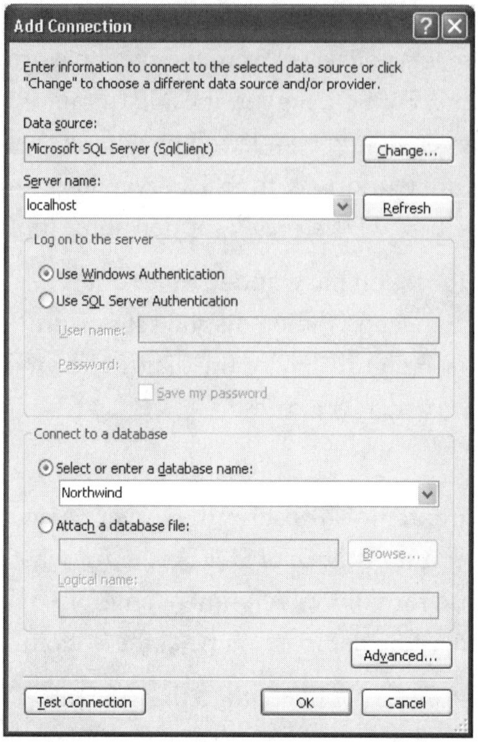

Add Connection

Enter information to connect to the selected data source or click
"Change" to choose a different data source and/or provider.

Data source:

Microsoft SQL Server (SqlClient)   Change...

Server name:

localhost   Refresh

Log on to the server

◉ Use Windows Authentication
○ Use SQL Server Authentication
  User name:
  Password:
  ☐ Save my password

Connect to a database

◉ Select or enter a database name:
  Northwind
○ Attach a database file:
                                        Browse...
  Logical name:

                                        Advanced...

Test Connection   OK   Cancel

FIGURE 2.5: Adding a New Data Connection for SQL Server

Add Connection

Enter information to connect to the selected data source or
click "Change" to choose a different data source and/or
provider.

Data source:

Microsoft SQL Server Database File (SqlClien   Change...

Database file name (new or existing):

C:\temp\northwnd.mdf   Browse...

Log on to the server

◉ Use Windows Authentication
○ Use SQL Server Authentication
  User name:
  Password:
  ☐ Save my password

                                        Advanced...

Test Connection   OK   Cancel

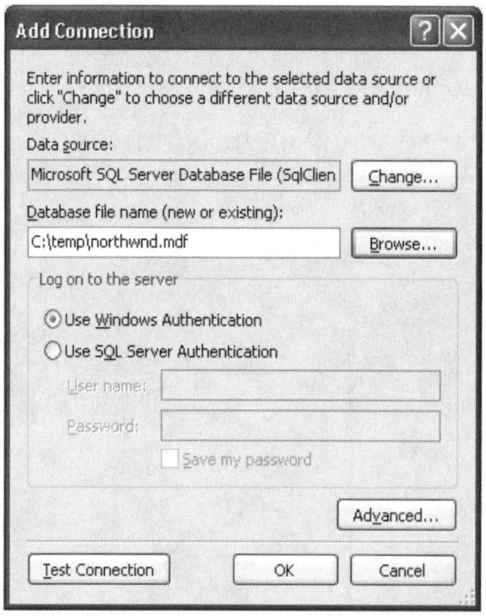

FIGURE 2.6: Adding a New Data Connection for SQL Server 2005 Express

10. Click and drag the Customers table onto the design surface. This creates a table definition that corresponds to the Customers table in the database (see Figure 2.7).

If you select any of the columns in the table definition in the data set designer and then look in the Properties window (in the bottom left in Figure 2.7), you will see that they are specified in terms of .NET types, not database types. The designer makes the translation between the database schema definitions of the columns and the corresponding types in .NET when you drag the table.

Also notice the `Name` and `Source` properties on a selected column in the data table as shown in Figure 2.7. The `Name` and `Source` properties (described earlier in this chapter) can be used to decouple the code property names from the database column names. There is also a `Caption`

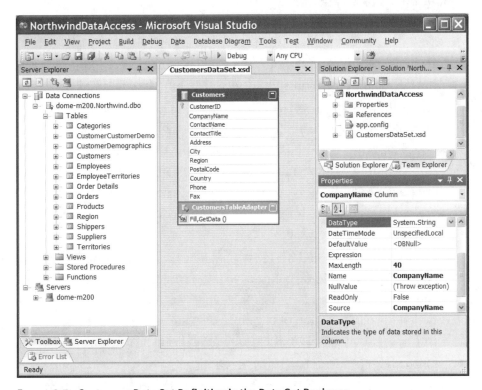

FIGURE 2.7: Customers Data Set Definition in the Data Set Designer

property not shown in Figure 2.7 that is used when a control is created by Visual Studio for data binding to that column.

Also notice that dragging the Customers table onto the design surface created a primary key in the data table definition for the `CustomerID` column. When the designer retrieves the schema information from the database to create the table and its columns, it also obtains the constraints from the database and adds those to the table definition as well.

You'll also see something attached to the bottom of the table definition that is labeled `CustomersTableAdapter` (in the center of Figure 2.7). This will be discussed later in this chapter, but for now it's enough to know that in addition to retrieving all the schema information when you drag a table out from Server Explorer, the data set designer also creates a table adapter class that lets you fill and update that table definition from the database with very little or no code.

Adding Tables to a Data Set

Now let's add a couple more tables to the data set.

1. Drag the Orders and Order Details tables from Server Explorer onto the design surface. You should see something like Figure 2.8.

   Notice that in addition to defining the data tables, Visual Studio 2005 also defined the data relations that correspond to the foreign key constraints between those tables in the database. This is a big improvement over Visual Studio .NET 2003, in which you had to create the relations for any multitable data sets yourself. It also generates table adapters for each table, as was done for the Customers table when it was added.

2. Once you have created a `DataTable` definition in your data set, you can also add additional columns to it if desired. For example, to add a column to the `Order Details` table that was named `Total` and contained the computation of `UnitPrice * Quantity * (1- Discount)`, right-click on the table in the designer and select Add > Column.

3. Once the column has been added, set the `Name` property to `Total`, and set the `Expression` property to the expression in step 2 involving `UnitPrice`, `Quantity`, and `Discount`. Now when the data table gets

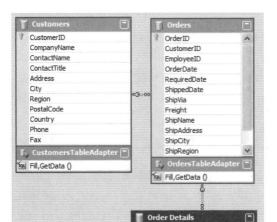

FIGURE 2.8: Defining Multiple Tables in a Data Set

filled, it will automatically compute that column's contents based on the expression.

Tip: Check the Visual Studio Help documentation to learn what constitutes a valid expression, because the `DataColumn` class supports a fairly complex syntax for computed column expressions.

Typed Data Set-Generated Code

Whenever you save your data set definition in the designer, a code generation tool runs to define a set of strongly typed classes behind the scenes. These classes correspond to the data set schema elements that you specify with the designer. Like the Windows Forms designer, this code is placed in files with .Designer.cs (or .Designer.vb for a VB project) extensions, and the file is shown in Solution Explorer as a child of the XSD file. Two other designer support files are also generated (with extensions of XSC and XSS). When you look at your typed data set definition in Solution Explorer, you should see something like Figure 2.9.

FIGURE 2.9: Typed Data Set Definition

If you open the CustomersDataSet.Designer.cs file, you will see that a whole ton of code has been generated for you (over a thousand lines of code per table in the data set). Scrolling through there and trying to make sense of it will be a little overwhelming at first, but Listing 2.3 highlights the most important parts, and you will get experience working with the rest of it throughout the book. Listing 2.3 shows a highly condensed version of the file with comments added for clarification.

LISTING 2.3: Typed DataSet Designer-Generated Code Sample

```
public partial class CustomersDataSet : System.Data.DataSet {
    private CustomersDataTable tableCustomers;
    private OrdersDataTable tableOrders;
    private System.Data.DataRelation relationFK_Orders_Customers;

    // Strongly typed table access
    public CustomersDataTable Customers {
        get {
            return this.tableCustomers;
        }
    }
    public OrdersDataTable Orders {
        get {
            return this.tableOrders;
        }
    }
    // ...

    // Nested typed DataTable definition
    public partial class CustomersDataTable : System.Data.DataTable,
        System.Collections.IEnumerable {
        // Strongly typed indexer for accessing rows
        public CustomersRow this[int index] { ... }
```

```
    // ...
    }

    // Strongly typed DataRow definition
    public partial class CustomersRow : System.Data.DataRow
    {
        // Strongly typed properties for each column in the row
        public string CustomerID { ... }
        public string CompanyName { ... }
// Strongly typed accessor methods for obtaining child rows
        public OrdersRow[] GetOrdersRows() { ... }
        // ...
    }

    public partial class OrdersRow : System.Data.DataRow
    {
        // ...
        // Strongly typed properties for obtaining parent row
        public CustomersRow CustomersRow { ... }
        // ...
    }
}
```

There are a number of things to note about the code in Listing 2.3. First, as described earlier, the typed data set class itself is just a derived class from the DataSet base class. The class definition uses the new partial classes feature that was introduced in .NET 2.0, which allows a class definition to span more than one file. Using partial classes lets you supplement the code in the typed data set with validation or business logic in a separate file in your project, and that file will be unaffected if you have to regenerate your typed data set definition. This was a big problem for many people in .NET 1.X; if they wanted to change the data set definition, they would lose those changes any time code generation was run, and this happened every time they saved the XSD file from which the code was generated.

Next you will notice that there are public properties at the data set level for each table contained within the data set, declared of a strongly typed class specific to that table. If there are relations defined between the tables, those show up as members as well; these can be accessed by name through the Relations property on the data set.

You can see that the skeleton of the CustomersDataTable definition toward the bottom of the listing uses inheritance as well to derive from

DataTable. Within the table class (along with a lot of other members not shown) is a strongly typed indexer into the rows collection of that table. Using that indexer, whenever you index into a given row number, you get back a reference of type CustomersRow. CustomersRow is itself a derived class from DataRow, which is also defined as a nested class inside the data set class. Using a CustomersRow reference, you then get strongly typed access to each of the columns in the row based on the Name property you set for the column in the data set definition (as described earlier in the discussion about Figure 2.7). Both the CustomersDataTable and CustomersRow type definitions are nested classes within the CustomersDataSet class. This means that to create a variable of that type in your code, you have to specify the outer class as well, in the form CustomersDataSet.CustomersRow as seen in Listing 2.2.

Beyond what is shown here, a lot more code is generated to support the public-facing members of the classes. Each class has a lot of initialization code that runs at construction time; this code sets up the underlying schema of the data set to contain the expected data tables, columns, relations, constraints, and so on. The initialization code also sets up some code to optimize the speed of accessing each individual column within the data set when accessed through the strongly typed properties. I encourage you to spend some time browsing through the typed data set code to get a sense of what is defined in there. The way you normally use typed data sets means that code is all just a black box to you, but it's a good idea to know how black boxes work if you really want to know how your program works and to be able to understand problems when your program doesn't work as expected. It may also come in handy when you are misusing the black box, and the debugger stops on a line of code inside the data set definition code where things are blowing up.

Introduction to Table Adapters

As you saw at the bottom of the table definition in Figure 2.7, there was something attached in the designer labeled CustomersTableAdapter that contains two displayed methods named Fill and GetData. This additional class that gets generated for each table in your typed data set is called a **table adapter**.

The table adapter, new in .NET 2.0, greatly enhances the experience of working with typed data sets. As discussed earlier in this chapter, prior to .NET 2.0, when you wanted to fill a data set or push updates back to the data source from the data set, you had to use a data adapter. This meant you had to make sure the commands for that adapter got created correctly to fill the columns appropriately and push changes back. It also meant that you had to construct separate adapters or change those commands programmatically if you wanted to use the same data set with different SELECT queries to fill it. In addition, you had to be careful to make sure that the data from the queries you defined got placed in the appropriate table within the typed data set. In other words, working with data adapters leaves a lot to be desired. Basically, you were left to your own devices to write a lot of code to create a consistent and well-designed data access layer that could work with your typed data sets.

Table adapters are designed to address most, if not all, of the common problems people experienced working with data adapters and strongly typed data sets, and they can save you considerable coding for managing your data through typed data sets. A table adapter gives you a prefabricated data access component for managing data from an individual table in your data source. When you drag a table from Server Explorer onto the data set designer surface, or when the typed data set is generated through the Data Source Configuration wizard (which is discussed in a later chapter), the table adapter class is generated along with the data set, data table, and data row classes in the designer-generated file. SELECT, INSERT, UPDATE, and DELETE queries are generated for the table and wrapped in command objects within the table adapter so that you can execute those queries through the table adapter's public methods. The table adapter also encapsulates a data adapter; the table adapter associates the command objects with that data adapter to work with the corresponding data table type to fill and update the database through the table adapter. All these details are hidden from you unless you go looking for them—you can just focus on the public methods that the table adapter exposes which let you execute queries on the corresponding table.

Listing 2.4 shows a trimmed-down version of the designer-generated code for a table adapter for the Customers table in Northwind. Some of the private members have been removed and the type names cleaned up to make it clear what is going on. The first thing you will notice is that the table adapter class is defined in a child namespace of the project namespace in which you create the typed data set. The project name is Northwind-DataAccess, and a child namespace, NorthwindDataAccess.Customers-DataSetTableAdapters, is declared and is where the table adapter classes are defined. The table adapter class is derived from the Component base class from the System.ComponentModel namespace by default. If you wanted to derive from a different base class, you could change the Base-Class designer property when that table adapter is selected in the data set designer in Visual Studio.

You can see from the private members depicted that the table adapter simply contains a data adapter, a connection, and an array of command objects that will be used to execute the queries represented by the table adapter methods. The public API exposed by the class includes type-safe Fill, GetData, and Update methods that will only work correctly with a CustomersDataSet.CustomersDataTable strongly typed table. There are also two Update methods defined; these let you work with untyped DataRow objects to support more dynamic situations, such as when you use the Select method to only get certain rows and want to use them for updates. The Select method returns an array of DataRow objects. This provides Update methods that accept a raw DataRow array, so you don't have to cast them to the specific DataRow derived class that is defined in the typed data set just to pass them to the Update method of the table adapter.

The table adapter class also exposes Insert, Update, and Delete methods that take individual parameters for each column, rather than a data row. These methods let you use a table adapter as a data access component even when you aren't working with an instance of a typed data set or data table. You can get the values used to execute the underlying query from wherever you need to within your application and then pass their values to these methods. Notice that the parameter list for the Update method includes both the values that will be used for the update as well as the original value of the corresponding columns. This is because the default queries generated for commands executed by the table adapter use the default designer optimistic concurrency checks. Specifically, they check the current value of every column in the database against the original values to see if any changes have been made since the data was retrieved, and if so, they will throw a DbConcurrencyException. If you don't want to use this approach to optimistic concurrency, you can generate custom queries on the table adapter as described later in this chapter to do something different, such as only checking a single timestamp or datetime column.

LISTING 2.4: Table Adapter Designer-Generated Code

```
namespace NorthwindDataAccess.CustomersDataSetTableAdapters {
    public partial class CustomersTableAdapter : Component {

        private SqlDataAdapter _adapter;

        private SqlConnection _connection;

        private SqlCommand[] _commandCollection;

        // Some other internal initialization

        internal SqlConnection Connection { get{...} set{...} }

        public virtual int Fill(CustomersDataSet.CustomersDataTable
            dataTable) {...}

        public virtual CustomersDataSet.CustomersDataTable GetData()
            {...}

        public virtual int Update(CustomersDataSet.CustomersDataTable
            dataTable) { ... }

        public virtual int Update(CustomersDataSet dataSet) {...}

        public virtual int Update(DataRow dataRow) {...}

        public virtual int Update(DataRow[] dataRows) {...}

        public virtual int Delete(string Original_CustomerID,
            string Original_CompanyName, string Original_ContactName,
            string Original_ContactTitle, string Original_Address,
            string Original_City, string Original_Region,
            string Original_PostalCode, string Original_Country,
            string Original_Phone, string Original_Fax) { ... }

        public virtual int Insert(string CustomerID,
```

continues

```
        string CompanyName, string ContactName, string ContactTitle,

        string Address, string City, string Region,
        string PostalCode, string Country, string Phone, string Fax)

        {...}

    public virtual int Update(string CustomerID,
        string CompanyName, string ContactName, string ContactTitle,
        string Address, string City, string Region,
        string PostalCode, string Country, string Phone, string Fax,

        string Original_CustomerID, string Original_CompanyName,
        string Original_ContactName, string Original_ContactTitle,
        string Original_Address, string Original_City,
        string Original_Region, string Original_PostalCode,
        string Original_Country, string Original_Phone,
        string Orsiginal_Fax) {...}
    }
}
```

Also notice that the class is marked as a partial class, just like the typed data set was. This lets you extend the class' functionality in a separate source file that won't be affected if the table adapter code is regenerated by the designer due to changes. We will use this fact in a little bit to add a helper method to the `CustomersTableAdapter` class so that you can control the transactions used during queries.

Filling and Updating a Typed Data Set with a Table Adapter

Once you have created a typed data set and its associated table adapter using the data set designer, you can easily fill the data set from the data source from which the data set definition was created. Listing 2.5 shows how easy coding with typed data sets and table adapters can be.

LISTING 2.5: Using a Table Adapter to Fill and Update a Data Set

```
partial class Form1 : Form
{
    CustomersTableAdapter m_Adapter = new CustomersTableAdapter();
    CustomersDataSet m_Customers = new CustomersDataSet();
```

```
public Form1()
{
    InitializeComponent();
}

private void OnFill(object sender, EventArgs e)
{
    m_Adapter.Fill(m_Customers.Customers);
    m_Grid.DataSource = m_Customers.Customers;
}

private void OnUpdate(object sender, EventArgs e)
{
    m_Adapter.Update(m_Customers.Customers);
}
}
```

The code in Listing 2.5 comes from a simple Windows Forms client application. The form has two buttons on it, labeled *Fill* and *Update*, and a DataGridView control named m_Grid. The form class declares and initializes two member variables at the top, one for the typed data set instance and one for the table adapter.

The OnFill and OnUpdate methods are the button click event handlers for the form, and you can see that filling the data set is a simple matter of calling Fill on the adapter and passing in the specific table in the typed data set you want to fill. Because the parameter to the Fill method only accepts a CustomersDataTable type in a CustomersDataSet, you would get a compiler error if you tried to pass in any other type, including an untyped data set or data table. This helps to ensure that the object you are trying to fill already has the correct schema for the data that will be returned by the SELECT query that is encapsulated in the table adapter. In the past, the developer had to ensure that the data set schema was aligned with the queries set on a data adapter; this was one of the most common places that mistakes occurred when filling data sets. By taking this strongly typed approach to table adapters, that problem is eliminated. So in Listing 2.5, Fill is passed the Customers property on the data set instance, which is a reference to the CustomersDataTable contained in the CustomersDataSet.

After the data set has been filled, it is data bound to the grid control using the grid's DataSource property. (I go into a lot more detail on the

`DataGridView` control and data binding in later chapters.) In the `OnUpdate` method, any changes that were made in the data set are pushed back into the underlying data source through the table adapter's `Update` method, which again accepts a strongly typed `CustomersDataTable` reference.

Connection Management

The table adapters that the designer generates contain code to initialize the connection to the database. By default, when you drag a table onto the data set designer surface from Server Explorer, an app.config configuration file is added to your project. The connection string to the database you are working with is added to the `connectionStrings` configuration section in that configuration file:

```
<connectionStrings>
    <add name="NorthwindDataAccess.Properties.Settings.
        NorthwindConnectionString"
        connectionString="Data Source=localhost;Initial
        Catalog=Northwind;Integrated Security=True"
        providerName="System.Data.SqlClient" />
</connectionStrings>
```

The `connectionStrings` section is a new part of the configuration file schema for .NET 2.0. The `add` element that you place under it adds a connection string that will be accessible in the project through a strongly typed `Settings` class. The `add` tag contains a `name` attribute that basically specifies a path to a property on a class that will contain the connection string at runtime. In this case, that is the `NorthwindConnectionString` property on the `Settings` class in the `Properties` child namespace within the `NorthwindDataAccess` project. The `add` element also contains a `connectionString` attribute that specifies the connection string that this entry corresponds to. Finally, the `providerName` attribute specifies the data access provider that the connection string corresponds to.

The `Settings` class that is specified in the connection string configuration setting is also created when you first drag a database object onto the data set designer. Visual Studio adds the class and defines the Settings.Designer.cs file under the Properties node in Solution Explorer, as shown in Figure 2.10.

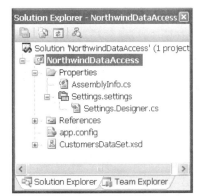

FIGURE 2.10: Settings and Application Configuration Files in Solution Explorer

The `Settings` class contains strongly typed properties to programmatically access the settings in your configuration files. The connection string that is set when you create your table adapters in the designer is also hard coded as a default into that `Settings` class, so if the corresponding setting cannot be found in the application configuration file, it at least has the original value of the connection string that it can try to use.

The table adapter generated with your typed data set uses this `Settings` class to obtain the connection string when the table adapter initializes the connection object that is encapsulated in it:

```
private void InitConnection() {
    this._connection = new System.Data.SqlClient.SqlConnection();
    this._connection.ConnectionString =
        NorthwindDataAccess.Properties.Settings.
        Default.NorthwindConnectionString;
}
```

The `Default` static property on the `Settings` class returns a singleton instance of the `Settings` class, through which the other properties, such as `NorthwindConnectionString`, can be used to get to the underlying configuration data.

Because the connection string information is embedded in the configuration file, and the table adapter calls through the `Settings` class to get the connection string out of the configuration file, if you need to change the target database in your application, you just have to change the connection string information in the application's configuration file.

At runtime in .NET, configuration files need to be named according to a particular convention and placed in the runtime folder on the application. For a Windows Forms application, the configuration file assumes the name of the executable file with a .config extension, such as MyDataApp.exe.config. For development in Visual Studio, a file named app.config is added to your project; this lets you set the configuration settings as part of your project. When you build a Windows Forms project that contains an app.config file, that file will be copied into the build output folder and renamed using the convention for the output executable file name.

If you place your data access code, including typed data set definitions, in a separate data access class library (as you always should for a good layered-application architecture), an app.config file will still be added to the project. This will contain the connection strings for your table adapters, and the Settings class in that project will contain a connection string property to access it. However, the app.config file won't be copied to the build output folder for the class library, because configuration files can only be associated with executable files in a Windows application. If you then set a reference to that class library from a Windows Forms project and call the table adapter methods from your application code, the table adapter connections will use the connection string information that was hard coded as a default into the Settings class in the data access class library project.

If you want to change the connection information used in your application, you need to add the connection string information to the application configuration file for the Windows Forms application. The easiest way to do this is to copy the app.config file from the data access layer project into the Windows Forms project if there isn't already one there. If there is already an app.config file in the Windows Forms project, then you can simply copy the connectionStrings section from the app.config file in the data access layer project into the app.config file in the Windows Forms project that will be using the data access layer. Then any changes you make to the connectionStrings configuration section in the Windows

Forms project will be used by the table adapters in the data access layer code, because it will be loaded through the `Settings` class in the data access layer.

If you want additional programmatic control of the connection at runtime, you have to add some code to the assembly where the typed data set definition resides. In Listing 2.4, an internal property exposed on the table adapter, named `Connection`, gives you access to set or get the `SqlConnection` object that is being used by the table adapter. If you add code to the project containing the typed data set that accesses that property, you can dynamically set or modify the connection object. There are two ways you could do this: in a separate helper class, or you could define your own partial class file for the table adapter class and add a method or a property with a different name to expose the underlying private member variable that holds the connection. You'll see an example of extending the partial class of the table adapter in the section on supporting transactions.

If you want to expose connection management on a table adapter by adding a separate class to the assembly, you can do it using a simple class like the following:

```
using System.Data.SqlClient;
using NorthwindDataAccess.CustomersDataSetTableAdapters;

namespace NorthwindDataAccess
{
    public class CustomersTableAdapterConnectionManager
    {
        public static SqlConnection GetConnection(
            CustomersTableAdapter adapter)
        {
            return adapter.Connection;
        }

        public static void SetConnection(CustomersTableAdapter adapter,

            SqlConnection connection)
        {
            adapter.Connection = connection;
        }
    }
}
```

The `GetConnection` and `SetConnection` static methods take a `CustomersTableAdapter` parameter that is used to access the members of the class. The `SetConnection` method also takes the `SqlConnection` object that you want to use to set the current connection for the adapter. Because the `Connection` property is declared as `internal` on the table adapter class, it can be accessed by the methods of other classes in the same assembly that include these helper class methods. So the helper class methods simply either get or set the connection through the table adapter reference, even though code external to the assembly could not do so. (I think they should have exposed the `Connection` property as public to avoid needing to do this, but the design choice was made to encapsulate it more rather than less; this requires you to write more code for the cases where you need to access it outside the assembly.)

Adding Transaction Support to a Table Adapter

If you want to execute multiple queries through a table adapter within the scope of a single transaction, you have a couple of options. You can use the `TransactionScope` class from the new `System.Transactions` namespace to execute the queries within a single transaction scope:

```
public void ExecuteTransaction(CustomersDataSet.CustomersDataTable
    customers)
{
    CustomersTableAdapter adapter = new CustomersTableAdapter();
    // Start the transaction
    using (TransactionScope scope = new TransactionScope())
    {
        // Save any changes currently in the data table
        adapter.Update(customers)        // First query
        customers[0].Phone = "030-0074321";  // make a change
        adapter.Update(customers);       // Second query
        scope.Complete();                // Commits the transaction
    }
}
```

However, doing this may result in this using a distributed transaction, and depending on the design of your application, this may have a higher performance cost than using a direct database transaction.

If you want to manage a transaction directly against a table adapter, you can extend the table adapter class by adding your own partial class definition to the project with the same name as the table adapter you want to modify, and then add some code to allow a client to establish a transaction that will encompass any queries executed through the table adapter.

If you add a new class file to the `NorthwindDataAccess` class library project and add the code in Listing 2.6 to it, the `CustomersTableAdapter` class will be extended to add capabilities to the code that was generated by the typed data set designer.

LISTING 2.6: CustomersTableAdapter Partial Class Definition

```
using System;
using System.Data;
using System.Data.SqlClient;

namespace NorthwindDataAccess.CustomersDataSetTableAdapters
{
    public partial class CustomersTableAdapter
    {
        public SqlTransaction BeginTransaction(SqlConnection connection)
        {
            if (connection.State != ConnectionState.Open)
            {
                throw new ArgumentException(
                    "Connection must be open to begin a transaction");
            }

            // Set the connection for all the contained commands
            Connection = connection;
            SqlTransaction transaction = connection.BeginTransaction();
            foreach (SqlCommand cmd in _commandCollection)
            {
                if (cmd != null)
                    cmd.Transaction = transaction;
            }
            if ((Adapter.InsertCommand != null))
            {
                Adapter.InsertCommand.Transaction = transaction;
            }
            if ((Adapter.DeleteCommand != null))
            {
                Adapter.DeleteCommand.Transaction = transaction;
            }
            if ((Adapter.UpdateCommand != null))
            {
```

continues

```
        Adapter.UpdateCommand.Transaction = transaction;
      }
      if ((Adapter.SelectCommand != null))
      {
          Adapter.SelectCommand.Transaction = transaction;
      }
      return transaction;
    }
  }
}
```

The code in Listing 2.6 performs the following steps.

1. It verifies that the connection is open, and throws an exception if the connection isn't open.

2. It sets the Connection property for the table adapter to that connection, which will set that connection for all the contained command objects in the designer-generated code.

3. The code loops through all the commands in the _commandCollection array, which is part of the designer-generated portion of the table adapter partial class. These commands are used for custom queries that have been added to the table adapter.

4. It checks and sets each of the commands held by the contained data adapter. These are the primary commands used for filling and updating from the corresponding table.

The BeginTransaction method lets you use this table adapter much like you work with transactions against the raw ADO.NET classes. When you work directly with database transactions in ADO.NET, you first have to:

1. Open a connection.

2. Call BeginTransaction on the connection.

3. Take the transaction object returned from that call and set it against each command that you want to execute as part of the transaction.

4. Finally, when you are done with the transaction, you call Commit on the transaction object itself.

The `BeginTransaction` method in the partial class extension to `CustomersDataSet` lets you follow a similar coding pattern when working with the table adapter. It allows you to pass in the connection that you'll be using to execute the queries, and it will start a transaction. It sets the `Transaction` property of all the commands encapsulated in the table adapter using the transaction returned from the call to `BeginTransaction` on the connection, and then returns it to the caller so that the calling code can call `Commit` or `Rollback` on that transaction object.

The following code shows a client that wants to use the table adapter to get back the contents of the `Customers` table, modify the first record in the table, and submit the change back to the database, all as part of a transaction.

```
public void ExecuteTransactionRetrieveAndUpdate()
{
    CustomersTableAdapter adapter = new CustomersTableAdapter();
    SqlConnection connection =
        new SqlConnection(Settings.Default.ConnectionString);
    using (connection)
    {
        connection.Open();
        SqlTransaction transaction =
            adapter.BeginTransaction(connection);
        CustomersDataSet.CustomersDataTable customers =
            adapter.GetData();
        customers[0].Phone = "030-0074321";
        adapter.Update(customers);
        transaction.Commit();
    }
}
```

As you can see, this code follows a similar pattern to the way you write transactional code with just the ADO.NET connection and command classes. First it opens a connection, and then it calls `BeginTransaction`. In this case, `BeginTransaction` is called against the table adapter instead of the connection using the table adapter extension method, which takes the connection as a parameter and returns the `SqlTransaction` object that is created. Once the transaction has been started, any number of query methods can be called on the table adapter instance, and they will all be enlisted in the database transaction that was started with the `BeginTransaction` call. When the code is ready to commit the transaction, `Commit` is called directly on the `SqlTransaction` object returned by the call to `Begin-Transaction`.

Adding Helper Data Access Methods

At this point, we have a data access layer class library with type definitions for a `CustomersDataSet`, which can contain `Customers`, `Orders`, and `Order_Details` table data and maintain the relations between those tables. We also have a table adapter for each table that lets us individually `Fill` and `Update` the tables in the data set. The designer wrote all of that code for us. We extended the table adapter for `Customers` to allow transactional updates, and we added a helper class that allows us to externally get or set the connection used by an instance of a `CustomersTableAdapter`.

What more could you possibly need? Well, in this case we have three tables in the data set that are related in a hierarchical manner. `Orders` is a child table for `Customers`, and `Order_Details` is a child table for `Orders`. In many situations, you will likely want to have all three tables populated at once, and it's a pain for a client to have to create three table adapter instances and make sure they fill them in the right order to ensure that they don't violate foreign key constraints. To avoid this, you can add some code to the data access layer to provide convenience methods to populate the whole data set in one simple method call. You could put this code in a couple of places. I am going to do it as a factory method on the `Customers-DataSet` class itself by adding to the partial class definition for that class.

If you add a new class file to the project and name it Customers-DataSet.cs, you can add the following partial class extension to the typed data set class:

```
using System;
using System.Data;
using NorthwindDataAccess.CustomersDataSetTableAdapters;

namespace NorthwindDataAccess
{
    public partial class CustomersDataSet : DataSet
    {
        public static CustomersDataSet GetCustomers()
        {
            CustomersTableAdapter custAdapter =
```

```
            new CustomersTableAdapter();
        OrdersTableAdapter orderAdapter = new OrdersTableAdapter();
        Order_DetailsTableAdapter detailsAdapter =
            new Order_DetailsTableAdapter();
        CustomersDataSet customers = new CustomersDataSet();
        custAdapter.Fill(customers.Customers);
        orderAdapter.Fill(customers.Orders);
        detailsAdapter.Fill(customers.Order_Details);
        return customers;
    }
  }
}
```

The GetCustomers static factory method is pretty straightforward in implementation. It simply creates an instance of each of the table adapters for the contained tables in the data set and uses them to fill the tables in the proper order to avoid foreign key constraint violations within the data set. This allows client code to simply call the factory method on the class to get back a fully populated instance of the data set to work with:

```
CustomersDataSet customers = CustomersDataSet.GetCustomers();
```

Updating a nested data set like this gets a little complicated, because you have to worry about performing the inserts, deletes, and updates to the database in the correct order so you won't violate constraints. Encapsulating the details of that in a helper method would be a good idea and will depend on the scenarios in which you are going to use master-details data sets for performing updates.

Basing Table Adapters on Stored Procedures or Views

Using stored procedures for all data access against a database has a number of advantages.

- It promotes looser coupling between the data access layer and the explicit schema of the database, because certain kinds of changes can be made to the underlying table schema, and the client code won't have to change if the signature of the stored procedure didn't change.

- Stored procedures improve your ability to secure the database to stored procedure-only access, which prevents clients from directly accessing tables and potentially violating data contracts through that access.

- You may benefit from improved execution performance in many scenarios.

You can also use views to expose logical tables of data that map to more complex schemas at the database level.

You can easily base your strongly typed data sets and table adapters on either stored procedures or views as well. If the stored procedure returns a result set (some combination of rows and columns), you can use that result set's schema to create a strongly typed data set that contains that schema and a table adapter capable of loading the rows returned from the stored procedure into the data set. If the stored procedure takes in parameters to perform an update, insert, or delete, but doesn't return any rows, it can also be used to configure the corresponding command on a table adapter to update the database from a data set. And finally, because a database view simply returns rows with a defined schema, it too can be used to fill a typed data set that matches the schema.

The method for using either stored procedures or views with typed data sets in the data set designer is very similar to what you have already seen with direct table access. Dragging a database view onto the data set designer surface gives you a strongly typed data table definition based on the schema of the rows that the view returns. It will also have a table adapter created to populate the data set from the database. However, because the views of data in underlying tables in the database are read-only in the general case, the created table adapter's insert, update, and delete commands are set to null, so you can only use the table adapter to fill or retrieve a data set. You will have to use some other means to perform updates.

When you drag a stored procedure onto the data set designer surface, what you get depends on the kind of stored procedure. If the stored procedure returns rows, then the schema of the first result set of rows that the stored procedure returns will be used to create a typed data table and corresponding table adapter for that schema, which only has its select command configured for filling the data set. If the stored procedure is one that doesn't return a result set, then a `QueriesTableAdapter` class will be created with methods exposed for each stored procedure that you drag onto the surface.

Adding Queries to Table Adapters

What if you want to execute other queries besides just selecting all rows to fill the data set and pushing entire rows back to the database for insert, update, and delete against the table that you are working with in a table adapter? The following procedure shows an easy way to define additional methods on the table adapter to perform other queries on that data table definition.

Adding a Custom Query to a Table Adapter

1. From the data set designer, right-click on the table adapter compartment of a data table definition.

2. On the pop-up menu, choose one of the following:

   – Select Add Query to start the TableAdapter Query Configuration wizard.

   This wizard steps you through defining an additional database query that you want the table adapter to be able to execute. You can use the wizard to create a new query based on a SQL statement, create a new stored procedure, or select existing stored procedures. This wizard helps you add methods to the table adapter that allow you to perform specialized selections to fill the data set differently, or specialized insert, update, or delete commands to modify the database based on specific conditions.

   – Select Configure to start the TableAdapter Configuration wizard.

   This wizard is similar to the one used for Add Query, but it lets you configure the SELECT, INSERT, UPDATE, and DELETE behavior of the table adapter all at once.

Let's step through a simple example to demonstrate how to use these wizards.

1. If you don't currently have the `CustomersDataSet` from the NorthwindDataAccess class library you created at the beginning of the chapter open in the designer, open it now.

2. Right-click on the `CustomersTableAdapter` at the bottom of the Customers table definition and select Add Query. This displays the Choose a Command Type page of the TableAdapter Query Configuration wizard (see Figure 2.11).

   You can choose whether to base the query method you are adding on a new SQL statement, on a new stored procedure, or on an existing stored procedure that is already defined in the database. For this example, let's define a new SQL statement.

3. After selecting or accepting the *Use SQL statements* option, click the *Next* button. This displays the Choose a Query Type page shown in Figure 2.12.

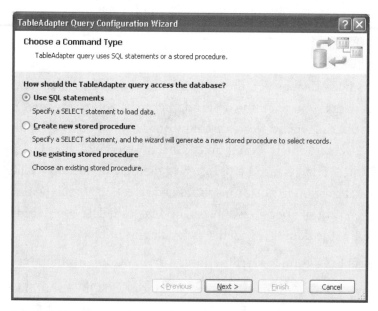

FIGURE 2.11: Choose a Command Type Page

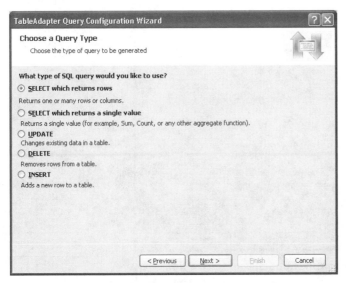

FIGURE 2.12: Choosing the SQL Statement Query Type

Here you can specify whether to add a query method to select rows into the data set (the default), select an individual value, or perform a delete, update, or insert. The last four options simply result in a new query method with a separate command object being added to the table adapter for performing the specified query against the underlying connection. They don't affect the data set in any way; they just take in parameters and return a value.

SELECT returns a single result set—the result set that is returned is whatever the SELECT statement you specify returns. The DELETE, UPDATE, and INSERT statement options return an integer that represents the number of rows affected. The wizard will complain at the completion step if the query you provide is incompatible with the expected result of the query; for example, if you select the default option but then enter a query that doesn't return a result set.

4. Click *Next* to accept the *SELECT which returns rows* option.

5. The next page lets you specify the exact query you'd like to add. Figure 2.13 shows the query that we are adding for this example, which is to perform a select on all columns with a WHERE clause that restricts the results based on a country parameter match against the Country column.

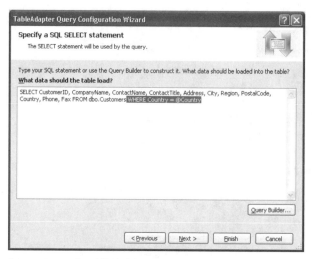

FIGURE 2.13: Providing the SQL Statement for the New Query

Using the Query Builder to Write a SQL Statement

There is a Query Builder that is similar to the one provided in Visual Studio .NET 2003 that you can access from the page in the wizard where you specify your SQL statement. This Query Builder lets you interactively specify the query you want to run and test it out. To use the Query Builder, follow these steps:

1. Click the *Query Builder* button (shown in Figure 2.13). Figure 2.14 shows the Query Builder in action.

   The Query Builder is a fairly complicated window. At the top is a diagram view pane; here you can add tables or remove them using the right-click pop-up menu. The Query Builder adapts its menus and what you are allowed to do depending on whether you entered it to build a SELECT, INSERT, UPDATE, or DELETE statement. For example, if you are building a SELECT statement, you can add multiple tables to build a JOIN query. However, if you are building an INSERT statement, only one table is allowed.

2. Once a table is displayed, check the boxes next to individual columns to include them in the query statement in the appropriate place based on the query type. Below the diagram pane is a grid pane—this lets you specify additional qualifiers for each selected column, such as default values and the direction of the parameter. Below the grid pane is the SQL statement itself, which dynamically changes based on your entries in the two panes above. You can also simply type the SQL text into that pane, and the other panes will update and the focus will change. At the bottom is a preview pane, where you can try to execute the query if it returns results to see what the results look like. You do this by clicking the *Execute* button.

6. After you have determined the SQL statement for the query that you want to add, you specify the name(s) of the method(s) that will be added to the table adapter. If you chose a SELECT statement that will return rows, and therefore can be used to populate the typed data set associated with the table adapter, you can generate two methods: one to fill the data set based on the query, and another that will construct a new data table, fill it, and return it as a return parameter from the method. These methods will default to being selected for generation and will start with a naming convention of `FillBy` and `GetBy`, respectively.

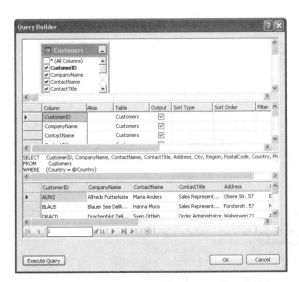

FIGURE 2.14: Using Query Builder to Specify a SQL Statement

7. Complete the method name with a meaningful addition based on the parameters that you are doing the select with. Figure 2.15 shows this step for the example, where we are performing a SELECT with a Country column WHERE restriction, so I named the methods `FillByCountry` and `GetByCountry`. If you are specifying one of the other types of queries that don't fill the data set, you will be given a text box to specify a single method name for the query method that is generated. Click *Next* to move to the final step of the wizard.

8. Assuming all went well and there were no errors, you will see a final feedback dialog (see Figure 2.16) that tells you what was done.

Configuring a Table Adapter to Use Stored Procedures

If you want to generate a new stored procedure and base the query method on that, the procedure is much the same as what was just covered for a SQL statement. You step through the wizard, and specify the SQL statement that the stored procedure should contain. The main difference is that when you complete the wizard, the stored procedure will also be created in the database that you are working with.

If you want to base your query method on an existing stored procedure, the wizard experience is a little different. Instead of the step shown in

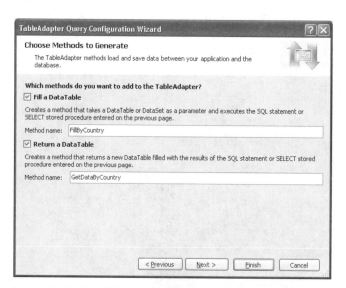

FIGURE 2.15: Specifying the Method Name(s) for the Table Adapter Query Methods

Figure 2.13 for specifying the SQL statement, the wizards displays the page shown in Figure 2.17 for choosing the stored procedure from the list of stored procedures in the database that you are connected to. Once you select a stored procedure, the dialog fills in and shows you what the parameters are and what result columns will be returned from the execution of that stored procedure.

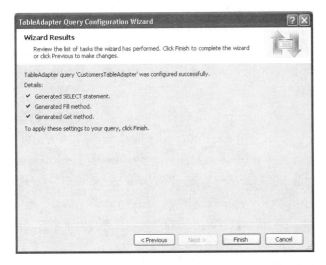

FIGURE 2.16: Results of Completing the Add Query Wizard

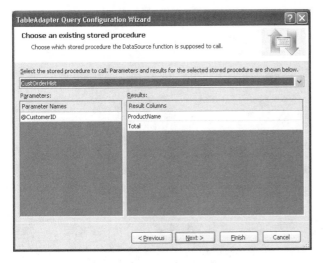

FIGURE 2.17: Selecting an Existing Stored Procedure to Create a Query Method

The next step in the wizard for a stored procedure is also a little different. It lets you specify the "shape," or schema, of the data returned from the stored procedure (see Figure 2.18). This is because stored procedures might return result sets, even though their primary purpose is to perform an insert, update, or delete. For example, a stored procedure might perform a SELECT statement to see if a row exists before trying to delete it. Because of the embedded SELECT statement, to the wizard the stored procedure looks like it returns a result set. However, it doesn't know if that result set is the intent of the stored procedure or just something that is generated as part of the execution of the stored procedure. So the wizard page shown in Figure 2.18 lets you choose whether the stored procedure returns rows, a single value, or no values.

As you can see, the data set designer, table adapters, and the Query wizard give you a great deal of power and flexibility to quickly generate a lot of data access code with just a few mouse clicks and drag-and-drop operations. For the simple example just covered with the Customers, Orders, and Order Details tables, the result is over 5,000 lines of generated code. And that is clean, well-factored code as well. With 5,000 fewer lines of tedious,

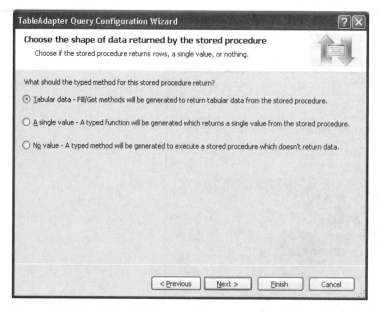

FIGURE 2.18: Specifying the Shape of the Data Returned from the Stored Procedure

error-prone data access code that you have to write, you can get on with implementing the specific logic and functionality of your application instead of writing a bunch of CRUD (Create-Retrieve-Update-Delete) methods in a data access layer. That fact, coupled with the type safety, IntelliSense, and clean design benefits of working with typed data sets, amounts to a huge win in my mind.

Creating Typed Data Sets with Command Line Tools

One other way to create typed data set definitions may make sense for some situations, but it means giving up some of the best features described so far. The command line tool XML Schema Support utility (xsd.exe) that comes with the .NET Framework SDK does a number of things, one of which is to let you run it against an XML Schema definition and generate a typed data set class definition from that schema. There are a number of limitations as to the shape of the schema provided—basically it has to be a schema that can be flattened into a relational schema within the data set definition that is generated.

The big limitation with the typed data set definition this tool generates is that the definition is just the data set definition itself—it doesn't have any associated table adapters. Because you are working from the command line, there is no direct tie to a database and its schema, and it would require a complicated syntax to include all the information that you easily specify through drag-and-drop and wizard operations in Visual Studio. You will also have to get the XML schema you are basing it on from somewhere; there is no autogeneration of the schema based on a database as in the Visual Studio environment.

Even with its limitations, this is still a useful tool to be aware of: There may be times you'll be building distributed applications that pass around data sets and you may not have direct access to the database that those data sets are going to be populated from. Or you may be specifically using typed data sets as simple but powerful business data entity definitions that are decoupled from the database schema by design. As long as someone can provide you with a schema that describes what the data sets will look like that you'll be working with—or you can define one yourself—you can easily generate a strongly typed data set class with xsd.exe for working with that data. The tool also supports other capabilities, such as the conversion of XML Data Reduced (XDR) schemas to XML Schema Definition (XSD) schemas, as well as the generation of classes from a schema that are simple data transfer classes that aren't related to data sets.

Using Typed Data Sets in Your Code

Because the typed data tables and rows in a data set definition are declared as nested types, they can become a little cumbersome when you are writing a lot of programmatic code against them. Needing the type name to be `CustomersDataSet.CustomersRow` for every row variable you declare, for example, can get a little hard to read, even though IntelliSense makes it fairly easy to type. In C# this is easy to address with the type aliasing capabilities of the `using` statement. For instance, to write some data access code to work with `CustomersRow` objects, you would first alias the full type name of that class with a `using` statement, and then declare your variables using the alias:

```
using System;
using NorthwindDataAccess.CustomersDataSetTableAdapters;
using CustomersRow =
    NorthwindDataAccess.CustomersDataSet.CustomersRow;

namespace NorthwindDataAccess
{
    class MyDataAccessComponent
    {
        public CustomersRow GetCustomer(string customerId)
        {
            CustomersTableAdapter adapter = new CustomersTableAdapter();
            CustomersRow row = adapter.GetDataByCustomerID(customerId)[0];
            return row;
        }
    }
}
```

This makes the code much more readable. The only downside to this approach is that the alias will have to be added to every individual source file where you want to use this shorthand notation. There is no clean and maintainable way to do this at a global scope level, because you would inevitably run into naming scope conflicts.

Where Are We?

In this chapter you learned about the strong Visual Studio support for creating typed data set definitions, as well as data access code in the form of table adapters that work with those data set definitions and fill and update them from their data source. You saw that you can use the data set designer directly to create definitions of tables from Server Explorer, and that you can add new tables and columns manually from the designer Toolbox. You also learned that you can define additional queries that are exposed as methods on the table adapters, so that your table adapters can provide most of the data access functionality you need in a data access layer without having to write any code.

Some key takeaways from this chapter are:

* Favor using typed data sets when you know the data schema at design time.
* Place your data access code (including typed data sets) in a separate class library, not in your Windows Forms project, for a decoupled, layered architecture.
* Dragging tables, stored procedures, or views from Server Explorer onto the data set designer generates typed data table classes and corresponding table adapters. Those table adapters can be used for strongly typed retrieval and updating of data from the tables.
* Add queries to your table adapters through the designer's Add Query context menu.
* Extend the partial classes created for data sets, table adapters, tables, or rows to add custom functionality that won't be destroyed if you need to regenerate the data set definition.

Now that you are well armed to create and use typed data sets, you are ready to launch into the real meat of this book—data binding.

■ 3 ■
Introducing Data Binding in Windows Forms

T HE PREVIOUS CHAPTER showed you how to define and use typed data sets and table adapters for getting data into your Windows Forms application. Now we'll get into the details of data binding to give you a solid foundation for understanding the rest of the material in the book.

In the past, developers often had to write a lot of custom code to present data and to take user input and put it into an underlying data source. At some point people realized it would make a lot more sense to encapsulate that functionality within the user interface framework, and automatic data binding was born. This chapter gives a quick introduction on how to bind sources of data to user interface controls in Windows Forms. It starts with the high-level concepts behind data binding introduced in Chapter 1 and dives a little deeper into each one, including how to set up data binding from code for various types of data-bound controls using `Binding` objects and the new `BindingSource` component, which is one of the most important additions to Windows Forms data binding in .NET 2.0.

The 40,000-Foot View of Data Binding

Data binding is a mechanism for automatically associating and synchronizing data objects in memory with controls for presenting and managing that data in the user interface. You can use data binding to make an association between a data source and a control, and then leave it to the control to figure out how to display the data. This leads to better encapsulation of the code required to display and manage the bound data, and also gives a consistent approach to data binding that can be implemented once in a base class and reused by any derived classes.

Data binding can assume different forms, depending on the data source and type of control that presents the data. As discussed in Chapter 1, this is data in the presentation tier, so the data sources being referred to are client-side data types, such as data sets and object collections.

Data Binding Concepts

Keep the following two concepts in mind when you think about data binding:

- The *direction* that data flows between data sources and the data-bound controls
- *When* the data flows

In **one-way data binding**, data flows only in one direction: values from properties of the data source are placed into properties on the user interface control, but there is no flow of data back from the control to the data source if those property values change within the control, at least not automatically.

In **two-way data binding**, changes to the bound properties of a control also result in those changed values updating the corresponding data source values in the object in memory on the client. Most data-binding mechanisms in Windows Forms are designed to be two-way. You present data in user interface controls that comes from a data source, but if changes are made to the control property values through user interaction with the control, you want those changes to be reflected in the underlying data source as well. The idea of two-way data binding is to have this happen without needing to write a bunch of code yourself that collects those changes and makes the updates.

The other aspect to consider is at what point in the execution of your program the data flows from the data source to the control, and back to the data source from the control if you have two-way data binding. To have data flow in a program, there has to be some executing code that makes it flow. There could be several different triggers:

- The line of code establishing the data binding was just executed.
- A line of code was called that tells the control, the data source, or the data-binding mechanism itself to refresh itself.
- An event handler is called because of a change in the data source or the control values.

Depending on the data-binding mechanism and the data sources and controls involved, these things may happen implicitly behind the scenes in base class or Framework code, or they may need to be invoked explicitly at points in the program where you need the data to flow. Understanding when the data is expected to flow based on the controls and mechanisms you are using is crucial to getting the data-binding mechanism to behave the way you expect.

There are two primary forms of data binding built into .NET Framework control classes: simple and complex data binding. **Simple data binding** maps a property on a control (or more accurately, a property on a component that implements `IBindableComponent`) to a property in a data source item:

```
Binding bind = new Binding("Text", m_CustomerCollection,
    "CompanyName", true);
m_TextBox.DataBindings.Add(bind);
```

The `Binding` object maps the `Text` property on a `TextBox` control to the `CompanyName` property on the current item within the `m_Customer-Collection` list data source. That `Binding` object is then added to the collection of data bindings for the control. Simple data binding isn't limited to any one property, and in general it can be used for binding any control property.

Complex data binding is list-based binding—a list of data items (a collection object that implements the IList interface) is bound to a control for presentation of more than one item at a time. Complex data binding typically uses a DataSource property to map the list to the control:

```
m_CustomersGrid.DataSource = m_CustomersCollection;
```

The names "simple" and "complex" don't necessarily indicate the diffi-cultly of using the two mechanisms; they are more an indication of the complexity of the data that is being bound. In fact, for routine cases, complex data binding requires about the same amount of code as simple data binding. The rich data-binding support built into the Windows Forms controls, combined with the powerful code generation support provided by the Visual Studio designer, makes presenting data through data-bound controls easier than it ever has been.

.NET Framework 2.0 Data Binding Enhancements

.NET Framework 1.0 introduced a number of data-binding mechanisms that still are valid in .NET 2.0. The Control base class (from which every Windows Forms control derives) implements IBindableComponent, which exposes a collection of data bindings that let you tie properties of that control to data source properties, as described earlier when I defined **simple data binding**. Additionally, some Windows Forms controls that support complex binding allow you to set other properties that determine what portion of the list is presented. For example, on a ComboBox control you can set a DisplayMember property to tell the control what property on the data items in the DataSource list it should use for displaying each item. You can also specify a ValueMember property that tells the control which property on the data items to track along with the display member. This latter value is often used to hold the primary key or object reference to the data item so that it can be used for subsequent queries or updates. Listing 3.1 demonstrates setting up data binding for a ComboBox.

LISTING 3.1: ComboBox Data Binding

```
public partial class MyForm : Form
{
    ComboBox m_Combo = new ComboBox();
    public void OnFormLoad(object sender, EventArgs args)
    {
        CustomersDataSet dataSource = new CustomersDataSet();
        CustomersTableAdapter adapter = new CustomersTableAdapter();
        adapter.Fill(dataSource);
        m_Combo.DataSource = dataSource.Customers;
        m_Combo.DisplayMember = "CompanyName";
        m_Combo.ValueMember = "CustomerID";
    }
}
```

Listing 3.1 sets the `DataSource` property on a `ComboBox` control to the `Customers` table within a typed data set, which implements the `IList` interface and is the complex binding data source. The `DisplayMember` property takes the name of the property (or column in the case of a data table) whose value will be extracted for each item in the list and displayed in the `ComboBox` as text. The `ValueMember` identifies an additional field that keeps the value for each item displayed in the `ComboBox`. In this case, the code points the `ValueMember` property to the `CustomerID` column, so this primary key value can be used to select the appropriate row from the database or data set when the user has selected an item in the `ComboBox`.

Another capability available since .NET 1.0 is that container controls include something called a `BindingContext`. This keeps track of all the data sources within the container that are bound to the container's controls, and ensures that changes within the individual controls and the data source are synchronized correctly.

Unfortunately, .NET 1.X had a lot of unnecessary complexity in how these mechanisms got surfaced to the programmer, and that made Windows Forms data binding a fairly painful process. While NET 1.X made it very easy to do some simple things—much more so than with UI technologies that preceded .NET—when you started trying to code slightly more complicated and real-world data-presentation scenarios, it was often difficult to get things to work consistently and correctly. This has been a major focus area for improvement in .NET 2.0, and things have gotten a lot better, both for the programmer and for the end user. Some of the data-binding improvements in .NET 2.0 include

- More of the complexity has been hidden from you unless you really need it.
- There are more options and flexibility.
- The code that you do need to write is more intuitive.
- You get more consistent results.

The designer does most of the grunt work for you, letting you use gestures and interactions with design-time UI to generate all the appropriate data-binding code for you. However, before you start to rely on the designer without understanding what it is doing for you, I will cover how things work at the code level.

Binding Data Collections to a Grid

One of the most common and visually satisfying things to do with data binding is to have a set of data presented in a grid. Most applications that deal with data need to present a collection of data in a grid so the user can see a summarized, compact view of that data. From there, the application may let users select individual rows and act upon them in some way. For now, we will just focus on the first step: taking a collection of data and presenting it in a tabular form to the user.

To present data in a tabular fashion, you need two things. First, you need the data that you want to present. The examples in this chapter use strongly typed data sets from the NorthwindDataAccess class library created in Chapter 2. The other thing you need is a control capable of presenting the data in a tabular form. In Windows Forms 2.0, you use the `DataGridView` control any time you want to present tabular data.

Let's take a quick look at the code required to present a data table within the `DataGridView` control. The code in Listing 3.2 is from a form's load event handler:

LISTING 3.2: DataGridView Data Binding

```
private void OnFormLoad(object sender, EventArgs e)
{
    CustomersDataSet nwData = CustomersDataSet.GetCustomers();
    m_CustomersGrid.DataSource = nwData.Customers;
}
```

As you can see, you need to obtain the data set from your data access layer and set the `DataSource` property on the grid to the desired table within the data set. This example uses a strongly typed data set, so you just set the `DataSource` property on the grid to the table reference returned from the `Customers` property on the data set. This property returns a `CustomersDataTable` reference, which is simply a derived class from `DataTable` (as discussed in Chapter 2). All it takes is those two lines of code—and the code in the data access layer to create and populate the data set—to have a rich presentation of data as shown in Figure 3.1. However, as you will see a little later in this chapter, you should never bind your controls directly to a data source like this in .NET 2.0; you should bind your controls to a `BindingSource` component, and bind the binding source to the data source.

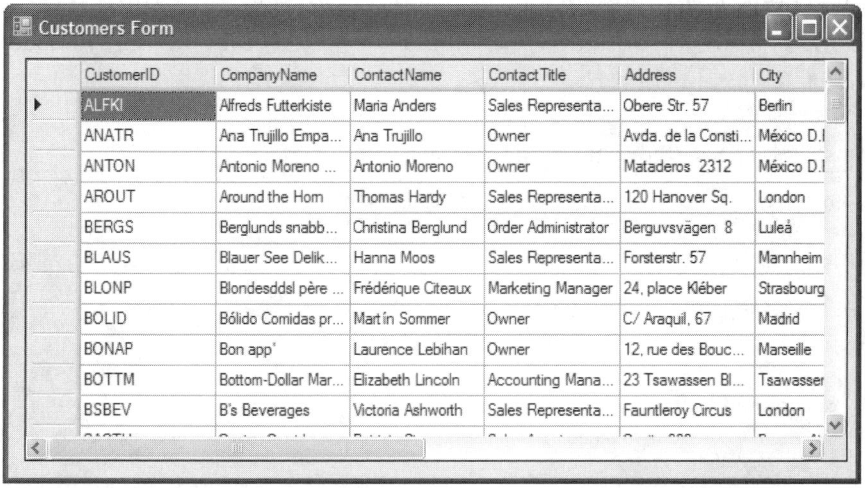

FIGURE 3.1: Presenting Bound Data in a Form

Binding Data Collections to Multi-Valued Controls

Another common scenario is to populate a list box or combo box from a property within a collection of data. Listing 3.1 showed an example of this. The code to bind a combo box or list box isn't all that different from the code to bind a collection of data to a grid. The difference lies in how you specify which property within the collection to use for presentation in the control (the `DisplayMember`), and which property to hold onto for each item as an associated value (the `ValueMember`).

The value of the property set as the `ValueMember` for the current item in the combo box or list box is accessible through the `SelectedValue` property on the control at runtime. For example, take a look at the form in Figure 3.2.

FIGURE 3.2: ComboBox SelectedValue Sample

If you hooked up the combo boxes and text boxes on this form as shown in Listing 3.3, the `SelectedValue` property on the combo boxes are used to drive the contents of the text boxes.

LISTING 3.3: Using SelectedValue from a Data-Bound ComboBox

```
public partial class SelectedValueForm : Form
{
   public SelectedValueForm()
   {
      InitializeComponent();
   }

   private void OnFormLoad(object sender, EventArgs e)
   {
      // Get the data
      m_CustomersDataSet = CustomersDataSet.GetCustomers();
      // Set up the bindings for the combo boxes
```

```
    m_CompanyNameCombo.DataSource = m_CustomersDataSet.Customers;
    m_CompanyNameCombo.DisplayMember = "CompanyName";
    m_CompanyNameCombo.ValueMember = "CustomerID";

    m_ContactNameCombo.DataSource = m_CustomersDataSet.Customers;
    m_ContactNameCombo.DisplayMember = "ContactName";
    m_ContactNameCombo.ValueMember = "Phone";

    // Hook up event handlers for selection change events
    m_CompanyNameCombo.SelectedIndexChanged
        += OnComboSelectionChanged;
}

private void OnComboSelectionChanged(object sender, EventArgs args)
{
    if (m_ContactNameCombo.SelectedValue == null ||
      m_CompanyNameCombo.SelectedValue == null)
        return;

    m_CustomerIDTextBox.Text =
        m_CompanyNameCombo.SelectedValue.ToString();
    m_ContactPhoneTextBox.Text =
        m_ContactNameCombo.SelectedValue.ToString();
}
}
```

In this example, the combo boxes are bound to the Customers table in the typed data set. The DisplayMember for each will show the Company-Name and ContactName properties (columns), respectively, as the text in the combo box for each item in the Customers table. Additionally, the ValueMember for the first combo box is set to the CustomerID property, and the second combo box is set to the Phone property. By doing this, the SelectedValue property on the combo box will give you back the value of the ValueMember property on the currently selected item in the combo box whenever it is called. In the code in Listing 3.3, the SelectedValue property for each of the combo boxes is accessed in an event handler for the SelectedIndexChanged event on the combo box, and it is used to set the Text property on the corresponding text boxes.

This same functionality could have been achieved better by simply data binding the text boxes as well, but the intent in this code was to demonstrate using the SelectedValue property and to show how it relates to the ValueMember. Instead of using the SelectedValue to populate a text box, a more common usage would be to perform a lookup query against the database for the `CustomerID` contained in the `SelectedValue` for the first combo box. You would typically do something like this if you have a large data set that you don't want to hold in memory just to display a single column in a combo box or list box, but you want to get the full row corresponding to a selection to act on it in your code.

Binding Data to Individual Controls on a Form

Another kind of data binding that you will commonly want to do is to bind properties on data items in a collection of data to properties on individual controls on a form. As mentioned earlier, this form of data binding is called simple data binding. To perform simple data binding, you use the `DataBindings` collection that every control inherits from the `Control` base class implementation of `IBindableComponent`. The `DataBindings` property exposes a collection of `Binding` objects, each of which represents an individual association between a data member within a data source and a property on the control itself.

A straightforward example of using simple data binding is to bind individual columns within a table to the `Text` property of `TextBox` or `Label` controls on a form, so the presented text in those controls shows the values from the current row of data in the table. If we extend the example shown in Figure 3.1 and add a set of text boxes to the form below the grid using the designer, we can add data binding so those text boxes will show the contents of some of the columns of the current row in the Customers table (see Listing 3.4).

LISTING 3.4: TextBox Data Bindings

```
private void AddTextBoxDataBindings(CustomersDataSet nwData)
{
   DataTable table = nwData.Customers;
   m_CustomerIDTextBox.DataBindings.Add("Text", table,
      "CustomerID", true);
   m_CompanyNameTextBox.DataBindings.Add("Text", table,
      "CompanyName", true);
   m_ContactNameTextBox.DataBindings.Add("Text", table,
      "ContactName", true);
   m_ContactPhoneTextBox.DataBindings.Add("Text", table,
      "Phone", true);
}
```

This code adds a new entry in the `DataBindings` collection for each of a series of text boxes on the form. The `DataBinding` property exposes a reference to an object of type `ControlBindingsCollection`. This collection class exposes an overloaded `Add` method that allows you to set up each data binding in a single line of code by providing the four parameters shown in Listing 3.4. This method constructs a `Binding` object under the covers and passes the parameters to its constructor, and then adds the `Binding` object to the `DataBindings` collection for the control.

- The first parameter to the `Add` method is the name of the property on the control that you want to bind to; it can be any of the public properties exposed on the control. In Listing 3.4, all of the bindings are created against the `Text` property of the `TextBox` controls.

- The second parameter is the data source containing the data you are binding to, and could be one of the many forms of data collections discussed in the Data Sources section of Chapter 1. It can also be a reference to a single data object. In this code example, the data source is the same for each of the bindings. The code first stores the table reference in a local variable of type `DataTable`, and then passes that local variable as the data source argument to the `Add` method.

- The third parameter to the `Add` method in Listing 3.4 is the name of the data member within the data source. This parameter can take on a number of forms, depending on what the data source is and where the data member can be found within that data source. This code example just specifies the column name, because the data source is the table that contains that column.

- The last parameter, which is set to `true` for each of the bindings, is a flag to indicate whether to automatically format the displayed values. The next chapter discusses automatic and custom formatting in detail, but in general this should always be turned on.

If you run the SimpleNorthwindClient sample application from the download code, you will see the application shown in Figure 3.1 with the text boxes and a combo box added. The data is bound to the grid, combo box, and text boxes using code similar to that shown in Listing 3.2, 3.3, and

3.4. If you click on different rows in the grid, you'll see that the content of the text boxes also automatically updates to reflect the contents of the bound fields in the data set based on the row that was selected. If you change the contents of one of the fields displayed in the text boxes and click on a different row in the grid, you'll see that the changes you entered in the text box automatically change the contents of the underlying data source and update the grid display of that same data. Wow! How the heck did that happen? We didn't write any code to keep the data in the grid and the data in the text boxes synchronized, or to propagate changes from the UI controls back into the underlying data source.

Well, that is part of the "magic" of the two-way complex data-binding mechanisms in Windows Forms. As mentioned earlier, when you set up a simple data binding between a control property and a data member within a data source, the control property would be set to the current item's bound property value. Any changes made to the bound control property (`Text` in the case of the text boxes) will also be automatically pushed into the underlying data source when focus leaves the control. Things are a little more complex for a grid, but the same basic process happens if you think of each cell within the grid being a control itself.

You might be wondering how the controls determine what the current item is within the collection. This is discussed later in this chapter, but the short answer is that something called a `CurrencyManager` for each list-based data source keeps track of what the current item is within the collection. The bound controls know about their own currency manager and can subscribe to an event raised by the currency manager when the current item changes. When that notification occurs, the bound controls can update their presentation of the data based on the contents of the new current item.

Data Paths Within Data Sources

Data sources specified in Windows Forms data binding are treated as hierarchical sources. The top-level object is a container for other collections of data (for example, data tables in a data set), and the collections themselves are containers for individual data items (the rows within a data table in a data set). Each data item then has values for each property in the object (the column values within the row). The data source can be even simpler: it could be an object containing properties, or it could be a simple array of objects. When dealing with custom object collections as your sources of data, the levels in the hierarchy can be arbitrarily deep. You could have a top-level object, Company, that contains a collection of Employees; each Employee could contain collections of Jobs, Tasks, and Contacts, as well as data items specific to the Employee; and each of the child collections could contain collections or data items themselves. To handle all these situations, data sources are treated as hierarchies, and a path syntax is used to specify data sources and data members. This accommodates specifying the exact location in a hierarchy of data where the desired collection, item, or value resides.

When I bound the TextBox controls to the data source in Listing 3.4, I specified the data source as the Customers table within the data set, and then I specified the data member as the column name within that table. You could also set the data source to the data set itself instead of the contained data table. But if you did that, you would also need to modify the way you specified the data member, because the data member represents a relative path within the data source hierarchy to the particular data object or value to which you are binding.

So an alternate approach to setting the text box data bindings could look like the code in Listing 3.5.

LISTING 3.5: Modified TextBox Data Bindings

```
private void AddTextBoxDataBindings(CustomersDataSet nwData)
{
    // Alternative approach:
    m_CustomerIDTextBox.DataBindings.Add("Text", nwData,
        "Customers.CustomerID", true);
    m_CompanyNameTextBox.DataBindings.Add("Text", nwData,
        "Customers.CompanyName", true);
    m_ContactNameTextBox.DataBindings.Add("Text", nwData,
        "Customers.ContactName", true);
    m_PhoneTextBox.DataBindings.Add("Text", nwData,
        "Customers.Phone", true);
}
```

In this case, since the data source is the data set itself, you have to specify the column to bind to by prefacing the column name with the table name, separated with a dot in the same way you use a dot with members of types in .NET code.

If you made just this change in the SimpleNorthwindClient sample application and ran it again, the data in the text boxes would initially present the data for the first row just fine. But if you clicked on another row in the grid, you would see that the text boxes no longer updated properly—because even though both the grid and the text boxes are working against the same underlying data source (the instance of the Customers-DataSet), the way that data source has been specified to the data-binding mechanisms was different for each of the two controls. For the grid, the data source was specified to be the Customers table within the data set. Effectively, the data member for the grid is empty or null because it wasn't specified, but now the data source for the text boxes is the data set itself, not the table within it.

This is an important concept that has tripped up a lot of developers when dealing with complex data-binding scenarios and trying to keep bound controls synchronized with one another. The data binding mechanisms create a separate synchronization object (either a CurrencyManager for list data sources or a PropertyManager for individual object data sources) for each data source that is specified. But even if two bindings use the same underlying logical data source, if that data source is specified differently between two bindings, then they will have separate synchronization objects created for each way the data source is specified, and you won't get synchronization as you might expect it.

To remedy that problem for the situation just described, all you need to do is be consistent in the way you specify your data sources and data members, and you should get nice synchronized behavior between controls that are bound to the same data source.

However, the recommended practice is to set your data source at the list level and to avoid compound data members (e.g., Customers.Phone). One exception to this would be if you are setting up data binding to a complex object that holds a single complex child object. For example, consider a Customer object that has an Address property on it. The Address property exposes a complex type instance with properties of City, State, and

Specify Data Sources and Data Members Consistently

It is important to specify your data sources and data members for bound controls on a form *consistently*. If you specify data sources using different reference types between different bound controls, you won't get synchronized updating of the controls when the current row selection changes on the form.

so on for that instance. In this case, you might use a compound data member for binding to a single `Customer` object's address information. You would probably set the data source to the `Customer` object, but then you might set a data member to `Address.City` if you were data binding to that piece of information within the `Customer` object.

If you wanted to violate this guidance and specify data bindings for your text boxes using the form just shown, but still wanted the text boxes to be synchronized with the data bound to the grid, then you'd also need to specify the data source and data member for the grid consistently. You would need to modify the form load event handler code to look like this instead:

```
private void OnFormLoad(object sender, EventArgs e)
{
    CustomersDataSet nwData = CustomersDataSet.GetCustomers();
    // Alternative approach:
    m_CustomersGrid.DataSource = nwData;
    m_CustomersGrid.DataMember = "Customers";
}
```

If you added this change in addition to the one shown in Listing 3.5 for the text boxes, you could run the application again and select rows in the grid, and the contents of the text boxes would be updated with each row selection in the grid as before.

Because the data sources are now specified to be exactly the same object reference (the data set), only one synchronization object gets created and used for all of the controls. Whereas the now-obsolete `DataGrid` control could be bound to a data set and it would present a hierarchical way of navigating the tables contained within the data set, the `DataGridView` control is designed to only be bound to a single list at a time. If you set the `DataSource` property on a `DataGridView` to a data set without specifying a table within that data set as the `DataMember` property, the grid will remain blank.

Synchronizing Data Between Controls

Let's take another look at what is going on when you bind a control or multiple controls to a set of data on a form. As mentioned earlier, when you create the data bindings, the form itself creates some synchronization objects to manage the fact that you may have multiple controls on the form bound to the same data source, and that you (probably) want them to be synchronized.

The form itself has a `BindingContext` property that holds a collection of synchronization objects for each data source that is being used for data binding on the form. For the most part in .NET 2.0, you don't have to deal directly with the binding context in your code, but it is still lurking under the covers making things work. (In .NET 1.X, you had to go through the binding context to get to the synchronization objects for a number of scenarios.) As discussed in the previous section, what gets created behind the scenes are instances of a `CurrencyManager` for list-based data sources or a `PropertyManager` for individual custom business objects. Each of these classes derives from `BindingManagerBase`, which is the type of object reference that the `BindingContext` is designed to contain. The `Currency-Manager` is the one you will deal with most often.

A container component (such as a `Form` or a `BindingSource`) creates a currency manager for each list-based data source that you specify for a control on a form, and it is added to the binding context for the form. The currency manager keeps track of both the underlying data source that controls are bound to and the controls that are bound to that data. You can use the currency manager to access the underlying data that is bound to controls, determine what the current row or object is, and change that current row and affect all of the controls that are bound to it. The currency manager notifies bound controls when items are added, removed, or changed in the bound collection, and controls can use these notifications to refresh their display of the data source.

Smarter Data Containment

So far we have been dealing exclusively with individual controls on a form and binding data sources directly to those controls. In .NET 1.X, this was basically the only way to do it. However, one problem with this approach is that if the underlying data source for multiple bound controls had to change at runtime, you had to write some code to reset the data source for each of the controls. Additionally, if you needed to figure out what the current item was in a bound collection or receive notifications when that data source changed, you had to dive deep into the guts of the form through the binding context to get access to the synchronization objects.

In .NET 2.0, the `BindingSource` component solves these problems. A **binding source** acts as a proxy between bound controls and their associated data source. It provides one-stop shopping for accessing or managing the data-binding context for one or more controls on a form. You bind controls on a form to a binding source, and then you bind the binding source to a data source. If you need to change the data source that controls are bound to, you only have to change the `DataSource` and `DataMember` properties on the binding source; all the controls bound to it will automatically update. If you need to know the current item in a data source, you can get it directly through the binding source. If you want to change the current item programmatically, the binding source exposes methods and properties to do so; if you want to be notified of changes in the data source, the binding source exposes events that you can subscribe to. The relationships between a binding source, bound controls, and a data source are depicted in Figure 3.3.

If we combined the code from Listings 3.2, 3.3, and 3.4 to hook up all the data bindings for a grid, combo box, and text boxes in one example, add a binding source to the form, and change the controls so they are bound to

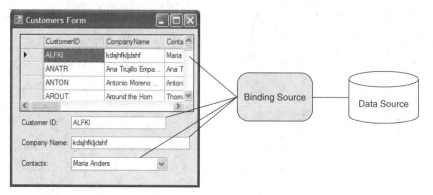

FIGURE 3.3: Data Binding Through a BindingSource

the binding source instead of the underlying data source, the code would look like this:

```
private void OnFormLoad(object sender, EventArgs e)
{
    CustomersDataSet nwData = CustomersDataSet.GetCustomers();
    m_CustomersGrid.DataSource = m_CustomersBindingSource;
    m_CustomersBindingSource.DataSource = nwData.Customers;
    AddTextBoxDataBindings(); // uses the binding source
    AddComboBoxDataBindings(); // uses the binding source
}
```

Now all it would take to change the bindings of all the controls is to set the `DataSource` property on the binding source object to some other collection, and all controls that are bound to the binding source would automatically update to the new data source. For example, you might retrieve a filtered list of customers from the data access layer and want to bind that new list to the same set of controls. If you are going to swap out a data source like this, the shape of the new data source (the schema) will have to be the same as the original data source if the controls are bound to specific properties on the contained items. For example, the `AddTextBoxData-Bindings` helper method adds data bindings for each text box to the `CompanyName` column, `ContactName` column, and so on. If you set the data source of the binding source to a collection of orders instead of customers, these data bindings would be broken—they wouldn't be able to find the bound properties in the new collection of data items, so they would throw exceptions.

I will discuss in greater depth throughout the book the many ways the `BindingSource` component comes into play in data-binding scenarios. In general, you should always use binding sources between your bound controls and their data sources, even if you don't anticipate changing the data source dynamically at runtime. The `BindingSource` also exposes functionality for controlling the current record in the data source and for monitoring changes in the data source through a set of events raised by the binding source.

Paging Through Data

Another common requirement is the need to be able to change the current record in a set of data programmatically, or in response to a user interaction that is outside of a data grid. In .NET 1.X, the way to do this was rather obscure: you had to obtain a reference to the `CurrencyManager` object for the data source you were working with, and then had to update the `Position` property on that object to change the current record:

```
private void SetNextRecord11Style()
{
    CurrencyManager currMgr =
        BindingContext[m_CustomersDataSet.Customers]
        as CurrencyManager;
    currMgr.Position++;
}
```

This mechanism still exists for backward compatibility and still works. However, as mentioned earlier, you should always favor binding your data-bound controls to a binding source. If you do so, the binding source itself contains a currency manager, and it exposes an easy-to-use API for controlling the current record position within the underlying data source.

The `BindingSource` class has a set of methods for explicitly navigating through the data source. The `MoveNext`, `MovePrevious`, `MoveFirst`, and `MoveLast` methods perform exactly what you would expect them to for positioning the current record within the data source. There is also a `Position` property exposed that lets you explicitly set the current position to an ordinal record number. In addition to these methods and the property, a series of events are raised whenever the position or data source changes; this allows other objects that may not be bound directly to the binding source or container to be notified when position changes occur so that they can react accordingly in their event handlers.

Using this functionality, programmatically moving to the next record is as simple as the following code:

```
m_CustomersBindingSource.Position += 1;
// or:
m_CustomersBindingSource.MoveNext();
```

The downloadable sample code contains an application called Paging-Sample that demonstrates both the basic use of the BindingSource for wiring a data source to bound controls, and the manual control of paging through a collection of data using the binding source. This application is shown in Figure 3.4.

In the PagingSample application, the m_CustomersBindingSource binding source was added to the form from the Toolbox without using any of the designer support for connecting it to a data source. The code once again uses the data access layer from Chapter 2 to get a data set containing customer data and sets the Customers table as the data source for the

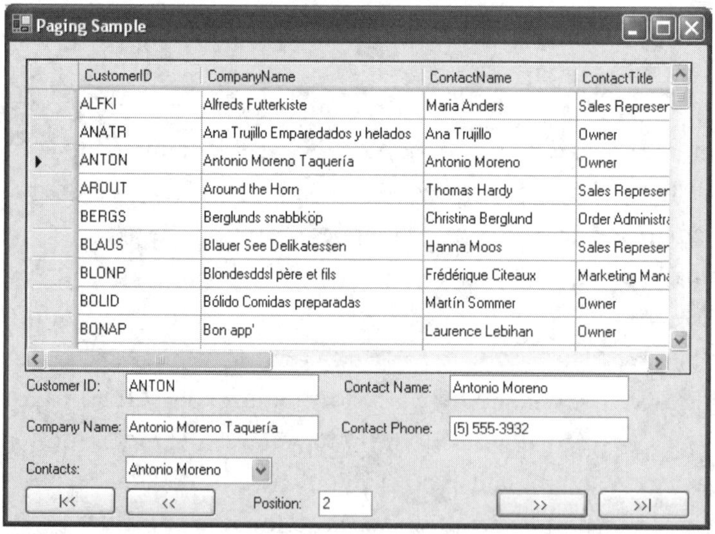

FIGURE 3.4: PagingSample Application

binding source. It then sets the data source for the grid, text boxes, and combo box to the binding source as shown in Listing 3.6.

LISTING 3.6: Connecting Data Sources to Controls with a BindingSource

```
private void OnFormLoad(object sender, EventArgs e)
{
    // Set up event handlers for connector position changed
    // and text box text changed events
    m_CustomersBindingSource.PositionChanged += OnPositionChanged;
    m_PositionTextBox.TextChanged += OnPositionTextChanged;
    // Set up data bindings
    CustomersDataSet nwData = CustomersDataSet.GetCustomers();
    m_CustomersGrid.DataSource = m_CustomersBindingSource;
    m_CustomersBindingSource.DataSource = nwData.Customers;
    AddTextBoxDataBindings();
    AddComboBoxDataBindings();

}

private void AddTextBoxDataBindings()
{
    m_CustomerIDTextBox.DataBindings.Add("Text",
        m_CustomersBindingSource, "CustomerID");
    m_CompanyNameTextBox.DataBindings.Add("Text",
        m_CustomersBindingSource, "CompanyName");
    m_ContactNameTextBox.DataBindings.Add("Text",
        m_CustomersBindingSource, "ContactName");
    m_ContactPhoneTextBox.DataBindings.Add("Text",
        m_CustomersBindingSource, "Phone");
}

private void AddComboBoxDataBindings()
{
    m_ContactsCombo.DataSource = m_CustomersBindingSource;
    m_ContactsCombo.DisplayMember = "ContactName";
    m_ContactsCombo.ValueMember = "CustomerID";
}
```

In addition to loading the data and hooking up the data binding, the OnFormLoad method also subscribes methods of the form to a couple of events. The first is the PositionChanged event of the binding source. This event will fire any time the current record position changes within its underlying data source. The form also subscribes a method to the TextChanged event of the position text box shown in Figure 3.4. The event subscriptions for the Click event of the forward and backward control buttons aren't shown because they were created in the designer using the Events view of the Properties window. The event handlers for the control buttons and the two events just described are shown in Listing 3.7.

LISTING 3.7: Event Subscriptions for PagingSample

```csharp
private void OnFirstRecord(object sender, EventArgs e)
{
    m_CustomersBindingSource.MoveFirst();
}

private void OnPreviousRecord(object sender, EventArgs e)
{
    m_CustomersBindingSource.MovePrevious();
}

private void OnNextRecord(object sender, EventArgs e)
{
    m_CustomersBindingSource.MoveNext();
}

private void OnLastRecord(object sender, EventArgs e)
{
    m_CustomersBindingSource.MoveLast();
}

void OnPositionChanged(object sender, EventArgs e)
{
    m_PositionTextBox.Text =
        m_CustomersBindingSource.Position.ToString();
}

private void OnPositionTextChanged(object sender, EventArgs e)
{
    int enteredPos;
    bool success = int.TryParse(m_PositionTextBox.Text, out enteredPos);
    if (success)
    {
        m_CustomersBindingSource.Position = enteredPos;
    }
}
```

As you can see from the code, the buttons on the form used for selecting records simply call the Move*XXX* methods on the binding source and let it worry about incrementing or decrementing the position within the data source appropriately. When the binding source has done so, all controls bound to it will automatically update their displays because of the changed current record. In addition, the OnPositionChanged event handler method is called when the PositionChanged event is raised by the binding source. This method uses that event to update the position text box to the current record number. The OnPositionTextChanged handler lets the user enter a new record number in the position text box, and will use it to set the Position property of the binding source explicitly.

Note the use of the new TryParse method that has been added to all of the primitives in .NET 2.0. This method lets you try to parse a string into a value of that type, but avoids having an exception thrown if the parsing fails. The code uses TryParse to check in case the user enters an invalid number.

You probably wouldn't want to have to write this code every time you needed to change the current record programmatically, and you wouldn't be alone. As a result, another new control available in .NET 2.0 is the BindingNavigator control, which implements the paging functionality against a binding source for you. The binding navigator is just a specialized version of the new ToolStrip control in .NET 2.0 (see Appendix C for more about this control). As you can see in Figure 3.5, the binding navigator control simply encapsulates the functionality that we created manually in the last example. It has toolbar buttons for moving forward or back by one record, and for moving to the very first or last record. It also has an edit box to enter a position explicitly, like the position text box in Figure 3.4. It also has buttons for adding a new row, deleting the selected row, or saving the bound data source back to the data persistence layer. All it takes to get the binding navigator control hooked up is to add it to the form and set the BindingSource property to a reference to a binding source that is managing the data source for a set of controls on the form. The Save button in the BindingNavigator (indicated by a floppy disk icon) is disabled by default until you add some code to persist the changes in the data source to wherever it came from. You will see more examples using the Binding-Navigator throughout the rest of this book.

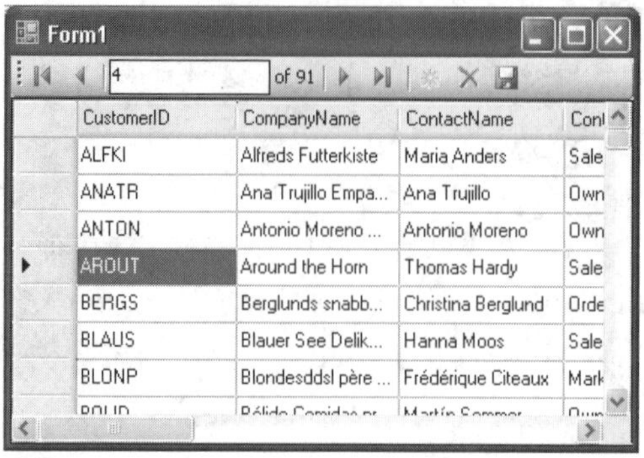

FIGURE 3.5: BindingNavigator Control in Action

Master-Details Data Binding

Often you will work with data collections that have parent-child relationships. For example, a Customer may have a collection of Orders that they have placed, and each Order will have a collection of Order Detail objects that describe the items in that Order. In this situation, you often want to provide users with a way to view the collection of parent objects, and when they select a parent object, for them to see just the associated child objects. This often involves two tables in a data set with foreign key relations providing the links between child rows and their respective parent row.

A common way to present this data and allow the user to navigate through it is to place the collection of parent objects in one grid (called the **master**), and display the set of related child objects in a second grid (called the **details**). You can easily accomplish this kind of data presentation using the Windows Forms `DataGridView` control and binding sources. To do this, you first need a data source that has the appropriate parent-child relations set up. Typically this is a data set with two (or more) tables in it that have a parent-child relation set up between the tables. You either do this manually using ADO.NET (described in Appendix D), or the data set designer will do it automatically for you when you add two related tables to a data set in the designer. You can also set up master-details binding with custom objects. To do so, each parent object must have a property that exposes a list (an implementation of `IList`) of related child objects.

Once you have a parent-child related set of data, you are ready to start hooking things up on the form. You can either read through these steps, or if you want to follow along, create a Windows Application project, and add two `DataGridView` controls, two `BindingSources`, and a `Binding-Navigator` to the form. One grid is for the parent collection of data; the other is for the related child rows of data. In the MasterDetailsSample application in the download code, this data comes from the Customers and Orders tables, respectively. The first binding source is just for populating the parent grid with the Customers data, much like you have seen in previous examples.

1. Set the `DataSource` property on the binding source to the data set containing the Customers and Orders tables.

2. Set the `DataMember` property on the binding source to "Customers" to identify the table within that data set by name.

3. Set the `DataSource` properties on the grids to their respective binding sources.

4. When you hook up the child grid, you still just set the `DataSource` property on the grid to its respective binding source, called `m_ChildOrdersBindingSource` in the MasterDetailsSample.

   The trick to making the master-details scenario work is that you set the `DataSource` property on the child binding source to the parent binding source, which is the `m_CustomersBindingSource` in the sample code. You then specify the name of the data relation that relates the parent rows to the child rows as the `DataMember` property for the child binding source, which is "FK_Orders_Customers" in the following sample:

```
private void OnFormLoad(object sender, EventArgs e)
{
    // Get the data set with parent / child tables into a data set
    CustomersDataSet customers = CustomersDataSet.GetCustomers();

    // Set up the data sources normally for the first grid
    m_CustomersBindingSource.DataSource = customers;
    m_CustomersBindingSource.DataMember = "Customers";
    m_CustomersGrid.DataSource = m_CustomersBindingSource;
```

```
    // Set up the data sources for the child source to point to
    // the parent source, and the contained relation
    m_ChildOrdersBindingSource.DataSource = m_CustomersBindingSource;
    m_ChildOrdersBindingSource.DataMember = "FK_Orders_Customers";

    // Child grid to child connector
    m_OrdersGrid.DataSource = m_ChildOrdersBindingSource;

    // Navigator to parent connector
    m_BindingNavigator.BindingSource = m_CustomersBindingSource;
}
```

That's all there is to it. The chaining of a child binding source to a parent binding source automatically synchronizes the current row in the parent collection to the set of related child rows in the child collection. You can see this application in action in Figure 3.6.

Updating Data Sources Through Data Binding

As you saw in Listing 3.4, when you have controls bound to a data source in Windows Forms, you can get automatic updating of the underlying

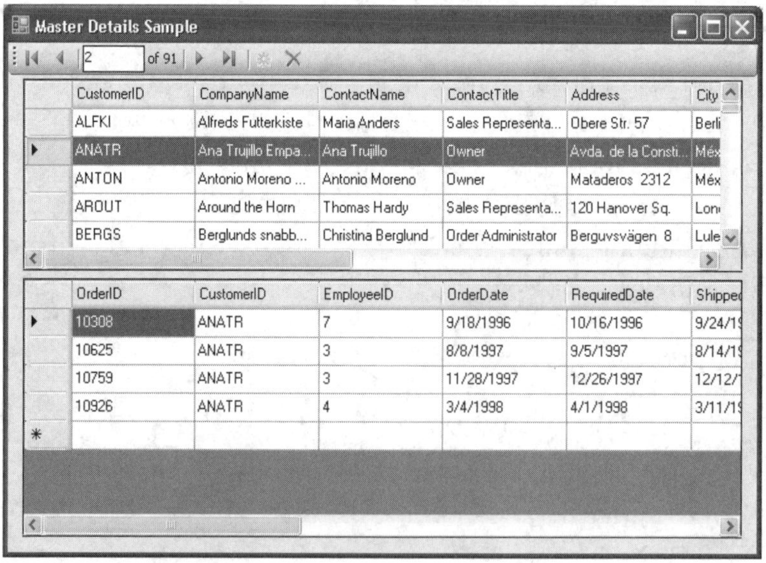

FIGURE 3.6: Master-Details Sample in Action

data source in memory (two-way data binding) if changes are made through the bound controls. This is true whether the data source is bound to a grid or to individual controls, such as text boxes, that let the user change the presented data values. The data source has to support certain interfaces to allow changes made in the bound control to be propagated into the underlying data source. Those interfaces and the requirements for implementing them is covered in Chapter 7; for now, just focus on the use of data sets, which implement all of the interfaces required for both simple and complex data binding, and for updating of the data set with changes made in the bound controls.

A number of things happen when a user makes a change to a control bound to a data source, such as a `TextBox`. First, events fire from the control itself based on the user's interaction with the control. Usually the action that gets the ball rolling is that the user changes a value, such as the text in a `TextBox` control, and then tabs out of the control or clicks on some other control, resulting in a change of focus on the form. The series of events that fire in response to that action depend on which action the user takes, what control the user changed, what property on that control changed, and where the focus is switching to.

Validation is discussed more in Chapter 10, but the bottom line is that if a control supports both data binding and editing the values presented (as do the `DataGridView`, `TextBox`, and most controls in Windows Forms), then any changes the user makes to the presented data will be automatically pushed down into the bound data source when the focus is lost by that control. There is no additional code to show you for this capability, because it is an inherent part of the bindings that you set up to display the data in the first place. As soon as the focus has switched to another control, any edits in the previous control are written to the data source used to bind the control.

However, if you want to persist those changes from the bound data source to its storage layer, then you need to write the appropriate data access code to do so. You typically do this in response to the user clicking a toolbar button, menu item, or button on the form, and you just need to call `Update` on the appropriate table adapter. The following example shows the update code the designer generates for the Save button on the `BindingNavigator`:

```
private void bindingNavigatorSaveItem_Click(object sender,
    EventArgs e)
{
    if (this.Validate())
    {
        m_CustomersBindingSource.EndEdit();
        m_CustomersTableAdapter.Update(m_NorthwindDataSet.Customers);
    }
    else
    {
        MessageBox.Show(this, "Validation errors occurred.", "Save",
            MessageBoxButtons.OK, MessageBoxIcon.Warning);
    }
}
```

The call to `Validate` ensures that validation occurs on the last control that had the focus. The call to `EndEdit` completes any changes made to the current data source item if that object supports transactional updates through the `IEditableObject` interface (discussed in Chapters 7 and 9). Finally, the call to `Update` on the table adapter iterates through any modified, deleted, or added rows in the `Customers` table and executes the appropriate commands in the table adapter to persist those changes to the database.

Where Are We?

In this chapter, you stepped through the basic mechanisms and code for creating two-way data binding between data sources and controls in a Windows Forms application. Thanks to the rich support for data binding embedded in the controls themselves, as well as the support provided by the form and `Binding` and `BindingSource` objects, you only have to write a miniscule amount of code to get rich data-bound scenarios running. And as you saw at the beginning of Chapter 1, you can often avoid writing even that miniscule amount of code for simple situations because the designer will write it all for you.

Some key takeaways from this chapter are:

- `Binding` objects set up a two-way data binding between a single property on a control and a single property on the data items in a collection.
- The `BindingSource` component acts as a proxy between bound controls and their data sources. In .NET 2.0, you should always bind controls to binding sources, and binding sources to data sources.
- The `BindingSource` component lets you change the data source for bound controls without having to update the bindings for the individual controls, and also exposes a number of events that allow you to keep track of what is happening in the data source.
- To set up master-details data binding, you bind the parent control(s) to a binding source, bind the child control(s) to a second binding source, set the second binding source's `DataSource` property to the first binding source, and the `DataMember` to the child collection property within the parent data source.

The next chapter dives deeper into the capabilities of `BindingSources` and `Binding` objects, and shows how to tackle a variety of more complex data-binding scenarios by coding things up by hand.

■ 4 ■

Binding Controls to Data Sources

T HE PREVIOUS CHAPTER gave you a quick introduction to data binding in Windows Forms and a quick preview of using the new `BindingSource` component to provide looser coupling between data sources and data-bound controls. This chapter further explores using binding sources and binding objects, and the numerous examples of binding data to Windows Forms controls will help you learn to conquer even the most challenging data-binding scenario. This chapter covers using the `BindingSource` component to bind data to controls programmatically. Chapter 5 then shows you how to use the Data Sources window and the Windows Forms designer to automate much of that coding process for common scenarios.

Getting to Know the BindingSource Component

The `BindingSource` component solves a number of tricky problems that surfaced with the approach of directly binding data sources to controls in .NET 1.X. It provides a layer of indirection between a data source and bound controls that makes a number of things easier. Additionally, it surfaces important control points and access to the underlying data source in a way that saves you from having to delve into the data-binding mechanisms of a form the way you had to in the past. A binding source also gives you a single API to program against from the form's perspective, and lets a lot of your form code remain decoupled from the specific data source type. This prevents you from having to adapt your programmatic coding patterns to each different type of data that your application works with, whether they are data sets, data readers, custom business objects, arrays, or other types of data. The `BindingSource` component also exposes a rich set of events that you can tap into to respond to changes in the underlying data coming from other controls or code in your application. I'll be stepping through the use of all of these features throughout this chapter.

Simple Data Binding with Binding Sources

The simplest possible use of a binding source component is as an intermediary between the data you are using for display and the controls that display the data. Consider the simple form class shown in Listing 4.1.

LISTING 4.1: Binding a Grid Through a BindingSource Component

```
partial class CustomersForm : Form
{
   BindingSource m_CustomersBindingSource = new BindingSource();
   DataGridView m_Grid = new DataGridView();
   public CustomersForm()
   {
      InitializeComponent();
      m_Grid.Dock = DockStyle.Fill;
      this.Controls.Add(m_Grid);
      m_Grid.DataSource = m_CustomersBindingSource;
   }

   // Form.Load event handler
   private void OnFormLoad(object sender, EventArgs e)
   {
      CustomersTableAdapter adapter = new CustomersTableAdapter();
      CustomersDataSet.CustomersDataTable customers = adapter.GetData();
      m_CustomersBindingSource.DataSource = customers;
   }
}
```

This form contains a single grid named m_Grid, which has its Dock property set to Fill so that it fills the client area of the form. It also has a member binding source component, to which the grid is data bound. This can all be set up in the constructor, and is typically done by dragging and dropping both the grid and the binding source onto the form and setting the appropriate properties in the designer. However, for now, let's focus on how to do things without the magic of the designer.

In the event handler for the form load, the code retrieves the Customers data through a table adapter (as discussed in Chapter 2), and then sets the DataSource property on the binding source to the Customers table. Because the grid was already set up with its DataSource property referencing the binding source in the constructor, this is all that is required to load and present the Customers data in the grid.

▪ NOTE   Binding to a `DataTable` Really Binds to a `DataView`

When you bind to a data table within a data set, whether or not it's strongly typed, you are really binding to the default data view exposed by that table. Every table exposes a default data view (an instance of the DataView class), and that is what is really used for data binding.

You can also explicitly construct a data view for a data table and bind to that, which gives you the flexibility to filter or sort that view to alter the presentation of the data. Alternatively, you can filter and sort data through a BindingSource, as long as the underlying data collection implements the IBindingList interface.

To change which data is displayed on the grid, you just set the Data-Source property on the binding source member and the grid automatically updates. This may not seem like a big win if you only have one control on the form as in this example, but you'll appreciate this if you have numerous controls on a form all bound to the same data source, and you need to programmatically switch the data source. Picture a data input form where you are editing all the columns for a customer or employee record. In the days before binding sources, if you needed to change the data source that each control was bound to, that meant programmatically resetting the data source binding on each individual control. Now you just need to change it in one place—on the binding source—and all of the controls bound to the binding source automatically switch to using the new data source.

A common situation when you might do this is while working with custom business objects. In that case, you might not retrieve an entire collection of objects, such as customers, into memory at once. You might get them one at a time as needed for editing or viewing the customer details. For example, if you were binding a form with input controls for a customer object's individual properties so the user could edit that customer, you might query individually for customer objects based on their name or some identifier, and then you could update the data source for the binding source to be the retrieved customer object. For the user to edit a different customer, you would retrieve that object and set it as the data source for the binding source, and all the controls would update automatically to this new data source's contents.

Binding sources can also be shared by more than one form. For example, to provide a simple form to let users edit certain columns of a customer record when they double-click on the row in the grid in Listing 4.1, you could design a simple form that looks like Figure 4.1.

You could have this form take the customer ID as a constructor parameter, retrieve the data into the form, edit it, and then save the data back to the database. You would then also need to refresh the main form with the grid after this dialog completes to reflect the change to the underlying data

FIGURE 4.1: Customer Editing Form

source. Depending on whether the grid itself was editable, this approach could introduce concurrency problems even for a single user in your application, and it is certainly not the most efficient approach in terms of round-trips to the database.

What you really want is for the two different forms to be working against the same data source in memory. This way you can pass the binding source that the editing form should bind to as a parameter to the editing form's constructor from the customer listing form that launches the editing form, and then the editing form can bind against the provided binding source, as shown in the following code.

```
public partial class CustomerEditForm : Form
{
    public CustomerEditForm(BindingSource bindingSource)
    {
        InitializeComponent();
        m_CompanyNameTextBox.DataBindings.Add("Text", bindingSource,
            "CompanyName");
        m_ContactNameTextBox.DataBindings.Add("Text", bindingSource,
            "ContactName");
    }

    private void OnSave(object sender, EventArgs e)
    {
        Close();
    }
}
```

This form uses simple data binding between the individual text boxes and the appropriate members in the data source through the binding source that was passed to the form. By doing this, as soon as the changes are made in the form, they are automatically reflected in the underlying data, so the grid from the form that launches this form will be synchronized with that data as well. All the Save button needs to do then is close the form and the data will be saved in the client-side data source. If you wanted to persist those changes to the database at that point, you could add code to also call through your data access layer to push the changes down into the database.

Chaining Binding Sources for Master-Details Data Binding

Simple data-binding scenarios are obviously very common, but situations where you need to display multiple related sets of data in a single form are too. When you do so, you'll want to keep the sets of data synchronized in terms of what the current record is in each data source. For example, consider the data schema shown in Figure 4.2. This schema has several tables defined with parent-child relations that cascade through several generations or layers of data.

As discussed in Chapter 3, it's easy to achieve master-details data binding using a binding source. You need to chain together two binding sources, with one binding source bound to the parent data source, and the child binding source bound to the parent binding source. You then set the data member of the child binding source to the property name on the parent objects that exposes the related child collection. In the case of a data set, this property is actually the name of the data relation that links the parent and child tables. Finally, you bind the respective controls to the parent and child binding sources. When completed, the child binding source automatically manages the filtering of presented data in the child control(s) based on the current item in the parent data source. This works whether the parent and child data sources are tables or object collections.

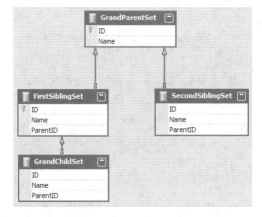

FIGURE 4.2: Hierarchical Data Schema

Figure 4.3 shows an application that has two levels of parent-child data binding, which means that the three binding sources are chained together. The grandparent data at the top of the form is just a grid that is bound to a binding source whose data source is the `GrandParentSet` table of the typed data set generated from the schema shown in Figure 4.2. The grandparent, first sibling, second sibling, and grandchild data tables have been populated with some sample data to show the automatic filtering in action.

The first and second sibling data tables have foreign keys into the grandparent data, and the grandchild data has foreign keys into the first sibling data. When a row is selected in the `GrandParentSet` table, the sibling tables update to only show those rows related to the currently selected grandparent row. Likewise, when a row is selected in the first sibling table, the grandchild table updates to only show the related grandchild rows.

This is all accomplished by chaining the binding sources. Listing 4.2 shows the code used to set up the data binding.

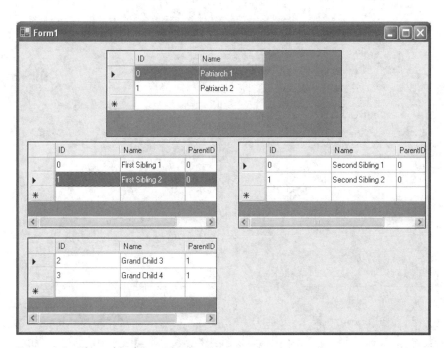

FIGURE 4.3: Hierarchical Data Viewing Form

LISTING 4.2: Master-Details Binding Source Chaining

```
partial class MasterDetailsChainingForm : Form
{
    MasterDetailsChainingDataSet m_Data =
        new MasterDetailsChainingDataSet();
    BindingSource m_GrandParentBindingSource = new BindingSource();
    BindingSource m_FirstSiblingBindingSource = new BindingSource();
    BindingSource m_SecondSiblingBindingSource = new BindingSource();
    BindingSource m_GrandChildBindingSource = new BindingSource();

    public MasterDetailsChainingForm()
    {
        InitializeComponent();
        InitData();
        m_GrandParentBindingSource.DataSource = m_Data;
        m_GrandParentBindingSource.DataMember = "GrandParentSet";
        m_GrandParentGrid.DataSource = m_GrandParentBindingSource;

        m_FirstSiblingBindingSource.DataSource =
            m_GrandParentBindingSource;
        m_FirstSiblingBindingSource.DataMember =
            "FK_GrandParentSet_FirstSiblingSet";
        m_FirstSiblingGrid.DataSource = m_FirstSiblingBindingSource;

        m_SecondSiblingBindingSource.DataSource =
            m_GrandParentBindingSource;
        m_SecondSiblingBindingSource.DataMember =
            "FK_GrandParentSet_SecondSiblingSet";
        m_SecondSiblingGrid.DataSource = m_SecondSiblingBindingSource;

        m_GrandChildBindingSource.DataSource =
            m_FirstSiblingBindingSource;
        m_GrandChildBindingSource.DataMember =
            "FK_FirstSiblingSet_GrandChildSet";
        m_GrandChildGrid.DataSource = m_GrandChildBindingSource;
    }

    private void InitData()
    {
        ...
    }
}
```

The InitData method programmatically populates the data set with several rows per table, with appropriate foreign key values from the child rows to the parent rows to set up the master-details relations. You can see that there is a separate binding source per data grid, and they are set up as described earlier in this section. The top-level binding source for the entire parental hierarchy is set with its data source to the `GrandParentSet` data table. The first and second sibling binding sources are each set to have the grandparent binding source as their data source, and the data member is set to the data relation's name that ties the child table to the parent table. For example, for the first sibling this is the `FK_GrandParentSet_First-SiblingSet` relation. The grandchild binding source is set to have the first sibling binding source as its data source, and its data member is set to the `FK_FirstSiblingSet_GrandChildSet` data relation.

You can use the same approach of chaining binding sources for binding to object collections that are hierarchical. Consider the object definitions in Listing 4.3.

LISTING 4.3: Hierarchical Object Definitions

```
public class ParentObject
{
   private BindingList<ChildObject> m_Children =
      new BindingList<ChildObject>();
   private string m_Greeting = "Hello there";

   public string Greeting
   {
      get { return m_Greeting; }
      set { m_Greeting = value; }
   }

   public BindingList<ChildObject> Children
   {
      get { return m_Children; }
      set { m_Children = value; }
   }
}

public class ChildObject
{
   private int m_DataItem1 = 42;
   private string m_DataItem2 = "yadda";

   public ChildObject() { }
   public ChildObject(int i, string s)
   {
      m_DataItem1 = i;
      m_DataItem2 = s;
   }
```

continues

```
   public string DataItem2
   {
      get { return m_DataItem2; }
      set { m_DataItem2 = value; }
   }

   public int DataItem1
   {
      get { return m_DataItem1; }
      set { m_DataItem1 = value; }
   }
}
```

Because there is a parent-child relationship represented by the `Children` collection on the parent object, you can use that for master-details data binding through a binding source as well. You could add two grids and two binding sources to a form, create a collection of the parent objects, and then data bind in a similar fashion to what you do when the data collections are tables:

```
partial class Form1 : Form
{
   ParentObject[] pos = new ParentObject[2];
   public Form1()
   {
      InitializeComponent();
      // Bind grids
      m_ParentGrid.DataSource = m_ParentBindingSource;
      m_ChildGrid.DataSource = m_ChildBindingSource;

      // Create data objects
      pos[0] = new ParentObject();
      pos[1] = new ParentObject();
      pos[0].Children.Add(new ChildObject());
      pos[1].Children.Add(new ChildObject(1,"foo"));

      // Bind connectors
      m_ParentBindingSource.DataSource = pos;
      m_ChildBindingSource.DataSource = m_ParentBindingSource;
      m_ChildBindingSource.DataMember = "Children";
   }
}
```

The key concept here is knowing that you need to set the data source for the parent binding source to be the parent object collection (in this case, an array held by the form), and the data source for the child binding source to reference the parent binding source. Then the data member of the child binding source needs to be the name of the property on the parent object that is a reference to the child collection. In this case, that is the `Children` property, which is of type `BindingList<ChildObject>`. `BindingList<T>` is a generic collection type in .NET 2.0 that is specifically designed for Windows Forms data binding. `ChildObject` is the type parameter that specifies what type of object the collection will contain. You can use this technique of chaining together binding sources to support arbitrarily deep hierarchies of parent and child data and their bound controls.

Navigating Data Through a Binding Source

In Chapter 3 you saw that you can change the current record in the underlying data source by using a set of `MoveXXX` methods and the `Position` property. I want to review those again here while I am in the process of making you an expert on binding sources, and point out a few other methods that assist in navigating through the data contained in a binding source. Table 4.1 shows the properties and methods related to navigating through the data in the underlying data collection and describes what each does.

TABLE 4.1: BindingSource Navigation Properties and Methods

Name	Description
Position	This property gets or sets the index of the current record within the underlying data source.
Contains	This method checks if the collection of data contains a particular item by passing in a reference to the object. It returns `true` if the object is found and `false` otherwise.
Find	This method looks up the index of an item that you think exists in the underlying data collection, where the item has a specific value on a specified property. You pass in the name of the property and a value that will be tested for equality against the value of the property for each row or object in the collection. The underlying data source must implement the `IBindingList` interface and return `true` from the `IBindingList.SupportsSearching` property for this method to work correctly.

continues

TABLE 4.1: BindingSource Navigation Properties and Methods (Continued)

Name	Description
IndexOf	This method looks for a known object within the collection by passing that object in by reference. It returns the index of the object in the collection if found. You could use this to then set the `Position` property to make that item current.
MoveFirst	This method sets the `Position` property to the zero index or the first item in the binding source's list.
MoveLast	This method sets the `Position` property to the last index in the binding source's list.
MoveNext	This method increments the `Position` property by one. If the current position is already the last item in the list, no change is made and no error is thrown.
MovePrevious	This method decrements the `Position` property by one. If the current position is already the first item in the list, no change is made and no error is thrown.

Manipulating Data Through a Binding Source

The binding source itself gives you indirect access to the data that is stored in the underlying client-side data source. Once you set the DataSource property on a binding source, you don't have to maintain a reference to the data source object itself, because one will be maintained by the binding source. You can always retrieve a reference to the data source by casting the DataSource property to the expected type. The only downside of this approach is that you have to make sure that at the point in the code where you are accessing the DataSource reference, you know exactly what type of data collection the binding source is holding onto.

You can also always get to the current data item in the collection through the Current property on the binding source. The Current property returns an object reference, and as long as you know the type of each item in the collection, you can again cast it to the appropriate type and work against its members. Remember, the type of object returned by the Current property will be a DataRowView object any time you are bound to a DataTable or DataView, and will be an instance of whatever object type you have stored in your object collection when dealing with custom objects.

Moving Between DataRowView and DataRow

A DataView is a wrapper around a DataTable that lets you sort or filter the rows exposed by the table. The DataView contains no data itself; it just exposes the data contained in the table in a different way. The individual rows in a DataView are instances of the DataRowView class. This class, like the DataView itself, is just a wrapper around the individual rows of the table that contain the data.

Because you are really binding to a DataView even when you specify a data table as the data source, the individual data items in the list are of type DataRowView. The DataView class implements all the necessary data-binding interfaces for collections, and the DataRowView class implements the interfaces needed for individual data item objects. This keeps the data binding specifics out of the basic data container classes of the DataSet, DataTable, and DataRow, so those collections consume less memory when they aren't being used for data binding.

If you access the items in a data-bound data table through the Current property on a BindingSource or through an IBindingList reference, you will get back a DataRowView instance. Often you do this because you want to work against the DataRow that it represents. To get to the data row, you can simply use the Row property on the DataRowView. For example, if you have a strongly typed data set of customers bound through a binding source, and you want to programmatically work with the current customer row, you can get to the strongly typed customer row through the DataRowView that is the current item:

```
private void OnGetCurrentRowValues(object sender, EventArgs e)
{
    DataRowView currentRowView = m_CustomersBindingSource.Current

        as DataRowView;
    CustomersDataSet.CustomersRow custRow = currentRowView.Row
        as CustomersDataSet.CustomersRow;
    string company = custRow.CompanyName;
    string phoneNo = custRow.Phone;
}
```

continues

> The data row instance itself is unaware of the `DataRowView` instance that wraps it, so there isn't any way to get from a row's reference directly to the `DataRowView`, but there aren't really any situations where you would need to do this.

To work with the underlying data for a binding source in a more loosely coupled way, you can access the data indirectly through the binding source without having to cast to the specific type at design time (because the `Current` property just returns an object reference for the current item without specifying its type). There is an indexer on the `Binding-Source` class, so you can pass an index in to access a particular item and get back an object reference:

```
object fifthItem = m_BindingSource[4];
```

You can access the `List` property, which returns an `IList` reference. You can then iterate through the items in the collection or index into it through the `IList` reference. Once you obtain an object reference by using any of these approaches, you could then use `PropertyDescriptors` (discussed in Chapter 7) to reflect on the objects and obtain information on them without having design-time insight into the specific type of object that the binding source is managing.

Using a Binding Source as a Data Storage Container

You can also use the binding source without actually binding a particular data source to it. If no data source has been set for an instance of a binding source, you can add objects directly to the list that is contained by the binding source. To do this, you use the `Add` or `AddNew` methods on the `Binding-Source` class. The `Add` method inserts an item in the underlying list. If nothing has been added to the list yet (through the `Add` method or implicitly through setting the `DataSource` property), then the first item added also determines the type of the objects contained in the `List` maintained by the binding source. Subsequent attempts to add an item to the list must add the same type of object, or an `InvalidOperationException` will be thrown because the items in the list must be homogeneous. Setting the `DataSource` property refreshes the entire collection with whatever collection of data the property is set to, so that results in the loss of any items that have been manually added to the list through the `Add` method.

The `AddNew` method lets you add a new item directly and get a reference to the new item back, allowing you to edit its properties. `AddNew` returns an instance of whatever type of object the binding source is set to contain. If no type has been set before calling `AddNew`, then an instance of type `Object` will be added, which is pretty useless. So calling `AddNew` only really makes sense after you have set a `DataSource` or you have added other objects of a specific type to the list with the `Add` method.

The `AddNew` method also causes the `EndEdit` method to be called (discussed later in this chapter) and commits any changes to the current row to the underlying data source. The new item becomes the current item after `AddNew` has been called. Finally, `AddNew` raises the `AddingNew` event, which you can use to either initialize the new object to a set of default values, or you can actually create the object that is used for the new object and return it through the event handler, as shown in Listing 4.4.

In Listing 4.4, the `OnAddingNew` event handler is subscribed to the `AddingNew` event on the binding source in the form's constructor. Note that the event subscription in the form constructor is using delegate inference in C#, rather than explicitly creating a new instance of the event delegate type. This new language feature provides a more compact syntax for creating delegates for event handlers or callback method parameters. The `AddingNew` handler constructs the new object and returns it through the event argument, and then the subsequent code in the form `Load` event handler modifies the property exposed on that object to some value other than its default.

LISTING 4.4: Handling the AddingNew Event to Create an Object

```csharp
public partial class Form1 : Form
{
    BindingSource m_CustomObjectSource = new BindingSource();
    public Form1()
    {
        InitializeComponent();
        m_CustomObjectSource.AddingNew += OnAddingNew;
    }

    private void OnFormLoad(object sender, EventArgs e)
    {
        object newObj = m_CustomObjectSource.AddNew();
        MyCustomObject mco = newObj as MyCustomObject;
        mco.Val = "yadda";
    }

    private void OnAddingNew(object sender, AddingNewEventArgs e)
    {
        e.NewObject = new MyCustomObject();
    }
}

public class MyCustomObject
{
    string m_Val = "foo";
    public string Val
    {
        get { return m_Val; }
        set { m_Val = value; }
    }
}
```

You can also remove items from the collection of data contained by the binding source using the Remove and RemoveAt methods. Remove takes an object reference and looks for an instance of that object in the list, and removes it if found. RemoveAt takes an index and removes the item found at that location. You can remove all of the items from the list using the Clear method.

Filling a Binding Source with a Data Reader

Another opportunity that opens up with the binding source that wasn't really an option before in Windows Forms is the ability to bind controls (indirectly) to data coming from a data reader. If you execute a data reader through a command object, you can set a binding source's `DataSource` property to that data reader. The binding source will iterate through the data reader's contents and use it to quickly populate the binding source's `List` collection. Then, as long as you execute the data reader using the `CommandBehavior.CloseConnection` flag, the connection will close and release back to the connection pool. Or you can close it explicitly or by disposing of the connection. See Appendix D if you are unfamiliar with data readers.

The code in Listing 4.5 shows using a data reader for binding. First the grid that the `BindingSource` is bound to has its `AutoGenerateColumns` property set to `true` in the constructor. This is required any time you will dynamically provide data to a `DataGridView` control without setting up its columns ahead of time. In the `Form.Load` event handler, after executing the reader, the code sets the binding source's data source property to the reader, which causes the binding source to iterate through all the items in the reader and add them to the internal `List` maintained by the binding source. In this case, the items added to the `List` of the binding source are instances of the `DbDataRecord` class from the `System.Data.Common` namespace. These objects have enough schema information embedded that it's easy for the `DataGridView` or other controls to use reflection to extract the column schema information just like it would for a `DataTable`.

LISTING 4.5: Populating a BindingSource Object with a DataReader

```
public Form1()
{
    InitializeComponent();
    m_Grid.AutoGenerateColumns = true;
}

private void OnFormLoad(object sender, EventArgs e)
{
    SqlConnection conn = new SqlConnection(
        "server=localhost;database=Northwind;trusted_connection=true");
    // SQL Server 2005 Express connection:
    // SqlConnection conn = new SqlConnection(
    //     @"server=.\SQLEXPRESS;AttachDbFileName=
    //     C:\temp\Northwind.mdf;trusted_connection=true");
```

continues

```
SqlCommand cmd = new SqlCommand("SELECT CustomerID, CompanyName,
    ContactName, Phone FROM Customers", conn);
using (conn)
{
    conn.Open();
    SqlDataReader reader = cmd.ExecuteReader();
    m_CustomersBindingSource.DataSource = reader;
}
}
```

Using a data reader in this way has several advantages and disadvantages. The advantage is speed—a data reader is about the fastest possible way to get data from a query into a collection in your application. The disadvantage is the tight coupling it introduces between your presentation tier and your data tier. I would recommend staying away from this approach for any large-scale application where maintainability is a concern, and only use it as a performance optimization technique for those places where you have identified a performance hotspot in your presentation of data.

Sorting, Searching, and Filtering Presented Data with a Binding Source

If the data source bound to the binding source implements the `IBinding-List` or `IBindingListView` interfaces (covered in detail in Chapter 7), then you may be able to sort, search, or filter the data through the binding source. The data source implementation of the `IBindingList` interface will have to return `true` from the `IBindingList.SupportsSorting` property in order to sort through the binding source. If it does, you can provide a sorting expression to the `Sort` property, and the data exposed through the binding source will automatically be sorted. This doesn't require any direct support for sorting in the control(s) to which the binding source is bound. The following example shows setting a sort expression for a binding source bound to a `CustomersDataTable`.

```
private void OnBindSortedCustomerGrid(object sender, EventArgs args)
{
    m_CustomersGrid.DataSource = m_CustomersBindingSource;
```

```
    CustomersTableAdapter adapter = new CustomersTableAdapter();
    CustomersDataSet.CustomersDataTable customers = adapter.GetData();
    m_CustomersBindingSource.DataSource = customers;
    m_CustomersBindingSource.Sort = "ContactName ASC";
}
```

In this code, a grid is bound to a binding source. The binding source is then bound to a `CustomersDataTable` instance returned from a table adapter. The `Sort` property on the binding source is then set to "Contact-Name ASC", which will sort the data from the table in ascending order based on the `ContactName` column. The grid will then display the data as sorted, because it sees the data as it is exposed by the binding source, regardless of the physical ordering in the underlying data table. The syntax for sort criteria is the name of the sort property, followed by `ASC` for ascending or `DESC` for descending. If no sort direction is specified, ascending is used as the default.

Data sources can use this advanced form of sorting through the `IBindingListView` interface. If a data source implements this interface and returns `true` from the `IBindingListView.SupportsAdvanced-Sorting` property, then you can pass a more complex sort expression with multiple sort criteria to the `Sort` property. This lets you sort on multiple columns or properties in the collection. For example, for a `Custom-ersDataTable`, you could pass a sort expression of "Region   ASC, CompanyName DESC". This would sort first on the `Region` column in an ascending order, then rows that had the same value for `Region` would be sorted by the `CompanyName` values in a descending order.

To search a data source through a binding source, you can call the `Find` method on the binding source. This method takes a property name and an `object` reference. The property name indicates which property on each of the collection's items should be checked, and the `object` reference contains the value that is being sought in that property. When the first item in the list is found whose property value for the specified property matches the specified value, its index will be returned. For this to work correctly, the underlying data source has to implement `IBindingList` and should return true from the IBindingList.SupportsSearching property. The following example shows how to use the Find method.

```
private void SetCurrentItemToSpecificCompany(string companyName)
{
    int index = m_CustomersBindingSource.Find("CompanyName",companyName);
    if (index != -1)
    {
        m_CustomersBindingSource.Position = index;
    }
}
```

This code searches the CompanyName property on each of the items in the list maintained by the binding source and seeks the one with a value that matches whatever was passed into this method. Note that there are no assumptions about the type of the underlying data source or its objects here. This method would work equally well for a CustomersDataTable or a custom collection of Customer objects, provided that the custom collection properly implements IBindingList with searching support. See Chapter 9 for an example of how to provide this support in your collections.

If the underlying collection implements the IBindingListView interface and returns true from the IBindingListView.SupportsFiltering property, the Filter property on the binding source can be set to a filter expression. When this is done, the data exposed through the binding source will be filtered to only show the matching data. Depending on the capabilities of the data source, this should work similarly to the filtering capabilities of a DataView in ADO.NET (see Appendix D for more details). The specific syntax and complexity supported in the filter expression is determined by the data source. The filter expression is just passed through the binding source to the data source, and the filtering is left up to that data source, as shown in the following example:

```
private void ShowGermanCustomers()
{
    m_CustomersBindingSource.Filter = "Country = 'Germany'";
}
```

This code filters the list exposed by the binding source to only those objects whose Country property (or column in the case of a data table) is equal to Germany. Any bound controls will automatically update to display only those items.

Monitoring the Data with Events

Another important capability of data-binding scenarios, especially when there are layers of decoupling involved, is getting notified when a change to the underlying data source occurs. Table 4.2 shows the events exposed by the `BindingSource`.

TABLE 4.2: BindingSource Events

Event	Description
AddingNew	Fires when the `AddNew` method is called to add a new item to the collection contained by the binding source. (This event was discussed earlier in this chapter.)
BindingComplete	Fires when each simple bound control has completed its data binding, meaning the bound control has read out the value from the current item of the collection or object to which the control is bound indirectly through the binding source. This will occur each time the data binding of the simple bound control needs to be refreshed, such as when the list is initialized or when the current position changes. If the binding source is bound to 10 controls, this event will fire 10 times—once for each data-binding operation.
CurrentChanged	Fires when some change occurs to the current item in the collection. This includes when a new item is placed into the current position, replacing the old item; the item is relocated due to an insertion or deletion of an item earlier in the list; the data source or data member changes; or the `Position` property changes, causing a new item to become current.
CurrentItemChanged	Fires when any of the values of the current item change. This could be triggered by a `ListChanged` event on the `IBindingList` interface with a change type of `ItemChanged`. It could also be triggered if the objects in the data source implement the `INotifyPropertyChanged` interface and raise the `PropertyChanged` event. These interfaces and events are discussed in more detail in Chapter 7.

continues

TABLE 4.2: BindingSource Events (Continued)

Event	Description
DataError	Is raised if the currency manager raises an exception because the binding source doesn't have internal code to handle an exception raised by the data source. Usually this occurs because of invalid changes to an item or property in the data source.
DataMemberChanged	Fires whenever the DataMember property is changed on the binding source.
DataSourceChanged	Fires whenever the DataSource property is changed on the binding source.
ListChanged	Fires any time a change occurs to the list managed by the binding source, including adding, editing, deleting, or moving items. Additionally, changes to properties that will alter the behavior of the list, such as changing the value of the AllowEdit property, should trigger this event. It is also fired if the list itself is replaced with a new collection of data. Whether this event is fired is dependent on the implementation of the IBindingList interface in the data source property. You can check the RaiseListChangedEvents property on the binding source to determine whether subscribing to the ListChanged event will do you any good. The binding source will also raise this event if changes are made to the underlying data source through the binding source, even if the data source does not support raising list changed events itself.
PositionChanged	Fires whenever the Position property changes, making a new item current.

You can use events like PositionChanged, ListChanged, and Current-Changed to control or synchronize the data binding of other controls on the form that aren't necessarily a strict parent-child relation that could be managed through chaining the binding sources as described earlier.

For example, imagine you had a data-bound combo box control on a form, and whenever a new value is selected in the combo box, you need to switch to a new data source on a second binding source that is controlling the data presented through another set of controls. Perhaps the combo box contains a collection of connection strings or database names. You could handle this situation with the switch on the `SelectedIndexChanged` event for the combo box. But what if there were multiple controls on the form that could cause the currently selected item in the collection of data sources to change? Using the `CurrentChanged` event on the binding source for the combo box and other controls, you could simply handle the situation at the binding source level instead of at the individual control level.

You can also use these events to synchronize data binding between collections of data beyond just master-details types of binding. This is demonstrated in Listing 4.7 (on page 166), where the `CurrentChanged` event updates the display of parent item data when a selection in a collection of child objects is made. You can also use the `CurrentChanged` event to achieve something like a master-details experience between object collections that are related through a many-to-many relationship, shown later in the section "Synchronizing Many-to-Many Related Collections."

Restricting Changes to the Data

The binding source can act as a gatekeeper for you to restrict access to the underlying data dynamically without the data source itself having to modify its behavior at all. By setting any of the `AllowEdit`, `AllowNew`, and `AllowRemove` properties defined on the `IBindingList` interface to `false`, you can prevent client code from making the respective modifications to the underlying data. Setting these properties makes the data items contained by the binding source appear as if they don't support the type of modification being attempted.

Any calls from bound controls to the `IBindingList` interface methods to determine whether their data source supports editing, adding, or removing are given the answer by the binding source instead of from the data source itself. The controls or code can then modify their behavior to present the data in a read-only mode, or disable, add, or remove controls. To restore the binding source to whatever behavior the underlying data source supports for allowing the addition of new items, call the `Reset-AllowNew` method. There are no corresponding reset methods for allowing editing or removing; you have to explicitly set the `AllowEdit` or `Allow-Remove` properties back to the desired value.

Underneath the Covers of Data Binding for Complex Types

Binding text and integer data to grids and controls rarely presents a challenge once you know the basic approach to Windows Forms data binding. But what does get a little trickier is presenting things like floating point numeric types, dates, and images that are stored in the database. The problem with these types is that their format in the database or in the custom objects doesn't necessarily map directly to the way that you would present them.

For example, when storing a graphic image in the database, you usually store the raw bytes of the saved image file or object into an `image` column in the database. To present that image, you need to transform it back into an image type that is compatible with the controls you are using to display it. You also may need to modify the raw stored image before presentation, such as scaling it down to present a thumbnail view of it. If it is a date or floating point numeric type, the database often stores greater precision than you plan to display, so the data needs to be formatted before presentation. You may also have a foreign key column in a table, and rather than just displaying that column value, you may want to retrieve a corresponding value from a column in the parent table for display purposes. For instance, you might want to get the customer name for display instead of just displaying a customer ID if you are displaying a collection of orders in a grid. Database columns can store NULL values for columns that translate to value types in the .NET type system, but because value types can never be `null`, what should happen when you try to data bind that column to a value type property on a control? The answer is going to depend on the design of the control, but a well-designed control will handle a `null` value gracefully and document what that behavior will be. You will see examples of how to control that behavior in the next few sections.

For all of these situations, there are easy ways to get what you want if you know where to look. Chapter 6 goes into more detail about handling situations like these for the `DataGridView` control. In this section, let's focus on binding these complex types to individual properties on controls (simple data binding, as defined in the last chapter). The key to handling these situations for individual control bindings is to understand how the `Binding` class works and how it controls the data-binding process.

In Listing 3.4, a `Binding` object was implicitly created and added to the `DataBindings` collection on a text box control by using an overload of the `Add` method on that collection:

```
private void AddTextBoxDataBindings(CustomersDataSet customers)
{
   DataTable table = customers.Customers;
   m_CustomerIDTextBox.DataBindings.Add("Text", table,
      "CustomerID", true);
}
```

This code binds the `Text` property on the `TextBox` control to the `CustomerID` column in the data table that is provided as the data source. This is actually equivalent to the following code, where you first explicitly create a `Binding` object and then add it to the collection:

```
private void AddTextBoxDataBindings(CustomersDataSet customers)
{
   DataTable table = customers.Customers;
   Binding customerIDBinding = new Binding("Text", table,
      "CustomerID", true);
   m_CustomerIDTextBox.DataBindings.Add(customerIDBinding);
}
```

The `Binding` object is a middleman between your data source and your data-bound control. It adapts its behavior for providing values to bound controls and accepting changes back from them based on

- The capabilities of the data source (determined by the interfaces the data source supports)
- The types of the data member and the bound control property
- The properties set on the `Binding` object itself

The binding object determines what value is set on the bound property of a control when the control is rendered or when the underlying data changes (referred to as **formatting the data**). It also determines what value is written back to the data member when updates occur (referred to as **parsing the data**) if the data source supports updating. The `Binding` object has been significantly enhanced in .NET 2.0, including more built-in capability to automatically handle formatting of data values when data binding occurs. Data binding occurs for a `Binding` object when it is added to a control's `DataBindings` collection.

There are several important overloads of the constructor for the `Binding` object that have a significant effect on what happens when data binding occurs. The parameters available to the various constructor overloads are shown in Table 4.3. Each of the parameters is also exposed as a property on the `Binding` class with the same name but PascalCased, which lets you set these values declaratively through properties instead of passing them as arguments to the constructor.

TABLE 4.3: Binding Class Constructor Parameters

Constructor Parameter	Type	Description
propertyName	String	The name of the property on the control to bind.
dataSource	Object	The data source to get the data from for data binding. You should always use a binding source for the data source of a `Binding` object in .NET 2.0.
dataMember	String	The property or column within the data source that contains the values to use when setting the control property value when data binding occurs. This can be a complex path into the object hierarchy maintained by the data source, but should normally just be the property name.
formattingEnabled	Boolean	When set to `true`, automatic formatting will be applied to convert from the data member type to the bound control property type and back. When `false`, the `FormatString`, `NullValue`, and `FormatInfo` properties will be ignored. In general, this value should always be provided as `true`.
dataSourceUpdate-Mode	DataSource UpdateMode	A flag that determines when changes in the bound control property will be pushed down into the data source if the data source supports updating. The values include `OnValidation` (the default), `OnProperty-Changed`, and `Never`.

TABLE 4.3: Binding Class Constructor Parameters (Continued)

Constructor Parameter	Type	Description
nullValue	Object	The value to be returned for data binding when the underlying data source property is logically null. This includes a value of DBNull, a CLR null, or a Nullable<T> object whose HasValue property returns false. Note that the value you specify to be used when the bound value is null has to be of the same type as the bound property on the control (e.g., a string for the Text property of a TextBox), because this value is applied after any type conversions are applied. See the sidebar on "Dealing with Nullable Types in .NET" for more information.
formatString	String	A format string to be passed to the format provider to modify the behavior of the type conversion process.
formatInfo	IFormat-Provider	A reference to an object that implements the IFormatProvider interface. This format provider is passed to the type converters used when formatting and parsing values if the type converter supports custom formatting.

The minimum constructor uses the first three parameters listed in Table 4.3. Overloads let you specify any of the additional parameters as needed for your data-binding scenario.

When you enable formatting by passing true in the formatting-Enabled parameter to the constructor, or by setting the Formatting-Enabled property to true, the binding object automatically performs type conversions between the type of the bound control property and the type of the data member when formatting occurs, and the reverse direction when parsing occurs. If automatic formatting fails, a FormatException will be thrown. Automatic formatting is an alternative to handling the Format and Parse events to manually control conversions. The default value for `FormattingEnabled` is `false`, but you should set this to `true` as a general rule unless you are specifically trying to avoid any changes to the data value from the underlying data source value.

The type conversion process is influenced by the types of the bound control property and data source property, as well as the `NullValue`, `FormatString`, and `FormatProvider` properties on the binding object. If `FormattingEnabled` is `false`, then the values for formatting and null values will be ignored. To understand how type conversion works, you need to know the basics of the standard approach to type conversions that are part of the .NET Framework. The sidebar "Type Conversions and Format Providers" discusses how these work.

Type Conversions and Format Providers

Each built-in .NET type has type conversion capabilities defined for it, either through a `TypeConverter`-derived class or through implicit conversions in the data-binding mechanisms in Windows Forms. `TypeConverter` classes are defined and associated with a particular type, and they are designed to support conversions from the associated type to one or more other types. For example, the `ImageConverter` class is associated with the `Image` type, and it can perform type conversions to and from a `byte` array. If a `TypeConverter` doesn't exist for a conversion that is needed for data binding, the Windows Forms implicit type conversions have additional capabilities that support the most common .NET types.

Additionally, the type conversion process can also modify the values that result based on a ***format provider***, which is an object that implements the `IFormatProvider` interface. For example, the `DateTimeConverter` class is associated with the `DateTime` type, and it can perform type conversions to and from strings. The `string` that is output by the type conversion process can be modified by a format provider. The `DateTimeFormatInfo` format provider is the default format provider for the DateTime type, and lets you easily specify what parts of the underlying date and time data to extract and return as the converted string.

You specify what parts you want in the converted string by specifying a case-sensitive formatting string that contains tokens that identify what part of the date and time to extract. There are predefined format strings that are localizable, such as `"d"`, which signifies that the returned string should just contain the date in short format (MM/DD/YYYY for en-US locale). The format provider can also support custom formatting strings that you can use to pass tokens that the format provider will parse to determine how to format the string. The same format for a date could also be returned if the custom formatting string `"mm/dd/yyyy"` was used, but these formatting strings won't be able to automatically adapt to changing locales the way the predefined format strings will.

The type conversion mechanism is designed to be extensible. When you define your own custom types, you can also define type converters for those types. You can associate a type converter with a type, property, or method with the `TypeConverterAttribute` attribute. The type converter is used by Windows Forms data binding and a number of other processes in the .NET Framework. You can also implement *custom formatters*, which are types that implement the `ICustomFormatter` interface, if you need to do formatting that goes beyond what the built-in formatters provide. Implementing custom type converters and custom formatters is beyond the scope of this book, but for almost all situations you encounter in data binding, the rich type converters and format providers in the .NET Framework should meet your needs.

For simple types like integers and strings, whose normal presentation includes the full contents of the data as they are stored, no type conversion is really needed. But for more complex database types, such as `image`, `datetime`, or floating point number, the formatters can transform the raw data into a completely different object type. The next few sections step through some examples of setting up data binding for complex types to help illustrate how this all works. The code for the next few sections is contained in the sample application ComplexTypeBinding in the download code.

Dealing with Nullable Types in .NET

The .NET Framework includes two types, `Nullable` and `Nullable<T>`, that help you manage the fact that a value type cannot be `null` in the .NET runtime. These types let you wrap a value type in an object that lets you express the value for a value type as a logical `null`. `Nullable<T>` is the generic version and is a better choice, because `Nullable` actually wraps the value type in a reference type wrapper, which puts additional pressure on the garbage collector if many of these are created. `Nullable<T>` keeps the instance on the stack as a value type, but still allows it to have a value of `null`.

C# 2.0 supports a special syntax for nullable types. You can declare a variable of value type with a trailing question mark (`int?`, `float?`, etc.), and that signals the compiler to declare that variable as an instance of type `Nullable<T>`, where `T` is the actual type specified in the shorthand notation.

The other special kind of null types you will deal with a lot when doing data binding is the `DBNull` class. This is a special placeholder class that is intended to represent a database `NULL`. Because there isn't 100 percent equivalence between a database `NULL` and a `null` in .NET, when you pull in data from a database, if the value of a column in the database is `NULL`, the corresponding .NET object that will be created is an instance of the `DBNull` class. This class has a single static property named `Value` that you can use for comparisons to check if something is equal to `DBNull`.

```
if (m_NorthwindDataSet.Employees[0].Country == DBNull.Value)
{
    // Handle null case here
}
```

However, if you are working with a typed data set like this, there is a better and recommended way. Part of the typed data row definitions includes the definition of a set of methods for every column that can accept `NULL`s. The first method is named `Is<ColumnName>Null`, where `<ColumnName>` is the strongly typed property name on the typed data row. Using this method, you could change the preceding code to this preferred approach:

```
if (m_NorthwindDataSet.Employees[0].IsCountryNull())
{
    // Handle null case here
}
```

The other related method that is defined for each column is Set<Col-umnName>Null. If you call this method, it assigns DBNull.Value to the underlying column value within the row. Then if you use that row to update a database through a data adapter or table adapter, the value set in the database will be a database NULL.

Keep in mind that having a value of DBNull and having a value of null are two separate and distinct things. Having a value of DBNull means you actually have a reference to a real object—one that represents a NULL in the database. Having a value of null means that you have an empty reference.

It's important to understand that if you use the NullValue property of a Binding object to specify a value that should be used when the bound data member is null, that value will be used whether you are bound to a custom data object and the bound property is null (empty reference), or whether you are bound to a data row and the corresponding column value is DBNull (logical database NULL). This also works if you are bound to a property that is of type Nullable<T>, and the value of that property is logically null (the HasValue property is false). The NullValue property on the Binding object will still be used for null values on Nullable<T> objects.

Binding an Image Column to a PictureBox Control

Let's start with a somewhat visually appealing example—binding an image column from a database to a PictureBox control on a form. This example assumes that the data stored in the database are the bytes of a saved bitmap image (or JPEG, GIF, PNG, or any other image type supported by the Bitmap class in .NET). An image column in the database gets stored in a data set as a byte array (byte[]). Because there is a built-in type conversion for converting from an Image type to a byte array and vice versa, the simplest way to achieve this is to enable automatic formatting on the binding object used to set up the data binding and let it do the work. The following code shows how to set up the binding object for a Picture-Box control to display an image.

```
m_PhotoPictureBox.DataBindings.Add("Image",
    m_EmployeesBindingSource, "Photo", true);
```

The code uses the overloaded Add method on the DataBindings collection of the PictureBox control and maps the Image property on the control to the Photo column in the m_EmployeesBindingSource data source. The m_EmployeesBindingSource has been set up with its data source set to the Employees table of the Northwind database. Passing true for the formattingEnabled parameter sets the FormattingEnabled property to true on the binding object. This tells the binding object to perform automatic type conversions and formatting based on the types of the bound control property and the data member as described earlier. When Visual Studio writes the data-binding code for you through drag-and-drop operations from the Data Sources window, it enables formatting in a similar fashion.

█ **NOTE** Image Conversion Handles OLE Images

The pictures stored in the Northwind database aren't stored in raw image file formats; they are stored as OLE image documents. There is an OLE header on the actual image bytes that you have to strip off to work with the image properly outside of an OLE document. Luckily, this logic is coded into the ImageConverter code in the .NET Framework, so you don't have to worry about stripping off that OLE header yourself. You can just bind the PictureBox.Image property to the column in the data table, and it will be rendered properly.

Binding a DateTime Column to a DateTimePicker

The DateTimePicker control is designed specifically for displaying date and time information and to give you a richer editing experience for the values by treating each of the parts of the displayed information (such as month, day, year, hours, minutes, and seconds) as individual values that can be set when editing through the control. Additionally, it provides a drop-down calendar control that lets a user select a date from a one-month calendar view (see Figure 4.4).

The `DateTimePicker` control had a number of problems in data-binding scenarios prior to .NET 2.0, but with the automatic formatting capabilities of the `Binding` object, it works very nicely with date and time values now. However, it still has problems if the property or column you are data binding to is equal to `null` or `DBNull`.

All it takes to get the `DateTimePicker` data bound is to create the binding object with formatting enabled and add it to the `DataBindings` collection on the control:

```
m_BirthDateTimePicker.DataBindings.Add("Value",
    m_EmployeesBindingSource, "BirthDate", true);
m_BirthDateTimePicker.Format = DateTimePickerFormat.Custom;
m_BirthDateTimePicker.CustomFormat = "MM/dd/yyyy";
```

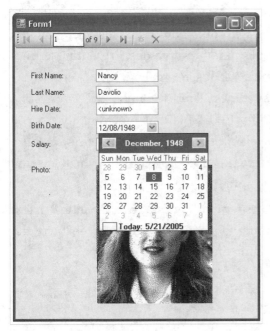

FIGURE 4.4: ComplexTypeBinding Sample Application with DateTimePicker Drop-Down Selected

Note that in the case of the `DateTimePicker`, the control itself has built-in formatting properties for how it presents the bound `DateTime` value. To specify what formatting the control should use, you set the `Format` property to an enumeration value of type `DateTimePickerFormat`. This enumeration has values of `Long`, `Short`, `Time`, and `Custom`. `Long` displays the date and time, `Short` just the date, `Time` just the time, and with `Custom` you can pass a custom formatting string through the `CustomFormat` property as shown in the code example. (You'll see in the next section how this works if the control doesn't directly support formatting.) I should point out that using a custom date format like this one will cause problems if you end up needing to localize your application to other cultures. Effectively this is a hard-coded dependency on the U.S. style for showing dates.

Binding a DateTime Column to a TextBox

Developers frequently choose to use a simple text box control for date and time display and input. In part this is due to the data-binding problems experienced with the `DateTimePicker` control in .NET 1.1 and to the remaining problems with dealing with nulls. But it can also be to simply have explicit control over the display and input values. Presenting a drop-down calendar as shown in Figure 4.4 doesn't make a lot of sense if the control is only going to display times. Unfortunately, the `DateTime-Picker` doesn't give you the ability to disable that functionality, so you may decide to display the time in a `TextBox` control. Another new control to consider for this scenario is the `MaskedTextBox` control, which lets you specify allowable patterns for the input into the text box.

The same basic approach applies for binding a `DateTime` value to a text box: you need to create the binding object with formatting enabled and add it to the `DataBindings` collection on the control.

```
Binding hireDateBinding = new Binding("Text",
    m_EmployeesBindingSource, "HireDate",true);
hireDateBinding.FormatString = "d";
hireDateBinding.NullValue = "<unknown>" ;
m_HireDateTextBox.DataBindings.Add(hireDateBinding);
```

This example explicitly creates an instance of the `Binding` class first, instead of using one of the overloads of the `Add` method on the `Data-Bindings` collection. The constructor for the `Binding` class has similar overloads, so you can choose whether to initialize all the relevant formatting properties inline as constructor parameters or to break them out as properties as shown in this code snippet. This example constructs the `Binding` object with automatic formatting turned on (the `formatting-Enabled` parameter to the constructor set to `true`) and then sets the `FormatString` property, which will be passed to the format provider that is being used for the control. In the example, the `NullValue` property is set to a string that will be displayed in the text box if the underlying bound property or column contains a `null` or `DBNull` value.

Because the value being used to set the `Text` property on the text box is a `DateTime` from the data source, the `DateTimeFormatInfo` provider is used. It supports a number of predefined and custom formatting strings as discussed earlier. This code example passes a format string of `d`, which translates to the short date predefined format. This displays the data only in the format MM/DD/YYYY in the United States, but will display it as DD/MM/YYYY in Europe. You could also pass a custom string such as MM/yy, which would display the date with only two digits each for month and year. Note that these formatting strings are case sensitive: MM will output a two-digit numeric month, and mm will output the minutes as two digits.

Binding a Numeric Column to a TextBox

Setting up binding for a numeric column to a `TextBox` control is very similar to doing it for a `DateTime` column. The main difference is in the formatting strings that you use to specify the output format in the text box. You can again provide the format string either through the `Binding` constructor or by setting the `FormatString` property on the `Binding` object. You can also use one of the overloaded `Add` methods on the `DataBindings` collection. The following code demonstrates the latter approach.

```
m_SalaryTextBox.DataBindings.Add("Text", m_EmployeesBindingSource,
    "Salary", true, DataSourceUpdateMode.OnValidation,
    "<not specified>", "#.00");
```

If you are an astute Northwind user, you know that there isn't a Salary column in the Employees table that we are using for this example. I added a Salary column to the Employees table in the typed data set after it was generated by the designer, with a column type of decimal. Then, in the sample code `Form.Load` event, I generated random salary values between 0 and 200,000 after retrieving the data from the database and injecting them into the rows:

```
Random rand = new Random((int)DateTime.Now.Ticks);
foreach (NorthwindDataSet.EmployeesRow row in employees)
{
    row.Salary = new Decimal(rand.Next(200000));
}
```

The `formattingEnabled` parameter to the `Add` method set to `true` turns on automatic formatting. You can use the `DataSourceUpdateMode` enumeration value to specify when automatic formatting occurs (`OnValidation`, `OnPropertyChanged`, or `Never`). The `nullValue` parameter maps to the `NullValue` property, and it's used here to specify that if the bound data member value is `null` or `DBNull`, then the text box should display the string `<not specified>`. Note that this null mapping works in both directions. If someone enters `<not specified>` in the salary text box, then the value that will be written to the data source will be `DBNull.Value`. The `formatString` parameter is the custom format string, which in this case specifies to display the number with two decimal places.

You can see the end result of the code from the previous few sections in Figure 4.5. You can get the code itself from the ComplexTypeBinding sample application in the download. I programmatically set the values of the `HireDate` and `Salary` columns to `DBNull` on the first record, and used the `SetHireDateNull` and `SetSalaryNull` methods exposed on the `EmployeesDataRow` class from the typed data set before data binding. This lets you see the effect of setting the `NullValue` property on the bindings for those columns.

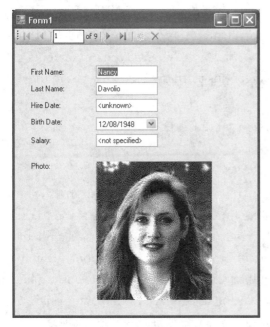

FIGURE 4.5: ComplexTypeBinding Application in Action

Automatic Formatting and Parsing Summary

This section summarizes what happens in the automatic formatting and parsing process. In the case of formatting, the source type is the type of the data source property involved in the binding, and the target type is the type of the bound control property. For parsing, the source type is the type of the bound control property, and the target type is the type of the data source property.

- If the target type of the conversion process is a string, and a format string has been provided, the formatting string is passed to the format provider to obtain the properly rendered version of the target string. Each built-in type has a default format provider defined for it.

- If the target type isn't a string or if there isn't a format provider associated with the source type, then the source and target types are inspected to see if one or the other has a type converter that can convert between the source and target types. If so, that type converter is used, such as the case of converting an image to a byte array or vice versa.

- If no type converter can be found, and the source or target type is a built-in .NET Framework type, the other type is checked to see if it implements the IConvertible interface. When a type implements this interface, it provides conversions to all the built-in types in the .NET Framework.

- Finally, if none those conversion processes can be done, a Format-Exception is thrown.

The whole story is actually even a little more complex than that. There are other conversion attempts made under the covers to use static Parse methods if the target type has a static Parse method defined and the source type is a string, and there are other implicit conversions for common types in a few other places in the formatting pipeline. The bottom line is that if you enable automatic formatting, the .NET Framework is going to try to do everything possible to come up with a sensible type conversion to render the data for you.

Going Beyond Built-In Type Conversion with Binding Events

When there is a built-in conversion and formatting process, the binding approach outlined so far is the easiest and most straightforward approach. However, there are always times when you need to do something a little different than the standard data-binding mechanisms support, so knowing how to go beyond the built-in type conversions is an important skill in your data-binding toolbox. Understanding the limitations of these custom approaches is also important.

For now, let's just focus on simple data binding. You can take control of the whole data-binding process for individual control properties by handling a number of different events, including events raised by the binding object itself and events raised by the control that is being bound. In fact, you often need to handle both control events and binding events to ensure that edited values in controls are pushed down into the data source before a form is closed.

The two `Binding` class events of interest are the `Format` and the `Parse` events. A number of other `Binding` class events are simple notifications that you can subscribe to if you are interested in knowing when any of the properties affecting data binding change, such as the `FormatString` and `NullValue` properties. As you might suspect from the preceding sections, the `Format` event is raised when the value is being pulled out of the data source property and before the bound control property is set using that value. The `Parse` event is the reverse: It is fired when the value has changed in the control property and is going to be written back into the corresponding data source property for two-way data binding.

The `Format` and `Parse` events give you explicit control over the values being set while data binding. Both events are declared using the same delegate type, a `ConvertEventHandler`, and they take two arguments. The first argument follows the pattern for most Windows Forms events and is an object reference that refers to the publisher of the event; the second argument is a `ConvertEventArgs` parameter, which lets you step in and provide whatever value you want when formatting and parsing occurs.

The `ConvertEventArgs` parameter has two properties that you will want to use to control the data-binding process. The `DesiredType` property tells you what type is needed for the object value being set. For the `Format` event, this represents the type of the property on the bound control and is an instance of the `Type` class that provides the metadata about the property type. For the `Parse` event, it specifies the type of the data source property that is being written to. The `Value` property gives you access to the object that is currently going to be used to try to set that property on the control or the data source. If you do nothing with the value, then the `Binding` class ends up just trying to set the property value using the current value. Normal type conversions will apply if automatic formatting is turned on (as discussed earlier in the section on automatic formatting). However, the `Value` property is an object reference, so you can replace the value with anything you like. If you do, whatever you set the `Value` property to is what will be used to set the value of the control or data source property. The `Format` and `Parse` events fire before automatic type conversions are applied. As a result, if you turn on automatic formatting and provide a different value through the `Value` property, the automatic formatting will be applied to the object that you set as the `Value`, instead of the one that was pulled out of the data source property or control property.

To demonstrate some of the things you can do through binding events, the download code for this chapter contains a project named Binding-Events, which contains the currency exchange rate application shown in Figure 4.6. To use this application, you first have to create a new database called MoneyDB. There is a script named MoneyDB.sql in the download code for Chapter 4 that you can run from SQL Query Analyzer to create and populate the database with some sample data. There is also an additional application called MoneyDBAdmin that you can use to edit, add, or delete data from the tables in this database.

The BindingEvents application performs numerous forms of data binding to demonstrate most of the concepts discussed so far in this chapter.

The application works on a database that contains two tables: Exchange-Rates and Countries. The Countries table contains the name of the country (e.g., United States, United Kingdom, etc.), the currency type name (dollars, pounds, etc.), and an image of the country's flag. The ExchangeRates table contains exchange rates between two countries with the rate information and the date the rate was based on. The country information is stored in the ExchangeRates table as foreign keys in the Countries table. Figure 4.7 shows the schema for this data in the data set designer diagram.

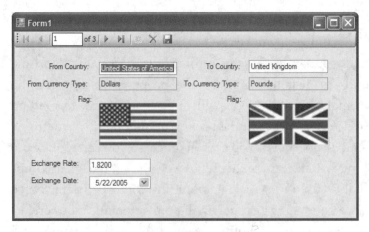

FIGURE 4.6: Currency Exchange Application

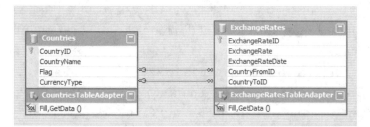

FIGURE 4.7: Currency Exchange Data Set

You can see that there are two foreign key relations from ExchangeRates to Countries, one for the CountryFromID column and one for the Country-ToID column.

The user interface shown in Figure 4.6 lets users browse through the records of exchange rate data, with the related country information for each exchange rate included in the form—as if it were all stored as a single table of data. However, the normalized format of the data in the data set requires some additional work to provide this appearance to the user. To support this display, each exchange rate record needs to retrieve two corresponding country records to display their data in place with the exchange data for the From Country and To Country text boxes. This example uses data-binding events to do this; in a later example, I will redo this to use additional `BindingSource` objects and their events.

In this example, the form is coded so that if a user types in a country name and tabs out of the country text box, the data in the text box is parsed, a lookup in the Countries table is made, and if the country is found, that country's currency type and flag will be displayed in the controls below the country text box. The code to support this for the two sets of country data controls is identical except for the controls and relations it works against.

There are a number of other controls on the form tied in with the data-binding mechanisms. First, there is a `BindingNavigator` control, which lets users page through the data records one at a time. (This was described in Chapter 3; it is simply a derived class from the `ToolStrip` control with controls and handlers for navigating the data. It also includes buttons for adding new records, deleting the current record, and saving changes in the data set.) The Exchange Rate and Exchange Date controls at the bottom of the form have their binding set up exactly as was discussed in the Binding a DateTime Column to a DateTimePicker and Binding a Numeric Column to a TextBox sections.

Here's what is going on in the binding of the country information at the top of the form. To start with, you need data to work on, so the sample loads the data from both the ExchangeRates and Countries tables into a data set in the form constructor:

```
public CurrencyExchangeForm()
{
    InitializeComponent();
    // Get the data
    CountriesTableAdapter countriesAdapter =
        new CountriesTableAdapter();
    ExchangeRatesTableAdapter exchangeRatesAdapter =
        new ExchangeRatesTableAdapter();

    m_ExchangeRatesDataSet = new ExchangeRatesDataSet();

    countriesAdapter.Fill(m_ExchangeRatesDataSet.Countries);
    exchangeRatesAdapter.Fill(m_ExchangeRatesDataSet.ExchangeRates);

    m_ExchangeRatesBindingSource.DataSource = m_ExchangeRatesDataSet;
    m_ExchangeRatesBindingSource.DataMember =
        m_ExchangeRatesDataSet.ExchangeRates.TableName;
    CreateBindings();
}
```

After filling each of the tables using their respective table adapter, the constructor code sets the data source on the binding source to the data set and sets the data member to be the ExchangeRates table. Notice that this uses strongly typed properties of the typed data table here to get the table name through a property, instead of having to code a string literal. Finally, it calls a helper method called CreateBindings, into which the code is separated for setting up the individual control bindings. The Create-Bindings method is shown in Listing 4.6.

LISTING 4.6: Creating the Individual Bindings

```
private void CreateBindings()
{
    // From Country TextBox
    Binding countryFromBinding = new Binding("Text",
        m_ExchangeRatesBindingSource, "CountryFromID");
```

```
countryFromBinding.Format +=
    new ConvertEventHandler(OnCountryFromFormat);
countryFromBinding.Parse +=
    new ConvertEventHandler(OnCountryFromParse);
m_CountryFromTextBox.DataBindings.Add(countryFromBinding);

// To Country TextBox
Binding countryToBinding = new Binding("Text",
    m_ExchangeRatesBindingSource, "CountryToID");
countryToBinding.Format +=
    new ConvertEventHandler(OnCountryToFormat);
countryToBinding.Parse +=
    new ConvertEventHandler(OnCountryToParse);
m_CountryToTextBox.DataBindings.Add(countryToBinding);

// From currency type text box
Binding currencyFromBinding = new Binding("Text",
    m_ExchangeRatesBindingSource, "CountryFromID");
currencyFromBinding.Format +=
    new ConvertEventHandler(OnCurrencyFromFormat);
m_CurrencyTypeFromTextBox.DataBindings.Add(currencyFromBinding);

// To currency type text box
Binding currencyToBinding = new Binding("Text",
    m_ExchangeRatesBindingSource, "CountryToID");
currencyToBinding.Format +=
    new ConvertEventHandler(OnCurrencyToFormat);
m_CurrencyTypeToTextBox.DataBindings.Add(currencyToBinding);

// Exchange rate
Binding exchangeRateBinding = new Binding("Text",
    m_ExchangeRatesBindingSource, "ExchangeRate", true,
    DataSourceUpdateMode.OnValidation, "1.0000", "#.0000");
m_ExchangeRateTextBox.DataBindings.Add(exchangeRateBinding);

// Exchange rate date
Binding exchangeRateDateBinding = new Binding("Value",
    m_ExchangeRatesBindingSource, "ExchangeRateDate", true);
m_ExchangeRateDateTimePicker.DataBindings.Add(
    exchangeRateDateBinding);

}
```

You can see from the `CreateBindings` method that this subscribes to the `Format` and `Parse` events on the binding object for each of the country name text boxes, and only the `Format` event for the currency type text boxes since they are read-only. Also note that both the country name and currency type text boxes for From and To information use CountryFromID and CountryToID from the ExchangeRates table, respectively. Because the country name, currency type, and flag are determined by the foreign key stored in the ExchangeRates table, the data-binding process effectively denormalizes the data back into a flat set of data for display.

Note that there are no data bindings set up for the `PictureBox` controls that display the flags. Those are manually bound through the `Format` event handlers for the country name text box, since the two pieces of information are linked through the country ID that is used to bind the country name. I could have used the same approach for populating the currency type text box since it is read-only, but I wanted to demonstrate that you can bind more than one control to the same data member, but handle the bindings completely differently if needed, through separate `Format` and `Parse` event handlers.

Handling the Format Event

The `Format` event for individual binding objects fires each time the property or column in the data source changes. As discussed earlier, the `Format` event is passed a `ConvertEventArgs`, which contains the `Value` that is to be used for setting the bound control property unless you decide to change it. In your event handler, you can transform that value, and you can do other processing or set properties on other controls as well:

```
void OnCountryFromFormat(object sender, ConvertEventArgs e)
{
    if (e.Value == null || e.Value == DBNull.Value)
    {
        m_FlagFromPictureBox.Image = null;
        return;
    }
    ExchangeRatesDataSet.CountriesRow countryRow =
        GetCountryRow((int)e.Value);
    e.Value = countryRow.CountryName;
    // Now set other control properties based on this same binding
    ImageConverter converter = new ImageConverter();
    m_FlagFromPictureBox.Image =
        converter.ConvertFrom(countryRow.Flag) as Image;
}
```

In this `Format` handler for the From Country text box, the code first checks to see if the value of the event argument is `null` or `DBNull`. This happens when paging to a new record that has not been populated yet. If the CountryFromId column is empty in the data set, it will be set to `DBNull`. However, the null case could happen if the data source were changed to an object collection instead of a data set, so it is best to program defensively. If the value is `DBNull` or `null`, the text box itself will just display an empty string, which is fine, but the code will also clear out the picture box containing the flag.

The normal case is that a country ID is passed in for the value. The handler code takes that country ID and calls a helper method that looks up the corresponding row in the Countries table using the `DataTable.Select` method.

Once the country row has been obtained, the value on the event argument is set to the country name. Doing this changes the value that will be used to set the `Text` property in the text box once the data-binding process completes. Instead of displaying the CountryFromId column value, it will display the text value set on the event argument. In addition, the `Format` handler retrieves the Flag column from the country row, uses the `Image-Converter` class to transform the byte array into an `Image` object, and sets the `Image` property on the `PictureBox` control to that object. This keeps the flag picture box synchronized with the displayed country name, all based on the country code that was originally bound to the country name text box. The `ImageConverter` class is the same one that is used by the automatic formatting type conversion process described earlier in the chapter.

The `Format` event handler for the currency type is simpler. It just does the lookup to obtain the country row, and then substitutes the currency type for the country ID that was passed in the value of the event argument:

```
void OnCurrencyFromFormat(object sender, ConvertEventArgs e)
{
    if (e.Value == null || e.Value == DBNull.Value)
    {
        return;
    }
    ExchangeRatesDataSet.CountriesRow countryRow =
        GetCountryRow((int)e.Value);
    e.Value = countryRow.CurrencyType;
}
```

Handling the Parse Event

As mentioned, the application also lets users type a country name into the From Country or To Country text boxes, and it will update the country information based on that input. The things that need to be updated are the currency type and flag for the entered country name, and the corresponding country ID that is set in the current ExchangeRates row. You could deal with this kind of situation by handling the TextChanged event on the text box and doing the lookup of the entered country name in that handler, but I wanted to show how you can accomplish this using data-binding mechanisms. The sample has the Parse event on the country name text box intercept the changed country name. The Parse event will be fired when the contents of the TextBox have changed and the focus changes to another control (after Validating and Validated events fire).

```
void OnCountryFromParse(object sender, ConvertEventArgs e)
{
    // Need to look up the Country information for the country name
    ExchangeRatesDataSet.CountriesRow row =
        GetCountryRow(e.Value.ToString());
    if (row == null)
    {
        string error = "Country not found";
        m_ErrorProvider.SetError(m_CountryFromTextBox, error);
        m_CountryFromTextBox.Focus();
        throw new ArgumentException(error);
    }
    e.Value = row.CountryID;
}
```

For the Parse event, the Value property of the event argument contains the value of the bound control property. When the parsing process is complete, the value set on the Value property will be used to set the content of the bound column in the data source. So the Parse handler needs to obtain the country ID corresponding to the entered country name, which it does using another helper method. The helper method again uses the DataTable.Select method on the Countries table, this time looking for the entered country name. If the country name is found, the Parse handler substitutes the country ID for the value on the event argument, and that

COMPLETING THE EDITING PROCESS   157

will set the corresponding CountryFromID column in the current ExchangeRates row to which this text box is bound.

If the country name isn't found, you need to let the user know and prevent an invalid value from being set in the data source. The way you do that is to throw an exception. When you throw an exception from a binding event handler, it terminates the binding process for that control and forces the control to refresh its bound property from the data member (triggering the Format event again). You also want to draw the user's attention to the problem, so the code also uses an error provider to alert the user of the problem and sets the focus back on the offending text box. The binding object handles the event, so the message that you provide in the thrown exception isn't important unless you are using instrumentation to monitor thrown exceptions at the runtime level.

Completing the Editing Process

If you coded the application as discussed so far, you will see there is still a problem with the data binding for the currency type text boxes. When you type in a new country name in the From Country or To Country text box and then press Tab, the flag for the country entered will be displayed. However, the currency type text box won't be updated unless you page to another record and then page back using the binding navigator. This problem is caused by the way a data row works when you edit the data contained in it.

The DataRowView class implements the IEditableObject interface. This interface lets an object support transactional changes to the object. This means that you can start to edit the object by setting values on its properties, and then you can either accept those changes or you can roll them back to the previous values before the object editing started. You commence changing an object like this with the BeginEdit method on the interface. You commit the changes by calling a method on that interface named EndEdit, and you roll the changes back with the CancelEdit method. Until the EndEdit method is called on the object, property value changes on that object are considered transient and aren't reflected in any other controls bound to that same object. Additionally, if EndEdit isn't called, those pending changes won't be persisted if you try to save the data source to its underlying data store.

Don't confuse EndEdit with the AcceptChanges method on a data set, data table, or data row. Data rows in a data table can maintain both a current version and the original version of the row values that were retrieved when the data set was filled. The IEditableObject caching described earlier goes beyond that capability; it says that there is really a third version when you are editing a row containing the uncommitted edits to the row. Until EndEdit is called on the row, any changes made programmatically or through bound controls to columns in the row aren't actually reflected in the current version of the row.

For example, say you have two text boxes bound to the same column in a data row, such as the CountryName column. If you change the value in one of the text boxes and tab to the other text box, you won't see the edited value reflected in the second text box. The changed value from the first text box has been parsed and written to the underlying data member in a transient state, but the changed value hasn't been committed to the data source yet, so other controls bound to that same data member don't see the change yet.

For the other text box to see the change and be updated, EndEdit needs to be called on the object, which is most easily done by calling EndEdit on the binding source that you are using for setting up the data binding. When you call EndEdit on a binding source, it calls EndEdit on the current item. The best place to call EndEdit if you want an edited value to be immediately committed is to handle the Validated event on the bound control and put the call to EndEdit in that handler. The Validated event is raised after the entered control value has passed validation and has been parsed, but focus hasn't yet changed to the next control. Calling EndEdit at this point commits the change; all other controls that are bound to that same data item will be notified that the data source has changed, and they will perform formatting on their respective data members.

EndEdit is also called implicitly if the current item changes. If you have a data navigator like in the BindingEvents application, when you page to another record, EndEdit will be called on the binding source, which calls

EndEdit on the current data item. This triggers other data bindings that are bound to properties in that current item to perform the formatting process and display any updates. Likewise, when working with a Data-GridView, when you change the current row through a selection in the grid, the EndEdit method is called on the row that was previously selected if any changes had been made to the row.

> **■ TIP** Call **EndEdit** on the data item to commit changes that have been made in simple bound controls.
>
> Developers are often confused when they change a value in one bound control and other controls bound to the same data source don't immediately update, or when they try to save the changes to the database and the old values are still persisted. This often happens because EndEdit needs to be called on the current item to commit the changes to the object if the object implements IEditableObject. Editing begins on the current item (through a call to the BeginEdit method on the interface) the first time one of its properties is edited through a data-bound control. (The IEditableObject interface is discussed in Chapters 7 and 9.)

Getting back to the problem with the currency type text boxes on the BindingEvents sample's form, when a user enters a new country name and tabs to another control, the currency type doesn't update because when you set the CountryFromID or CountryToID column value in the Parse event handler for the text box, you have made a transient programmatic change to that row. Until the change is committed with a call to EndEdit, other controls bound to that same property won't be notified that the value has changed.

To fix this problem, the Validated event handlers on the Country From and Country To text boxes need to call EndEdit on the binding source and get it to commit the changes to the current row. This will cause

`Format` to fire again on the currency type text boxes, allowing them to update their contents based on the new CountryFromID or CountryToID:

```
public CurrencyExchangeForm()
{
    // Other constructor code ...
    m_CountryFromTextBox.Validated += OnCountryFromValidated;
    m_CountryToTextBox.Validated += OnCountryToValidated;
}
private void OnCountryFromValidated(object sender, EventArgs e)
{
    m_ExchangeRatesBindingSource.EndEdit();
}

private void OnCountryToValidated(object sender, EventArgs e)
{
    m_ExchangeRatesBindingSource.EndEdit();
}
```

Making the User's Life Easier with AutoComplete

If you run the BindingEvents sample, you will see that if you start to type in a country name that is in the database, the text box controls for From Country and To Country will actually provide AutoComplete functionality—a drop-down list of the available countries based on the characters that have been typed in so far displays. Any time you are going to provide a `TextBox` or `ComboBox` input control that is likely to take on repeated or predictable values, you should consider providing AutoComplete functionality for your users. In this case, for example, when users start by typing the letter U, they will immediately get a drop-down with United Kingdom and United States of America in it (using the sample data in the MoneyDB.sql script). They can use the arrow keys to select an item in the list, and the list will continue to refine as they type more characters. When they tab out of the text box, the currently selected item will be accepted and entered as the text in the box. If they press the Esc key, the list disappears and they can type whatever they like.

This slick new feature in Windows Forms 2.0 is easy to use. The following steps show you how to enable AutoComplete.

1. Select the `TextBox` control in the designer, and set the `AutoComplete-Source` property to a value other than `None` (the default) through the Properties window. Other modes are available, including `File-System`, `HistoryList`, `RecentlyUsedList`, and a few others that map to built-in collections of strings that are either provided by the system or are managed by the Framework.

2. Because you want to provide the list of values yourself, set the `AutoCompleteSource` property to `CustomSource`.

3. Set the `AutoCompleteMode` to `SuggestAppend`. This means that as the users type, the drop-down list will display matches and append any missing letters for the selected item when users tab out of the `TextBox`. You can also set the mode to `Suggest` or `Append` if desired.

4. If you aren't using one of the built-in sources, you need to write a little code to create the list of strings that will be checked against for suggested values. Create an instance of the `AutoCompleteString-Collection` class and include each value you want to have in the collection against which the AutoComplete functionality checks for matches.

5. After you build that collection, set it as the `AutoCompleteCustom-Source` property for the `TextBox`.

Here's the code that creates and attaches the custom list of Auto-Complete values:

```
private void BuildAutoCompleteList()
{
    AutoCompleteStringCollection filterVals =
        new AutoCompleteStringCollection();
    foreach (ExchangeRatesDataSet.CountriesRow countryRow in
        m_ExchangeRatesDataSet.Countries)
    {
        filterVals.Add(countryRow.CountryName);
    }
    m_CountryFromTextBox.AutoCompleteCustomSource = filterVals;
    m_CountryToTextBox.AutoCompleteCustomSource = filterVals;
}
```

This method is called from the constructor of the BindingEvents sample application after data binding is set up. You can find the complete code for BindingEvents in the download code for this chapter.

Data Binding Lifecycle

As mentioned earlier in the book, it's important to keep in mind the *direction* of data flows in data binding and *when* the data flow occurs. Formatting sends data from the data member to the control property, and parsing sends data from the bound control property to the data member. But when do these processes happen?

The trigger for formatting is usually when the current item in a data source is being set, or when the property in the current item for a given binding object is changed. The current item in the data source is set when the data first loads, and again at any time the `Position` property on the `CurrencyManager` for the data source changes. For a tabular data source, such as a data set, the current item is the current row of the data table. For an object collection, the current item is an object reference to one of the objects in the list. If you use the binding source to separate your bound controls from your data sources as recommended, then you don't have to worry about the `CurrencyManager`; just think of it in terms of the `Position` and `Current` properties on the binding source. The `Binding-Source` component encapsulates a currency manager and exposes its properties and events in an easy-to-use API, so you almost never need to worry about the currency manager.

You can expect the formatting process to get called whenever

- You set the data source on a binding source that is bound to controls
- The current item in the binding source is set to a different position
- The data member that a binding object is tied to changes in the under-lying data source (possibly through programmatic code or through a change from another control bound to that same data member)

The exception is if you set the `ControlUpdateMode` property on the binding object to `Never`. This prevents the control from being formatted automatically when the value of the data member changes. Effectively, this makes the data member write-only through data binding. This supports certain advanced error handling scenarios, especially when you want one control to support writing data to the data source, but you don't want that control to update with the current value of the data member if another control bound to the same item in the data source triggers the formatting process. Normally you will want to leave this property set to its default value of `OnPropertyChanged`.

The trigger for the parsing process depends on the binding object's `DataSourceUpdateMode` property. This property supports three enumerated values: `OnValidating`, `OnPropertyChanged`, and `Never`. The default, `OnValidating`, means parsing will occur after the `Validating` event on the bound control fires. For example, if you edit the value in a data-bound `TextBox` control that has a `DataSourceUpdateMode` value of `OnValidating`, and then tab off the control, the order of events is `TextBox.Leave`, `TextBox.Validating`, `Binding.Parse`, and `TextBox.Validated`. If you set the `CausesValidation` property on the control to `false` in conjunction with the `OnValidating` value, then neither validation nor parsing will ever occur.

If the value of the `DataSourceUpdateMode` property is set to `OnPropertyChanged`, then `Binding.Parse` will fire every time the bound control property changes. For a `TextBox`, that means it will fire for every character entered. Finally, setting the `DataSourceUpdateMode` property to `Never` means the parsing process will never be triggered, making the control a read-only control from a data-binding perspective.

Smarter Child-Parent Data Binding

If you've spent any time looking at the BindingEvents application, you are probably thinking that there must be a better way to handle this particular data-binding scenario than what has been presented in the preceding sections—and you're right. What I've showed so far was more to illustrate the use of the formatting and parsing events, not the cleanest way to address the scenario.

If you step back from the existing code and analyze the data-binding scenario, what you really need for the BindingEvents application are three data items that stay synchronized:

- The ExchangeRates row that is the current record being browsed with the data navigator

- The Countries row corresponding to the From Country information

- The Countries row corresponding to the To Country information

The functionality you are trying to achieve here is that when paging through the exchange rate data rows, the corresponding country information should be displayed at the top of the form. And if you edit one of the country names, you want the flag and currency type to update to the entered country.

Countries and ExchangeRates are related by a couple of parent-child relations, so you may be thinking of chaining the binding sources. Unfortunately, that won't really work here because you are displaying child rows, but you want the parent data items to be synchronized to the child, not the other way around.

There is a fairly straightforward way to do this, and it again relies on events. Whenever the current exchange rate record changes, you want to update the two pieces of country information based on the foreign key columns in the exchange rate table. However, you'd probably rather not have to do so much manual data binding for the controls that contain the two parent data items as you did in the BindingEvents sample. What you really want is to have those two sets of country information controls data bound to the country rows themselves, but to keep those bindings synchronized with the data binding of the exchange rows being browsed.

`BindingSource` components raise a number of events throughout their data binding lifecycle, as described earlier. The one you would be interested in for this scenario is the `CurrentChanged` event. If you simply handle the `CurrentChanged` event for the ExchangeRates binding source, you can add code to set the current record for the country information and you will get exactly the behavior described here.

One other change you might want to consider is making the user interface a little friendlier by replacing the text boxes for From Country and To Country with combo box controls that display all the countries currently in the data set. Selecting the country from the combo box should update all the controls displaying country information on that side of the form and should also update the corresponding foreign key column in the exchange rate row being displayed. This new user interface design is shown in Figure 4.8.

Binding to Multiple Copies of Data

The first trick that some people get hung up on for an application like this is dealing with displaying two sets of data-bound controls that are bound to the same set of data (the two sets of country controls), but wanting them to display different items. Your first instinct might simply be to create a single binding source for the Countries table and bind each of the controls in the two sets to their respective columns in that data source. Unfortunately, if you do this, the From Country will always reflect the same information as the To Country and vice versa. Whichever one is selected last will update the other set of controls to match it.

If you read and understood the discussion of currency managers in the last chapter, you probably already understand the problem. If both sets of controls are bound to the same data source, there is one currency manager

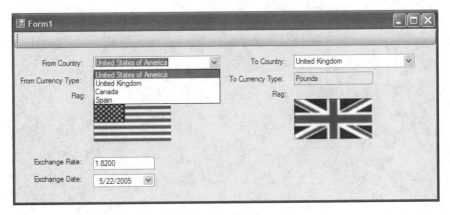

FIGURE 4.8: Updated Currency Exchange Application

created for that data source, and there is only one current item *ever* in that currency manager. Updating the current item in one of the sets of controls immediately updates the controls in the other set because they are bound to the same data source, and the currency manager for that data source keeps all controls bound to the data source synchronized to the current item. So to fix that problem you need to maintain two separate currency managers for the two sets of controls. You could get two separate copies of the data, and each would have its own currency manager as separate data sources. However, a better approach is to have two separate country binding sources, each bound to the same underlying single Countries table in the data set. This does exactly what's needed without requiring you to maintain two copies of the data. Because each binding source encapsulates its own currency manager, even if bound to the same set of data, it gives you just the layer of indirection you need.

As shown in Listing 4.7, the revised sample application includes three binding sources corresponding to the three sets of displayed data—one for the exchange rate data, one for the From Country data, and one for the To Country data. Only one set of data is retrieved and used, and the two country binding sources are both bound to the same table in that data set.

LISTING 4.7: Initializing the Three BindingSource Components

```
public CurrencyExchangeForm()
{
    InitializeComponent();
    // Get the data
    CountriesTableAdapter countriesAdapter =
        new CountriesTableAdapter();
    ExchangeRatesTableAdapter exchangeRatesAdapter =
        new ExchangeRatesTableAdapter();
    m_ExchangeRatesDataSet = new ExchangeRatesDataSet();
    countriesAdapter.Fill(m_ExchangeRatesDataSet.Countries);
    exchangeRatesAdapter.Fill(m_ExchangeRatesDataSet.ExchangeRates);

    m_CountriesFromBindingSource.DataSource = m_ExchangeRatesDataSet;
    m_CountriesFromBindingSource.DataMember =
        m_ExchangeRatesDataSet.Countries.TableName;
    m_CountriesFromBindingSource.CurrentChanged +=
        OnCountryFromChanged;

    m_CountriesToBindingSource.DataSource = m_ExchangeRatesDataSet;
    m_CountriesToBindingSource.DataMember =
```

```
        m_ExchangeRatesDataSet.Countries.TableName;
    m_CountriesToBindingSource.CurrentChanged += OnCountryToChanged;

    m_ExchangeRatesBindingSource.DataSource = m_ExchangeRatesDataSet;
    m_ExchangeRatesBindingSource.DataMember =
        m_ExchangeRatesDataSet.ExchangeRates.TableName;
    m_ExchangeRatesBindingSource.CurrentChanged +=
        OnCurrentExchangeRateChanged;
    CreateBindings();
}
```

The code hooks up the data source and member for each binding source, sharing the Countries table in the data set across two binding sources. It also hooks up event handlers to the CurrentChanged event on each binding source and uses those handlers to help enforce synchronization between the different data sources. By using binding sources like this, the data-binding code for the individual controls is lot more straightforward. You no longer need to hook up to the Format and Parse events, and can simply let the normal data-binding mechanisms and automatic formatting do all the work for you. You could even hook up all the rest of the data binding in the designer; the code to do it programmatically is shown in Listing 4.8 so that you can see what is going on at the individual control level.

LISTING 4.8: CreateBindings Method

```
private void CreateBindings()
{
    m_CurrencyTypeFromTextBox.DataBindings.Add("Text",
        m_CountriesFromBindingSource, "CurrencyType", true);

    m_CurrencyTypeToTextBox.DataBindings.Add("Text",
        m_CountriesToBindingSource, "CurrencyType", true);

    m_FlagFromPictureBox.DataBindings.Add("Image",
        m_CountriesFromBindingSource, "Flag", true);

    m_FlagToPictureBox.DataBindings.Add("Image",
        m_CountriesToBindingSource, "Flag", true);

    m_ExchangeRateTextBox.DataBindings.Add("Text",
        m_ExchangeRatesBindingSource, "ExchangeRate", true,
        DataSourceUpdateMode.OnValidation, "1.0000", "#.0000");
```

continues

```
m_ExchangeRateDateTimePicker.DataBindings.Add("Value",
    m_ExchangeRatesBindingSource, "ExchangeRateDate", true);

m_FromCountryCombo.DataSource = m_CountriesFromBindingSource;
m_FromCountryCombo.DisplayMember = "CountryName";
m_FromCountryCombo.ValueMember = "CountryID";

m_ToCountryCombo.DataSource = m_CountriesToBindingSource;
m_ToCountryCombo.DisplayMember = "CountryName";
m_ToCountryCombo.ValueMember = "CountryID";

// Twiddle the position to get the CurrentChanged
// event to sync things up initially
m_ExchangeRatesBindingSource.Position = 1;
m_ExchangeRatesBindingSource.Position = 0;
}
```

Most of the code in Listing 4.8 just adds data bindings to the individual controls and ties the appropriate control property to the corresponding column in the table through the binding source with automatic formatting turned on. The end of the method shows the data binding setup for the combo boxes. As discussed in Chapter 3, the ComboBox control uses complex binding and lets you specify both a DisplayMember and a Value-Member within the data source. In this case, set the ValueMember to the CountryID column so that you can later use that to update the exchange rate row when the parent item changes.

The code also does a little "twiddle" at the end by setting the position on the exchange rate binding source to one and then back to zero. This is needed to make things work correctly on the initial presentation of the form. The reason for this twiddle is to get the CurrentChanged event (discussed next) to fire again after all the data bindings are set up, because it is the CurrentChanged handler that takes care of synchronizing the three sets of controls.

Updating Parent Data-Bound Controls from Child Data-Bound Controls

The trick to reversing master-details scenarios like this is to synchronize the controls bound to parent data items based on the selection of child data items. In this case, the individual data items are rows in two different tables. Those tables have a parent-child relation from the parent Country table to the child ExchangeRates table based on the foreign key constraints from the CountryFromID and CountryToID columns of the Exchange-Rates table to the CountryID column of the Countries table. The `Current-Changed` event on the child data source gives you the perfect opportunity to perform that synchronization. The following code shows the handler for the `CurrentChanged` event on the exchange rates binding source:

```csharp
private void OnCurrentExchangeRateChanged(object sender, EventArgs e)
{
    // Get the strongly typed row for the exchange rate table
    ExchangeRatesDataSet.ExchangeRatesRow currentRow =
        (ExchangeRatesDataSet.ExchangeRatesRow)
        ((DataRowView)m_ExchangeRatesBindingSource.Current).Row;

    // Get the related parent rows through the properties generated
    // on the typed data rows
    ExchangeRatesDataSet.CountriesRow fromCountryRow =
        currentRow.CountriesRowByFK_ExchangeRates_CountriesFrom;
    ExchangeRatesDataSet.CountriesRow toCountryRow =
        currentRow.CountriesRowByFK_ExchangeRates_CountriesTo;

    // Update the parent row controls based on this record change
    if (fromCountryRow != null && toCountryRow != null)
    {
        m_FromCountryCombo.SelectedValue = fromCountryRow.CountryID;
        m_ToCountryCombo.SelectedValue = toCountryRow.CountryID;
    }
    else // New record
    {
        currentRow.CountryFromID = 0;
        m_CountriesFromBindingSource.Position = 0;
        currentRow.CountryToID = 0;
        m_CountriesToBindingSource.Position = 0;
        currentRow.ExchangeRate = 1.0M;
        currentRow.ExchangeRateDate = DateTime.Now;
        // Commit the changes to notify other controls
        m_ExchangeRatesBindingSource.EndEdit();
    }
}
```

The first thing the code does is to obtain a strongly typed reference to the current exchange rate row through the binding source. It does this by casting the `Current` item to a `DataRowView`, then using the `Row` property on that to obtain a `DataRow` reference to the row, which it then casts to the strongly typed row. After the code gets the current exchange rate row, it uses the strongly typed row properties exposed on the `Exchange-RateRow` to obtain the two country parent rows. These properties are named by the data set code generation based on the relations in the XSD file that defines the data set. If there is just one parent-child relation between the tables, it will be named for the parent table (e.g., `Countries-Row`). However, in this case there are two parent-child relations between the Countries table and the ExchangeRates table, so it appends the specific relation name to distinguish between the two (e.g., `CountriesRow-ByFK_ExchangeRates_CountriesTo`). These properties simply call the `GetParentRow` method for you with the appropriate relation name. You could also call this method directly, providing the relation names, but you'd get back an untyped data row and have to do more casting. Thus the parent row properties are a better option.

As long as the parent rows are found, all it takes to synchronize the two sets of parent data is to set the `SelectedValue` property on the country combo boxes to the corresponding foreign key values from the child row. Alternatively, you could have gone through the individual binding sources for the two sets of country data, done a lookup to find the corresponding item in the data source, then set that as the current item, but that would be a lot more work. Setting the `SelectedValue` property on the combo box is just like the user selecting the item in the list, which updates the current record in the data source, so this results in much more straightforward code.

The code also handles the situation wherein, if you have paged to an item that has just been added to the exchange rates table, none of the columns are initialized yet, so the code sets some simple defaults. Notice that it also calls the `EndEdit` method after making those changes. You need to call this method any time you programmatically update values in the data source to get the bound controls to update (discussed earlier in the section "Completing the Editing Process").

> **▪ NOTE** **Working with Strongly Typed Data Sets Requires Tradeoffs**
>
> The downside of working with the strongly typed data rows is that you end up having to do a lot of casting to get them into their appropriate type from methods that return loosely typed rows. The tradeoff is that when you access the columns of that row—like the code does at the end of the method—you can get compile-time error information if any of the columns get renamed or go away. That compile-time information has saved me countless hours, and so the tradeoff is well worth the extra casting hassle to me.

You need two more `CurrentChanged` handlers to get the whole form functioning in an intuitive way that keeps the three sets of data synchronized. Any time the user selects a new country in one of the two sets of country data controls at the top of the form, they are effectively editing the exchange rate item that is currently being displayed (specifically, setting the CountryFromID or CountryToID columns). But those controls are bound to different sets of data. To get those changes pushed down into the exchange rates table, you can handle the `CurrentChanged` event on each of the binding sources for the two sets of country controls. The following code is for the `m_CountriesFromBindingSource`. The code for the other country binding source is identical except for the names of the objects involved, which reflect the other set of country controls:

```
private void OnCountryFromChanged(object sender, EventArgs e)
{
    // Get the current From Country row
    ExchangeRatesDataSet.CountriesRow fromCountryRow =
        (ExchangeRatesDataSet.CountriesRow)
        ((DataRowView)m_CountriesFromBindingSource.Current).Row;

    // Get the current exchange rate row
    ExchangeRatesDataSet.ExchangeRatesRow currentExchangeRateRow
        = (ExchangeRatesDataSet.ExchangeRatesRow)
        ((DataRowView)m_ExchangeRatesBindingSource.Current).Row;

    // Set the foreign key column in the child
    currentExchangeRateRow.CountryFromID = fromCountryRow.CountryID;
}
```

Again, most of the code here has to do with obtaining and casting the current country and exchange rate rows to the appropriate type so that you can do a strongly typed assignment from the parent row primary key to the child row foreign key.

This code is all included in the BindingParentData sample application in the download code.

Synchronizing Many-to-Many Related Collections

Binding source events also come in handy for managing complex synchronization scenarios when you want to present data that has many-to-many relationships between the data items. In these situations, you might want to present the related items with multiple controls in a way that gives the user a similar experience to master-details data binding.

For example, take a look at the data schema depicted in Figure 4.9. It shows the Orders, Order Details, and Products tables from Northwind. The Order Details table has foreign key relations into both the Orders and Products tables. As a result, in addition to containing other data related to each order detail item, it also forms a many-to-many relationship between Orders and Products. In other words, each Order contains a collection of Products, and each Product belongs to many Orders.

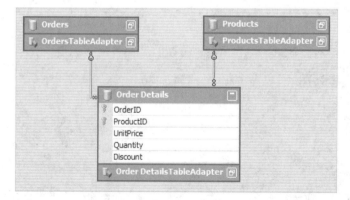

FIGURE 4.9: Many-To-Many Relationship Between Orders and Products

Assume you want to present a user interface that lets the user browse through orders and see which products were contained within those orders. You could present the collection of orders in one grid, and when the user selects an order row in the grid, you could present all the products that are part of that order in another grid, as shown in Figure 4.10.

The application shown in Figure 4.10 is named ManyToManyBinding and is contained in the download code for this chapter. It contains a data set with the relations shown in Figure 4.9 and uses a set of binding sources to drive the user interface behavior we are trying for here. Specifically, the form has a grid for orders and a grid for products. In the sample I applied some formatting of the columns in the grid using the designer to get the specific set of columns shown. The form also has three binding sources: one for the Orders grid, one for the products grid, and one is just used to help synchronize the data that will be presented through the other two binding sources.

The code supporting the Orders grid is just like many of the other data-binding examples shown so far. The grid is bound to the binding source, and the binding source is bound to the Orders table in the data set. The code that sets up the data binding for the Products grid actually does much

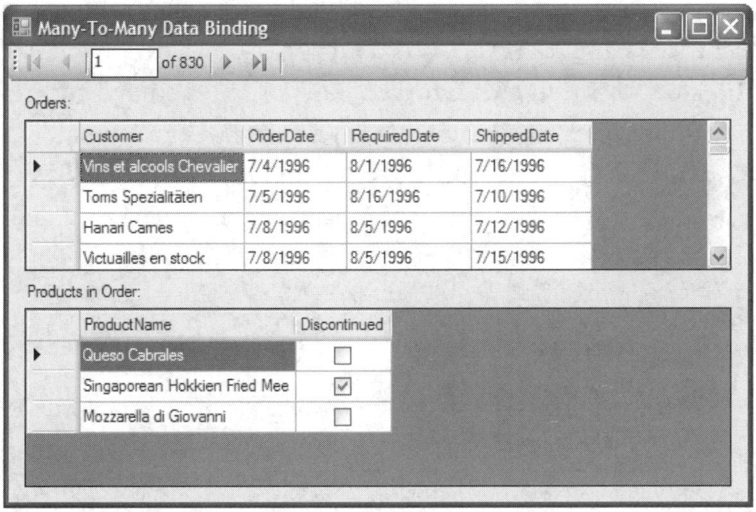

FIGURE 4.10: Browsing Related Many-To-Many Records

the same, binding the grid to its binding source, and the binding source to
the Products table:

```
void InitDataBindings()
{
   // Hook the grids to their binding sources
   m_OrdersGrid.DataSource = m_OrdersBindingSource;
   m_ProductsGrid.DataSource = m_ProductsBindingSource;

   // Hook up the orders and products binding sources
   m_OrdersBindingSource.DataSource = m_OrdersProductsDataSet;
   m_OrdersBindingSource.DataMember =
      m_OrdersProductsDataSet.Orders.TableName;
   m_ProductsBindingSource.DataSource =
      m_OrdersProductsDataSet.Products;

   // Set up the order details binding source
   // for master-details binding
   m_OrderDetailsBindingSource.DataSource = m_OrdersBindingSource;
   m_OrderDetailsBindingSource.DataMember = "FK_Order_Details_Orders";

   // Hook up the ListChanged event on the details source
   m_OrderDetailsBindingSource.ListChanged += OnDetailsListChanged;
}
```

The data binding hook-up code then sets up master-details binding
between the Orders binding source and the Order Details binding source,
so whenever a new Order row is selected, the data contained by the
m_OrderDetailsBindingSource will be updated to just show the order
detail rows for the selected order. The code then hooks up an event handler
for the ListChanged event on that Order Details binding source so that
you can react to that changing list of details, each of which contains a
ProductID that identifies the product the detail item represents.

The following code shows the handler for that ListChanged event:

```
void OnDetailsListChanged(object sender, ListChangedEventArgs e)
{
   if (m_OrderDetailsBindingSource.Count < 1)
      return;
   PropertyDescriptor productIdPropDesc =
      TypeDescriptor.GetProperties(
      m_OrderDetailsBindingSource.Current)["ProductID"];
   // Extract the parent item identifier from each order detail item
   // and add to a filter string
   StringBuilder builder = new StringBuilder();
```

```
    foreach (object detailItem in m_OrderDetailsBindingSource.List)
    {
        int productId = (int)productIdPropDesc.GetValue(detailItem);
        if (builder.Length != 0) // Adding criteria
        {
            builder.Append(" OR ");
        }
        builder.Append(string.Format("ProductID = {0}", productId));
    }

    // Set a filter on the products binding source to limit
    // what is shown in the products grid
    m_ProductsBindingSource.Filter = builder.ToString();
}
```

This event handler first has a guard statement to see if there are any detail rows to work with. If not, it does nothing. The event handler next gets the type information for the ProductID property from the current item in the Order Details binding source. I could have simply cast the items to the DataRowView type as in some previous samples, but I wanted to write the code in a way that would work even if the data source was composed of an object hierarchy with many-to-many relations. When you use the TypeDescriptor class to retrieve property descriptor information, it will work whether the underlying collection is a data table or some other custom collection of custom objects. In this case, as long as the objects in the collection have a ProductID property (or column), it will work just fine (see Chapter 7 for more details about property descriptors).

The event handler then loops through each of the Order Details items and extracts the value of the ProductID property using the property descriptor. It uses that value to build up a filter string using the String-Builder class. Note that any time you are doing string concatenation in a loop like this, you should use the StringBuilder class or String.Format to avoid creating unnecessary temporary strings that make the garbage collector work harder.

Once the filter string has been constructed from the product IDs of all the detail rows, the filter string is set on the Filter property of the binding source. The Filter property, as discussed earlier, restricts the items presented through the binding source based on the filter criteria, as long as the underlying data source supports filtering. As a result of setting that filter, the only rows that will be presented in the Products grid are the ones that have order details related to the current order, which gives us just what we were looking for.

Where Are We?

This chapter covered the BindingSource component in detail and discussed how to use it as an intermediary between your data sources and your data-bound controls. You learned how to set up binding objects to bind control properties to sources, using either automatic formatting or binding events to control the formatting and parsing yourself. It also covered some event handling at the BindingSource level, which gives you more control over related items on a form that don't have a parent-to-child relationship you can directly bind to.

Some key takeaways for this chapter are the following:

- You create simple data bindings by using the Binding class to associate a single property on a control with a single property in a data source.

- To set up master-details data binding, you point the child collection binding source to the parent collection binding source and specify which property within the parent collection identifies the child relation.

- The BindingSource component is a rich data container that encapsulates a currency manager and a data source. It exposes numerous methods and properties that let you manage the contained data collection, as well as events to let you track what is happening to the data source. You can use these events to support updating controls bound to parent objects when the child objects are selected.

The next chapter shows you how to generate most of the data-binding code covered in this chapter using the designer, which saves an immense amount of time. I think it is important to understand the code that is being generated, which is why I covered how to do it manually first. Now you will learn how to shave days or weeks off your Windows Forms data-binding schedules using Visual Studio 2005.

5

Generating Bound Controls with the Visual Studio Designer

B Y NOW, YOU are hopefully getting a firm grasp on the code involved
for setting up data binding between controls and data sources using
`BindingSource` components or `Binding` objects as middlemen. However,
writing all that code can become tedious and error prone, especially for the
more common scenarios. It would be really nice if someone else could
write that code and you could just focus on the core logic of your application. Thanks to a number of new designer features in Visual Studio 2005,
you will rarely have to write the data-binding code by hand for common
scenarios. The Data Sources window combined with the Properties window, Smart Tags, and wizards in the designer let you tell Visual Studio
what you want in an intuitive and declarative point-and-click manner, and
it will write all the tedious data-binding code for you.

Working with the Data Sources Window

The Data Sources window is a new designer support window in the Visual
Studio 2005 IDE. This window lets you quickly set up data binding
between controls and data sources using just a few selection and drag-and-
drop mouse gestures in the designer. You can create new data sources,

generate bound controls from those data sources, and bind data sources to existing controls. You can use the Data Sources window to create data sources from databases, Web services, or objects. Figure 5.1 shows the Data Sources window with the following data sources:

- A data set data source based on the MoneyDB database used for the currency exchange samples in Chapter 4.

- A Web service data source named localhost that references the CustomersService Web service that is included in the download samples for this chapter.

- An object data source based on a CustomersBusinessLayer object hierarchy included in the download samples.

If you have multiple projects in a solution, the contents of the Data Sources window reflect the current project based on the current selection in Solution Explorer. To view the data sources for another project within the solution, select the project or any of its child items in Solution Explorer,

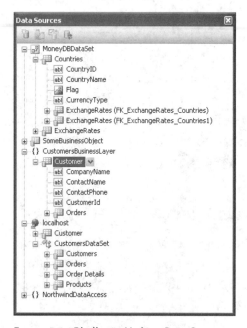

FIGURE 5.1: Binding to Various Data Sources

then switch back to the Data Sources window. The view that is presented will be slightly different depending on whether the current document in the editor is a form in Design view. The Data Sources window is designed to generate data-bound controls in Windows Forms through the designer, so you usually won't work with the Data Sources window except when the Forms designer is displayed.

Adding Data Sources to a Project

Visual Studio automatically adds any typed data set definitions that are part of your project to the Data Sources window. It also adds objects returned from any Web references that are part of your project to the Data Sources window. However, you don't necessarily have to add these things to your project before you start using the Data Sources window, because you can create connections to data sources directly from the window itself.

When you add a data source through the Data Sources window to a Web service or object data source, you aren't actually creating the data source itself; you are just creating an association or connection to the data source type that you can use for data-binding purposes in your project. When you add a database data source to your project, you are in fact generating a new type definition that will be part of your project. To add a data source, you launch the Data Source Configuration wizard. There are three ways to do this:

- If no data sources exist in your project yet, click the *Add New Data Source* link in the Data Sources window.

- Click the *Add New Data Source* icon in the Data Sources window (see Figure 5.2).

- From the *Data* menu in Visual Studio, select *Add New Data Source*.

In addition to letting you create new data sources, if the data source is a typed data set, the Data Sources window toolbar lets you edit the data set in the designer or configure it with the Data Source Configuration wizard (which we'll be stepping through shortly). The toolbar also lets you refresh

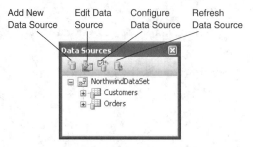

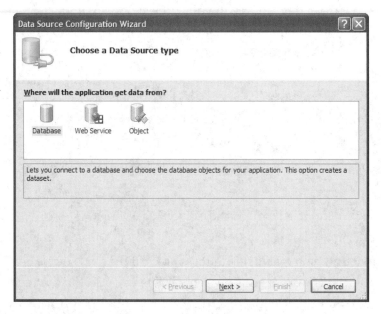

FIGURE 5.2: Data Sources Toolbar

the data source if something about it has changed while the Data Sources window is displayed.

Choosing the Type of Data Source

The first step in the wizard lets you choose the type of data source you want to create: database, Web service, or object types (see Figure 5.3).

Let's start with databases, since they are easier to understand if you have worked with data binding in the past in .NET.

FIGURE 5.3: Choose a Data Source Type Step

Adding a Database Data Source

When you select *Database* for the data source type, what you really are doing is adding a typed data set definition to your project that is ready to contain data from the database objects that you select in the wizard. You could accomplish the same thing by selecting a data set from the Add New Item dialog, then dragging and dropping database objects on the designer surface from Server Explorer. The Data Source Configuration wizard steps you through the process in a little different way. The following procedure outlines this process.

1. Choose your database connection (see Figure 5.4).

   The drop-down list shows the data connections that have been configured in Visual Studio through this wizard or through the Server Explorer window. These same items appear in the Data Connections node in the Server Explorer tree.

   Depending on the options selected when the connection was created, the section below the drop-down list may indicate that the connection

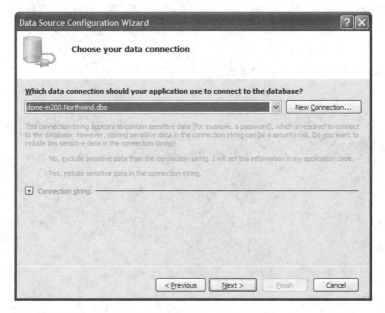

FIGURE 5.4: Choose Your Database Connection Step

string contains sensitive information (specifically, a username and password). If so, it gives you the option to leave that information out of the connection string so that the sensitive information doesn't get embedded in your configuration file. You can also view the resulting connection string by clicking on the plus sign next to the Connection String group header. This displays the connection string that will be used in a selectable text box. You can select the string (in case you need to copy it to the Clipboard), but you cannot edit the string directly.

2. If you click the *New Connection* button, what you see depends on whether you have configured any connections before. The first time you add a connection, you are prompted to select a data source and provider (see Figure 5.5). You also get the same dialog if you click the *Change* button from the Add Connection dialog (see Figure 5.6). The Add Connection dialog lets you create a new connection based on any of the available providers, and once you do, it too will be added to the list of data connections in Server Explorer.

The Add Connection dialog is new in Visual Studio 2005, but it's very similar to the one that existed in previous versions. The items presented in this dialog change based on the provider selected. Figure 5.6 shows the settings for the managed SQL Server provider. To configure a SQL Server connection, you specify a server name—this can be a SQL Server instance name on the network or an IP address. If you are referring to the local machine's default instance of SQL Server, you can use one of three shorthand addresses: localhost, (local), or just the

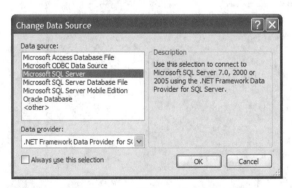

FIGURE 5.5: Data Source and Provider Selection

dot (.) character. You also provide authentication information and specify the database name. This configures the connection string that is used to connect to the database.

If you had selected a SQL Server database file as the data source in Figure 5.5, the dialog would be different and would only let you specify a path to the database file and authentication information. This is the way to specify a data connection for a SQL Server 2005 Express Edition database.

3. Choose whether to save the connection information in your application configuration file (Figure 5.7). Doing so lets you easily modify the connection string when you deploy your application without needing to change any of the source code.

Visual Studio adds code to the table adapter definitions to read in the connection string from the .config file if it can be found; otherwise, the

FIGURE 5.6: Add Connection Dialog

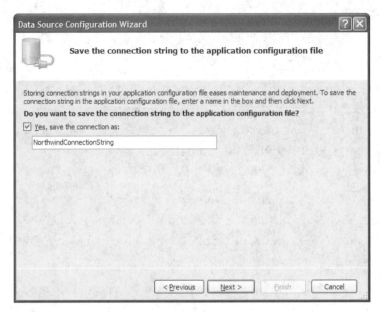

FIGURE 5.7: Save Connection String Step

table adapter tries to use a hard-coded default (the one specified at design time through this process).

4. In the next window you select the objects from the database that you want to include in the typed data set that will be generated as the output of this wizard process (see Figure 5.8). As mentioned earlier in the book, you can include tables, views, stored procedures, or functions in the data set simply by checking the boxes next to them in the tree of database objects. This is analogous to dragging these objects onto the data set designer surface from Server Explorer. At the bottom of the dialog you can specify the type name for the generated typed data set class.

5. When you click the *Finish* button, the typed data set definition will be added to your project as an XML Schema Definition (XSD) file with an associated typed data set definition source file that is hidden by default. You can view the actual typed data set code by expanding the Solution Explorer tree underneath the XSD file. Underneath the XSD file is a .Designer.cs file for the data set that contains the autogenerated class definitions for the data set and its associated table adapters. Additionally, the Data Sources window will update to show the objects in your data set.

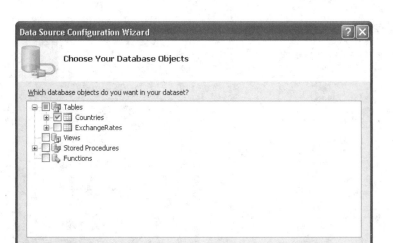

FIGURE 5.8: Choose Database Objects Step

Adding a Web Service Data Source

Windows Forms applications are often just a user interface for front-end functionality that resides on a middle-tier server somewhere out on the network. As the use of the Internet and widely distributed networks grow, a common model for distributing functionality and data is through Web services. As such, consuming data returned from a Web service is a common need for Windows Forms applications, and one way to consume data is to bind controls to it. The Data Sources window makes this much easier by generating all the appropriate code for you based on a Web reference that you add to your project.

As mentioned earlier, if you add a Web reference to your project directly, the object types returned by methods on that Web service will show up in the Data Sources window automatically. If you need to add a Web reference for the purposes of data binding and you haven't already added the reference, you can easily do so by selecting a Web service as the data source type when you are in the Data Source Configuration wizard. This displays the Add Web Reference dialog as the next step in the wizard (see Figure 5.9). Note that this is the same dialog you get when you select *Add Web Reference* from Solution Explorer.

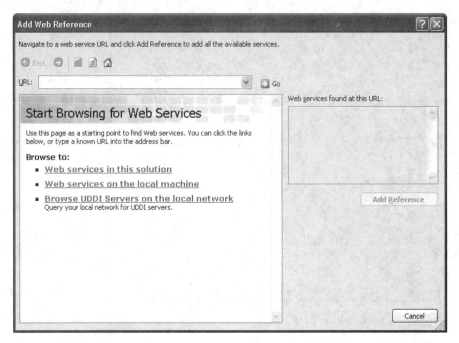

FIGURE 5.9: Add Web Reference Dialog

You can type in a URL to a Web service or browse for one using the available links in the embedded browser window. When you enter or select a Web service, the browser window displays information about the Web service. If you provide a name for the Web service in the Web Reference Name box after selecting a Web service, this will be used as the namespace that wraps the Web service proxy class and type information within the project. This namespace will be generated as a child namespace of the default project namespace. In addition to the proxy class that lets you make calls to the Web service, class declarations are also generated for all the types that the Web service methods return. It is these type definitions that the Data Sources window lets you use for data binding.

Adding an Object Data Source

In addition to working with database objects and Web service return types, you also often want to perform data binding against objects returned from your business layer or data access layer classes. Note that these include typed data set definitions that reside in a separate assembly, which should be the normal way you design your data access components.

1. To set up data binding to these objects through the designer, select the *Object* data source type in the wizard's first step (see Figure 5.3).

2. Select the object type that you would like to bind to (see Figure 5.10). The wizard displays the objects in a tree view that lets you drill down from the assembly level, through the namespaces, and to the types defined in those namespaces.

3. If the type you want to bind to resides in an assembly that you don't yet have a reference to, click the *Add Reference* button to display the corresponding dialog that lets you add a reference to the assembly to your project. This is the same Add Reference dialog that you use from Solution Explorer. When you select an assembly in it, a normal reference is added to your project.

All public types in a referenced assembly are displayed in the tree of bindable objects, and they can be displayed in the Data Sources window if

FIGURE 5.10: Object Type Selection Step

selected. However, if the object type doesn't expose any public properties, the type will be useless in the Data Sources window. By design, the Data Sources window only lets you set up data binding to public properties on an object, even if fields (member variables) are exposed as public. This is deliberate—to encourage you to follow the .NET design guidance that fields should always be private and should be wrapped by properties if they are meant for external consumption. Additionally, if there is no way to obtain an instance of an object type that has been populated with data through methods on that type or other types in the external library, then it may not be very useful for data binding anyway, unless you are going to programmatically populate instances of that type.

You can use the Data Sources window from any kind of project, including a class library project. However, since the main purpose of the Data Sources window is to generate data-bound controls or to generate the data-binding code for existing controls on a form, the window has limited utility in non-Windows Forms projects.

When you add an object data source through the Data Sources window, a couple of things happen in your project. Behind the scenes, Visual Studio adds a .datasource file under the Properties subfolder. This file contains type information about each data source object type that has been added to the project. That file is just an XML file that complies with a schema defined by Microsoft. A separate file will be created for each referenced assembly and type within it that is added as a data source. The file naming convention for these files is <namespace>.<typename>.datasource, and the content looks like the following:

```
<GenericObjectDataSource DisplayName="Customer" Version="1.0"
    xmlns="urn:schemas-microsoft-com:xml-msdatasource">
  <TypeInfo>CustomersBusinessLayer.Customer, CustomersBusinessLayer,
      Version=1.0.0.0, Culture=neutral, PublicKeyToken=null</
TypeInfo>
  </GenericObjectDataSource>
```

If you perform your data access from a data access layer class library—which I recommend for any serious application—you will need to set up data binding for controls in your Windows Forms application based on the data that your data access layer will return. That data might be in the form of typed data sets, custom business objects, data readers, or untyped data sets. The only object types that the Data Sources window can work with are those that provide enough type information about the data that they contain to generate the appropriate data-binding code. Thus, these can only be typed data sets and custom business objects that define public properties to expose the contained data.

Even if you are dealing with a typed data set, when it comes from outside your Windows Forms project, the Data Sources window considers it just another object. So to get a typed data set definition from your data access layer to display in the Data Sources window for data-binding purposes, do the following:

1. Add a reference to the data access layer assembly.
2. Use the Data Source Configuration wizard to add a new data source.
3. Select the *Object* data source type.
4. Select the typed data set out of the type tree shown in Figure 5.10.

Once you do this, you can use the table and field information in that data set to set up control bindings using the Data Sources window.

However, when it comes time to use that data type, you will have to populate it with data from somewhere, so you will have to write a little bit of code to obtain an instance of the object and set it as the data source on the control or component you are bound to.

Generating Bound Controls from Data Sources

One of the most tedious things to do in Windows Forms programming is to lay out a bunch of controls on a form that you intend to bind to data sources, name all the controls, and then get all the binding code wired up correctly. Luckily, because this is such a common thing you need to do, the Data Sources window automates most of it for you. You saw an example of this in Chapter 1 when we generated an entire data-bound details form for Employees through a single drag-and-drop operation from the Data Sources window.

Once you have added data sources to your project as described in the preceding sections, they display as icons in the Data Sources window. The icons displayed depend on what the current document is in the editor window of Visual Studio. You can't really do anything with the items in the Data Sources window except browse through them if you are in a code window. It can be a handy way to refresh your memory about the data members for a particular table or object that you are coding against without having to declare a member to get IntelliSense assistance. But the main purpose of the Data Sources window is to work with the Windows Forms design surface. If you display a form in the designer, the icons next to the data sources and members change to represent the kind of controls that they will generate if you drag data items from the Data Sources tree onto a form.

There are default control associations for different types, and those associations can be customized. At the collection level (such as a data table, list of objects, or array), the default control association is a `DataGridView` control. At the individual data member level, the default control depends on the type of the member. Things like strings, numeric types, and `Guids` default to a control type of a `TextBox`; `DateTime` types default to a `DateTimePicker` control; and Booleans default to a `CheckBox` control. Custom types don't default to a specific control, but you can set them to use a specific control type as long as there is a suitable format conversion for the default property on that control type from the data member type.

If you look back at Figure 5.1, you will see the icons for these controls depicted for the MoneyDB tables and fields, and for the parent and child objects covered earlier in this chapter. These built-in control icons used in the Data Sources window are the same as their corresponding control icon from the Toolbox window. Table 5.1 illustrates these icons and describes them.

When you drag an item from the Data Sources window tree of controls, a number of controls and components are generated as members of the form in the designer. First off, if the item you are dragging is a data table or a field from a data table, a typed data set member is added to the form and displayed in the component tray. Additionally, a table adapter and a binding source are generated and added to the form as well.

If the data source was created as an object data source type, then only a binding source will be generated. The binding source has its `DataSource` property set a `Type` class instance describing the actual bound object type

TABLE 5.1: Data Sources Control Icons

Icon	Icon Type	Description
⊘	No mapping	Default icon used when Visual Studio cannot determine an appropriate control to use based on the type. Doesn't generate any control if dragged onto the design surface.
{ }	Namespace	Top-level icon for custom object data sources contained within a namespace. Doesn't generate any control if dragged onto the design surface.
	Web reference	Top-level icon for types defined through a Web service reference. Doesn't generate any bound controls if dragged onto the design surface.
	`DataSet`	Top-level icon for a typed data set data source. Doesn't generate any control if dragged onto the design surface.
	`DataGridView`	Default icon used for collections of data. Generates a `DataGridView` control bound to the data collection. The cell types will be determined by the child data member control mappings.
	Details view	Generates a collection of form controls of the types mapped to the child data members.
abl	`TextBox`	Generates a `TextBox` control with its `Text` property bound to the data member.
A	`Label`	Generates a `Label` control with its `Text` property bound to the data member.
☑	`CheckBox`	Generates a `CheckBox` control with its `Checked` property bound to the data member.
	`PictureBox`	Generates a `PictureBox` control with the `Image` property bound to the data member.

continues

TABLE 5.1:   Data Sources Control Icons (Continued)

Icon	Icon Type	Description
	ComboBox	Generates a `ComboBox` control with its `Text` property bound to the string representation of the data member. It doesn't give you a way to set up the `DataMember` and `ValueMember` properties, so you probably won't use this much.
	ListBox	Generates a `ListBox` control with its `Text` property bound to the string representation of the data member. It doesn't give you a way to set up the `DataMember` and `ValueMember` properties, so you probably won't use this much.
	NumericUpDown	Generates a `NumericUpDown` control with its `Value` property bound to the data member.
	DateTimePicker	Generates a `DateTimePicker` control with its `Value` property set to the data member.
A	LinkLabel	Generates a `LinkLabel` control with its `Text` property set to the data member.

(using the `typeof` operator). This gives the designer enough information about the bound object type's metadata to let you configure data member bindings in the designer. Specifically, the metadata that matters are which public properties the object exposes. Additionally, the first collection data source that is dragged onto the form will have a binding navigator created for it, and that navigator will be associated with the binding source.

It is a little difficult to describe all of this with static pictures and text because it is a very dynamic process. Figure 5.11 shows a form in the designer after the ExchangeRates table has been dragged from the Data Sources window onto the form.

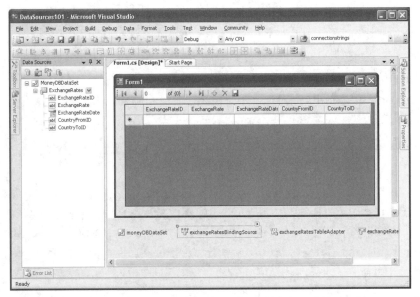

FIGURE 5.11: Generated Form Controls and Components from a Data Table

From that single mouse gesture, the following things happen:

- A `MoneyDBDataSet` instance is added to the form to contain the data for the table.

- An `ExchangeRatesTableAdapter` is added to the form to fill the data set with data.

- A `BindingSource` is added to the form to bind the data set to the grid control, its data source set to the data set, and its data member set to the `ExchangeRates` table within the data set.

- A `BindingNavigator` is added to the form and associated with the binding source.

- A `DataGridView` control is added to the form because the control mapping set in the Data Sources window for the ExchangeRates data table defaults to a `DataGridView` control because it is a list-based data source. The `DataSource` property for the grid is also set to the binding source.

- Columns are added to the grid for each of the child data item properties, and their column types and column names are set according to the type of the data item property.

- All of the instances of controls and components are given names based on the name of the data source item it was generated from (e.g., `exchangeRatesBindingSource`).

- A line of code is added to the `Form.Load` event handler in the main form code file to fill the data table using the table adapter.

- Finally, an event handler is added for the *Save* button in the binding navigator to persist changes to the data set back to the database through a call to the `Update` method on the table adapter.

As a result of that single mouse gesture and all the resulting designer code generated, you have a fully functioning, complex data-bound application with running data—without writing a single line of code yourself. That's pretty cool!

Because we haven't covered the `DataGridView` control in any detail yet, I'll save describing that example and how to customize it until the next chapter. For now, let's look at the other kind of generated controls for data collection—the Details view. You saw a quick example of using the Details view control mapping in Chapter 1.

When you set the control type to Details for a business object or a data table in the Data Sources window, and then drag the item out onto the designer surface, a collection of controls are generated: one control for each data member that has a control mapping set for it in the Data Sources window. You also get a `Label` control for each data member, with its `Text` property set to the name of the data member. This gives you a form view like that shown in Figure 5.12.

Each data member gets a control generated based on the control mapping in the Data Sources window, and the name of the control is set to correspond to the data member name (e.g., `someBitmapPictureBox` for the `SomeBitmap` property on the `SomeBusinessObject` class in the figure, `someStringTextBox` for the `SomeString` property, `someIntegerNumeric-UpDown` for the `SomeInteger` property, and so on). Basically, what you get is a fully laid-out form with bound controls for each of the data members. This saves a ton of time dragging and dropping controls from the Toolbox and setting their properties to get them all wired up. The form will also automatically resize to fit the controls when you drag-and-drop the Details

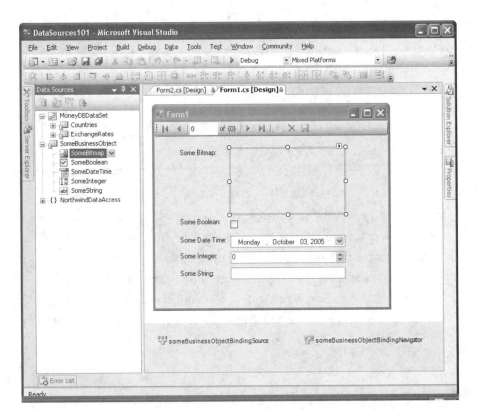

Figure 5.12: Details View Generated Controls for Custom Business Object

view, which keeps all of the controls nicely aligned and easy to grab within the form. Immediately after the drop, all of the generated controls are selected so that clicking and dragging on any of them will drag the entire bunch, letting you get them all positioned in the form as you like.

Like with the `DataGridView` mapping, you also get other objects created to manage the data source. In this case, since the data source was a business object instead of a data table, the generated components include a binding source and binding navigator, but no data set or table adapter. The binding source is only created if needed. So if a binding source already exists that is bound to the same data source, the existing binding source will be used for the data source for creating the `Binding` objects for the generated controls. The binding navigator is only created for the first collection that is dragged onto the form from the Data Sources window. You can always add and configure your own binding navigators later from the Toolbox.

When you set up bindings to custom objects, the `DataSource` of the binding source is set using the object's type information, so it knows what the data members and types of the properties are on the object for code generation and designer purposes. However, to actually use the binding source at runtime, you have to write the code to obtain an instance of the object and set that instance as the data source of the binding source. The bound controls will then display the data contained in that object. This is true whether the object represents a business object, an object returned by a Web service, or a typed data set that is defined in another assembly.

You can also generate the controls one at a time from the Data Sources window if you prefer. If you drag an individual property from a custom object, or an individual column from a data table's data source onto the form, only the individual corresponding control and its associated label will be created. A binding source and navigator will also be created if needed, along with a data set and table adapter if the bound data property is a member from a data table.

Selecting the Bound Control Type

As discussed earlier, the control types you first see for individual data members are defaults. You can change the control type in the Data Sources window by selecting the data member and selecting a different control type from the drop-down list (see Figure 5.13).

The list of controls presented is based on the data member's type. Visual Studio ships with a predefined set of mappings, but you can customize those mappings. You can also set the control mapping to [None], so when you perform a drag-and-drop of that member or its parent object, no controls or columns will be generated for that member.

Customizing the Bound Control Types

The built-in controls and mappings give you a lot of flexibility for creating data-bound controls, but inevitably there will be situations where you want something different than what is set up as the defaults, or you will want to plug in your own data-bound controls. The details of how to create

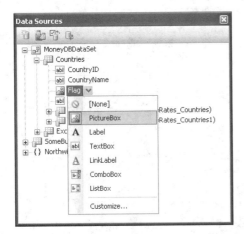

FIGURE 5.13: Selecting the Bound Control Type for a Data Member

custom data-bound controls are discussed later in this book; let's focus here on how to change the list of controls presented as options for items in the Data Sources window and how you can make your own controls capable of being plugged in for use in the Data Sources window.

If you select the *Customize* option at the bottom of the list shown in Figure 5.13, the Visual Studio Options dialog displays (see Figure 5.14). (This is the same as choosing Tools > Options in Visual Studio.) The Data UI Customization node of the Windows Forms Designer is selected in the tree of option categories. This is where you can set the mappings between data member types and the control options presented by the Data Sources window. As you can see in Figure 5.14, when you select a built-in .NET type on the left, you can select from a list of associated controls on the right. The controls selected on the right will be the ones presented as control mapping options in the Data Sources window (see Figure 5.13) for any data members of the associated type. The list also shows which control type is set as the default (indicated by *(default)* next to the control type name), and you can change this by using the *Set Default* and *Clear Default* buttons to the right of the list.

There is also an item in the *Data type* drop-down list at the top named *[List]*, which displays the list of controls available for collections of data, such as data tables or object types that contain properties as their data members (specifically, objects that implement the IList interface). This

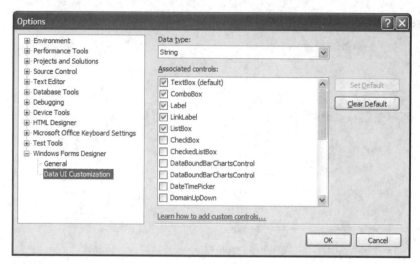

FIGURE 5.14: Customizing Control Mappings

list only contains the `DataGridView` control by default, because the Details view isn't really a control type, but a Data Sources-specific control generation mechanism that will always be available for any complex type that exposes public properties.

Additionally, the *Data type* drop-down list contains a type of *[Other]*, which lets you specify a list of controls that should be presented for data members that are a custom type. When you use the *[Other]* type and add control types to the list of options presented in the Data Sources window, you could potentially generate data-binding code that won't compile. The type of the default binding property on the control type you select (determined by the `DefaultBindingProperty` attribute set on the control class definition) needs to match the data type of the bound data member to ensure that data binding will successfully compile and run. If there is a suitable type converter between the data member type and the bound control property type, you should also be okay.

To have your own custom controls available for selection in the list of control options, there are several things you have to do. First, you have to develop a custom Windows Forms control that supports either simple or complex data binding. Simple binding means that the control will have individual properties bound to individual data members. These controls will also need to support a default binding property. You can think of complex data binding being broken into two types for this discussion: lookup and table-oriented complex binding. **Lookup complex data binding** is the kind that `ComboBox` and `ListBox` controls support, including a data source, display member, value member, and selected item. **Table-oriented complex data binding** assumes the whole collection is going to be rendered in some form, so the control only needs the data source and data member. Developing controls that support these aspects is discussed in detail in Chapter 10.

If you have a custom or third-party control that is decorated with the appropriate attributes that allow it to work correctly with the Data Sources window (specifically, the control has a `DefaultBindingProperty`, `LookupBindingProperties`, or `ComplexBindingProperties` attribute on the class), you will need to add it to the Toolbox in Visual Studio before it becomes available for selection in the Data UI Customization settings shown in Figure 5.14.

You add a control to the Toolbox in one of two ways.

- The easier way is to simply drag the DLL that contains the controls onto the Toolbox from a Windows Explorer window.
- The second way is to right-click in the Toolbox and select *Choose Items*. This displays the Choose Toolbox Items dialog shown in Figure 5.15. Click on the *Browse* button and find the assembly containing your custom controls. Once you select that assembly, the controls within it will be added to the list and checked for inclusion in the Toolbox.

Once your control has been added to the Toolbox, it should show up in the list of available controls in the Data UI Customization options. You can then select the control for inclusion in the drop-down list of controls in the Data Sources window for a data member of the appropriate type.

Binding Existing Controls to Data Sources

Using the Data Sources window to generate bound controls is one easy way to set up your form and have the designer write the data-binding code for you. However, your development team may have user interface

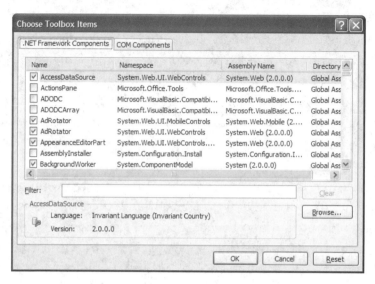

FIGURE 5.15: Customizing the Toolbox Using the Choose Toolbox Items Dialog

designers who lay out your forms and don't know a thing about data binding, and other programmers who will do the coding to hook up the functionality for the forms. Or you may just prefer to do the UI design step first, getting all your controls laid out, named, and so on, and then worry about connecting them to the data later. Perhaps the data access and business layers from which your data is going to come are being developed in parallel, and the type definitions are not yet available to generate your controls from them. Whatever the case, the Data Sources window also supports generating the data-binding code for controls that already exist on a form.

The process for using this capability is very simple. If you have an existing control on the form, such as a text box or grid, you can drag an item from the Data Sources window onto that control. If the item you are dragging is of a compatible type with the binding properties of the control, the designer generates the data-binding code to bind that control's default binding property to the data item. This process works pretty much the same when the designer creates the control too, but it uses the existing control instead of generating the control instance on the form too. So the designer still generates all the supporting components to support that data-binding scenario, including a binding source, binding navigator, as well as a data set and table adapter if the data item being dragged is a data table.

When you drag an item from the Data Sources window onto a control on the form, the mouse cursor changes to indicate what the resulting drop operation will do. When you drag a Data Sources window item onto a blank area of the form, as discussed in the beginning of this chapter, the mouse cursor shows a little plus sign to indicate that controls will be added to the form. When you drag a data item onto an existing control on the form, and that data item is compatible with the control for the purposes of data binding, the mouse cursor will display a small shortcut arrow, indicating that the drop will result in linking the data source item to the control. Finally, if the data item being dragged is not compatible with the control the mouse is over, the mouse cursor will change to a circle with a slash to indicate that drop isn't allowed and will result in no action. Compatibility is again driven by the type of the data item or member combined with what the default data-binding properties of the control are.

For example, if you drag a data member that is a string, numeric field, or property from a data source object onto a `TextBox` control that is already on the form, the designer will generate a binding source with the `DataSource` property set to the data source object, as well as a binding navigator tied to the binding source. The designer will also generate the code to create a binding object tying the `TextBox.Text` property to the data member using the binding source as the data source and will add that binding object to the textbox's `DataBindings` collection. If the data member's parent object is a data table, a data set and table adapter will also be added to the form, along with the line of code in the form's `Load` event handler to fill the data set using the table adapter.

If you try to drag that same field onto a `DataGridView` control, you'll see a circle with a slash mouse cursor, indicating that a single-valued data member isn't compatible for data binding with a control intended for displaying collections of data. However, if you drag the parent data table onto the grid, all the same supporting components described earlier in this section would be generated, and the grid's `DataSource` property would be set to the binding source that was generated and bound to the table.

Behind the Scenes: Designer Code and Data Sources Files

Understanding what is going on behind the scenes is always important, especially when the designer-generated code isn't doing exactly what you want. The first thing to understand is that all of the controls and components generated by the designer actions, along with the supporting code to set up data-binding objects and properties, are part of the standard Windows Forms designer-generated code. With Visual Studio 2005, this code is now placed in a separate code file using partial classes, and it isn't displayed by default in the Solution Explorer project tree. To inspect the code that was generated as a result of designer interactions, you need to click the plus sign (+) next to the form class file in your project. Under that item, you will see a file named <formname>.Designer.cs (or .vb, depending on your language flavor), which contains all the designer-generated code. Most of the code is inside a collapsed region within that file, inside the definition for the InitializeComponent method.

The other thing that is going on behind the scenes is that any time you add a data source from outside your project using the Web server or object data source types, a data source file is added to your project to provide the ties between the type information for the object(s) in that data source and the Data Sources window. Additionally, if you customize which controls are mapped to a particular data member by selecting another control type from the drop-down list of bound control types, Visual Studio has to save that information somewhere so that you don't have to keep reselecting it. This information is saved in those same data source files.

Data source files are XML files that are added to several different places in your project, depending on the kind of data source you are customizing the UI mappings for. If the data source type is an object, the data source files get created under a DataSources folder under the Properties folder in your Visual Studio project. The files are named based on the namespace and type of the data source object, and they have a .datasource file extension.

- If the data source type is a Web service, the .datasource files are placed in the subfolder of the Web References folder that is created to contain the Web service proxy code.

- If the data source is a typed data set definition that is part of your project, a .xsc file is generated and associated with the .schema definition that defines the data set.

To access this information for Web service data sources, select the *Show All Files* button, expand the Web reference node, drill down to the *Reference.map* item, and you will see the sub-items in the tree for that reference. In addition to the Reference.cs (or .vb) file that contains the generated proxy class for calling the Web service, there will also be a collection of .datasource files for each of the return types of the Web methods that are part of that service. These types also may be complex types with child object collections and data members, but only the top-level object types defined as return values from the Web service methods get data source files generated. The type definitions themselves get added to the Reference.cs file where the proxy class is placed. The Data Sources window can infer the rest of the type information about the child object types through reflection.

The following XML shows an example of a simple .datasource file for a Web service data source type:

```
<GenericObjectDataSource DisplayName="LonLatPt"
    Version="1.0" xmlns="urn:schemas-microsoft-com:xml-msdatasource">
    <TypeInfo>DataSources101.net.terraservice.LonLatPt</TypeInfo>
</GenericObjectDataSource>
```

The .datasource file contains an XML document whose root element is named `GenericObjectDataSource`. This is the case whether you set up the data source as an Object data source type or a Web service type. The only difference is where the .datasource file gets placed in your project. As you can see, the root element can contain several attributes that provide versioning information, a display name for the Data Sources window, and the schema information that specifies the allowable schema of the .datasources XML. The main thing that a data source file contains is a `TypeInfo` element, which specifies the fully qualified type name of the object that is being treated as a top-level data source. This shows up as a root node in the tree presented by the Data Sources window. Child objects and properties are determined through reflection by the Data Sources window when you expand a data source.

In addition to the `TypeInfo` information contained in a data source file, the file can also contain control mapping information for those data items or members that have had their control mapping changed from the default. To support this, a `TypeUISetting` element is added to the data source root element. A fairly complex XML schema underneath this element allows each data item or member that has a custom control mapping to have the information describing that mapping specified. This schema consists of a collection element named `PropertyUISettings` that contains individual `PropertyUISetting` elements. One of these elements is specified for each data member that has a custom control mapping set up. Underneath the `PropertyUISetting` element is a collection of control settings and bindable control information that sets up the mapping:

```
<GenericObjectDataSource DisplayName="SomeBusinessObject"
Version="1.0"
   xmlns="urn:schemas-microsoft-com:xml-msdatasource">
   <TypeInfo>DataSources101.SomeBusinessObject, DataSources101,
     Version=1.0.0.0, Culture=neutral, PublicKeyToken=null</TypeInfo>
   <TypeUISetting>
     <PropertyUISettings>
        <PropertyUISetting Name="SomeInteger" SimpleProperty="True">
           <ControlSettings>
             <ControlSetting
             ArtifactName="Microsoft:System.Windows.Forms:Form">
               <BindableControlInfo Name="NumericUpDown"
               Type="System.Windows.Forms.NumericUpDown"
               AssemblyName="System.Windows.Forms,
               Version=2.0.0.0, Culture=neutral,
               PublicKeyToken=b77a5c561934e089" />
             </ControlSetting>
           </ControlSettings>
        </PropertyUISetting>
     </PropertyUISettings>
   </TypeUISetting>
</GenericObjectDataSource>
```

If the data source is a typed data set within your Windows Forms project, you can select *Show All Files* in Solution Explorer, expand the typed data set (.xsd) file node, and you will see an .xsc file under it. If you have customized the control mappings for any of the data members of that data set definition through the Data Sources window, that file will contain XML similar to the following code to record those custom control mappings as part of your project:

```
<DataSetUISetting Version="1.00"
    xmlns="urn:schemas-microsoft-com:xml-msdatasource">
  <TableUISettings>
    <TableUISetting Name="Countries">
      <ColumnUISettings>
        <ColumnUISetting Name="Flag">
          <ControlSettings>
            <ControlSetting
             ArtifactName="Microsoft:System.Windows.Forms:Form">
              <BindableControlInfo Name="PictureBox"
               Type="System.Windows.Forms.PictureBox"
               AssemblyName="System.Windows.Forms,
               Version=2.0.0.0, Culture=neutral,
               PublicKeyToken=b77a5c561934e089" />
            </ControlSetting>
          </ControlSettings>
        </ColumnUISetting>
      </ColumnUISettings>
    </TableUISetting>
  </TableUISettings>
</DataSetUISetting>
```

You should never have to hand-code this stuff, though you may want to look at it if things aren't working correctly so you can understand where the Data Sources window is getting the information that is driving the display. Usually regenerating the data source reference through the Data Source Configuration wizard is a better way to go than trying to hand-modify the XML yourself. In the case of the .xsc file, you can simply delete the file, and it will be regenerated the next time you customize the UI control mappings for any of the data set members.

Other Designer Data-Binding Code Generation

You can perform several other designer interactions that generate data-binding code but that don't involve the Data Sources window, for example, using the Properties window and using Smart Tags on the designer form. The Properties window lets you declaratively set properties on controls in the designer, which is ultimately an interactive way of writing the code that sets those properties. But some of the interactions in the Properties window actually do a little more than just set a property; they end up writing a few lines of code that create and manage the binding objects as well. Smart Tags provide direct access to commonly used features and properties of individual controls and components.

Setting Control Data Binding Through the Properties Window

If you select a control such as a `TextBox` in the Forms designer, and then show the Properties window (using the View menu or the F4 default keyboard shortcut), all of the properties that can be set at design time in the designer are available in that window. There are also a number of pseudo-properties presented in the Properties window that don't correspond one-to-one with individual properties of a control, but that let you generate or modify code through a similar interaction. For example, when you set the `(Name)` pseudo-property for a control in the Properties window, you aren't actually changing a property on the instance of the class, but changing the name of the instance member variable itself. This is why it is surrounded by parentheses in the Properties window, because it doesn't correspond to a true property on the control instance. Setting the `(Name)` pseudo-property results in the designer changing every designer-generated line of code using that member variable to reflect the new name. In fact, Visual Studio 2005 goes beyond that and uses its refactoring features to also locate the use of that named instance in all other code in the project and update it there as well.

Likewise, you can set several properties in the Properties window that give you a rich design experience and that also generate more than one line of code in many cases. These properties include the `DataSource` and `DataMember` properties for any complex bound control, the `Display-Member` and `ValueMember` properties for a lookup bound control like a `ComboBox` or `ListBox`, and the `(DataBindings)` set of pseudo-properties for any control. When you select the `DataSource`, `DataMember`, `Display-Member`, or `ValueMember` properties of a control in the Properties window, a pop-up window that looks like a miniature version of the Data Sources window displays. This window is docked to the property you are setting in the Properties window (see Figure 5.16).

This property editor lets you navigate through the data sources in the project much like you do in the Data Sources window. However, what is presented in the data sources tree is tailored based on the property that you are setting and what the compatible data members are within the data source. For example, Figure 5.16 shows setting the `DataSource` property of a `ComboBox` control, which is designed to be bound only to list data sources. So the tree only presents those items that implement the appropriate `IList` interface to be bound to that property. Notice that this includes the foreign key relationships for related data tables in a data set, as well as child object collections on other data objects. You can even create new data sources through the Data Source Configuration wizard directly from the link control at the bottom of the pop-up property editor window as well.

The current selection in other data-binding properties will further restrict what is presented while setting a particular data-binding property. For example, the `DisplayMember` property in Figure 5.17 only presents the

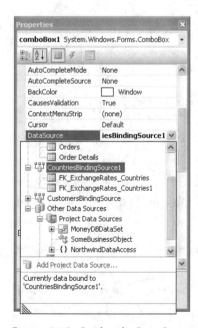

FIGURE 5.16: Setting the Data Source in the Properties Window

FIGURE 5.17: Setting the DisplayMember in the Properties Window

individual columns or properties of the list source selected for the Data-Source property of that control.

When you select items from the data sources tree, the designer performs similar actions to when you drag items to the form from the Data Sources window. Specifically, it creates a binding source for the data source if one doesn't already exist. If that data source is a typed data set, the designer creates an instance of the data set as a member of the form, along with a table adapter to fill the table that was bound to the control. If a suitable binding source is already present on the form, it shows up in the data sources tree as well, and you can select that binding source as the source to prevent a second (and redundant) binding source instance from being added to the form.

Another pseudo-property that is useful for setting up data binding, especially for simple bound controls like text boxes, labels, and picture boxes, is the (DataBindings) pseudo-property. When you expand (DataBindings) in the Properties window with a control selected in the designer, the Properties window will determine what the default bound property is for the control and display that Property as a subproperty under (DataBindings) in the Properties window (see Figure 5.18).

If you click on the bound property, or on the Tag property that is also displayed as a subproperty under (DataBindings), a window for selecting data source items (similar to the one shown in Figure 5.17) displays. Here you can select a different data member for the binding.

You can also click on the (Advanced) subproperty, and a button with ellipses (…) will display in the subproperty. When you click that button, the Formatting and Advanced Binding dialog (shown in Figure 5.19) displays. You can use this dialog to customize the current binding or add other bindings for that control to other properties. The *Binding* drop-down list in the middle of the dialog allows you to select the data member for a binding using the same drop-down window that is used for DataMember properties in the Properties window. The *Data Source Update Mode* drop-down list lets you pick when formatting occurs; it uses the same values from the DataSourceUpdateMode enumeration that was discussed in Table 4.3 for automatic formatting using the Binding class. Depending on the type of the data member selected in the *Binding* drop-down list, you can select a format type from the list in the middle at the bottom, along with a corresponding type from the list on the right. This is basically setting up a formatting string for the format provider for the selected data member type. Finally, you can provide a value in the *Null value* text box that will be used if the data member value is null or DBNull at runtime.

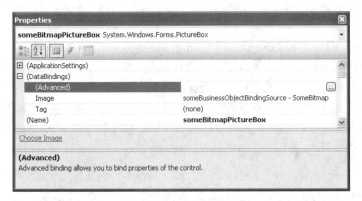

FIGURE 5.18: (DataBindings) Properties in the Properties Window

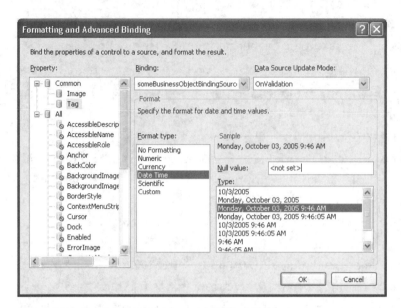

FIGURE 5.19: Formatting and Advanced Binding Dialog

Ultimately, all these settings are a designer-oriented way to provide the information for the automatic formatting capabilities of the `Binding` class that were discussed in detail in Chapter 4. When you accept any changes made in this dialog with the *OK* button, code will be added to the designer code file to create appropriate `Binding` objects, and you should set the corresponding formatting properties on those bindings before adding them to the control's `DataBindings` collection.

Generating Data Bindings with Smart Tags

Smart Tags, a new feature in the Visual Studio 2005 Forms designer, let you access commonly used property settings and actions on a control or component in the designer, instead of having to go through the Properties window or a menu item. You access a Smart Tag by clicking on the small triangular glyph that displays on the upper right edge of the control or component when you click on it (see Figure 5.20).

Depending on the control or component type that you select, the Smart Tag may be simple, complex, or the control may have no Smart Tag at all.

The Smart Tag in Figure 5.20 shows two options at the bottom that are available in the Smart Tag of any control or component whose data source is set directly or indirectly to a typed data set. The *Add Query* item displays the Search Criteria Builder dialog (shown in Figure 5.21); this dialog lets you add a new query to the typed data set to which the control is bound.

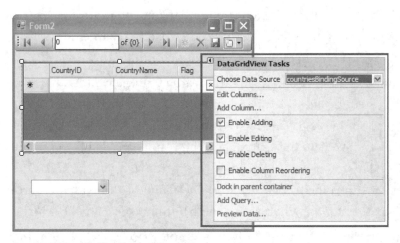

FIGURE 5.20: Binding Source Smart Tag

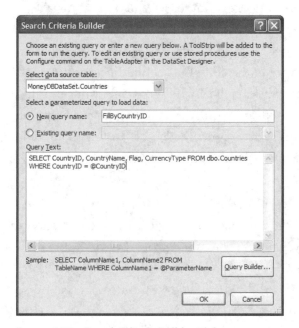

FIGURE 5.21: Search Criteria Builder Dialog

When you enter a new query and accept it using this dialog, a new query is added to the bound table's table adapter. You can use this query to fill the table. This query lets you specify parameterized queries that will return a set of rows to fill the table based on search criteria. If you try to enter a query that doesn't return rows, you will get an error when you click *OK* that says it failed to get the schema for the query. This means that it saw that there wasn't any data returned based on the query that you entered. You can also design the query using the Query Builder described in Chapter 2 by clicking the *Query Builder* button in the Search Criteria Builder dialog.

When you enter a new query using the Search Criteria Builder dialog, a new `ToolStrip` control is added to the form, and some supporting code is added to your source file for the form (e.g., Form1.cs). This lets you enter search criteria and execute the search, and the results are displayed in the bound control that you generated the new query from (see Figure 5.22). The generated `ToolStrip` includes a label for the name of the search criteria field, a text box to enter the criteria into, and a button to execute the search.

The Add Query functionality only works for typed data sets that are part of your Windows Forms projects. If you want to set up the same functionality for a data set that is defined in another assembly, such as a data access layer assembly, you will have to manually add the query to the table adapter (as described in Chapter 3), add the `ToolStrip` and its controls to the form manually, and then write the code to execute the query method on the table adapter and put the results in the corresponding binding source on the form. In other words, the designer is only going to help you on this one if you follow the bad design practice of putting your data access code inside your Windows Forms project. Bummer, huh?

The other item at the bottom of the Smart Tag for any control or component bound to a typed data set within the Windows Forms project is a *Preview Data* option. When you click on this, the Preview Data dialog shown in Figure 5.23 is presented. When you click the *Preview* button in the middle of the dialog, the corresponding `GetData` method of the table adapter will be executed and the data will be displayed in the Results section so you can preview it.

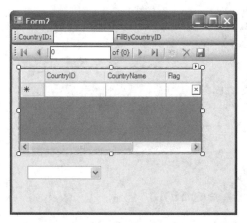

FIGURE 5.22: Form with Search ToolStrip Added by the Designer

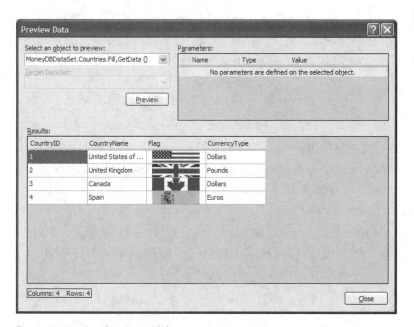

FIGURE 5.23: Preview Data Dialog

ComboBox and ListBox controls have Smart Tags on them that you can use to set up their data-binding properties (see Figure 5.24). You first have to check the *Use data bound items* box, and then the four combo boxes below that display. These each let you open the Data Sources window, as described for the DataSource and DataMember properties in the Properties window earlier.

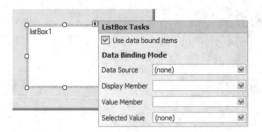

FIGURE 5.24: ListBox Smart Tag

Generating Master-Details Data-Bound Controls with the Designer

You learned how to set up master-details data binding in code in previous chapters. The designer will write all that code for you based on a couple of simple drag-and-drop gestures from the Data Sources window. Let's step through an example to demonstrate.

1. Start a new Windows Forms project in Visual Studio 2005.

2. After the project is created, add a new Database data source from the Data Sources window.

3. Select the existing Northwind database connection created earlier in the chapter, and select the Customers and Orders tables within that database in the wizard.

4. Accept `NorthwindDataSet` as the data set type name in the last step of the wizard. (Review the steps at the beginning of this chapter if you need help stepping through that wizard.)

   This adds a typed data set to the project that is suitable for master-details data binding, because the Orders table has a foreign key relationship (details) to the Customers table (master), and both of those tables now display in the Data Sources window under Northwind-DataSet.

5. If you expand the Customers table in the tree, you will see that in addition to each of the columns of the table being shown with the corresponding control type that will be generated for them (all `TextBoxes` in this case), there is another `DataGridView` item for the Orders table.

6. Drag the Customers table from the Data Sources window onto the form, about a half-inch down and in from the top left of the form. This will generate a `DataGridView` control, and `BindingSource`, `BindingNavigator`, `CustomersTableAdapter`, and `Northwind-DataSet` members on the form with their data-binding code all hooked up in the designer code file.

It also adds code to the `Load` event handler to fill the data set, as you have seen several times by now. This grid will be bound to the binding source, and the binding source will be bound to the Customers table in the `NorthwindDataSet` instance through its `DataSource` and `DataMember` properties.

7. Grab the Orders table that is shown as a child member of the Customers table in the Data Sources window (note that there is an Orders table at the same level as Customers in the Data Sources tree, but that isn't the one you want; you want the one that is shown as a child item under Customers, because this is the one that is exposed through the data relation linking child rows in Orders to parent rows in Customers). Drag the table onto an empty area at the bottom of the form.

This adds another `DataGridView` control to the form for the Orders table, and another `BindingSource` and `OrdersTableAdapter` will be added to the form as well. The second grid will be bound to the second binding source, and the second binding source will have its `DataSource` property set to the first binding source, which was bound to the Customers table. The `DataMember` for the second binding source will be set to Orders, the name of the child collection within the first binding source. An additional line of code was also added to the form `Load` event handler to fill the Orders table as well as the Customers table.

The net result is that by simply dragging two related items from an object hierarchy onto the form, the designer wrote master-details data-binding code for you. The same thing would happen if instead of using Customers and Orders from a typed data set, you were using a custom collection as the master, and the details were a child collection property exposed by the objects in the parent collection. Once again, this is pretty cool! Before Visual

Studio 2005, you had to write a fair amount of unintuitive code to get this kind of thing working. Now, the designer writes this all for you.

Where Are We?

In the last few chapters, you have read about the basics of the data-binding mechanisms in Windows Forms and the underlying details. You have seen a number of examples of binding sets of data to grids, combo boxes, text boxes, and `PictureBox` controls. You learned to use binding sources to decouple your controls from the specific data sources they are bound to, giving a number of benefits for maintaining and evolving your application and for controlling the context of the data binding on the form. You saw how to set up the bindings to individual controls manually and how to configure master-details bindings by chaining together binding sources. You also learned how to avoid having to write most of that code by using the designer and the Data Sources window to generate data-binding code and controls through a few simple gestures and interactions in Visual Studio.

Some key takeaways from this chapter are:

* The Data Sources window is your new drag-and-drop control panel for setting up Windows Forms data binding.
* The Data Sources Configuration wizard lets you define database, Web service, and object data sources, and it creates the appropriate glue code in your Windows Forms project to be able to set up data binding to those object types.
* Avoid using the database data source type in any large real-world project because it embeds data access code in your Windows Forms project, which tightly couples your presentation tier application to the data tier—a bad idea from a design perspective.
* To add custom controls to the controls presented in the Data Sources window, you must first add them to the Toolbox, then customize the Data UI Customization settings by choosing Tools > Options.

I kept deferring getting into any detail on the `DataGridView` control because it is a complex and powerful enough control to warrant a dedicated chapter, which is where we are headed next.

6

Presenting Data with the DataGridView Control

T HE PRECEDING CHAPTERS showed many detailed examples of data binding to simple bound controls and list bound controls. However, one of the most common ways of presenting data is in tabular form. Users are able to quickly scan and understand large amounts of data visually when it is presented in a table. In addition, users can interact with that data in a number of ways, including scrolling through the data, sorting the data based on columns, editing the data directly in the grid, and selecting columns, rows, or cells. In .NET 1.0, the `DataGrid` control was the primary Windows Forms control for presenting tabular data. Even though that control had a lot of capability and could present basic tabular data well, it was fairly difficult to customize many aspects of the control. Additionally, the `DataGrid` control didn't expose enough information to the programmer about the user interactions with the grid and changes occurring in the grid due to programmatic modifications of the data or formatting. Due to these factors and a large number of new features that customers requested, the Windows Client team at Microsoft decided to introduce a replacement control for the `DataGrid` in .NET 2.0. That new control, the `DataGridView` control, is the focus of this chapter.

DataGridView Overview

The `DataGridView` control is a very powerful, flexible, and yet easy-to-use control for presenting tabular data. It is far more capable than the `Data-Grid` control and is easier to customize and interact with. You can let the grid do all the work of presenting data in tabular form by setting the data-binding properties on the control appropriately. You can also take explicit control of presenting data in the grid through the new features of unbound columns and virtual mode. **Unbound columns** let you formulate the contents of the cell as the cells are being added to the grid. **Virtual mode** gives you a higher degree of control by allowing you to wait until a cell is actually being displayed to provide the value it will contain.

You can make the grid act like a spreadsheet, so that the focus for interaction and presentation is at the cell level instead of at the row or column level. You can control the formatting and layout of the grid with fine-grained precision simply by setting a few properties on the control. Finally, you can plug in a number of predefined column and cell control types, or provide your own custom controls, and you can even mix different control types within different cells in the same row or column.

Figure 6.1 shows an example of a `DataGridView` control in action with some of the key visual features highlighted. You can see that the grid picks up the visual styles of Windows XP; they are much like many of the Windows Forms controls in .NET 2.0. The grid is composed of columns and rows, and the intersection of a column and a row is a cell. The cell is the basic unit of presentation within the grid, and is highly customizable in

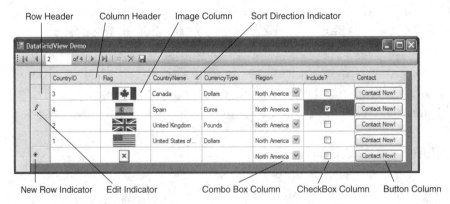

FIGURE 6.1: DataGridView in Action

appearance and behavior through the properties and events exposed by the grid. There are header cells for the rows and columns that can be used to maintain the context of the data presented in the grid. These header cells can contain graphical glyphs to indicate different modes or functions of the grid, such as sorting, editing, new rows, and selection. The grid can contain cells of many different types, and can even mix different cell types in the same column if the grid isn't data bound.

Basic Data Binding with the DataGridView

The easiest way to get started using the DataGridView control is to use it in basic data-binding scenarios. To do this, you first need to obtain a collection of data, typically through your business layer or data access layer. You then set the grid's data-binding properties to bind to the data collection, as described in Chapters 4 and 5. Just like with other Windows Forms controls, the recommended practice in .NET 2.0 is to always bind your actual client-side data source to an instance of the BindingSource class and then bind your controls to the binding source. The following code shows this process.

```
private void OnFormLoad(object sender, EventArgs e)
{
    // Create adapter to get data source
    CustomersTableAdapter adapter = new CustomersTableAdapter();
    // Bind table data source to binding source
    m_CustomersBindingSource.DataSource = adapter.GetData();
    // Bind the binding source to grid control
    m_Grid.DataSource = m_CustomersBindingSource;
}
```

Alternatively, if the binding source is bound to a collection of data collections, such as a data set, then you can refine what part of the data source you want to bind to using the DataMember property:

```
private void OnFormLoad(object sender, EventArgs e)
{
    // Create adapter to get data source
    CustomersTableAdapter adapter = new CustomersTableAdapter();
    // Get data set instance
    CustomersDataSet customers = new CustomersDataSet();
    // Fill data set
```

```
adapter.Fill(customers);
// Bind binding source to the data set
m_CustomersBinding source.DataSource = customers;
// Bind grid to the Customers table within the data source
m_Grid.DataSource = m_CustomersBinding source;
m_Grid.DataMember = "Customers";
}
```

For basic data-binding scenarios, the DataGridView functions exactly like the DataGrid control did in .NET 1.0, except that the combination of DataSource and DataMember must resolve to a collection of data items, such as a DataTable or object collection. Specifically, they need to resolve to an object that implements the IList interface.

The DataGrid could be bound to a collection of collections, such as a DataSet, and if so, the DataGrid presented hierarchical navigation controls to move through the collections of data. However, this capability was rarely used, partly because the navigation controls that were presented inside the DataGrid were a little unintuitive and could leave the user disoriented. As a result, the Windows Client team that developed the DataGridView control decided *not* to support hierarchical navigation within the control. The DataGridView is designed to present a single collection of data at a time. You can still achieve an intuitive hierarchical navigation through data, but you will usually use more than one control to do so, adopting a master-details approach as discussed in previous chapters.

The DataSource property can be set to any collection of objects that implements one of four interfaces: IList, IListSource, IBindingList, or IBindingListView. (These interfaces will be discussed in more detail in Chapter 7.) If the data source is itself a collection of data collections, such as a data set or an implementer of IListSource, then the DataMember property must identify which data collection within that source to bind to. If the DataSource property is set to an implementer of IList (from which both IBindingList and IBindingListView derive), then the DataMember property can be null (the default value). When you bind the DataGridView to a binding source, the BindingSource class itself implements IBindingListView (as well as several other data-binding related interfaces), so you can actually bind a grid to any kind of collection that a binding source can work with through a binding source, which includes simple collections that only implement IEnumerable.

Any time the `DataSource` and/or `DataMember` properties are set, the grid will iterate through the items found in the data collection and will refresh the data-bound columns of the grid. If the grid is bound to a binding source, any change to the underlying data source to which the binding source is bound also results in the data-bound columns in the grid being refreshed. This happens because of events raised from the binding source to any bound controls whenever its underlying collection changes.

Like most properties on the `DataGridView` control, any time the `DataSource` and `DataMember` properties are set, they fire the `DataSourceChanged` and `DataMemberChanged` events, respectively. This lets you hook up code that responds to the data binding that has changed on the grid. You can also react to the `DataBindingComplete` event, since that will fire after the data source or data member has changed and data binding has been updated. However, if you are trying to monitor changes in the data source, you usually are better off monitoring the corresponding events on the `BindingSource` component rather than subscribing to the events on the grid itself. This is especially true if the code you are using to handle the event affects other controls on the form. Because you should always bind your controls to a binding source instead of the data source itself if possible, the binding source is the best place to monitor changes in the data source.

Controlling Modifications to Data in the Grid

The `DataGridView` control gives you explicit control over whether users can edit, delete, or add rows in the grid. After the grid has been populated with data, the user can interact with the data presented in the grid in a number of ways, as discussed earlier. By default, those interactions include editing the contents of cells (fields) in a row, selecting a row and deleting it with the Delete keyboard key, or adding a new row using an empty row that displays as the last row in the grid.

If you want to disallow any of these interactions, set the `AllowUserToAddRows` or `AllowUserToDeleteRows` properties to `false`, or set the `ReadOnly` property to `true` for adding, deleting, or editing, respectively. Each of these properties also raise corresponding *XXX*Changed property changed events whenever their values are set. When you support adding, editing, or deleting, you may need to handle certain additional events to accept new values for unbound rows or for virtual mode, as described later in this chapter.

Programmatic DataGridView Construction

The most common way of using the grid is with data-bound columns. When you bind to data, the grid creates columns based on the schema or properties of the data items, and generates rows in the grid for each data item found in the bound collection. If the data binding was set up statically using the designer (as has been done in most of the examples in this book), the types and properties of the columns in the grid were set at design time. If the data binding is being done completely dynamically, the `Auto-GenerateColumns` property is `true` by default, so the column types are determined on the fly based on the type of the bound data items. You may want to create and populate a grid programmatically when working with a grid that contains only unbound data. To know what code you need to write, you need to know the `DataGridView` object model a little better.

The first thing to realize is that like all .NET controls, a grid on a form is just an instance of a class. That class contains properties and methods that you can use to code against its contained object model. For `DataGridView` controls, the object model includes two collections—`Columns` and `Rows`—which contain the objects that compose the grid. These objects are cells, or more specifically, objects derived from instances of `DataGridViewCell`. The `Columns` collection contains instances of `DataGridViewColumn` objects, and the `Rows` collection contains instances of `DataGridViewRows`.

Programmatically Adding Columns to a Grid

There are a number of ways to approach programmatically adding columns and rows to the grid. The first step is to define the columns from which the grid is composed. To define a column, you have to specify a cell template on which the column is based. The cell template will be used by default for the cells in that column whenever a row is added to the grid. Cell templates are instances of a `DataGridViewCell` derived class. You can use the .NET built-in cell types to present columns as text boxes, buttons, check boxes, combo boxes, hyperlinks, and images. Another built-in cell type renders the column headers in the grid. For each of the cell types, there is a corresponding column type that is designed to contain that cell type. You can construct `DataGridViewColumn` instances that provide a cell type as a template, but in general you'll want to create an instance of a derived column type that is designed to contain the specific type of cell you want to work with. Additionally, you can define your own custom cell and column types (discussed later in this chapter).

For now, let's stick with the most common and simple cell type, a `DataGridViewTextBoxCell`—a text box cell. This also happens to be the default cell type. You can programmatically add a text box column in one of three ways:

- Use an overloaded version of the `Add` method on the `Columns` collection of the grid:

```
// Just specify the column name and header text
m_Grid.Columns.Add("MyColumnName", "MyColumnHeaderText");
```

- Obtain an initialized instance of the `DataGridViewTextBoxColumn` class. You can achieve this by constructing an instance of the `Data-GridViewTextBoxCell` class and passing it to the constructor for the `DataGridViewColumn`, or just construct an instance of a `DataGrid-ViewTextBoxColumn` using the default constructor. Once the column is constructed, add it to the `Columns` collection of the grid:

```
// Do this:
DataGridViewTextBoxColumn newCol = new DataGridViewTextBoxColumn();
// Or this:
DataGridViewTextBoxCell newCell = new DataGridViewTextBoxCell();
DataGridViewColumn newCol2 = new DataGridViewColumn(newCell);
// Then add to the columns collection:
m_Grid.Columns.Add(newCol);
m_Grid.Columns.Add(newCol2);
```

If you add columns this way, their name and header values are null by default. To set these or other properties on the columns, you can access the properties on the column instance before or after adding it to the `Columns` collection. You could also index into the `Columns` collection to obtain a reference to a column, and then use that reference to get at any properties you need on the column.

- Set the grid's `ColumnCount` property to some value greater than zero. This approach is mainly used to quickly create a grid that only contains text box cells or to add more text box columns to an existing grid.

```
// Constructs five TextBox columns and adds them to the grid
m_Grid.ColumnCount = 5;
```

When you set the `ColumnCount` property like this, the behavior depends on whether there are already any columns in the grid. If there are existing columns and you specify fewer than the current number of columns, the `ColumnCount` property will remove as many columns from the grid as necessary to create only the number of columns you specify, starting from the rightmost column and moving to the left. This is a little destructive and scary because it lets you delete columns without explicitly saying which columns to eliminate, so I recommend to avoid using the `ColumnCount` property to remove columns.

However, when adding text box columns, if you specify more columns than the current number of columns, additional text box columns will be added to the right of the existing columns to bring the column count up to the number you specify. This is a compact way to add some columns for dynamic situations.

Programmatically Adding Rows to a Grid

Once you have added columns to the grid, you can programmatically add rows to the grid as well. In most cases, this involves using the `Add` method of the `Rows` collection on the grid. When you add a row this way, the row is created with each cell type based on the cell template that was specified for the column when the columns were created. Each cell will have a default value assigned based on the cell type, generally corresponding to an empty cell.

```
// Add a row
m_Grid.Rows.Add();
```

Several overloads of the `Add` method let you add multiple rows in a single call or pass in a row that has already been created. The `DataGridView` control also supports creating heterogeneous columns, meaning that the column can have cells of different types. To create heterogeneous columns, you have to construct the row first without attaching it to the grid. You then add the cells that you want to the row, and then add the row to the grid. For example, the following code adds a combo box as the first cell in the row, adds some items to the combo box, adds text boxes for the remaining four cells, and then adds the row to the grid.

```
private void OnAddHeterows(object sender, EventArgs e)
{
    m_Grid.ColumnCount = 5; // Create 5 text box columns
    DataGridViewRow heterow = new DataGridViewRow();
    DataGridViewComboBoxCell comboCell = new
DataGridViewComboBoxCell();
    comboCell.Items.Add("Black");
    comboCell.Items.Add("White");
    comboCell.Value = "White";
    heterow.Cells.Add(comboCell);
    for (int i = 0; i < 4; i++)
    {
        heterow.Cells.Add(new DataGridViewTextBoxCell());
    }
    m_Grid.Rows.Add(heterow); // this row has a combo in first cell
}
```

To add a row to a grid this way, the grid must already have been initialized with the default set of columns that it will hold. Additionally, the number of cells in the row that is added must match that column count. In this code sample, five text box columns are implicitly added by specifying a column count of five, then the first row is added as a heterogeneous row by constructing the cells and adding them to the row before adding the row to the grid.

You can also save yourself some code by using the grid's existing column definitions to create the default set of cells in a row using the `Create-Cells` method, then replace just the cells that you want to be different from the default:

```
DataGridViewRow heterow = new DataGridViewRow();
heterow.CreateCells(m_Grid);
heterow.Cells.RemoveAt(0);
heterow.Cells.Insert(0, new DataGridViewComboBoxCell());
m_Grid.Rows.Add(heterow);
```

To access the contents of the cells programmatically, you index into the Rows collection on the grid to obtain a reference to the row, and then index into the Cells collection on the row to access the cell object.

Once you have a reference to the cell, you can do anything with that cell that the actual cell type supports. If you want to access specific properties or methods exposed by the cell type, you have to cast the reference to the actual cell type. To change a cell's contents, you set the Value property to an appropriate value based on the type of the cell. What constitutes an appropriate value depends on what kind of cell it is. For text box, link, button, and header cell types, the process is very similar to what was described for the Binding object in Chapter 4. Basically, the value you set on the Value property of the cell needs to be convertible to a string, and formatting will be applied in the painting process. To change the formatting of the output string, set the Format property of the style used for the cell. The style is an instance of a DataGridViewCellStyle object and is exposed as another property on the cell, not surprisingly named Style. The cell's style contains other interesting properties that you can set (described later in the section "Formatting with Styles").

For example, if you want to set the contents of a text box cell to the current date using the short date format, you could use the following code:

```
m_Grid.Rows[0].Cells[2].Value = DateTime.Now;
m_Grid.Rows[0].Cells[2].Style.Format = "d";
```

This sets the value of the third cell in the first row to an instance of a DateTime object, which is convertible to a string, and sets the format string to the short date predefined format string "d" (which is the short date format—MM/YYYY). When that cell gets rendered, it will convert the stored DateTime value to a string using the format string.

Custom Column Content with Unbound Columns

Now that you understand how to programmatically create columns and rows, and populate them with values, you may be wondering if you have to go to all that trouble any time you want to present content in a cell that isn't bound to data. The good news is that there is a faster way for most scenarios where you want to present unbound data. You will need to programmatically create all the columns in the grid (although you can get the designer to write this code for you too, as shown later), but you can use events to make populating the values a little easier, especially when you mix bound data with unbound columns.

An **unbound column** is a column that isn't bound to data. You add unbound columns to a grid programmatically, and you populate the column's cells either programmatically as shown in the previous section or by using events as shown in this section. You can still add columns to the grid that are automatically bound to columns or properties in the data items of the data source. You do this by setting the `DataPropertyName` property on the column after it is created. Then you can add unbound columns as well. The rows of the grid will be created when you set the grid's `Data-Source` property to the source as in the straight data-binding case, because the grid will iterate through the rows or objects in the data collection, creating a new row for each.

There are two primary ways to populate the contents of unbound columns: handling the `RowsAdded` event or handling the `CellFormatting` event. The former is a good place to set the cell's value to make it available for programmatic retrieval later. The latter is a good place to provide a value that will be used for display purposes only and won't be stored as part of the data retained by the grid cells collection. The `CellFormatting` event can also be used to transform values as they are presented in a cell to something different than the value that is actually stored in the data that sits behind the grid.

To demonstrate this capability, let's look at a simple example.

1. Start a new Windows application project in Visual Studio 2005, and add a new data source to the project for the Customers table in the Northwind database (this is described in Chapter 1—here are the basic steps):
   a. Select Data > Add New Data Source.
   b. Select *Database* as the data source type.
   c. Select or create a connection to the Northwind database.
   d. Select the *Customers* table from the tree of database objects.
   e. Name the data set **CustomersDataSet** and finish the wizard.

At this point you have an empty Windows Forms project with a typed data set for Customers defined.

2. Add a `DataGridView` and `BindingSource` to the form from the Toolbox, naming them `m_CustomersGrid` and `m_Customers-BindingSource` respectively.

3. Add the code in Listing 6.1 to the constructor for the form, following the call to `InitializeComponents`.

LISTING 6.1: Dynamic Column Construction

```
public Form1()
{
    InitializeComponent();

    // Get the data
    CustomersTableAdapter adapter = new CustomersTableAdapter();
    m_CustomersBindingSource.DataSource = adapter.GetData();

    // Set up the grid columns
    m_CustomersGrid.AutoGenerateColumns = false;
    int newColIndex = m_CustomersGrid.Columns.Add("CompanyName",
        "Company Name");
    m_CustomersGrid.Columns[newColIndex].DataPropertyName =
        "CompanyName";
    newColIndex = m_CustomersGrid.Columns.Add("ContactName",
        "Contact Name");
    m_CustomersGrid.Columns[newColIndex].DataPropertyName =
        "ContactName";
    newColIndex = m_CustomersGrid.Columns.Add("Phone","Phone");
    m_CustomersGrid.Columns[newColIndex].DataPropertyName = "Phone";
    newColIndex = m_CustomersGrid.Columns.Add("Contact", "Contact");

    // Subscribe events
    m_CustomersGrid.CellFormatting += OnCellFormatting;
    m_CustomersGrid.RowsAdded += OnRowsAdded;

    // Data bind
    m_CustomersGrid.DataSource = m_CustomersBindingSource;
}
```

This code first retrieves the Customers table data using the table adapter's `GetData` method. As discussed earlier in the book, the table adapter was created along with the typed data set when you added the data source to your project. It sets the returned data table as the data source for the binding source. The `AutoGenerate-Columns` property is set to `false`, since the code programmatically populates the columns collection. Then four text box columns are added to the grid using the overload of the `Add` method on the `Columns` collection, which takes a column name and the header text. The first three columns are set up for data binding to the Customers table's CompanyName, ContactName, and Phone columns by setting the `DataPropertyName` property on the column after it is created. The fourth column is the unbound column and is simply created at this point through the call to the `Add` method. It will be populated later through events.

Finally, the events of interest are wired up to the methods that will handle them using delegate inference. Using this new C# feature, you don't have to explicitly create an instance of a delegate to subscribe a handler for an event. You just assign a method name that has the appropriate signature for the event's delegate type, and the compiler will generate the delegate instance for you. In Visual Basic, you use the `AddHandler` operator, which has always operated similarly.

When the data source is set on the grid and the grid is rendered, the grid iterates through the rows of the data source and adds a row to the grid for each data source row, setting the values of the bound column cells to the corresponding values in the data source. As each row is created, the `RowsAdded` event is fired. In addition, a series of events are fired for every cell in the row as it is created.

4. Add the following method as the handler for the `CellFormatting` event:

```
private void OnCellFormatting(object sender,
    DataGridViewCellFormattingEventArgs e)
{
    if (e.ColumnIndex == m_CustomersGrid.Columns["Contact"].Index)
    {
        e.FormattingApplied = true;
        DataGridViewRow row = m_CustomersGrid.Rows[e.RowIndex];
        e.Value = string.Format("{0} : {1}",
            row.Cells["ContactName"].Value,
            row.Cells["Phone"].Value);
    }
}
```

As previously mentioned, you can use the `CellFormatting` event if you are programmatically setting the displayed values for the cells. The event argument that is passed in to the `CellFormatting` event exposes a number of properties to let you know what cell is being rendered. You can use the `ColumnIndex` to determine which column the event is being fired for. It is checked against the index of the Contact column using a lookup in the `Columns` collection.

Once it is determined that this is the column you want to supply a programmatic value for, you can obtain the actual row being populated using the `RowIndex` property on the event argument. In this case, the code just concatenates the ContactName and Phone from the row to form a contact information string using the `String.Format` method, and sets that string as the value on the Contact column.

In other situations, you may use the `CellFormatting` event to do something like look up a value from another table, such as using a foreign key, and use the retrieved value as the displayed value in the unbound column. It also sets the `FormattingApplied` property on the event argument to `true`. This is very important to do; it signals the grid that this column is being dynamically updated. If you fail to do this, you will get an infinite loop if you also set the column to have its size automatically determined, as discussed in a later section.

> **■ NOTE** Always Set `FormattingApplied` to True When Dynamically Formatting Cell Content
>
> If you fail to set the `FormattingApplied` property on the event argument to the `CellFormatting` event, the grid won't know that the content is being determined dynamically and may not work properly for certain other grid behaviors.

It should be noted that the code example for the `CellFormatting` event is fairly inefficient from a performance perspective. First, you wouldn't want to look up the column's index by name in the column collection every time. It would be more efficient to look it up once, store it in a member variable, and then use that index directly for comparison. I went with the lookup approach in this sample to keep it simple and easy to read—so you could focus on the grid details instead of a bunch of performance-oriented code. Besides, this is a somewhat contrived example anyway; it's just meant to demonstrate how to create an unbound column.

If you want to set the actual stored cell values of unbound columns in the grid, a better way to do this is to handle the RowsAdded event. As you might guess from the name, this event is fired as rows are added to the grid. By handling this event, you can populate the values of all the unbound cells in a row in one shot, which is slightly more efficient than having to handle the CellFormatting event for every cell. The Rows-Added event can be fired for one row at a time if you are programmatically adding rows in a loop, or it can be fired just once for a whole batch of rows being added, such as when you data bind or use the AddCopies method of the rows collection. The event argument to RowsAdded contains properties for RowIndex and RowCount; these properties let you iterate through the rows that were added to update the unbound column values in a loop. The following method shows an alternative approach for populating the grid's Contact column from the previous example, using the RowsAdded method instead of the CellFormatting event:

```
private void OnRowsAdded(object sender,
    DataGridViewRowsAddedEventArgs e)
{
    for (int i = 0; i < e.RowCount; i++)
    {
        DataGridViewRow row = m_CustomersGrid.Rows[e.RowIndex + i];
        row.Cells["Contact"].Value = string.Format("{0} : {1}",
            row.Cells["ContactName"].Value,
            row.Cells["Phone"].Value);
    }
}
```

This code obtains the current row being set in the loop by indexing into the Rows collection with the RowIndex property from the event argument and a loop index offset up to the number of rows that are affected when this event fires. It then uses the existing data in that row's other columns to compute the contents of the current row. For a real-world application, you could obtain or compute the value of the unbound columns in the row in the loop instead.

■ TIP　Use the `CellFormatting` event to control displayed cell content and the `RowsAdded` event to control stored cell content

The `CellFormatting` event is fired for every cell as it is rendered, giving you a chance to inspect and possibly modify the value that will be presented for any of the cells in the grid. If you want to modify the actual value of an unbound column that is stored in the grid cells collection, use the `RowsAdded` event to set all the unbound column values in one shot when the row is added, instead of requiring a separate event firing for each cell. If the data that you are presenting is purely computed data, instead of data that you are retrieving or deriving from bound data, consider using virtual mode to populate those cells, as discussed in the next section.

■ NOTE　Generate Computed Columns Where It Makes Sense

The example presented in this section simply computed a new column based on the contents of other columns. If this was needed just for display purposes, then using an unbound column might be the best approach. However, if that computed column value might be needed anywhere else in your application, it would make more sense to make it part of your application data entities by making it a custom data column based on an expression in the data set itself.

It is easy to add a custom column to a typed data set table using the data set designer, and there are a number of custom expressions to compute that column's values from other data in the table. If you need to generate the column data based on other tables or data in the database, doing so in a stored procedure might make even more sense.

The bottom line is that you need to pick the appropriate scope for your computed data. Don't use unbound columns with repeated code to display something that could have been computed once and made an actual member of the data you are working with.

Displaying Computed Data in Virtual Mode

Another scenario where you may want to take explicit control over providing a display value for each cell is when you are working with data that contains computed values, especially in combination with bound data and large sets of data. For example, you may need to present a collection of data that has tens of thousands or even millions of rows in a grid. You really ought to question the use case first before supporting such a thing, but if you really need to do this, you probably don't want to clobber your system's memory by creating multiple copies of that data. You may not even want to bring it all into memory at one time, especially if this data is being dynamically created or computed. However, you will want users to able be to smoothly scroll through all that data to locate the items of interest.

Virtual mode for the `DataGridView` lets you display values for cells as they are rendered, so that data doesn't have to be held in memory when it's not being used. With virtual mode you can specify which columns the grid contains at design time, and then provide the cell values as needed, so they display at runtime but not before. The grid will internally only maintain the cell values for the cells that are displayed; you provide the cell value on an as-needed basis.

When you choose to use virtual mode, you can either provide all of the row values through virtual mode event handling, or you can mix the columns of the grid with data-bound and unbound columns. You have to define the columns that will be populated through virtual mode as described earlier in the "Programmatic DataGridView Construction" section. If you also data bind some columns, then the rows will be populated through data binding and you just handle the events necessary for virtual mode for the columns that aren't data bound. If you aren't data binding, you have to add as many rows as you expect to present in the grid, so the grid knows to scale the scrollbar appropriately. You then need a way to get the values corresponding to virtual mode columns when they are needed for presentation. You can do this by computing the values dynamically when they are needed, which is one of the main times that you would use virtual mode. You might also use cached client-side data in the form of an object collection or data set, or you might actually make round-trips to the server to get the data as needed. With the latter approach, you'll need a smart preload and caching strategy, because you could quickly bog down the application if data queries have to run between the client and the server while the user is scrolling. If the data being displayed is computed data, then it really makes sense to wait to compute values until they are actually going to be displayed.

Setting Up Virtual Mode

The following steps describe how to set up virtual mode data binding.

1. Create a grid and define the columns in it that will use virtual mode.

2. Put the grid into virtual mode by setting the `VirtualMode` property to `true`.

3. If you aren't using data binding, add as many rows to the grid as you want to support scrolling through. The easiest and fastest way to do this is to create one prototype row, then use the `AddCopies` method of the `Rows` collection to add as many copies of that prototype row as you would like. You don't have to worry about the cell contents at this point, because you are going to provide those dynamically through an event handler as the grid is rendered.

4. The final step is to wire up an event handler for the `CellValue-Needed` event on the grid. This event will only be fired when the grid is operating in virtual mode, and will be fired for each unbound column cell that is currently visible in the grid when it is first displayed and as the user scrolls.

The code in Listing 6.2 shows a simple Windows Forms application that demonstrates the use of virtual mode. A `DataGridView` object was added to the form through the designer and named `m_Grid`, and a button added to the form for checking how many rows had been visited when scrolling named `m_GetVisitedCountButton`.

LISTING 6.2: **Virtual Mode Sample**

```
partial class VirtualModeForm : Form
{
    private List<DataObject> m_Data = new List<DataObject>();
    private List<bool> m_Visited = new List<bool>();
    public VirtualModeForm()
    {
        InitializeComponent();
        m_Grid.CellValueNeeded += OnCellValueNeeded;
        m_GetVisitedCountButton.Click += OnGetVisitedCount;
        InitData();
        InitGrid();
    }

    private void InitData()
    {
        for (int i = 0; i < 1000001; i++)
        {
            m_Visited.Add(false);
            DataObject obj = new DataObject();
            obj.Id = i;
            obj.Val = 2 * i;
            m_Data.Add(obj);
        }
    }

    private void InitGrid()
    {
        m_Grid.VirtualMode = true;
        m_Grid.ReadOnly = true;
        m_Grid.AllowUserToAddRows = false;
        m_Grid.AllowUserToDeleteRows = false;
        m_Grid.ColumnCount = 3;
        m_Grid.Rows.Add();
        m_Grid.Rows.AddCopies(0, 1000000);
      // Uncomment the next line and comment out the
      // the rest of the method to switch to data bound mode
      //    m_Grid.DataSource = m_Data;
    }
    private void OnCellValueNeeded(object sender,
        DataGridViewCellValueEventArgs e)
    {
        m_Visited[e.RowIndex] = true;
        if (e.ColumnIndex == 0)
        {
            e.Value = m_Data[e.RowIndex].Id;
        }
        else if (e.ColumnIndex == 1)
        {
```

continues

```csharp
                e.Value = m_Data[e.RowIndex].Val;
            }
            else if (e.ColumnIndex == 2)
            {
                Random rand = new Random();
                e.Value = rand.Next();
            }
        }

        private void OnGetVisitedCount(object sender, EventArgs e)
        {
            int count = 0;
            foreach (bool b in m_Visited)
            {
                if (b) count++;
            }
            MessageBox.Show(count.ToString());
        }
    }
    public class DataObject
    {
        private int m_Id;
        private int m_Val;

        public int Val
        {
            get { return m_Val; }
            set { m_Val = value; }
        }

        public int Id
        {
            get { return m_Id; }
            set { m_Id = value; }
        }
    }
```

The form constructor starts by calling InitializeComponent as usual, to invoke the code written by the designer from drag-and-drop operations and Properties window settings. For this sample, that just declares and creates the grid and the button controls on the form. The constructor code then subscribes two event handlers using delegate inference.

The first event handler is the important one for virtual mode—the CellValueNeeded event. As mentioned earlier, this event is only fired when the grid is in virtual mode and is called for each unbound column cell that is visible in the grid at any given time. As the user scrolls, this event fires again for each cell that is revealed through the scrolling operation. The constructor also subscribes a handler for the button click, which lets you see how many rows the `CellValueNeeded` event handler was actually called for.

After that, the constructor calls the `InitData` helper method, which creates a collection of data using a `List<T>` generic collection that contains instances of a simple `DataObject` class, defined at the end of Listing 6.2. The `DataObject` class has two integer values, `Id` and `Val`, which are presented in the grid. The collection is populated by the `InitData` helper method with one million rows. The `Id` property of each object is set to its index in the collection, and the `Val` property is set to two times that index.

■ TIP **Favor object collections for large data collections**

Object collections that are easily defined using the generic collections in .NET 2.0 are inherently lighterweight and perform better than storing your data in a data set. Typed data sets are a great way to go for smaller sets of data, particularly when you need to support updates, inserts, and deletes. But for simply presenting a large collection of data, you will pay a significant performance and memory cost for using a data set compared to a custom object collection.

Choosing Data Sets or Custom Collections

When you are dealing with very large collections of data in memory like the one in Listing 6.2, one of your primary concerns should be memory impact. Based on the other samples presented in this book so far, you may be inclined to use a typed data set as your data collection object. However, you should think twice before doing this. Even though improvements in the `DataSet` class (and therefore derived typed data set classes) in .NET 2.0 significantly improve its scalability and performance for large data sets, the `DataSet` class is still a fairly heavyweight object because of all the hierarchical, change tracking, and updating capability that is built into a data set.

continues

If you are thinking of presenting millions of rows of data in a grid, and you expect to let users edit the rows in the grid and let the data set updating capabilities propagate those changes back to your data store, then the `DataSet` class may actually be what you need. However, I would discourage you from designing your application this way. Displaying large collections of data should be a special use case that focuses on presentation—you are just letting the user scroll through large numbers of rows to locate a data item of interest. If you need to support editing of those data items, I suggest you send the user to a different form for editing. However, you can let them edit the values in the grid without needing the extra overhead of a data set, as described shortly.

Object collections like the `List<T>` generic collection are significantly more lightweight than a data set and result in less memory consumption and quicker construction times. If you are going to cache a large collection in memory, you should try to design the form to use a lightweight object collection to cache the values for display only.

Initializing the Grid

After the data is initialized, the constructor calls the `InitGrid` helper method, which does the following:

- Sets the grid into virtual mode.
- Turns off editing, adding, and deleting.
- Adds three text box columns to the grid by setting the `ColumnCount` property.
- Adds one row to the grid as a template.
- Uses the `AddCopies` method on the `Rows` collection to add one million more rows. This method also contains a commented-out line of code that can be used to change the VirtualMode download sample to be data bound against the object collection so that you can see the difference in load time and memory footprint.

After that, Windows Forms event handling takes over for the rest of the application lifecycle. Because the grid was set to virtual mode, the next thing that happens is the OnCellValueNeeded handler will start to get called for each cell that is currently displayed in the grid. This method is coded to extract the appropriate value from the data collection based on the row index and column index of the cell that is being rendered for the first two columns. For the third column, it actually computes the value of the cell on the fly, using the Random class to generate random numbers. It also sets a flag in the m_Visited collection—you can use this to see how many rows are actually being rendered when users scroll around with the application running.

Understanding Virtual Mode Behavior

If you run the VirtualMode sample application from Listing 6.2, note that as you run the mouse over the third column in the grid, the random numbers in the cells that the mouse passes over change. This happens because the CellValueNeeded event handler is called every time the cell paints, not just when it first comes into the scrolling region, and the Random class uses the current time as a seed value for computing the next random number. So if the values that will be calculated when CellValueNeeded are time variant, you will probably want to develop a smarter strategy for computing those values and caching them to avoid exposing changing values in a grid just because the mouse passes over them.

The OnGetVisitedCount button Click handler displays a dialog that shows the number of rows rendered based on the m_Visited collection. If you run the VirtualMode sample application, you can see several things worth noting about virtual mode. The first is that the biggest impact to runtime is the loading and caching of the large data collection on the client side. As a result, this is the kind of operation you would probably want to consider doing on a separate thread in a real application to avoid tying up the UI while the data loads. Using a BackgroundWorker component would be a good choice for this kind of operation.

When dealing with very large data sets, if the user drags the scrollbar thumb control, a large numbers of rows are actually skipped through the paging mechanisms and latency of the scroll bar. As a result, you only have to supply a tiny percentage of the actual cell values unless the user does an extensive amount of scrolling in the grid. This is why virtual mode is particularly nice for computed values: you can avoid computing cell values that won't be displayed.

If you run this example and scroll around for a bit, then click the *Get Visited Count* button, you will see how many rows were actually loaded. For example, I ran this application and scrolled through the data from top to bottom fairly slowly several times. While doing so, I saw smooth scrolling performance that looked like I was actually scrolling through the millions of rows represented by the grid. However, in reality, only about 1,000 rows were actually rendered while I was scrolling.

What if you want to support editing of the values directly in the grid? Maybe you are just using virtual mode to present a computed column with a relatively small set of data, and you want to use that column's edited value to perform some other computation or store the edited value. Another event, `CellValuePushed`, is fired after an edit is complete on a cell in a virtual mode grid. If the grid doesn't have `ReadOnly` set to true, and the cells are of a type that supports editing (like a text box column), then the user can click in a cell, hesitate, then click again to put the cell into editing mode. After the user has changed the value and the focus changes to another cell or control through mouse or keyboard action, the `CellValuePushed` event will be fired for that cell. In an event handler for that event, you can collect the new value from the cell and do whatever is appropriate with it, such as write it back into your data cache or data store.

Virtual Mode Summary

That's all there is to virtual mode: Set the `VirtualMode` property to `true`, create the columns and rows you want the grid to have, and then supply a handler for the `CellValueNeeded` event that sets the appropriate value for the cell being rendered. If you need to support the editing of values directly in the grid, then also handle the `CellValuePushed` event and do whatever is appropriate with the modified values as the user makes the changes. Hopefully, you won't need to use virtual mode often in your applications, but it's nice to have for presenting very large data collections or computing column values on the fly. There are no hard and fast rules on when virtual mode will be needed. If you are having scrolling performance problems in your application, or you want to avoid the memory impact of holding computed values for large numbers of rows in memory, you can see if virtual mode solves your problems. You will still need to think about your data retrieval and caching strategy, though, to avoid seriously hampering the performance of your application on the client machine.

Using the Built-In Column Types

Using a text box column is straightforward enough: you data bind to something that can be rendered as text, or set the `Value` property on a cell to something that can be converted to a string, and you are done. Using some of the other cell types may not be as easy to figure out, so this section steps through each of the built-in column types, pointing out its capabilities and how to use it.

The first thing to realize is that even though most of the functionality is surfaced at the cell level in a `DataGridView` and it can support spreadsheet-like behavior (as described later in this chapter), the grid is still primarily a tabular control. The columns in the grid usually represent information that can be determined at design time—specifically, the schema of the data that will be presented. The rows are usually determined dynamically at runtime and map to the structure specified by the columns. You may occasionally programmatically create columns for rendering based on dynamic data schemas at runtime, but even then you are first defining the data's shape (the columns) and then providing the data (the rows).

As a result, for each of the built-in cell types that the grid is capable of displaying, there is a corresponding column type designed to contain cells of that type. Each cell type is derived from the `DataGridViewCell` class, and each of the corresponding column types is derived from `DataGrid-ViewColumn`. Each of the column types expose properties to aid in the data's data binding, and each column type corresponds to the expected content for the type of cells that the column contains. Likewise, each derived cell type may expose additional properties based on the type of content it is designed to display.

Because each built-in column type is different in subtle ways, it's best to cover them one at a time. However, since all of the cell types contained by the column types derive from the same base class, there are a number of properties from the base class that you'll use for controlling and accessing cell content. The properties of the `DataGridViewCell` base class are described in Table 6.1.

TABLE 6.1:   DataGridViewCell Properties

Property Name	Type	Description
ColumnIndex	Int32	Gets the position index of the containing column within the grid.
ContentBounds	Rectangle	Gets the bounding rectangle for the content of the cell. The upper left corner will be relative to the upper left corner of the cell, and the width and height represent the area available for rendering content within the cell.
ContextMenuStrip	ContextMenu-Strip	Gets or sets the context menu associated with the cell. If the user right-clicks in the cell, this property's context menu displays. If a context menu has been assigned at the column level, setting a different one at the cell level will replace the one used for the rest of the column, but only for this cell.
DefaultNew-RowValue	Object	Gets the value that will be used if no value has been provided for the cell. The base class returns `null` from this property, but derived classes can provide a more meaningful value based on their expected content. For example, the image cell type returns a red X bitmap when no image has been provided for a value.

TABLE 6.1: DataGridViewCell Properties (Continued)

Property Name	Type	Description
Displayed	Boolean	True if the cell is currently displayed in the viewable area of the grid, false otherwise. This is a read-only property.
EditedFormatted-Value	Object	Gets the formatted version of the transient edited value of the cell, after any formatting or type conversion has been applied, and before the edited value has been made the current value through a focus change to a different cell.
EditType	Type	Gets the type of the control that will be rendered in the cell when in editing mode.
ErrorIconBounds	Rectangle	Gets the rectangle that bounds where the error icon will be presented so you can do any custom rendering based on that.
ErrorText	String	Gets or sets the text that can be displayed if an error is associated with the cell.
FormattedValue	Object	Gets the formatted version of the current value of the cell, after any formatting or type conversion has been applied.
FormattedValue-Type	Type	Gets the type that will be set on the cell for rendering, after formatting or type conversion has been applied.
Frozen	Boolean	True if either the row or column containing this cell is Frozen, false otherwise. (See the later section "Column and Row Freezing" for details on the meaning of this value.) This is a read-only property.

continues

TABLE 6.1: DataGridViewCell Properties (Continued)

Property Name	Type	Description
HasStyle	Boolean	True if a style has been explicitly set for this cell, false otherwise. This is a read-only property.
InheritedState	DataGridView ElementState	Gets the state enumeration that describes the states provided by the cell base class.
InheritedStyle	DataGridView CellStyle	Gets the style that will be applied based on the styles of the grid, row, column, and default cell style. (See the later section on styles for details.)
IsInEditMode	Boolean	True if the cell is being edited by the user, false otherwise. This is a read-only property.
OwningColumn	DataGridView Column	Gets a reference to the cell's column.
OwningRow	DataGrid-ViewRow	Gets a reference to the cell's row.
PreferredSize	Size	Gets the preferred size of the cell based on the cell template, which can be used in custom cell painting.
ReadOnly	Boolean	True if the contents of this cell are editable, false otherwise. This is a read/write property.
Resizable	Boolean	True if either the containing row or column is resizable, false otherwise.
RowIndex	Int32	Gets the index of the containing row within the grid.
Selected	Boolean	True if the cell is rendered as being selected and is marked as part of the selected cells collection, false otherwise. This is a read/write property.

TABLE 6.1: DataGridViewCell Properties (Continued)

Property Name	Type	Description
Size	Size	Gets the size of the entire cell.
Style	DataGridView CellStyle	Gets or sets the Style object used for rendering this cell. (See the later section on styles for details on this property.)
Tag	Object	This simple placeholder reference, like other Windows Forms controls, lets you get or set an associated object reference for the cell. Typically, the tag is used as a place to stash a unique identifier for the control that can be used in lookup scenarios, such as looping through cells.
ToolTipText	String	Gets or sets the text that is rendered when the mouse hovers over a cell.
Value	Object	Probably the most important property on any cell. This property lets you get or set the value that the cell renders when it is displayed, but formatting and type conversion may occur automatically if the value set is different from the expected type of the cell.
ValueType	Type	Gets or sets the type of the value that is set against this cell, before formatting or type conversion applies. If the type hasn't been explicitly set, it is derived from the type of the containing column.
Visible	Boolean	True if both the containing row and column are visible, false otherwise. This is a read-only property.

The `DataGridViewColumn` (discussed earlier in this chapter) is the base class from which built-in column types derive. This class also has a number of useful properties that you can set to drive the behavior of the grid and that the type-specific column classes inherit. These properties are described in Table 6.2.

TABLE 6.2: DataGridViewColumn Properties

Name	Type	Description
AutoSizeMode	DataGridView-AutoSizeColumnMode	Gets or sets the autosizing behavior of the column (described in the later section on autosizing columns).
CellTemplate	DataGridViewCell	Gets or sets the cell type that will be used as a template for new cells that are created. Derived column types should limit the setting of a cell type to only the cell type they were designed to contain.
CellType	Type	Gets the type of cells this column was designed to contain.
ContextMenuStrip	ContextMenuStrip	Gets or sets the context menu object that will be presented when the user right-clicks in the column.
DataPropertyName	String	Gets or sets the property's name on bound data that will be used to set the value when data binding occurs.
DefaultCellStyle	DataGridView-CellStyle	Gets or sets the cell style that will be used by default for rendering the column's cells.

TABLE 6.2: DataGridViewColumn Properties (Continued)

Name	Type	Description
DisplayIndex	Int32	Gets or sets the display index of the column within the grid. This can be different than the ColumnIndex when column reordering is enabled (described later in this chapter).
DividerWidth	Int32	Gets or sets the width, in pixels, of the divider line that is drawn between this column and the next one to the right.
FillWeight	Float	Gets or sets the value used to determine the width of the column when in AutoSize-Mode of Fill.
Frozen	Boolean	True if the column is frozen, false otherwise. (Freezing columns and rows is discussed later in this chapter.) This is a read/write property.
HeaderCell	DataGridViewCell	Gets or sets the header cell (rendered at the top of the column).
HeaderText	String	Gets or sets the text that is rendered in the header cell as its value.
InheritedAuto-SizeMode	DataGridViewAuto-SizeColumnMode	Gets the autosize mode that is set for the base column class.
InheritedStyle	DataGridView-CellStyle	Gets the style that is inherited from the grid that will be used if none is assigned at the column, row, or cell level.

continues

TABLE 6.2: DataGridViewColumn Properties (Continued)

Name	Type	Description
IsDataBound	Boolean	True if the grid is operating in data-bound mode (a data source has been set), false otherwise. This is a read-only property.
MinimumWidth	Int32	Gets or sets the number of pixels used for a minimum width. This restricts the resizing of the column at runtime to be no less than this number.
Name	String	Gets or sets the name of the column. This is used for indexing into the columns collection on the grid and for data-binding purposes.
ReadOnly	Boolean	True if the cells in the column can be edited, false otherwise. This is a read/write property.
Resizable	Boolean	True if runtime resizing of the column is allowed by the user, false otherwise. This is a read/write property.
Site	ISite	Gets the ISite interface reference for the column, if any. This is used when the column is hosting a component.
SortMode	DataGridView-ColumnSortMode	Gets or sets the sort mode used for sorting the rows of the grid based on this column. This enumerated value can be set to NotSortable, Automatic, or Programmatic.

TABLE 6.2: DataGridViewColumn Properties (Continued)

Name	Type	Description
ToolTipText	String	Gets or sets the text that is shown as a tooltip pop-up when the mouse hovers over a cell in the column. If this property is set at the cell level, the value set for the cell is the one displayed.
ValueType	Type	Gets or sets the type of the values stored in the cells of this column type.
Visible	Boolean	True if the column will be displayed in the grid, false otherwise. This is a read/write property.
Width	Int32	Gets or sets the width, in pixels, of the column in the grid.

There are a number of built-in column types that are available for using with the `DataGridView` control corresponding to the most common control types that developers want to include in a grid. The following subsections describe each of the built-in column types and what is involved in using them.

DataGridViewTextBoxColumn

This is the default type of column (as described earlier in this chapter), and it displays text within the contained cells, which are of type `DataGrid-ViewTextBoxCell`. Data that is bound to this column type and values set on the cell have to be of a type that can be converted to a string.

This column type supports editing if the `ReadOnly` property is `true` (the default) and the focus in on the cell. To enter editing mode, press F2, type in characters, or click in the cell. This embeds a separate editing control of type `DataGridViewTextBoxEditingControl`, which derives from

`TextBox`. This type enables in-place editing for the grid value, like you are used to for text box controls. The value in the text box is treated as a transient value until the focus leaves the cell; then the `CellParsing` event fires, and the value is pushed into the underlying data store if data bound or the `CellValuePushed` event fires if in virtual mode.

DataGridViewButtonColumn

This column type displays cells of type `DataGridViewButtonCell`, which is sort of a fancy form of read-only text cell. A button cell lets you have a button-push experience embedded in the grid, which you can use to trigger whatever action makes sense for your application. The button cell renders itself with a border that looks like any other button control, and when the user clicks on it, the cell renders again with a depressed offset so that you get an action like a button. To handle the "button click," you need to handle the `CellClick` event on the grid, determine if it was a button cell that was clicked, and then take the appropriate action for your application. This involves taking the event argument from the `CellClick` event, checking its `ColumnIndex` property against the column index of button columns in your grid, and then calling the button click handling code from there based on the row index, or the contents of that cell or others in that row.

DataGridViewLinkColumn

Like the button column, this is another form of rendering a text cell that gives the user a visual cue that clicking on it will invoke some action. This column type contains cells of type `DataGridViewLinkCell` and renders the text in the cell to look like a hyperlink. Typically, clicking on a link "navigates" the user somewhere else, so you might use this kind of column if you are going to pop up another window or modify the contents of another control based on the user clicking on the link. To do so, you handle the `CellClick` event as described previously for the button, determine if you are in a cell containing a link, and take the appropriate action based on that link. You will have to derive the context of what action you should take either from the cell's contents or other cells in that row or column.

DataGridViewCheckBoxColumn

By now you are probably picking up the pattern, and as you would guess, this column type contains cells of type `DataGridViewCheckBoxCell`. This cell type renders a `CheckBox`-like control that supports tri-state rendering like a `CheckBox` control.

The values that this cell type supports depend on whether you set the cell or column type into `ThreeState` mode or not. If the `ThreeState` property is set to `false` (the default), then a value of `null` or `false` will leave the check box unchecked; a value of `true` will check the box. If `ThreeState` is set to `true`, then the `Value` property of the cell can be `null` or one of the `CheckState` enumeration values. If `null` and `ThreeState` is `true`, then the check box will be rendered in the indeterminate state (a square filling it). The `CheckState` enumeration values are `Unchecked`, `Checked`, and `Indeterminate`, which are self-explanatory. The cell's `Value` property can be set explicitly through programmatic code that accesses the cell in the `Cells` collection of the row, or it can be set through data binding.

DataGridViewImageColumn

This column, not surprisingly, contains cells of type `DataGridView-ImageCell`, which support the rendering of images directly within the grid's cells. This cell type provides a very handy and easy-to-use capability in the `DataGridView` control that used to be fairly painful to achieve with the `DataGrid` control. This column type exposes `Image` and `ImageLayout` properties in addition to the usual base class properties. Setting the column's `Image` property results in that image being displayed by default for all the cells in that column. The `ImageLayout` property takes a `DataGrid-ViewImageCellLayout` enumeration value. The values of this enumeration and their effect on the rendering of an image in the grid are described in Table 6.3.

In addition to setting a default image at the column level, you can set the `Value` property at the cell level, either explicitly through code or implicitly through data binding. The value can be set to any type that can be converted to an `Image` object for display in the cell. Natively in .NET, this means that the value can either be an `Image` or a `byte` array that contains a serialized `Image`.

TABLE 6.3: DataGridViewImageCellLayout Enumeration Values and Effects

Value	Effect
`NotSet`	This is the default and indicates that the layout behavior has not been explicitly specified. The resulting behavior of the cell is the same as if `Normal` had been explicitly set.
`Normal`	The image is rendered at its native size and centered in the cell. Depending on the size of the cell, any portions of the image that are outside the bounds of the cell will be clipped.
`Stretch`	The image is stretched or shrunk in both width and height so that it fills the cell and no clipping occurs. No attempt is made to maintain the aspect ratio (width/height) of the image.
`Zoom`	The image is resized so that it fits within the cell without clipping, and the aspect ratio (width/height) is maintained so that no distortion of the image occurs.

DataGridViewComboBoxColumn

This column type contains cells of type `DataGridViewComboBoxCell`, which renders itself like a standard `ComboBox` control within the cell. This column type is definitely the most complex built-in column type for the `DataGridView`, and it exposes a number of properties that drive its behavior, as described in Table 6.4.

TABLE 6.4: DataGridViewComboBoxColumn Properties

Name	Type	Description
`AutoComplete`	`Boolean`	True if `AutoComplete` functionality is enabled when the cell is in edit mode, false otherwise. This lets users type in characters, and the combo box will select matching items in the list based on the characters typed. This is a read/write property.
`CellTemplate`	`DataGridViewCell`	Gets or sets the cell type being presented in the column. The cell type must be a derived class from `DataGridView-ComboboxCell`.

TABLE 6.4: DataGridViewComboBoxColumn Properties (Continued)

Name	Type	Description
DataSource	Object	Gets or sets the object being used as the data source for data binding the column. Setting this property to a data collection has the same data-binding effect as it does with a normal combo box—it will display items from the collection as the items in the drop-down list, using the `Display-Member` property to determine which data member or property within the items in that collection to use for the text in the list.
DisplayMember	String	Gets or sets which data member or property within the data source to display as the text items in the list.
DisplayStyle	DataGridView-ComboBox-DisplayStyle	Gets or sets the style that the combo boxes in the column are using. The values for this enumeration include `ComboBox`, `DropDown-Button`, and `Nothing`.
DisplayStyleFor-CurrentCellOnly	Boolean	True if the `DisplayStyle` value only applies to the current cell in the column, false if it is being used for all cells within the column. This is a read/write property.
DropDownWidth	Int32	Gets or sets the width of the drop-down list that is displayed when the user clicks on the down arrow or presses F4.
FlatStyle	FlatStyle	Gets or sets the `FlatStyle` enumerated value that determines the visual appearance of the combo box when it is rendered.

continues

TABLE 6.4:   DataGridViewComboBoxColumn Properties (Continued)

Name	Type	Description
Items	ObjectCollection	Gets the collection of objects that are set for the cell template.
MaxDropDownItems	Int32	Gets or sets the maximum number of items to display in the drop-down list.
Sorted	Boolean	True if the items in the list will be sorted alphabetically, false otherwise. This is a read/write property.
ValueMember	String	Gets or sets the data member or property within the data source that will be kept with the items in the list. Lets you keep track of additional information, such as the record primary key.

The combo box cells support edit mode, and users can type in a value for autocompletion purposes or select values from a drop-down list. When in edit mode, this cell type hosts a control that derives from the `ComboBox` control, so all of its functionality is exposed when the cell is switched into edit mode.

The `Value` property represents the currently selected value in the combo box. It may contain the displayed text value in the combo box, or it may contain the underlying `ValueMember` value for the selected item, depending on what you set for the `DataSource`, `DisplayMember`, and `ValueMember` properties. The `FormattedValue` property, inherited from the base class, always contains the formatted text for the selected item that is being displayed in the combo box.

Data binding this column type or the cells in it works just like data binding a standalone `ComboBox` control. You set the `DataSource`, `Display-Member`, and `ValueMember` properties, and the items in the data source collection are rendered in the drop-down list using the value of the data member that is identified as the display member:

```
toCountryColumn.DataSource = m_CountriesBindingSource;
toCountryColumn.DisplayMember = "CountryName";
toCountryColumn.ValueMember = "CountryID";
```

The sample code that accompanies this chapter contains a simple application called ColumnTypes that demonstrates how the code interacts with each of the built-in column types described in this chapter.

Built-In Header Cells

Header cells are the cells rendered at the top and left sides of the grid. They provide the context or a guide to what the cells in the grid contain. Column header cells are of type DataGridViewColumnHeaderCell, and their header text indicates the content of the column cells. The cell contains an up or down triangle when the column supports sorting; users can sort the column by clicking on the column header. Usually the header text is set through the HeaderText property on the column, either explicitly through code or implicitly through data binding based on the data's schema. You can also access the header cell directly from the column through the HeaderCell property and use its Value to set the text displayed.

The row header cells are of type DataGridViewRowHeaderCell. They indicate row selections with a triangle glyph, editing mode with a pencil glyph, and the new row with a star glyph. Row header cells can display text as well; you set the cell's Value to a string value by accessing the row's HeaderCell property.

Both column and row headers can be further customized by implementing custom painting by handling the CellPainting event on the grid. Note that if you do custom painting, you must do all the painting of the header cell yourself, and then set the Handled property on the event argument to true:

```
private void OnCellPainting(object sender,
    DataGridViewCellPaintingEventArgs e)
{
    if (e.ColumnIndex < 0)
    {
        e.Graphics.FillRectangle(Brushes.Aqua, e.CellBounds);
        e.Handled = true;
    }
}
```

This code checks to see if the column being painted has an index less than zero, which indicates that the row header is being painted. The column index of the row headers is –1, and the row index of the column headers is also –1. You cannot index into the `Cells` collection on the row with these values, but you can use them as a flag in the `CellPainting` event to know when it is a header that is being painted.

Additionally, you can set the `CellHeader` property to an instance of a class that derives from `DataGridViewCell`, and then that cell type will be used when the header cells are rendered. You can derive your own class from the cell base class and do whatever kind of custom painting, formatting, or setting of styles there that makes sense.

Handling Grid Data Edits

How you handle grid edits is going to depend on the following:

- The type of column or cell you are dealing with
- Whether the data is data bound
- Whether you are in virtual mode

As mentioned earlier, when working with a text box column, users can start editing a cell by putting the focus into the cell with the mouse, arrow keys, or by pressing the F2 key when the mouse pointer is in the cell. If users then start typing characters, the current contents of the cell will be overwritten. When they change the focus to another cell, this completes the editing process.

The first thing that happens that you might want to handle is that the `CellParsing` event fires. Like its `CellFormatting` counterpart, this event gives you an opportunity to intercept the value that was entered into the cell while in edit mode, either to handle storing that value somewhere yourself or to transform it into some other value before it is stored.

If the cell is data bound, and if the data source supports editing the data objects in the collection, the data will automatically be pushed back into the underlying data source. If the cell is a button or link cell, however, you won't be able to edit the contents in the first place because they don't support editing. If the cell is a combo box cell, editing is done by selecting a value in the drop-down list or overtyping the current selection if the cell has its `DisplayStyle` property set to `ComboBox`. This changes the cell's value when editing is complete (when the focus moves off the cell) and results in the same action as if that value had been typed into a text box cell. If the grid is in virtual mode, you will need to handle the `CellValue-Pushed` event to grab the value that was entered and do what you need to with it.

When a cell switches into edit mode, an event named `Editing-ControlShowing` fires. This event passes an event argument that lets you get a reference to the editing control itself. The built-in cell types that support editing (text box, combo box, and check box cell types) create an instance of an editing control that derives from their normal Windows Forms counterparts (`TextBox`, `ComboBox`, and `CheckBox`, respectively) and display that control as a child control inside a panel inside the cell. If you create a custom cell type that supports editing, then you will want to follow a similar approach. Through the `EditingControlShowing` event, you can get a reference to the editing control in use and can tap into its event model to respond to edits in realtime. For example, if you want to dynamically react to selections in a combo box column while the control is still in edit mode and the selected value hasn't been pushed yet into the cell's underlying value (meaning the `CellParsing` event hasn't yet fired), you could use the `EditingControlShowing` event to hook things up:

```
public Form1()
{
    InitializeComponent();
    m_Grid.EditingControlShowing += OnEditControlShowing();
}

private void OnEditControlShowing(object sender,
    DataGridViewEditingControlShowingEventArgs e)
{
    if (m_Grid.CurrentCell.ColumnIndex == 2)
    {
```

```
        m_HookedCombo = e.Control as ComboBox;
        if (m_HookedCombo == null)
            return;
        m_HookedCombo.SelectedIndexChanged += OnCountryComboChanged;
    }
}


void OnCountryComboChanged(object sender, EventArgs e)
{
    string countryName =
        (string)m_Grid.CurrentCell.EditedFormattedValue;
    if (string.IsNullOrEmpty(countryName))
        return;
    DataRow[] countries = m_MoneyData.Countries.Select(
        string.Format("CountryName = '{0}'", countryName));
    if (countries != null && countries.Length > 0)
    {
        MoneyDBDataSet.CountriesRow row =
            countries[0] as MoneyDBDataSet.CountriesRow;
        int flagColIndex = m_Grid.Columns["TargetCountryFlag"].Index;
        DataGridViewCell cell = m_Grid.CurrentRow.Cells[flagColIndex];
        cell.Value = row.Flag;
    }
}
```

This code does the following:

1. The constructor subscribes the OnEditControlShowing method to
   the grid's EditControlShowing event.

2. When the EditControlShowing event fires, the OnEditControl-
   Showing method uses the Control property on the event argument
   to get a reference to the ComboBox control that is embedded in the cell
   that is being edited.

3. The OnEditControlShowing method then subscribes the
   OnCountryComboChanged method to the SelectedIndexChanged
   event on that ComboBox control.

4. When the SelectedIndexChanged event fires, the OnCountry-
   ComboChanged method retrieves the country name from the cell
   containing the drop-down list using the current cell's Edited-
   FormattedValue property. This lets you get the edited value before
   the cell has left editing mode.

5. The `OnCountryComboChanged` method then uses the country name to retrieve the corresponding row in the Countries table and extracts the flag image from the Flag column.

6. Finally, it sets the flag image as the value on the cell corresponding to the country's flag.

Keep in mind that the Flag column in the Countries table is actually a byte array containing the bits of the saved image file. The automatic formatting of the image column kicks in here to present the image in the same way that was discussed for a `PictureBox` control in Chapter 4. The ColumnTypes sample in the download code demonstrates this technique.

Automatic Column Sizing

One of the `DataGridView` control's new features is its ability to automatically calculate the width of the columns to fit the content of the columns based on several different criteria. Like many of the grid's features, all you need to do to take advantage of this feature is to set the appropriate property on a given column—and then the grid does the rest. Specifically, the property that takes care of this for you is the `AutoSizeMode` property of the `DataGridViewColumn` class. By setting this property to one of the enumerated values of the `DataGridViewAutoSizeColumnMode` enumeration shown in Table 6.5, you can drive how to set the width of columns in the grid.

TABLE 6.5: DataGridView AutoSizeMode Values

Value	How the Column Width Is Calculated
NotSet	By the value set on the `AutoSizeColumnsMode` property at the grid level. This is the default value.
None	Set explicitly by setting the column's `Width` property.
ColumnHeader	By the width of the content in the header cell only.
AllCellsExcept-Header	By the width of the widest cell in the grid, whether it is displayed or not, but the header cell content size is ignored.

continues

TABLE 6.5:   DataGridView AutoSizeMode Values (Continued)

Value	How the Column Width Is Calculated
AllCells	By the width of all cells in the column, including those not displayed and the header cell content.
DisplayedCells-ExceptHeader	Based only on displayed cells in the column, ignoring the width of the header cell content.
DisplayedCells	By the width of the content in displayed cells, including the header cell.
Fill	Automatically calculated to fill the displayed content area of the grid so the contents can be viewed without scrolling. The actual value used depends on the mode of the other columns in the grid, and their Minimum-Width and FillWeight properties. If all the columns in the grid are set to Fill mode, and their minimum width requirements are met, then the columns will each have equal width, filling the grid, but not requiring any horizontal scrolling.

One of the most useful values is AllCells. I recommend that this be your default, unless you see a performance hit from using it for large data sets or if you have some cell values that will be very long. This setting ensures that the content of cells never wraps. Additionally, remember to set the FormattingApplied property on the event argument to the Cell-Formatting event if you are dynamically populating cell values. Otherwise, setting the AutoSizeMode to one of the row values will result in an infinite loop.

As a simple example of using this feature, the following code modifies the code from Listing 6.1 to set the column width of the Full Name computed column:

```
newColIndex = m_AuthorsGrid.Columns.Add("FullName", "Full Name");
m_AuthorsGrid.Columns[newColIndex].AutoSizeMode =
    DataGridViewAutoSizeColumnMode.AllCells;
```

The Fill mode is very powerful for automatically maximizing the use of the grid real estate, but it can be a little complicated to understand. Basically, if you set the mode for all columns to Fill, each of the columns will have their width set equally, and the columns will fill the grid boundary with no horizontal scrollbar needed. If the `MinimumWidth` property of any column set to `Fill` mode is wider than the width that was computed using the fill algorithm, then the `MinimumWidth` value will be used instead, and the other columns just end up being narrower so that they all still fit in the grid without a horizontal scrollbar. If the `MinimumWidth` values of multiple columns make it so that all columns cannot be displayed, then the columns that cannot be displayed will be set to their minimum width value, and a scrollbar will be displayed. The default value for minimum width is only 5 pixels, so you will definitely want to set a more sensible `Minimum-Width` value when working with `Fill` mode.

Each column also has a `FillWeight` property, which takes effect when that column's `AutoSizeMode` is set to `Fill`. The `FillWeight` can be thought of as the percentage of the remaining available grid width that the individual column will take up compared to other columns that are set to `Fill`. It is a weight instead of a percentage, though, because you can use values that don't add up to 100. For example, suppose you wanted to display the CustomerID, CompanyName, and ContactName columns from the Northwind Customers table in a grid. The following code sets the column width of the CustomerID column to 75 pixels, and then sets the remaining two columns to `Fill` mode with weights of 10 and 20, respectively.

```
public Form1()
{
    InitializeComponent();
    m_CustomersGrid.Columns["CustomerID"].Width = 75;
    m_CustomersGrid.Columns["CompanyName"].AutoSizeMode =
        DataGridViewAutoSizeColumnMode.Fill;
    m_CustomersGrid.Columns["CompanyName"].FillWeight = 10;
    m_CustomersGrid.Columns["ContactName"].AutoSizeMode =
        DataGridViewAutoSizeColumnMode.Fill;
    m_CustomersGrid.Columns["ContactName"].FillWeight = 20;
}
```

As a result, the remaining two columns occupy 33 percent and 67 percent of the remaining grid width, respectively, after the CustomerID column has taken up its fixed width space. Figure 6.2 illustrates this.

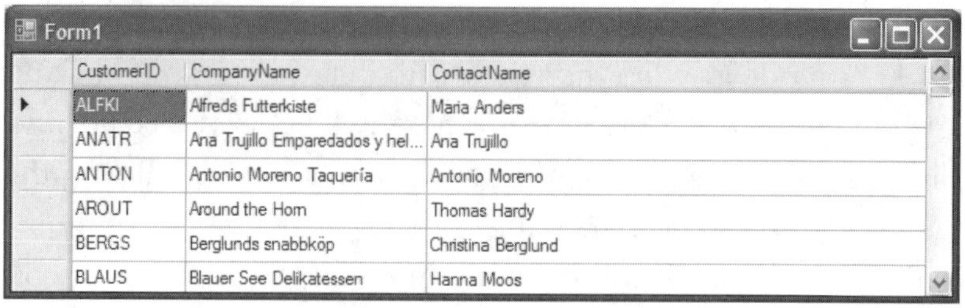

FIGURE 6.2: Columns Using AutoSizeMode of Fill and FillWeights

Column and Row Freezing

Scrolling is inevitable when dealing with lots of rows or columns of data. Often when you scroll through data, it is easy to lose the context of what rows or columns you are looking at, especially if that context is based on the values in some other rows or columns. Let's say you are browsing through a grid filled with product information. If there are a lot of columns of data associated with each product, as you scroll to the right to view columns that aren't currently displayed, you will lose the context of the product name as it gets scrolled off the left of the screen. What you would really want in this situation is to be able to freeze the product name column so that it is always shown and only have the remaining columns scroll. Likewise, there may be situations where you need to present one or more rows at the top of the grid that need to remain in place as you scroll down to additional rows in the grid.

Accomplishing this with the `DataGridView` control is simple: You just set the `Frozen` property to `true` on any row or column to get this behavior. Specifically, if you freeze a column, then that column, and all the columns to the left of it, won't scroll when you scroll to the right in the grid. Similarly, if you freeze a row, then that row and all the rows above it won't scroll when you scroll down in the grid. If you are going to freeze a column or row, then you will probably want to provide a visual cue to the user indicating the logical boundary that exists between the frozen item and the nonfrozen ones next to it. The easiest way to do this is to set the `Divider-Width` property on the column or row to something other than the default. This property is an integer that specifies the number of pixels used to draw

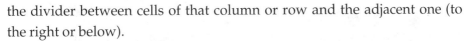

the divider between cells of that column or row and the adjacent one (to the right or below).

The following code shows a simple example of freezing both a column and a row and setting the divider width:

```
m_ProductsGrid.Columns["ProductName"].Frozen = true;
m_ProductsGrid.Columns["ProductName"].DividerWidth = 3;
m_ProductsGrid.Rows[1].Frozen = true;
m_ProductsGrid.Rows[1].DividerHeight = 3;
```

Using the Designer to Define Grids

Now that you understand how to code most of the common uses of the grid, let's cover how to avoid having to write a lot of that code yourself. The `DataGridView` control supports a very rich experience while working in the Visual Studio designer through a combination of the designer Smart Tags, dialogs, and the Properties window.

For starters, if you have defined a data source in your project, you can simply drag a data collection source like a data table onto the form designer and a `DataGridView` instance will be created with all of its supporting objects. Additionally, the column definitions based on the grid's data source properties let you set other properties, such as the `AutoSize-Mode`, using the designer. If you select the grid and display its Smart Tag, as shown in Figure 6.3, you can modify the most common options of the grid's appearance and behavior from there.

The *Choose Data Source* drop-down displays a data sources selection window similar to the one described in Chapter 5 for the Properties window. The presented data sources will be tailored to only those that implement the `IList` interface and thus are suitable for binding to the grid.

The *Edit Columns* and *Add Column* links display dialogs that let you define the columns that the grid will contain, shown in Figures 6.4 and 6.5 respectively.

The Edit Columns dialog lets you add and remove columns, set the order of the columns within the grid, and set all the design-time properties for a defined column in a focused dialog. The properties shown in the dialog will be tailored based on whether the column is a bound or unbound

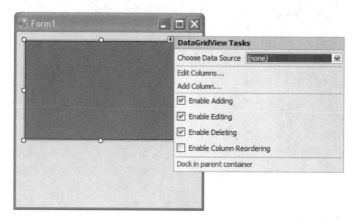

FIGURE 6.3: DataGridView Smart Tag

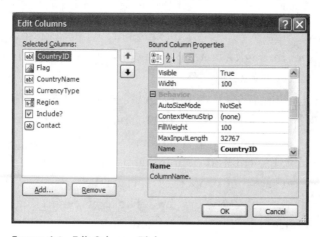

FIGURE 6.4: Edit Columns Dialog

column, and will expose additional properties based on the column type and cell type. If you define custom column types and include them in your project, they will show up as options for new columns or for configuring columns through this dialog.

The Add Column dialog (see Figure 6.5) lets you add a new data-bound or unbound column to the grid. If you are adding a data-bound column, you can select from the columns available in the currently selected data source. You will first have to set the data source to an appropriate collection of data either through the Smart Tag or through the `DataSource` property in the Properties window. If you are adding an unbound column,

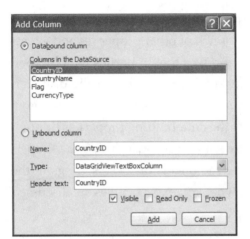

FIGURE 6.5: Add Column Dialog

then you just specify the name of the column, the type of the column, and the header text. When you click the *Add* button, the column is added to the grid, and the dialog remains open so you can quickly define multiple new columns.

Configuring the columns through these dialogs writes all the code for you that has been covered earlier in this chapter for defining columns and controlling their runtime behavior.

The *Enable Adding* check box on the `DataGridView` Smart Tag sets the `AllowUserToAddRows` property to `true` if checked, which displays a new empty row at the bottom of the grid. This lets users add a new row to the data collection by typing new values into the cells. The ability to support this depends on whether the grid is data bound, and, if so, whether the underlying object collection supports adding new items to the collection (see the discussion in Chapter 7). Likewise, the *Enable Editing* check box sets the `ReadOnly` property, which affects whether users can edit the contents of the grid in place, and *Enable Deleting* sets the `AllowUserToDeleteRows` property. The *Enable Column Reordering* check box sets the `AllowUser-ToOrderColumns` property, whose behavior is described in the next section.

The *Dock in parent container* link is only available if you first drag and drop a grid control onto a form. It does exactly what it says—it simply sets the `Dock` property to `Fill`.

In addition to the common properties and behaviors that you can configure through the Smart Tag, there are a bunch of other properties and events that you can configure at design time through the Properties window. Setting any of these properties generates appropriate code in the designer-generated partial class for the form in the `InitializeComponent` method. Most notably, you can configure any of the data-binding properties through the Properties window. You'll probably want to set styles using the Properties window, because you can preview the results of those settings in the designer to make sure you are getting what you expect. Styles are discussed in more detail at the end of this chapter.

Column Reordering

Column reordering is a slick built-in behavior of the grid that lets users change the display order of columns in the grid at runtime. Because different users of an application often pay more attention to some columns in a grid than others, users commonly request to set the order of the columns displayed in the grid themselves. While you could support this functionality by programmatically removing columns from the grid and then inserting them back in the new position, that requires a fair amount of tedious code to have to write for a common use case. So the Windows Client team was nice enough to build functionality for this right into the grid control.

The way this works is that if the `AllowUserToOrderColumns` property is set to `true` and the user clicks and drags on a column header, the grid lets them drag and drop the column to the position where they would like it to display. The columns to the right of the drop position will move one position to the right, and the columns surrounding the original location of the dragged column will move to be adjacent after the column has been moved. Figure 6.6 shows this in action. In this case, the QuantityPerUnit column was clicked on and is being dragged to the left. A gray box is drawn the size of the column's header cell you are dragging. When you move the cursor to one side of another column, the border between that column and the adjacent one darkens, indicating where the column you are dragging will be placed if you release the mouse button.

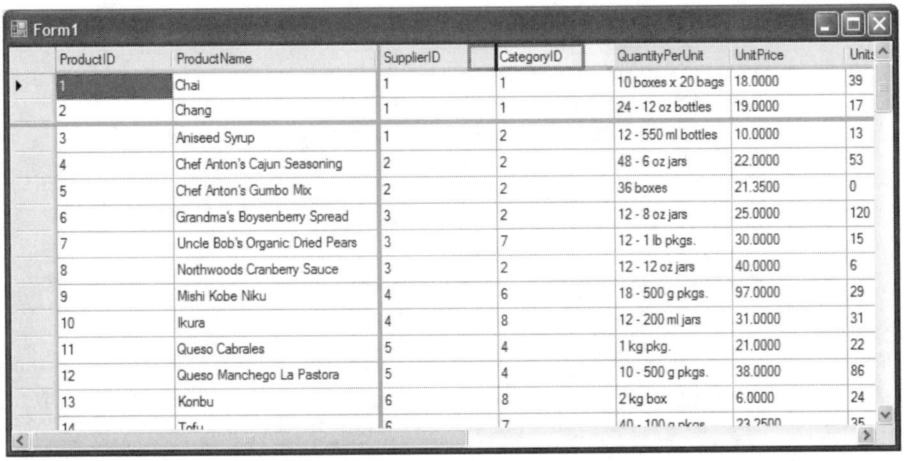

FIGURE 6.6: Column Reordering in Action

When a column has been moved through column reordering, its
ColumnIndex doesn't change, but the DisplayIndex property indicates
its current display order within the grid. By default, the display order of
the grid is not persisted between application runs, but it's a simple matter
to persist that information yourself and reinstate the display order by writing the display order to a file. The code in Listing 6.3 demonstrates persisting the data into a file in isolated storage using the XmlSerializer class.

LISTING 6.3: Persisting Display Order of Columns

```
public partial class Form1 : Form
{
    public Form1()
    {
        InitializeComponent();
    }


    private void Form1_Load(object sender, EventArgs e)
    {
        m_Grid.AllowUserToOrderColumns = true;
        SetDisplayOrder();
    }

    private void OnFormClosing(object sender, FormClosingEventArgs e)
    {
        CacheDisplayOrder();
    }
```

continues

```csharp
private void CacheDisplayOrder()
{
   IsolatedStorageFile isoFile =
      IsolatedStorageFile.GetUserStoreForAssembly();
   using (IsolatedStorageFileStream isoStream = new
      IsolatedStorageFileStream("DisplayCache", FileMode.Create,
         isoFile))
   {
      int[] displayIndices =new int[m_Grid.ColumnCount];
      for (int i = 0; i < m_Grid.ColumnCount; i++)
      {
         displayIndices[i] = m_Grid.Columns[i].DisplayIndex;
      }
      XmlSerializer ser = new XmlSerializer(typeof(int[]));
      ser.Serialize(isoStream,displayIndices);
   }
}


private void SetDisplayOrder()
{
   IsolatedStorageFile isoFile =
      IsolatedStorageFile.GetUserStoreForAssembly();
   string[] fileNames = isoFile.GetFileNames("*");
   bool found = false;
   foreach (string fileName in fileNames)
   {
      if (fileName == "DisplayCache")
         found = true;
   }
   if (!found)
      return;
   using (IsolatedStorageFileStream isoStream = new
      IsolatedStorageFileStream("DisplayCache", FileMode.Open,
         isoFile))
   {
      try
      {
      XmlSerializer ser = new XmlSerializer(typeof(int[]));
      int[] displayIndicies =
         (int[])ser.Deserialize(isoStream);
      for (int i = 0; i < displayIndicies.Length; i++)
      {
         m_Grid.Columns[i].DisplayIndex = displayIndicies[i];
      }
      }
      catch { }
   }
}
}
```

This code isn't specific to the data source in any way. The key facets here are that the code in the form `Load` event handler sets the `AllowUserToOrderColumns` property to `true`, allowing the dynamic changing of `DisplayIndex` for columns through drag-and-drop operations. I then added a `CacheDisplayOrder` helper method that is called by the `Form.Closing` event handler, and a `SetDisplayOrder` helper method that is called when the form loads.

`CacheDisplayOrder` first collects all the display index values for each of the grid's columns and puts them into an integer array. It then creates an isolated storage file stream and writes the array to that stream using the `XmlSerializer` class. The `SetDisplayOrder` method does the reverse: it first checks to see if the file exists, and if so, reads the array back in and uses it to set the `DisplayIndex` on each column in the grid.

Defining Custom Column and Cell Types

With the `DataGridView`, you are already leaps and bounds ahead of the `DataGrid` for presenting rich data because of the built-in column types that it supports out of the box. But there are always custom scenarios that you will want to support to display custom columns. Luckily, another thing the `DataGridView` makes significantly easier is plugging in custom column and cell types.

If you want to customize just the painting process of a cell, but you don't need to add any properties or control things at the column level, you have an event-based option rather than creating new column and cell types. You can handle the `CellPainting` event and draw directly into the cell itself, and you can achieve pretty much whatever you want with the built-in cell types and some (possibly complex) drawing code. But if you want to be able to just plug your column or cell type in a reusable way with the same ease as using the built-in types, then you can derive your own column and cell types instead.

The model you should follow for plugging in custom column types matches what you have already seen for the built-in types: You need to create a column type and a corresponding cell type that the column will contain. You do this by simply inheriting from the base `DataGridViewColumn` and `DataGridViewCell` classes, either directly or indirectly, through one of the built-in types.

The best way to explain this in detail is with an example. Say I wanted to implement a custom column type that lets me display the status of the items represented by the grid's rows. I want to be able to set a status using a custom-enumerated value, and cells in the column will display a graphic indicating that status based on the enumerated value set on the cell. To do this, I define a `StatusColumn` class and a `StatusCell` class (I disposed of the built-in type naming convention here of prefixing `DataGridView` on all the types because the type names get sooooooooooo long). I want these types to let me simply set the value of a cell, either programmatically or through data binding, to one of the values of a custom-enumerated type that I call `StatusImage`. `StatusImage` can take the values `Green`, `Yellow`, or `Red`, and I want the cell to display a custom graphic for each of those based on the value of the cell. Figure 6.7 shows the running sample application with this behavior.

Defining a Custom Cell Type

To achieve this, the first step is to define the custom cell type. If you are going to do your own drawing, you can override the protected virtual `Paint` method from the `DataGridViewCell` base class. However, if the cell content you want to present is just a variation on one of the built-in cell types, you should consider inheriting from one of them instead. That is what I did in this case. Because my custom cells are still going to be presenting images, the `DataGridViewImageCell` type makes a natural base class. My `StatusCell` class isn't going to expose the ability to set the image at random, though; it is designed to work with enumerated values.

FIGURE 6.7: Custom Column and Cell Type Example

I also want the cell value to be able to handle integers as long as they are within the corresponding numeric values of the enumeration, so that I can support the common situation where enumerated types are stored in a database as their corresponding integer values. The code in Listing 6.4 shows the `StatusCell` class implementation.

LISTING 6.4: Custom Cell Class

```
namespace CustomColumnAndCell
{
    public enum StatusImage
    {
        Green,
        Yellow,
        Red
    }

    public class StatusCell : DataGridViewImageCell
    {
        public StatusCell()
        {
            this.ImageLayout = DataGridViewImageCellLayout.Zoom;
        }

        protected override object GetFormattedValue(object value,
            int rowIndex, ref DataGridViewCellStyle cellStyle,
            TypeConverter valueTypeConverter,
            TypeConverter formattedValueTypeConverter,
            DataGridViewDataErrorContexts context)
        {
            string resource = "CustomColumnAndCell.Red.bmp";
            StatusImage status = StatusImage.Red;
            // Try to get the default value from the containing column
            StatusColumn owningCol = OwningColumn as StatusColumn;
            if (owningCol != null)
            {
                status = owningCol.DefaultStatus;
            }
            if (value is StatusImage || value is int)
            {
                status = (StatusImage)value;
            }
            switch (status)
            {
                case StatusImage.Green:
                    resource = "CustomColumnAndCell.Green.bmp";
                    break;
```

continues

```
            case StatusImage.Yellow:
                resource = "CustomColumnAndCell.Yellow.bmp";
                break;
            case StatusImage.Red:
                resource = "CustomColumnAndCell.Red.bmp";
                break;
            default:
                break;
        }
        Assembly loadedAssembly = Assembly.GetExecutingAssembly();
        Stream stream =
            loadedAssembly.GetManifestResourceStream(resource);
        Image img = Image.FromStream(stream);
        cellStyle.Alignment =
            DataGridViewContentAlignment.TopCenter;
        return img;
    }
  }
}
```

The first declaration in this code is the enumeration StatusImage. That is the value type expected by this cell type as its Value property. You can then see that the StatusCell type derives from the DataGridViewImage-Cell, so I can reuse its ability to render images within the grid. There is a default status field and corresponding property that lets the default value surface directly. The constructor also sets the ImageLayout property of the base class to Zoom, so the images are resized to fit the cell with no distortion.

The key thing a custom cell type needs to do is either override the Paint method, as mentioned earlier, or override the GetFormattedValue method as the StatusCell class does. This method will be called whenever the cell is rendered and lets you handle transformations from other types to the expected type of the cell. The way I have chosen to code Get-FormattedValue for this example is to first set the value to a default value that will be used if all else fails. The code then tries to obtain the real default value from the containing column's DefaultValue property if that column type is StatusColumn (discussed next). The code then checks to see if the current Value property is a StatusImage enumerated type or an integer, and if it is an integer, it casts the value to the enumerated type.

Once the status value to be rendered is determined, the GetFormatted-Value method uses a switch-case statement to select the appropriate resource name corresponding to the image for that status value. You embed bitmap resources in the assembly by adding them to the Visual Studio project and setting the Build Action property on the file to *Embedded Resource*. The code then uses the `GetManifestResourceStream` method on the `Assembly` class to extract the bitmap resource out of the assembly, sets the alignment on the `cellStyle` argument passed into the method, and then returns the constructed image as the object from the method. The object that you return from this method will be the one that is passed down-stream to the `Paint` method as the formatted value to be rendered. Because this doesn't override the `Paint` method, the implementation of my `Data-GridViewImageCell` base class will be called, and it expects an `Image` value to render.

Defining a Custom Column Type

So now you have a custom cell class that could be used in the grid, but you also want to have a custom column class that contains `StatusCells` and can be used for setting up the grid and data binding. If you were going to use the custom cell type completely programmatically, you could just con-struct an instance of the `DataGridViewColumn` base class and pass in an instance of a `StatusCell` to the constructor, which sets that as the `CellTemplate` for the column. However, that approach wouldn't let you use the designer column editors covered in Figures 6.4 and 6.5 to specify a bound or unbound column of `StatusCells`. To support that, you need to implement a custom column type that the designer can recognize. As long as you're implementing your own column type, you also want to expose a way to set what the default value of the `StatusImage` should be for new rows that are added. The implementation of the `StatusColumn` class is shown in Listing 6.5.

LISTING 6.5: Custom Column Class

```
namespace CustomColumnAndCell
{
    public class StatusColumn : DataGridViewColumn
    {
        public StatusColumn() : base(new StatusCell())
        {
        }
```

continues

```
        private StatusImage m_DefaultStatus = StatusImage.Red;

        public StatusImage DefaultStatus
        {
            get { return m_DefaultStatus; }
            set { m_DefaultStatus = value; }
        }

        public override object Clone()
        {
            StatusColumn col = base.Clone() as StatusColumn;
            col.DefaultStatus = m_DefaultStatus;
            return col;
        }

        public override DataGridViewCell CellTemplate
        {
            get { return base.CellTemplate; }
            set
            {
                if ((value == null) || !(value is StatusCell))
                {
                    throw new ArgumentException(
    "Invalid cell type, StatusColumns can only contain StatusCells");
                }
            }
        }
    }
}
```

You can see from the implementation of StatusColumn that you first need to derive from the DataGridViewColumn class. You implement a default constructor that passes an instance of your custom cell class to the base class constructor. This sets the CellTemplate property on the base class to that cell type, making it the cell type for any rows that are added to a grid containing your column type.

The next thing the class does is define a public property named DefaultStatus. This lets anyone using this column type to set which of the three StatusImage values should be displayed by default if no value is explicitly set on the grid through data binding or programmatic value setting on a cell. The setter for this property changes the member variable that keeps track of the current default. The DefaultStatus property on the column is accessed from the `StatusCell.GetFormattedValue` method, as described earlier.

Another important thing for you to do in your custom column type is to override the `Clone` method from the base class, and in your override, return a new copy of your column with all of its properties set to the same values as the current column instance. This method is used by the design column editors to add and edit columns in a grid through the dialogs discussed in Figures 6.4 and 6.5.

The last thing the custom column class does is to override the `Cell-Template` property. If someone tries to access the `CellTemplate`, the code gets it from the base class. But if someone tries to change the `Cell-Template`, the setter checks to see if the type of the cell being set is a `StatusCell`. If not, it raises an exception, preventing anyone from programmatically setting an inappropriate cell type for this column. This doesn't prevent you from mixing other cell types into the column for a heterogeneous grid (as shown earlier in the section on programmatically creating the grid).

Now that you have defined the custom cell and column types, how can you use them? Well, you can define them as part of any Windows application project type in Visual Studio, but generally when you create something like this, you are doing it so you can reuse it in a variety of applications. Whenever you want reuse code, you need to put that code into a class library. So if you define a class library project, add the classes just discussed to the class library, along with the images you want to use for displaying status as embedded resources in the project. This creates an assembly that you can then reference from any Windows application that you want to use the column and cell type within. All you need to do is set a reference to that assembly from the Windows Forms project in which you want to use them, and the custom column types will display in the Add Column dialog, as shown in Figure 6.8 (`StatusColumn`, in this case).

Within your Windows Forms application, you can programmatically add `StatusColumns` to a grid, or use the designer to do so. If you add the column through the designer and then look at it in the Edit Columns dialog, you will see that `DefaultStatus` appears in the property list and is settable as an enumerated property with its allowable values (see Figure 6.9).

With a column of this type added to the grid, you can either populate the grid programmatically with either of the types that the cell is able to handle for values (either StatusImage values or integers within the value range of StatusImage), or you can data bind to it with a collection of data that contains those values. Here is a simple example of setting the values programmatically on a grid containing two columns: a text box column

FIGURE 6.8: Custom Column Types in the Add Column Dialog

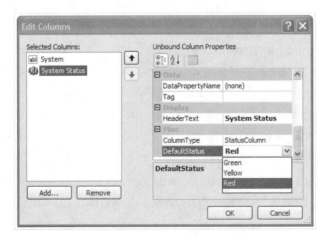

FIGURE 6.9: Custom Column Properties in the Edit Columns Dialog

and a `StatusColumn`. Note that you can set the values with either the enumerated value or with an appropriate integer value.

```
m_Grid.Rows.Add("Beer Bottler", StatusImage.Green);
m_Grid.Rows.Add("Beer Bottle Filler", 1); //StatusImage.Yellow = 1
m_Grid.Rows.Add("Bottle capper", StatusImage.Red);
```

The CustomColumnAndCell sample application in the download code also demonstrates creating a data set and data binding against the status column.

Utilizing Cell-Oriented Grid Features

You have probably noticed that the `DataGridView` is much more focused at the cell level that its `DataGrid` predecessor was. Part of the reason for this is that a frequent use of grids is where columns don't necessarily dictate the structure of the grid's content. Specifically, users want spreadsheet-like functionality that mimics the interaction model millions of people have become accustomed to with programs like Microsoft Excel and other spreadsheet applications.

Once again, the `DataGridView` comes to the rescue and makes supporting that model fairly easy. You have already seen some of the cell-level events that let you control what is displayed at the cell level (`Cell-Formatting` event) and that tell you when users interact with a cell by editing the contents (`EditControlShowing` event) or simply click on it (`CellClick` event). You can set different context menus and tooltips down to the cell level, so that every cell can become a distinct entity in the grid from the users' perspective. There are actually over 30 events raised by the `DataGridView` that expose interactions and modifications at the cell level that you can subscribe to for providing cell-oriented features.

Additionally, there are different selection modes that you can use to change the way the grid highlights cells, columns, or rows when the user clicks in different places in the grid. The `SelectionMode` property on the grid determines the selection behavior and is of type `DataGridView-SelectionMode`. The `DataGridView` control supports the selection modes (described in Table 6.6). While you can't combine these modes (the

TABLE 6.6: DataGridViewSelectionMode Enumeration Values

Value	Description
CellSelect	This mode lets you select one or many cells in the grid using the mouse or keyboard. If you click in any cell, just that cell will be selected. You can click and drag, and contiguous cells that you drag over will also be selected. If you click in one cell, then Shift-click in another, you will select the entire contiguous set of cells from the first click to the second. You can even select noncontiguous cells by holding down the Ctrl key while you click cells. This is the default selection mode.
FullRowSelect	Clicking in any cell in the grid will select all of the cells in the entire row that contains the cell and will deselect any cells outside the row.
FullColumnSelect	Clicking in any cell in the grid will select all of the cells in the entire column that contains the cell and will deselect any cells outside the column.
RowHeaderSelect	Clicking on the row header cell will select the entire row, but otherwise this selection mode behaves like CellSelect. This is the mode set by the designer for a grid when you add it to a form.
ColumnHeaderSelect	Clicking on the column header cell will select the entire column, but otherwise this selection mode behaves like CellSelect.

enumeration isn't a Flags enumerated type), you can achieve a combination of modes by using the SelectionMode property on the grid plus some additional event handling. Regardless of which of these modes you select, clicking on the upper left header cell (the one that is above the row header cells and to the left of the column header cells) selects all the cells in the grid.

As an example of a more cell-oriented application, the download code includes an application called SimpleSpread. This application mimics a simple spreadsheet and lets you do summations of the numeric values in a cell. It uses a combination of selection mode and some event handling to give you a similar selection experience to most spreadsheets—specifically, it acts like a combination of `RowHeaderSelect` and `ColumnHeaderSelect`, even though you can't achieve that through the `SelectionMode` property alone. The SimpleSpread sample application is shown in Figure 6.10.

As you can see, the application lets you enter numbers into the cells; then you can select a sequence of cells and press the *Sum* button in the tool strip control at the top to get it to calculate the sum and place that in the next cell to the right or below the sequence of selections. As Figure 6.10 shows, this application even supports selecting rectangular groups of cells, and it will compute the summation in both the row and column directions. The logic is nowhere near complete to handle all combinations of selections and cell contents, but it gives you a good idea of how to set something like this up.

To code this up (as shown in Listing 6.6), I had to do a few things that are different from your average `DataGridView` application. As I mentioned, I wanted to support a spreadsheet-like selection model, where you can select individual cells, but that selecting a column or row header would select the entire column or row, respectively. To do this, I set the `SelectionMode` for the grid to `RowHeaderSelect`, turned off sorting for all the columns as I created them and added them to the grid, and then handled the `ColumnHeaderMouseClick` event to manually select all the cells in a column when the user clicks on a column header.

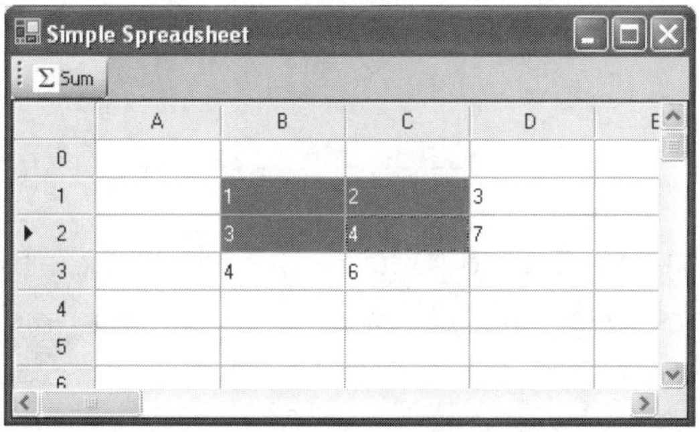

FIGURE 6.10: SimpleSpread Sample Application

LISTING 6.6: Spreadsheet-Oriented Grid Column Selection Support

```
public partial class SimpleSpreadForm : Form
{
    public SimpleSpreadForm()
    {
        InitializeComponent();
        m_Grid.SelectionMode =
            DataGridViewSelectionMode.RowHeaderSelect;
    }

    private void OnFormLoad(object sender, EventArgs e)
    {
        int start = (int)'A';
        for (int i = 0; i < 26; i++)
        {
            string colName = ((char)(i + start)).ToString();
            int index = m_Grid.Columns.Add(colName, colName);
            m_Grid.Columns[i].SortMode =
                DataGridViewColumnSortMode.NotSortable;
            m_Grid.Columns[i].Width = 75;
        }
        for (int i = 0; i < 50; i++)
        {
            m_Grid.Rows.Add();
        }
    }

    private void OnColumnHeaderMouseClick(object sender,
        DataGridViewCellMouseEventArgs e)
    {
        m_Grid.ClearSelection();
        foreach (DataGridViewRow row in m_Grid.Rows)
        {
            row.Cells[e.ColumnIndex].Selected = true;
        }
    }
    ...
}
```

In this case, I just programmatically added some rows and columns to the grid, set the column headers to be the letters of the alphabet, and turned off sorting on the column by setting the SortMode property to Not-Sortable. If you were going to support very large spreadsheets, you might need to maintain an in-memory sparse array, and only render the cells as you need them (which you could do with virtual mode) to avoid the overhead of maintaining a large number of cells, their contents, and their selections if the grid will be sparsely populated.

To get the row numbers to display in the row headers, I handled the `RowAdded` event and set the header cell value in that handler:

```
private void OnRowAdded(object sender, DataGridViewRowsAddedEventArgs e)
{
    m_Grid.Rows[e.RowIndex].HeaderCell.Value = e.RowIndex.ToString();
}
```

Another selection mode you might want to support is to have **hot cells**, meaning that the selection of cells changes as you move the mouse around the grid without having to click. To do this, you could just handle the `CellMouseEnter` and `CellMouseLeave` events, selecting and deselecting the cell under the mouse in those handlers, respectively.

Formatting with Styles

The last topic I want to cover about the `DataGridView` is how to handle custom formatting of cells. As mentioned earlier, the grid supports a rich formatting model. The styles in the grid work in a layered model, which lets you set styles at a more macro level, then refine it at a more micro level. For example, you might set a default cell style that applies to all cells in the grid, but then have one entire column that has a different cell formatting, and have selected cells within that column have yet a different cell formatting. You do this by setting a series of default cell style properties that are exposed on the grid, which you can then refine by setting cell styles at the individual cell level.

As can be seen in Figure 6.11, the lowest layer in the model is the `DefaultCellStyle` property. This style will be used by default for any cells in the grid that haven't had their style set to something else by one of the other style layers. The next layer up contains the `RowHeaders-DefaultCellStyle` and `ColumnHeadersDefaultCellStyle`, which affect the way the header cells are presented. Above that layer sits the `DataGridViewColumn.DefaultCellStyle` property, followed by the

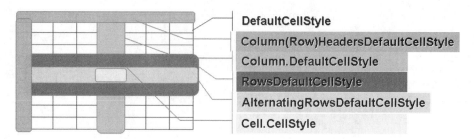

FIGURE 6.11: Cell Style Layering

`DataGridViewRow.DefaultCellStyle` property, representing the default styles on a column-by-column or row-by-row basis. The grid also supports an alternating row cell style that is set through the `AlternatingRows-DefaultCellStyle` property on the grid. Finally, the top-level layer that will override the settings of any of the lower layers if set is the `DataGrid-ViewCell.CellStyle` property.

You can set these properties programmatically by accessing the appropriate property member on the instance of the grid, column, row, or cell. All of these properties are of type `DataGridViewCellStyle`, which exposes properties for setting fonts, colors, alignment, padding, and formatting of values. You can also configure the cell styles through the designer. Whenever you access one of the cell style properties on the grid or a column through the Properties window or Smart Tag property editors in the designer, you will see the CellStyle Builder dialog shown in Figure 6.12.

Using the property fields in this dialog, you can set fine-grained options for how the cell will display its content, and you can even see what it is going to look like in the Preview pane at the bottom of the dialog.

You can also set border styles for cells using the grid's `CellBorder-Style`, `ColumnHeadersBorderStyle`, and `RowHeadersBorderStyle` properties. Using these styles, you can achieve some fairly sophisticated grid appearances, as seen in Figure 6.13. In this sample, default cell styles were set at the column and row level, and then the filling in of the shape was done through individual cell selection.

However, you will still hit some limitations in using cell styles. For example, a natural next step for the grid shown in Figure 6.13 would be to

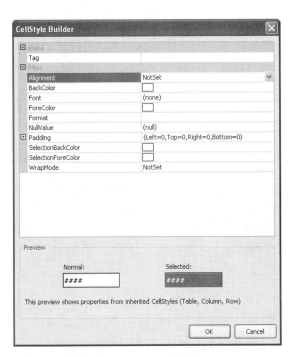

FIGURE 6.12: CellStyle Builder Dialog

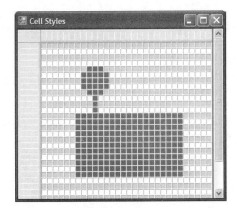

FIGURE 6.13: Cell and Border Styles Applied

set the border colors on the cells that have been colored in to show a black border. However, there is really no way to accomplish this just through cell styles, since the border styles available are only 3D effects and are applied at the grid level for entire cells, not for individual sides of a cell. But, as always, you can almost always accomplish what you need through custom painting or custom cell type definition.

Where Are We?

This chapter has covered all the main features of the `DataGridView` control. It focused a lot on the code involved and what the capabilities were. For most common cases, you'll be able to get what you need simply by defining the columns in the designer, setting up some data binding with the Data Sources window, and maybe mixing in some custom code and event handlers. The `DataGridView` control is considerably simpler to use and more flexible and powerful than the `DataGrid` control from .NET 1.0, and you should always favor using the `DataGridView` for new applications that will present tabular data or something that needs to be presented in a grid format.

Some key takeaways from this chapter are:

- Setting the `DataSource` and `DataMember` properties on the `DataGridView` to a `BindingSource` that binds to the data source is the standard way of using the grid.

- Use the Edit Columns functionality in the designer Smart Tag for the easiest way to edit and customize the bound and unbound column types and properties.

- Bound columns will use automatic type conversion and formatting similar to the `Binding` object, as discussed in Chapter 4.

- To add a custom cell type, you create a custom column type derived from `DataGridViewColumn`, and a custom cell type derived from `DataGridViewCell` or one of the derived built-in cell types.

Next we'll go deeper into the data-binding mechanisms used in Windows Forms, specifically the interfaces that you need to understand and implement in order to create any custom data objects or collections that you want to use for data binding. You will gain a better understanding of what the data-bound controls are looking for when you set up data binding, and how they use what they find.

■ 7 ■
Understanding Data-Binding Interfaces

T O REALLY UNDERSTAND data binding and how to implement either custom data sources or custom data-bound controls, you first have to understand the interface-based contracts that drive data binding. This chapter describes each of the key interfaces that are involved in data binding from the perspective of the contract that the interface represents. It discusses the purpose of the interface, when it is used, and what the interface defines. This chapter is less hands-on than most of the other chapters, and is meant to familiarize you with the interfaces and provide a reference for using and implementing them. Probably the best strategy for reading this chapter is to first skim through each section, reading the portion that highlights the purpose and use of each interface. Then if you want to know more about that interface, read the following details on the members and implementation of that interface. A certain amount of coupling in the definitions of the interfaces is unavoidable, so in some cases I have to mention an interface's relationship to some other interface that hasn't been described yet. When that is the case, feel free to jump ahead to read the summary for that other interface to get a sense of it, then return to the one that you are focusing on.

The interfaces involved in data binding are designed to set up a two-way contract between data-bound controls and collections of data objects that are used by those controls. Those collections may be custom business object collections containing business objects, or they may be one of a number of .NET Framework collection and object types, such as a `DataView` collection containing `DataRowView` objects. By using these interfaces to define the communications between bound controls and data objects, data-bound controls don't need to know the specific types of the objects they bind to, and the data objects don't need to know anything about the specific capabilities of the controls that will bind to them. Once you understand these interfaces and what they are designed to support, the "magic" of data binding should be no more than smoke and mirrors to you—or rather just interfaces at work that aren't magic at all, but very powerful nonetheless.

Although this stuff may seem like raw plumbing to you, there are several good reasons for reading and understanding the information in this chapter. The first is that to really understand what is going on when data binding occurs and to be able to troubleshoot problems, you need to understand what's happening behind the scenes. Data binding is driven by the interfaces covered in this chapter, and the .NET Framework controls and components work against objects that implement those interfaces. The second reason is that if you plan to use custom object collections for data binding, you have to implement some of these interfaces to make your collection bindable and your objects editable through bound controls. Finally, if you are going to implement custom controls that support data binding or just code against the collection in the logic of your application, you will be a consumer of these interfaces to implement your data-binding code and logic code.

What Does Data Binding Have to Do with Interfaces?

When you deal with data, you typically work with collections of data items, where each of those items is an object that contains the data values or properties that represent the discrete pieces of data that you are binding to. When dealing with **relational data**—the collection of data in a table—the data items are rows within the table, and the properties are the columns within the rows. You usually focus at the table level, and think of the rows and columns as the details of the tabular data. In reality, any time you data bind to a `DataTable`, you are actually data binding to the table's default view. So the `DataView` class is really the key class to focus on for data binding when working with data sets in .NET, and its data items are instances of `DataRowView`.

When dealing with custom business objects, the focus is more at the data item level, where each data item is an instance of a business object. These objects may be contained within some sort of collection object that acts as a container or parent object for the data items in the same way that a `DataView` is a container for `DataRowView` objects. These collection objects let you maintain a grouping of object instances, so you can hold on to a reference to the collection itself and use that reference to get to the individual objects when you need them.

Because everything is an object and the term is so overloaded, it can get confusing when talking about data or business objects. As a result, I will often use the term *data item* instead of *object* to describe the individual objects in a collection. A **data item** could be a custom business object instance, an instance of a .NET Framework type that contains some data of interest, such as a `FileInfo` object, or a relational data object, such as a `DataRowView` instance that belongs to a `DataView`.

The .NET Framework has a number of built-in collection types, and you can implement your own collection types if you need your collection to support features that the available collection types don't support. Before .NET 2.0, it was fairly common to need to create custom collections if you wanted to have type-safe collections of data or business objects. With the introduction of **generics** in .NET 2.0, the need to implement custom collection classes should be fairly rare. The `List<T>`, `Dictionary<T>`, `Queue<T>`, `Stack<T>`, `LinkedList<T>`, and `SortedDictionary<T>` classes should address most situations where you want to implement a custom strongly typed object collection. Additionally, there is the `BindingList<T>` class for data binding in Windows Forms that implements most of the interfaces you will need. `BindingList<T>` is covered in detail in Chapter 9, but you have already seen it in action in many of the samples in earlier chapters.

Given all of that, there are potentially infinite numbers of collection and object types to which you might want to data bind in your applications. So how can you possibly cover all the possibilities? You do it by defining a common contract that you expect all types that want to play nicely together in data binding to support. The best way to specify a contract for code that is decoupled from the implementation of that contract is through an interface.

Interface definitions have to be considered from two perspectives: from that of the implementer and of the consumer.

- The **implementer** is the class that provides an implementation of the members defined on the interface.
- The **consumer** is the code that obtains an interface reference to an object and invokes the functionality represented by that interface through the reference.

This chapter describes each of the interfaces involved in data binding and the contract that it represents, followed by the details of that interface's members. There are a number of examples of consuming the interface to demonstrate the concepts, but the full details for implementing or consuming the interfaces will be demonstrated and discussed in Chapters 8 and 9. Table 7.1 lists the interfaces discussed in this chapter and the kind of object responsible for implementing the interface. The consumers of all of these interfaces are either data-bound controls or client code that is programmatically interacting with the data collections.

One of the most important interfaces for data binding is the `IList` interface. This interface derives from two base interfaces, `IEnumerable` and `ICollection`, so these are discussed first, as well as their cousin generic interfaces and what they do for you and when you need to worry about them. Then some additional collection-oriented interfaces that further enhance data binding capabilities are covered, including the `IListSource`, `ITypedList`, `IBindingList`, `IBindingListView`, `ICancelAddNew`, and `IRaiseItemChangedEvents` interfaces. Next are the four interfaces that individual data objects can implement to support editing and design-time features through bound controls: `IEditableObject`, `INotifyProperty-Changed`, `IDataErrorInfo`, `ICustomTypeDescriptor`. The last interfaces covered control oriented interfaces, the `ISupportInitialize`, `ISupport-InitializeNotification`, and `ICurrencyManagerProvider` interfaces.

TABLE 7.1: Data Binding Interfaces

Interface	Implemented By
IEnumerable	Collection
IEnumerator	Collection helper object
ICollection	Collection
IList	Collection
IListSource	Collection, or collection of collections
ITypedList	Collection
IBindingList	Collection
IBindingListView	Collection
ICancelAddNew	Collection
IRaiseItemChangedEvents	Collection
IEditableObject	Data object
INotifyPropertyChanged	Data object
IDataErrorInfo	Data object
ICustomTypeDescriptor	Data object
ISupportInitialize	Data source or control
ISupportInitializeNotification	Data source or control
ICurrencyManagerProvider	Data source container (BindingSource)

The IEnumerable and IEnumerator Interfaces: Supporting Iteration Through Collections

Implement IEnumerable *to allow consumers of your collection to iterate through all of the objects in the collection in various ways. When you implement* IEnumerable, *you also have to implement* IEnumerator *on at least one class and return an instance of that class from the* IEnumerable.GetEnumerator

method. The implementation of IEnumerator *provides the methods and proper-*
ties that let you iterate over the collection. You can provide multiple implementa-
tions of IEnumerator *to allow different kinds of iteration over the collection.*

The need to iterate through collections of objects goes well beyond data
binding. In past languages and technologies, the way you provided support for iteration and the way you actually performed iterations was not at
all consistent. The architects of the .NET Framework addressed this by
specifying a pattern and implementation for iteration that all collections in
.NET are expected to support, regardless of the implementation language.
Additionally, most .NET languages have added direct support for iteration
based on this pattern, so you rarely have to deal directly with the
IEnumerable and IEnumerator interfaces, even though they are what are
driving the iteration behind the scenes.

This pattern is based on two interfaces: IEnumerable and
IEnumerator. A collection type should implement the IEnumerable
interface, which indicates that it supports iteration through its contained
objects.

The IEnumerable interface contains only one method that the type
needs to implement: GetEnumerator. This method is expected to return
an object that implements the IEnumerator interface.

The IEnumerator interface has three members (described in Table 7.2)
and works like a logical cursor in the collection of data. It starts out initialized to a position just before the first item in the collection. You start using
it by calling the MoveNext method on the enumerator, which positions the
cursor on the first item if there is one and returns true. If the collection is
empty, the first call to MoveNext returns false. Subsequent calls to
MoveNext move the cursor to the next logical item in the collection until
there are no more items. MoveNext continues to return true as long as the
cursor is positioned on an item in the collection at the completion of the
call. When there are no more items, MoveNext returns false. This pattern
lets you put the call to MoveNext in a while loop to set up the iteration in a
nice compact way.

The order that the logical cursor moves is up to the implementer of the
IEnumerator interface and doesn't have to be tied to the physical order of

TABLE 7.2: IEnumerator Members

Member	Description
bool **MoveNext**()	This method increments the logical cursor of the collection to the next item and returns `true` if there is an item in that position to work with, and returns `false` otherwise.
void **Reset**()	This method sets the logical cursor back to its initial position, readying the collection to reiterate through the items.
object **Current**	This property returns an object reference to the current item in the collection.

the items in the collection. For example, if you were implementing an enumerator for a sortable collection, you would want to modify the order that the cursor moved through the collection based on the sort order. However, if you plan to support sorting, you should look into implementing the `IBindingList` interface as well.

You access the items that are being iterated over through the `Current` property. The `Current` property on the `IEnumerator` interface returns an `Object` reference that should point to the current item at the logical cursor's position in the collection. The `IEnumerator` interface also includes a `Reset` method, which returns the cursor to its initial position, allowing you to iterate over the same collection again using the same enumerator.

The following code snippet shows a typical loop using the `IEnumerable` and `IEnumerator` interfaces to iterate over a collection.

```
List<int> myvals = new List<int>();
myvals.Add(42);
myvals.Add(38);
myvals.Add(13);

IEnumerable enumerable = myvals;
IEnumerator enumerator = enumerable.GetEnumerator();
while (enumerator.MoveNext())
{
    int val = (int)enumerator.Current;
}
enumerator.Reset();
```

The `List<T>` generic collection implements the `IEnumerable` interface (and its `IEnumerable<T>` generic counterpart), so the code obtains an `IEnumerable` interface reference to the collection through an implicit cast. It then calls `GetEnumerator` on that interface reference, which returns an interface reference of type `IEnumerator`. Once you have an enumerator, you set up a `while` loop on its `MoveNext` method. The first call to `Move-Next` positions the cursor on the first item and returns `true` if anything is in the collection and enters the loop block. If the collection is empty, `MoveNext` returns `false` and never enters the loop. Each time through the loop, the cursor's position is advanced when `MoveNext` is called until the last item is reached. Then the next time the `while` statement call to `Move-Next` returns `false` and exits the loop. Figure 7.1 depicts what is going on in this process.

Because the `IEnumerable` and `IEnumerator` interfaces are a fundamental pattern in .NET, support for them is baked in at the language level. Both C# and VB.NET support a `foreach` construct that lets you conveniently iterate through a collection like this:

```
List<int> myvals = new List<int>();
myvals.Add(42);
myvals.Add(38);
myvals.Add(13);
foreach (int val in myvals)
{
    Console.WriteLine(val.ToString());
}
```

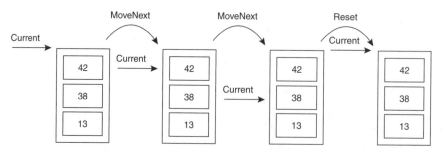

FIGURE 7.1: Moving Through a Collection with IEnumerator

Under the covers, the `foreach` operator uses the `Current` property and `MoveNext` method defined by the `IEnumerator` interface on the object returned from `GetEnumerator` to iterate through the collection, as described earlier. The generated Intermediate Language (IL) code doesn't actually use the `IEnumerator` interface reference to access the current item; it just calls the `Current` property on the object itself. As a result, if the type implementing the `IEnumerator` interface contains a `Current` property that returns a specific type instance (such as `Int32` or `Double`), then the `foreach` loop can avoid boxing and unboxing those values as it iterates through the collection. See the sidebar "The Problem with Type Unsafe Enumeration" for details on why `foreach` is implemented this way.

When implementing collections in .NET 2.0 that will contain specific types, you should also implement the generic versions of these interfaces, `IEnumerable<T>` and `IEnumerator<T>`. Generic interface types are used in .NET 2.0 to provide type safety for the contained types and to avoid performance penalties that could result for collections that contained value types when using the `IEnumerable` and `IEnumerator` interfaces. The untyped interfaces still have a place; they are used by the data-bound controls in .NET because they don't want to make assumptions about the specific types contained in collections that you will use in data binding, which would limit the scenarios that data-bound controls could support.

The `IEnumerator<T>` interface doesn't include a `Reset` method in order to simplify the implementation of enumerator objects. For simple collections where you use an explicit index into an array of objects, resetting the enumerator is a simple matter. But for more intricate scenarios, implementing a `Reset` method can get more complicated than it is worth. If you need to iterate over a collection multiple times, you can simply obtain multiple enumerators by calling `GetEnumerator` more than once. `IEnumerator<T>` is also different from `IEnumerator` in that it derives from `IDisposable` because of this assumption that enumerators are designed to be used once and then disposed of. If your enumerator maintains any internal state to manage the current context of the logical cursor, the `Dispose` method of the `IDisposable` interface is where you should clean them up. You should also implement a finalizer to perform that same clean up if your collection's client fails to call `Dispose`.

The Problem with Type Unsafe Enumeration

Prior to .NET 2.0, the enumeration pattern was supported by the `IEnumerable` and `IEnumerator` interfaces. The problem with the `IEnumerator` interface is that its `Current` property only returns an `Object` reference, and you have to cast to the object's actual type to use it correctly. Besides the lack of type safety this represents, it also can induce performance problems when your collection contains value types, and the casting itself doesn't come for free. Value types have to be boxed to be passed as an object reference, which means that an object has to be allocated in garbage-collected memory to contain the value, the value needs to be copied into that object from the stack, and a reference to that memory is what you get back as the object reference.

Typically what you do next when accessing an item from a collection through the `IEnumerator.Current` property is to cast it back to its appropriate type. If that type is a value type, the object reference has to be unboxed to cast it back to the appropriate type (such as `int` or `DateTime`) and then copied into the stack-allocated variable. Then the object that was allocated becomes available for garbage collection, which increases the workload of the garbage collector. All of this has performance costs associated with it that you should avoid.

As a result, always favor using the generic collection types and interfaces to avoid this problem when operating directly on a collection of a particular type. The `foreach` operator avoids the problem by calling the `Current` property and `MoveNext` method directly on the enumerator object instead of doing it through the `IEnumerator` interface. This allows that object's enumerator to return the actual type of the item instead of a vanilla object reference. In addition, the `foreach` operator can operate directly against the actual type of the collection's items, thus avoiding boxing and unboxing for value types if they implement their enumerators correctly.

You might be wondering why two separate interfaces are needed. Why not just define one interface that the collection itself implements that directly supports iterating through the collection? The answer is that you might want to support more than one form of iteration on a collection, so separating the iteration logic into a separate object lets you plug in additional forms of iteration if you need to. You can then expose those additional iteration approaches through properties on the collection class that return an `IEnumerator` interface reference to an object that iterates through your collection in a different way. This pattern also allows you to provide multiple enumerators to the same collection, so your code can maintain more than one current position in the collection. If your code will iterate over the collection using multiple threads, then you'll want to look into implementing the `ICollection` interface to provide thread-safe access to the collection.

Typically, the object that implements the iteration methods of `IEnumerator` are created as a nested class within the collection class, but you are free to implement things however you want. It should be fairly rare that you would need to do a raw implementation of `IEnumerable` and `IEnumerator`, because the built-in collection classes in .NET already do that for you.

`IEnumerable` and its related `IEnumerator` interface are really all that is needed to support a read-only presentation of bound data. If you can provide a collection reference to a control, it can iterate over the items in the collection and use specific type information—helper classes like the `PropertyDescriptor` class—or reflection to access the properties on the data items and display them. This is how the `BindingSource` component lets you bind to anything that implements `IEnumerable`.

The ICollection Interface: Controlling Access to a Collection

You can use the `ICollection` interface to find out how many items exist within a collection, copy the items from a collection into an array, discover whether the collection provides synchronization for multithreaded scenarios, or access the synchronization object for the collection to implement your own synchronization locking.

The next collection-oriented interface up the inheritance hierarchy from `IEnumerable` is the `ICollection` interface. `ICollection` is derived from `IEnumerable`, so to implement `ICollection`, you have to implement `IEnumerable` as well. This interface adds a few members that define some additional attributes about a collection to help control access to the collection items, as described in Table 7.3 and the following paragraphs.

Probably the most important and frequently used member that is part of the `ICollection` interface is the `Count` property. If you have a collection that only implements `IEnumerable`, the only way to figure out how many items are in the collection is to obtain an enumerator for it and iterate through all of the elements, counting how many there are in your own loop. That kind of code gets very tedious and is expensive, so collections that implement `ICollection` let users of the collection obtain the number of items in the collection directly from the `Count` property, which puts the burden of determining that value on the collection implementer—where it belongs. Usually when you implement `ICollection`, you will maintain an internal count of the items as they are added and removed, so that the implementation of `Count` will be fast and easy.

The `CopyTo` method lets the consumer of a collection obtain a copy of all the items in the collection in the form of a typed array so that the consumer can operate on those items without worrying about affecting other

TABLE 7.3: ICollection Interface Members

Member	Description
int **Count**	This read-only property returns the number of items in the collection.
object **SyncRoot**	This read-only property returns the object used for performing synchronization locks on the collection.
bool **IsSynchronized**	This method returns true if the collection is safe for multithreaded access, false otherwise.
void **CopyTo**(Array array, int index)	This method lets you copy the items in the collection into an array starting with the item at the specified index.

consumers of the collection. CopyTo takes two arguments: a reference to an array and an index that indicates which item in the collection the copying should start with. The array that is passed in by the caller has to be of an appropriate type to contain the collection's items and needs to be of sufficient size for all of the items in the collection, starting with the provided index, to be copied into the array. Of course, you need to take into account the performance impact of creating a copy of every item in the collection before you use this method. If it is acceptable to directly manipulate the items in the collection, don't bother copying them to a separate array first.

If a collection supports being accessed by multiple threads at a time, it needs to be synchronized. This means that it has to implement a locking mechanism to ensure that race conditions cannot arise, such as one thread trying to access an item in the collection that might have been removed by another thread just moments before. The details involved in doing this are beyond the scope of this chapter, but there are a number of other books that provide information on that topic. (I would suggest *Programming .NET Components*, second edition, by Juval Löwy as the definitive source for multithreaded programming and synchronization in .NET.)

The IsSynchronized property indicates whether the collection supports synchronous access from multiple threads. If this property returns true, then the collection is expected to ensure that it is safe for multiple threads to add, remove, and access items in the collection concurrently. If it returns false, then it's up to the user of the collection to ensure that only one thread at a time accesses the collection. The latter is the more common case, because adding locking mechanisms to a collection to support concurrent access can have a significant performance penalty for everyone who uses the collection. It is usually better to make the few who need concurrent access pay for it in the form of writing more code than to make the many who consume it in a single-threaded way suffer in performance.

The SyncRoot property provides an object reference that consumers of the collection can use to implement their own locking to support concurrent access. The collection is expected to return an object reference that can be used with a Monitor or lock statement, and if the consumer locks on the returned object, then the lock should prevent any other thread from accessing the collection's members while the lock is in place. Usually the collection just returns a reference to itself if it is a reference type, and locking on the object itself blocks access to any of the members of the class from another thread until the lock is released. However, in certain situations you might use a contained object for locking purposes instead of the collection object itself. The bottom line to consumers is that they should be able to take the object reference returned from `SyncRoot`, lock on it, and know that other threads won't be able to access, add, or delete items in the collection while the lock is in place.

`ICollection<T>` is a generic version of the same interface. You should also implement this interface if you are creating a strongly typed collection that exposes its count and supports copying and multithreaded access scenarios. The factoring of the `ICollection<T>` and `IList<T>` interfaces are a little different from their untyped cousins. Several of the members of the `IList` interface are implemented on `ICollection<T>` in the generic interface inheritance hierarchy, including `Add`, `Remove`, `Contains`, `Clear`, and `IsReadOnly` (these are discussed in the next section). These all really would make sense to be down at the collection level, since they aren't specific to the ordered, indexed collection notion that `IList` represents. But Microsoft cannot refactor the `ICollection` and `IList` interfaces at this point, since they have been around since .NET 1.0 and would break immense amounts of legacy code.

The IList Interface: Enabling Data Binding

The `IList` *interface lets you treat a collection as an ordered, indexed set of data items. The* `IList` *interface is one of the most important interfaces in data binding, because complex data-bound controls can only be bound to collections that implement* `IList`*. Using an* `IList` *interface reference to a collection, you can manage the collection's data by adding, removing, inserting, and accessing items.*

The `IList` interface is a key interface that enables runtime data binding in most Windows controls. `IList` derives from `ICollection`, so you need to also implement `ICollection` and `IEnumerable` to support `IList`. `IList` defines a set of members that further defines a collection as an ordered, indexed collection of data that can be accessed and modified in a random order. The good news is that you should never have to implement the `IList` interface yourself in a .NET 2.0 application, because the `List<T>` generic type provides a full implementation for any type that you want to contain in a collection. However, you many need to consume the interface to use a collection within your application code or in a custom data-bound control. The members of the `IList` interface are described in Tables 7.4 and 7.5 and in the following paragraphs.

TABLE 7.4: IList Interface Properties

Name	Type	Description
IsFixedSize	Boolean	True if items cannot be added or removed from the collection, false otherwise. If true, the collection size is pre-allocated at construction time and cannot be changed. If that is the case, the collection should throw an exception if the `Add`, `Insert`, `Remove`, `RemoveAt`, or `Clear` methods are called. False indicates that the collection can be modified by the consumer. This is a read-only property.
IsReadOnly	Boolean	True if the items in the collection cannot be edited after the collection is constructed, false otherwise. If `IsReadOnly` is true, then the constraints implied by `IsFixedSize` also apply. When this property is false, the items in the collection can be edited by the consumer. This is a read-only property.
this[int index]	Object	Lets you index into the collection using array notation with an index position to read or assign objects into the collection. Also know as the `Item` property, because the convention in Visual Basic is to expose a parameterized `Item` property that is the default property, which is how indexers are exposed in Visual Basic that are written in C#.

TABLE 7.5: IList Interface Methods

Method	Description
int **Add** (object item)	Adds a new item into the collection at the end of the list and returns the index of the new item in the collection.
void **Clear**()	Empties the collection of all items, removing the references to all the contained objects, thus making them eligible for garbage collection.
bool **Contains** (object item)	Checks to see if it can find the object instance passed in as a parameter within the collection. If it finds the object, the method returns true. If no matching object reference is found, the method returns false.
int **IndexOf** (object item)	Tries to locate the object reference passed in as a parameter within the collection. If the object is in the collection, the index of it within the collection is returned. If the object isn't in the collection, the method should return –1.
void **Insert** (int index, object item)	Adds a new item to the collection by inserting it at a particular location. The desired index is provided as a parameter, along with a reference to the object. The item currently residing at that index and any that follow it have their position incremented by one. If the specified index is the size of the collection, the item is appended at the end of the list, which is the same effect as calling Add.
void **Remove** (object item)	Removes an object reference from the collection by matching against the object reference passed in. If the specified object is found, it is simply removed from the list, and any items that follow it in the list have their index decremented by one.
void **RemoveAt** (int index)	Removes an item from the collection based at the index specified by the method parameter. Any items that follow it in the collection will have their index decremented by one.

The IList interface adds the methods and properties to a collection that make it behave like a full-fledged random access, editable, and modifiable collection of data. As discussed in an earlier chapter, Windows Forms data binding is two way—many data-bound controls not only support presenting data for viewing, but also let the user edit the data within the control, resulting in updates to the underlying data source. You can access any item in the collection through the bound control at any time because of the stateful model of Windows Forms and controls, so random access to the collection's contents becomes important.

If you only need to support one-way data binding (forward-only, read-only iteration through the data items), IEnumerable would be enough to get to all the data items, and late bound discovery could be used to display the data. As mentioned before, the BindingSource component is able to iterate over collections that only implement IEnumerable to put those objects into its own internally maintained list of items, at which point you can data bind in Windows Forms to the BindingSource component because it implements the IList interface.

The Add, Insert, Remove, RemoveAt, and Clear methods make it easy to manage the items in the collection as a variable-length ordered list (this should be fairly intuitive from the descriptions in Table 7.4). The Contains and IndexOf methods, in conjunction with the indexer, let you have random access to the collection's contents to either read data out for presentation or to modify the contents of a given position in the list.

The IsFixedSize and IsReadOnly properties are intended to give you an indication of whether you can modify the contents of the collection, and if so, to what degree. Because the other members of IList are specifically designed to support modifying the list, it is rare that you will run into a collection that is never modifiable, and usually the default is that they are modifiable. However, you might find collections that support switching the collection into a read-only mode or a frozen-size mode. Those properties let you check for the presence of that mode before trying to modify the contents of the collection, which should result in an exception if the collection is marked as read-only or fixed-size.

Working with a collection that implements IList from code is straightforward. You can declare an instance of the collection, add items to it with the Add method, locate items with IndexOf, determine how many are in the collection through the implemented Count member of the inherited ICollection interface, iterate over all of the collection's items and index into the collection with the IList indexer, or access the items through the inherited support from the IEnumerable interface, all in a very few lines of code:

```
List<int> myCollection = new List<int>();
myCollection.Add(42);
myCollection.Add(38);
Debug.Assert(myCollection.IndexOf(42) == 0);
for (int i = 0; i < myCollection.Count; i++)
{
    myCollection[i] = 99;
}
foreach (int val in myCollection)
{
    Console.WriteLine("Value = {0}", val);
}
```

This code uses an instance of the List<T> generic type, which implements IList and all of its base interfaces for you for any type parameter that you specify. As mentioned earlier in the book, when you declare a variable of a generic type with a type parameter, such as the declaration of myCollection in this code with int as the type parameter, you are really creating a new type that is a strongly typed list of integers, as well as declaring an instance of that type, all in one line of code.

As long as a collection supports the IList interface, you will be able to bind it to any of the .NET Framework Windows Forms controls that support data binding, using either simple binding (Binding objects) or complex data binding (DataSource and DataMember properties). If the control supports modifying the collection (such as the DataGridView), you can add items to the collection, remove them, or edit the values of an item exposed through properties on the contained objects. Internally, the data-binding code of a control iterates over the collection's contents and indexes into it using the IList methods and properties. Once the control has obtained access to an item in the collection, it can use the Property-Descriptor class to dynamically discover information about the properties of the items in the collection and can use those to populate whatever properties or display elements of the control are bound to the data. See the later section on property descriptors for more information and the samples in Chapter 8 for implementing custom data-bound controls.

One limitation of the `IList` interface with respect to data binding is that although it is sufficient to allow the data to be displayed and support updates, additions, and deletions from the bound control, it doesn't support all scenarios for the collection's modifiable data. Specifically, if the data collection is changed programmatically by code outside of the bound control, the control won't know of those changes, and the data it displays will be out of sync with the actual data contained by the collection (see the examples in Chapter 9 for more information on this). To remedy this shortcoming, you have to implement `IBindingList` in collections that you want to use for data binding (described later in this chapter). You will also want to implement the `INotifyPropertyChanged` interface on the data item's object type.

Like its parent interfaces, `IList` also has a generic cousin interface, `IList<T>`, that you should implement if your collection will be a strongly typed collection of objects. `IList<T>` only defines the `Insert`, `IndexOf`, `RemoveAt`, and indexer members, because the other `IList` members are inherited from `ICollection<T>`. The `List<T>` generic collection type implements these generic interface versions for you as well.

The IListSource Interface: Exposing Collections of Collections

The `IListSource` *interface allows a type to indicate whether it contains a collection of collections and to expose a default collection for use in data binding. Data-binding code can use the* `IListSource` *interface implementation on an object to obtain a list to bind against when the data source itself is not a list, or to obtain a list of collections that the object contains.*

Frequently you will need to work with collections of data that are related to one another. The most common case of this is working with data sets in .NET. A data set can be thought of as a *collection of collections* because it can contain multiple data tables. Each `DataTable` is a *collection of data items*, which are the rows of data (of type `DataRow`). You might also implement your own custom container type that contains other collections, such as a list of lists. Or perhaps your container type only contains a single list, but you want to let consumers use your object as their data source and obtain the list from your object for the purposes of data binding.

For example, suppose you had a business class called `Inventory-Manager` that lets you manage your inventory items and gain access to them for various use cases. You might want to allow applications to data bind to your inventory manager and have the manager control what gets exposed for data binding based on some other criteria that the class exposes:

```
public class InventoryManager : IListSource
{
    public string InventoryFilter { get { ... } set { ... } }

    public IList GetList()
    {
        // Lazy load inventory items based on current filter criteria
    }

    public bool ContainsListCollection { return false; }
}
```

You might also have a container with multiple collections, such as an inventory manager class that contains lists of in-stock inventory items, on-order items, and suppliers. In that case you might want to provide an easy way for consumers to get a list of the lists that your object contains.

The `IListSource` interface supports these scenarios through its two members (described in Table 7.6). It lets you return a default collection (specifically, an object that implements `IList`) from a call to `GetList`. That list could either be a simple list of objects for data binding or a list of lists contained by the object. If you return `true` from the `ContainsList-Collection` property, then it is assumed that the list you return from `GetList` is itself a list of lists.

TABLE 7.6: IListSource Interface Members

Member	Description
IList **GetList**()	This method returns an object that implements the IList interface that represents the default collection of data managed by a collection of collections container class.
bool **ContainsListCollection**	This property is expected to return true if the object implementing the interface contains collections itself. You would return false if your object only contains a single list collection that is accessed through the GetList method.

Property Descriptors: Allowing Dynamic Data Item Information Discovery

An important class for allowing data-binding code to work against any collection and data item type is the PropertyDescriptor class. This class is defined in the System.ComponentModel namespace and provides dynamic discovery of type information about the individual properties of an object. You can obtain a property descriptor in a number of ways. As discussed in the following sections, some of the data-binding interfaces have methods or properties that will return property descriptors. You can also obtain them for an object any time you have a reference. The Type-Descriptor class, also in the System.ComponentModel namespace, lets you request the property descriptors for an object's properties with the GetProperties method. In fact, the TypeDescriptor class has a bunch of other methods that let you dynamically discover almost anything there is to know about an object, including its methods, properties, events, attributes, and so on.

As their name implies, property descriptors are used to describe information about an object's property. The PropertyDescriptor class derives from MemberDescriptor, which provides many of the properties that you can use to discover information about the described property on the object. You can find out the name of the property, its type, what its type converter is, and what attributes have been applied to its declaration in the type that it belongs to.

For the most part, when it comes to data binding, you will mainly be interested in four properties exposed on the `PropertyDescriptor` class: `Name`, `PropertyType`, `ComponentType`, and `Converter`. Each of these is a read-only property.

- The `Name` property tells you the name of the property as it was declared in the data object type definition. You can use this for display purposes, such as setting the column headers in a grid, or you can use its reflection to get or set the value of the property.

- The `PropertyType` gives you the type of the property itself.

- The `ComponentType` gives you the type of the component (or data item type) on which the property is defined.

- The `Converter` property gives you back a reference to a `Type-Converter` object for the property type, if there is one. As discussed in Chapter 4, the `Binding` class uses type converters to perform automatic formatting of bound-data values to corresponding types. Other complex data-bound controls, such as the `DataGridView`, can use type converters to do the same thing internally when rendering the values of data members within a data source.

Additionally, you can use the `PropertyDescriptor` to access the value of the property for instances of your data objects. The `GetValue` method takes an object reference to the data item for which you want to obtain the value of the property described by the property descriptor. It returns an object reference that contains the value of that property on the data object's instance that you pass in. See Listing 7.1 later in this chapter for an example of using `GetValue` to obtain the values of a data item's properties. The `SetValue` method works in a similar fashion, allowing you to set the value of an object's specific property without having any compile-time type information about that object.

Property descriptors also support providing change notifications for changes to property values, if those changes are made through the

SetValue method exposed by the property descriptor. When data-bound controls let the user edit a bound data item through the control, they do so with the SetValue method on that item's property descriptors without being coupled to the particular object type. If some other piece of code needs to be notified when property values are changed in this way, you can use the AddValueChanged method to provide a callback object and method (through a delegate). This will be called whenever that property's value is changed by the property descriptor's SetValue method. The BindingSource component uses this capability to be notified any time a property changes on one of the data items in the collection it contains. It then raises the ListChanged event on its IBindingList implementation, enabling it to keep multiple controls that are bound to the same data source synchronized when the values are edited through those controls.

The ITypedList Interface: Exposing Data-Binding Properties

The ITypedList interface lets you expose or access type information about the properties that the items in a collection define. It allows consuming code to say to a collection, "Tell me all about the data items that you contain." This information is used extensively by the Visual Studio designer to let you declaratively configure bound controls at design time, such as configuring columns on a DataGridView control based on the typed properties of the items in the bound collection. It can also be used at runtime to modify behavior based on the dynamically discovered types of the properties of a collection's data items.

Types that implement the ITypedList interface can support design-time or runtime discovery of type information about the contained data items. Both the DataView class and the BindingSource class implement ITypedList, and the information exposed through their implementations let you dynamically discover type information about the contained data items. Because every DataTable exposes a default DataView, this makes the type information about the data in a DataTable available through ITypedList. The members of the ITypedList interface are shown in Table 7.7.

TABLE 7.7: ITypedList Interface Members

Member	Description
PropertyDescriptorCol- lection **GetItemProperties**(PropertyDescriptor[] listDescriptors)	This method returns a collection of PropertyDescriptor objects that describe the properties of the data items in the list. The PropertyDescriptor[] parameter lets you specify a set of descriptors that the collection can use to select which properties to return.
string **GetListName**(PropertyDescriptor[] listDescriptors)	This method returns the list name that corresponds to the set of property descriptors that are passed in.

The GetItemProperties method may look a little like a circular definition—you pass in an array of property descriptors to get back a collection of property descriptors. It is easiest to understand how this works if you understand the DataView implementation of this interface.

If you obtain an ITypedList interface reference to a DataView and then call GetItemProperties on that reference with a null parameter, you get back a collection of PropertyDescriptors that describe each field in the data table to which the data view refers. See Listing 7.1 later in this chapter for an example of using GetItemProperties to obtain property descriptors for the columns in a table.

If you call GetItemProperties with a null parameter, you get back the property descriptors for the list's data items. What is the parameter good for, then? Well, that depends on what collection is implementing it, but in the case of a DataView, you can use it to obtain property descriptors for related tables. If the table that the DataView wraps has a related table (defined through a DataRelation), there will be a property descriptor in the returned collection for the view that represents the relation that exposes child rows in some other table. If you pass that property descriptor to the view's GetItemProperties method, you will then get back the property descriptors for the related view (table).

The GetListName method just returns the name of the list that will be returned by the GetItemProperties method. The DataView behavior for this is that if you pass in a complete array of descriptors that matches the collection that is returned from `GetItemProperties`, you get back the table's name. If you have a complex container of collections, like a `DataSet`, you can return the names of other collections in the container when their property descriptors are passed in. This method isn't really used anywhere except in the old `DataGrid` control for displaying the names of child lists when you navigate through a hierarchical collection of collections.

The following is a simple implementation of `ITypedList` on a `BindingList` that sorts the property descriptors.

```
public class SortedTypesBindingList<T> : BindingList<T>, ITypedList
{
    public PropertyDescriptorCollection
        GetItemProperties(PropertyDescriptor[] listAccessors)
    {
        PropertyDescriptorCollection pdc = null;

        if (null == listAccessors) // Told to get all properties
        {
            // Get browsable properties only
            pdc = TypeDescriptor.GetProperties(typeof(T),
                new Attribute[] { new BrowsableAttribute(true) });
            // Sort the properties alphabetically
            pdc = pdc.Sort();
        }
        else // Expect only one argument representing a child collection
        {
            // Return child list shape
            pdc = ListBindingHelper.GetListItemProperties(
                listAccessors[0].PropertyType);
        }

        return pdc;
    }

    public string GetListName(PropertyDescriptor[] listAccessors)
    {
        // Not really used anywhere other than in DataTable and
DataGrid
        return typeof(T).Name;
    }
}
```

The IBindingList Interface: Providing Rich Binding Support

The IBindingList interface is the most important data-binding interface for supporting full-featured data binding. It defines capabilities for controlling changes to the list, sorting and searching the list, and providing change notifications when the contents of the list change. You can easily create a partial implementation of IBindingList (minus sorting and searching) using the BindingList<T> generic collection class in .NET 2.0.

As mentioned earlier, implementing the IList interface is the minimum bar to pass to support Windows Forms control data binding. However, just implementing that interface isn't sufficient to support the kind of rich data binding that developers are accustomed to when working with a collection like a DataView. The IBindingList is the most important interface for supporting data binding with modifications to the data collection. This can be done either through the bound control itself or through programmatic modifications to the collection behind the scenes. IBinding-List also lets the collection specify whether it supports sorting or searching, and provides the methods that will drive those processes. IBindingList derives from IList, so you will need to implement all of the members of IList, ICollection, and IEnumerable as well when you implement IBindingList. The best way to do this is to use or derive from the BindingList<T> generic class. Chapter 9 develops a full sample showing how to do this, as well as adding implementations for IBinding-ListView, ITypedList, and IRaiseItemChangedEvents. For more information on consuming the IBindingList interface and what functionality each of its members provide, read on.

Getting to Know the IBindingList Members

The properties of the IBindingList interface are read-only and are described in Table 7.8. The methods of IBindingList are described in Table 7.9, and the one event in Table 7.10.

TABLE 7.8: IBindingList Interface Properties

Name	Type	Description
AllowEdit	`Boolean`	True if the collection supports modification of the items in the collection, false otherwise. This is a read-only property.
AllowNew	`Boolean`	True if the collection supports the addition of new items, false otherwise. This is a read-only property.
AllowRemove	`Boolean`	True if the collection supports the removal of items from the collection, false otherwise. This is a read-only property.
IsSorted	`Boolean`	True if the collection is sorted, false otherwise. This is a read-only property.
SortDirection	`ListSort-Direction`	Specifies the sort direction if the collection is sorted. The `ListSort-Direction` enumeration can take the values `Ascending` or `Descending`.
SortProperty	`Property-Descriptor`	Lets you determine which property on the data items is used to perform sorting.
SupportsChange-Notification	`Boolean`	True if the collection will raise `ListChanged` events when an item in the collection has changed or when items in the collection are added or removed, false if no `ListChanged` events will be raised. This is a read-only property.
Supports-Searching	`Boolean`	True if the collection can be searched based on an index property, false otherwise. This is a read-only property.
SupportsSorting	`Boolean`	True if the collection can be sorted, false otherwise. This is a read-only property.

TABLE 7.9: IBindingList Interface Methods

Member	Description
void **AddIndex**(PropertyDescriptor indexProperty)	Adds the specified property to the set used for indexing the collection when it is searched.
object **AddNew**()	Creates a new item in the collection and returns a reference to it.
void **ApplySort**(PropertyDescriptor sortProperty, ListSortDirection direction)	Specifies what property to sort on and the direction to sort. ListSortDirection can be Ascending or Descending.
int **Find**(PropertyDescriptor matchProperty, object propValue)	Searches the collection, looking for items whose matchProperty value equals the propValue, using the indexes created with AddIndex.
void **RemoveIndex**(PropertyDescriptor indexProperty)	Removes a property from the index set used for searching when the Find method is called.
void **RemoveSort**()	Removes a sort criteria from the collection, reverting it to unsorted mode.

TABLE 7.10: IBindingList Interface Event

Name	Type	Description
ListChanged	ListChangedEventHandler	This event is raised if the collection supports change notifications whenever an item is added or removed from the collection, and when an item in the collection has been modified. The latter also requires an implementation of INotifyPropertyChanged by the object type that the collection contains.

Raw changes to the collection, in the form of adding items directly, removing items, or accessing individual items, are all done through the methods and properties of the `IList` inherited interface, as described in the section on `IList`. The change functionality of the `IBindingList` interface lets you control whether changes can be made to the list, as well as the construction of new items in the list.

The `AddNew` method provides a convenient way for a data-bound control to add a new item to the collection that can then be edited directly through the control, without the control needing to know anything about the item type at compile time. This method returns an object reference to the created item that can then be used with late-bound methods or reflection to discover that item's properties for presentation.

The `AllowEdit`, `AllowNew`, and `AllowRemove` properties let the collection tell a bound control what kinds of modifications it supports, so a bound control can render itself differently to match the capabilities of the underlying collection. For example, it wouldn't make sense to have a button that adds a new item to a collection in a bound control if the collection that is currently bound is read-only. These properties are read-only, so it is up to the collection itself to decide whether it supports those things. Although not part of the `IBindingList` interface, the collection could expose other methods that allow the consuming code to switch the collection in and out of read-only or fixed-size modes; this way, the values that the collection returns from these properties could change over time. These properties are primarily designed with the expectation that these aspects of a collection won't change: either the collection supports changes or it does not. Other controls can be used at a presentation level to decide whether you are going to let users make modifications at any given time.

Notifying Consumers of Changes to the Collection

If the collection supports changes, it should also support firing a `ListChanged` event when the collection changes. To indicate that, it should return `true` from the `SupportsChangeNotification` property. The collection itself should be able to raise `ListChanged` events when items are added or removed from the collection. Ideally, it will also be able to provide `ListChanged` notifications when existing items in the collection change because their properties have changed. However, the collection's ability to do this will be dictated by how the properties are changed and what support the contained object types provide.

As mentioned earlier, if changes are made through a property descriptor's `SetValue` method, a container can call the `AddValueChanged` method on the property descriptor and provide a callback delegate so that the container will be notified when the property changes. It can then raise the `ListChanged` event in response to notification from the property descriptor that the property changed. This is exactly what an implementation of the `IRaiseItemChangedEvents` interface, discussed in a later section, is expected to do. However, if the property is changed directly through its property setter through a reference to the object, there is no way for the collection to know about the change unless the object itself notifies the collection. The support for that comes from the `INotifyPropertyChanged` interface.

Another form of change that a collection can support is a dynamically changing schema, where new properties are added to the collection items at runtime or design time. The `ListChanged` event also supports notification of this type of change through its event arguments.

The `ListChanged` event is of type `ListChangedEventHandler`, which carries an event argument of type `ListChangedEventArgs` along with it. This event argument's properties, listed in Table 7.11, give you more information on the changes to the list.

TABLE 7.11: ListChangedEventArgs Properties

Name	Type	Description
List-ChangedType	List-ChangedType	Indicates what was changed about the list. The values of the `ListChangedType` enumeration are shown in Table 7.12. This is a read-only property.
NewIndex	Integer	Indicates the index of the item in the list that was affected by the change. The default value is −1 if not applicable to the change type. This is a read-only property.
OldIndex	Integer	Gives the old index of the item that was changed in case the change type is a move. The default value is −1 if not applicable to the change type. This is a read-only property.

TABLE 7.11: ListChangedEventArgs Properties (Continued)

Name	Type	Description
Property-Descriptor	Property-Descriptor	Gives the property's property descriptor that was affected by the change. This is a read-only property.

TABLE 7.12: ListChangedType Enumeration Values

Value	Description
Reset	Indicates a major change in the list and is a signal to bound controls that they should completely rebind to the collection.
ItemAdded	Indicates a new item was added to the collection. The NewIndex property of the event argument indicates the location of the new item in the collection.
ItemDeleted	Indicates an item was removed from the collection. Strangely, the NewIndex property of the event argument indicates the index of the item that was removed. (OldIndex would seem more appropriate for this case, but is not used.)
ItemMoved	Indicates that an item was relocated to a new index position in the collection. The NewIndex property of the event argument contains the new index position and the OldIndex property shows where it was before.
ItemChanged	Indicates that an item in the collection was modified directly. This requires that the data item object type supports notifying the collection of the change so that it can raise the ListChanged event.
Property-Descriptor-Added	Indicates that the schema of the items in the collection changed by adding a property (or column) to the data items. If this is the ListChangedType, then the PropertyDescriptor property of the event arguments will contain the property information about the new property.
Property-Descriptor-Deleted	Indicates that the schema of the items in the collection changed by deleting a property (or column) from the data items. If this is the ListChangedType, then the PropertyDescriptor property of the event arguments will contain the property information about the property that was deleted.
Property-Descriptor-Changed	Indicates that something changed about a property in the schema. The PropertyDescriptor will contain the new property information after the change.

Exercising IBindingList Change Notifications

The following simple console application shows the results of List-
Changed events being raised from a data view as the underlying data collection is modified in several ways.

```
class Program
{
    static void Main(string[] args)
    {
        // Get some data to work with
        NorthwindDataSet nwData = new NorthwindDataSet();
        CustomersTableAdapter adapter = new CustomersTableAdapter();
        adapter.Fill(nwData.Customers);

        // Get an IBindingList interface reference
        IBindingList list = nwData.Customers.DefaultView;
        // Subscribe to change events
        list.ListChanged += new ListChangedEventHandler(OnListChanged);

        // Delete a row
        list.RemoveAt(1);

        // Add a column
        nwData.Customers.Columns.Add("New Column", typeof(string));

        // Change an item in the collection
        nwData.Customers[0].CompanyName = "IDesign";
    }

    static void OnListChanged(object sender, ListChangedEventArgs e)
    {
        Console.WriteLine("ListChangedType Value: {0}",
            e.ListChangedType);
        Console.WriteLine("NewIndex value: {0}",e.NewIndex);
        Console.WriteLine("OldIndex value: {0}",e.OldIndex);
        if (e.PropertyDescriptor != null)
        {
            Console.WriteLine("PropertyDescriptor Name: {0}",
                e.PropertyDescriptor.Name);
            Console.WriteLine("PropertyDescriptor Type: {0}",
                e.PropertyDescriptor.PropertyType);
        }
        Console.WriteLine();
    }
}
```

In this code, a typed data set is created and filled with customer data. An
IBindingList interface reference to the default view of the Customers

table is then obtained and used to subscribe to the `ListChanged` event. The collection is then modified in three ways:

- A row (a data item) is deleted from the table (the collection).
- A new column (property) is added to the table.
- The value of one of the columns (properties) of a row is modified.

Running this program results in the following output:

```
ListChangedType Value: ItemDeleted
NewIndex value: 1
OldIndex value: -1

ListChangedType Value: PropertyDescriptorAdded
NewIndex value: 0
OldIndex value: 0
PropertyDescriptor Name: New Column
PropertyDescriptor Type: System.String

ListChangedType Value: ItemChanged
NewIndex value: 0
OldIndex value: 0
PropertyDescriptor Name: CompanyName
PropertyDescriptor Type: System.String
```

From this you can see that deleting items gives the deleted item's index in the `NewIndex` property of the event arguments; the property descriptor is returned for a new column, describing that column; and when an item in the collection changes, its index is returned, along with a property descriptor for the property that changed.

Supporting Sorting with IBindingList

The next category of functionality specified by the `IBindingList` members is sorting. The `SupportsSorting` property lets the collection specify whether it even supports sorting. If it doesn't, then a bound control shouldn't even expose sorting controls to the user. If the collection does support sorting, then the `ApplySort` and `RemoveSort` methods let a control invoke or remove the sorting functionality provided by the collection. The `ApplySort` method takes two parameters: the `PropertyDescriptor` identifies the property on which you want to sort, and the ListSort-Direction enumeration, whose value can be either Ascending or Descending. The sorting support defined by the IBindingList interface only supports sorting on a single property at a time. For multi-property sorts, you need to implement the IBindingListView interface, as described in the next section.

Listing 7.1 shows an example of using the IBindingList interface sorting properties and methods to sort a collection in various ways.

LISTING 7.1: Sorting a List Through IBindingList

```
class Program
{
    static void Main(string[] args)
    {
        // Get some data to work with
        object dataCollection = GetData();
        IBindingList list = dataCollection as IBindingList;
        ITypedList typedList = dataCollection as ITypedList;
        // Dump the raw data view
        DumpList(list, "Raw Data");
        // Check to see if the list supports sorting
        if (list.SupportsSorting)
        {
            // Get property descriptors for table
            PropertyDescriptorCollection props =
                typedList.GetItemProperties(null);
            // Apply Sort on column 1
            list.ApplySort(props[0], ListSortDirection.Ascending);
            DumpList(list, "Sorted Key1 Ascending");
            // Apply Sort on column 2
            list.ApplySort(props[1], ListSortDirection.Descending);
            DumpList(list, "Sorted Key2 Descending");
            // Remove Sort
            list.RemoveSort();
            DumpList(list, "Unsorted");
        }


    }

    private static object GetData()
    {
        // Create a data set with some sortable sample data
        DataSet data = new DataSet();
        // Add a table
```

```
    DataTable table = data.Tables.Add();
    // Add two columns, Key1 and Key2
    table.TableName = "TestTable";
    table.Columns.Add("Key1", typeof(string));
    table.Columns.Add("Key2", typeof(int));
    // Add some data rows
    table.Rows.Add(".NET", 2005); // Row 1
    table.Rows.Add("ZZZZ", 9999); // Row 2
    table.Rows.Add("Rocks",2);     // Row 3
    return data.Tables[0].DefaultView;
  }


private static void DumpList(IBindingList list, string prompt)
{
    Console.WriteLine(prompt);
    // Loop through each data item without knowing its type
    // Use a type descriptor to obtain the property descriptors
    PropertyDescriptorCollection props =
       TypeDescriptor.GetProperties(list[0]);
    foreach (object dataobject in list)
    {
        StringBuilder builder = new StringBuilder();
        // Loop through the properties, outputting name
        // and value for this data object
        foreach (PropertyDescriptor prop in props)
        {
           builder.Append(prop.Name);
           builder.Append(" = ");
           builder.Append(prop.GetValue(dataobject).ToString());
           builder.Append("; ");
        }
        // Write it out to screen
        Console.WriteLine(builder.ToString());
    }
    Console.WriteLine();
  }
}
```

The code in Listing 7.1 first constructs a simple data set on the fly to work against and then returns the table's default view as the data collection. The DataView class implements both IBindingList and ITypedList, which lets us dynamically determine the data collection's behavior and content. Obviously, in production code you should check the cast's results to see if it succeeded and do something appropriate if it doesn't succeed. After obtaining the interface references to the data collection, the code first calls the `DumpList` helper method to output the list's contents before any sorting has been applied.

The `DumpList` method uses the `TypeDescriptor` class (described earlier in this chapter) to obtain the collection of property descriptors for one of the data items in the collection. Usually the lists you deal with will be homogeneous collections of objects; otherwise, you aren't likely to be able to data bind with them in the first place. As a result, you only need to obtain the property descriptors once using one of the objects in the collection. Using those property descriptors, the consuming code can output the name and value of each data object as it iterates over the list with a `foreach` loop (which is enabled by the base interface `IEnumerable`). Note that this method has no specific type information about the list or its data items, other than that the collection is represented by an interface reference of type `IBindingList`.

After the raw list is dumped, the code uses the `IBindingList` reference to see if the collection supports sorting. If so, the sample enters the block of code that applies sorts. The code first uses the `ITypedList` interface reference to get the property descriptors for the data view's columns through the `GetItemProperties` method. It then uses the property descriptors for the first and second columns to apply an ascending and descending sort on each one, respectively. After applying each sort, it calls `DumpList` again to show that the list's iteration order has in fact changed to reflect the sort. Finally, it calls `RemoveSort` to show that the list order is restored to its original order.

If you run this sample, you will see the following results of sorting in the output:

```
Raw Data
Key1 = .NET; Key2 = 2005;
Key1 = ZZZZ; Key2 = 9999;
Key1 = Rocks; Key2 = 2;

Sorted Key1 Ascending
Key1 = .NET; Key2 = 2005;
Key1 = Rocks; Key2 = 2;
Key1 = ZZZZ; Key2 = 9999;
```

```
Sorted Key2 Descending
Key1 = ZZZZ; Key2 = 9999;
Key1 = .NET; Key2 = 2005;
Key1 = Rocks; Key2 = 2;

Unsorted
Key1 = .NET; Key2 = 2005;
Key1 = ZZZZ; Key2 = 9999;
Key1 = Rocks; Key2 = 2;
```

This example demonstrates that sorting should modify the order that the list returns items when it is iterated over. If you are creating your own object collection type, how you apply sorting is up to you, but it is usually nontrivial to support sorting effectively. The RemoveSort method removes just the current sort. You can check whether a collection is sorted using the IsSorted property. You can also obtain the sort direction and property with the SortDirection and SortProperty properties, respectively, on the binding list.

There are a couple of important things to note from this example. The first is that this is a good example of the power of the data-binding interfaces. Once the data collection is constructed by the helper method, the main part of the code has no specific type information about the collection or the data items it is working on. Yet the sample code is able to iterate over the data, output the data, and modify the sorting of the data all based on the various data-binding interfaces. This is what you want, because in data-binding situations you are going to be given an object reference for a collection, and you have to take it from there without knowing or assuming any specific type information other than the data-binding interfaces. The way you will typically do that is to try to cast to the various data-binding interface types, and if the cast succeeds, then you can count on using the behavior defined on that interface. If the cast fails, then you will have do whatever is appropriate for your control—either downgrade the functionality of the control or throw an exception if the minimum required interface support isn't met.

Supporting Searching with IBindingList

The final category of functionality described by the IBindingList interface is searching. To search effectively, you usually need to apply some sort of indexing over the collection. The SupportsSearching property indicates whether a collection even supports searching. If it returns true, then you should be able to safely call the Find method with a property descriptor for the property you want to match against and an object reference that contains the value to match with.

If you are implementing a collection that supports searching and you will have large sets of data, you might want to also support indexing of the data for more efficient searches. If the collection supports indexing, you can call AddIndex to direct the collection to establish an index on a particular property, and you can call RemoveIndex to remove one that has been previously added. For example, you could add the following code to the end of the Main method in Listing 7-1 to perform a search for a particular item, using indexing to speed the search (although in this simple case, the cost of establishing the index would probably greatly outweigh the performance benefit for the search over three items):

```
if (list.SupportsSearching)
{
    // Get property descriptors for table
    PropertyDescriptorCollection props =
        typedList.GetItemProperties(null);
    list.AddIndex(props[0]);
    int index = list.Find(props[0], ".NET");
    list.RemoveIndex(props[0]);
    Debug.Assert(index == 0);
}
```

Implementing a collection supporting IBindingList from scratch is a ton of work, and most of it is stock code for all the straight collection-oriented things like adding items, clearing them, firing ListChanged events when the collection or items change, and so on. Before .NET 2.0, there weren't a lot of options to avoid that work. However, the BindingList<T> class in .NET 2.0 makes this a lot easier, and it will be explored further in Chapter 9.

The IBindingListView Interface: Supporting Advanced Sorting and Filtering

The IBindingListView *interface supplements the data-binding capabilities of the* IBindingList *interface by adding support for multi-property sorts and filtering of the list.*

As described in the previous section, IBindingList gives you simple sorting and searching capability. However, sometimes you need additional functionality. You may want to be able to sort on multiple properties or columns in a data collection at the same time, or you may want to filter the items presented by the collection based on some criteria without having to search for matches one at a time. The IBindingListView interface is designed exactly to address these needs. IBindingListView derives from IBindingList, so all the stuff described for IBindingList and all of its base interfaces applies here as well. The properties and methods of IBindingListView are described in Tables 7.13 and 7.14.

TABLE 7.13:   IBindingListView Interface Properties

Name	Type	Description
Filter	String	Gets or sets the string used as filter criteria for changing the data objects exposed by the collection.
Sort-Descriptions	ListSort-Description-Collection	Lets you inspect the current collection of sort descriptions that are applied to the collection. This is a read-only property.
Supports-Advanced-Sorting	Boolean	True if the collection allows you to perform multi-property sorts, false otherwise. This is a read-only property.
Supports-Filtering	Boolean	True if the collection allows you to filter it by setting the Filter property, false otherwise. This is a read-only property.

TABLE 7.14: IBindingListView Interface Methods

Method	Description

`void ApplySort(`
`  ListSortDescriptionCollection`
 	
`  sortDescriptions)`
	Lets you apply complex sort criteria that are based on one or more properties on the collection's data objects. You can remove the sort with the `RemoveSort` method inherited from the base `IBindingList` interface.

`void RemoveFilter()`	Lets you remove the current filter criteria and restore the list to the full collection of data. You can accomplish the same thing by setting the `Filter` property to a `null` string.

To support advanced sorting, a collection must be able to set the order based on multiple properties on the data objects simultaneously. Before attempting to apply advanced sorting, the client code should check the `SupportsAdvancedSorting` property to see if it is `true`. If so, then the sort criteria are specified by constructing a collection of `ListSortDescription` objects and passing those to the `ApplySort` method on the `IBindingList-View` interface. The `ListSortDescription` type is pretty straightforward: it is just a container for a pair containing a `PropertyDescriptor` property and a `SortDirection` property. Typically, the order of these items in the `ListSortDescriptionCollection` determines the order in which the sort criteria are applied. To remove an advanced sort that has been applied, just call the `RemoveSort` method that was inherited from the `IBinding-List` base class. If you want to access the sort descriptions that are currently in use for the collection, you can check the `IsSorted` property from the base interface, and then use the `SortDescriptions` property to obtain the collection of `ListSortDescriptions` currently in play.

If a collection supports filtering, it should return `true` from the `SupportsFiltering` property. You can then set a filter string using the `Filter` property, which should immediately modify what data objects are exposed by the collection if you were to iterate over it. The format of the filter string is going to be an implementation detail that will be specified by each collection type. For example, the `DataView` class supports

SQL-like filter strings that match the strings permissible on the `Data-Column.Expression` property. If you are implementing your own collection type, you have to decide on syntax for filter strings that makes sense for your scenario, and then document it well so your collection's users know what filter strings they can provide.

If a filter has been applied to a collection, you can remove it with the `RemoveFilter` method. If you want to check what the current filter criteria is, just read the `Filter` property. This property should be `null` if there is no filter applied. In fact, this is an alternate way of removing a filter: just set the `Filter` property to `null`.

See Chapter 9 for a sample implementation of the `IBindingListView` interface on the `BindingListView<T>` generic type developed there.

The ICancelAddNew Interface: Supporting Transactional Inserts in a Collection

The `ICancelAddNew` *interface lets you add and edit new items to a collection with the item in a transient state, which allows you to remove the new item before finalizing the addition if desired (if a problem occurs while initializing the object's properties). This interface was added in .NET 2.0 to break an implicit coupling that occurs with the* `IEditableObject` *interface when adding new items to a collection. Prior to adding this interface, objects in the collection that implemented the* `IEditableObject` *interface had to notify their parent collection if editing was canceled on a newly added item so the collection could remove that item from the collection. With* `ICancelAddNew`, *the collection can take care of the removal, and the contained object no longer has to have a direct coupling to its containing collection for backing out a newly added item if initialization is canceled.*

Another capability that can come in handy for a richer data-binding experience is to support transactional adding of items to the collection. To understand this, consider a data table bound to a grid. The grid presents a blank line at the bottom of the grid that lets you add new rows to the table. But what if there are constraints on the columns of that row or if there is validation that needs to occur based on the input to multiple fields *before* the item should be added to the data collection? How can you prevent inconsistent data from being added to the collection? After all, there needs to be an object instance somewhere to accept the data being input by the user as they tab from field to field. A new row in the data source is the most logical kind of object to create. But you don't want to actually add the object until the addition is considered "complete"—whatever that means based on the collection and the data objects that go within it.

To support this scenario, the ICancelAddNew interface has been defined to allow a collection to decide whether to accept or reject a new item that has been added to the collection through this interface's methods. If a collection supports transactional adding of items to the collection, it should implement the ICancelAddNew interface. Bound controls can then call EndNew(int index) to commit the transaction of adding a new item or CancelNew(int index) to roll back the addition. This lets the control call AddNew on the list, get a new item back, and start setting values on the new object. If the code calls CancelNew with the index of the item that was added, the new object can be discarded without actually adding it to the collection for good. If the code calls EndNew with the index or performs any other operation on the collection, the addition should be committed. The object itself never needs to know about its transient state with respect to membership in the collection; that is all handled by the collection itself.

This is a little different behavior than what you might expect. In the world of distributed and database transactions, you are expected to explicitly commit the transaction or it should roll back. In the case of ICancel-AddNew, committing is the default behavior even if EndNew isn't explicitly called based on the contract specified by the Framework. So inserting or removing other items, or setting the current item to another item in the collection, is considered to take the focus off the item being added and will commit the item to the collection.

Both the BindingList<T> class that will be discussed in detail in Chapter 9 and the BindingSource class implement this interface for the collections they manage. Because the BindingList<T> generic class cannot know what to do about the transactional semantics of a call to AddNew or CancelNew, you will need to derive a class from BindingList<T> and override the base class methods AddNewCore and CancelNewCore to provide the implementation that makes sense for your scenario.

The IRaiseItemChangedEvents Interface: Providing Item Modification Notifications on Collections

The IRaiseItemChangedEvents *interface lets a collection indicate that it will monitor changes to the properties of the contained objects made through the* SetValue *method of their property descriptors. You would want to do this if you expected your collection type to contain objects that might not implement the* INotifyPropertyChanged *interface but wanted to provide some opportunity to notify bound controls that the underlying data item properties had changed. This interface doesn't make any guarantees about notifying of changes if the properties change through any means other than the* SetValue *method of their property descriptors.*

This interface is used as a signal to consuming code that your collection will raise ListChanged events when the property values contained in your objects change due to changes made through property descriptors—which is how all property updates are done through data-bound controls that support editing. This interface defines a single member, the RaiseItemChangedEvents Boolean property. If your collection returns true from this property, then consuming code can expect to be notified when some object in the collection has changed through a data-bound control.

The BindingSource component uses this internally to provide better currency of the presented data in bound controls, even if the underlying objects don't support property change notifications themselves. To implement support for raising the ListChanged event in response to property value changes on the collection objects, you have to provide a callback delegate to the property descriptor for each property on each object in a collection, so that your collection will be notified when those properties change through the property descriptor. You do this through the AddValueChanged method on the PropertyDescriptor class. See the BindingListView<T> class implementation in Chapter 9 for an example and more discussion of this.

The IEditableObject Interface: Supporting Transactional Item Modifications

The IEditableObject interface lets you defer committing changes to object properties until the editing process is complete. Consuming code can then explicitly declare when an edit operation has commenced on an object, and then later choose to commit or reject the changes made to one or more properties on the object before those changes are made visible to other code that may be working with the object. Specifically, using this interface defers change notifications to bound controls while an object is being edited until the editing operation is completed through a call to EndEdit. You would typically want to implement this interface if your object has co-dependent properties, or if you need to validate multiple property values before declaring an edit to be a legal combination of values.

If you understood the discussion of the ICancelAddNew interface, then understanding IEditableObject should be easier. This interface lets you support the same kind of transactional semantics at the individual data item level for modifying an object in the collection. If you have ever edited a row in a data table that is bound to a grid as well as to other controls on a form, you have seen this interface in action. If you change a column value in the grid and then tab to another column, that changed value isn't reflected in other bound controls on the form until the focus leaves the row that you are editing (typically by setting the current row to another row). If you press the Esc key before moving the focus off the row, the changes you made are rolled back and the old values are put back into the columns that you edited. If you switch the focus to another row, the changes to the row being edited are committed at that point, and the other bound controls on the form will then be updated to reflect the new values. This is because the edits to the column (property) values are all treated as part of a single editing transaction against the object, and the edits aren't considered complete from the perspective of other controls until the editing operation is explicitly committed. This happens through a call to the object's EndEdit method, either because the grid calls this method when the row is changed or because you explicitly call EndEdit to commit the changes.

The IEditableObject interface includes three methods: BeginEdit, EndEdit, and CancelEdit. None of these take any parameters, and they don't return anything.

This interface is useful when an object is going to be edited by a data-bound control or other client code; that code can then check to see if the object implements this interface. If so, it can call BeginEdit before starting to modify the object, and either call CancelEdit to roll back the changes or EndEdit to commit them. The object that implements this interface is expected to maintain a temporary copy of the property values being edited so that it can roll back to the original version if CancelEdit is called. Chapter 9 shows an example of implementing this interface.

The INotifyPropertyChanged Interface: Publishing Item Change Notifications

The INotifyPropertyChanged *interface lets an object notify its container any time a property on the object changes. This allows the containing collection to raise a* ListChanged *event when an item in the collection has one or more of its property values changed. The* BindingList<T> *class uses this interface to bubble up* ListChanged *events when contained objects are edited either through programmatic code or data-bound control. This results in consistent synchronization of object values that are bound to multiple controls.*

The IBindingList interface defines a ListChanged event that is designed to notify a collection's client when anything about the list has changed. One kind of change it is designed to support is modifications to the data items that are contained in the collection. However, there needs to be a way for the list itself to be notified when an item within the collection changes. A control can index into a collection and obtain a direct reference to an object. The control can use the object in a variety of ways and maintain the reference to it for a long period of time. Other controls also bound to that object will want to know when the object has changed so they can refresh the way they are rendered or react to the change. The INotify-PropertyChanged interface provides a contract for objects to notify their containers that they have changed, so the container can bubble that information up to any bound controls.

It is a very simple interface. It defines a single event member, `Property-Changed`, of type `PropertyChangedEventHandler`. The event signature includes the usual `object` as the first parameter for the sender and a `PropertyChangedEventArgs` second parameter. The `PropertyChanged-EventArgs` is itself simple: it tells the name of the property that was changed. Once you have been notified that a particular property has changed, your consuming code can refresh whatever dependencies you have on that property. The main consumer of this interface is the `Binding-List<T>` class, and it uses this to raise `ListChanged` events to any bound controls, or to the `BindingSource` component when properties are modified on the collection's items. You will see this interface in action in the samples in Chapter 9 as well.

The IDataErrorInfo Interface: Providing Error Information

The `IDataErrorInfo` interface lets an object store and expose error information that can be used by bound controls to notify the user when errors were encountered while using the object. It exposes a top-level error message for the object as a whole, as well as an indexer that can expose per-property error messages. Controls such as the `DataGridView` can use this information to expose in-place error indications and messages to the user.

When a control is bound to a collection of data items, and the data items can be modified either by the control itself or through other code in the application, things can go wrong. Someone could try to stuff a value of an inappropriate type into a business object's loosely typed property. Someone could pass in a value that is outside of an allowable validation range. An error could occur when the value contained in the object is used to try to persist the data to a database. In any of these situations, the bound control might want to know that an error occurred and may be designed to present some information to the user about the error.

A good example of this is a `DataGridView` control that is data bound to a `DataView`. If an error occurs in any of the columns of a row in the underlying data table, the `DataRow` class can store the error information in its `Errors` collection. When this occurs, it stores not only what the error was, but specifically what column within the row was affected by the error. When an error occurs in a data row, it is reflected in the grid with an error icon next to the offending cell. When a user's mouse cursor hovers over an error icon, the error message for the problem that occurred displays in that column in that row.

This all happens when a `DataRowView` (the row objects within a `DataView`) implements the `IDataErrorInfo` interface, and the `DataGridView` is coded to look for that interface on the data items in any collection it is bound to. If the grid sees that the data items it is presenting in the grid's rows implement this interface, the grid will use the interface's properties shown in Table 7.15 to determine if any of the columns have errors that should be presented or whether the object itself has a general error to be displayed.

By implementing this interface on your custom data objects, and storing error information at the object or property level that you expose through these interface properties, you enable data-bound controls to provide a richer error-handling experience to the user. Likewise, if you implement a custom data-bound control, you can check the object your control is bound to for an implementation of this interface, and then use the information you obtain and present it to the user in some form that makes sense for your control.

TABLE 7.15: IDataErrorInfo Properties

Property Name	Type	Description
`Error`	String	Displays a top-level error message for the data object itself. This is a read-only property.
`this[string propertyName]`	String	Lets you retrieve the error message related to a particular property or column on the data object. This is a read-only property.

The ICustomTypeDescriptor Interface: Exposing Custom Type Information

The ICustomTypeDescriptor *interface lets an object provide custom type information for the information it wants to expose publicly, so that consuming code can ask the object to describe itself, rather than using raw reflection against the type definition. If you don't implement this interface, the* TypeDescriptor *class can describe the public properties that are defined on your object using reflection for data binding and other purposes. But if you implement this interface, you can take control of providing the* PropertyDescriptors *to the* TypeDescriptor *class yourself. By doing this, you can expose things for data-binding purposes that may not even be declared as public properties on your class, and you can hide properties that you don't want exposed to code that doesn't have explicit type information about your object. The* DataView *does this to expose child row collections in some other table that are defined through a* DataRelation *as child collection property on the* DataView.

The ICustomTypeDescriptor interface isn't one that you should normally have to implement. But if you need to take explicit control over which properties are exposed through the TypeDescriptor class when it reflects on your object type, then implementing this interface gives you that control. When the TypeDescriptor class goes to obtain the properties implemented on an object, it first checks to see if that object type implements the ICustomTypeDescriptor interface. If so, it will ask the object to provide its own PropertyDescriptors through this interface's Get-Properties method.

In fact, the ICustomTypeDescriptor interface goes well beyond just allowing you to describe your properties. When you implement this interface, you have to provide implementations for all of the methods shown in Table 7.16, most of which won't be directly used in data-binding scenarios.

TABLE 7.16: ICustomTypeDescriptor Interface Methods

Signature	Description
AttributeCollection GetAttributes()	Returns the collection of attributes that are defined at the class level.

TABLE 7.16: ICustomTypeDescriptor Interface Methods (Continued)

Signature	Description
`string GetClassName()`	Returns the class name.
`string GetComponentName()`	Returns a name for the component. Lets you name the object differently when used as a component as opposed to a basic class.
`TypeConverter GetConverter()`	Returns the `TypeConverter` that should be used to perform type conversions between this and other types.
`EventDescriptor GetDefaultEvent()`	Returns the event that is used as a default. This is the event the designer will hook up, based on a double-click if the component supports designer interaction.
`PropertyDescriptor GetDefaultProperty()`	Returns the property descriptor for the default property. This property is used for setting up certain data-binding actions when no property is explicitly specified, such as setting up a simple data binding to an object through the Data Sources window.
`Object GetEditor(Type type)`	Returns an object that can be used to edit the type in the designer and property grid.
`EventDescriptorCollection GetEvents()`	Returns the collection of events exposed by the object.
`EventDescriptorCollection GetEvents(Attribute[] attributes)`	Returns the collection of events exposed by the object that have the specified attributes applied to their declarations.
`PropertyDescriptorCollection GetProperties()`	Returns the collection of properties exposed on the object.
`PropertyDescriptorCollection GetProperties(Attribute[] attributes)`	Returns the collection of properties exposed on the object that have the specified attributes applied to their declaration.

continues

TABLE 7.16:   ICustomTypeDescriptor Interface Methods (Continued)

Signature	Description
`Object GetPropertyOwner( PropertyDescriptor prop)`	Returns an instance of an object that has the specified property defined on it. This can be used for pseudo-properties to return a reference to a related object that is exposed as a property.

The ISupportInitialize Interface: Supporting Designer Initialization

The `ISupportInitialize` *interface lets controls defer acting on values set on interdependent properties until the container tells the control that all values have been set. This avoids having a control try to take actions based on a property's setting if those actions might fail if another property needs to be set first, and those properties can be set in any order. The Windows Forms designer uses this interface, so the code it generates to set properties doesn't need any insight into the correct order to set interdependent properties.*

Sometimes components have interdependent properties that all need to be logically set at the same time for things to work correctly. But because only one line of code can execute at a time, supporting this notion of having multiple properties set simultaneously becomes a problem. For example, if you specify a `DataMember` property for a `BindingSource` component or a `DataGridView` control, that property provides information about what part of the object that you set as the `DataSource` property should be used for data binding. Any change to the `DataMember` property necessitates refreshing the data bindings. However, the `DataMember` property doesn't understand this unless the `DataSource` has been set first. You can't be sure that they will be set in the right order, with `DataSource` first and then `DataMember` second. Also, what if you want to take a component or control that was already bound to some other data source and change it to a new data source? You might change the `DataSource` property first, or you might change the `DataMember` property first. When the designer writes code for you based on interactions in the designer such as selections in Smart Tags or setting properties in the Properties window, there is no way to be sure what order the code will be written to initialize those properties.

So there needs to be a way to signal a control or component to tell it that you will be entering a period of initialization, and then notify it again when you are done with that period of initialization. If you can do that, then the component can defer enforcing any interdependencies or using the values of any of the properties until you signal it that initialization is complete. This is precisely what the ISupportInitialize interface is designed for.

ISupportInitialize defines two methods: BeginInit and EndInit. Neither takes any parameters or returns anything; they are just signal methods to the implementing class of when initialization is starting and when it is complete from some consuming code's perspective. The Visual Studio designer is aware of this interface and looks for it on any component or control that you drag and drop onto a designer surface. If it sees that something you added through the designer implements this interface, the designer adds calls to BeginInit and EndInit that bracket the setting of any properties for that component in the designer-generated code. Doing so ensures that the order that properties are set by the designer is not important, just that it properly signals when it is starting to set properties, and when it is done setting them. The following code shows a trimmed down version of the InitializeComponent method from the designer code file for a form in a Windows Forms application.

```
private void InitializeComponent()
{
  // Code to create component instances omitted…

  // BeginInit calls
  ((System.ComponentModel.ISupportInitialize)
     (this.bindingSource1)).BeginInit();
  ((System.ComponentModel.ISupportInitialize)
     (this.northwindDataSet1)).BeginInit();

  // Property initialization—order not important
  this.bindingSource1.DataMember = "Customers";
  this.bindingSource1.DataSource = this.northwindDataSet1;
  this.northwindDataSet1.DataSetName = "NorthwindDataSet";

  // EndInit calls
  ((System.ComponentModel.ISupportInitialize)
     (this.bindingSource1)).EndInit();
  ((System.ComponentModel.ISupportInitialize)
     (this.northwindDataSet1)).EndInit();
}
```

Notice that it calls BeginInit on each component at the beginning of the initialization phase (after casting the component variable to the ISupportInitialize reference type), then sets properties, and then calls EndInit. Doing this allows the control or component to internally defer acting on the properties that are being set until EndInit is called, which avoids the challenges of setting interdependent properties in the correct order.

Listing 7.2 shows a simple implementation of ISupportInitialize on a class that contains a string collection. For demonstration purposes, the class is designed to support initialization by caching any values that are set on the StringCollection property until initialization is complete. To support this, the class does a number of things.

- It implements the ISupportInitialize interface and its methods BeginInit and EndInit.

- Member variables are defined to hold the primary string collection that the class encapsulates, as well as a flag to indicate when the class is being initialized, and another string collection to hold onto a temporary copy of a value that is being set for the string collection during initializing.

- The StringCollection property sets block checks to see if the class instance is being initialized through the flag, and if so, places any values set for that property into a temporary copy. If the class isn't initializing, then it just writes the value into the primary string collection member variable.

- The implementation of BeginInit sets the flag to indicate to the rest of the class that it is in initialization mode.

- The EndInit method copies the reference to the last value set for StringCollection from the temporary variable into the primary string collection variable and resets the flag.

You will see a real-world implementation of ISupportInitialize in Chapter 8 for a custom data-bound control.

LISTING 7.2: ISupportInitialize Implementation

```
public class SomeContainerClass : ISupportInitialize
{
    private List<string> m_Data = null;
    private bool m_Initializing = false;
    private List<string> m_TempData = null;

    public List<string> StringCollection
    {
        get
        {
            return m_Data;
        }
        set
        {
            if (m_Initializing)
                m_TempData = value;
            else
                m_Data = value;
        }
    }

    void ISupportInitialize.BeginInit()
    {
        m_Initializing = true;
    }

    void ISupportInitialize.EndInit()
    {
        m_Data = m_TempData;
        m_Initializing = false;
    }
}
```

The ISupportInitializeNotification Interface: Supporting Interdependent Component Initialization

The ISupportInitializeNotification *interface lets interdependent child objects be notified when other objects have completed initialization. This allows an object that depends on another object's state to wait until the other object has completed its own initialization before the dependent object tries to complete its own initialization.*

The ISupportInitialize interface just discussed helps you work with components with interdependent properties on a single component. But what if you have multiple components that are interdependent in terms of the order that those components are initialized? For example, when you set up data binding, you often bind a control to a Binding-Source, and then bind the BindingSource to a data set. The properties being set during initialization on the BindingSource will probably reference a table in the data set. But the table in the data set may be getting created as part of the initialization steps for the data set. So if EndInit is called on the binding source before EndInit is called on the data set, the data set won't have completed the initialization that makes that table available to the binding source. Therefore, when the binding source tries to start iterating over the data in the table, users will get an error message because the referenced table isn't there.

To make this more concrete, let's use the SomeContainerClass from Listing 7.2 as a data source for a binding source. The following code shows a Load event handler for a form that uses the initialization methods of the components, but calls EndInit in the wrong order, with unexpected results.

```
private void OnFormLoad(object sender, EventArgs e)
{
    SomeContainerClass dataContainer = new SomeContainerClass();
    ISupportInitialize bindSourceInit = m_BindingSource;
    ISupportInitialize dataInit = dataContainer;

    bindSourceInit.BeginInit();
    dataInit.BeginInit();

    dataContainer.StringCollection = new List<string>();
    m_BindingSource.DataSource = dataContainer;
    m_BindingSource.DataMember = "StringCollection";

    // Binds against the null default value for the collection,
    // not the collection just set above
    bindSourceInit.EndInit();
    // Now the new string collection is set on the container class,
    // but binding is already complete, so unexpected results
    dataInit.EndInit();
}
```

The problem with this code is that because `EndInit` is called on the binding source *before* the data object, the binding will be done against incomplete initialization of the data object.

What's needed here is a way for interdependent objects like this to ensure that they get initialized in the correct order. The `ISupport-InitializeNotification` interface is new in .NET 2.0, and it's designed to address these kinds of initialization order dependencies.

Specifically, the `ISupportInitializeNotification` interface allows one component (call it ComponentA) to ask another component (ComponentB) to notify it when ComponentB has completed its initialization. This allows ComponentA to wait until ComponentB is done with its initialization before ComponentA completes its own initialization.

`ISupportInitializeNotification` defines one property and one event. The `IsInitialized` property returns a Boolean value that indicates whether the component that implements the interface has completed initialization. The `Initialized` event, of type `EventHandler`, is fired by the implementing component when initialization completes. So if a component might depend on another component's initialization, the first component can check that other component for this interface's implementation. If it finds that interface, it can see if the component is already initialized, and if not, can subscribe to the `Initialized` event to be notified when that occurs. The code in Listing 7.3 shows an example where `ISupportInitializeNotification` is used in the `EndInit` method for the `BindingSource` component.

LISTING 7.3: Use of ISupportInitializeNotification in BindingSource

```
void ISupportInitialize.EndInit()
{
  // See if data source implements ISupportInitializeNotification
  ISupportInitializeNotification notification1 =
    this.DataSource as ISupportInitializeNotification;

  // If so, and not initialized
  if ((notification1 != null) && !notification1.IsInitialized)
  {
    // Subscribe to notification event
    notification1.Initialized += new
      EventHandler(this.DataSource_Initialized);
  }
```

continues

```
        else
        {
            EndInitCore(); // Complete initialization
        }
    }

    // End initialization event handler
    private void DataSource_Initialized(object sender, EventArgs e)
    {
        ISupportInitializeNotification notification1 =
            this.DataSource as ISupportInitializeNotification;
        if (notification1 != null)
        {
            // Unsubscribe from the event—one time process
            notification1.Initialized -=
                new EventHandler(this.DataSource_Initialized);
        }
        // Complete initialization now
        this.EndInitCore();
    }
```

The comments I added in Listing 7.3 describe what is going on. When EndInit is called on the BindingSource component, it checks the object that was set as its DataSource to see if it implements the ISupport-InitializeNotification interface (through an attempted cast with the as operator). If so, it checks the object through the IsInitialized property to see if it has already completed initialization. If not, it then subscribes to the object's Initialized event and does no further work in EndInit. If the data source object has already completed initialization or doesn't implement the interface, then the method completes the initialization process by calling the EndInitCore method, which is where the real work of completing initialization is done. If the object did support the interface and indicated that it wasn't complete with its own initialization, then BindingSource waits until the object fires the Initialized event to complete its own initialization through EndInitCore. In addition, the event handler for Initialized unsubscribes from that event, since it shouldn't fire more than once in a given initialization scenario.

So if you implement a class that can be used as a data source, and that class requires an ISupportInitialize implementation to control interdependencies among properties, then you should also implement ISupport-InitializeNotification, return false from the IsInitialized property while you are in the initialization process (signaled by a call to your `BeginInit` method), and fire the `Initialized` event to any subscribers when you are done with initialization (signaled by a call to your `EndInit` method).

The ICurrencyManagerProvider Interface: Exposing a Data Container's CurrencyManager

The `ICurrencyManagerProvider` interface lets a container indicate whether it provides its own currency manager for any contained data collections. This interface is implemented by the `BindingSource` component, and you shouldn't have to implement it yourself. However, you may occasionally need to use this interface to access the `CurrencyManager` for a container from a custom bound control.

The `ICurrencyManagerProvider` interface has two members: a method named `GetRelatedCurrencyManager` and a property named `CurrencyManager`. The `CurrencyManager` property is the main thing you'll use to get a reference to the underlying currency manager to subscribe to change notifications on that currency manager. (An example using this is shown in Chapter 8 on the `FilteredGrid` control.) The `GetRelatedCurrencyManager` method lets you specify a data member parameter, which lets you get a child collection's currency manager in a master-details data-binding scenario.

Where Are We?

This chapter has covered all the major data-binding interfaces that you might need to either implement or consume. I presented them from the perspective of describing the contract that the interface represents, followed by the details represented by the interface's members. I used a few examples to describe and demonstrate the more complex concepts, and also described some things in terms of the implementations and use of the interfaces as they exist in the .NET Framework controls and collections that you should already be getting familiar with, such as the `DataView` and `DataGridView`. There are a few more interfaces at work behind the scenes, such as the

`IBindableComponent` interface implemented on the base `Control` class of Windows forms. But because you really shouldn't have to mess with these interfaces directly, I didn't bother going into any detail on them.

Some key takeaways from this chapter are:

- `IList` is the minimum interface implementation that lets you bind a collection directly to a control.

- The `BindingSource` component can iterate through a collection that only implements `IEnumerable` and add the items to its own internal list collection, so `IEnumerable` is sufficient to support data binding through a `BindingSource`.

- `IBindingList` is the minimum support you should strive for on a data-bound collection, because it allows synchronization between bound controls when items are added or removed from the collection.

- `INotifyPropertyChanged` is important for rich data binding on custom objects—it lets the UI stays up to date when the objects are modified through programmatic code.

- `PropertyDescriptor` objects are the key to runtime getting and setting of property values on a data object, regardless of whether that object is a row in a data table or a custom business object in a custom collection.

To really gain a full appreciation of these interfaces and how to use them, you have to assume one of two perspectives—that of the interface's consumer or that of the interface's implementer. The consumer could be any form of client code that interacts with the collection, but will often be data-bound controls. The implementer will be a collection, a data object, or a control.

The next two chapters further explore these different perspectives. Chapter 8 shows how to implement custom data-bound controls and uses some of the interfaces defined in this chapter to consume the data to which they are bound. Chapter 9 shows how to implement custom collections and objects that support rich data binding, and how to implement all of the collection- and object-level interfaces described in this chapter.

8

Implementing Custom Data-Bound Controls

T HE .NET FRAMEWORK provides a rich set of Windows Forms controls for presenting data in your applications. The controls in the Framework are by necessity and design very general purpose and flexible, and with the addition of the `DataGridView` in .NET 2.0, they can be used to address most common requirements. However, there are certain advanced scenarios where the Framework controls might not meet your needs, as well as other times when developing custom controls can make sense as well.

You might choose to implement your own custom data-bound controls for a number of reasons, including:

- You need similar special-purpose functionality in more than one place in your application or across multiple applications.
- You can contain the complexity of the special-purpose code, even if you don't see a strong potential for reuse. Encapsulation is a good thing, both for providing the potential for reuse and for isolating portions of your code so that only those who need to know and work with the internal details of an implementation have to deal with that portion of the code.

- You want to create a custom control that encapsulates the code required to bend the Framework controls to your will.

- You can code and debug your custom functionality and code as a custom control once, and then reuse it in many places in the same way that you use the controls provided by the Framework.

- You need to provide functionality or a presentation rendering of data that is not already available through the Framework controls.

The code required to implement custom data-bound controls depends on how customized the control is. This chapter covers several examples of custom controls that demonstrate different approaches to custom controls and discusses the considerations for each approach. It describes how to subclass existing Framework controls, how to use containment to use existing custom controls while gaining an additional level of flexibility and ease of development from the subclassing case, and how to develop a custom data-bound control that doesn't use any of the built-in data-bound controls or components. You don't need to write much data-binding-related code yourself for subclassed controls and control containment, but if you step into the deep end and create a totally custom data-bound control, you will have to consume the data-binding interfaces described in Chapter 7. I'll be demonstrating how to do that in the latter half of this chapter.

Extending Framework Data-Bound Controls

Depending on the kind of custom data-bound functionality you need to support, inheriting from one of the existing controls in the .NET Framework might be your best option. Specifically, if you want to tailor the presentation of the data in a control, many of the Windows Forms Framework controls expose rich event models and virtual methods in the base class that let you integrate your own code to customize the appearance and/or behavior of the control as it is presented to the user or while they interact with it.

The data-binding behaviors of the Windows Forms controls are pretty tightly woven into the controls; they aren't exposed in a way that lets you easily override that data-binding behavior by inheriting from the control. If you need to vary the data that gets presented by a Windows Forms control, you are better off doing that by changing the data source that you bind to the control, rather than trying to make the control change what data in the bound data source it presents.

For example, if you wanted to only show selected items in a collection of data within a data-bound control, you could just bind that control to a binding source and use the `Filter` property on a binding source to modify which data items are presented by the control. Alternatively, you could requery for new data based on the user's interactions.

However, if you want to customize the appearance of the data within a control, most of the data-bound Windows Forms controls let you take over some or all of the painting or rendering logic of the control and do the data rendering yourself. For text boxes, combo boxes, and the `DataGridView`, there are ways to handle the painting events that are raised by the Framework, and in your handler you can take over the painting of data yourself. You also have opportunities to customize the formatting of the data as it is rendered by the control. (See the discussion in Chapter 4 of the `Format` and `Parse` events of the `Binding` object, and the description in Chapter 6 of the`DataGridView` control's `CellFormatting` event, and how to use those to modify the data presented within the control to be something different than what it is in the underlying data source.)

Most of these capabilities can be done on a case-by-case basis inside the forms where you use the controls. But many times it will make sense to encapsulate that logic, either to separate it from the other code in your form or to package it for reuse. Deriving a class from one of the Windows Forms control classes is one way to accomplish this encapsulation in an easily reusable way.

Creating a Grouped Column DataGridView

As an example of creating a custom data-bound control by deriving a class from an existing Framework control, let's create a specialized

`DataGridView` control that presents its bound data as grouped data items within each column. For example, say you have a table containing summary data of all the products ordered by each customer by date. Each customer may have multiple orders for the same product, and multiple orders might have been placed by each customer on a given date. If you sort the data by customer and product name, it would be easier to read the data in the grid if the repeated customer names and products weren't shown in every row of the table. It would be much easier to read if only new values were shown, and rows with the same value as previous rows were presented with blank cells, and the borders of the cells also helped to indicate the grouping of data values (see Figure 8.1).

Because this example specifies some behavior and altered rendering of the data in the grid, it makes a decent candidate for subclassing (deriving from) the `DataGridView` control. To achieve this functionality doesn't require a ton of code, just a few overrides of base class methods and tapping into the formatting and painting behavior of the base class.

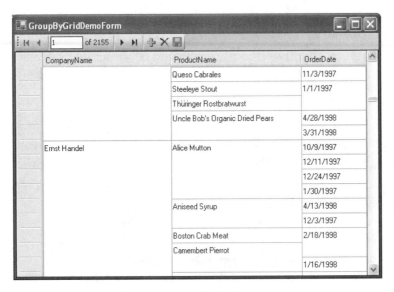

FIGURE 8.1: GroupByGrid Sample Application

Deriving from DataGridView and Handling the CellFormatting Event

The first step is to declare a class that derives from the `DataGridView` class:

```
public class GroupByGrid : DataGridView
{
    ...
}
```

To support the requirement to render blank cells when the cell content will be the same as the previous cell in the column, you need to override the `OnCellFormatting` base class method, as shown in Listing 8.1.

LISTING 8.1: DataGridView OnCellFormatting Method Override

```
protected override void OnCellFormatting(
    DataGridViewCellFormattingEventArgs args)
{
    // Call home to base
    base.OnCellFormatting(args);

    // First row always displays
    if (args.RowIndex == 0)
        return;


    if (IsRepeatedCellValue(args.RowIndex, args.ColumnIndex))
    {
        args.Value = string.Empty;
        args.FormattingApplied = true;
    }
}

private bool IsRepeatedCellValue(int rowIndex, int colIndex)
{
    DataGridViewCell currCell =
        Rows[rowIndex].Cells[colIndex];
    DataGridViewCell prevCell =
        Rows[rowIndex - 1].Cells[colIndex];

    if ((currCell.Value == prevCell.Value) ||
        (currCell.Value != null && prevCell.Value != null &&
        currCell.Value.ToString() == prevCell.Value.ToString()))
    {
        return true;
    }
```

continues

```
        else
        {
            return false;
        }
    }
}
```

In almost all cases, when you override one of the base class On*XXX* methods, you should call the base class method from your override either at the beginning or the end, depending on what you are doing in your override. The reason is that it's the base class method that fires the corresponding event that can be handled in client code. Additionally, the base class method may do some additional work that usually needs to be performed even if you are doing other processing in your derived control method. Whether you put your custom code before or after the call to the base class method depends on if your custom code will act on other members of the class that might have side effects based on what the base class method does to them. This requires either understanding what the base class method is going to do by using a tool like Reflector to inspect the implementation of that base class method or just experimenting with the calling order to get the behavior you expect.

So the first thing this override of OnCellFormatting does is to call the base class implementation. Next it checks if the row index is zero, and if so, the handler just returns without doing anything else. This ensures that the first row cell values are always formatted normally. For rows beyond the first row, the handler calls a helper method to check whether the current cell's value is the same as the previous cell's value from the same column. If so, then it sets the cell value to an empty string so the cell will render blank. As discussed in Chapter 6, any time you change the formatted value of a cell, you should set the FormattingApplied flag to true, so this is done in Listing 8.1 after setting the Value property on the event argument.

Modifying the Painting Behavior of the Cell

That takes care of rendering the cell contents as blank when the value is the same as the previous row. The next thing is to handle painting the cell borders so that the blank cells for repeated values appear as one big cell in the grid. To do this, you need to override the OnCellPainting base class method as shown in Listing 8.2.

LISTING 8.2: DataGridView OnCellPainting Method Override

```
protected override void OnCellPainting(
    DataGridViewCellPaintingEventArgs args)
{
    base.OnCellPainting(args);

    args.AdvancedBorderStyle.Bottom =
        DataGridViewAdvancedCellBorderStyle.None;

    // Ignore column and row headers and first row
    if (args.RowIndex < 1 || args.ColumnIndex < 0)
        return;

    if (IsRepeatedCellValue(args.RowIndex, args.ColumnIndex))
    {
        args.AdvancedBorderStyle.Top =
            DataGridViewAdvancedCellBorderStyle.None;
    }
    else
    {
        args.AdvancedBorderStyle.Top = AdvancedCellBorderStyle.Top;
    }
}
```

The overridden method does the following:

1. It calls the base class implementation to ensure that subscribers of the
   CellPainting event still get notified.

2. It sets the event argument's AdvancedBorderStyle.Bottom property to a border style of None. This ensures that no cells will draw a
   bottom border.

3. It checks to see if it is being called for the column or row headers (in
   which case the column or row index will be –1) or for the first row. If it
   is being called for a header cell it just returns and performs no further
   custom painting.

4. Finally, it calls the same helper method as the formatting method to
   determine if the current cell value is the same as the previous cell's
   value from the same column. If so, it sets the top border to None; if
   not, it sets it to the value on the default AdvancedCellBorderStyle
   property from the base class.

That is all there is to it. If you duplicate this code or run the Custom-ControlsHost sample program from the download code, you should see the custom grid in action. This example is fairly straightforward, but it's not even close to a bulletproof implementation. It doesn't correctly handle if the user customizes the default cell borders, and there are other properties on the base class that can be set that could result in undesired effects running this code. This is a hazard of deriving a class directly from a Framework control: Any modifications you make to its behavior through the access you gain to protected members of the base class assume you have intimate knowledge of how the changes you make will affect the base class behavior. With a complex control like the DataGridView, that requires you to have far too much insight into the inner workings of the control. A better approach is to go with containment of the control and customizing its behavior through its public API, which is discussed shortly.

Using Custom Controls

Once you have developed a custom control, you need to add it to a form or another user control to test it and verify that it works as expected. To test this, do the following:

1. Open the custom control project within the same solution as a Windows application project in which you want to test the control.
2. Open a form in the designer, and you will see a tab added dynamically to the top of the Toolbox for each custom control library in the solution.
3. Drag and drop your custom controls from the Toolbox onto a form to use and test them.

For production purposes, you don't want others to have access to your projects and source code, so the way to use a custom control library without opening its project in the consuming solution is to customize the Toolbox. To do this, perform the following:

1. Open a new or existing Windows application project.
2. Bring up a form in the designer.

3. Display the Toolbox. From here, there are two ways you can add your custom controls to the Toolbox.

   – You can locate the DLL that contains your custom controls through Windows Explorer and drag and drop the DLL onto the Toolbox. This will add all of the controls in that DLL to the Toolbox.

   – If you want to have more explicit control over which controls are added, right-click in an existing tab within the Toolbox (such as the *All Windows Forms* tab), or create your own by choosing *Add Tab* from the context menu, then select *Choose Items* from the context menu. Click the *Browse* button in the lower right of the Choose Toolbox Items dialog and navigate to the location of the DLL containing your custom controls. Once you select that file and click *Open*, the dialog will check the boxes of all custom controls it finds in that library (see Figure 8.2). If you want to exclude certain controls from being added, simply uncheck their boxes. Click *OK* to add the selected controls to the Toolbox.

4. Once the controls are in the Toolbox (see Figure 8.3), you can drag and drop them onto forms and user controls like any other built-in Framework control in the Toolbox.

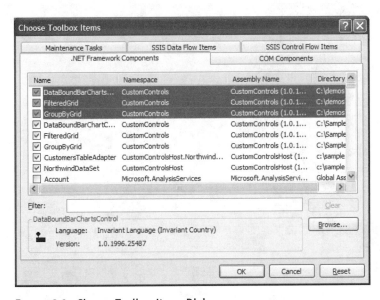

FIGURE 8.2: Choose Toolbox Items Dialog

FIGURE 8.3: Customized Toolbox Tab and Controls

The User Control Test Container

A new capability in Visual Studio 2005 is to run and debug a Windows user control without having to develop a forms application and add it to a form. Visual Studio now includes a test container (see Figure 8.4) for presenting user controls. This lets you test many of their behaviors directly from the Windows Control Library project that they live in. You display this by running a debug session from a project of type Windows Control Library.

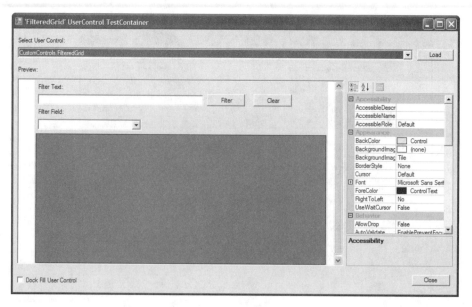

FIGURE 8.4: User Control Test Container

The test container renders the user control in a simple host container that exposes the control properties in the container's properties panel that you can use to tweak properties and verify that they work correctly. Unfortunately, for data-bound controls, the control's key behaviors are all based around providing runtime data through a data source. Although those properties are exposed in the test container (like they are in the designer for a hosting form), there is no data available in the test container's runtime context to bind the control to. So for most data-bound control testing, you still need to create a test application form to host the control in and provide it with some data to bind to. But if you just want to test the way certain parts of your control will render themselves, the test container can be a quick way to check that out.

Developing Data-Bound Container Controls

As mentioned earlier, the problem with deriving a new control from an existing Framework control type is that if you access or override any protected members of the base class, you need to have a great deal of insight into what the side effects will be. The public members exposed by a control are a lot easier to understand, are better documented, and provide greater protection from introducing unexpected side effects. As a result, you'll usually have better success customizing the behavior of Framework data-bound controls from the outside through their public members rather than from the inside through their protected members.

However, if there are particular customizations you need to make that will be used in more than one location, repeating those customizations in all the forms that use the control is tedious, error-prone, and introduces an unnecessary maintenance burden. To avoid this repetition, you can customize the built-in Framework controls through containment in user controls. This lets you encapsulate all the customizations inside your user control, so that users of your control don't have to worry about the messy implementation details at all. They just focus on the (often simplified) API of your control and add it to as many forms as they like.

Your user control can contain a collection of Framework controls, custom controls, and custom code to integrate those controls. You expose public properties and methods on your user control to enable users of your control to code against it in a fashion similar to the Framework controls. Another advantage of taking this approach is that you can use the new `BindingSource` component to greatly simplify exposing data-binding capabilities from your custom control. By containing a `BindingSource` (or several) inside your user control, you can easily hook up external data sources passed in by the users of your custom control, yet still have the built-in mechanisms of the Framework controls and components do all the dirty work for you.

The following sections develop a custom data-bound user control to demonstrate these concepts and techniques.

Building a Filtered Grid Control

Assume that you need a `DataGridView` control in several places in your application that is going to present tabular data coming from various data sources. Once the grid is data bound, you want users to be able to input filter conditions into a text box and have it autocomplete the filter text based on the contents of a specified filter field within the table. This kind of grouping of functionality is a good example of where creating a custom user control is a perfect choice. You can reap the benefits of a good design-time experience in laying out the controls and setting their properties in the user control designer, and then you can add it to a form and test it out. Once it is all coded and working correctly, other developers can just add your control to their forms, set a few properties, and have a rich, consistent use case implemented in many places. Figure 8.5 shows the filtered grid in action, and Figure 8.6 shows the autocomplete functionality helping in the selection of filter criteria.

To get this kind of scenario working correctly requires a good understanding of binding sources and grids, as well as control and data-binding lifecycles. You also need to understand other Windows Forms concepts like working with `ComboBox` controls and using autocomplete functionality on a text box. I'll step through all of this in the following sections. If you want to follow along to create a control like this, you need to create a Windows

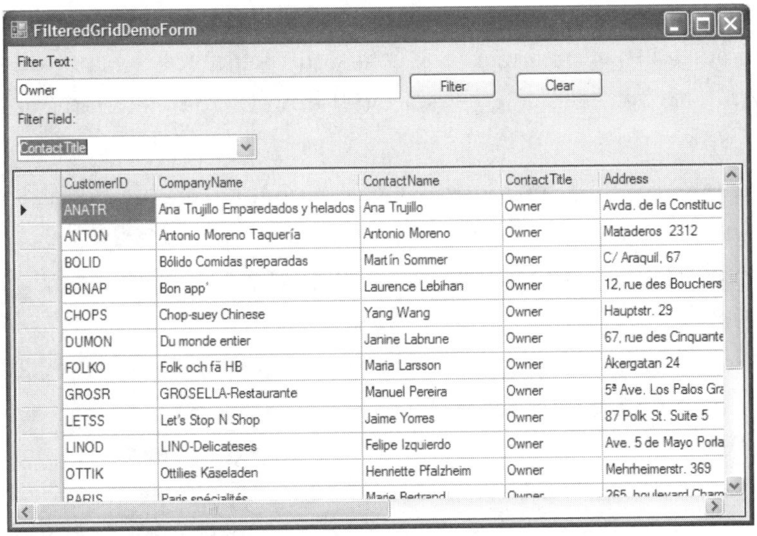

FIGURE 8.5: Filtered Grid in Action

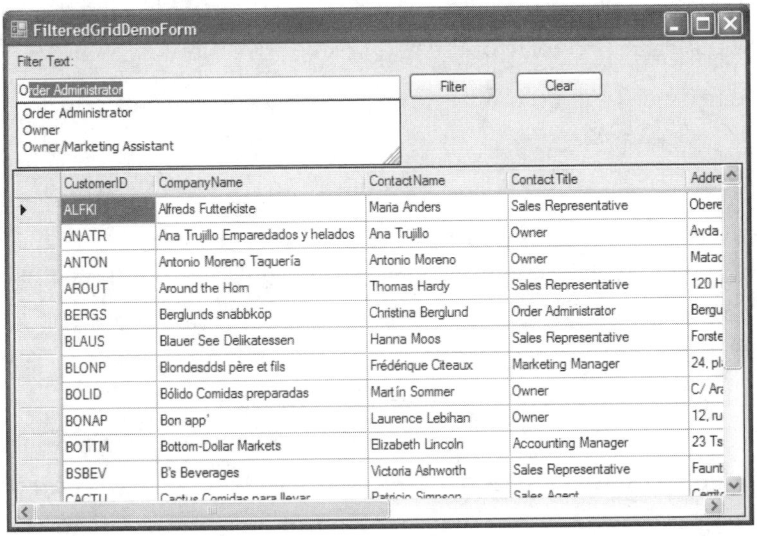

FIGURE 8.6: Filter Textbox Autocomplete

Control Library project. This is really a class library project that has references added to it for the `System.Windows.Forms` and `System.Drawing` namespaces. The project wizard also adds a blank user control named `UserControl1` to the project. You can either rename that to get started, or delete it and add a new user control named what you want. (To add one, right-click on the project and choose Add > User Control.)

1. Name the control `FilteredGrid`. This results in a new user control file being added to your project and a design surface for the control that is similar to a form design surface (without the title bar and borders) is displayed.

2. Expand the size of the user control by grabbing the edge of it in the designer and dragging it down and right until it is about 600 x 350 pixels (you can monitor the size in the bottom right of the designer as you drag).

3. Using Figure 8.5 as a model, add two labels, a text box, two buttons, a combo box, a binding source (`BindingSource` component), and a DataGridView control to the user control by dragging them out from the Toolbox. Arrange them like you see the controls presented in Figure 8.5. The binding source will be shown in the nonvisual components tray at the bottom of the designer.

4. Set the `Text` property for the labels and button as shown in Figure 8.5, and leave the `Text` property of the text box control blank.

5. Name the text box, combo box, buttons, binding source, and grid controls `m_FilterTextBox`, `m_FieldsCombo`, `m_FilterButton`, `m_ClearButton`, `m_BindingSource`, and `m_Grid`, respectively.

6. Set the grid's `Anchor` property to include the `Top`, `Bottom`, `Left`, and `Right` anchor values so that it will resize automatically to fill the bottom portion of the user control regardless of the size of the control.

At this point, all the code is being injected into the designer code partial class (FilteredGrid.Designer.cs), which is hidden from you in Solution Explorer by default. If you go to Code view on the `FilteredGrid` control now, you should just see the partial class definition with a call to the `InitializeComponent` method (which is in the designer partial class file):

```
public partial class FilteredGrid : UserControl
{
    public FilteredGrid()
    {
        InitializeComponent();
    }
}
```

Adding Data-Binding Capability to a Custom Control

This procedure will add the functionality to the control incrementally, just like you normally should while developing such a control. Let's start with the simplest part—letting users of your control provide a data source and data member to bind the contained grid to a set of data. Because the Data-GridView control is a child control of your user control, it is declared as a private member of your user control class. This is true for any controls you drag onto the designer surface of a form or control by default. You can alter this through the Modifiers property in the Properties window, if desired, or by editing the designer-generated code directly. In general, you should avoid directly modifying designer-generated code because your changes can be overwritten by subsequent designer actions, which is why it is all placed in a separate partial class code file in Visual Studio 2005.

One way to support data-binding to the grid in your user control would be to simply allow users to access the contained grid directly and set its data source. This wouldn't work well for the filtered grid requirements though, because the whole point is to create a control that modifies what is bound to the grid based on input from the filter text box and field list. So the right way to set up data binding in this case is to mimic the data-binding API exposed by other data-bound controls on your custom user control. For displaying tabular data, that means exposing Data-Source and DataMember properties that can be set to establish the data binding on your control.

Thanks to the contained binding source component in your control, you won't have to do any grunt work for the data-binding yourself—you can just delegate the data binding to the binding source, and let it handle the dirty work. Continuing from the procedure in the last section, do the following:

1. Set the DataSource property on the grid (m_Grid) to the binding source (m_BindingSource) through the designer's Properties window. By doing this, any time the data source on the binding source is modified, the grid will automatically update. Now you can expose

DataSource and DataMember properties on the FilteredGrid control and delegate to the binding source in their implementations:

```
public object DataSource
{
    get { return m_BindingSource.DataSource; }
    set { m_BindingSource.DataSource = value; }
}

public string DataMember
{
    get { return m_BindingSource.DataMember; }
    set { m_BindingSource.DataMember = value; }
}
```

2. Because this control is being designed for bound data to be supplied to the grid externally through the user control, you also want to make sure the AutoGenerateColumns property on the grid is set to true, which you can do by adding a call to the constructor for your control:

```
public FilteredGrid()
{
    InitializeComponent();
    m_Grid.AutoGenerateColumns = true;
}
```

3. Add an instance of the FilteredGrid control to a Windows Forms application by dragging it from the Toolbox onto a form, and set its data source programmatically in the form Load event handler. When you run the application, you should see the data presented in the form:

```
private void Form1_Load(object sender, EventArgs e)
{
    CustomersTableAdapter adapter = new CustomersTableAdapter();
    filteredGrid1.DataSource = adapter.GetData();
}
```

CustomersTableAdapter here was generated by creating a typed data set with the Customers table in it (as described in Chapter 2).

If you tried to set up the data binding through the designer instead of doing it programmatically, you would run into a few problems. First, if you tried to drag the Customers table from the Data Sources window, you would see that it wouldn't consider the `FilteredGrid` control a valid drop target for the data source. Second, if you went to the Properties window with the `FilteredGrid` control selected in the designer, you would see the `DataSource` and `DataMember` properties exposed there, but the `DataSource` property would be grayed out because it is declared as an object reference type, so the designer doesn't know enough to let you select something as a data source.

Supporting Designer Initialization of Data Binding

You want your `DataSource` and `DataMember` properties to behave just like those of the built-in Windows Forms controls, letting you select data sources and members using the graphical pop-up windows that allow browsing of project data sources, as described in Chapter 5. To do this, you need to adorn these properties with some attributes that let the designer know how to treat them in the designer.

1. Add the `AttributeProvider` attribute to the `DataSource` property and the `Editor` attribute to the `DataMember` with the appropriate arguments. This lets you tell the designer to treat your properties just like the Framework controls `DataSource` and `DataMember` properties get treated.

```
[AttributeProvider(typeof(IListSource))]
public object DataSource
{
    get { return m_BindingSource.DataSource; }
    set { m_BindingSource.DataSource = value; }
}

[Editor("System.Windows.Forms.Design.DataMemberListEditor,
    System.Design, Version=2.0.0.0, Culture=neutral,
    PublicKeyToken=b03f5f7f11d50a3a", typeof(UITypeEditor))]
public string DataMember
{
    get { return m_BindingSource.DataMember; }
    set { m_BindingSource.DataMember = value; }
}
```

2. Add a `using` statement to bring in the `System.Drawing.Design` namespace for the `UITypeEditor` type name.

Just by adding these attributes and rebuilding the control library, now when you work with the `FilteredGrid` control in a form's designer, you get the same drag-and-drop data-binding experience as you do for a `Data-GridView`, `ComboBox`, or any of the other data-bound Framework controls, as shown in Figure 8.7. You may need to close and reopen the form you are editing the `FilterGrid` on after rebuilding the solution to see the Properties window changes.

This gets you the interaction you are looking for in the Properties window, but if you try to drag and drop a data source from the Data Sources window, you will still get a mouse cursor indicating the drop is not allowed (circle with a slash). To remedy this, you need to add an appropriate binding attribute to the class itself.

Specifying Binding Properties on a Control

When you want the designer to be able to set up data bindings for your control through drag-and-drop operations, the designer needs to know

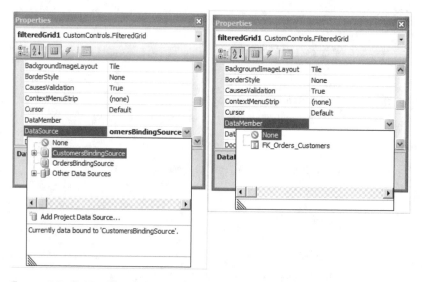

FIGURE 8.7: Setting DataSource and DataMember Properties on the FilteredGrid Control

whether your control is designed for simple or complex data binding and which properties on the control it is supposed to be setting in response to drag-and-drop operations. To identify these items on a custom control that you want to use through the Data Sources window, you have to add an appropriate attribute to the control class definition so that the Data Sources window can work with it. The attributes used are described in Table 8.1.

Because your `FilteredGrid` control represents a complex bound control, you need to add a `ComplexBindingProperties` attribute to the class itself:

```
[ComplexBindingProperties("DataSource", "DataMember")]
public partial class FilteredGrid : UserControl, ISupportInitialize
{
...
}
```

The two parameters of this attribute's constructor specify the names of the properties for setting the data source and data member, respectively, on the control. I recommend that you stick to the convention of naming these `DataSource` and `DataMember`, respectively, which is what is done in the `FilteredGrid` control.

TABLE 8.1: Data Sources Binding Attributes

Attribute	Control Type	Description
DefaultBind-ingProperty	Simple bound control	Identifies the name of the property on the control that will be used as the default for binding. This property type has to match the type of the data member it is used for, or a suitable type converter has to be available, or the data binding will fail at runtime.
LookupBinding-Properties	Lookup complex bound control	Identifies the control's properties that should be used as the data source, display member, value member, and selected item.
ComplexBind-ingProperties	Table-oriented complex bound control	Identifies the control's properties that should be used as the data source and data member.

Now you should be able to drag and drop data sources from the Data Sources window onto the control, and the designer will generate all the appropriate objects (typed data set, table adapter, binding source, and data navigator in the case of a typed data set source) and hook them up to your `DataSource` and `DataMember` properties appropriately.

Supporting Delayed Initialization with ISupportInitialize

One other thing you should do at this point is to implement the `ISupport-Initialize` interface, defined in the `System.ComponentModel` namespace.

This interface, as discussed in Chapter 7, lets you defer certain initialization steps until all the dependent properties on your control that might be set through the designer are initialized in a batch and then makes them take effect all at once. This interface is kind of like the `IDisposable` interface, in that if you create a class that contains disposable objects, you should make your class disposable and delegate to the contained objects in the `Dispose` method.

If your control contains objects that can be initialized, you should make your control initializable and delegate to the contained initialized objects. To do this, add the `ISupportInitialize` interface to your class definition, and add implementations of the interface's methods to your class, delegating to the binding source and grid implementations:

```
public partial class FilteredGrid : UserControl, ISupportInitialize
{
    private bool m_Initializing = false;
    void ISupportInitialize.BeginInit()
    {
        m_Initializing = true;
        ((ISupportInitialize)(m_Grid)).BeginInit();
        ((ISupportInitialize)(m_BindingSource)).BeginInit();
    }

    void ISupportInitialize.EndInit()
    {
        m_Initializing = false;
        ((ISupportInitialize)(m_BindingSource)).EndInit();
        ((ISupportInitialize)(m_Grid)).EndInit();
    }
}
```

This lets you control the initialization order of the controls, as well as giving you a place to control your own batch initialization if needed. I added a Boolean flag, m_Initializing, to the class as well. This lets you use this as a signal in your methods to indicate when you are in this initialization process, which will come in handy in a little while. I also chose to complete initialization on the contained binding source first, then the grid, which makes sense: to get the grid's data source initialized before the grid tries to complete its data-binding process against the binding source.

To test everything you have so far, do the following:

1. Create a new Windows application project in the same solution as the Windows Control Library project that you created earlier.

2. In the Form1 that is added to the new project, drag and drop a FilteredGrid control from the *CustomControls Components* tab in the Toolbox onto the form.

3. Go to the Data Sources window, and add a new data source to the Northwind database (as described in Chapter 5).

4. Add the Customers table to the resulting typed data set and name it CustomersDataSet.

5. Drag the Customers table from the Data Sources window onto the FilteredGrid on the form.

   The designer should create several objects on the form for you: an instance of the data set named customersDataSet, a binding source named customersBindingSource, and a table adapter named customersTableAdapter. It will also hook all these up appropriately, will set the DataSource and DataMember properties of your control to work with the generated data objects, and will add the line of code to the Form Load event handler to fill the data set using the data adapter.

   If you run the application at this point, you should see the grid filled with data. However, you aren't quite all the way there yet.

6. Add a BindingNavigator control to the form, and set its Binding-Source property to the customersBindingSource.

7. Run the application, and select the navigation controls on the data navigator control. You will see that it is changing the position in the toolbar, but the caret on the grid inside the filtered grid control isn't updating to match that position.

To understand how to fix this, you have to think about what controls and components are on the form and how they relate to one another.

When you add controls to a form, you are just adding instances of the controls that are members of the class to the `Controls` collection of the base class. So the `FilteredGrid` control that is added to the form is just one control on the form from the form's perspective. Because `Filtered-Grid` derives from `UserControl`, which derives from `Control` indirectly, it too has its own `Controls` collection, and this is the collection into which the grid and binding source inside the user control go. When you hooked up all the data binding in the form through the designer, what you effectively end up with is what is depicted in Figure 8.8 (minus the controls not directly involved in data binding yet).

The `customersBindingSource` instance in the form is hooked up to the `customersDataSet` as its data source, with its `DataMember` set to the `Customers` table within that source. The `filteredGrid1` instance has its `DataSource` set to the `customersBindingSource`, which just implicitly hooks the user control's contained `m_BindingSource` instance up to that same binding source. The `m_Grid` instance inside the user control has its `DataSource` set to the `m_BindingSource` instance in the user control. When the data set gets filled out in the form's `Load` event handler, the data

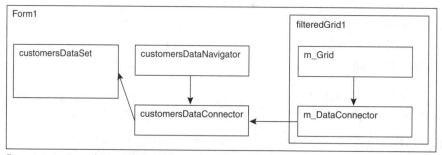

FIGURE 8.8: Bound Controls in the Hosting Form and User Control

shows up automatically in the grid through the handy work of the binding sources.

The problem with the data navigator is that it is hooked directly to the customersBindingSource in the form, and there is no automatic way for it to cascade the changes in the position for that binding source down into the one in the user control (m_BindingSource). This is because each binding source has its own currency manager under the covers, and they aren't hooked up in a way that lets the binding sources know they are supposed to stay synchronized. To fix this, you need to do a little more work when you hook up the data source in the user control.

Chapter 7 briefly covered the ICurrencyManagerProvider interface, which is implemented by objects that host their own currency manager, as is the case with a BindingSource component. To be notified when the currency manager's position in the form's binding source changes within the user control's binding source, you need to use the ICurrencyManager-Provider interface to detect when something will maintain its own currency manager, and you need to subscribe to that currency manager's CurrentItemChanged event to keep things synchronized yourself. Listing 8.3 shows the modifications required to the set block of the DataSource property on the FilteredGrid control, as well as the event handler method that gets called.

LISTING 8.3: **Handling Position Changes in the Bound Data Source**

```
public partial class FilteredGrid : UserControl, ISupportInitialize
{
    // Add a member to track parent currency manager
    private CurrencyManager m_CurrencyManager = null;

    [AttributeProvider(typeof(IListSource))]
    public object DataSource
    {
        get
        {
            return m_BindingSource.DataSource;
        }
        set
        {
            // If there is an existing parent currency manager,
            // unsubscribe from its event and get rid of the ref
            if (m_CurrencyManager != null)
```

continues

```
            {
                m_CurrencyManager.CurrentItemChanged -=
                    new OnCurrencyManagerPositionChanged;
                m_CurrencyManager = null;
            }
            m_BindingSource.DataSource = value;
            // Check to see if the new data source provides its own
            // currency manager
            ICurrencyManagerProvider currmgr =
                value as ICurrencyManagerProvider;
            // If so, subscribe to be notified when the parent current
            // item changes
            if (currmgr != null)
            {
                m_CurrencyManager = currmgr.CurrencyManager;
                m_CurrencyManager.CurrentItemChanged +=
                    OnCurrencyManagerPositionChanged;
            }
        }
    }

    // Update your position based on the parent position
    void OnCurrencyManagerPositionChanged(object sender, EventArgs e)
    {
        if (m_CurrencyManager != null)
        {
            m_BindingSource.Position = m_CurrencyManager.Position;
        }
    }
    ...
}
```

As shown in Listing 8.3, each time a new data source is assigned, you have to check to see if it implements the ICurrencyManagerProvider interface. If so, you subscribe to the CurrentItemChanged event on the CurrencyManager exposed through the interface property. You also need to hold on to a reference to the currency manager, so you can unsubscribe from that event before releasing the reference to the data source when a new data source is assigned. The event handler updates the position of the binding source inside the user control to match the position of the currency manager that is set as the data source. Now if you ran the sample application, when you change the position with the data navigator, the cursor in the grid will be updated as well.

Dynamically Determining the Properties of a Data Source

The next requirement we will tackle is to be able to dynamically populate the m_FieldCombo control in the FilteredGrid control with the columns or properties of the data items in the bound data source. When you create custom controls that support data binding like this, you should make as few assumptions as possible about the actual data types being bound to your control. For example, one way to support this functionality would be to say that your control can only be bound to DataTable objects (in which case you wouldn't even need a DataMember property), and therefore you could just cast the DataSource to a DataTable, access its Columns collection, and obtain the column names from each of the DataColumn objects in that collection.

The problem with that approach is that you have just prevented anyone from using your control with a collection of custom business objects, which is a use case that you should support in the same way that the data-bound Framework controls do. Because the data-bound portion of your user control is a grid bound to a binding source, you can let the binding source worry about all the details of handling various kinds of data collections, which it does quite nicely. However, you need to be able to reach into whatever collection is bound to the binding source and determine what the names of the columns or properties are on each of the data items in the collection, and you need to do it in a way that makes no assumptions about the object type. Whether the data source is a data set, data table, or custom collection of business objects, your code needs to handle it properly, and preferably without writing a bunch of conditional tests to check for specific types.

Luckily, the Framework has some built-in support for doing exactly this through property descriptors (the PropertyDescriptor class—see Chapter 7 for a discussion of property descriptors). By using the Get-Properties static method on the TypeDescriptor class, you can get back a PropertyDescriptorCollection instance containing all the property descriptors for all of an object's properties, whether that object is a row in a table or an instance of a Foo business object.

Dynamically Populating a Combo Box Control

To dynamically populate the combo box control with the field or property names in the data source collection items, add the helper method to the `FilteredGrid` class shown in Listing 8.4.

LISTING 8.4: BindFilterFields Helper Method

```
private void BindFilterFields()
{
   if (m_Initializing)
      return;

   List<string> cols = new List<string>();
   // Check if you have something to work with
   if (m_BindingSource.List.Count > 0)
   {
      object dataItem = m_BindingSource.List[0];
      // Get the property descriptors for the object type
      // currently contained in the collection
      PropertyDescriptorCollection props =
         TypeDescriptor.GetProperties(dataItem);
      foreach (PropertyDescriptor prop in props)
      {
         // Exclude any properties that are references to
         // child collections
         if (prop.PropertyType.GetInterface("IList") == null)
         {
            cols.Add(prop.Name);
         }
      }
   }
   // Populate the combo box with the column/property names
   m_FieldsCombo.DataSource = cols;
}
```

The first thing this helper method does is to check your `m_Initializing` flag to see if this method is being called while you are in the initialization stage, based on your implementation of the `ISupport-Initialize` interface. If so, the method just returns without doing anything, because it will assume that the data source itself might not be done initializing yet.

Next, a list of strings is created using the `List<T>` generic type to hold the field names as they are discovered. The binding source exposes a `List` property that gives you direct access to whatever list of objects it contains as a data source. You could just go through the `DataSource` property of the binding source, but then you would have to manually resolve the data member within that data source if there was one. Using the `List` property gives you direct access to the resolved collection of data, which returns an `IList` reference.

As long as the list contains some items, the method then accesses the first item in the collection. Binding sources only support lists containing a homogeneous collection (objects of a single type), so accessing the first item should give you all the information you need to know. The method then obtains the collection of property descriptors for the properties on the first object in the list and loops through them.

The code checks each property descriptor to see if the property it represents implements the `IList` interface itself by using the `PropertyType` property on the property descriptor, which returns a `Type` instance describing the actual type of the property. The code calls the `GetInterface` method on the `Type` instance to determine if the property represents a child collection. If so, it doesn't add the property to the list. This protects against two scenarios.

- If you have a data source that is a data set with data tables that have relations between them, and the binding source is bound to one of the tables with the data relation, the relation will show up as a property on the list through the property descriptors. However, it doesn't make sense to show the relation in the filter fields list, because the data relation doesn't represent a single-valued property that can be filtered through the text box entry.
- If the list contains business objects, those objects can have properties that are collections of data as well, and those properties wouldn't be displayed by the grid, so they shouldn't be included in the combo box.

So, as long as the property isn't a list property, the property's name is added to the string collection and the loop continues on through the rest of the data item's properties. When the method ends, it sets the string collection as the data source on the `m_FieldsCombo`, which will automatically display those strings as the items in the combo box.

Handling the ListChanged Event

You need to call this helper method from somewhere appropriate, which is whenever you know that the underlying data collection has changed. You can be notified of this by the `ListChanged` event raised by the binding source. To continue in the vein of letting the designer do as much coding as possible for you, take the following steps.

1. Open the `FilteredGrid` control in the designer, and select the `m_BindingSource` in the components tray.

2. Go to the Events view of the Properties window and type `OnListChanged` into the text box next to the `ListChanged` event.

3. When you press the Enter key, the designer declares the event handler for you with the appropriate signature in your user control code file and subscribes the handler to the event in the designer-generated code partial class file behind the scenes.

4. Add the following code to the `OnListChanged` method:

```
private void OnListChanged(object sender, ListChangedEventArgs e)
{
    if (e.ListChangedType == ListChangedType.Reset ||
        e.ListChangedType == ListChangedType.PropertyDescriptorAdded ||
        e.ListChangedType ==
ListChangedType.PropertyDescriptorDeleted)
    {
        if (!m_FilterInProgress) // Don't reinit when filtering
        {
            // Fill the combo box with the column names
            BindFilterFields();
            // Populate the autotext string collection with the
            // contents of the filter column values
            BuildAutoCompleteStrings();
        }
        else
        {
            m_FilterInProgress = false;
        }
    }
}
```

The `ListChangedType` property of the event arguments passed to this event let you filter those changes that affect the schema of the contained objects. A reset means the entire source has changed, and the `Property-DescriptorAdded` and `PropertyDescriptorDeleted` change types let you handle the case if the data source is being programmatically modified at runtime. The guard condition checking the `m_FilterInProgress` flag keeps the combo box from resetting when the list has reset due to a filter being applied. This lets the combo box keep the current selection, and the autocomplete string list (discussed next) will remain as it was before the filter was applied.

If you run the Windows application that contains the filtered grid at this point, you should see that the combo box gets populated with the data source's field names—just what you were looking for.

Autocompleting Input in a TextBox Control

The next requirement to tackle is not directly related to data binding, but is a common requirement for data input applications: the capability to auto-complete user input as they type it within input controls such as a `TextBox` or `ComboBox` control. This is a new capability provided in .NET 2.0, so let's use it to enhance the filtered grid functionality.

1. To enable autocomplete for a text box, you need to set the `Auto-CompleteMode` property to something other than its default value of `None`. The options are `Suggest`, `Append`, or `SuggestAppend`.

   - `Suggest` means that the text box will provide a drop-down list of potential matching string candidates to select from.

   - `Append` means that it will append the best matching string candidate to the end of the characters that the user has typed so far, with those additional letters selected, allowing the user to overtype the additional characters.

   - `SuggestAppend` gives you the combination of these behaviors, which is what you will probably want in most cases.

2. You also need to set the `AutoCompleteSource` property to one of its enumerated values. The choices for this include most recently used lists, file system lists, URL lists, and other built-in sources. Because you are going to be generating the list dynamically based on the

data source, you need to select CustomSource as the value for this property.

3. Because you selected CustomSource, there is a third property provided on the control, AutoCompleteCustomSource, that is prepopulated with an instance of a AutoCompleteStringCollection that you can use to populate with your autocomplete values.

4. To set all these for the FilteredGrid control, open the control in the designer, select the m_FilterTextBox control, and go to its Properties window.

5. Set AutoCompleteMode to SuggestAppend, and set AutoComplete-Source to CustomSource.

6. You have to populate the AutoCompleteCustomSource collection programmatically. You do this by building a list of the current contents of each row for the filter field selected in the combo box. To populate the autocomplete string collection, I added the helper method to the class shown in Listing 8.5.

LISTING 8.5: BuildAutoCompleteStrings Helper Method

```
private void BuildAutoCompleteStrings()
{
    if (m_Initializing || m_BindingSource.List.Count <= 0
        || m_FieldsCombo.Items.Count <= 0)
        return;

    // Clear what is in there now
    m_FilterTextBox.AutoCompleteCustomSource.Clear();
    // Get the column name
    string filterField = m_FieldsCombo.SelectedItem.ToString();
    // Build the list of filter values
    AutoCompleteStringCollection filterVals =
        new AutoCompleteStringCollection();
    foreach (object dataItem in m_BindingSource.List)
    {
        PropertyDescriptorCollection props =
            TypeDescriptor.GetProperties(dataItem);
        PropertyDescriptor propDesc = props.Find(filterField, true);
        string fieldVal = propDesc.GetValue(dataItem).ToString();
        filterVals.Add(fieldVal);
    }
    // Set the list on the collection
    m_FilterTextBox.AutoCompleteCustomSource = filterVals;
}
```

The first step in the helper method is to verify that it is being called while initializing or while the collection of data or the filter field combo box is empty. If any of those are true, then the method simply returns because there isn't enough information available to build the autocomplete string collection. If there is data to work with, it first clears the current collection of strings, which again is accessible through the `AutoComplete-CustomSource` property on the text box.

Next, an instance of an `AutoCompleteStringCollection` is created to add your new filter values to. The method then enters a loop to step through each row in the data collection, and uses property descriptors and the `Find` method to locate the field or property on each item with the name of the field selected in the combo box. It then extracts the current value of that field with the `GetValue` method on the property descriptor and adds it to the collection of filter strings. Once the loop is complete, the code replaces the `AutoCompleteCustomSource` string collection with the one just created.

As with the `BindFilterFields` method, you need to call this helper method from an appropriate place, which includes two places.

- The first happens to be the same place as for the `BindFilterFields` method, in the `ListChanged` event handler (as you saw in the previous section).

- The other place is the `SelectedIndexChanged` event on the filter field combo box. Any time the filter field changes, you need to rebuild your autocomplete list by calling the `BuildAutoCompleteStrings` method from that handler as follows:

```
private void OnFilterFieldChanged(object sender, EventArgs e)
{
    BuildAutoCompleteStrings();
}
```

If you run the sample at this point, the grid and filter field combo box should populate with data and column names respectively, and if you select a particular field in the combo box and start typing a value, you should see autocomplete kick in, as shown in Figure 8.6.

You are almost done with the filtering capabilities. The last thing you need to do is to make the selected filter take effect on the presented rows in the grid. To do this, add a handler for the `Filter` button named `OnFilterClicked`, with the code shown in Listing 8.6.

LISTING 8.6: OnFilterClicked Event Handler

```
private void OnFilterClicked(object sender, EventArgs e)
{
    if (m_BindingSource.List.Count <= 0 ||
        m_FieldsCombo.Items.Count <= 0)
        return;

    if (string.IsNullOrEmpty(m_FilterTextBox.Text))
    {
        m_BindingSource.Filter = null;
        return;
    }
    // Set filtering flag
    m_FilterInProgress = true;

    // Determine the filter column
    string filterMember = m_FieldsCombo.SelectedItem.ToString();
    object dataItem = m_BindingSource.List[0];
    PropertyDescriptorCollection props =
        TypeDescriptor.GetProperties(dataItem);
    PropertyDescriptor propDesc = props.Find(filterMember, true);

    m_BindingSource.Filter = string.Format("{0} = '{1}'",
        propDesc.Name, m_FilterTextBox.Text);
}
```

To do the actual filtering, use the inherent capability of the `Binding-Source` itself to do the dirty work. All you need to do in your `Filter` button `Click` event handler is to tell it what to filter on, which needs to be a valid `Filter` expression. The filter expressions supported by the `Binding-Source` are simpler than those used by the `DataColumn.Expression` property, in that you don't have different delimiters for different data types. You just delimit the value of the filter property or field with single quotes, and it will work fine for numeric and date types as well. However, the underlying data source does need to support filtering, meaning it needs to implement the `IBindingListView` interface (discussed in Chapters 7 and 9).

The first thing the filter method does is to check to make sure there is data to work with; if not, it returns. The next thing is that if a blank filter expression is entered, it is treated as clearing the filter expression, so the code checks to see if the text box is empty and if so, sets the binding source's `Filter` property to `null`. Notice the call to `string.IsNullOr-Empty`. This is a new method added to the string class in .NET 2.0, and it saves having to declare a long conditional statement that checks both for an empty string and for a null string, a very common requirement in code dealing with strings. In this case it is somewhat unnecessary, since the `TextBox` control always returns an empty string when blank (but I decided to include it here so you'd be aware of it).

After that, the code grabs the field name from the combo box and the filter string from the text box, and uses them to construct a filter expression with the `string.Format` method and set that as the `Filter` property on the binding source. With this in place, you should be able to type in filter values into the text box at runtime, see autocomplete kick in to help you select appropriate values, and then tailor the grid to matching values when you click the `Filter` button.

Autosizing Columns in the Grid

I want to add one more feature to this control before we declare it done. Because programmers using your `FilteredGrid` control won't have direct access to the `DataGridView` that it contains, there is no opportunity for them to declaratively set the column names, widths, and such through the designer—this just automatically generates the columns based on the data. One of the most common desires when this is done is to have the column widths also set automatically to display the contained content without wrapping. As discussed in Chapter 6, the `DataGridViewColumn` class has an `AutoSizeMode` property that you can set to `AllCells` (or a number of other settings) to achieve this presentation effect. So what you need to add to your `FilteredGrid` is some code to set that property on the automatically generated columns of data. You probably also want to allow programmers using your control to turn this feature off as well.

To set that property on the columns, the columns naturally have to exist, which doesn't happen until after data binding is complete. Luckily, the DataGridView control raises an event called DataBindingComplete when that occurs, giving you the perfect place to do this kind of post-databinding processing.

1. Add an event handler for the DataBindingComplete event by selecting the grid in the FilteredGrid control design surface, and name the handler OnGridDataBindingComplete.

2. Add a property and a corresponding private member to let users of your control set whether to autosize columns or not:

```
private bool m_AutoSizeColumns = false;
public bool AutoSizeColumns
{
    get { return m_AutoSizeColumns; }
    set { m_AutoSizeColumns = value; }
}

private void OnGridDataBindingComplete(object sender,
    DataGridViewBindingCompleteEventArgs e)
{
    if (m_AutoSizeColumns)
    {
        foreach (DataGridViewColumn col in m_Grid.Columns)
        {
            col.AutoSizeCriteria =
                DataGridViewAutoSizeColumnCriteria.HeaderAndRows;
        }
    }
}
```

The code for the DataBindingComplete event handler loops through each of the columns in the grid, setting the AutoSizeCriteria property to the appropriate enumerated value.

Winding Up the Filtered Grid Example

With that, you have a fairly complete functioning example of a custom data-bound control, created as a user control, containing other data-bound controls, and managed through a contained binding source. Approaching things this way gives you a clean way to encapsulate functionality in a single control that can be reused in many places, and lets you harness the powers of the built-in Framework data-bound controls to their full extent without having to know anything about them beyond their public properties, methods, and events.

You could certainly continue to enhance the capabilities of this control by surfacing additional properties on your control that you then delegate in appropriate ways to the contained controls and components. You might want to expose the contents of the filtered list so that other programmers can grab those filtered data items and do something with them as their own list. Obviously, caching all the autocomplete values of every row for the selected filter field in the grid in memory can be a scalability concern if you try to use this control for very large data sets. To address that, you would need to come up with a more robust way of populating the auto-complete list—or do away with that requirement. By doing things like this, you add capabilities to your control with minimal code, but limit what is exposed to the user of your control, which is a good approach to component-oriented development from an encapsulation point of view.

If you really want to expose the full API or a significant subset of it from the grid to the users of your control, you may want to expose just a property on your control that gives them direct access to a reference to the grid. However, that still won't give them access to the designer capabilities of working with a `DataGridView` control, so if you need to support that as well, you might need to step back to deriving a class from the `DataGrid-View` control. At that point you have to tackle the full complexities of integrating custom code into the processing model of the Framework control, which again requires pretty intimate knowledge of all of the control's internal details. An alternate approach would be to create a custom designer class for your control that provides similar capabilities to that of the `DataGridView`, as discussed in the sidebar "Supporting Rich Design-Time Declarative Programming."

The full `FilteredGrid` example and a sample hosting Windows Forms application are available in the CustomControls project download code for this book.

Supporting Rich Design-Time Declarative Programming

Selecting a control in the designer and setting properties or using context menus to alter the behavior of that control is a form of declarative programming. This is something that Windows Forms programmers have grown to expect from rich controls due to the support for this programming paradigm that Visual Studio provides. You have seen a few simple examples of providing rich designer support in the attributes that you added to the `Data-Source` and `DataMember` properties in the `FilteredGrid`. You will see a few others with the `ToolboxItem` and `ToolboxBitmap` attributes in the next example.

You should also include `Description` and `Category` attributes for any properties that will be exposed in the Properties window. You have seen that any properties added to your control that have types recognized by Visual Studio will be automatically displayed in the Properties window when your control is selected. You will be able to edit those properties with the editors associated with that type in Visual Studio.

Visual Studio provides a great deal of capability that enables you to go well beyond this. You can use a variety of other attributes to influence other design-time behaviors, and you can create custom type converters that allow the Properties window to convert input strings into complex types that the Properties window wouldn't ordinarily recognize. You can design custom editors that can plug into the Properties window so you can edit your complex types in a rich graphical way, similar to the `Anchor` property on form controls or the Color selection dialog that is presented for properties of type `Color`.

You can also create separate designer classes that you associate with your control to provide alternative or supplemental rendering of your control when it is hosted in the designer as opposed to how it presents itself at runtime. These capabilities are outside the scope of this book, but you can read more about them in a variety of sources on Windows Forms designer support programming. For adding design-time features to controls, I recommend *Windows Forms Programming in C#* by Chris Sells. Chris Sells and Mike Weinhardt wrote a two-part series on the topic for *MSDN* magazine in the April and May 2003 issues.

Building a Custom Data-Bound Control from Scratch

So far I have presented examples of deriving from a built-in Framework control or developing a user control that contains other controls and exposing a data-binding interface on that user control. However, sometimes you may need to build custom controls that aren't simple containment scenarios for existing Framework controls, and you may want to support data binding on these controls as well. If you can at least handle containing a binding source component as a child component of your control, you can let it do most of the data-binding dirty work, as you saw in the last example with the `FilteredGrid`. That control inherently supports all the myriad forms of data collections that the Framework controls do, simply because it is using a binding source to sort the data from whatever is provided as a data source and data member.

In case you need to be more directly in the loop for rendering your control and accessing the data that is bound to it, you may have to eschew the support of the binding source and drop back to dealing with different forms of data collections yourself. If you do this, one approach would be to handle all the different interface types described in Chapter 7 directly, figuring out whether you have a list, a list of lists, a list of lists of lists, and so on, and figuring out type information and sorting and filtering capabilities on your own. There is still some other support in the Windows Forms classes that can save you some of this grunt work without using a binding source, as you will see in the next example. So to demonstrate getting a little "closer to the metal" and how to implement a data-bound control that doesn't rely on any Framework controls for its data binding, let's jump right into another example.

Building a Data-Bound Charting Control for Decision Support

The scenario for this sample control is that you need to build a data-bound charting control that will render bar chart data for comparative purposes to help decision makers...well, make decisions based on that data. You can call this decision support, knowledge management, business intelligence, or whatever your favorite buzzword is for this kind of functionality.

Obviously, to create a production-capable rich graphic control that executives would use to make billion dollar decisions is going to take a little more code than I have room or time for in this chapter. So I am going to limit the functionality and presentation graphics to a fairly crude and simple set of bar charts that can be generated dynamically from data with an appropriate shape.

This example will support users who are going to provide sets of data to the control. The sets of data contain numeric data series representing categories that I want to compare on two axes. Each row of data represents some entity; within each row will be sets of numeric fields, which each represent some category of data supported by each entity that the row represents. By presenting each row as a series of graphical bars, decision makers can quickly scan complex numerical data looking for trends and indicators. For example, consider a set of data where each row represents a sales year, and then within that row are data fields containing the net sales amounts for each sales region in your organization. If you had that kind of scenario and wanted to let executives quickly review that data for comparison purposes between years and regions, you could present it as shown in Figure 8.9.

As soon as you start designing for specialized data-binding scenarios like this, you step out of the realm of the generalized data binding that the Framework controls support. In this case, we have specified that the data

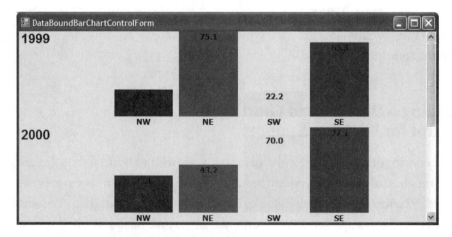

FIGURE 8.9: DataBoundBarChartControl in Action

that the control supports needs to have a particular shape. We could make this more explicit by perhaps defining a specific interface that the data collections have to support, say `IDecisionSupportDataList`, and then program against methods or properties exposed by that interface. This would model what the Framework controls do with respect to assuming that the data supports the `IList` interface. However, for many scenarios that may be overkill, and you will just want to support a particular shape of data based on assumptions of what you should find in data sources bound to the control, and then handle errors accordingly if those assumptions aren't met. That is how we'll approach things in this example. Defining a separate interface that describes a certain kind of data collection might make sense if you were going to define multiple controls that made the same assumptions about the shape of the data, but that would impose an additional nonstandard implementation burden on any data collections you want to use with your controls, which would limit its usability.

So let's design a control that looks like Figure 8.9. It should provide the data that drives the presentation dynamically in a way that models the data-binding support in the Framework Windows Forms controls. Additionally, it should support both relational data sources, such as data sets, as well as custom business object collections. The data collections provided as a data source and data member are expected to have a single column or property that is the row identifier and will be used to label the row. They are also expected to have any number of additional columns or properties of numeric types that will be used to generate the bars with their values and property names.

Creating a Custom Control That Draws Itself

To get started, you need to write the code that will do the graphical rendering of the bars for each row. Because this functionality is going to be invoked repeatedly for each row, and it is separable from the code that worries about the data binding to the collections of data that provide each row, it makes sense to separate out the rendering functionality into its own control. This control will be a custom control derived from the `Control` base class, because it is responsible for doing all its own drawing of its client area and will be named `BarChartControl`. Because this control won't be used outside of the containing data-bound control (called `DataBound-BarChartControl`) that will render instances of the `BarChartControl`, you will make this class internal to the `CustomControls` assembly and won't expose it in the Toolbox for other programmers to add directly to their forms.

Most of the implementation of the `BarChartControl` is a bunch of mundane geometric and graphics rendering code that I won't go into the details of here. You can see all the details if you download the Custom-Controls sample code for the book. The basic skeleton of the `BarChart-Control` class is shown in Listing 8.7.

LISTING 8.7: BarChartControl Class

```
[ToolboxItem(false)]
internal class BarChartControl : Control, IDisposable
{
    BindingList<ChartPair> m_Data = new BindingList<ChartPair>();
    Font m_LabelFont = new Font("Tahoma", 10, FontStyle.Bold);

    internal BarChartControl() { ... }

    public IList<ChartPair> Data
    {
        get
        {
            return m_Data;
        }
    }

    private void UpdateCoordinates() { ... }

    protected override void OnPaint(PaintEventArgs e)
    { ... }

    protected override void Dispose(bool disposing)
    {
        try
        {
            m_LabelFont.Dispose();
        }
        finally
        {
            base.Dispose(disposing);
        }
    }
}
```

```
~BarChartControl()
{
    m_LabelFont.Dispose();
}
}
```

The class is declared as internal with a `ToolboxItem` attribute set to `false`, which prevents it from being added to the Toolbox, and the class is marked as `internal` to prevent using it outside of the declaring assembly. The `BarChartControl` class derives from both the base `Control` class and the `IDisposable` interface. The `IDisposable` interface implementation is needed (as well as a finalizer) because the class contains a member variable containing a `Font` object, which is itself a disposable object. To ensure that the `Font` object gets properly cleaned up when users of your `BarChart-Control` are done with the control, you need to release that `Font` object when your control is released, which is what the `Dispose` and finalizer methods take care of.

Defining a Custom Data Structure for Rendering

The data that the control uses to render the bars is contained in a member data collection created from a generic `BindingList<T>` type (the `Binding-List<T>` type is discussed in the next chapter). In this case, the `BindingList<T>` is used as a container for pairs of data contained in instances of `ChartPair` objects. The `ChartPair` object is a simple container for a value and a label associated with each bar:

```
internal class ChartPair
{
    public string m_Label;
    public double m_Value;

    public ChartPair(string label, double value)
    {
        Label = label;
        Value = value;
    }

    public string Label
    {
        get {return m_Label; }
        set {m_Label = value;}
```

```
    }
    public double Value
    {
        get {return m_Value; }
        set {m_Value = value;}
    }
}
```

Again, this type is an implementation detail of the control, so it too is marked as `internal`. The data used by the control is exposed through an `IList` property named `Data`, so that the data can be populated and accessed by its containing control. There are some other member variables not shown here that are used for storing the bar and label rectangles, as well as minimum and maximum values used by the drawing code.

The control has an `UpdateCoordinates` method that is called to recalculate the coordinates of the bars and labels when needed based on the data, and an override of the `Control.OnPaint` method, which is where it does all the rendering of the bars based on the coordinates computed in `UpdateCoordinates`. Again, if you want to see the details of how it does all this, grab the download code. It is not super-involved; it only has about 100 lines of code.

Coding a Data-Bound Custom Control

Once the `BarChartControl` control has been coded and debugged (by making it public and allowing a containing form to populate the data directly), you can create the data-bound containing control that creates and populates an instance of the `BarChartControl` for each row of analysis data. In this example I created this as a user control to be able to automatically provide a scroll bar to use when more rows of data (`BarChartControl` instances) are added that can be presented within the control's size.

Because the control is supposed to support data binding in a fashion similar to other data-bound controls, it will need `DataSource` and `DataMember` properties. The control presentation's coupling to part of the individual data items in the bound collection (the need to use one of the fields in each data item as a label for the row) requires that the control also needs a property that lets users of the control specify what the field or property name is that contains the row identifier. This is similar in concept to the function of the

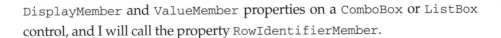

DisplayMember and ValueMember properties on a ComboBox or ListBox control, and I will call the property RowIdentifierMember.

Defining the Custom Control Skeleton

The basic skeleton of the class definition is shown in Listing 8.8.

LISTING 8.8: DataBoundBarChartControl Class

```
[ToolboxBitmap(typeof(DataBoundBarChartControl), "IDesignIcon.bmp")]
public partial class DataBoundBarChartControl : UserControl,
    ISupportInitialize
{
    private object m_DataSource;
    private string m_DataMember;
    private string m_RowIdMember;
    private bool m_Initializing = false;

    public DataBoundBarChartControl()
    {
        InitializeComponent();
    }

    [Editor("System.Windows.Forms.Design.DataMemberListEditor,
        System.Design, Version=2.0.0.0, Culture=neutral,
        PublicKeyToken=b03f5f7f11d50a3a", typeof(UITypeEditor))]
    public string DataMember
    {
        get { return m_DataMember; }
        set
        {
            m_DataMember = value;
            UpdateDataBinding();
        }
    }

    [AttributeProvider(typeof(IListSource))]
    public object DataSource
    {
        get { return m_DataSource; }
        set
        {
            m_DataSource = value;
            UpdateDataBinding();
        }
    }

    public string RowIdentifierMember
```

continues

```
      {
          get { return m_RowIdMember; }
          set
          {
              m_RowIdMember = value;
              UpdateDataBinding();
          }
      }


      private void UpdateDataBinding() { ... }

      public void BeginInit()
      {
          m_Initializing = true;
      }

      public void EndInit()
      {
          m_Initializing = false;
          UpdateDataBinding();
      }
  }
```

The DataBoundBarChartControl class is derived from UserControl and implements the ISupportInitialize interface, which lets it control its data binding when in an initialization phase. The ToolboxBitmap attribute is applied to the control class and sets what the icon is that will be used for the control when it is added to the designer's Toolbox. The file name specified is the name of a 16 x 16 bitmap that is added to the project and marked as an embedded resource.

The DataSource and DataMember properties are declared in a fashion similar to that described for the FilteredGrid example, except that in this case you aren't containing a binding source that you can delegate to. Instead, this control saves the DataSource and DataMember properties in member variables on the control class that it can use to do the data binding whenever it is appropriate. The set portions of these properties also call the UpdateDataBinding method, which is where the actual data-binding code lives. (We will get to the implementation of that method shortly.) A RowIdentifierMember property is also exposed to identify which property on the data items should be used for rendering the labels next to each bar chart instance.

Initializing and Updating the Data Bindings

The implementation of the `ISupportInitialize`, `BeginInit`, and `EndInit` methods prevents data binding from occurring during initialization by setting a flag that is checked by the `UpdateDataBinding` method (`m_Initializing`), and data binding is deferred until initialization is complete by calling that method explicitly from the `EndInit` method.

The implementation of the `UpdateDataBinding` method requires you to reach into the data source, locate the data collection specified by the data member (if there is one), and iterate through the data items to render the bar charts. Although that doesn't sound overly complicated, it can get very involved if you consider that the data source could be a data set, a data table, an array, a custom collection, a list of lists of lists, and so on. Covering all those different scenarios can get very complex. It basically involves taking the data source and trying to cast it to one of the various interfaces described in Chapter 7. Once you discover what kind of a collection it is, based on the interfaces it implements, you can use the interface implementations and the `DataMember` to determine the actual list of data that you want to bind to. Luckily, most of the grunt work of doing this has been exposed through a static method on the `ListBindingHelper` class called `GetList`.

Listing 8.9 shows the implementation of the `UpdateDataBinding` method.

LISTING 8.9: UpdateDataBinding Method

```
private void UpdateDataBinding()
{
    if (m_Initializing)
        return;
    if (m_DataSource == null || m_RowIdMember == null)
        return;

    IList list = ListBindingHelper.GetList(m_DataSource, m_DataMember)

        as IList;
    if (list == null || list.Count < 0)
        return;

    // Get the property descriptors for the items
```

continues

```
PropertyDescriptorCollection objProps =
   TypeDescriptor.GetProperties(list[0]);

// Loop through the items, extracting the row identifier member
// and binding each of the other numeric columns as ChartPairs
int vertPos = 0;
for (int index = 0; index < list.Count; index++)
{
    object obj = list[index];
    // Locate the row identifier property in the object
    PropertyDescriptor propDesc =
       objProps.Find(m_RowIdMember, true);
    if (propDesc == null)
    {
        continue; // Not a valid row
    }

    // Code to add a label based on the row identifier omitted...

    AddBarChartControl(index, 150, vertPos,obj,objProps);
    vertPos += 150;
}
}
```

This method first checks to see if the control is initializing; if so, it does nothing. If it isn't initializing, the method checks to make sure that, at a minimum, there is a data source and row identifier to work with. Then it calls the `GetList` method on the `ListBindingHelper` class. This method does a lot of complex work for you, based on the various data-binding interfaces discussed in Chapter 7. Basically what it does is to first check the data source to see if it implements the `IListSource` interface. If so, it uses the `GetList` method on that interface to get back a list. It then checks the data member and tries to resolve that data member on the data source and return that as a list. It goes through a few other gyrations, handling different combinations of lists of lists, data member vs. no data member, and so on, but basically it takes care of trying to find a valid `IList` collection from the provided data source and data member. If it fails to find a valid collection to work with, the data-binding method gives up and returns `null`.

Once the list has been determined from the data source and member, the code reaches into the list, again using property descriptors, and locates the field or property containing the row identifier label and gets its value. The method then creates an instance of a `Label` control, sets appropriate properties on that control, and adds it to the Controls collection of your custom control to render the row identifier label. The code for this is omitted because it is just rudimentary Windows Forms control initialization code like that the designer generates every time you drag and drop a Label control onto a form and set its Text property. Next the loop calls the AddBarChartControl method.

Adding Bar Chart Instances to the Container

The AddBarChartControl method gets the property descriptors for all of the columns or properties in the corresponding data item, determines if the field is a numeric type based on the property descriptor's PropertyType property, and then extracts the field name and value and adds a corresponding ChartPair to the Data property of the bar chart. This method is shown in Listing 8.10.

LISTING 8.10: AddBarChartControl Method

```
private void AddBarChartControl(int index, int xpos, int ypos,
    object dataItem, PropertyDescriptorCollection objProps)
{
    BarChartControl bar = new BarChartControl();
    m_BarIndexes.Add(bar, index);
    bar.Location = new Point(xpos, ypos);
    bar.Size = new Size(ClientSize.Width-250, 150);
    Controls.Add(bar);
    bar.Data.Clear();

    foreach (PropertyDescriptor propDesc in objProps)
    {
        Type propType = propDesc.PropertyType;
        string propName = propDesc.DisplayName;
        if (propName == m_RowIdMember)
            continue;

        double propVal;
        if (propType == typeof(int) ||
                propType == typeof(short) ||
                propType == typeof(float) ||
                propType == typeof(double) ||
                propType == typeof(long))
        {
            object val = propDesc.GetValue(dataItem);
            propVal = Convert.ToDouble(val);
```

continues

```
    }
    else if (propType == typeof(string))
    {
        bool converted =
            double.TryParse((string)propDesc.GetValue(dataItem),
            out propVal);
        if (!converted)
            continue;
    }
    else
    {
        continue;
    }
    bar.Data.Add(new ChartPair(propName, propVal));
    }
}
```

The AddBarChartControl method creates an instance of a BarChart-Control, initializes it size and location, and adds it to the Controls collection of the container user control. It then loops through each of the properties on the data item that was passed in, and if it is a numeric type, or is a string that can be converted to a numeric type, then a corresponding ChartPair is added to the Data collection of the bar chart control.

Notice the use of the new TryParse method on the double class. Each primitive class in .NET has a Parse method that has been there since version 1.0 of the Framework. The problem with the Parse method is that it will throw an exception if it fails to convert the string passed in—and throwing an exception is a very expensive operation and can seriously hinder your performance if it is done frequently. As a result, in version 2.0 of the Framework, each of the primitive types has had a TryParse method added, which lets you try to parse a string value into a value of the primitive type without throwing an exception. If the parsing succeeds, it returns a Boolean value of true, and you can use the value you passed in as the second (out) parameter to the method. If the return value is false, parsing was unsuccessful and should ignore the value that you passed in.

As you can see, there isn't a ton of code involved to handle the data binding yourself for basic iteration through a data source and presenting the data without a binding source, but there are a lot of things that aren't handled in the code so far, such as support for sorting, filtering, editing, adding new rows, and so on, which the binding source handles for you.

The `ListBindingHelper.GetList` method handles the initial probing and discovery aspects of locating an appropriate list in a data source. To handle all those other things requires working with a number of other interface types. You will usually want to harness the support of the binding source for these.

Adding Editing Support to a Custom Data Bound Control

Presenting data is really only one-way data binding—from the data source to the screen. Most Windows Forms data-bound controls support some sort of two-way data binding—letting the user modify values in the control, which directly modifies the values in the underlying data collection. There are a number of different levels to which you can take this. If you recall from Chapter 7, the `IList` interface contains a Boolean property named `IsReadOnly`, which returns `true` if the list isn't intended to be modified by the consumer of the list. The meaning of `IsReadOnly` can be interpreted in a number of ways, so the `IBindingList` interface refines this by adding `AllowEdit`, `AllowNew`, and `AllowRemove` properties to explicitly indicate whether the collection allows the editing of individual items in the collection, the addition of items, or the removal of items, respectively.

If you want to design a control to allow editing of the presented values, you need to use these interfaces to decide whether you should be trying to edit the collection of data represented by your data source and what kinds of edits you should allow.

As a simple example, let's add some modifications to the `BarChart-Control` and `DataBoundBarChartControl` to let users edit the presented values in a crude fashion. Specifically, end users can left-click on a bar to increase its value by 10 percent, or right-click on a bar to decrease its value by 10 percent. The control should only allow this interaction when the data is editable, meaning that the list is not read-only, and that if the collection supports the `IBindingList` interface, it specifically says that it allows editing of the contained values.

To support this functionality, the first step is to modify the `BarChart-Control` to support the form of editing described earlier. This involves adding a property to indicate whether the bar should be editable based on the data it was created from, and a mouse-click handler to detect and react to mouse clicks if the control is in editable mode. There also needs to be a way to propagate the changed values back out to the containing control, which will be responsible for pushing them into the underlying data collection.

The modifications to the `BarChartControl` are shown in Listing 8.11.

LISTING 8.11: Changes to the BarChartControl for Edit Support

```
internal delegate void BarChartChangedEventHandler(
    object sender, int barIndex);

internal class BarChartControl : Control, IDisposable
{
    //... other members
    BindingList<ChartPair> m_Data = new BindingList<ChartPair>();
    public event BarChartChangedEventHandler DataValueChanged;

    internal BarChartControl()
    {
        ...
        m_Data.ListChanged += new
            ListChangedEventHandler(OnDataListChanged);
    }

    public bool AllowEdit
    {
        get { return m_Data.AllowEdit; }
        set { m_Data.AllowEdit = value; }
    }

    protected override void OnMouseClick(MouseEventArgs mea)
    {
        base.OnMouseClick(mea);
        if (!m_Data.AllowEdit)
            return;

        for (int index = 0; index < m_BarRects.Count; index++)
        {
            Rectangle barRect = m_BarRects[index];
            if (barRect.Contains(mea.Location))
            {
                ChartPair pair = m_Data[index];
                if (mea.Button == MouseButtons.Left)
                {
                    pair.Value = pair.Value + pair.Value * .1;
```

```
        }
        else
        {
            pair.Value = pair.Value - pair.Value * .1;
        }
        m_Data[index] = pair;
        UpdateCoordinates();
        break;
        }
    }
}
void OnDataListChanged(object sender, ListChangedEventArgs e)
{
    UpdateCoordinates();
    if (DataValueChanged != null &&
        e.ListChangedType == ListChangedType.ItemChanged)
    {
        DataValueChanged(this, e.NewIndex);
    }
}
}
```

The way that the control supports editing is to add a handler for mouse-click events and to modify the values of the chart pairs contained in the control directly. However, to support two-way data binding, those changes have to be propagated outside of the control to the containing control so that the data-bound container control can update the data source from whence the values came. To support that, the control needs to raise an event that indicates that the bar was changed and which value within it changed. To support raising that event, the code in Listing 8.11 starts with a delegate definition called `BarChartChangedEventHandler`. This delegate's parameters include a reference to the object (the control) that is firing the event, as well as the index of the data item that was modified. A corresponding event is declared on the `BarChartControl` class called `DataValueChanged`; it is this event that will be subscribed and handled by the containing data-bound charting control.

The data presented in the control can change in one of two ways: an end user clicking on a bar in the control, or programmatically outside the control through the `Data` property reference to the collection of `ChartPairs`. For the changes that are made directly to the data in the mouse-click event handler, you could raise the `DataValueChanged` event handler yourself.

But how are you supposed to know when a data value has changed *inside* of the data collection of chart pairs if it is done *outside* of the control?

This is the reason that I implemented the collection using the `Binding-List<T>` generic type. That type can automatically provide support for `ListChanged` events, even for modifications to the contained data values through bound controls. So by simply containing your data values inside a `BindingList<T>` type, and then handling the `ListChanged` event from that type, you can be notified any time a contained value changes, whether you did it yourself or whether it is done externally through the `Data` property reference. This lets you centralize your handling for changing values to one place, which is simply to tell the control to update itself (through the `UpdateCoordinates` method), and to fire the `DataValueChanged` event if the change type is an edited value and if there are any subscribers.

The `AllowEdit` property gets or sets the corresponding property on the contained `BindingList<T>` collection, which is checked by the mouse-click event handler to decide whether to process the mouse click as an edit. The mouse-click event handler does some simple hit detection on the rectangles calculated and stored by the `UpdateCoordinates` method, and if it sees that a mouse click is inside one of the bars, it increases or decreases the value by 10 percent, depending on which mouse button was clicked.

Now you need to add the corresponding support to the `DataBound-BarChartControl` control to update the corresponding data source if appropriate and control the editability of the individual bar chart controls. The modified portions of the control are shown in bold in Listing 8.12.

LISTING 8.12: Changes to DataBoundBarChartControl for Editing Support

```
public partial class DataBoundBarChartControl :
   UserControl, ISupportInitialize
{
   //... other members
   private bool m_UpdateableDataSource = false;
   private Hashtable m_BarIndexes = new Hashtable();
   private IList m_BoundList = null;

   private void UpdateDataBinding()
   {
      //... guard conditions
```

```
        IList list = CurrencyManager.GetList(m_DataSource,
    m_DataMember) as IList;
        if (list == null)
            return;
        m_BoundList = list;

        m_UpdateableDataSource = !list.IsReadOnly;
        IBindingList blist = list as IBindingList;
        if (blist != null)
        {
            // we have more fine grained info about editability

            m_UpdateableDataSource = blist.AllowEdit;
        }
        // The rest of the implementation...
    }

    private void AddBarChartControl(int index, int xpos,
        int ypos, object dataItem,
        PropertyDescriptorCollection objProps)
    {
        BarChartControl bar = new BarChartControl();
        m_BarIndexes.Add(bar, index);
        bar.DataValueChanged += OnBarChartChanged;
        bar.AllowEdit = m_UpdateableDataSource;
    // rest of implementation...
    }

    void OnBarChartChanged(object sender, int barIndex)
    {
        BarChartControl bar = (BarChartControl)sender;
        // Get the index of the bar in the collection
        int index = (int)m_BarIndexes[sender];
        // Get the corresponding item out of the data collection
        object item = m_BoundList[index];
        // Get the data value that changed
        ChartPair pair = bar.Data[barIndex];
        // Find the property on the data item
        PropertyDescriptorCollection props =
            TypeDescriptor.GetProperties(item);
        PropertyDescriptor prop = props.Find(pair.Label, true);
        if (prop == null)
            throw new ArgumentException("Unable to find " +
            pair.Label + " property on data item to make change.");

        if (prop.PropertyType == typeof(double))
        {
            prop.SetValue(item, pair.Value);
```

continues

```
        }
        else if (prop.PropertyType == typeof(float))
        {
            prop.SetValue(item, (float)pair.Value);
        }
        else if (prop.PropertyType == typeof(int))
        {
            prop.SetValue(item, (int)pair.Value);
        }
        else if (prop.PropertyType == typeof(long))
        {
            prop.SetValue(item, (long)pair.Value);
        }
        else if (prop.PropertyType == typeof(short))
        {
            prop.SetValue(item, (short)pair.Value);
        }
        else if (prop.PropertyType == typeof(string))
        {
            prop.SetValue(item, pair.Value.ToString());
        }
        else
        {
            throw new InvalidCastException("Cannot convert to type "
                + prop.PropertyType.ToString());
        }
    }
}
```

To keep track of enough information to change the bound data list when a change occurs inside an individual instance of a bar chart control, several new members had to be added:

- A flag to indicate whether you are dealing with an updatable data source
- A Hashtable to contain mappings between each instance of a bar chart control and its corresponding item index in the list of data
- A reference to the data list itself, to avoid having to resolve it through the currency manager more than once

When the data source is updated and UpdateDataBinding is called, you hold on to a reference to the bound list and set the flag that indicates whether the source is updated based on either the IList.IsReadOnly flag or the `IBindingList.AllowEdit` property, depending on whether the list's data source implements `IBindingList`.

When each bar chart control is added to your `Controls` list, the containing control subscribes to its `DataValueChanged` event and sets its editability based on that of the list. Finally, the handler for the `DataValueChanged` event on any of the contained bar chart controls uses the sender object reference to the control, along with the changed bar index, to reach back into that control, extract the changed value, find the corresponding value in the bound data list based on the index stored in the `Hashtable` for that object, and set its value depending on the actual type of the value in the list.

With those changes, you now have a data-bound custom control that supports presenting and editing data from a bound data source. Obviously there are a lot of things that you would want to add to a production control, such as a little better look-and-feel, more customizability, and better designer support as discussed earlier. If you expected other controls in a form to be bound to the same set of data, you would want to monitor other forms of `ListChanged` events on the data (based on the `ListChangedType` event argument property) and possibly subscribe to the currency manager's `CurrentItemChanged` event, as was done in the filtered grid example, to monitor context changes to the data from other bound controls.

Where Are We?

This chapter explored three ways to create custom data-bound controls: subclassing Framework controls, creating a user control that contains Framework data-bound controls, and creating a data-bound control from scratch. In the process, you got some exposure to how many of the interfaces described in the last chapter were used from a control's perspective as a consumer.

Some key takeaways from this chapter are:

- Inheriting from Framework controls is great for customizing simple presentation aspects of the control, but it is difficult to modify the data-binding behavior without a great deal of study of the protected members and interrelated behavior of those members in the class.

- Control containment is a better way to go for most custom controls, as shown in the filtered grid example.
- Building a generalized data-bound control from scratch is a lot of work, but building one that is specific to a given use case and a specific shape of data is much easier to tackle.
- The `ListBindingHelper` class makes it easy to obtain an appropriate `IList` reference from a data source without having to test for all the various related interface types yourself.

In the next chapter we'll jump to the other side of the data-binding fence—to the data collection and object side, and you'll see how to create custom objects and collections of objects that are suitable for data binding in Windows Forms.

9

Implementing Custom Data-Bound Business Objects and Collections

T HROUGHOUT MOST OF the samples in this book I have used relational data sources, specifically typed data sets, as the data source to which you connect binding sources and controls from the form's perspective. There are several reasons for this. One is that the predominate way of storing application data is in relational databases, and thus bringing the data into your application as a relational data collection provides a low impedance mismatch between the data that your application operates on and the data that your application persists and loads. Another is that the use of relational data in the presentation tier is still the most common way of presenting collections of data and letting users interact with that data. And the final reason is that in the past, it has typically been easier to work with relational data in data-binding scenarios than it was to work with custom business objects, partly because of the tools and the effort required to properly define business objects and collections of those objects that are suitable for data binding.

The problem with using relational data in the presentation layer is that it makes it more likely that your application will be tightly coupled from the data tier all the way into the presentation layer. When you are tightly coupled in this way, small changes in the data schema at the database level require changes all the way through your data access, business, and presentation layers. You are forced to go find all the places in your application that touched a particular part of your database so that you can update the data access that is working against that data. This doesn't have to be the case, because you can decouple your business layer through a combination of stored procedures and defining separate data set types in the business layer from those defined in the data access layer. But sometimes defining custom business objects makes more sense than to decouple your business layer and give you more explicit control of everything that is going on in the objects that you use for data presentation and manipulation.

Luckily in .NET 2.0, in both the Windows Forms and ASP.NET portions of the Framework, it is far easier than in previous versions of the Framework to work with custom object collections and still get a rich data-binding experience, both at design time and runtime. It still requires more work than using data sets, but the tooling and the classes in the .NET Framework have significantly reduced the amount of work involved.

Chapter 5 showed how you can use the Data Sources window to add an object data source, which allows you to bind to collections of objects and follow the same process of connecting and configuring that data source to your bound controls. This chapter focuses on what it takes from the perspective of the data objects and collections to be suitable for use in data binding, and how to implement custom objects and collections to maximize their capabilities in a data-binding scenario.

Defining and Working with Data-Bound Business Objects

A lot of people object to the term *business object* (pun intended). What *is* a business object? If your application is a game, are your objects really "business" objects? Probably not. But for the purposes of this book, it helps to have a common term to use to refer to "those objects that are part of your application that are neither presentation nor data access; that usually have some logic, rules, validation, or workflow embedded; may contain data themselves; and live somewhere between what the user sees on the screen and the code that executes queries against your data store." So I'll use the term *business object*, but you can expand it to this more detailed definition every time mentally if you prefer.

Business objects come in many forms. Some may be pure data containers, others may just contain logic—code that manipulates data that comes from somewhere else—and some may be a mix of the two. The bottom line for the purposes of presenting data in Windows applications is that some business objects can contain data, and you may want to use that object directly to present that data. If that's the case, you would really like to use them in the same way that you use a data set—point the data source to a collection of these objects or a single instance, and have the control do the work from there.

Achieving this data binding with business objects in .NET 2.0 is quite easy. As discussed in previous chapters, Windows Forms data binding is all based on a set of interfaces that define different capabilities of objects and collections within the context of accessing and navigating through data. As long as the objects that you are using for data binding support the appropriate interfaces, it will be transparent to data-bound controls that they are working with custom objects instead of the intrinsic .NET Framework relational data objects.

Just to make things more concrete, let me define a simple business object to use for some of the examples in this chapter. I will stick to a common construct and draw the parallels to the relational data used throughout the rest of the book. Specifically, let's say you want to work with `Customer` objects. These objects will define the data associated with a customer and may include some behavior, or logic, that operates on that data.

The following is a simple representative definition of a `Customer` object:

```
class Customer
{
    private string m_CustomerID;
    private string m_CustomerName;
    private string m_PhoneNumber;
    private string m_ContactName;

    public string CustomerID
    {
        get { return m_CustomerID; }
        set { m_CustomerID = value; }
    }
}
```

```
public string CustomerName
{
    get { return m_CompanyName; }
    set { m_CompanyName = value; }
}
// more properties...
}
```

As defined so far, the `Customer` class is a simple strongly typed container for some data values associated with a single business entity. Each of those data values is a primitive in .NET; in fact, they are all the easiest type of primitive to use for data binding—strings. If this were all there was to most business objects, our lives would be easy. But the reality is that when you transition to managing everything as business objects, there is usually a whole complex hierarchy of objects—and relationships between those objects—that are part of the object model and that you have to account for and manage when it comes to using those objects in a databinding scenario.

For the purposes of demonstration, this next example expands the `Customer` definition to include a couple of other related objects.

```
class Order
{
    private int m_OrderID;
    private Customer m_Customer;
    private DateTime m_OrderDate;
    private Employee m_SalesPerson;

    public int OrderID
    {
        get { return m_OrderID; }
        set { m_OrderID = value; }
    }

    public Customer Customer
    {
        get { return m_Customer; }
        set { m_Customer = value; }
    }

    public DateTime OrderDate
    {
        get { return m_OrderDate; }
        set { m_OrderDate = value; }
    }
```

```
    public Employee SalesPerson
    {
        get { return m_SalesPerson; }
        set { m_SalesPerson = value; }
    }

}

class Employee
{
    private int m_EmployeeID;
    private string m_Name;

    public int EmployeeID
    {
        get { return m_EmployeeID; }
        set { m_EmployeeID = value; }
    }

    public string Name
    {
        get { return m_Name; }
        set { m_Name = value; }
    }
}
```

This code models the way that a relational store manages object relationships: the child objects hold references to the parent objects through properties, specifically, the `Customer` and `SalesPerson` properties on the `Order` class. However, depending on the way you plan to use the objects, it is usually much more natural in an object-oriented system to allow easy navigation from the parent object down to the child objects through a collection property. The following code adds the modification to the `Customer` class to allow this.

```
class Customer
{
    // other members
    private BindingList<Order> m_Orders;

    public BindingList<Order> Orders
    {
        get { return m_Orders; }
        set { m_Orders = value; }
    }
    // other properties...
}
```

The `Orders` property on the `Customer` class uses the member `m_Orders` (which is a `BindingList<Order>`, a generic strongly typed collection of `Order` references) to allow direct access to all the related orders from a customer object. This may or may not make sense based on the way your objects are going to be used. If you are going to use `Customer` objects in a number of contexts, and in some of those contexts orders aren't relevant or wouldn't be in scope, then having `Orders` as a property on your `Customer` class could be considered to be polluting your `Customer` class definition with details that don't always belong there. However, if there are a number of use cases in your application where you need to iterate through the orders associated with a customer, or you need to perform data binding against them for presentation purposes, then this is probably exactly what you want.

So when it comes to business object definitions and data binding, the main thing that you are concerned with is the properties that they expose that represent the state or data contained in that entity. Those properties may represent single valued objects, such as numbers, strings, or dates, or they may represent references to other entities, single or multi-valued.

There could also be any number of methods and events exposed on the object related to the logic that is embedded that operates on the object state. Those methods aren't usually directly involved in the data binding of that object to the UI, but there are several ways that they may be tied in. Properties exposed on a class can invoke any amount of functionality they need to in their get and set blocks—either other methods in the class, or even other methods on other objects that are held through member variables on the class. For example, you might call methods from the set blocks of your properties that check the values being set against business or validation rules before letting the property value change. Additionally, the other methods on the class can in general be invoked from anywhere at any time, and those methods can potentially alter the state of the object that is being used for data binding.

In a Windows Forms application, you usually want any changes in state in a data-bound object to be immediately updated and accessible in the application. So with data-bound business objects, you have to account for the fact that the contained data in the object could change at any time through mechanisms other than the data-bound UI, and you have to decide whether those changes should be immediately reflected in the bound controls. Once again, the ways these considerations manifest themselves is through the interfaces that the individual classes implement, as well as those that their containing collections implement. These will be discussed through the remaining sections in this chapter.

Defining and Working with Data-Bound Business Object Collections

When dealing with data, objects rarely exist as single instances of an object type in a system. Usually there are collections of objects of a particular type, and you often want to present those collections of objects together through a tabular interface or one where you can navigate through the objects to view them through the same interface and interact with them. To do that, you need some way to keep them all together and make them easily accessible within the same context. The way you do that is through an object type that contains a collection of other objects.

A good background in data structures is essential to becoming a good object-oriented systems programmer. If you aren't comfortable with the differences and core concepts of lists, sets, stacks, queues, and hash tables, I suggest picking up a good data structures book. As you have seen from the other chapters, the main collection data structure you will deal with in data binding is the list. Some of the other collection types have other semantics, such as the key-value pairs of a hash table, or the order that things go onto and come off of stacks and queues. Ultimately they are all just sets of data objects in memory that have some ordering to them and that can be accessed in a variety of ways. Most of the other collection types have ways to access their contents (such as the Keys and Values properties on a Hashtable) as collections as well.

The DataSet type is itself just a fancy collection class. It is a class that contains a collection of data tables (of type DataTable). The data tables contain collections of rows (of type DataRow) and columns (of type Data-Column). The equivalent to a business object with a data set is an instance of a row, and that row could be untyped (a DataRow instance) or typed, such as a `CustomersRow` in a typed data set containing customer data. So from that perspective, a typed data set row is really just an autogenerated business object that contains no logic associated with the contained data. However, because typed data rows and tables are defined as partial classes in the autogenerated code in .NET 2.0, you could even add business logic to them as well.

For other types of business objects, though, you will need to come up with an appropriate collection class to contain those objects. You could use some of the .NET Framework collection classes that have been available since .NET 1.0. Better yet, you can use the generic collection classes that are being introduced in .NET 2.0. Finally, in some specialized situations, you might need to implement your own custom collection classes. When you work with the Framework collection classes, you don't have to do much work at all, because in general they already implement most of the interfaces that you need for your collections to work nicely in a data-binding situation. But if you need to step into the deep end and implement completely custom collections, you will have a fair amount of work to do to implement the appropriate interfaces, depending on how rich the data-binding scenarios are that you want your class to support.

.NET Framework Generic Collection Classes

In .NET 1.1, you implemented custom collection classes using the `Collection-Base` class and its underlying `ArrayList`. This had some problems, because everything was stored and accessed as a raw `Object` reference under the covers, which incurs performance problems due to boxing and unboxing of value types and casting of any type. One of the most important new features at a Framework level in .NET 2.0 is the introduction of generics. You have already seen the use of generics in a number of samples in this book, and a full discussion of generics is beyond the scope of this book. However, the use of generic collection classes is core to building data-bound Windows Forms applications with custom business objects, because generic collections solve all of the problems discussed earlier in this chapter. (For a good understanding of generics and how they fit into other Framework programming capabilities, check out *Programming .NET Components*, second edition, by Juval Löwy.)

When you use generic collection classes, you effectively declare a new strongly typed collection class just by declaring an instance of the generic class with a parameterized type. For example, consider the following line of code:

```
List<Customer> m_Customers = new List<Customer>();
```

This line of code declares a member variable of type `List<Customer>` and creates an instance of that type. The generic type parameter is `Customer`, specifying that a new generic `List` type that contains `Customer` objects should be created. Generics are similar to C++ templates in syntax and concept, but the implementation is very different and more efficient. This simple declaration is equivalent in function, but far more efficient in storage and execution, to declaring a whole class such as that shown in Listing 9.1. It provides you with a type-safe collection class for containing any kind of object, just by declaring a new instance of the generic `List<T>` type with an appropriate type parameter (`T`) specifying the type of objects the collection is intended to hold. In fact, the `List<T>` class is more powerful than the `ArrayList` class in other ways. It includes advanced searching, sorting, and read-only options that you typically had to manually implement prior to .NET 2.0.

The `List<T>` type implements `IList`, `ICollection`, and `IEnumerable` for untyped data-binding support, and it implements generic versions of these interfaces as well (`IList<T>`, `ICollection<T>`, and `IEnumerable<T>`), giving you strongly typed access to the collection contents through interface-based programming. This lets you write more strongly typed and loosely coupled code to manipulate the contents of the collections programmatically through interface references, rather than programming directly against the specific collection type.

Because of the `IList` implementation on the `List<T>` type, you can easily data bind a collection of objects of any type by creating an instance of `List<T>` using the custom object type as the type parameter to the `List<T>` instance, as was shown earlier for the `Customer` type. Therefore, you can use an instance of a `List<T>` as the data source for binding to controls on a form, and you can also keep track of collections of child objects through a List<T> member on an object that contains references to the child objects.

Other generic collection classes have been added through the System.Collections.Generic namespace, including Dictionary<T>, Queue<T>, Stack<T>, and SortedDictionary<T>. An additional generic collection class that is extremely useful in data-binding scenarios is the BindingList<T> type, discussed later in this chapter. The Binding-List<T> type should actually be your first choice for collections of objects that you intend to use for data binding.

The CustomBusinessObjects Example

Let's look at a simple example. Say you have an application that needs to track customers and their related orders. You want to have a form that has two grids: one that shows a list of customers, and another that shows the list of orders associated with the selected customer in the first grid. This is a standard master-details kind of data-binding scenario, but now you want to support it with custom business objects instead of data sets. You first need to define the custom business object types that will contain the application's data, as shown in Listing 9.1.

LISTING 9.1: Customer and Order Classes

```
public class Customer
{
   private int m_CustomerId;
   private string m_Name;
   private List<Order> m_Orders = new List<Order>();

   public int CustomerId
   {
      get { return m_CustomerId; }
      set { m_CustomerId = value; }
   }

   public string CustomerName
   {
      get { return m_Name; }
      set { m_Name = value; }
```

```
        }

        public List<Order> Orders
        {
            get { return m_Orders; }
        }
    }

    public class Order
    {
        private int m_OrderId;
        private string m_ProductName;
        private Customer m_Customer;
        private DateTime m_OrderDate;

        public Customer Customer
        {
            get { return m_Customer; }
            set { m_Customer = value; }
        }

        public int OrderId
        {
            get { return m_OrderId; }
            set { m_OrderId = value; }
        }

        public string ProductName
        {
            get { return m_ProductName; }
            set { m_ProductName = value; }
        }

        public DateTime OrderDate
        {
            get { return m_OrderDate; }
            set { m_OrderDate = value; }
        }
    }
```

In this case, `Customer` objects contain a `CustomerName` and a `CustomerId` property, as well as an `Orders` property that contains the collection of orders associated with the customer. Note that the collection property `Orders` on the `Customer` class is a read-only property. Typically, if your class encapsulates a collection, you will want to maintain the lifetime of that collection internally. By exposing the collection through a `List<Order>` reference in this case, users of the `Customer` class can easily access the `Orders` collection, add `Order` object references to it, and basically use any part of the public API of the `List<T>` class. However, because it is a read-only property on the `Customers` class, they cannot replace that collection with a new one (which might result in the unintentional loss of order information) or set the collection reference to `null` (which might violate certain assumptions the `Customer` class code might make about the underlying `m_Orders` variable always containing a live instance of a collection).

`Order` objects consist of an `OrderId`, an `OrderDate`, and a `Product-Name`. They also contain a reference back to the `Customer` object to which they belong. Because you are dealing with object references, rather than copies of the data that they contain, there is nothing stopping you from maintaining references in both directions—from the parent to the children, and from the child to the parent as this example is doing. This tight coupling between the `Customer` and `Order` objects is often something you want to avoid, but it may make sense if you frequently need to navigate from the parent down to the children and from the children back to their parent. This is similar to the two-way navigation enabled by `Data-Relations` in related tables of a data set.

To support master-details types of data binding, the collection of children has to show up on the parent objects, as is the case with this `Customer` object. The link back from the `Order` to the `Customer` is just done for demonstration purposes in this case, but it does have some effect on the data-binding process, as you will see shortly.

Binding the Customers and Orders Objects to Form Controls

To demonstrate the use of these object types with data-bound controls, I put together the form shown in Figure 9.1. I used the designer to add the controls and components, but the rest is wired up in code—there is no magic being done by the designer-generated code other than declaring the members for the controls and components you see in the designer in Figure 9.1.

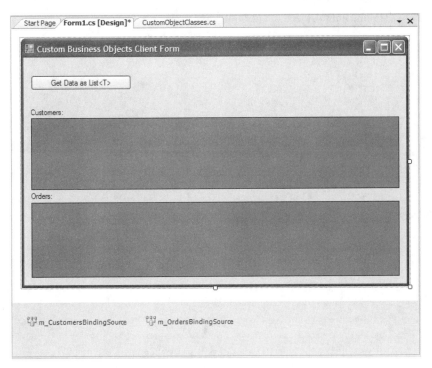

FIGURE 9.1: CustomBusinessObjectClient Sample Application

The two grids, `m_CustomersGrid` and `m_OrdersGrid`, top and bottom repectively, are intended to show a list of customers in the top grid with the orders for the selected customer shown in the bottom grid. Two binding sources, `m_CustomersBindingSource` and `m_OrdersBindingSource`, will be used to hook up their respective grids.

The `m_CustomersBindingSource` will be bound directly to a collection of `Customer` objects, and more specifically, starting with a `List<Customer>` collection. The `m_OrdersBindingSource` will be bound to the `m_CustomersBindingSource` as its `DataSource` property, with `DataMember` set to Orders—the `Orders` property on the `Customer` object, which is itself a `List<Order>` and therefore implements the `IList` interface, making it a candidate for data binding to a table.

To hook all this up and bind to some sample data, the form code looks like Listing 9.2.

LISTING 9.2: CustomBusinessObjectsClient Form Class

```
partial class Form1 : Form
{
  public Form1()
  {
    InitializeComponent();

    // Set up grid data binding
    m_CustomersGrid.DataSource = m_CustomersBindingSource;
    m_CustomersGrid.AutoGenerateColumns = true;

    m_OrdersGrid.DataSource = m_OrdersBindingSource;
    m_OrdersGrid.AutoGenerateColumns = true;
  }

  private void OnGetList(object sender, EventArgs e)
  {
    m_CustomersBindingSource.DataSource =
       TestDataGenerator.GetTestCustomers();
    // Set up expected relations between connectors
    m_OrdersBindingSource.DataSource = m_CustomersBindingSource;
    m_OrdersBindingSource.DataMember = "Orders";
  }
}
```

The constructor starts by setting each grid's DataSource to its respective binding source and then setting the AutoGenerateColumns to true. The rest of the data-binding initialization has to be deferred until the actual data is populated, because you cannot set up master-details type relations or refer to data members within a data source until that data member has been populated.

The OnGetList method is called based on a button-click from the form, and goes out to a test class within the project containing the Customer and Order object definitions shown earlier. It sets the data source of the m_CustomersBindingSource to the list of customers that is returned, then sets the child m_OrdersBindingSource data source and data member to set up the master-details data binding. This results in the data-binding graph shown in Figure 9.2.

In Figure 9.2, each grid is bound to its own binding source with its DataSource property pointing to that component. The customers binding

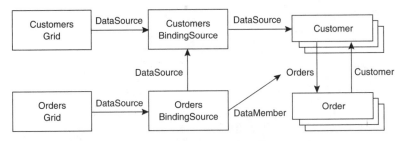

FIGURE 9.2: CustomBusinessObjectsClient Data-Binding Relationships

source is the one that is actually bound to the data source, by setting its `DataSource` property to the `List<Customer>` returned from the `GetTestCustomers` method. Its `DataMember` is left set to `null`. The orders binding source has its `DataSource` set to the customers' binding source and its `DataMember` set to Orders. This sets up the master-details binding so that it will only show the related collection of orders for whichever `Customer` object is the current object in the collection maintained by its parent binding source, as described in Chapters 3 and 4.

Generating Some Test Data to Bind Against

The `GetTestCustomers` static method on the `TestDataGenerator` static class that provides the runtime sample data is shown in Listing 9.3.

LISTING 9.3: GetTestCustomers Data Generation Method

```
public static List<Customer> GetTestCustomers()
{
    List<Customer> results = new List<Customer>();
    Customer c = new Customer();
    c.CustomerId = 1;
    c.CustomerName = "Barney's Biscuits";
    results.Add(c);

    Order o = new Order();
    o.Customer = c;
    o.OrderDate = new DateTime(2004, 12, 22);
    o.OrderId = 1;
    o.ProductName = "12 Pack Lambchops";
    c.Orders.Add(o);

    o = new Order();
    o.OrderId = 2;
```

continues

```
o.Customer = c;
o.OrderDate = new DateTime(2004, 7, 6);
o.ProductName = "2000 yards cellophane";
c.Orders.Add(o);

c = new Customer();
c.CustomerName = "Fred's Fritters";
c.CustomerId = 2;
results.Add(c);

o = new Order();
o.Customer = c;
o.OrderDate = new DateTime(2004, 9, 8);
o.OrderId = 3;
o.ProductName = "Deep fryer fat";
c.Orders.Add(o);
return results;
}
```

The `GetTestCustomers` method is a simple test data generation method, which creates a `List<Customer>` collection and then populates it with two `Customer` objects, each of which has some associated `Order` objects. Notice that the way client code uses the `Orders` collection on the `Customer` class is to just call methods on the `List<T>` class, such as `Add`, by referencing the `Orders` property itself and calling the methods on it. Also notice that the code sets the back reference from the `Order` object to its parent `Customer` object simply by setting the `Customer` property on the `Order` object to the instance of the `Customer` that is being created. Once the list has been constructed, the list is returned to the calling form and can be used for data binding.

If you code all this up, or download the CustomBusinessObjects sample from the book's download site, and run it, you should see the data populating both grids. Whatever the current customer is in the top grid should drive which orders are shown in the bottom grid, and the text boxes at the bottom should continue to show the current customer's properties, as shown in Figure 9.3.

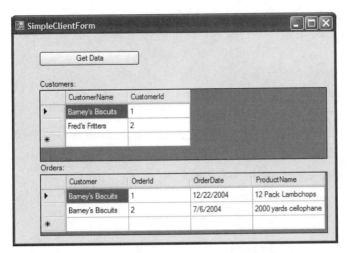

FIGURE 9.3: CustomBusinessObjectsClient in Action

Setting the Textual Data-Binding Behavior of Custom Objects

One thing that you will notice right off the bat is that if a single-valued property on a class is a reference type, such as the Customer property in the Order class, it will show up in the grid by default since this example autogenerates columns. Unfortunately, the values that show up there are not particularly meaningful, because what happens is that the grid calls the ToString method on those objects to get a string value for presentation in the grid cell as part of the formatting process. The same thing would happen if you bound that property for display in a ComboBox, ListBox, or TextBox control. The default ToString method inherited from the System.Object base class returns the fully qualified type name as a string, which probably isn't what you want to display.

You could handle this by not autogenerating columns and skipping the display of the Customer property in the grid. But depending on the situation, you may want the Customer property to be able to be used for data-binding scenarios, in which case you would want it to display something meaningful when it is used for binding to a textual control. The way to do this is to simply override the ToString method in your custom business object. In this example, this means adding a ToString override in the

Customer class, which you can implement by simply returning the customer name:

```
public override string ToString()
{
    return m_Name;
}
```

Now when you run the sample, the customer name for the parent customer will show up in the Customer column of the orders grid, instead of just the fully qualified type name repeating in every cell of that column.

Supporting Transacted Object Editing with IEditableObject

If you ran the CustomBusinessObjects sample from the last section, and edited a property on either a Customer or Order object in the grid, then tabbed into the next field, the edit to that property is immediately written to the underlying bound object property. If there are any other controls that are data bound to the same object and displaying it, you should see their display immediately update to the new value as well. This is because the change was made through a data-bound control, which notifies the currency manager controlling the data binding of the change, and that change will then be rippled to any other bound controls that are in communication with the same currency manager.

This behavior may or may not be what you want. Sometimes when you are editing an object, you want changes to that object to be treated in a transacted way, with all changes to properties of a single object being done all together or not at all. Say you have a custom object with three properties bound to controls on a form. You edit properties one and two of the object, and then something goes wrong while editing property three. Do you want the changes to properties one and two to remain in effect, or do you want them to revert to what they were before the editing operation on that object was initiated? Or perhaps you have interdependencies between properties, where the first property can only be between 1 and 10 if it is Tuesday, but otherwise must be between 10 and 20. If the second property tells you what day it is, you won't know whether you have a valid combination of row values until they have all been edited. In a transacted world, the changes to those properties could be rolled back to their previous values automatically if something went wrong or if you decided you wanted to abort the object editing process.

The `DataRowView` class has built-in support for this kind of thing, as does the `DataGridView`. If you have a data set bound to a grid and start editing the fields in a row and then press the Esc key, the changes you made to that row will be rolled back, changing the values back to their original values before the editing of that row commenced. If you shift the focus to a new row with the arrow keys, tab off the last field in a row, press the Enter key, or click on a different control or row in the form, the changes are accepted (committed), and you will no longer have the opportunity to revert them to their previous values.

Likewise, if your grid is set up to let users add new rows, and they commence entering values for a new row, those entered values have to go somewhere, and the grid is only displaying rows that are actually part of the bound table. So once you start editing fields within the empty row at the bottom of a grid that is marked with an asterisk in the row header cell, a new `DataRow` is actually added to the table and you are editing the fields in that row as you edit the row in the grid. But if you press the Esc key during the editing of the new row, the grid is able to remove the row from the table and pretend that it never existed. This is another form of transacted object editing, where a new object isn't considered to be fully part of the collection until the initial editing of that newly created object is complete. However, for data-binding display purposes, you usually need that object to physically be added to the collection before the editing is complete, so that the entered field or property values have an object in memory on which they can be set and which can be displayed by the normal data-binding mechanisms.

To support this kind of transacted editing of your objects in a form, you need to implement the `IEditableObject` interface on the custom object definition. This interface includes three methods that you need to implement on your class: `BeginEdit`, `EndEdit`, and `CancelEdit`. As you might expect, from a transaction perspective, these operations logically correspond to beginning a transaction, committing the transaction, and rolling back the transaction.

- `BeginEdit` should be called by a data-bound control when an editing operation is commenced against a single instance of an object.
- `EndEdit` should be called when the editing process is complete.
- If `CancelEdit` is called anytime between `BeginEdit` and `EndEdit`, any changes made since `BeginEdit` was called should be rolled back.
- `CancelEdit` shouldn't be called after `EndEdit` unless `BeginEdit` is called again to initiate a new transaction.

What you typically need to do inside the implementation of the interface methods is to cache changes to the object using some temporary variables to keep track of the property's original values before the editing operation commenced from the `BeginEdit` method. Then if editing is completed normally with a call to `EndEdit`, you can discard the cached original values and treat the current values of the properties as permanent. If `CancelEdit` is called, you should use the cached original values to reset the values of the object properties to their original values.

To do this on your simple `Customer` object type requires the following additions to the class:

```
public class Customer ( : IEditableObject )
{
    private int m_OldCustomerId;
    private string m_OldName;
    private bool m_Editing;
    // other fields, properties, and methods ...

    public void BeginEdit()
    {
        if (!m_Editing)
        {
            m_OldCustomerId = m_CustomerId;
            m_OldName = m_Name;
        }
        m_Editing = true;
    }

    public void CancelEdit()
    {
```

```
    if (m_Editing)
    {
        CustomerId = m_OldCustomerId;
        CustomerName = m_OldName;
    }
    m_Editing = false;
}

public void EndEdit()
{
    m_Editing = false;
}
}
```

First, you add the `IEditableObject` interface to your class definition. You then need somewhere to stuff the cached original values of properties when an edit operation is in progress. To keep the sample simple, this just caches the values of the object's name and ID properties in additional private fields on the class named `m_OldCustomerId` and `m_OldName`. For a more complex object with many fields, having two of every field would get cluttered, so you could also simplify this process by creating a new instance of your custom object type, populating its fields with the original values, and holding a private reference to that object as the original values to revert to if `CancelEdit` is called. Note that this sets the current values through the properties, rather than directly on the member variables. The reason for this will become apparent in the next section.

As you can see from the code, the `BeginEdit` method stores the current values of the fields in the cached fields and sets a flag to indicate that you are in edit mode. This is necessary because depending on how data binding is hooked up, `BeginEdit` will likely be called multiple times by the form, and you want to store the old values just when the edit operation really begins, not repeatedly as the rest of the editing process gets going.

`EndEdit` effectively accepts the current values by setting the editing flag back to `false`. `CancelEdit` rolls back the changes by setting the current property values back to the original value using the cached values.

By implementing `IEditableObject` like this, your custom business objects will now behave like a data set when being edited in a grid like the `DataGridView`. Specifically, if several properties of a given row have been edited, and the user presses the Esc key, the changes will be rolled back and the original values will be reset on the object.

This simple implementation doesn't account for the fact that conceptually the `Orders` collection could also be changed as part of the logical editing of a `Customer` object. You would want to be able to roll back those changes as well since they are child objects, and conceptually they are "part of" a `Customer` object. However, since the `IEditableObject` interface is primarily used in a data-binding context, you would have to switch the focus to the `Orders` grid to modify the `Orders` collection associated with the selected `Customer`, and that change of control focus is going to call `EndEdit` on the `Customer` object anyway. There may be more advanced scenarios where you might want to use the `IEditableObject` implementation to support fully transacted editing of an object, whether through a bound control or through programmatic edits, but that isn't really what it was designed for.

Supporting Object Edit Notifications with Property Change Events

Another problem people frequently encounter when first trying to use collections of objects as their data source is detecting changes in the bound data objects if those changes aren't made directly through the bound control getting or setting properties on the object. When you change an object property by editing it through a bound control, the control will change the values through the property descriptors for the object. Containers for those objects, such as the binding source, can hook up a callback to be notified when the property values are changed through the property descriptor (as discussed in Chapter 7 and demonstrated later in this chapter). When this happens, other controls that are bound directly or indirectly to the same source can be updated by the container raising `ListChanged` events on the `IBindingList` interface implementation.

However, if an object property's value changes behind the scenes due to other means, the values presented in a bound control won't automatically be updated. For example, you could have a background thread that is continuously updating the objects based on some activity that it is monitoring, or you could have another control in the form, such as a button, invoke some code that modifies an object in memory directly.

For example, if you add a button to your form in the CustomBusiness-ObjectsClient example, and call the following code from that button's Click event handler, the first object in the customers list collection would have its CustomerName property changed to IDesign. However, the customers grid would not immediately update with the changed value. You would have to perform some interaction with the grid or form to make it refresh its data binding to see the changed customer value.

```
private void button1_Click(object sender, EventArgs e)
{
    List<Customer> custs = m_CustomersBindingSource.DataSource
        as List<Customer>;
    custs[0].CustomerName = "IDesign";
}
```

One way to address this problem is to implement property change events on the Customer object (or any object that you plan to support data binding against). **Property change events** are events that you define on an object that notify anyone who is interested any time a particular property on the object changes. For the data-binding mechanisms in Windows Forms, the expected naming convention for these events is to publish a <propertyname>Changed event for each property, where <propertyname> is replaced with the name of the property in question.

For your Customer object and your limited support for changes against the CustomerName and CustomerId properties, this means defining two events on the class: CustomerNameChanged and CustomerIdChanged. These events need to be of type EventHandler and should be fired whenever the corresponding properties change. This can easily be done from the set blocks of the properties themselves, as shown in the following modified code for the Customer class:

```
public class Customer : IEditableObject
{
    // other fields...
    public event EventHandler CustomerIdChanged;
    public event EventHandler CustomerNameChanged;

    public int CustomerId
```

```
    {
      get { return m_CustomerId; }
      set
      {
        m_CustomerId = value;
        if (CustomerIdChanged != null)
          CustomerIdChanged(this, EventArgs.Empty);
      }
    }

    public string CustomerName
    {
      get { return m_Name; }
      set
      {
        m_Name = value;
        if (CustomerNameChanged != null)
          CustomerNameChanged(this, EventArgs.Empty);
      }
    }

    // other methods and properties...
  }
```

By making this simple change to the class, any bound controls will be automatically notified whenever an object's properties change, whether it is due to editing those objects in a data-bound control or due to some other code execution that sets the properties in memory. Basically, the data-binding mechanisms detect the presence of these methods and set up subscriptions to them so that they can refresh their values when the data values change. Note that if you write your own data-bound controls from scratch as discussed in the last chapter, you will have to take responsibility for performing these subscriptions yourself.

So with this code in place, if you press the button added earlier that directly modified properties on objects in the collection of customers, the grid would immediately reflect the change. You will also see that if you edit a cell in the customers grid, then press Esc to abort the change, the Customer field in the orders grid will also update based on that rollback, because the control will call CancelEdit. If you hadn't done the rollback by setting the properties in the implementation of CancelEdit as mentioned earlier, then the property change events wouldn't fire, and any other controls bound to the same objects wouldn't be immediately updated. You could alternatively have fired the appropriate property change events from CancelEdit instead, but that would result in more code duplication than just setting the properties in CancelEdit, which call whatever related behavior is needed through the property set block.

Supporting Object Edit Notifications with INotifyPropertyChanged

Adding a separate event for each property on an object can significantly clutter up your object. In .NET 1.1 and 1.0, this was the only way that you could ensure that bound controls would be updated when the underlying object properties changed. However, a more elegant approach has been introduced in .NET 2.0 with the INotifyPropertyChanged interface. This interface has a single member, an event named PropertyChanged. If you implement this interface on your custom business objects and then fire the event whenever any property changes, the net effect will be the same as implementing a separate event for each property. The BindingSource and Binding classes will look to see whether an object type implements this interface when the data binding is set up through one of these object types, and if so, they will update any bound controls if a property changes. Additionally, if the object is contained in a BindingList<T> collection, the collection will raise a ListChanged event if any of its contained objects raises a PropertyChanged event.

Implementing this interface on your Customer object from the earlier examples changes the class code as follows:

```
public class Customer : IEditableObject, INotifyPropertyChanged
{
    public event PropertyChangedEventHandler PropertyChanged;

    public int CustomerId
    {
        get { return m_CustomerId; }
        set
        {
            m_CustomerId = value;
            FirePropertyChangedNotification("CustomerId");
        }
    }
}
```

```
public string CustomerName
{
   get { return m_Name; }
   set
   {
      m_Name = value;
      FirePropertyChangedNotification("CustomerName");
   }
}

private void FirePropertyChangedNotification(string propName)
{
   if (PropertyChanged != null)
      PropertyChanged(this,
         new PropertyChangedEventArgs(propName));
}
// other members...
}
```

With this code in place, each time someone programmatically sets a property on the custom object, the PropertyChanged event will be fired. Containers can subscribe to the PropertyChanged event on those objects so that they will be notified and can refresh the display or bubble up ListChanged events when the bound object's properties change.

Using BindingList<T> to Create Rich Object Collections

So far we have been using the List<T> class for many of the custom business object collections in data-binding scenarios. And for many scenarios, creating a customer collection type using the List<T> generic type may be all you need. However, when you are doing data binding in Windows Forms, the BindingList<T> class is more powerful than the List<T> type, and should be the one you favor in general.

One of the biggest differences is that the BindingList<T> class takes care of raising ListChanged events any time objects from a collection are programmatically added or removed. If you make similar changes to a bound List<T> collection, bound controls will *not* update automatically, because they have no way of knowing that the contents of the list changed. So if you added the following code to a button Click event handler on the CustomBusinessObjects form, the customers grid wouldn't update to show the new item in the list unless you interact with the form in a way that causes it to refresh the data binding, such as using the arrow keys to move down rows within the grid.

```
private void AddCustomer(object sender, EventArgs e)
{
    IList custs = m_CustomersBindingSource.DataSource as IList;
    Customer c = new Customer();
    c.CustomerName = "Brian";
    c.CustomerId = 99;
    custs.Add(c);
}
```

The BindingList<T> generic class is not only capable of fixing this problem, but also gives you more control over the data-bound collection and provides a way to support sorting and searching. For whatever type you supply as a type parameter, the BindingList<T> generic class provides a generic implementation of the IBindingList interface, which enables sorting, searching, and change notifications.

By simply declaring a type based on BindingList<T> instead of List<T>, you get automatic support for ListChanged events being fired by the collection whenever an item is added, removed, or replaced within the collection. For example, if you add the following method to the TestData-Generator class to return the test data as a BindingList<Customer> instead of a List<Customer>, and modify the data-binding code to call this method instead of GetTestCustomers, then when you programmatically add an item to the collection as shown in the AddCustomers method, the grid will immediately update to show the new item in the collection.

```
public static BindingList<Customer> GetCustomersBindingList()
{
    List<Customer> coll = GetTestCustomers();
    BindingList<Customer> custs = new BindingList<Customer>(coll);
    return custs;
}
```

In addition to firing events for additions, removals, or replacements of items in the collection, the BindingList<T> class also supports transacted additions to the collection through the ICancelAddNew interface implementation. This interface defines two methods, EndNew and CancelNew.

When `AddNew` is called on the `IBindingList` interface, a new item is created in the collection. If `CancelNew` is called, the item is removed from the collection. Once `EndNew` is called, the new item is considered a completed addition to the collection. It can always be removed later, but this lets a new object be created and incrementally initialized. However, if any part of the initialization process fails, this lets you rollback the addition to the collection. This is conceptually very similar to the `IEditableObject` interface implementation that was discussed in an earlier section, but it solves an implicit coupling that occurs with objects that implement `IEditable-Object` and their container collections, as was described in Chapter 7.

The `BindingList<T>` class implementations for sorting and searching aren't implemented, and the `SupportsSearching` and `SupportsSorting` properties return `false`. If you call the `ApplySort` or `Find` methods on an instance of a `BindingList<T>` type, they will throw exceptions of type `NotSupportedException`, because there isn't a general-purpose way for the class to figure out what kind of algorithm it should use for sorting and searching properties of arbitrary types.

If you want to support searching and sorting, you will need to implement a custom type that derives from `BindingList<T>` with the appropriate type parameter. The base class will still do most of the work for you for containing the objects and supporting data binding; you just need to override a couple of methods to provide the actual sorting and searching algorithms. By implementing your own custom type, you can also take over the construction process when objects are dynamically added to the collection through a bound control, such as when a user starts typing into the row at the bottom of a `DataGridView` control that lets them add items to the collection, as you will see later in this chapter.

Creating a Custom Collection Type Based on BindingList<T>

Say you want to create a strongly typed collection of `Customer` objects that support searching and sorting, and that you want to take over the construction process of instances of `Customers` that get added to the collection through data-binding mechanisms. The first step in this process is to declare a class derived from `BindingList<T>` with the appropriate type parameter:

```
public class CustomerCollection : BindingList<Customer>
{
}
```

Taking Over the Construction Process

For a next step, let's take over the process of adding new `Customer` objects to the collection when called by the data-binding mechanism. When you add a new row to a `DataGridView`, or call `AddNew` on a `BindingSource`, the `AddNew` method gets called on the `IBindingList` implementation of your collection class. The default implementation of `AddNew` on the `BindingList<T>` base class creates a new instance of your object type using its default constructor, places that into the collection, and passes a reference to that new object back to the caller.

You can take over the construction process and do whatever custom initialization you want. You might need to do this if the objects that will go in the collection don't have a default constructor. For example, say that when each new `Customer` object is created, you want to initialize its `CustomerId` to a value that is one greater than the largest `CustomerId` currently in the collection (similar to an autoincrementing feature for an integer data set field). Also, you want to set the `CustomerName` to the prompt "<Enter Customer Name>". To do this, you need to override the base class `AddNewCore` method.

The `BindingList<T>` class takes the approach of making the `IBindingList` methods and properties nonvirtual, and its implementation of the members call virtual members that you can override in your derived class. These virtual members have a naming convention of the name of the corresponding member on the base class, with Core appended, such as `AddNewCore`, `ApplySortCore`, and `IsSortedCore`.

The following is the `AddNewCore` implementation for the `Customers-Collection` class:

```
public class CustomerCollection : BindingList<Customer>
{
    public CustomerCollection() : base() {}

    public CustomerCollection(List<Customer> custs) : base(custs) {}
```

```
protected override object AddNewCore()
{
    Customer c = new Customer();
    c.CustomerId = FindMaxId() + 1;
    c.CustomerName = "<Enter Customer Name>";
    this.Add(c);
    return c;
}

private int FindMaxId()
{
    int maxId = -1;
    foreach (Customer c in this)
    {
        if (c.CustomerId > maxId)
            maxId = c.CustomerId;
    }
    return maxId;
}
}
```

This code declares a number of things:

- It declares default and parameterized constructors that delegate to the base class constructors. This is done so that you can initialize an instance of the CustomerCollection class using a preexisting List<Customer>, modeling what the base class is capable of.
- It defines the AddNewCore method, which performs the following:
  - It constructs an instance of a Customer object.
  - It calls a helper method to determine what the maximum CustomerId value is by iterating through the collection.
  - It uses the value returned from the helper method to set the new Customer object's CustomerId to one greater than that maximum value.
  - It sets the CustomerName text to the prompt "<Enter Customer Name>".
  - It adds the customer object to the collection.
  - It returns the new Customer object as an object reference, which will be handed back to the caller of the AddNew method on the base class.
- It defines the FindMaxID helper method called by AddNewCore.

Getting Some Test Data to Work With

If you now add a method to the `TestDataGenerator` class to return a `CustomerCollection`:

```
public static CustomerCollection GetCustomerCollection()
{
   List<Customer> coll = GetTestCustomers();
   CustomerCollection custs = new CustomerCollection(coll);
   return custs;
}
```

you can call this method in the CustomBusinessObjectsClient form when the button is clicked to get the data, and bind to the returned `Customer-Collection` instead of directly to a `List<T>` or `BindingList<T>` as was done before. If you do so, as soon as you click in the new row of the Customers grid, you will see that the code has done its work, as shown in Figure 9.4.

A nice little side effect of this functionality is that the `DataGridView` is smart enough to look at the values of the fields in the new row, and if they haven't changed since it was added, it will remove the row if you change the focus from it if no editing has been done. So even though you set the `CustomerName` to "<Enter Customer Name>" and calculated a new `CustomerId`, if users click off the row without having edited either of those fields, the grid will remove it. This is probably exactly what you want to happen if users haven't filled in the prompted field, instead of

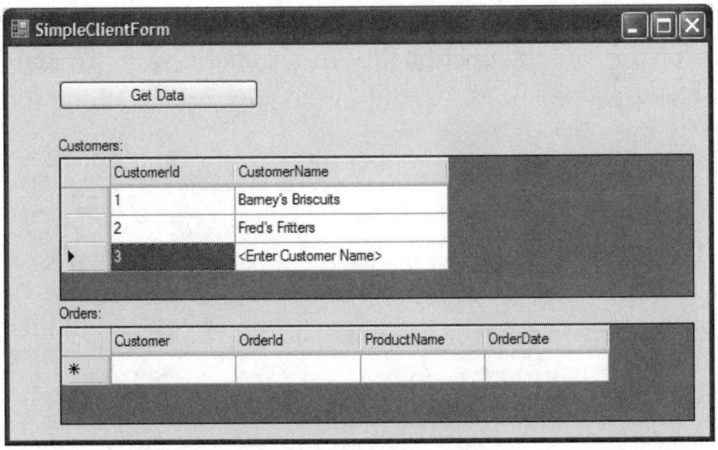

FIGURE 9.4: AddNew Functionality in Play

having it become a valid new row. However, if this isn't the behavior you want, you could handle events on the grid and call `EndNew` on the collection to get it to accept those values as valid.

Adding Search Functionality to the Collection

The next functionality we will add is also fairly simple—the ability to search the collection to find a particular `Customer` object. There are, of course, a lot of different algorithms that you could use for performing a search, and there are also a lot of different approaches that you could use for declaring a match. The `Find` method of the `IBindingList` interface is designed to let you search the collection for an object and specify which property on those objects to inspect. The method should return the object's index in the collection when it finds one whose property value matches that of the key value passed into the `Find` method.

To provide search capability, you need to override both the `Supports-SearchingCore` property and the `FindCore` method. Instead of continuing with a specific collection class for customers, however, you want to provide a generic implementation for sorting and searching that can be reused for any kind of custom data object. To do this, you can define a new generic class called `BindingListView<T>` that derives from `Binding-List<T>`. You will implement the sorting and searching functionality on this, and you will implement the `IBindingListView` interface on this later in this chapter. You can then derive the `CustomersCollection` class from `BindingListView<T>`, specifying `Customer` as the type `T` as was done earlier with the `BindingList<Customer>` base class. You can then start taking advantage of the added functionality in a generic way. To start building up that class, use this initial definition to support searching the collection:

```
public class BindingListView<T> : BindingList<T>{

    public BindingListView() : base() { }

    public BindingListView(List<T> list) : base(list) { }

    protected override bool SupportsSearchingCore
    {
        get { return true; }
```

```
    }

    protected override int FindCore(PropertyDescriptor property,
        object key)
    {
        for (int i = 0; i < Count; i++)
        {
            T item = this[i];
            if (property.GetValue(item).Equals(key))
            {
                return i;
            }
        }
        return -1; // Not found
    }
}
```

The `BindingListView<T>` class so far does the following:

1. Defines the same two constructors as for the `CustomerCollection` earlier, a default constructor and a parameterized constructor that lets you initialize the list with an instance of `List<T>`.

2. Overrides the `SupportsSearchingCore` method and returns `true`, indicating that you are adding that capability to the collection class.

3. Overrides the `FindCore` method, which iterates over the collection, using the `GetValue` method of the `PropertyDescriptor` class to extract the value of the current object's specified property, and compares it to the `key` value. If they match, the `FindCore` method returns the index of that object in the collection. If no match is found, it returns –1, a standard convention in .NET.

The CustomBusinessObjects download sample shows an alternative implementation for the `FindCore` method that uses the `FindIndex` method of the `List<T>` class. That approach uses generics and anonymous delegates, and it leaves the iteration up to the `List<T>` class implementation. Both approaches will work fine, though the simple iteration shown in this code is easier to understand. The `List<T>` implementation includes support for defining indexes, which would be more efficient for searching large collections.

Adding Sorting Capabilities to the Collection

Implementing sorting is a little more involved. First off, there are a number of base class methods and properties that you must override. The code and algorithm used for sorting is necessarily a little more complex as well. There are four properties you need to override: `SupportsSortingCore`, `IsSortedCore`, `SortDirectionCore`, and `SortPropertyCore`. There are two methods you also need to override: `ApplySortCore` and `Remove-SortCore`.

If you just needed to support sorting of the collection, things wouldn't be too complicated. It is the ability to remove the sort that complicates things. When you sort the collection, you need to make it so that any code that uses the collection from that point forward sees the collection in its new order. That means that you have to actually change the contents of the collection to be in a different order, so that when any code iterates over the collection using its base `IEnumerator` interface implementation, it sees the sorted order. Because you have to support removing the sort, you also need a way to get the contents of the collection back into their original order.

The simplest way to do this is to create a copy of the collection in its unsorted state before you apply the sort, and then you can restore that original collection when the sort is removed. However, this too introduces another level of complexity—what happens if a new item is added or an item is removed while the collection is being sorted? That item will be added to the sorted collection, but unless you intercept every modification to the collection, the new item or the removed item won't be reflected in the copy of the original collection that you are going to restore when you remove the sort.

To intercept the additions and removals, you need to override some more methods from the `BindingList<T>` base class, such as `InsertItem`, `RemoveItem`, and `ClearItems`, and make sure that the same changes get made to the unsorted collection as well as the primary collection. You also have to worry about transacted additions to the collection, so you will need overrides of `EndNew` and `CancelNew`, as well as transacted removals from the unsorted collection. As you can see, things can get complicated pretty quickly.

To demonstrate some basic sorting capability, let's not support the addition or removal of items in the collection when it is sorted. You still have to make a copy of the existing collection before applying the sort and revert to that collection when the sort is removed, but you don't have to worry about items being added or removed and maintaining the parallel collection while sorted.

The List<T> class has sorting capability built in, as mentioned before, and you can use that to do the actual sorting for you. It does the sort based on a generic implementation of the IComparer<T> interface that you provide to the method. To implement this interface, you create a class with a method named Compare that compares to objects of type T and returns an integer that indicates whether the first object is equal to, greater than, or less than the second object. What criteria you use to decide which value to return is up to you and your implementation of the interface.

The implementation in Listing 9.4 was inspired by the "Wonders of Windows Forms" column by Michael Weinhardt in *MSDN Online*, which itself was inspired by an earlier article by Rocky Lhotka. I chose a different implementation strategy and added capability for multiproperty sorts, as discussed later in the implementation of the IBindingListView interface, but some of the basic details of the following implementation were based on Michael's Custom Data Binding series from the winter of 2004.

The SortComparer class shown in Listing 9.4 provides the basic comparison implementation to be used with the List<T>.Sort method.

LISTING 9.4: SortComparer Simple Implementation

```
class SortComparer<T> : IComparer<T>
{
   private PropertyDescriptor m_PropDesc = null;
   private ListSortDirection m_Direction =
      ListSortDirection.Ascending;

   public SortComparer(PropertyDescriptor propDesc,
      ListSortDirection direction)
   {
      m_PropDesc = propDesc;
      m_Direction = direction;
   }

   int IComparer<T>.Compare(T x, T y)
   {
```

continues

```
        object xValue = m_PropDesc.GetValue(x);
        object yValue = m_PropDesc.GetValue(y);
        return CompareValues(xValue, yValue, m_Direction);
    }

    private int CompareValues(object xValue, object yValue,
        ListSortDirection direction)
    {

        int retValue = 0;
        if (xValue is IComparable) // Can ask the x value
        {
            retValue = ((IComparable)xValue).CompareTo(yValue);
        }
        else if (yValue is IComparable) //Can ask the y value
        {
            retValue = ((IComparable)yValue).CompareTo(xValue);
        }
        // not comparable, compare String representations
        else if (!xValue.Equals(yValue))
        {
            retValue = xValue.ToString().CompareTo(yValue.ToString());
        }
        if (direction == ListSortDirection.Ascending)
        {
            return retValue;
        }
        else
        {
            return retValue * -1;
        }
    }
}
```

The SortComparer class lets you construct an instance of the class and specify what property on the objects will be compared to determine equality, greater than, or less than values by passing in a PropertyDescriptor and a ListSortDirection enumeration value. When the List<T> class iterates over the list, applying its internal sort algorithm, it calls the Compare method, and passes in two objects that it is currently working with to set up the sort. The Compare implementation in Listing 9.4 tries a number of ways to compare the objects. It first extracts the specified property's current value for each of the objects using the GetValue method on the property descriptor. It then sees if the object that those values represent implements the IComparer interface. This is a standard interface in the .NET Framework. It implements a CompareTo method that embeds the same logic that we are looking for—specifically, that if the object itself decides it is equal to the other object passed in, it will return 0; if it is greater, it will return 1; and if it is less than, it will return –1.

If the property values don't implement IComparer, but the Equals method on the value says that it is equal to the other object, then Compare returns 0, indicating equality. Finally, if none of those tests succeed, the property values are converted to strings and their string representations are compared using the CompareTo method, which the String class implements. The final thing the method does is to look at the sort direction, and if it indicates that it should be a descending sort, it multiplies the returned value by –1 to reverse the greater than/less than meaning.

To perform the sort from your BindingListView<T> class, you need to provide the overrides of all the sort-related methods and properties from the base class. These are shown in Listing 9.5.

LISTING 9.5: Sorting Functionality on CustomerCollection Class

```
public class BindingListView<T> : BindingList<T>
{
   private bool m_Sorted = false;
   private ListSortDirection m_SortDirection =
      ListSortDirection.Ascending;
   private PropertyDescriptor m_SortProperty = null;
   private List<T> m_OriginalCollection = new List<T>();

   // constructors, AddNew, etc... omitted

   protected override bool SupportsSearchingCore
   {
      get { return true; }
   }

   protected override bool SupportsSortingCore
   {
      get { return true; }
   }

   protected override bool IsSortedCore
   {
      get { return m_Sorted; }
```

continues

```
   }

   protected override ListSortDirection SortDirectionCore
   {
      get { return m_SortDirection; }
   }

   protected override PropertyDescriptor SortPropertyCore
   {
      get { return m_SortProperty; }
   }

   protected override void ApplySortCore(PropertyDescriptor property,

      ListSortDirection direction)
   {
      m_SortDirection = direction;
      m_SortProperty = property;
      SortComparer<T> comparer = new
         SortComparer<T>(property,direction);
      ApplySortInternal(comparer);
   }

   private void ApplySortInternal(SortComparer<T> comparer)
   {
      // store the original order of the collection
      if (m_OriginalCollection.Count == 0)
      {
         m_OriginalCollection.AddRange(this);
      }
      List<T> listRef = this.Items as List<T>;
      if (listRef == null)
         return;

      // Let List<T> do the actual sorting based on your comparer
      listRef.Sort(comparer);
      m_Sorted = true;
      OnListChanged(new ListChangedEventArgs(
         ListChangedType.Reset, -1));
   }

   protected override void RemoveSortCore()
   {
      if (!m_Sorted)
         return;

      Clear();
      foreach (T item in m_OriginalCollection)
      {
         Add(item);
```

```
        }
        m_OriginalCollection.Clear();
        m_SortProperty = null;
        m_Sorted = false;
    }
}
```

The additions to the class include the following:

- An override of `IsSortedCore`, which indicates whether the collection is currently sorted.
- An override of `SortDirectionCore`, which provides the sort direction.
- An override of the `SortPropertyCore`, which indicates which property the sort is based on.
- An `ApplySortCore` method override, which sets the above properties when it is called by the base class in response to an `IBindingList.ApplySort` call. This method delegates to an `ApplySortInternal` helper method to do most of the work of the sorting.
- A `RemoveSortCore` method override that resets the properties appropriately when it is called by the base class in response to an `IBindingList.RemoveSort` call.
- A member variable of type `List<T>` is declared to hold the unsorted collection when a sort is applied.

The `ApplySortCore` method creates a `SortComparer` object for the specified sort property and direction, and passes that to the helper `ApplySortInternal` method. The `ApplySortInternal` method checks the unsorted collection to see if it has been populated, and if not, adds all the current values to it in the order that they exist in the collection at the time that `ApplySort` is called. The check for the list being populated is in case the list is sorted several times in succession. `ApplySortInternal` then casts the `Items` collection that your class inherited to a `List<T>` reference and calls the `Sort` method on it, passing in the `SortComparer` object. This causes the items in the collection maintained by the base class to be sorted according to the criteria provided to the `SortComparer` class and the comparison logic implemented in that class. Finally, the `ApplySortInternal` method sets the flag that indicates that the collection is sorted and fires an event through a call to the base class `OnListChanged` method indicating that the list has changed. The `Reset` type of change is most appropriate, since potentially every item in the list has been moved around.

The `RemoveSortCore` method clears the current collection again and refills it with the values that were stored in the original collection list. It then clears the original collection list and sets the member variables used by the algorithm appropriately to indicate that no sort is currently applied.

To make the list so that items cannot be changed when the collection is sorted, you need to add overridden implementations of the appropriate `IBindingList` methods:

```
bool IBindingList.AllowNew
{
    get
    {
        return CheckReadOnly();
    }
}


bool IBindingList.AllowRemove
{
    get
    {
        return CheckReadOnly();
    }
}


private bool CheckReadOnly()
{
    if (m_Sorted || m_Filtered)
    {
        return false;
    }
    else
    {
        return true;
    }
}
```

This code conditionally returns a different value for `AllowAdd` and `AllowRemove` based on whether the collection is sorted or filtered (the filtering support is added later in this chapter).

With that code in place, you can now change your `Customers-Collection` derivation, as well as the `Orders` collection contained in the `Customer` class. Now both the `CustomersCollection` (bound to the first grid) and the child collection named `Orders` on each `Customer` object (bound to the second grid) will support sorting:

```
public class CustomerCollection : BindingListView<Customer>
{
  // AddNew implementation shown earlier
}

public class Customer : IEditableObject, INotifyPropertyChanged
{
   private BindingListView<Order> m_Orders =
      new BindingListView<Order>();
   // The rest of the Order class implementation
}
```

Managing Transacted Additions to a Collection

If you are supporting transacted editing of an object, you will usually also want to support transacted addition of the object type to whatever collection it belongs to. As mentioned before, if you are using the `Binding-List<T>` class for your custom collections, you already get transacted additions for free through the combination of the `AddNew` method and the implementation of the `ICancelAddNew` interface methods `EndNew` and `CancelNew`. However, if the control that you are bound to doesn't know to call those methods—and many controls may not, since this is a new interface in .NET 2.0—you may still be able to support transacted editing through the `IEditableObject` interface implementation.

To do this, you need to introduce some coupling between your custom collection class that contains a specific object type and the object type itself. The modification requires that each `Customer` object hold a reference to its containing collection, so it can remove itself when `CancelEdit` is called if it knows that `EndEdit` hasn't been called yet on this instance of the object.

You need two more member variables on the Customer class to support this: another Boolean flag to indicate when an object is "new," meaning that it hasn't had EndEdit called since it was created, and a reference to the parent collection instance. You then need to modify CancelEdit and EndEdit to use the flag and the reference to remove the object from the parent collection if CancelEdit is called before EndEdit on any new object. The following code shows the modifications needed to set up this relationship between the collection and the contained object.

```
public class Customer : IEditableObject, INotifyPropertyChanged
{
    // other member variables...
    internal CustomerCollection m_ParentList;
    private bool m_NewObject = true;

    // other member properties and methods...

    public void CancelEdit()
    {
        if (m_Editing)
        {
            CustomerId = m_OldCustomerId;
            CustomerName = m_OldName;
        }
        if (m_NewObject && m_ParentList != null)
        {
            m_ParentList.Remove(this);
        }
        m_Editing = false;
    }

    public void EndEdit()
    {
        m_Editing = false;
        m_NewObject = false;
    }
}
```

The m_NewObject flag is set to true when an object is constructed. The only code that uses this is the IEditableObject methods CancelEdit and EndEdit. EndEdit sets the flag to false, meaning the object has been accepted by the bound control. The CancelEdit method has code added to check whether the current object is a new object. If the object is in a new state and has a valid reference to a parent collection, the object removes itself from the collection if `CancelEdit` is called.

The other modification that is required to complete this functionality is to add code to the `AddNewCore` method in the `CustomerCollection` class to set that parent reference in the object that it creates:

```
protected override object AddNewCore()
{
    Customer c = new Customer();
    c.CustomerId = FindMaxId() + 1;
    c.CustomerName = "<Enter Customer Name>";
    c.m_ParentList = this;
    this.Add(c);
    return c;
}
```

Now the `Customer` objects will remove themselves from the parent collection if added through a bound control, and that bound control calls `CancelEdit` before calling `EndEdit`. The code works fine even in combination with the `ICancelAddNew` interface implementation, which also ensures that objects are removed from the collection if the addition wasn't accepted through a call to `EndAdd`.

Raising Item Changed Events

One other interface is implemented on the `BindingList<T>` class that you might want to override for advanced scenarios in your custom collection classes: the `IRaiseItemChangedEvents` interface. This interface has a single Boolean property, `RaiseItemChangedEvents`, defined on it. In the `BindingList<T>` class implementation, this property returns `false`, but you can override it in a derived class if desired.

If you return `true` to indicate that you do raise item changed events, it is expected that you will raise `ListChanged` events when the items in your collection change. If the items in your collection implement the `INotifyPropertyChanged` interface as described earlier, this will happen automatically. But there is a way that you can continue to support item changed events even if the objects in your collection don't support `INotifyPropertyChanged`. However, you should be judicious about implementing the `IRaiseItemChangedEvents` interface: it can cause a significant performance hit for large collections, because you have to reflect on each object as it is added to your collection.

To implement the `IRaiseItemChangedEvents` interface, you need to provide the property descriptor a callback delegate for each property on the objects that are in your collection. Your callback will be invoked when the property value is set through the descriptor. Strangely enough, this isn't exposed as an event that you can explicitly subscribe to; you have to call the `AddValueChanged` and `RemoveValueChanged` methods, passing in a delegate to the method to call back. Calling `AddValueChanged` makes the method that the delegate points to be called whenever the value of an object's property is changed through its property descriptor's `SetValue` method, which is how data-bound controls edit the data source. This won't do anything for you if some code obtains a reference to the object and directly sets the property through its setter on the property definition. However, the callback will invoke the target method any time a property is changed through a data-bound control, because that is how data-bound controls set properties, since they don't have compile-time information about the objects to which they are bound. The following code shows the additional methods added to the `BindingListView<T>` class to support item changed notifications.

```
protected override void InsertItem(int index, T item)
{
    foreach (PropertyDescriptor propDesc in
TypeDescriptor.GetProperties(item))
    {
        if (propDesc.SupportsChangeEvents)
        {
            propDesc.AddValueChanged(item, OnItemChanged);
        }
    }
    base.InsertItem(index, item);
}

protected override void RemoveItem(int index)
{
    T item = Items[index];
    PropertyDescriptorCollection propDescs =
        TypeDescriptor.GetProperties(item)
```

```
    foreach (PropertyDescriptor propDesc in propDescs)
    {
        if (propDesc.SupportsChangeEvents)
        {
            propDesc.RemoveValueChanged(item,OnItemChanged);
        }
    }
    base.RemoveItem(index);
}

void OnItemChanged(object sender, EventArgs args)
{
    int index = Items.IndexOf((T)sender);
    OnListChanged(new ListChangedEventArgs(
        ListChangedType.ItemChanged, index));
}
```

The `BindingList<T>` class already implements `IRaiseItemChanged-Events`, but returns `false` indicating no support. To indicate that you have added support, you need to reimplement the interface and return `true` from the `RaisesItemChangedEvents` property:

```
public class BindingListView<T> : BindingList<T>, IBindingListView,
    IRaiseItemChangedEvents
{
    // other members...
    bool IRaiseItemChangedEvents.RaisesItemChangedEvents
    {
        get { return true; }
    }
}
```

Adding IBindingListView Functionality

If you remember from Chapter 7, there is a level of data-binding functionality defined through the `IBindingListView` interface that you can support to make your collections even richer. The `IBindingListView` specifically adds the ability to perform sorting on more than one property at a time, and to filter the collection based on some filter expression to only show parts of the underlying collection at a time.

The `IBindingListView` interface defines four additional properties and two methods you will need to implement on your collection to fully support this interface.

- The `SupportsAdvancedSorting` and `SupportsFiltering` Boolean properties indicate which of the two capabilities you support.

- The `SortDescriptions` property returns a `ListSortDescription-Collection` that contains whatever sort criteria is currently in effect. Each `ListSortDescription` object within that collection is just a pair associating a `PropertyDescriptor` and a `ListSortDirection` for each of the properties on which sorting is applied.

- The `Filter` property supports getting and setting a string filter expression that you are using to tailor the collection contents that are presented to anyone using the collection.

- The `ApplySort` method is similar to the one defined on the `IBindingList` interface, except that it takes a `ListSort-DescriptionCollection` as a parameter instead of a single `PropertyDescriptor` and `ListSortDirection`. Each `ListSort-Description` in that collection contains a property descriptor and a sort direction, which enable you to sort on each criteria in turn.

- The `RemoveFilter` method removes whatever filter is in effect and restores the collection to its full contents.

Although this sounds straightforward, implementing this interface is no trivial matter. Sorting on multiple properties actually is fairly easy to implement, but requires some extensions to the `SortComparer<T>` class and sorting logic presented earlier. Filtering can be done in a number of ways, but this further complicates matters if you want to allow additions and removals from the collection while it is in the filtered state (for the same reasons that those operations present difficulties when sorted, as discussed earlier). With a filtered list, your collection could also potentially be sorted, so you need to be able to get back to the original, possibly altered, list from sorted/unfiltered, filtered/unsorted, and filtered/sorted states.

To show a reasonable implementation that you can reuse if you can live with not adding and removing items from the list when it is sorted or filtered, I enhanced the `BindingListView<T>` class to provide an implementation of `IBindingListView`. The first step is to enhance the `SortComparer<T>` to support multiproperty comparisons. The full class listing is shown in Listing 9.6.

LISTING 9.6: SortComparer Class

```
class SortComparer<T> : IComparer<T>
{
   private ListSortDescriptionCollection m_SortCollection = null;
   private PropertyDescriptor m_PropDesc = null;
   private ListSortDirection m_Direction =
      ListSortDirection.Ascending;

   public SortComparer(PropertyDescriptor propDesc,
      ListSortDirection direction)
   {
      m_PropDesc = propDesc;
      m_Direction = direction;
   }

   public SortComparer(ListSortDescriptionCollection sortCollection)
   {
      m_SortCollection = sortCollection;
   }

   int IComparer<T>.Compare(T x, T y)
   {
      if (m_PropDesc != null) // Simple sort
      {
         object xValue = m_PropDesc.GetValue(x);
         object yValue = m_PropDesc.GetValue(y);
         return CompareValues(xValue, yValue, m_Direction);
      }
      else if (m_SortCollection != null &&
               m_SortCollection.Count > 0)
      {
         return RecursiveCompareInternal(x,y, 0);
      }
      else return 0;
   }

   private int CompareValues(object xValue, object yValue,
      ListSortDirection direction)
```

continues

```
        {
            int retValue = 0;
            if (xValue is IComparable) // Can ask the x value
            {
                retValue = ((IComparable)xValue).CompareTo(yValue);
            }
            else if (yValue is IComparable) //Can ask the y value
            {
                retValue = ((IComparable)yValue).CompareTo(xValue);
            }
            // not comparable, compare String representations
            else if (!xValue.Equals(yValue))
            {
                retValue = xValue.ToString().CompareTo(yValue.ToString());
            }
            if (direction == ListSortDirection.Ascending)
            {
                return retValue;
            }
            else
            {
                return retValue * -1;
            }
        }

        private int RecursiveCompareInternal(T x, T y, int index)
        {
            if (index >= m_SortCollection.Count)
                return 0; // termination condition

            ListSortDescription listSortDesc = m_SortCollection[index];
            object xValue = listSortDesc.PropertyDescriptor.GetValue(x);
            object yValue = listSortDesc.PropertyDescriptor.GetValue(y);

            int retValue = CompareValues(xValue,
                yValue,listSortDesc.SortDirection);
            if (retValue == 0)
            {
                return RecursiveCompareInternal(x,y,++index);
            }
            else
            {
                return retValue;
            }
        }
    }
```

The additions to what was shown in Listing 9.4 are in bold.

- A new parameterized constructor is added that lets you create a `SortComparer<T>` with a `ListSortDescriptionCollection` instead of a single property descriptor and sort direction.
- Depending on which constructor was used, the `Compare` method calls either the `CompareValues` method directly as shown in Listing 9.4, or calls the new `RecursiveCompareInternal` method, which recursively compares the two values, starting with the first property specified in the `ListSortDescriptionCollection`.
- If that property is equal between the two objects, then it proceeds to the next property, and then the next one, until all properties have been compared or a difference has been found.

With this in place, you can make the additions to the `BindingList-View<T>` class to support multiproperty sorting. Filtering is completely separate, but it is also implemented in this version. For simplicity, the filtering code only supports filtering on a single property at a time, based on the string representation of that property's value, and uses quotes to delimit the value that is being filtered. A filter expression that is supported would look something like:

```
IBindingListView listView = m_OrdersCollection as IBindingListView;
if (listView == null)
   return;

listView.Filter = "ProductName='Deep fryer fat'";
```

The full `BindingListView<T>` class is shown in Listing 9.7.

LISTING 9.7: BindingListView<T> Class

```
public class BindingListView<T> : BindingList<T>, IBindingListView,
   IRaiseItemChangedEvents
{
   private bool m_Sorted = false;
   private bool m_Filtered = false;
   private string m_FilterString = null;
   private ListSortDirection m_SortDirection =
```

continues

```csharp
            ListSortDirection.Ascending;
        private PropertyDescriptor m_SortProperty = null;
        private ListSortDescriptionCollection m_SortDescriptions =
            new ListSortDescriptionCollection();
        private List<T> m_OriginalCollection = new List<T>();

        public BindingListView() : base()
        {
        }

        public BindingListView(List<T> list) : base(list)
        {
        }

        protected override bool SupportsSearchingCore
        {
            get { return true; }
        }

        protected override int FindCore(PropertyDescriptor property,
            object key)
        {
            // Simple iteration:
            for (int i = 0; i < Count; i++)
            {
                T item = this[i];
                if (property.GetValue(item).Equals(key))
                {
                    return i;
                }
            }
            return -1; // Not found

            // Alternative search implementation
            // using List.FindIndex:
            //Predicate<T> pred = delegate(T item)
            //{
            //    if (property.GetValue(item).Equals(key))
            //        return true;
            //    else
            //        return false;
            //};
            //List<T> list = Items as List<T>;
            //if (list == null)
            //    return -1;
            //return list.FindIndex(pred);
        }

        protected override bool SupportsSortingCore
        {
```

```
      get { return true; }
}

protected override bool IsSortedCore
{
      get { return m_Sorted; }
}

protected override ListSortDirection SortDirectionCore
{
      get { return m_SortDirection; }
}

protected override PropertyDescriptor SortPropertyCore
{
      get { return m_SortProperty; }
}

protected override void ApplySortCore(PropertyDescriptor property,

      ListSortDirection direction)
{
      m_SortDirection = direction;
      m_SortProperty = property;
      SortComparer<T> comparer =
         new SortComparer<T>(property,direction);
      ApplySortInternal(comparer);
}

private void ApplySortInternal(SortComparer<T> comparer)
{
      if (m_OriginalCollection.Count == 0)
      {
         m_OriginalCollection.AddRange(this);
      }
      List<T> listRef = this.Items as List<T>;
      if (listRef == null)
         return;

      listRef.Sort(comparer);
      m_Sorted = true;
      OnListChanged(new ListChangedEventArgs(
         ListChangedType.Reset, -1));
}

protected override void RemoveSortCore()
{
      if (!m_Sorted)
         return;
```

continues

```
        Clear();
        foreach (T item in m_OriginalCollection)
        {
            Add(item);
        }
        m_OriginalCollection.Clear();
        m_SortProperty = null;
        m_SortDescriptions = null;
        m_Sorted = false;
    }


    void IBindingListView.ApplySort(ListSortDescriptionCollection sorts)
    {
        m_SortProperty = null;
        m_SortDescriptions = sorts;
        SortComparer<T> comparer = new SortComparer<T>(sorts);
        ApplySortInternal(comparer);
    }


    string IBindingListView.Filter
    {
        get
        {
            return m_FilterString;
        }
        set
        {
            m_FilterString = value;
            m_Filtered = true;
            UpdateFilter();
        }
    }


    void IBindingListView.RemoveFilter()
    {
        if (!m_Filtered)
            return;
        m_FilterString = null;
        m_Filtered = false;
        m_Sorted = false;
        m_SortDescriptions = null;
        m_SortProperty = null;
        Clear();
        foreach (T item in m_OriginalCollection)
        {
            Add(item);
        }
        m_OriginalCollection.Clear();
    }
```

```
ListSortDescriptionCollection IBindingListView.SortDescriptions
{
   get
   {
      return m_SortDescriptions;
   }
}

bool IBindingListView.SupportsAdvancedSorting
{
   get
   {
      return true;
   }
}

bool IBindingListView.SupportsFiltering
{
   get
   {
      return true;
   }
}

protected virtual void UpdateFilter()
{

   int equalsPos = m_FilterString.IndexOf('=');
   // Get property name
   string propName = m_FilterString.Substring(0,equalsPos).Trim();
   // Get filter criteria
   string criteria = m_FilterString.Substring(equalsPos+1,
      m_FilterString.Length - equalsPos - 1).Trim();
   // Strip leading and trailing quotes
   criteria = criteria.Substring(1, criteria.Length - 2);
   // Get a property descriptor for the filter property
   PropertyDescriptor propDesc =
      TypeDescriptor.GetProperties(typeof(T))[propName];
   if (m_OriginalCollection.Count == 0)
   {
      m_OriginalCollection.AddRange(this);
   }
   List<T> currentCollection = new List<T>(this);
   Clear();
   foreach (T item in currentCollection)
   {
      object value = propDesc.GetValue(item);
      if (value.ToString() == criteria)
      {
         Add(item);
```

continues

```
            }
        }
    }

    bool IBindingList.AllowNew
    {
        get
        {
            return CheckReadOnly();
        }
    }

    bool IBindingList.AllowRemove
    {
        get
        {
            return CheckReadOnly();
        }
    }

    private bool CheckReadOnly()
    {
        if (m_Sorted || m_Filtered)
        {
            return false;
        }
        else
        {
            return true;
        }
    }

    protected override void InsertItem(int index, T item)
    {
        foreach (PropertyDescriptor propDesc in
            TypeDescriptor.GetProperties(item))
        {
            if (propDesc.SupportsChangeEvents)
            {
                propDesc.AddValueChanged(item, OnItemChanged);
            }
        }
        base.InsertItem(index, item);
    }

    protected override void RemoveItem(int index)
    {
        T item = Items[index];
        PropertyDescriptorCollection propDescs =
            TypeDescriptor.GetProperties(item)
        foreach (PropertyDescriptor propDesc in propDescs)
```

```
    {
        if (propDesc.SupportsChangeEvents)
        {
            propDesc.RemoveValueChanged(item,OnItemChanged);
        }
    }
    base.RemoveItem(index);
}

void OnItemChanged(object sender, EventArgs args)
{
    int index = Items.IndexOf((T)sender);
    OnListChanged(new ListChangedEventArgs(
        ListChangedType.ItemChanged, index));
}

bool IRaiseItemChangedEvents.RaisesItemChangedEvents
{
    get { return true; }
}
```

```
}
```

Binding to Business Objects Through the Data Sources Window

Now that we have stepped through how to declare business objects and collections that support the full range of functionality for data binding, let's look again at the easiest way to use them in data-binding scenarios using the Data Sources window. The CustomBusinessObjects sample actually declared the `Customer`, `Order`, `CustomerCollection`, and `TestData-Generator` classes in a separate class library assembly from the Windows application project that was being used to test them. To show how easy it is to use these types with data binding, let's add a new form, called `CustomersForm`, to the Windows application project CustomBusinessObjectsClient.

1. Set a reference to the CustomBusinessObjects class library in that project.
2. Bring up the Data Sources window, which is initially blank.
3. Click on the *Add New Data Source* link, which displays the Data Source Configuration wizard.

4. Select *Object* as the *Data source* type in the first step.

5. On the next page, Select the Object you wish to bind to,"navigate to the `CustomerCollection` type, as shown in Figure 9.5.

6. Click *Finish*.

A data source for the `CustomerCollection` with the `CustomerId`, `CustomerName,` and `Orders` properties will display, as shown in Figure 9.6.

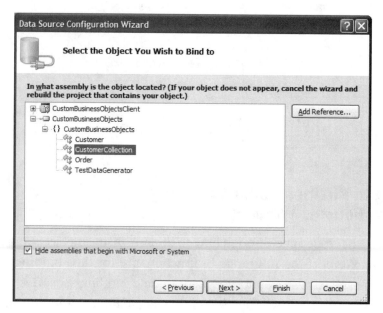

FIGURE 9.5: Selecting the Object Type for a Data Source

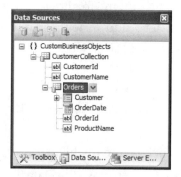

FIGURE 9.6: Data Sources Window with Custom Object Collection

7. Drag the `CustomerCollection` onto the `CustomerForm` design surface from the Data Sources window, and a `DataGridView`, `BindingSource`, and `BindingNavigator` are added and wired up so that the grid is ready to present customer collections.

8. Add enough code to get an instance of the `CustomersCollection` (through the `TestDataGenerator` class), and set the `DataSource` of the `BindingSource` to that live instance of a `CustomersCollection`:

```
private void OnFormLoad(object sender, EventArgs e)
{
    m_CustomerCollectionBindingSource.DataSource =
        TestDataGenerator.GetCustomerCollection();
}
```

With these few steps, you can see that it is just as easy to set up data binding to custom objects and collections using the designer as it is to set up data binding for a data set. However, as you saw in the rest of this chapter, there is certainly a lot more work involved in defining the custom object and collection types themselves so that they will work properly in a data-binding scenario.

Where Are We?

In this chapter, you stepped through the concepts behind defining and using custom business objects for data binding in Windows Forms 2.0. It all comes down to supporting the various data-binding interfaces at the object and collection level. You learned how to define objects that support transacted editing and property change notifications, and about the various kinds of collections you can define and use in data-binding scenarios. The bottom line to take away is that you should favor using the `BindingList<T>` generic type, or a derived class from it, to define collections of business objects that you expect to use for data binding. You may also want to provide implementations for sorting, searching, and filtering depending on your needs through your derived collection class implementation.

In case it isn't clear by now, creating collections and objects that support the full spectrum of data binding is a lot of work. I am a big proponent of using typed data sets as containers for business entity data, rather than defining custom objects when they will be used in data-binding scenarios. One of the main reasons why is because the data set and its contained objects already do all of this for you in a well-tested and proven way. Specifically, the `DataView` and `DataRowView` classes provide full implementations of all of the interfaces covered, and the classes will work fine for just about any kind of data that you need to put into them. If you are bringing data into your presentation layer for the purposes of data binding, your first instinct should be to use the power of the data set to contain that data, rather than needing to go to a lot of work to properly implement the objects and collections just to make them suitable for data binding in the interest of object-oriented purity.

Some key takeaways from this chapter are:

- The `DataSet` class and its contained objects already do all of this for you, so use typed data sets whenever you can to save having to try and recreate the rich data containment functionality that is already written for you.
- Favor using `BindingList<T>` for a strongly typed collection class that supports rich data binding.
- Inherit from `BindingList<T>` to add support for sorting, searching, and filtering.
- Add implementations of `INotifyPropertyChanged` to support `ListChanged` notifications from a `BindingList<T>` collection when property values change.

The next chapter finishes the coverage of the concepts behind building data-bound Windows Forms applications with a discussion of validation and error handling—two things that are key to building rich and robust data applications that do what the user expects them to do. It discusses both the built-in mechanisms for validation and error handling in the Windows Forms controls, and how to supplement what is provided to save repetition in writing your validation and error-handling code.

■ 10 ■
Validating Data Input and Handling Errors

A
N IMPORTANT PART of any data-driven application is ensuring data consistency and handling errors when they occur. Ensuring data consistency requires a combination of data input validation and concurrency protections at the data access level. Validation means ensuring that any user input meets the application's expectations for what that data should contain. Data concurrency issues arise when two or more users or pieces of code can access and modify the same data at the same time. Whenever dealing with data, errors can occur at a number of levels, and you need to be prepared to deal with those errors in a way that minimizes the impact on users and yet ensures the consistency and correctness of the data. This chapter describes the mechanisms that are built into the .NET Framework for dealing with validation and error handling, and mentions some ways to go beyond what is provided out of the box.

Unfortunately, error handling is one of those arenas where it is difficult to generalize very much. Every application is different, and how it needs to react to errors will be different based on the particular type of error, who the users are, and what the application requirements say the application should do in the face of certain kinds of errors. Error handling is definitely something you want to be thinking about upfront and designing for all along the way. You need to anticipate where things could go wrong and what to do about them when they do. Once you know what errors you need to protect against, the validation and error handling mechanisms in Windows Forms provide a standardized way that you can detect input errors and display them to the user. Failing to validate data early in your application processing can have severe performance and reliability impacts by transmitting data across the network that will cause failures or inconsistency downstream.

Windows Forms Validation

Validation is all about checking input from the user and making sure it is valid, based on some criteria that you, as the application designer, determine. Examples of validation checks include

- Checking for required input in a particular field
- Checking whether input data is a valid numeric value
- Checking for input to be within some range of values
- Checking for particular patterns within an input string
- Invoking complex business rules that check dependencies between other business entities and values in your application

Validation can and should occur at multiple levels in a large application. The first line of defense is to check the input from users at the point where they put it in—at the form and control level. However, in a large application, that data is often passed down into a business layer and/or data access layer through some remote technology such as a Web service. There could be any amount of intervening code through which the values have to pass before they are persisted to a data store. Data validation should occur when the user inputs data, and it should also occur at boundary crossings, such as when the data is submitted from a smart client application into the middle tier that provides the business services for that application.

How much intelligence is embedded in the presentation tier (Windows Forms) application is a design decision, but in general, in a layered application architecture, you want to keep your presentation layer or tier as thin as possible. You will want to enforce validation checks at the form level that are relatively invariant, but defer complex checks that may vary over time to the business layer. Regardless of how much validation logic you put at the forms level, there is a rich infrastructure built into Windows controls and forms to allow you to perform the checking that you need when you need it.

As with most aspects of Windows Forms programming, validation is based around controls and events. Data-bound controls raise events when validation occurs, giving you an opportunity to write custom code to perform the validation. In addition to events that are raised by the controls, an `ErrorProvider` control that is part of the Framework makes it straightforward to notify the user of any validation problems in a standardized and easy way to understand, from the perspective of both the end user and the programmer who hooks it up. Complex controls like the `DataGridView` control have built-in support for displaying validation errors in-situ to notify the user of a problem right where it occurs. There is built-in support at the forms level to cascade checks for validation up and down the control hierarchy. This prevents you from needing to write a ton of code to check and make sure the controls on a form are all happy with the data that they are containing. All of these things come together to give you a number of ways and opportunities to make sure that only good data gets into your application, and that when errors do occur, you can give clear indications to users to help them correct the problem.

Handling Validation Events

Every Windows Forms control exposes two events, `Validating` and `Validated`, which they inherit from the base `Control` class. When or whether these events ever fire depends on the design of the derived control, certain properties in the container control to which a control belongs, and what programmatic code is invoked with respect to validation. The `Validating` event is intended to fire immediately after input has been completed, but before it has been accepted as valid. The `Validated` event fires after the input has been accepted as valid.

The Validating event is the one you will handle most often for data-binding scenarios. When a control decides that input is complete, typically because the focus is shifting to another control on the form, it should fire the Validating event. This event is of type CancelEventHandler, which takes an event argument of type CancelEventArgs. The CancelEvent-Args class contains a single Boolean property named Cancel that you can set to signal that the event being fired shouldn't be completed. Setting Cancel to true is a signal back to the control that validation failed in the code that handles the event.

For example, say you want to write some code in a login form that checks a username field. A simple example that you could write to confirm that some value was entered would be to subscribe to the Validating event for the TextBox control that takes the username with the following handler:

```
private void OnUsernameValidating(object sender,
    CancelEventArgs e)
{
    if (string.IsNullOrEmpty(m_UsernameTextBox.Text))
    {
        e.Cancel = true;
        MessageBox.Show("Username is a required field");
    }
}
```

This code is part of the form that contains the m_UsernameTextBox control and gets invoked by the form when the focus switches from that control to some other control on the form. The code uses the IsNullOr-Empty method on the String class to check whether the text box is empty. If so, it sets the CancelEventArgs argument's Cancel property to true. Setting this argument to true is a signal to the validation infrastructure of Windows Forms that validation has failed on that control, which will ter-minate the validation process by default. The default value of Cancel is false, which allows the Validation process to continue. A message box is then shown to give the user some (crude) feedback about what the problem is.

By default, a couple of things happen when you set the CancelEvent-Args.Cancel property to true in your Validating event handler. The first is that the focus won't leave that control, forcing the user to correct the problem before being able to move on to input data in other controls (see Figure 10.1). This may be a good thing in many situations, because it makes it so users can't get too far out of context from where they made an input error before correcting it. This will also prevent the `Validated` event from firing since the validation process didn't complete.

However, there are several problems with this approach. First, you may not always want to force users to correct their errors immediately; you may want to let them complete an entire form of entries and just force them to resolve any problems before submitting or saving the data. This allows rapid data entry for people who spend their days repeatedly filling out the same form over and over. In those cases, if they are tabbing from field to field, they don't have to constantly look at the form to see if the focus wasn't allowed to shift to the next control because of a validation failure.

Another problem with this approach is that if users try to close a form that has validation errors that are being handled by canceling the `Validating` event, by default they won't be able to close the form. The act of clicking on another control, such as the window frame buttons (the X button), causes a focus change, which triggers validation, which fails and sets the focus back onto the control that failed. Finally, this approach requires that the control first obtain the focus, then give up the focus to another control before the validation process will be invoked.

Luckily .NET 2.0 introduces the `AutoValidate` property on the `Form` class that lets you specify exactly what the behavior should be when a

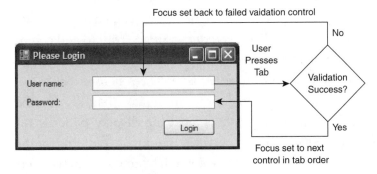

FIGURE 10.1: Control Validation Process

validation error occurs at the control level. This property is discussed later in this chapter.

DataGridView Validation Events

The `DataGridView` control is a Windows Forms control derived from the `Control` base class, and it is a complex data container. The `DataGridView` control lets you handle validation at several levels. The grid itself is a control, and thus raises `Validating` and `Validated` events when the focus shifts away from the grid. However, usually you will want to handle validating a little closer to the data that is being validated, either at the individual row or cell level. To allow this, the `DataGridView` fires `RowValidating` and `RowValidated` events each time the selected row changes within the grid. Likewise, as the focus shifts from cell to cell within the grid, `CellValidating` and `CellValidated` events fire as well.

These events follow the same pattern as the control validating events, letting you cancel validation by setting their event argument `Cancel` property to `true`. In the case of the `RowValidating` event, the event argument type is `DataGridViewCellCancelEventArgs`; for `CellValidating`, the event argument type is `DataGridViewCellValidatingEventArgs`. Both of these types give you access to the current `RowIndex` and `ColumnIndex`, and they have a `Cancel` property that can be set to `true` to cancel validation. The `DataGridView` control is designed to keep the focus on the current cell if validation fails.

As you may remember from earlier in the book, each time you shift focus in a data-bound grid, a `CellParsing` event fires for the cell you are leaving, and a `CellFormatting` event fires for the cell you have moved to. These events let you modify the displayed data as it goes out to and comes in from the data source, respectively. With respect to validation, you should be aware that the `CellValidating` event fires before the `CellParsing` event. So the validation logic you apply in a handler for the `CellValidating` event should validate against the display patterns for the cell, which don't necessarily map directly to the storage patterns for the corresponding data member in the data source. If you are doing conversions or formatting for display purposes, and want to validate the data before it gets pushed back into the underlying data source but after the parsing process has occurred, you will want to call that logic in the Cell-Parsing event handler, not the CellValidating event handler.

Validation Up the Control Hierarchy

The ContainerControl class (which Form and UserControl derive from) defines a Validate method that will validate the currently focused control in the container, and then will walk up the control hierarchy to each of its ancestors in the control tree, validating each of them as well. For a typical dialog-style form, each control is a child of the form, so the only ancestor of every control on the form is the form itself. The Form class does nothing in response to validation itself, because it doesn't directly contain input data. If you have a form that contains other container controls, such as user controls or split containers, then the container control will be the immediate ancestor of any controls it contains, and the form will be the ancestor for the container control.

The Validate method was often used in .NET 1.1 applications to let you programmatically check whether all the controls on the form were valid. However, because the Validate method only checks the currently focused control and its ancestors, you had to check all controls on the form to iterate through the Controls collection on the form, set the focus to each one, and then call Validate. This approach was tedious and problematic, so a better approach was needed. You can still call Validate on the form or on a user control to programmatically invoke validation on the currently focused control if needed, but you will probably want to use the new ValidateChildren method more often.

If you choose to use the Validate method, it returns true if validation is successful, which again is determined by whether the focused control, or any of its ancestor controls, sets the Cancel property on the Validating event argument to true. If the focused control or any control up the control hierarchy from that control votes no by setting Cancel to true, then the Validate method will return false, and your code should take appropriate measures to make users aware of the problem, and you will usually want to prevent them from moving on until the problem is corrected.

Displaying Validation Errors with the ErrorProvider Control

In the example of handling the Validating event at the beginning of this chapter, I used the crude approach of popping up a message box when a validation error occurred. Although this works, it is extremely disruptive to most users to use pop-up dialogs for something like this. Windows Forms 1.0 included the ErrorProvider control that provides a standard and less obtrusive way to notify a user of an error.

The error provider (the ErrorProvider class) control is a special kind of control, called an **extender provider control**, that lets you add properties to other controls on the form from a single instance of the extender provider. When you use an error provider control, you only need to add one to your form, and it shows up in the nonvisual components tray at the bottom of the designer (see Figure 10.2).

The error provider control maintains a mapping of error messages associated with each control on the form. If you set an error message for a

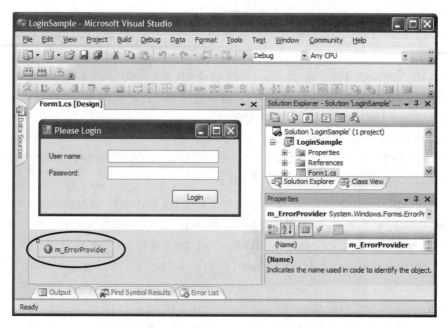

FIGURE 10.2: ErrorProvider Control in Designer

control that isn't `null` or an empty string, the error provider extender control will draw an error icon next to that control and will also display a tooltip when you hover the mouse over the error icon, as shown in Figure 10.3. You set an error message for a control by calling the `SetError` method on the error provider control instance in your form. The `SetError` method takes two arguments: a reference to the control for which you are setting the error, and the error message to set.

Typically, you will set the error provider error message in response to the `Validating` event discussed earlier. For example, if you want to validate the user's password when the focus leaves the password text box, you could have a handler for the `Validating` event that looks like this:

```
private void OnPasswordValidating(object sender,
    CancelEventArgs e)
{
    if (!string.IsNullOrEmpty(m_UsernameTextBox.Text) &&
!CheckPasswordForUser())
    {
        m_ErrorProvider.SetError(m_PasswordTextBox, "Password is
incorrect");
    }
    else
    {
        m_ErrorProvider.SetError(m_PasswordTextBox, null);
    }
}
```

This handler will be invoked by default when the focus shifts from the password text box to some other control on the form. The first thing the code does is to see if the username text box is empty. If so, it doesn't have enough

FIGURE 10.3: ErrorProvider Control in Action

information to make a decision about the password. If the username has been provided, it calls a helper method to check the user's password. This method could go out to a database or look up the user in some other credential store. If the username has been provided, and the password checks out, then the error provider error message is set to `null` for the password text box control. Otherwise, it is set to an appropriate error message. The error provider will display the notification icon adjacent to the text box, as shown in Figure 10.3, and will use the provided error message for the tooltip.

The icon shown in Figure 10.3 is the default icon used by the control, but you can customize this by setting the `Icon` property to an instance of a `System.Drawing.Icon` object. Additionally, the default behavior is for the icon to blink initially at a blink rate of 250 milliseconds to grab the user's attention. These settings can be easily changed through the `Blink-Style` and `BlinkRate` properties. If you want different behavior for different controls on the form, you will need to use separate instances of the error provider control with the appearance properties set statically, and then only set error messages for a specific control against the appropriate instance of the error provider.

You can also tie the error provider to a data source and let it extract any error information from the data source. The `ErrorProvider` class exposes `DataSource` and `DataMember` properties that let you tie it into a data source the same way as other bound controls on the form. If an error gets set through the data source, and the data items in the data source implement the `IDataErrorInfo` interface (as described in Chapter 7 and later in this chapter), then the error provider will display as described here next to any controls that are bound to the data items that have errors in the data source. You can do this in lieu of explicitly calling `SetError` on the error provider for each control in the `Validating` event handler, as long as the data source objects support providing their own error information. However, you may still want to supplement the error messages that the data source provides by calling `SetError` on the error provider when you detect certain kinds of validation errors in your forms, because the data source doesn't have context information about where and how it is being used that your form code would be aware of.

DataGridView Error Displays

Once again, the `DataGridView` requires special treatment with respect to displaying error information because of the complexity of data it is capable of displaying. The `DataGridView` control has built-in support for displaying error information at both the row and cell levels. The way it works is quite simple. Just like working with an error provider at the form level, you set the `ErrorText` property on either a row or a cell. When you do, an error provider-like icon will appear on the row or cell, with its tooltip set to whatever error text you set (see Figure 10.4).

Typically you will want to set only one or the other. As you can see in Figure 10.4, the icon shows up in the row header when you set the `Error-Text` property on a row, and in the far right side of a cell when you set it on a cell.

These same error indications will be displayed by the `DataGridView` if there are errors returned from the data source itself, instead of being set directly on the grid's cells or rows. Data source errors are discussed later in this chapter.

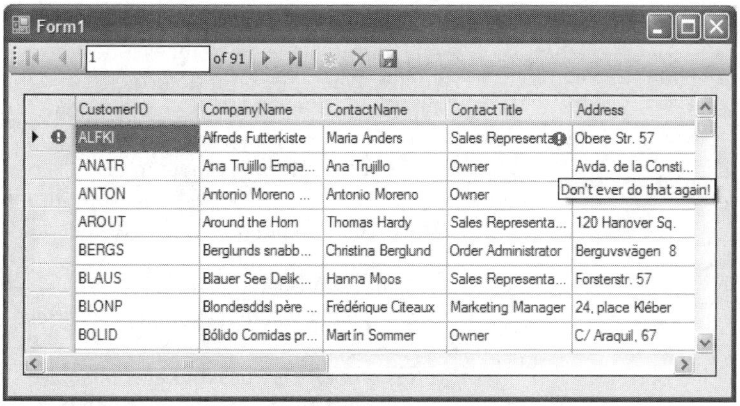

FIGURE 10.4: Row and Cell Errors in a DataGridView

DataGridView DataError Event

There are a lot of different places that things can go wrong with bound data in a `DataGridView` control. The data that goes into the grid could come from direct input from the user if you allow the grid to support editing and adding new rows, or it could be programmatically changed behind the scenes. You could have complex cell types that have some error in their processing or presentation of their values.

The `DataError` event on the `DataGridView` lets you provide centralized processing code for handling errors of many different types that can occur to the data within a `DataGridView` control or from the underlying data source. The event passes an event argument of type `DataGridView-DataErrorEventArgs`, which carries a bunch of context information about the error along with it. This event argument type has the properties shown in Table 10.1.

TABLE 10.1: DataGridViewDataErrorEventArgs Class Properties

Name	Type	Description
Cancel	Boolean	If you set this property to true, other subscribers for this event will not be called; if false, they will. The default is false. This property is inherited from the `Cancel-EventArgs` base class.
ColumnIndex	Integer	The cell's column index that caused the error.
Context	DataGridView DataError-Contexts	An enumerated value that describes the context where the error occurred (see Table 10.2). This is a flags enumeration type, so it can take on any combination of the values shown in Table 10.2.
Exception	Exception	The exception that was thrown to cause the error.
RowIndex	Integer	The row index where the problem occurred.
Throw-Exception	Boolean	If this property is true, your event handler should rethrow the exception after processing it. If false (the default), your handler shouldn't rethrow the exception.

TABLE 10.2: DataGridViewDataErrorContexts Flags Enumeration Values

Value	Description
ClipboardContent	An error occurred copying the cell contents to the Clipboard because it couldn't be converted to a string.
Commit	An error occurred when the grid tried to write the parsed value to the underlying data source.
CurrentCellChange	This error is caused by trying to change to a different cell when there is already an error in the current cell that hasn't been corrected yet.
Display	An error occurred when trying to paint the cell or the tooltip text. This usually means there is something wrong with the mapping of the column to the property or field in the data source.
Formatting	An error occurred when trying to format data as it is taken out of the data source and before it is displayed, possibly from any custom formatting code.
InitialValueRestoration	An error occurred when trying to roll back the cell value to its previous value, typically by the user pressing the Esc key.
LeaveControl	An error occurred as the focus was leaving the grid, because the control couldn't save pending changes in the grid to the data source.
Parsing	An error occurred when trying to take the entered value from a cell and save it to the underlying data source, possibly from any custom parsing code.
PreferredSize	An error occurred when the grid tried to calculate the desired size of a cell based on its formatted contents.
RowDeletion	An error occurred when the grid tried to remove a row from the data source based on a deletion in the grid (usually by the user pressing the Del key).
Scroll	An error occurred when scrolling a cell into view, because of the formatting or display code invoked based on the cell becoming visible.

For example, if a property's get or set blocks in a custom data object that is bound to a row in the DataGridView control throw an exception, the DataError event will fire with a context value of Display or Commit, respectively.

As an example, consider if you bound a DataGridView control to a binding source, which was bound to a List<SimpleDataItem>. The SimpleDataItem class is defined as:

```
class SimpleDataItem
{
    private int m_SomeVal;

    public int SomeVal
    {
        get { throw new ArgumentException("foo"); }
        set { m_SomeVal = value; }
    }

    private string m_SomeVar;

    public string Var
    {
        get { return m_SomeVar; }
        set { m_SomeVar = value; }
    }
}
```

Then assume you added a handler to your form for the DataError event on the grid as follows:

```
private void OnDataError(object sender,
    DataGridViewDataErrorEventArgs e)
{
    string msg =
        string.Format(
            "DataError occurred:\n{0}\n{1}\nDataErrorContext: {2}",
            e.Exception.GetType().ToString(),e.Exception.Message,
            e.Context);
    MessageBox.Show(msg);
}
```

As the DataGridView attempted to render the contents of the SomeVal property for each row, you would get the MessageBox shown in Figure 10.5.

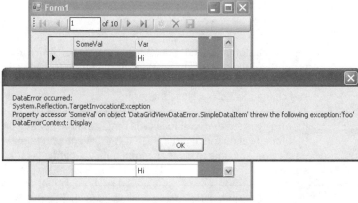

FIGURE 10.5: DataError Event Handling

The context value may be combined with one of the other flags if additional context can be determined by the grid. There are lots of other subtle things that can go wrong internally in the grid as it is parsing input values and trying to put them into the data source as edited values. These too can raise the `DataError` event, letting you trap the information and either log it or possibly conditionally handle the problem based on the context argument.

Controlling Validation Behavior with the AutoValidate Property

By default, Windows Forms 2.0 applications will behave just like previous versions if you set the `Cancel` property of the `Validating` event's `CancelEventArgs` argument to `true`—this prevents the focus from leaving that control and terminates the validation process, so `Validated` won't fire. This is done for backward-compatibility reasons.

However, a new property has been introduced to the `Container-Control` class that will let you modify this behavior if desired. If you plan to perform validation programmatically for the entire form, or just don't want to force users to correct problems one control at a time, you can change the value of the `AutoValidate` property for the form. This property takes a value of the `AutoValidate` enumeration type, which can be set to any of the values described in Table 10.3. The default value for this

TABLE 10.3: AutoValidate Enumeration Values

Value	Description
Disable	Disables automatic validation. When you set the Cancel property of the Validating event argument to true, it will still keep the Validated event from firing, but users can still change focus and close the form.
EnablePrevent-FocusChange	If Cancel is set to true, focus will remain on the control that failed validation and the Validated event won't fire. Users won't be able to close the form until validating is successful.
EnableAllow-FocusChange	If Cancel is set to true, focus is allowed to change to other controls on the form, but the Validated event won't fire, and users won't be able to close the form until validation is successful.
Inherit	The control's behavior is determined by the AutoValidate setting of its parent. If there is no parent control, then the behavior is the same as if EnablePreventFocusChange was set.

property is EnablePreventFocusChange, which models the .NET 1.1 behavior.

Typically, you will set AutoValidate equal to EnableAllowFocus-Change or Disable if you plan to perform manual validation at a form level using the ValidateChildren method, which is described in the next section.

Validation down the Control Hierarchy

As mentioned earlier, the Validate method performs validation on the currently focused control and each of its ancestors. However, a more common need is to validate all of the controls on the form in response to some event, such as the user pressing a Save or Submit button. In .NET 2.0 this becomes extremely easy, and you have a number of options to control the scope of what happens as part of the validation process.

If you want to perform validation for all the controls on a form, or a subset based on some common attributes, you can call the `ValidateChildren` method of the `ContainerControl` class. The `Form`, `UserControl`, and several other classes derive from `ContainerControl`, so they inherit this validation functionality. There are two overloads of the `ValidateChildren` method, one with no argument and one with a `ValidationConstraints` enumeration value (see Table 10.4).

The `ValidationConstraints` enumeration is a flags enumeration, which means its values can be combined with Boolean operators. So if you want to validate all child controls on a form that are selectable, visible, and tab stops, you would call `ValidateChildren` like this:

```
ValidateChildren(ValidationConstraints.Selectable |
    ValidationConstraints.Visible |
    ValidationConstraints.TabStop);
```

TABLE 10.4: **ValidationConstraints Enumeration Values**

Value	Description
None	Validates all controls within the container (including child controls of other containers).
Selectable	Validates only controls that have a control style of selectable (`ControlStyles.Selectable = true`). This is the default behavior when `Validate-Children` is called with no arguments.
Enabled	Validates only controls that are enabled.
Visible	Validates only controls that are currently visible (`Visible = true`).
TabStop	Validates only controls that are set as a tab stop (`TabStop = true`), meaning that they can be navigated to with the Tab key.
ImmediateChildren	Validates only the immediate children of the container. If any children are themselves container controls, their children won't be validated (no recursion).

Extended Validation Controls

The good thing about the validation events model and the `ErrorProvider` control is that they are simple and straightforward to use. The bad thing about them is that to cover every control in a complex form requires a ton of separate event handlers, and each one has to contain the custom code that looks at the value being validated and makes a decision about its validity and what to do about it.

Validation code can do any number of things, but it typically takes on certain patterns for most cases. The following are the four common validation checks that you will often need.

- **Required input validation**: Checks to make sure some value was put in to a specific control, without making a judgment about whether it is an appropriate value at the UI level.

- **Input range validation**: Checks the input value against a range of acceptable values.

- **Input comparison validation**: Compares the values in two or more input controls and ensures that they all have the same value.

- **Input pattern validation**: Checks the input to ensure it complies with some textual pattern, such as a Social Security Number or phone number having dashes in the right place, a string having the appropriate case or length, and so on. You can easily perform that kind of checking using the power of regular expressions.

If you have done any ASP.NET development, you know that all of these kinds of validation are covered by a set of Web server validation controls that you can place on a Web page to perform input validation against other controls on the page. ASP.NET includes a `RequiredField-Validator`, `CompareValidator`, `RangeValidator`, and `Regular-ExpressionValidator` to cover the four kinds of validation described earlier in this section. There is also a `ValidationSummary` control that lets you display the error messages caused by validation failures all together in one location on the page, rather than needing to reserve space by each control to display the error information. Unfortunately, Windows Forms doesn't include any corresponding controls for you out of the box.

Several great articles have been written by Billy Hollis and Michael Weinhardt describing techniques for extending the validation capabilities of Windows Forms in .NET 1.1. Many of the things they describe in their articles are still applicable in .NET 2.0, such as the creation of additional controls or components to simplify the process of validating input from controls on Windows Forms. Billy Hollis describes an approach in his article in MSDN Online that involves creating an extender provider control that covers all four forms of validation mentioned previously (see the article "Validator Controls for Windows Forms" at http://msdn.microsoft.com/library/default.asp?url=/library/en-us/dnadvnet/html/vbnet04082003.asp).

Michael Weinhardt takes a different approach in his series of three articles and uses classes derived from `Component` to provide individual controls for the four forms of validation mentioned, as well as providing a mechanism to centralize the validation of controls on a form (see his article "Extending Windows Forms with a Custom Validation Component Library" at http://msdn.microsoft.com/library/default.asp?url=/library/en-us/dnforms/html/winforms03162004.asp). The approach described in parts 2 and 3 of Weinhardt's article is somewhat obsolete because of the introduction of the `ValidateChildren` method and the `AutoValidate` property in .NET 2.0. However, his approach for required field, range, comparison, and regular expression validation more closely models the ASP.NET approach, so if you have to build both Web and Windows applications, you might find his approach more to your liking, although Billy Hollis' approach taps the power of Windows Forms extender provider controls in a clever way that is more consistent with the `ErrorProvider` approach. Hollis' approach also reduces the number of additional components that you have to add to a form for each control on the form. I strongly suggest that you check out both of these approaches to decide which of them is to your liking.

Capturing Data Errors on Data Sets

Data sets and their child data objects, such as data tables and rows, have built-in support for keeping track of data errors. The `DataRow` class exposes a string `RowError` property that you can set to an error message to indicate that an error has occurred somewhere in that row and give descriptive information about the error.

To be more specific, you should also set error information associated with the individual data fields that are the cause of the error if appropriate. To do that, you call the `SetColumnError` method on the `DataRow` class. This method has three overloads.

- The first takes a `DataColumn` reference and an error message as a string.

- The second takes a column index as an integer and an error message as a string.

- The third takes a column name as a string and the error message as a string.

The result of calling any of these overloads is to associate an error message with a particular column value within the row (a field). The following is an example of setting errors against a row:

```
private void OnCauseDataError(object sender, EventArgs e)
{
    northwindDataSet.Customers[0].SetColumnError(1,
        "Manual column error");
    northwindDataSet.Customers[0].RowError = "Row error";
}
```

Typically, these errors are going to be set by ADO.NET in response to an error when executing queries against the database, but you can set them manually, as shown in this example, for advanced scenarios.

When any errors have been set within a data set that is the data source for a `DataGridView` control, even if indirectly through a `BindingSource` component, then the grid will display row error and cell error icons based on those errors, as described earlier in this chapter. This is because the `DataRowView` class that is the actual source of display data for a grid implements the `IDataErrorInfo` interface to make this error information readily accessible to any data-bound control without having to know the object model for the specific data source type to discover errors within that data source.

If an error has been set for any column in a row, or for the row itself, then the table itself is considered to have errors, as does the data set that contains it. If you know you are programming against a data set, you can use the data set's object model to extract the error information within that data set. Both the `DataSet` and `DataTable` classes expose a `HasErrors` Boolean property that you can check to see if there are any rows with errors. If `HasErrors` returns `true` on the data set, you can iterate over the data set's `Tables` collection to determine which table has problems by checking the `HasErrors` property on each table.

For a table that returns `true` from `HasErrors`, if you want to programmatically explore what errors occurred, you can call the `GetErrors` method on that `DataTable` object, which will return an array of `DataRow` objects containing the rows that have errors. You can check the `RowError` property on each row for a nonempty string. Additionally, you can call the `GetColumnsInError` method to get back an array of `DataColumns`, which you can then use to call `GetColumnError` to extract the individual error messages. An example of some code to perform this drill-down process and display the errors in a separate grid is shown in Listing 10.1 and is contained in the DataErrorInfo sample in the chapter's download code.

LISTING 10.1: Discovering Data Source Errors

```
private class DataErrorInfo
{
   private string m_TableName;
   private int m_RowNumber;
   private int m_ColumnNumber;
   private string m_ErrorMessage;


   public string TableName
   {
      get { return m_TableName; }
      set { m_TableName = value; }
   }

   public int RowNumber
   {
```

continues

```
      get { return m_RowNumber; }
      set { m_RowNumber = value; }
   }

   public int ColumnNumber
   {
      get { return m_ColumnNumber; }
      set { m_ColumnNumber = value; }
   }

   public string ErrorMessage
   {
      get { return m_ErrorMessage; }
      set { m_ErrorMessage = value; }
   }

   internal DataErrorInfo(string tableName, int rowNo,
      int columnNo, string errorMsg)
   {
      m_TableName = tableName;
      m_RowNumber = rowNo;
      m_ColumnNumber = columnNo;
      m_ErrorMessage = errorMsg;
   }

}

private void OnDisplayDataSourceErrors(object sender, EventArgs e)
{
   if (northwindDataSet1.HasErrors)
   {
      List<DataErrorInfo> errors = new List<DataErrorInfo>();
      foreach (DataTable table in northwindDataSet1.Tables)
      {
         if (table.HasErrors)
         {
            string tableName = table.TableName;
            DataRow[] errorRows = table.GetErrors();
            for (int rowIndex = 0; rowIndex < errorRows.Length;
               rowIndex++)
            {
               DataRow errorRow = errorRows[rowIndex];
               int tableRowIndex = table.Rows.IndexOf(errorRow);
               if (!string.IsNullOrEmpty(errorRow.RowError))
               {
                  errors.Add(new DataErrorInfo(tableName,
                     tableRowIndex,-1, errorRow.RowError));
               }
               DataColumn[] colErrors = errorRow.GetColumnsInError();
               for (int colIndex = 0; colIndex < colErrors.Length;
```

```
            colIndex++)
        {
            DataColumn errorCol = colErrors[colIndex];
            int tableColumnIndex =
                table.Columns.IndexOf(errorCol);
            string errorMsg =
                errorRow.GetColumnError(errorCol);
            errors.Add(new DataErrorInfo(tableName,
                tableRowIndex,tableColumnIndex, errorMsg));
        }
    }
}
m_ErrorsGrid.DataSource = errors;
}
}
```

Providing Error Information from Custom Objects with IDataErrorInfo

If you are using custom business objects for data binding as described in the last chapter, you may want to have those objects be responsible themselves for determining what is valid data and what is not. For example, if you had a PurchaseOrder class, that class could contain logic that determined what a valid range was for purchase dates (such as not allowing ones to be entered before the company was in business). Or perhaps the validation logic could involve complex business logic that determined if the order is being placed by a particular kind of sales associate on a particular day of the week, and if so, then the price of all items should be discounted 10 percent. In that case, the prices input should be compared to the catalog prices for the order items and the discount applied based on that price. Whatever the case, there needs to be a standardized way for data-bound business objects to notify data-bound controls when there is a validation error at the object level.

Once again, interfaces come to the rescue. The IDataErrorInfo interface (introduced in Chapter 7) is designed exactly for this scenario. If the individual data items (objects) in your data collections implement the IDataErrorInfo interface, then data-bound controls can use that interface to determine if an error has occurred, what that error is, and which property on the object the error is related to.

The `IDataErrorInfo` interface has two members: a string property named `Error`, and an indexer (named `Item`) that takes a string parameter and returns a string. The parameter takes a property or column name within the data object and is expected to return an error corresponding to that property, if there is one. This corresponds to the way the `DataGrid-View` displays errors. As discussed in an earlier section, the `DataGridView` can display errors both at the row level (data object) and at the cell level (property or column on a data object). The `Error` property on the `IData-ErrorInfo` interface corresponds to the row-level error, and the error messages returned from the `Item` indexer correspond to cell-level errors.

As an example, I will make some minor modifications to the `Customer` class that was used in Listing 9.1. Specifically, I'll add some bounds checking on the `CustomerId` property to prevent a value greater than 99,999 from being entered. I'll also implement the `IDataErrorInfo` interface on the class so that it can support reporting errors to bound controls. The code modifications to the `Customer` class are shown in Listing 10.2.

LISTING 10.2: Customer Class Supporting IDataErrorInfo

```
public class Customer : IEditableObject,
   INotifyPropertyChanged, IDataErrorInfo
{
    // Other member variables...
    private string m_Error = string.Empty;
    private Hashtable m_PropErrors = new Hashtable();

    public int CustomerId
    {
        get
        {
            return m_CustomerId;
        }
        set
        {
            if (value > 99999)
            {
                m_PropErrors["CustomerId"] =
                    "Maximum Customer ID is 99999";
                m_Error = "Customer data may be invalid";
            }
            else
            {
```

```
                m_CustomerId = value;
                FirePropertyChangedNotification("CustomerId");
            }
        }
    }


    string IDataErrorInfo.Error
    {
        get
        {
            return m_Error;
        }
    }


    string IDataErrorInfo.this[string columnName]
    {
        get
        {
            return (string)m_PropErrors[columnName];
        }
    }


    // Other members...
}
```

In addition to the functionality described in Chapter 9, the `Customer`
class now adds an implementation of the `IDataErrorInfo` interface with
some simple error handling as an example. To support this, the class needs
somewhere to store the error information until a client (bound control)
asks for it. For the object-level error information exposed by the `Error`
property of the `IDataErrorInfo` interface, the `m_Error` string member
provides a storage location. An empty or null string is treated as if there is
no object-level error. For the per-property errors supported by the indexer
on the `IDataErrorInfo` interface, the `m_PropErrors` member stores the
error messages in a hash table, indexed on the property name.

If some code in the class decides a data error has occurred, it can populate the `Error` text, a property's error text, or both. This is what the property set block for the `CustomerId` property does. If the `CustomerId` that is
set is greater than 99,999, the property set block sets the error text for both
the object and the `CustomerId` property, and these errors will be detected

by any controls bound to an instance of the object when that property value is exceeded through the IDataErrorInfo implementation.

Figure 10.6 shows a sample application running with the errors kicking in. In the sample application, the grid and the text boxes are bound to a BindingSource component that is bound to a CustomerCollection containing two instances of a Customer object. There is also an Error-Provider control on the form that is bound to the same BindingSource with the error provider's DataSource property. When a user tries to type in a CustomerId greater than 99,999 in either the grid or the Customer ID text box, the property set block assigns the corresponding errors within the object. The property set block also raises the PropertyChanged event, which signals any bound controls to check for errors. The bound controls use the IDataErrorInfo interface to look for errors for any properties they are bound to on the object, as well as an error at the object level itself. If errors are found, the bound controls can update their displays accordingly. As a result of the errors set inside the Customer object in the CustomerId property, the grid immediately displays the error icons and tooltips on the row of the grid for the affected object, and any other bound controls, such as the text boxes, get an error provider icon displayed next to them, because the error provider checks for these errors in the same way as the grid.

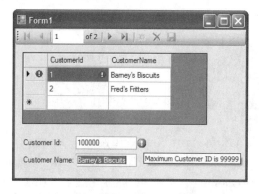

FIGURE 10.6: IDataErrorInfo Errors Exposed

Data Concurrency Resolution

Data concurrency issues can surface in a number of situations, particularly in distributed, multi-user systems. The basic problem with data concurrency is that when working with disconnected data, like you do most of the time through ADO.NET, the same data can be edited by two different users or pieces of code at the same time. When those changes are persisted back to the data store, you have to decide whose changes to keep and what to do about conflicts.

As described in Appendix D, when a concurrency error occurs in ADO.NET, a DBConcurrencyException is thrown in the data access layer. In large-scale enterprise systems, these errors often will be trapped in the business layer or below it, and handled in some automated fashion, possibly raising some other kind of error to the presentation layer for display to the user. In smaller systems, you may allow the DBConcurrency-Exception to propagate all the way up to the presentation layer for handling there. It is also possible that you will choose to have the business layer raise a custom exception in response to a concurrency error.

Whichever approach you take, there is no "built-in" functionality for resolving these errors or presenting them to a user. The sophistication of users varies widely across different application domains, and thus the degree of complexity that you can present to users to resolve such issues varies accordingly, so this precludes a general-purpose solution that would be applicable to everyone. If your users are fairly sophisticated, you might present a UI that lets them pick between the values that they are submitting and the values that are currently in the database when concurrency exceptions occur, as shown in Figure 10.7.

For less sophisticated users, you might just reject their submission and force them to re-enter things. You will have to analyze how often this might occur and the impact on users, but sometimes forcing them to do extra work by re-entering their data is less confusing and stressful for them than trying to figure out what they are supposed to do with a more complex interface.

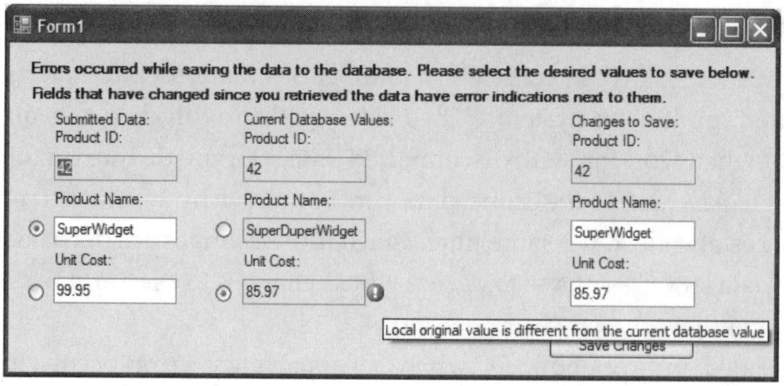

FIGURE 10.7: Resolving Concurrency Errors

The optimistic concurrency that is used for the queries generated by Visual Studio is designed for the most general case possible. As a result, if a table adapter is generated for a table in a database, the queries for updates and deletes in a table adapter check the table's current value for every column in a row that is being updated against the value that was there when the row was originally retrieved. This can be horribly inefficient, and a recommended practice for real-world applications is to include a column in your transactional tables that is of type `timestamp`, `rowversion`, or `datetime` that you can use to detect when the row has been updated without having to carry along twice as many parameters for every update.

Where Are We?

Data input validation and error handling are an important part of any data application. Even though I have waited until the last chapter to address the topic, don't wait until the end of your project to think about what to do about errors. You should be designing for this and integrating the code throughout the project. The Windows Forms Validation Framework provides a great starting point and mechanisms for handling input validation in a consistent way that gives a good user experience. You can build on this by adding custom validators that save repetitive coding for things like required fields, comparisons, range checking, and pattern checking. Validation errors aren't the only kind of data errors that can occur in your application, so you need to be prepared to deal with data concurrency errors, formatting and parsing errors, and other kinds of errors. Your business objects may contain error checking themselves, and if you are binding those objects to controls, you will want to surface that information in a consistent way with the IDataErrorInfo interface.

Key takeaways from this chapter are:

- Handle the Validating event and set the event argument Cancel property to true if you detect a validation error.
- Use the ErrorProvider control to present in-situ error information to the user in a standardized way.
- Look into the validation control libraries created by Michael Weinhardt and Billy Hollis in their *MSDN Online* articles for reusable controls for required fields, range checking, field comparisons, and regular expression validation.
- Implement the IDataErrorInfo interface on custom business objects to provide rich error information to bound controls.

◼ A ◼
Binding to Data in ASP.NET

MANY DEVELOPERS ARE faced with the challenge of having to build user interfaces using both Windows Forms and ASP.NET. Windows Forms is the ideal choice to provide the richest, most interactive application interface to your users possible. However, deploying Windows Forms applications requires some control over the configuration of the client desktop computer, and in some applications you need to reach users who may not have standard or controlled configurations. Rather than dumbing down your whole UI, you might provide a rich user interface with Windows Forms for users who live inside the firewall on your corporate network, and if you have to expose some functionality to a broad audience on the open Internet, where you have no control over the software configuration of the client machines, using ASP.NET is a good choice as a Web user interface development platform.

If you are designing your application architecture well, exposing a Web UI doesn't mean completely duplicating your whole application. With good decoupling of the application logic and data access through a layered application architecture, you should be able to focus on adding a new UI that happens to be a Web UI built with ASP.NET. In this situation, you will often want to provide data-bound user interfaces in a similar fashion to what you built for your Windows Forms application, and maximize the reuse of your business logic and data access code.

ASP.NET provides many of the same conceptual data-binding features as Windows Forms, although they manifest themselves in different ways to your code. Additionally, whenever you are programming a user interface that will live in a browser on the user's desktop, your hands are tied by the request-response model of the Web. The only way the user interface gets updated is if the client browser requests a refresh. So there is no way to achieve true two-way data binding in a browser-based application, because changes to the bound data on the server side will only be seen by users if they request a refresh of their page explicitly or implicitly. Likewise, any changes made to one control in a page don't immediately reflect in other controls in the page, because the page has been statically rendered to the browser. A client-side script is needed to achieve synchronization between controls on the client side, which isn't part of the ASP.NET processing model. However, in ASP.NET 2.0, you can still get pretty close to true two-way binding with postbacks, and you can easily present and update data through bound controls.

This appendix isn't intended to be a tutorial or comprehensive coverage of how to build Web applications with ASP.NET. The intent here is just to cover how to create some simple data-bound interfaces in ASP.NET to get you started if you need to build both Window Forms and ASP.NET Web applications, and to give you a sense of the similarities and differences between the ways of doing it in Windows Forms and in ASP.NET. The material in this appendix assumes that you have some familiarity with building simple Web forms with ASP.NET. I will give a quick introduction to the page processing model of ASP.NET to lay the groundwork if you don't have this experience, and then will dive right into how data binding works with some examples. We'll start with an example and walkthrough in ASP.NET 1.1, because the basic mechanisms of page processing and data binding haven't changed in ASP.NET 2.0, then cover the specific ways that you should approach data binding in ASP.NET 2.0 in the rest of this appendix. This should whet your appetite and help get you started with doing the same kinds of things the rest of this book has discussed, but in ASP.NET.

ASP.NET Page Processing Basics

ASP.NET Web form processing is based on a postback model. When a page first gets visited by a user (either by directly addressing it in the browser address bar or by following a link on another page or a favorite), the page is rendered by ASP.NET. This involves creating an instance of the page class, firing some events that are part of the page processing, and having each of the controls on the page render themselves into the response stream in the form of HTML that a browser can then render on the user's desktop. If a page is designed to be interactive (rather than just a plain rendering of content), then the ASP.NET processing model is designed to have a page postback. This means that the user takes some action in the page, such as clicking a button or selecting a control, and this results in a new request being sent from the browser to the ASP.NET Web application for the same page. The new request is an HTTP POST request for the same page, and it may carry along any number of parameters from the embedded controls on the page. The page processing code and the controls themselves may then choose to render the page content differently based on the posted back parameters.

Typically, ASP.NET pages built with Visual Studio are constructed of a combination of the page itself, which is an ASPX file containing the markup describing the page and its contents, and a code-behind class that gets defined in a separate source file and compiled at design time to an assembly that is loaded by ASP.NET at runtime. The markup code in the ASPX file gets compiled into a class along with the code from the code-behind class, which will either be a partial class definition that gets blended with the ASPX file definition (the default model in ASP.NET 2.0), or the page class can derive from the code-behind class, which itself derives from the ASP.NET `Page` base class (the ASP.NET 1.1 model). The code that handles postback processing and event handling typically resides in the code-behind class, although ASP.NET also supports putting all supporting code for the page in script blocks in the ASPX file itself. The ASPX markup file can also contain embedded script blocks of various types for inline computation of content that will be emitted as HTML.

Data Binding in ASP.NET 1.X

Data binding in ASP.NET 1.X involved a combination of data-bound controls, data-binding expressions in the page markup, data sources, and data-binding event processing that was part of the page-rendering lifecycle. The mechanisms for data binding in .NET 1.X still work in .NET 2.0 for backward-compatibility reasons, and you will still use many of the same constructs. However, the approach has changed quite a bit, and there are a number of new controls that support the new process that are discussed in the rest of this appendix. Additionally, there have been some significant changes in the Visual Studio experience when developing ASP.NET Web applications in Visual Studio 2005 compared to Visual Studio .NET 2003. You no longer use projects to manage Web applications; you just work on individual files and artifacts that are part of a Web folder. There are also new features, like dynamic code compilation for support code and script callbacks that let server controls refresh their contents in the browser without performing a full postback of the entire page. However, it is worthwhile to review how data binding worked in ASP.NET 1.X to understand the differences between the Web data-binding model and that of Windows Forms, in case you get exposed to any existing ASP.NET applications that were built before .NET 2.0 came out. You can still use the ASP.NET 1.X controls in ASP.NET 2.0 applications, but it is recommended that you adopt the new approach to data binding to reduce the amount of code you need to write and maintain.

ASP.NET 1.X data-bound controls follow a similar data-binding process to their Windows Forms counterparts. For example, the ASP.NET `Data-Grid` control is a complex tabular control that lets you show tables of data, select rows, edit them, sort columns, and page through the data. The `Data-Grid` has a `DataSource` property that you set to a collection of data and a `DataMember` property that you can use to refine what collection of data within that collection you want to use for complex containers of data like a data set. The `DataGrid` default behavior involves iterating over the table specified by its `DataSource` and `DataMember` properties and will render each row in the collection as an HTML table on the page. There is a great deal of flexibility in formatting the output HTML, both from a look-and-feel perspective and in terms of which columns of data get included. To handle things like sorting, selecting, and editing requires handling events fired by the control on postback. The `DataGrid` control, like many ASP.NET server controls, are template driven, allowing you to customize exactly what gets rendered for each cell of the resulting table, although the code to do so can become somewhat arcane and isn't intended for beginners.

Presenting Tabular Data in a Grid

As a simple example, assume you want to present a table of customers on a page, with the ability to select a customer from the list. When the customer is selected, the customer's company name is to be displayed at the top of the page. The code to accomplish this is shown in Listings A.1 and A.2. The running application is shown in Figure A.1 (with some autoformatting changes applied so that you can see what is going on).

LISTING A.1: Default.aspx Markup

```
<%@ Page language="c#" Codebehind="Default.aspx.cs"
AutoEventWireup="false" Inherits="Simple10DataBinding._Default" %>
<!DOCTYPE HTML PUBLIC "-//W3C//DTD HTML 4.0 Transitional//EN" >
<HTML>
    <HEAD>
            <title>Simple Data Binding Example</title>
    </HEAD>
    <body MS_POSITIONING="FlowLayout">
            <form id="Form1" method="post" runat="server">
                    <asp:Label id="m_SelectedCustomerPromptLabel"
                    runat="server">Selected Customer:</asp:Label>
                    <asp:Label id="m_SelectedCustomerLabel"
                      runat="server" />
                    <asp:DataGrid id="m_CustomersGrid" runat="server">
                        <Columns>
                                <asp:ButtonColumn Text="Select"
                            CommandName="Select" />
                        </Columns>
                    </asp:DataGrid>
            </form>
    </body>
</HTML>
```

An ASP.NET Web form always contains HTML that marks the HEAD and body elements, which are part of the HTML standard for a Web page. Each Web form should contain a single form element that contains all of the ASP.NET-specific markup. Within the form element, other markup tags define the controls that the page is composed of, along with attributes or child elements for those tags that drive their behavior when rendered to the browser. Intermixed with the markup tags can be any amount of inline script in several different forms of script blocks.

In the code in Listing A.1, you can see that three ASP.NET controls are declared—two `Labels` and a `DataGrid`. Each tag is prefixed by `asp:`, which scopes the tag name to the namespace in which Web server controls are defined. They also each have an `id` attribute and a `runat="server"` attribute. The `id` is used to map the tag to a server control instance at run-time, and the `runat` attribute identifies the control as a server control that will have an instance created and called while the page is being processed on the server.

Complex controls like the `DataGrid` have an intricate schema of allow-able child attributes and elements that can be used to customize their run-time rendering behavior. Any properties that are exposed on the control class as public or private can also be set to values in the markup by specify-ing those properties as attributes on the control's markup tag. In the `Data-Grid` in Listing A.1, a single column control of type `ButtonColumn` is specified as a child element in the `Columns` collection. Additional columns will be dynamically added in this sample when the grid is data bound.

Hooking Up Dynamic Behavior in a Code-Behind Class

After you have specified the layout of the page through the ASPX markup file, you then hook up the dynamic behavior of the page through a code-behind file, as shown in Listing A.2.

LISTING A.2: Default.aspx.cs Code-Behind

```
public class _Default : System.Web.UI.Page
{
    protected Label m_SelectedCustomerPromptLabel;
    protected Label m_SelectedCustomerLabel;
    protected NorthwindDataSet m_CustomersDataSet;
    protected DataGrid m_CustomersGrid;

    private void Page_Load(object sender, EventArgs e)
    {
        if (!IsPostBack)
        {
```

```
            NorthwindDataAccess dac = new NorthwindDataAccess();
            m_CustomersDataSet = dac.GetCustomers();
            m_CustomersGrid.DataSource = m_CustomersDataSet;
            m_CustomersGrid.DataMember = "Customers";
            DataBind();
        }
    }

    private void OnSelectedIndexChanged(object sender, EventArgs e)
    {
        int rowNumber = m_CustomersGrid.SelectedIndex;
        string customerName =
            m_CustomersGrid.SelectedItem.Cells[2].Text;
        m_SelectedCustomerLabel.Text = customerName;
    }
}
```

The code in Listing A.2 shows the code-behind for the sample, and it is typical of a simple ASP.NET 1.1 Web form. Any server controls that are defined in the markup of the ASPX file are also included as member variables in the code-behind class. The ASP.NET runtime will associate the

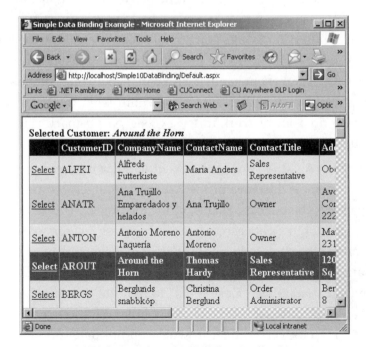

FIGURE A.1: Simple Data-Bound ASP.NET 1.1 Application

control created at runtime based on the markup with these member variables by matching the member variable name with the control tag ID in the ASPX file. The member variables of the code-behind class can then be used to programmatically access and modify those controls while the page is processing. You can see one additional member here that wasn't visible in the page markup for a `NorthwindDataSet` typed data set. This was added by dragging a `DataSet` item from the Toolbox onto the page in the designer, but because it has no visible rendering of its own, it doesn't add anything to the markup, just the code-behind.

Most ASP.NET pages will do a lot of their processing in their `Page.Load` event handler, which is named `Page_Load` by default in Visual Studio. This is often the place that you will go to retrieve any data that is needed by the page for rendering, and you will often store that data in member variables so that it is available for other methods in the page that are called while the page is being processed. Keep in mind that a new instance of the page is created for each request that comes in, so the member variables are only in scope for as long as a single request is processing.

Additionally, you may have any number of helper methods to factor out the code that initializes page controls and members, and you may have any number of event handlers for events that are raised by controls on the page on postback. You will typically do the first rendering initialization of page controls in the `Page_Load` event handler, and will then do most of the postback processing in the event handlers for the controls on the page, although you can also do a lot of work in `Page_Load` on postback if it makes sense for your scenario.

In the code in Listing A.2, the `Page_Load` event handler retrieves the customer data into a member instance of the `NorthwindDataSet` typed data set using a data access helper class that is part of the project. This kind of call will typically call out to a data access layer or business layer in real-world applications. After the page code gets the data into the member variable, it uses that data set to set the `DataSource` property on the `DataGrid` control and sets the `DataMember` to "Customers" to indicate that it is the Customers table within the data set that is the real tabular data source for the grid. This should all look very similar to what you normally do in a Windows Form. Finally, it calls `DataBind`, which is always required in

ASP.NET 1.X, and is still required in ASP.NET 2.0 when you programmatically set the `DataSource` property. All of this code is wrapped in a check for the page's `IsPostBack` property, which means that it will only be executed when the page is initially rendered, and it won't be re-executed on postbacks.

Handling Row Selecting in the Grid

The grid is designed to support selecting of rows by adding a `Button-Column` to the grid with the link text set to `Select`, as shown in Listing A.1. When that link is clicked, the code that is rendered to the browser causes the form to post itself back to the server with the same address (default.aspx), and it will carry with it enough information so that the grid on the server side can detect that a postback has occurred. It will know the selected row index based on the form's post parameters generated from the code emitted to the browser by the grid control. The grid will also fire an event named `SelectedIndexChanged`, and the page code-behind class has an event handler hooked up to that event named `OnSelectedIndex-Changed`.

The handler code for the `SelectedIndexChanged` event extracts the text from the third cell (index 2) of the currently selected item, which is a row in the grid, and presents it by setting the `Text` property of a `Label` control on the page. When the page rerenders itself back to the browser based on this postback, the label will display the selected customer, and the selected row will be rendered differently in the grid based on its own internal rendering and formatting code (see Figure A.1).

Note that when the postback occurs, the `Page_Load` event handler will still be called in the page processing, but the data-binding code in that method won't be called again because the `IsPostBack` property on the page will be `true`. The grid will still render the previously retrieved table data because by default the `DataGrid` carries all of the data in `ViewState` for the page, and so it can rerender the grid using that data, which comes back to the server with the post parameters for the page.

`ViewState` is really just a hidden input field that is rendered to the page and that contains base64-encoded data for the controls on the page. `ViewState` can have a significant negative impact on performance, so if you want to avoid the round-trip transmission cost of all that data in ViewState, you can turn off ViewState for the grid, but then you will have to requery for the data on every postback, or obtain it from a server-side cache.

Using Data-Binding Expressions

Instead of explicitly setting the DataSource and DataMember properties through the code-behind as shown in Listing A.2, you can use the designer in Visual Studio to set up the binding based on the data set member that was added to the page through the designer. Doing so results in a different form of data-binding syntax supported by ASP.NET—data-binding expressions in the markup code. The following code shows the modified DataGrid tag that sets the DataSource property using a data-binding script expression.

```
<asp:DataGrid id="m_CustomersGrid" runat="server"
    DataSource="<%# m_CustomersDataSet %>" DataMember="Customers">
...
</asp:DataGrid>
```

The <%# ... %> syntax marks a data-binding expression in the markup code. Data-binding expressions aren't evaluated until their control's DataBind method is called, either directly or by the page's DataBind method or event. Properties on controls can be set directly in the markup by specifying them as an attribute on the tag with the value to be set. The value can be static, as in the case of the string "Customers" for the DataMember property in the preceding sample code, or it can be dynamic in the form of an ASP.NET script or data-binding expression, as is the case for the DataSource property. You will still need to have code in the code-behind class that goes out and retrieves the data from the source and places it in the instance of the data set to which the grid is bound through the data-binding expression. You will also need to make an explicit call to DataBind on the control or page to trigger the data-binding expression in the markup to execute, which sets the DataSource property on the page to the data set. When you call DataBind at the page level, the page calls DataBind on all of its child controls.

Other controls follow different data-binding approaches. For example, the `ListBox` and `DropDownList` controls let you show a collection of items, and you can keep a hidden value associated with them as well, much like the Windows Forms `ListBox` and `ComboBox` controls. For the `ListBox` and `DropDownList` controls, you set a `DataSource` and option-ally a `DataMember` to define what the collection of data is that you are working with. You then set the `DataTextField` property to the field's name within each row of the collection that you want displayed in the list. You can also set the `DataValueField` property to the name of another field within that collection, and its value will be associated with each item in the list as well. Just like with Windows Forms, this lets you keep track of a primary key or object identifier that can be used for subsequent queries based on selections in the list. Think of `DataTextField` in an ASP.NET `DropDownList` as being the same as the `DisplayMember` property for a `ComboBox` control in Windows Forms and the `DataValueField` property as being the same as `ValueMember`.

For single-valued controls like a `TextBox`, you will usually use data-binding expressions to set the `Text` property or set the value programmat-ically from code-behind methods. You can also explicitly call code-behind methods or properties from a data-binding expression as long as they are protected or public members on the code-behind class. For example, to set the `Text` property of a `TextBox` on a page using a property in the code-behind class named `CurrentCustomerID`, you could use code like this in the ASPX page:

```
<asp:TextBox id=TextBox1 runat="server"
   Text='<%# CurrentCustomerID) %>' />
```

Notice that everything discussed so far has to do with rendering the data bound to a control, which is one-way data binding. What about receiving updates from the bound controls if the user edits the data? Well, this is where you become constrained by the Web request-response model. There is no way for the server to know whether the user will ever submit changes, and it doesn't make sense to keep instances of controls hanging around in server memory, tying up resources in case they do. So each time a page gets rendered, the page and all of its child controls get created, used, and discarded. If the user makes changes to the rendered data through the controls in the browser and sends them back, it will come in the form of a new request, typically a postback to the same page in an ASP.NET application. The changed data will come back as form post parameters for the page's input controls, and the page will have to reassociate those values with the new instances of the controls it creates while processing the postback. This creates the appearance, from a programming perspective, that you are working with the same instance of the control that you did when initially rendering the page, although that isn't really the case. As a result, it is difficult to achieve the appearance of true two-way data binding, because that requires persistent instances of data-bound controls throughout the interaction with the user, as well as the data sources that feed them.

There is obviously a lot more that you will need to learn to be able to tackle complex data-binding scenarios in ASP.NET 1.X applications, but this should give you a general sense of the approach and how things get tied together, and most of it still applies to ASP.NET 2.0.

Data-Binding Overview in ASP.NET 2.0

One of the big goals for ASP.NET 2.0 was to dramatically reduce the amount of application code programmers had to write when designing rich, interactive, data-bound Web user interfaces. To accomplish this, a bunch of new controls and components were added to the .NET Framework for ASP.NET Web forms, many of them focused on data-bound scenarios. Additionally, the designer in Visual Studio 2005 has been improved to the point that for many common scenarios, you can get exactly what you want without writing a line of programmatic code, and this is done without causing unnecessary coupling between your data sources and your bound controls.

The biggest change in terms of how you approach data binding in ASP.NET 2.0 is the use of **data source controls**, which are a new kind of control that are conceptually very similar to a `BindingSource` component in Windows Forms 2.0. Data source controls provide a layer of decoupling between a data source and the controls to which it gets bound. However, the similarities stop at the conceptual level. The way that you define and employ data source controls in ASP.NET is quite different from the way that you use `BindingSources` in Windows Forms, and will be the subject of the following sections in this appendix.

There are also a number of additions to the set of controls available for data-bound scenarios in ASP.NET pages, as well as enhancements to existing controls. The most significant new data-bound controls that I will cover are the `GridView`, `DetailsView`, `FormView`, and `TreeView` controls. Existing controls such as `DropDownList`, `ListBox`, `TextBox`, and `Label` are used in much the same way as they were in ASP.NET 1.X, except that you should bind them to data source controls instead of directly to data sources to provide the same indirection and a consistent model with the new data controls. Additionally, the need to set up individual control bindings is greatly reduced due to the capabilities of the `DetailsView` and `FormView` controls, as you will see later in this appendix.

Data Sources

As mentioned earlier, data source controls play a crucial role in building data-bound ASP.NET 2.0 Web forms. There are a number of data source controls that ship with ASP.NET 2.0, and they are tailored to different kinds of data. Each data source control implements a common interface called `IDataSource`, which provides the shared behavior of the data sources as well as defines the interface that derived data source controls must implement to work properly with data-bound controls in Web forms.

A data source control forms a layer of abstraction between a bound control and the data that is being presented. It lets you easily bind multiple controls to the same data source and update all of those controls simply by changing the data in one place—at the data source control. Data source controls encapsulate all the details of connecting to their respective data sources and exposing the underlying data as a collection suitable for binding.

Data source controls, as well as a number of other capabilities in ASP.NET 2.0, follow a design pattern referred to as the **provider model**. This lets you plug in new capabilities by implementing new components that comply with the interface defined as part of the provider model and integrating them through configuration file entries. As a result, you can define custom data source controls if the built-in controls don't meet your needs.

To use a data source control, you add an instance of one to your Web forms, and set any appropriate properties on the control to drive the way it retrieves and updates data from the underlying source. You then set the `DataSourceID` property for a data-bound control, such as a `GridView` or `DropDownList`, to the data source control's ID. Each of the ASP.NET data-bound controls has been extended to include a `DataSourceID` property in addition to a `DataSource` property. You can still set the data source through the `DataSource` property, but then you will still be responsible for calling the `DataBind` method on the control or the page at the appropriate time. When you set the data source through the `DataSourceID`, the binding will be automatic as the page is loaded. Let's take a quick look at each of the data source controls that ship with ASP.NET 2.0 and what they are designed for, and then we will get into a couple of examples.

SqlDataSource Control

The `SqlDataSource` data source control is designed to let you execute queries against a SQL Server database to retrieve and update data through bound controls. When you add a `SqlDataSource` object to your page, you populate its `ConnectionString` and `ProviderName` properties to tell it what to connect to. You then populate its `SelectCommand`, `InsertCommand`, `UpdateCommand`, and `DeleteCommand` properties with the SQL statements or stored procedure names that are to be executed when data is retrieved or updated. Each command can have a set of child `Parameter` objects that identify their types along with the parameters in the queries or stored procedures. The `SelectCommand` will automatically be executed when data binding occurs to retrieve the data and make it available to any bound controls as a collection. Additionally, the insert, update, and delete queries are exposed by the data source control through a standard interface that all bound controls understand and can use to persist changes that are returned through a postback to the underlying data source without requiring any programmatic code.

The easiest way to get familiar with the code required to use a `SqlDataSource` is to let the Visual Studio designer write it for you.

1. Start by creating a new Web site in Visual Studio (File > New > Web Site).

2. When you see the source code for the default.aspx page, change to Design view by clicking the *Design* tab at the bottom left of the content window. You will then see the design surface for the Web page, which should be blank.

3. Bring up Server Explorer (View > Server Explorer), and create a new data connection for the Northwind database if you don't already have one.

4. Expand the tree for Northwind down to the Customers table, and drag and drop the Customers table onto the design surface for the Web page.

After you do these steps, Visual Studio will add a `GridView` control and a `SqlDataSource` control to your page, populate them with all the information needed to retrieve the data from the Customers table, and present it in the grid—without you needing to write a single line of code. If you look at your code-behind file at this point, you will see that it is still empty. All of the code needed to set up the binding is added in the markup code of the ASPX file itself, as shown in Listing A.3.

LISTING A.3: Data-Bound GridView Sample

```
<%@ Page Language="C#" AutoEventWireup="true"
CodeFile="Default.aspx.cs" Inherits="_Default" %>

<!DOCTYPE html PUBLIC "-//W3C//DTD XHTML 1.1//EN" "http://www.w3.org/
TR/xhtml11/DTD/xhtml11.dtd">

<html xmlns="http://www.w3.org/1999/xhtml" >
<head runat="server">
    <title>Untitled Page</title>
</head>
<body>
    <form id="form1" runat="server">
    <div>
```

continues

```
<asp:GridView ID="GridView1" runat="server"
AutoGenerateColumns="False" DataKeyNames="CustomerID"
    DataSourceID="SqlDataSource1"
    EmptyDataText="There are no data records to display.">
    <Columns>
        <asp:BoundField DataField="CustomerID"
          HeaderText="CustomerID" ReadOnly="True"
          SortExpression="CustomerID" />
        <asp:BoundField DataField="CompanyName"
          HeaderText="CompanyName"
          SortExpression="CompanyName" />
        <asp:BoundField DataField="ContactName"
          HeaderText="ContactName"
          SortExpression="ContactName" />
        <asp:BoundField DataField="ContactTitle"
          HeaderText="ContactTitle"
          SortExpression="ContactTitle" />
        <asp:BoundField DataField="Address"
          HeaderText="Address" SortExpression="Address" />
        <asp:BoundField DataField="City" HeaderText="City"
          SortExpression="City" />
        <asp:BoundField DataField="Region"
          HeaderText="Region"
          SortExpression="Region" />
        <asp:BoundField DataField="PostalCode"
          HeaderText="PostalCode"
          SortExpression="PostalCode" />
        <asp:BoundField DataField="Country"
          HeaderText="Country" SortExpression="Country" />
        <asp:BoundField DataField="Phone" HeaderText="Phone"
          SortExpression="Phone" />
        <asp:BoundField DataField="Fax" HeaderText="Fax"
          SortExpression="Fax" />
    </Columns>
</asp:GridView>
<asp:SqlDataSource ID="SqlDataSource1" runat="server"
  ConnectionString=
  "<%$ ConnectionStrings:NorthwindConnectionString1 %>"
    DeleteCommand="DELETE FROM [Customers] WHERE [CustomerID] =
                @original_CustomerID"
    InsertCommand="INSERT INTO [Customers] ([CustomerID],
                [CompanyName], [ContactName],
                [ContactTitle],[Address], [City], [Region],
                [PostalCode],[Country], [Phone], [Fax])
                VALUES (@CustomerID, @CompanyName,
                @ContactName, @ContactTitle, @Address,
                @City, @Region, @PostalCode, @Country,
                @Phone, @Fax)"
        ProviderName=
"<%$ ConnectionStrings:NorthwindConnectionString1.ProviderName %>"
```

```
            SelectCommand="SELECT [CustomerID], [CompanyName],
                         [ContactName], [ContactTitle], [Address],
                         [City], [Region], [PostalCode], [Country],
                         [Phone], [Fax] FROM [Customers]"
            UpdateCommand="UPDATE [Customers] SET [CompanyName] =
                         @CompanyName, [ContactName] =
                         @ContactName, [ContactTitle] =
                         @ContactTitle, [Address] = @Address,
                         [City] = @City, [Region] = @Region,
                         [PostalCode] = @PostalCode, [Country] =
                         @Country, [Phone] = @Phone, [Fax] = @Fax
                         WHERE [CustomerID] = @original_CustomerID">
            <InsertParameters>
                <asp:Parameter Name="CustomerID" Type="String" />
                <asp:Parameter Name="CompanyName" Type="String" />
                <asp:Parameter Name="ContactName" Type="String" />
                <asp:Parameter Name="ContactTitle" Type="String" />
                <asp:Parameter Name="Address" Type="String" />
                <asp:Parameter Name="City" Type="String" />
                <asp:Parameter Name="Region" Type="String" />
                <asp:Parameter Name="PostalCode" Type="String" />
                <asp:Parameter Name="Country" Type="String" />
                <asp:Parameter Name="Phone" Type="String" />
                <asp:Parameter Name="Fax" Type="String" />
            </InsertParameters>
            <UpdateParameters>
                <asp:Parameter Name="CompanyName" Type="String" />
                <asp:Parameter Name="ContactName" Type="String" />
                <asp:Parameter Name="ContactTitle" Type="String" />
                <asp:Parameter Name="Address" Type="String" />
                <asp:Parameter Name="City" Type="String" />
                <asp:Parameter Name="Region" Type="String" />
                <asp:Parameter Name="PostalCode" Type="String" />
                <asp:Parameter Name="Country" Type="String" />
                <asp:Parameter Name="Phone" Type="String" />
                <asp:Parameter Name="Fax" Type="String" />
                <asp:Parameter Name="original_CustomerID"
                   Type="String" />
            </UpdateParameters>
            <DeleteParameters>
                <asp:Parameter Name="original_CustomerID"
                   Type="String" />
            </DeleteParameters>
        </asp:SqlDataSource>

    </div>
    </form>
</body>
</html>
```

Obviously, having Visual Studio write all this code for you is preferable and less error-prone than trying to write it all yourself. You can also accomplish the same thing by programming against the objects themselves. For example, if you don't need to support updating, you don't have to provide insert, update, and delete commands and their parameters. You can also use the default behavior of the GridView to autogenerate the columns based on the data it is bound to. So the code generated by Visual Studio in Listing A.3 can be trimmed down to the code in Listings A.4 and A.5.

LISTING A.4: Programmatic Read-Only Grid Markup

```
<%@ Page Language="C#" AutoEventWireup="true"
   CodeFile="ProgrammaticGrid.aspx.cs" Inherits="ProgrammaticGrid" %>

<!DOCTYPE html PUBLIC "-//W3C//DTD XHTML 1.1//EN"
   "http://www.w3.org/TR/xhtml11/DTD/xhtml11.dtd">

<html xmlns="http://www.w3.org/1999/xhtml" >
<head runat="server">
    <title>Untitled Page</title>
</head>
<body>
    <form id="form1" runat="server">
    <div>
        <asp:GridView ID="m_CustomersGrid" runat="server">
        </asp:GridView>
        <asp:SqlDataSource ID="m_CustomersDataSource"
            runat="server"></asp:SqlDataSource>
    </div>
    </form>
</body>
</html>
```

LISTING A.5: Programmatic Read-Only Grid Code-Behind

```
public partial class ProgrammaticGrid : System.Web.UI.Page
{
    protected void Page_Load(object sender, EventArgs e)
    {
        m_CustomersDataSource.SelectCommand =
            "SELECT * FROM Customers";
        m_CustomersDataSource.ConnectionString =
            "server=localhost;database=Northwind;trusted_connection=true";
        m_CustomersGrid.DataSourceID = m_CustomersDataSource.ID;
    }
}
```

The advantage of the SqlDataSource is expediency. You can drag and drop objects from Server Explorer onto the designer surface and it will generate the appropriate code as part of your page. You can also use the Configure Data Source wizard (see Figure A.2) to set up the query associated with a data source control after it has been added to the page. This allows you to simply drag and drop a SqlDataSource control from the Toolbox onto the page, and then generate the binding code through the wizard.

The problem with the SqlDataSource control is that it introduces a tight coupling between your pages and your database, something that violates the concept of a layered application architecture and that is generally to be avoided in large applications. However, for smaller applications or rapid prototypes, using this capability can save a lot of time coding up infrastructure code that you may or may not need.

ObjectDataSource Control

The ObjectDataSource control is the solution to the tight coupling that is caused by using SqlDataSources in your pages. Using the ObjectData-Source control, you can easily bind controls on your page to any source of

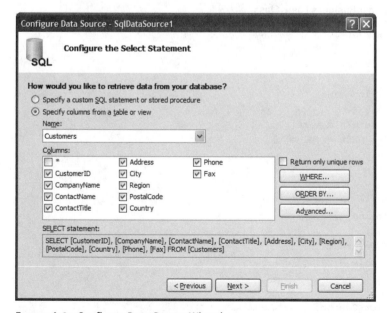

FIGURE A.2: Configure Data Source Wizard

data, such as custom business objects and collections in a layered application architecture. You set the `ObjectDataSource` control's `TypeName` property to the fully qualified type name of a class, and that class should have a method that returns a collection of the objects you want to bind to.

As an example, say that you have a layered application with a data access layer, a business layer, and the ASP.NET presentation layer. You want to bind a grid on a Web form to a collection of `Customer` objects that are returned by a method in your business layer, but the details of how those `Customer` objects are constructed are hidden from you through the encapsulation of the business layer.

The data will need to come from somewhere, so for the example I added a `CustomersDataSet` to the project as a typed data set using the techniques described in Chapter 2. The business layer classes include the `Customer` business entity class definition, which contains a factory method for returning a collection of `Customers` as shown in Listing A.6. The `GetCustomers` method uses the `CustomersTableAdapter` defined in the typed data set to retrieve a collection of customer data, and uses it to populate the simple business class entities and return them as a `List<Customer>`.

LISTING A.6: Customer Business Logic Class

```
public class Customer
{
    private string m_Name;

    public string Name
    {
        get { return m_Name; }
        set { m_Name = value; }
    }

    private string m_ID;

    public string CustomerID
    {
        get { return m_ID; }
        set { m_ID = value; }
    }

    public List<Customer> GetCustomers()
    {
```

```
        List<Customer> results = new List<Customer>();
        CustomersTableAdapter adapter = new CustomersTableAdapter();
        CustomersDataSet.CustomersDataTable custs = adapter.GetData();
        foreach (CustomersDataSet.CustomersRow row in custs)
        {
            Customer c = new Customer();
            c.Name = row.CompanyName;
            c.CustomerID = row.CustomerID;
            results.Add(c);
        }
        return results;
    }
}
```

To use this data from an ASP.NET Web form requires that you add an `ObjectDataSource` control to the page, and something to bind that to, such as a `GridView`. The following code is from the code-behind for such a page.

```
protected void Page_Load(object sender, EventArgs e)
{
    m_CustomerDataSource.TypeName = "Customer";
    m_CustomerDataSource.SelectMethod = "GetCustomers";
    m_CustomerGrid.DataSourceID = m_CustomerDataSource.ID;
}
```

AccessDataSource Control

The `AccessDataSource` control provides simplified support for binding to data coming from a Microsoft Access database. To use this control, you set the file path for the database file through the `DataFile` property. This class derives from `SqlDataSource` and only supports reading data; if you need to update data, you should use a `SqlDataSource`. The `AccessData-Source` uses the OLE DB provider under the covers, so you can only parameterize queries by position using the `?` (question mark) character for parameter placeholders in the query.

XmlDataSource Control

The `XmlDataSource` control lets you perform data binding against a hierarchical XML data document. This is particularly powerful with a control that allows you to present hierarchical data, such as the `TreeView` and

Menu controls, but it can also be used when the XML data represents tabular data that is received as an XML document.

SiteMapDataSource Control

The SiteMapDataSource control is a specialized hierarchical data provider. Its primary use is for mapping navigation controls to a site map that defines the structure of your site. A site map is defined using a particular schema of nodes in an XML file. Because of the limited scenario for which this data source control was designed, it doesn't support sorting, filtering, paging, caching, or updating like the other data source controls do.

Data-Binding Expressions

To include an expression in your markup code that is evaluated when data binding occurs, you have enclosed it in the special <%# ... %> syntax. The code that you enclose in these data-binding expressions can include code that gets evaluated directly, as if it were in the code-behind, such as referencing a property or method on the code-behind class as discussed earlier.

```
<asp:TextBox ID="TextBox3" runat="server"
    Text=<%# SomeProperty %>"></asp:TextBox>
<asp:TextBox ID="TextBox2" runat="server"
    Text="<%# GetSomeTextValue() %>"></asp:TextBox>
```

Another common expression within a data-binding expression in ASP.NET is to reference the container's data item:

```
<%# Container.DataItem["CustomerID"] %>
```

The data item means the current row or object within the collection that is being bound to, which is associated with the container control. This syntax can be used when the control is designed to be bound against a strongly typed collection of data, so the compiler can resolve the [. . .] indexer operator against the current data item for the container of data (the collection). Because most controls are designed to be bound to a wide variety of collection and data item types, you usually have to use a more dynamically typed resolution of the item you are trying to bind to. To do this, you can use the `DataBinder.Eval` method:

```
<%# DataBinder.Eval(Container.DataItem, "CustomerID") %>
```

This uses reflection to attempt to locate a `CustomerID` property or field on the current item in the bound data collection and return its value.

ASP.NET 2.0 supports a simplified syntax of the `DataBinder.Eval` that uses the `Eval` method. The following expression:

```
<%# Eval("CustomerID") %>
```

gets you the same result as if you used the lengthier syntax with the `Data-Binder.Eval` method.

There is also a `Bind` method that is new in .NET 2.0 that you will want to use instead of the `Eval` method for expressions that work against data sources that support updates on postback. If you plan to let the user edit the data in a bound control, and that control is bound to a data source that supports persisting updates, then the `Bind` method will also call the update method on the bound data source when a postback occurs with edited data. Specifically, the `GridView`, `DetailsView`, and `FormView` classes support this kind of automatic updating.

```
<%# Bind("CompanyName") %>
```

You should use the `Bind` method instead of `Eval` whenever you are setting properties inside a template for one of the new bound controls, and when you are setting the data source using the `DataSourceID` property, which allows automatic updating on postback.

GridView Control

Probably the most common control used in data-bound ASP.NET Web applications prior to ASP.NET 2.0 was the `DataGrid` control, which allows the presentation of tabular data. Like the Windows Forms `DataGrid` control, the ASP.NET `DataGrid` control was easy to use for simple scenarios, but it left a lot to be desired for more advanced scenarios. As a result, the

ASP.NET team followed the same approach as the Windows Client team—instead of trying to "fix" or improve the existing control while maintaining backward compatibility, they decided to replace it outright. The result is the GridView control.

The GridView control functions much like the DataGrid control did for simple scenarios. You set a data source, apply some styling, and when data binding occurs, the items in the bound collection are rendered as rows in an HTML table, with each column or property in the data source items displayed in a column in the row.

However, the GridView capabilities go way beyond that and make common and more advanced scenarios far easier. For example, as mentioned earlier, to support editing, selecting, sorting, and paging with the DataGrid control required handling events on postback that weren't particularly easy or intuitive to get right until you had done it a few times. In the GridView control, you just set a control's property and specify that you want it to support one or several of those functions, and this control takes care of it. All of the postback handling is encapsulated for you for the most common scenarios, but the events are still raised, letting you handle custom situations in a consistent way. The grid's styling capabilities have been improved, as well as its ability to use templates for containing custom cell contents.

The GridView is also designed to work with the data source controls to allow it to communicate changes back through the data source control it is bound to when the user edits data through the control. The data source can then ensure that changes are persisted automatically. Working with the GridView control in the designer has been beefed up; you can handle most common scenarios declaratively through designer interactions and wizards, so that you often can get very complex data binding and formatting set up without writing a single line of code by hand.

To hook up simple data binding, you set the control's DataSourceID property to the ID of the corresponding page's data source control. As shown earlier, you can also still set the DataSource and DataMember properties and programmatically call DataBind to have explicit control over the data-binding process if desired.

You have already seen some simple uses of the `GridView` in the code examples in this appendix. For a slightly more complex example, the code in Listing A.7 shows the markup for a `GridView` that supports the sorting, editing, paging, deleting, and selecting of rows.

LISTING A.7: GridView Control Example

```
<asp:GridView ID="GridView1" runat="server"
    AllowPaging="True" AllowSorting="True"
    AutoGenerateColumns="False" DataKeyNames="CustomerID"
    DataSourceID="SqlDataSource1"
    EmptyDataText="There are no data records to display.">
    <Columns>
        <asp:CommandField ShowDeleteButton="True"
            ShowEditButton="True" ShowSelectButton="True" />
        <asp:BoundField DataField="CustomerID"
            HeaderText="CustomerID" ReadOnly="True"
            SortExpression="CustomerID" />
        <asp:BoundField DataField="CompanyName"
            HeaderText="CompanyName" SortExpression="CompanyName" />
        <asp:BoundField DataField="ContactName"
            HeaderText="ContactName" SortExpression="ContactName" />
        <asp:TemplateField HeaderText="Phone" SortExpression="Phone">
            <ItemTemplate>
                <asp:Label ID="Label1" runat="server"
                  Text='<%# Eval("Phone") %>'></asp:Label>
            </ItemTemplate>
            <EditItemTemplate>
                <asp:TextBox ID="TextBox1" runat="server"
                    Text='<%# Bind("Phone") %>'></asp:TextBox>
            </EditItemTemplate>
        </asp:TemplateField>
        <asp:BoundField DataField="Fax" HeaderText="Fax"
            SortExpression="Fax" />
    </Columns>
</asp:GridView>
```

To support paging, all that is required is to set the `AllowPaging` property to `true`. For sorting, you set the `AllowSorting` property to `true`, and then specify a `SortExpression` property for each of the bound columns. Editing, deleting, and selecting are supported by adding a `CommandField` to the grid and setting the Show*XXX*Button properties to `true` for each of the kinds of command buttons you want to support. Note also the use of a template column for the Phone column, and the use of the `Eval` and `Bind` methods to set the data-binding expression.

DetailsView Control

The `DetailsView` control is a handy new control that sets up a table to display the details of a single data item for easier viewing. You can think of the formatting of a `DetailsView` control as if it flipped a row from a tabular grid on its side, presenting the column headers as row headers, and the field values from the desired row as adjacent cells in each of those rows. An example is shown in Figure A.3.

To use the `DetailsView`, you set up a data source control as described earlier, and set its ID as the `DataSourceID` on the `DetailsView` control. You can restrict which row is chosen within the data source either by restricting the data source query to return only a single data item (using a WHERE clause in the case of a `SqlDataSource`), or you can set the `FilterExpression` property to a value that will filter to the desired row. The code for the page illustrated in Figure A.3 (minus its formatting) is shown in Listing A.8.

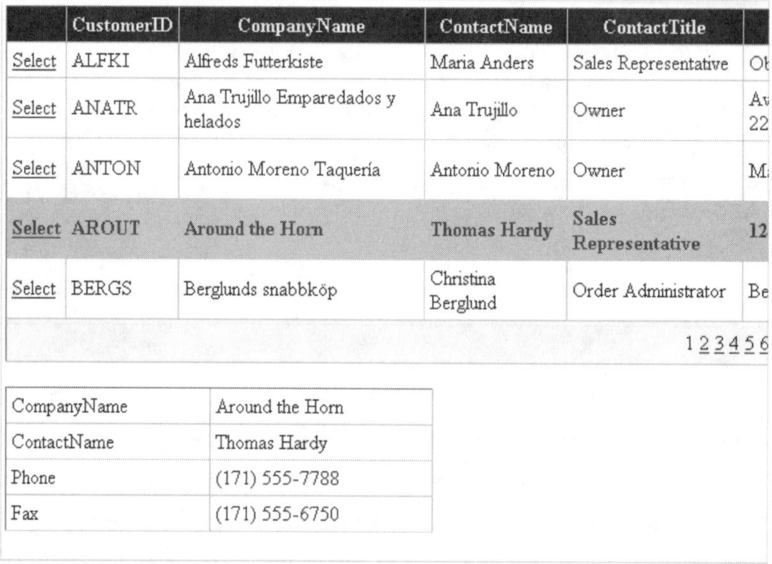

	CustomerID	CompanyName	ContactName	ContactTitle	
Select	ALFKI	Alfreds Futterkiste	Maria Anders	Sales Representative	Ob
Select	ANATR	Ana Trujillo Emparedados y helados	Ana Trujillo	Owner	Av 22
Select	ANTON	Antonio Moreno Taquería	Antonio Moreno	Owner	Ma
Select	AROUT	Around the Horn	Thomas Hardy	Sales Representative	12
Select	BERGS	Berglunds snabbköp	Christina Berglund	Order Administrator	Be

1 2 3 4 5 6

CompanyName	Around the Horn
ContactName	Thomas Hardy
Phone	(171) 555-7788
Fax	(171) 555-6750

FIGURE A.3: DetailsView Control

LISTING A.8: Integrated GridView and DetailsView

```
<%@ Page Language="C#" AutoEventWireup="true"
   CodeFile="GridViewSample.aspx.cs" Inherits="GridViewSample" %>

<!DOCTYPE html PUBLIC "-//W3C//DTD XHTML 1.1//EN"
   "http://www.w3.org/TR/xhtml11/DTD/xhtml11.dtd">

<html xmlns="http://www.w3.org/1999/xhtml" >
<head runat="server">
    <title>DetailsView Sample</title>
</head>
<body>
    <form id="form1" runat="server">
    <div>
        <asp:GridView ID="m_CustomersGrid" runat="server"
           AllowPaging="True" DataKeyNames="CustomerID"
           DataSourceID="m_CustomersDataSource" PageSize="5">
            <Columns>
                 <asp:CommandField ShowSelectButton="True" />
            </Columns>
        </asp:GridView>
        <asp:SqlDataSource ID="m_CustomersDataSource" runat="server"
           ConnectionString=
           "<%$ ConnectionStrings:NorthwindConnectionString1 %>"
            SelectCommand="SELECT * FROM Customers">
        </asp:SqlDataSource>
        <br />
        <asp:DetailsView ID="m_CustomerDetails" runat="server"
           AutoGenerateRows="False" DataKeyNames="CustomerID"
           DataSourceID="m_ CustomerDetailsDataSource"
           Height="50px" Width="348px">
            <Fields>
                <asp:BoundField DataField="CompanyName"
                   HeaderText="CompanyName"
                   SortExpression="CompanyName" />
                <asp:BoundField DataField="ContactName"
                   HeaderText="ContactName"
                   SortExpression="ContactName" />
                <asp:BoundField DataField="Phone" HeaderText="Phone"
                   SortExpression="Phone" />
                <asp:BoundField DataField="Fax" HeaderText="Fax"
                   SortExpression="Fax" />
            </Fields>
        </asp:DetailsView>
        <asp:SqlDataSource ID="m_CustomerDetailsDataSource"
           runat="server" ConnectionString=
           "<%$ ConnectionStrings:NorthwindConnectionString %>"
            SelectCommand="SELECT * FROM [Customers]
```

continues

```
                WHERE ([CustomerID] = @CustomerID)">
            <SelectParameters>
                <asp:ControlParameter ControlID="m_CustomersGrid"
                    Name="CustomerID" PropertyName="SelectedValue"
                    Type="String" />
            </SelectParameters>
        </asp:SqlDataSource>
    </div>
    </form>
</body>
</html>
```

Note that there are two `SqlDataSource` controls. The first is set as the grid's data source and gets all customer records from the database. The second is set as the `DetailsView` control's data source, and uses a `SELECT... WHERE` clause to restrict which row is selected. The selection parameter is dynamically determined using a `SelectParameter` that points to the grid control, and its `SelectedValue` property gets the value of the selected row's data key field, which is set to the `CustomerID`.

The `DetailsView` control also supports paging, editing, and many of the features supported by the `GridView` itself. It is designed to operate on a single row at a time, so the data source has to be set up appropriately based on the way it is going to be used.

FormView Control

The `FormView` control provides similar capability to the `DetailsView` control, but it also lets you provide templates for all aspects of its display, which gives you a lot more flexibility in the way a single row of data or an object is presented. You provide an item template that specifies the form's content for each record in the bound data source. The template's contents can contain static markup and binding expressions that result in the output of each row or object in the data collection in the format that you provide. The following code is a simple example of a `FormView` control with an `ItemTemplate`. It shows the company name and phone information of each item in the Customers table that gets bound to the control:

```
<asp:FormView ID="FormView1" runat="server"
    DataKeyNames="CustomerID" DataSourceID="SqlDataSource1">
```

```
<ItemTemplate>
    CompanyName:
    <asp:Label ID="CompanyNameLabel" runat="server"
        Text='<%# Bind("CompanyName") %>'></asp:Label><br />
    Phone:
    <asp:Label ID="PhoneLabel" runat="server"
        Text='<%# Bind("Phone") %>'></asp:Label><br />
</ItemTemplate>
</asp:FormView>
```

If you have worked with ASP.NET controls before, you can think of the FormView being related to the DetailsView much like the Repeater control is related to the DataList. The DetailsView gives you more built-in data presentation capability, but you cannot customize the content quite as easily or directly. In contrast, the FormView is more primitive, providing almost no automatic presentation of data, but it gives you much more flexibility in specifying the way the data gets presented and how it gets laid out on the page.

The FormView also supports editing and adding new records, as well as paging. These things are enabled in a similar fashion to other controls, by setting properties on the control or by providing subelements in the markup. Specifically, if you want to support paging, set the AllowPaging property to true. If you want to support editing and inserting, you provide additional templates under the EditTemplate and InsertTemplate elements as child elements of the FormView tag.

Master-Details Binding

Master-details data binding is accomplished much differently from how you do it in Windows Forms. You saw a simple example earlier in Listing A.8. You set up separate data source controls for each bound control that will participate in the master-details presentation. The first data source binds to the parent collection of data in a normal fashion.

If the child data source is a SqlDataSource, it sets its SelectCommand to an appropriate query to get the child collection of data. You can then choose between either providing a parameterized WHERE clause in the SelectCommand as shown earlier, or you can set the FilterExpression property on the data source control to a valid filter criteria and provide any

FilterParameters that feed it. An example of this approach is shown in
Listing A.9.

LISTING A.9: Master-Details Binding Using Filtering

```
<%@ Page Language="C#" AutoEventWireup="true"
   CodeFile="MasterDetails.aspx.cs" Inherits="MasterDetails" %>

<!DOCTYPE html PUBLIC "-//W3C//DTD XHTML 1.1//EN"
   "http://www.w3.org/TR/xhtml11/DTD/xhtml11.dtd">

<html xmlns="http://www.w3.org/1999/xhtml" >
<head runat="server">
    <title>Master Details Sample</title>
</head>
<body>
    <form id="form1" runat="server">
    <div>
        <asp:GridView ID="m_CustomersGrid" runat="server"
            AutoGenerateColumns="False"
            DataSourceID="m_CustomersDataSource"
            EmptyDataText="There are no data records to display."
            DataKeyNames="CustomerID" AllowPaging="True">
            <Columns>
                <asp:CommandField ShowSelectButton="True" />
                <asp:BoundField DataField="CompanyName"
                    HeaderText="CompanyName"
                    SortExpression="CompanyName" />
                <asp:BoundField DataField="ContactName"
                    HeaderText="ContactName"
                    SortExpression="ContactName" />
                <asp:BoundField DataField="Phone"
                    HeaderText="Phone" SortExpression="Phone" />
                <asp:BoundField DataField="CustomerID"
                    HeaderText="CustomerID" ReadOnly="True"
                    SortExpression="CustomerID" />
            </Columns>
        </asp:GridView>
        <asp:SqlDataSource ID="m_CustomersDataSource" runat="server"
            ConnectionString=
                "<%$ ConnectionStrings:NorthwindConnectionString1 %>"
            SelectCommand="SELECT [CompanyName], [ContactName], [Phone],
                [CustomerID] FROM [Customers]"></asp:SqlDataSource>
        <asp:GridView ID="m_OrdersGrid" runat="server"
            AutoGenerateColumns="False" DataSourceID="m_OrdersDataSource"
            EmptyDataText="There are no data records to display.">
            <Columns>
                <asp:BoundField DataField="CustomerID"
                    HeaderText="CustomerID"
                    SortExpression="CustomerID" />
```

```
            <asp:BoundField DataField="OrderDate"
                HeaderText="OrderDate"
                SortExpression="OrderDate" />
            <asp:BoundField DataField="ShipAddress"
                HeaderText="ShipAddress"
                SortExpression="ShipAddress" />
            <asp:BoundField DataField="ShipCity"
                HeaderText="ShipCity"
                SortExpression="ShipCity" />
            <asp:BoundField DataField="ShipRegion"
                HeaderText="ShipRegion"
                SortExpression="ShipRegion" />
            <asp:BoundField DataField="ShipPostalCode"
                HeaderText="ShipPostalCode"
                SortExpression="ShipPostalCode" />
            <asp:BoundField DataField="ShipCountry"
                HeaderText="ShipCountry"
                SortExpression="ShipCountry" />
        </Columns>
    </asp:GridView>
    <asp:SqlDataSource ID="m_OrdersDataSource" runat="server"
        ConnectionString=
            "<%$ ConnectionStrings:NorthwindConnectionString1 %>"
        SelectCommand="SELECT [CustomerID], [OrderDate],
        [ShipAddress], [ShipCity], [ShipRegion], [ShipPostalCode],
        [ShipCountry] FROM [Orders]"
        FilterExpression="CustomerID='{0}'">
        <FilterParameters>
            <asp:ControlParameter ControlID="m_CustomersGrid"
                PropertyName="SelectedValue" Name="CustomerID"
                DefaultValue="ALFKI"/>
        </FilterParameters>
    </asp:SqlDataSource>
    </div>
    </form>
</body>
</html>
```

In this example, the customers grid is bound to the SqlDataSource in the same way shown in previous examples. The orders grid is bound to its own data source, whose query selects all order records from the Orders table. The data source then sets the FilterExpression property to a string with a placeholder in it ('{0}'). The placeholder gets populated from the filter parameter that is provided by a ControlParameter object. This object extracts the value to use for filtering from some other control on the page, in this case the customers grid, using the specified property name on that control (SelectedValue). The result is that all order records are pulled down to the Web page, but a filter is placed on a data view under the covers to limit which records are rendered through the data source.

Using select parameters, as shown earlier, will be more efficient if you aren't caching the data. But if you cache the data, then you would want to get all the records in this way so that they are being filtered in memory from the entire collection, saving a round-trip to the database. There are additional properties you can set on the data source to have it cache the data automatically.

To do master-details binding to an object collection using an Object-DataSource instead of a SqlDataSource, you would need to have a SelectMethod that takes parameters to limit the result set that is returned in the same way that a WHERE clause does for SQL. It would depend on the capabilities of the collection returned as to whether filtering would work.

Hierarchical Binding

One capability that ASP.NET has that Windows Forms does not is the ability to bind a hierarchical data source, such as an XML file, to a hierarchical control, such as the TreeView control. To do this, you can use an XmlData-Source pointed to an XML file, and set that as the data source for the TreeView. You can then set TreeNodeBindings within the TreeView to pick out particular fields from the elements in the hierarchy. The following example will display each element name in the books.xml file as a tree node, and when a tree node named book is found, it will show child items based on the value of the title attribute of each book node:

```
<form id="form1" runat="server">
<div>
    <asp:XmlDataSource ID="XmlDataSource1" runat="server"
       DataFile="~/App_Data/books.xml"></asp:XmlDataSource>
    <asp:TreeView ID="TreeView1" runat="server"
       DataSourceID="XmlDataSource1">
        <DataBindings>
            <asp:TreeNodeBinding DataMember="book"
               TextField="title" />
        </DataBindings>
    </asp:TreeView>
</div>
</form>
```

Where Are We?

This appendix has given you a very quick introduction to coding data-binding scenarios using ASP.NET 2.0, and an idea of what capabilities exist and how to approach them. It isn't intended as a comprehensive lesson in data binding, but it should help get you started. This information will be important to you if you need to code similar data-bound UIs for an application when you are also building a Windows Forms version for a subset of your users.

▪ B ▪

Binding Data in WinFx Applications

WINDOWS PRESENTATION FOUNDATION (WPF), formerly code-named *Avalon*, is the presentation (user interface) subsystem of the WinFx development platform for Windows Vista, Windows XP, and Windows Server 2003. WinFx is the successor to the Win32 development platform and is based on the .NET Framework. Also part of WinFx is the Windows Communication Foundation (formerly code-named *Indigo*). WinFx presentation capabilities are designed to revolutionize the development of rich user interfaces for both the desktop and the browser. The WinFx rendering engine is designed to better harness the power of modern graphics cards and displays.

WinFx doesn't make Windows Forms programming or applications obsolete. Windows Forms applications will continue to run fine on current Windows platforms and on Windows Vista as well. Windows Forms is the best option for developing desktop applications today and will remain the best choice for portable applications until you no longer want to support Windows 2000 clients. However, WinFx provides a lot of new capabilities that you may want to start taking advantage of, particularly if you are writing graphics-intensive applications or need a lot of control and customization of the look-and-feel of your applications. Many books and articles will be written on WinFx programming in the future, and you will need to dive into those to really become a WinFx programmer (one great resource is *Programming Windows Presentation Foundation* by Chris Sells and Ian Griffiths). In this appendix, I want to give you a quick introduction to WinFx user interface development and an idea of how data binding works there as compared to Windows Forms.

At the time of this writing, I am using the WinFx SDK Beta 1 with Visual Studio 2005 Beta 2. To work with Beta development tools like this, I strongly recommend you use a virtual machine, such as Microsoft Virtual PC or VMware Workstation. If you want to run the samples for this appendix, you will need to first install the WinFx Beta 1 Runtime Components, then the WinFx SDK Beta 1, then Visual Studio 2005 Beta 2, then the Visual Studio 2005 Extensions for WinFx Beta 1.

▪▪ NOTE

One big caveat about this appendix is that it is written against these volatile early Beta bits. Every Beta and Community Technology Preview (CTP) that comes out will see significant changes in class names, class member names, functionality, and the like. It is very possible that by the time this book goes to print, the sample code in this appendix won't run against current bits as is, and you will have to do some tweaking to migrate the code to where WinFx has evolved to.

However, the basic principals discussed and demonstrated through the code in this appendix should remain roughly the same, so learning the material in this appendix will give you a good jump-start for building data-bound WinFx applications, even if you have to do some playing to get it all to work.

WinFx UI Programming and Capabilities Overview

WinFx introduces a number of new concepts and approaches to developing user interface applications for Windows. WinFx takes a new approach to targeting the display device and rendering graphics, introduces several new approaches to programming UI elements, and provides a new declarative language for specifying UI applications.

One of the first things that WinFx does is to try to break out of the pixel-based programming model for low-level graphics rendering on users' desktops. Current and near-future displays are capable of rendering at incredibly high resolution. If you base the size of elements rendered to the display on pixels, as is commonly done in Windows applications today, you will get vastly different UI element sizes when applications run on different devices and displays. Although there are ways to do size transformations in GDI and GDI+ today to logical units, the primary programming model is based on pixels. In WinFx, that model is reversed; the primary APIs for performing drawing operations are based on logical units.

Additionally, the primary graphics rendering approach in Windows today is based on raster operations—drawing items on the display based on a matrix of pixels. But most things being drawn represent geometric shapes, such as rectangles and curves, which are more easily specified and rendered using vector graphics. As such, WinFx makes vector graphics the primary rendering technique for low-level drawing. This makes it much easier to do something like put UI elements on the screen and then perform transformations on them, such as to rotate, scale, or move them. This makes programming animated effects much easier and more natural.

Under the covers, WinFx uses the DirectX graphics engine to do all drawing to the screen, which significantly boosts performance of many graphics operations and enables programming of complex multimedia applications using a single, managed, object-oriented API instead of having to choose between the simpler GDI+ API or low-level DirectX API. In WinFx, you will have a similar and simpler programming experience whether you are drawing custom user controls to the screen, embedding an animation or video in a document, or writing a complex simulation or game. WinFx applications can be run either as a standalone desktop application or as embedded controls or pages within a Web browser.

In addition to the rendering engine differences in WinFx programming, there are some significant differences in the way you program WinFx applications. WinFx uses a control composition model that lets you achieve rich effects and a consistent look and feel across Windows and Web applications using far less code than is required in current presentation technologies. You can layer styles onto controls within a container to avoid recoding look-and-feel aspects over and over. You can also create data-binding contexts that automatically affect child elements to achieve a rich compositional approach to data-bound controls. You'll get more of a feel for this in the coming sections.

When you program WinFx applications, you have two approaches that you can choose from or intermix. WinFx is based on a complex but easy to understand object model, so you can write entire WinFx applications using the managed programming language of your choice (e.g., C# or Visual Basic). You can also use a completely new declarative, XML-based programming language, called Extensible Application Markup Language (XAML), to code the UI elements and objects from which your application is composed. You can embed logic code within a XAML file as script blocks using C# or Visual Basic, or you can place the logic code in a separate code file and only declare the markup that describes UI elements in the XAML file. XAML basically provides a similar declarative approach to creating user interfaces as is used in ASP.NET markup, but it can be used for both Web and Windows applications. Like ASP.NET, you have the option of tying code-behind logic code from compiled source files to the objects declared in XAML, and the runtime will merge the compiled results when it dynamically compiles the markup and script found in an XAML file.

For most of this appendix, I am going to stick to just programming C# code against the WinFx object model to present a few samples. I chose to do this for several reasons. First off, if you are a Windows programmer, you may not be very comfortable with XML, schemas, and the declarative approach that XAML represents for creating WinFx applications. Even if you are, XAML represents a whole new dialect of XML that you probably aren't familiar with yet, and learning about both the objects you need to deal with along with new syntax might be a bit overwhelming for a quick overview appendix.

There's a reasonable argument made that no one in their right mind should ever end up writing XAML code by hand. XAML has some distinct advantages from a developer tools-and-compilation model perspective over source code and can end up being much more compact than the corresponding programmatic code. In fact, I expect that most WinFx user interface applications will be written using XAML for declaratively creating the

UI elements. But ideally, by the time you really start programming WinFx applications in earnest, there will be tools that generate XAML based on designer interactions, and you will rarely, if ever, edit XAML directly yourself. However, if you are an XML-lover or have a strong ASP.NET programming background, you might be quite comfortable diving in and swimming in the angle brackets, and might thus enjoy XAML programming. There are some XAML applications at the end of this appendix to give you a sense of what the corresponding XAML code looks like for one of the samples developed in code earlier in the appendix.

Writing a Simple WinFx Application

To get started programming WinFx applications, you have to get used to some of the object types you will use to compose an application. The type hierarchy for WinFx user interfaces is rooted at the `System.Windows` namespace (as opposed to `System.Windows.Forms` for Windows Forms). At the top level, there is an `Application` object, similar to a Windows Forms application, except that it is a separate type defined in the `System.Windows` namespace. There are several derived application classes that are specialized for specific kinds of applications, such as the `NavigationApplication` class you will see in a later example. Within an application, you create `System.Windows.Window` objects that will contain the pages and controls that compose the UI of the application. Controls are assembled into a hierarchy of elements called a **visual tree**, where any given element may either render its own client area, contain other controls, do both, or render nothing.

This approach leads to a very flexible and powerful approach to declaring and designing your UI, because you can effectively extend the control's functionality by adding different content to it. For example, in Windows Forms, the `Button` class lets you add a button to your forms that can contain a text prompt, an image, or both. You determine what it will contain by setting explicit properties on the class corresponding to those visual aspects that the control was designed to support in rendering its client area. With a WinFx button, and many other WinFx controls, you can add arbitrarily complex child elements to the button, and they will each be called to render themselves within their own area. Through styles, you can dynamically determine the content elements and set properties on them that affect the look-and-feel and behaviors.

Most of the WinFx controls you will deal with for simple applications are declared in the `System.Windows.Controls` namespace. The names don't map one-for-one with those found in Windows Forms, but there are similar controls for most of the simple controls you are used to dealing with. For example, there are `Button`, `TextBox`, and `ListBox` classes that are conceptually very similar to their Windows Forms cousins, although they can do quite a bit more, because you can add complex content to them. There is a `TextBlock` control that is like a `Label` on steroids, and there are a number of layout controls including `Canvas`, `StackPanel`, `Table`, and `Grid` that let you explicitly determine the layout of controls within your windows and pages. However, at the time of this writing, there is one big gaping hole from the perspective of data binding—there is no rich grid control that supports simple data binding. I'm sure this will be remedied in future builds, but as you will see later in the appendix, to achieve a `DataGrid`-like experience, you have to get low level and dynamically compose it from other controls for the time being.

Getting Started with a "Hello World" Application

To work your way up to that example, let's start with a simple WinFx "Hello World" application using only code. To create this, you will need to create a project in Visual Studio 2005. There are WinFx project types that are added to Visual Studio 2005 Beta 2 by the Visual Studio Extensions for WinFx, so you will need to have that installed, as well as the runtime components and the WinFx SDK.

1. Start by creating an Avalon application project type. You can delete the MyApp.xaml and Window1.xaml files from the project through Solution Explorer since you will be writing everything in code for now. I'll give an example in XAML later on, and the download code for this appendix includes XAML versions of all the applications discussed in this appendix.

2. Add a class to the project and name it `Program` (or something like that—the name of the class is unimportant in this example).

3. Add a `using` statement for the `System.Windows` namespace to the top of the file.

4. Add a static `Main` method. In that method, add the following code:

```
using System;
using System.Windows;
class Program
{
    [STAThread]
    static void Main()
    {
        Application app = new Application();
        Window win = new Window();
        win.Content = "Hello WinFx";
        win.Show();
        app.Run();
    }
}
```

In this simple application, you can see that first you need an application object. You also need a main window, which you can create for simple scenarios by creating an instance of the `Window` class.

In real applications, you will usually be creating an instance of a class that you define that will derive from `Window` or one of its WinFx Framework-derived classes, such as `NavigationWindow`. A window is a visual tree element like controls are, so the way you modify what is shown in the window is by setting its `Content` property. In this case, set it to a simple string, and the `Window` class is capable of rendering that string for you. Typically, you will compose a window's UI contents by constructing a tree of other elements (controls) and setting that tree's top-level object as the `Content` property for the window.

Once you have set the content of the window to the string "Hello WinFx," you show the window by calling the `Show` method. You then call the `Run` method of the `Application` object, which sets up the message processing loop that Windows really uses under the covers to communicate with your running application, just as is done in Windows Forms applications today.

Note the `STAThread` attribute on the `Main` method. This is still required in WinFx on Windows XP, because WinFx still wraps some of the system-provided controls that are designed to run in a single-threaded apartment.

Building a Slightly More Involved Application

A "Hello World" application isn't going to get you very far in understanding the WinFx object model and how to compose an application, so let's look at a slightly more complex example. Say you are building a WinFx application that will use authentication and authorization to determine what a user is allowed to do based on a custom membership database and roles. In that case, you need to authenticate the user, so you need a login window. So let's code a WinFx window that looks like the crude login dialog shown in Figure B.1.

1. Set up an empty WinFx project as described earlier in this appendix. Start with a WinFx application project and delete the MyApp.xaml and Window1.xaml files from the project.

2. Add a new class and name it `LoginApp`.

3. Add `using` statements for `System.Windows` and `System.Windows.Controls` to the top of the file.

4. Add `Application` as the base class for `LoginApp`, and add a static `Main` method that creates an instance of the application and calls the `Run` method on that instance:

```
using System;
using System.Windows;
using System.Windows.Controls;

namespace LoginSampleCode
{
   class LoginApp : Application
   {
      [System.STAThread()]
      static void Main()
      {
         LoginApp app = new LoginApp();
         app.Run();
      }

   }
}
```

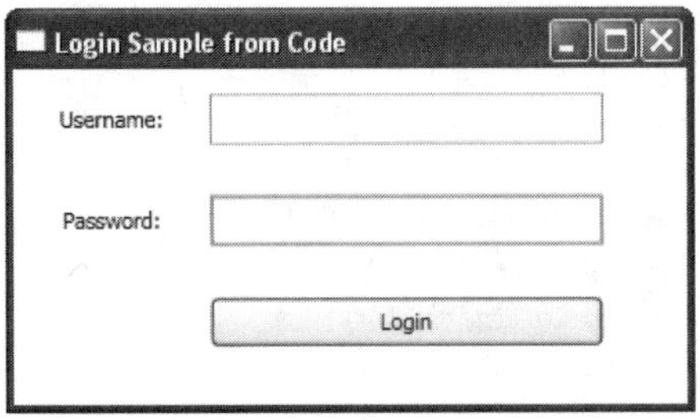

FIGURE B.1: Simple Login Dialog

5. Add an override for the base class OnStartingUp method, which is where you will do all of your window construction. Listing B.1 shows the entire implementation.

LISTING B.1: OnStartingUp Method

```
protected override void OnStartingUp(StartingUpCancelEventArgs e)
{
    Window win = new Window();
    win.Width = 350;
    win.Height = 200;
    win.Text = "Login Sample from Code";

    // Create the controls
    Grid grid = new Grid();
    TextBlock userNameLabel = new TextBlock();
    userNameLabel.TextContent = "Username:";
    userNameLabel.VerticalAlignment = VerticalAlignment.Center;
    userNameLabel.HorizontalAlignment = HorizontalAlignment.Center;

    TextBlock passwordLabel = new TextBlock();
    passwordLabel.TextContent = "Password:";
    passwordLabel.VerticalAlignment = VerticalAlignment.Center;
    passwordLabel.HorizontalAlignment =
    HorizontalAlignment.Center;TextBox userNameInput = new TextBox();
    userNameInput.Height = 25;
    PasswordBox pwdInput = new PasswordBox();
    pwdInput.Height = 25;
    Button loginButton = new Button();
    loginButton.Height = 25;
    loginButton.Content = "Login";

    // Set up the grid layout
    grid.ColumnDefinitions.Add(new ColumnDefinition());
    grid.ColumnDefinitions.Add(new ColumnDefinition());
```

continues

```
grid.RowDefinitions.Add(new RowDefinition());
grid.RowDefinitions.Add(new RowDefinition());
grid.RowDefinitions.Add(new RowDefinition());
grid.ColumnDefinitions[0].Width = new GridLength(100);
grid.ColumnDefinitions[1].Width = new GridLength(200);
grid.RowDefinitions[0].Height = new GridLength(50);
grid.RowDefinitions[1].Height = new GridLength(50);
grid.RowDefinitions[2].Height = new GridLength(50);

// Add the controls to the grid
AddControlToGrid(grid, userNameLabel, 0, 0);
AddControlToGrid(grid, passwordLabel, 1, 0);
AddControlToGrid(grid, userNameInput, 0, 1);
AddControlToGrid(grid, pwdInput, 1, 1);
AddControlToGrid(grid, loginButton, 2, 1);

// Set the grid as content for the window and show it
win.Content = grid;
win.Show();
}

private void AddControlToGrid(Grid grid, FrameworkElement ctl, int
rowPos, int colPos)
{
    Grid.SetColumn(ctl,colPos);
    Grid.SetRow(ctl,rowPos);
    grid.Children.Add(ctl);
}
```

The code first creates the main `Window` object and sets its `Width`, `Height`, and `Text` properties. There is nothing mystical going on here; the code is similar to what the Windows Forms designer writes in the designer code file for each form that you create.

Next it creates the following controls: a `Grid`, two `TextBlocks`, one `TextBox`, one `PasswordBox`, and a `Button`. Each instance is created with a default constructor, and then certain properties are set on it. For the `Text-Blocks`, the `TextContent` property is set to the prompt string that the `TextBlock` is there for—this is acting like a `Label` control in Windows Forms. The `HorizontalAlignment` and `VerticalAlignment` properties are also set to `Center` to make things align nicely in the form. For the `TextBox`, `PasswordBox`, and `Button`, their `Height` property is set; for the `Button`, the `Content` property is set to a string, resulting in that string being displayed on the surface of the button as you are used to in setting the `Text` property of a `Button` control in Windows Forms.

The `Grid` control is a container control, and it lets you easily lay out controls in a rectangular grid on the rendering surface of some other element by setting the grid as the content of that element. The next block of code in Listing B.1 creates the column and row definitions for the grid and sets their `Width` and `Height` properties to get the layout you desire.

The next block of code calls a helper method at the bottom of the listing to add each control to a specific position within the grid. Unfortunately, with the current programming model in WinFx, it takes three lines of code for each control to perform the simple action of placing the control in a cell in the grid:

```
Grid.SetColumn(someControl, 0);
Grid.SetRow(someControl, 0);
gridInstance.Children.Add(someControl);
```

The `AddControlToGrid` helper method encapsulates these steps, which makes the calling code a little more compact. But basically that method sets the column and row for each control, and then adds it to the grid. Note that the way a control position is set within a grid is by using static methods on the `Grid` class itself, rather than methods or properties on an instance of a grid.

After adding each control to the grid in its respective cell, the grid is set as the content element on the window, and the window is shown. The net result is a window that looks like Figure B.1.

This example gives you a little better idea of how controls get layered into the content of each other to form a visual tree of controls. At this point, the programmatic approach probably seems a little cumbersome to you. I mean, come on, all that code just to lay out a simple login form? The thing to keep in mind is that there isn't significantly less code to achieve the same thing in Windows Forms, but almost no one writes Windows Forms from scratch by hand; they let the designer write most or all of that code. Well, the same will be true for WinFx by the time it ships. There isn't a designer to work with at this point, and understanding the code will help you out once the designer starts writing it and you find things not working quite the way you want.

WinFx Data Binding 101

So now you have seen a couple of simple programmatic WinFx applications, but there wasn't really any data stuff going on in them. WinFx has a rich model for setting up data-bound controls as well. It works a little different from how Windows Forms works, with the intent of being more flexible and requiring less code.

WinFx elements support the concept of a data-binding context that is flowed down to child elements automatically: from the application, down to window objects, and down to child controls. So if you have a source of data that needs to be bound to multiple controls, potentially even in separate windows, you can establish a data context that lets you initialize and set the data source in one place, and it will automatically cascade down the element tree to any child elements that don't explicitly set their own context.

If you have read the chapters in this book carefully, this should be sounding a little familiar. The binding approach in WinFx is somewhat similar to BindingSource objects in Windows Forms. They set up a one-stop-shopping object for a source of data to which multiple controls can be bound. There are some distinct differences, though, both in the way that you declare and initialize a binding in WinFx, and in the way that they flow to other elements. In Windows Forms, you have to explicitly set DataSource properties on controls to point to a BindingSource, or add a Binding object to the DataBindings collection on a control to make the association between a specific BindingSource and a control. You then also specify the data member path within that data source to which you want to bind. In the case of WinFx bindings, you only need to specify the path within the data context that you want, and a control will automatically pick up the data context (the data source) that is set on its parent element tree.

For example, consider a Window in which you have a grid containing a set of text boxes that are intended to be bound to the fields of a row of customer data. You could set the data context of the Window to be the collection of customers, and you could then specify the bindings at the control level to identify the path to each field (such as CompanyName, Contact-Name, etc.). Because the text boxes are designed to display a single value at a time, the values from the current record within the data source set at the Window level would be displayed.

You could then set a new data context at the grid level to a different collection of customers from the one that is currently set at the window level. As long as the shape of the objects in the collection set at the grid level was the same as the objects in the collection at the Window level (same field or property names), the text boxes in the grid would automatically switch to using the binding specified at the grid level. This happens because it is the closest parent that has specified its own data context.

If you set out to implement an application that bound customer data to rows of text boxes in a grid as just discussed, it might look something like Figure B.2.

Listing B.2 shows the application class for this example. The Main method again creates an instance of your derived application class and then sets it running. The OnStartingUp override gets called as the application is starting up, letting you create the main window and populate it with controls. In this sample, I am using a StackPanel as the top-level container control within the window to stack the controls in a vertical column, as you can see in Figure B.1. One of the child controls in the Stack-Panel is a Grid that contains the TextBlocks and TextBoxes that display the bound fields of the rows. Most of the code is basic WinFx control creation and layout, and is similar to the code in Listing B.1. The lines of code related to data binding are in bold.

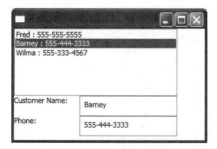

FIGURE B.2: Simple Data-Bound Application

LISTING B.2: Data-Bound Application

```
class MyApp : Application
{
    [STAThread]
    static void Main()
    {
        MyApp app = new MyApp();
        app.Run();
    }

    protected override void OnStartingUp(StartingUpCancelEventArgs e)
    {
        Window win = new Window();
        win.Width = 300;
        win.Height = 200;
        StackPanel stack = new StackPanel();
        stack.VerticalAlignment = VerticalAlignment.Top;
        stack.HorizontalAlignment = HorizontalAlignment.Left;
        ListBox custList = new ListBox();
        custList.Height = 100;
        custList.IsSynchronizedWithCurrentItem = true;
        custList.SetBinding(ListBox.ItemsSourceProperty, new Binding());

        Grid grid = new Grid();
        grid.ColumnDefinitions.Add(new ColumnDefinition());
        grid.ColumnDefinitions.Add(new ColumnDefinition());
        grid.RowDefinitions.Add(new RowDefinition());
        grid.RowDefinitions.Add(new RowDefinition());
        grid.ColumnDefinitions[0].Width = new GridLength(100);
        grid.ColumnDefinitions[1].Width = new GridLength(150);
        grid.RowDefinitions[0].Height = new GridLength(30);
        grid.RowDefinitions[1].Height = new GridLength(30);

        TextBlock custNameLabel = new TextBlock();
        custNameLabel.TextContent = "Customer Name:";
        TextBlock custPhoneLabel = new TextBlock();
        custPhoneLabel.TextContent = "Phone:";
        TextBox custNameInput = new TextBox();
        custNameInput.SetBinding(TextBox.TextProperty, "Name");
        TextBox custPhoneInput = new TextBox();
        custPhoneInput.SetBinding(TextBox.TextProperty, "Phone");
        AddControlToGrid(grid, custNameLabel, 0, 0);
        AddControlToGrid(grid, custNameInput, 0, 1);
        AddControlToGrid(grid, custPhoneLabel, 1, 0);
        AddControlToGrid(grid, custPhoneInput, 1, 1);
        stack.Children.Add(custList);
        stack.Children.Add(grid);

        win.Content = stack;
```

```
      win.Loaded += WindowLoaded;
      win.Show();
   }

   private void AddControlToGrid(Grid grid, FrameworkElement ctl,
      int rowPos, int colPos)
   {
      Grid.SetColumn(ctl, colPos);
      Grid.SetRow(ctl, rowPos);
      grid.Children.Add(ctl);
   }

   private void WindowLoaded(object sender, EventArgs e)
   {
      Window win = (Window)sender;
      CustomersCollection custs = new CustomersCollection();
      win.DataContext = custs;
   }
}
```

The calls to the `SetBinding` method on the list box and the text boxes are what sets up the path within whatever the data context is for those controls. In the case of the list box, the property that sets up the binding is the `Items-Source` property, and it is bound to a default instance of the `Binding` class. The `SetBinding` method takes a `DependencyProperty` argument, which provides type information about the property on a bound type to which the binding applies and a path within the data context. The path will be used at runtime to try to resolve the binding dynamically based on the current data context and the path information provided by the `Binding` instance. When you create a default instance of a `Binding` object, it sets the path to the root of the data context. Alternatively, as in the case of the `TextBoxes`, the path to a subobject or collection can be provided. For the `TextBoxes`, the name of the property within the objects in the collection is identified and used to populate the corresponding `Text` property on the `TextBox`.

The data used in this example is a custom collection of `Customer` objects, which is created in the `WindowLoaded` event handler and set as the data context for the `Window` through the `DataContext` property. The `CustomersCollection` class default constructor populates the collection with three test objects, which is what is seen at runtime. After the data context is set, the data bindings of all child controls are refreshed and their paths within that data context sought out.

Data Contexts and Data Sources

The CustomersCollection class in Listing B.2 is derived from the ObservableCollection<T> class, which provides implementation for the interface INotifyCollectionChanged. This interface is necessary to have synchronization between multiple controls bound to the collection, and it is similar in function to the ListChanged event on the IBinding-List interface. Because this interface type is new to WinFx, current .NET Framework collection classes and data sets don't support full data-binding capabilities against WinFx controls. (By the time WinFx releases, though, I would expect the built-in data collection classes of the .NET Framework to support WinFx data binding.)

You can use any collection of data for data binding that at least supports the IEnumerable interface, which lets the data-binding code in WinFx to iterate over the collection of objects to present values from them using Bind objects. You can also use individual objects if the data context will only be used for binding against single-valued controls. You set the data source through the DataContext property on any element, which can be done at the Application, Window, or any child-control level. Again, when data binding occurs, any bound controls use the data context of the closest parent that has a data context set to perform its data binding. The DataContext property is declared on the FrameworkElement class and is of type System.Object, which lets you set it to anything.

For more robust data-binding features, such as the ability to edit the data in the objects that are bound, detect changes to a collection when it is changed by another control or programmatic code, or the ability to sort and filter the data collection, you will need to have objects and a data collection that support a variety of interfaces, similar to those discussed in Chapter 7. Those interfaces are likely to change quite a bit by the time WinFx releases, so I won't go into any detail on them here. The most capable collection to place your objects in today is the ObservableCollection<T> class that is part of the System.Windows.Data namespace. Hopefully by the time WinFx ships, DataViews and other generic collection classes will support the necessary interfaces to allow rich data binding in WinFx.

What About XAML?

Most WinFx user interfaces will probably be programmed using XAML. I started this appendix with the objects and programmatic code to make it clear that the objects you deal with in WinFx are just a different set of controls and classes from a new set of namespaces that supplement the existing .NET Framework. However, in addition to the objects that support the new WinFx user interface capabilities, there is also a new language to specify your user interface code with. XAML brings the declarative markup capabilities that Web developers have had for years to Windows UI programmers using XML markup, which is often easier and more concise for specifying the layout and properties of UI elements. Ideally, no one should ever have to edit XAML or any other form of XML directly. Tools should overlay the XML and let you manipulate designer objects in a more intuitive way, and the tools should generate the appropriate XML as a result of those interactions. Hopefully by the time WinFx ships, that will be the case in Visual Studio as well.

For now, you have to code the XAML by hand using the text editor. You do at least get some support in Visual Studio 2005 with the schema-bound IntelliSense of the XML editor, in that it will prompt you with the allowable elements and attributes based on where you are in an XAML element tree. But you are still just cranking out XML by hand, which leaves a lot to be desired.

As an example, I will recreate the same functionality shown earlier in the DataBinding101 example and Figure B.2—a window with a list box of customers and two text boxes that are bound to the same collection to display the customer name and phone number of the current item in the collection—but I will implement it using a mix of XAML and programmatic code.

XAML is good for declaratively specifying the elements that the application is composed of, along with setting any of their properties that can be statically defined. Some things will still require programmatic code, which can either be placed as script blocks in the XAML file itself, or you can write a separate partial class file containing a partial class definition that is pointed to by the `Class` attribute on the top-level element within the corresponding XAML file. The latter model is very similar to code-behind in ASP.NET and is the preferred model in Visual Studio.

To declare an application class using XAML, you can use the following code:

```
<Application x:Class="DataBinding101.MyApp"
    xmlns="http://schemas.microsoft.com/winfx/avalon/2005"
    xmlns:x="http://schemas.microsoft.com/winfx/xaml/2005"
    StartingUp="AppStartingUp"
    >
    <Application.Resources>

    </Application.Resources>
</Application>
```

Having an XAML file with an `Application` element in it will result in the creation of an instance of the application class at runtime. In this case, the `Application` element specifies that its class name is `Data-Binding101.MyApp`, which will be created as a partial class. The namespaces define the schemas used in the XAML markup, and the `StartingUp` attribute lets you hook up an event handler for the `StartingUp` event by specifying the name of the method within your application class that will handle the event. The `Application.Resources` element is a container for application-scoped resources that you can declare as part of your file. Things such as static data and configuration settings, styles, and other elements can be declared in that section and will be accessible to any child elements of the application.

The code-behind for the application goes in a file named MyApp.xaml.cs, although the file could be named anything, and contains a partial class declaration with the programmatic code that goes along with the application class defined in the XAML:

```
public partial class MyApp : Application
{
    void AppStartingUp(object sender, StartingUpCancelEventArgs e)
    {
        Window1 mainWindow = new Window1();
        mainWindow.Show();
    }
}
```

The handler method for the `StartingUp` event has to comply with the signature of the event's delegate, which in this case is the `StartingUp-CancelEventHandler` type. The handler simply creates an instance of the

`Window1` class, which will be discussed soon, and calls the `Show` method on that window to present it.

The `Window1` class is declared using a combination of XAML and code as well. Here's Window1.xaml:

```xml
<Window x:Class="DataBinding101.Window1"
    xmlns="http://schemas.microsoft.com/winfx/avalon/2005"
    xmlns:x="http://schemas.microsoft.com/winfx/xaml/2005"
    xmlns:def="Definition"
    Text="DataBinding101"
    Loaded="WindowLoaded"
    Width="300"
    Height="200"
    >
  <StackPanel HorizontalAlignment="Left" VerticalAlignment="Top">
    <ListBox ID="custList" ItemsSource="{Binding}"
      IsSynchronizedWithCurrentItem="true"  Width="150"
      Height="50" Grid.Column="0" Grid.Row="0"/>
    <Grid Grid.Column="0" Grid.Row="1">
      <ColumnDefinition Width="100" />
      <ColumnDefinition Width="150" />
      <RowDefinition Height="30" />
      <RowDefinition Height="30" />
      <TextBlock Grid.Column="0" Grid.Row="0">
        Customer Name:</TextBlock>
      <TextBlock Grid.Column="0" Grid.Row="1">Phone:</TextBlock>
      <TextBox Grid.Column="1" Grid.Row="0" Text="{Binding Path=Name}"
        Height="25"/>
      <TextBox Grid.Column="1" Grid.Row="1" Text="{Binding Path=Phone}"
        Height="25"/>
    </Grid>
  </StackPanel>
</Window>
```

Like the application class XAML, the window class XAML declares a root `Window` element and identifies the class name with the `Class` attribute. It hooks up the `Loaded` event to a method named `Window-Loaded`, sets the title bar text through the `Text` attribute, and sets the `Width` and `Height` properties to drive the size of the window.

The window's controls are then created by declaring them as child elements under the `Window` element. In this case, the outermost element is a `StackPanel`, which contains the list box and a grid containing the labels and text boxes for the customer name and phone. You can see that to set properties on the instances of the controls that will be created, you simply add attributes to their XAML elements. To set up the grid layout, `Column-Definition` and `RowDefinition` elements are specified as child elements of the grid, and then the controls are placed in the desired column or row by making them a child element and adding the `Grid.Column` and `Grid.Row` attributes to the control's element tag.

Note also the binding statements for the list box and two text boxes. The list box simply sets its `ItemsSource` property to `{Binding}`. This is a special syntax in XAML that effectively creates a default instance of a `Binding` object, setting the current data context as the bound source. The text boxes set their `Text` property to a similar `Binding` statement, except one that sets the `Path` property on the resulting `Binding` object to the desired member name within the objects in the data context.

The code-behind for the window is in the file Window1.xaml.cs, and contains a default constructor that calls the `InitializeComponent` method, and an event handler named `WindowLoaded` for the `Loaded` event. Unlike Windows Forms, there is no designer code file that contains `InitializeComponent`. Instead, that method and the rest of the code corresponding to the XAML file markup is generated on the fly as part of the compilation process. `InitializeComponent` still needs to be called, because it is where all the code to set the properties specified in the XAML file resides after compilation. The implementation of the `Window1` class is shown below:

```
public partial class Window1 : Window
{
    public Window1() : base()
    {
        InitializeComponent();
    }

    private void WindowLoaded(object sender, EventArgs e)
    {
        CustomersCollection custs = new CustomersCollection();
        DataContext = custs;
    }
}
```

The `WindowLoaded` event handler creates an instance of the `Customers-Collection` class, whose default constructor populates the collection with some test data. The method then sets the `DataContext` property on the window to that collection, which initiates the data-binding process for any elements with `Binding` objects associated with their properties.

That's all there is to it. The combination of XAML and code-behind shown in this section is functionally equivalent to the programmatic code shown in the WinFx Data Binding 101 section. You will probably find that the resulting XAML for any given set of controls is generally more compact and concise than the corresponding programmatic code, but it does require you to look at XML instead of clean, imperative code.

Binding a Collection to a Grid with Templates

You might expect to be able to bind the collection of `Customer` objects to a grid or table control and get a tabular rendering of that data the way you can today with the `DataGridView` or `DataGrid` controls. Unfortunately, a rich, tabular, data-bound control has not been added to the WinFx control suite yet, so you have to do a fair amount of work to generate a UI that contains a data-bound grid of controls that simulates a `DataGridView`-like experience.

One approach would be to programmatically loop through the collection of data and dynamically add child controls to a grid control. That can get a little messy, tedious, and error prone. A more elegant but slightly less intuitive way is to use item templates in WinFx. You can use item templates to define a template for the content of other controls, and that content can be arbitrarily complex and contain other elements. For example, to create a grid of text boxes on the fly in response to data binding, you can set up the XAML in Listing B.3. Instead of a `Window` object, this example defines a `Page` as part of a `NavigationApplication`. In a `Navigation-Application`, a `NavigationWindow` gets created automatically, and the `Page` specified as the `StartupUri` in the `NavigationApplication` element is loaded into that window as the starting page. This gives you a navigation experience like a browser, but in a rich Windows application.

LISTING B.3: Dynamic Grid with Templates

```
<Page x:Class="CustomersViewerXAML.Page1"
    xmlns="http://schemas.microsoft.com/winfx/avalon/2005"
    xmlns:x="http://schemas.microsoft.com/winfx/xaml/2005"
    Loaded="PageLoaded"
    >
<Page.Resources>

</Page.Resources>
<Grid HorizontalAlignment="Left" VerticalAlignment="Top">
  <ColumnDefinition Width="400" />
  <RowDefinition Height="50"/>
  <RowDefinition />
  <Grid Grid.Row="0">
    <ColumnDefinition Width="100*" />
    <ColumnDefinition Width="100*" />
    <ColumnDefinition Width="100*" />
    <TextBlock Grid.Column="0">Company</TextBlock>
    <TextBlock Grid.Column="1">Contact</TextBlock>
    <TextBlock Grid.Column="2">Phone</TextBlock>
  </Grid>
<ItemsControl Grid.Row="1" Margin="20,0,20,20"
        ItemsSource="{Binding}">
  <ItemsControl.ItemTemplate>
    <DataTemplate>
      <Grid>
            <ColumnDefinition Width="100*" />
            <ColumnDefinition Width="100*" />
            <ColumnDefinition Width="100*" />
            <TextBox Text="{Binding Path=CompanyName}"
              Grid.Column="0" />
            <TextBox Text="{Binding Path=ContactName}"
              Grid.Column="1" />
            <TextBox Text="{Binding Path=Phone}" Grid.Column="2" />

        </Grid>
      </DataTemplate>
    </ItemsControl.ItemTemplate>
  </ItemsControl>
  </Grid>
</Page>
```

In Listing B.3, the `ItemTemplate` is defined under the `ItemsControl`. The `ItemsControl` is bound to the default data context, which gets set in the code-behind on page load as described shortly. What happens is that for each item in the bound collection, an instance of the contents of the

`DataTemplate` gets injected into the `ItemsControl`. So this creates an instance of a `Grid`, with its content controls each bound to the appropriate part of the current item, rendered for each row in the data source.

The data context in this sample is set to a data set of customers through the `PageLoaded` event handler:

```
private void PageLoaded(object sender, EventArgs e)
{
    SqlConnection conn = new SqlConnection(
      "server=localhost;database=Northwind;trusted_connection=true");
    SqlDataAdapter adapter = new SqlDataAdapter(
      "SELECT * FROM Customers", conn);
    DataSet ds = new DataSet();
    adapter.Fill(ds, "Customers");
    DataContext = ds.Tables["Customers"].DefaultView;
}
```

Templates in XAML allow you to specify the shape of the content that is rendered for individual items in a control collection. The controls can be rendered based on data items in a collection as was done here. This gives you a lot of flexibility for dynamically constructing a form based on bound data.

Control Styling in WinFx

Styles let you declaratively determine what the content of a given WinFx element will contain. Styles can also be used to dynamically alter the content of an element at runtime. Using styles, you can set look-and-feel properties such as background colors, fonts, and the like. But you can also dynamically inject child elements into the content of another element using a style. A style basically sets up a template that can be applied to a control or to its content.

Styles cascade down the element tree in a similar fashion to data contexts. This is a wonderful thing, because it means you no longer have to repetitively apply the same property to a collection of controls to get them all behaving or looking the same. You can simply apply a style to that control at an element level above where the multiple controls live, and they will all pick up that style automatically. You can also explicitly set a style to a named style instance if the style defines a `Key` attribute.

Take the case of a `TextBlock` control. Say that you have a set of three `TextBlock` controls, and you want them all to have a background color of light blue and a font of Comic Sans 14. Rather than having to set the `Font` and `Background` properties on each of the `TextBlock` controls as you would in Windows Forms, you can instead simply define a style at the window or grid level that contains style settings for `TextBlocks`, and all of the child `TextBlock` elements below the level where that style was defined will automatically pick up whatever property settings and content that style defines. You can also define a style for a `TextBlock` or other control that has a `Key` attribute, and then use that style to explicitly set the style for one or more controls without having to set all of the associated properties one by one.

The following is some XAML that does this for a window with three `TextBlocks` in a grid. It uses the cascading style for `TextBlocks` from the window level for two of the controls and then explicitly sets the style of another `TextBlock` to a different style based on its key.

```
<Window x:Class="SimpleSyles.Window1"
    xmlns="http://schemas.microsoft.com/winfx/avalon/2005"
    xmlns:x="http://schemas.microsoft.com/winfx/xaml/2005"
    Text="SimpleStyles"
    >
<Window.Resources>
    <Style TargetType="{x:Type TextBlock}">
            <Setter Property="FontFamily" Value="Comic Sans MS"/>
            <Setter Property="FontSize" Value="14" />
            <Setter Property="Background" Value="LightBlue" />
    </Style>
        <Style x:Key="ExplicitStyle">
            <Setter Property="Control.FontFamily"
            Value="Times New Roman"  />
            <Setter Property="Control.FontSize" Value="24" />
    </Style>
</Window.Resources>
<Grid>
    <ColumnDefinition />
    <RowDefinition />
    <RowDefinition />
    <RowDefinition />
    <TextBlock Grid.Column="0" Grid.Row="0">Label1</TextBlock>
    <TextBlock Grid.Column="0" Grid.Row="1"
        Style="{StaticResource ExplicitStyle}">Label2</TextBlock>
    <TextBlock Grid.Column="0" Grid.Row="2">Label3</TextBlock>
</Grid>
</Window>
```

The first `Style` defined in the `Window.Resources` element says that any child elements of type `TextBlock` that don't explicitly set their style to something else should inherit the style settings of a light blue background and Comic Sans MS size 14 font. The second `Style` element defines a different style that applies to any controls, but that needs to be set explicitly using its key. The first and third `TextBlocks` in the grid don't explicitly set a style, so they are automatically styled based on the default style for `TextBlocks` at that scope, which translates to the first style declared at the window level. The second `TextBlock` explicitly sets its style to the `ExplicitStyle` key, and therefore gets set with Times New Roman size 24 font with the default white background.

Where Are We?

This appendix has given you a quick and dirty introduction to WinFx UI programming and data binding in WinFx. There is a lot more to be said, and many more books on the topic to follow. The intent here was to just give you some quick exposure so that you could get a sense of how data binding works in WinFx, and how it is similar and different from data binding in Windows Forms.

▎C ▪

Programming Windows
Forms Applications

T HE FIRST PLACE many programmers start when developing applications with .NET is with Windows Forms. Windows Forms represents
an application framework within the .NET Framework for developing
desktop user interface applications and their supporting components. Getting started with programming Windows Forms applications is very easy,
especially when using Visual Studio 2005. If you have programmed with
Visual Basic 6 or earlier, the process for designing Windows Forms in
Visual Studio 2005 will feel very comfortable and familiar. If you come
from a C++ background, you will find that designing with Windows
Forms is familiar but easier than the process of programming views and
dialogs in Microsoft Foundation Class (MFC), but that you sacrifice almost
none of the power and control you had when programming Windows
from C++. If you have been developing Windows Forms applications in
.NET, then you are probably already familiar with most of what is covered
in this appendix. The bottom line is that Windows Forms programming is
intuitive and fun, and it is easier and faster to put together rich user interface applications in Windows Forms than with any other technology that I
have encountered.

Despite the name, Windows Forms can be used to create any style of
Windows application that you need; the UI doesn't necessarily have to be

oriented toward the presentation of actual forms. In earlier Windows UI development frameworks, everything was treated as a window. Each top-level window was a window, each dialog was a window, and even each control within a window was itself a window. In .NET, the common underlying construct for developing Windows Forms is the *control*. In Windows Forms, every UI element presented by your application will generally be derived from the `Control` base class. Even forms are derived from the `Control` base class and are therefore controls as well. But the term *form* in Windows Forms is used to describe any class that derives from the `System.Windows.Forms.Form` base class and which presents a window or dialog. Any other classes that derive from the `Control` base class and are intended to be contained within a window are called *controls*.

This appendix isn't intended to be a comprehensive treatise on Windows Forms programming. I just want to give you enough background on the basics of Windows Forms programming so that if you haven't done any Windows Forms programming, you don't have to go read another book first. For a comprehensive treatment of Windows Forms programming, I recommend the forthcoming *Windows Forms 2005 Programming in C#* by Chris Sells and Mike Weinhardt (tentatively scheduled for publication by Addison-Wesley in early 2006).

This appendix covers the basic structure of a Windows Forms application, the architecture of the supporting Framework classes, some of the most common controls you will deal with in developing data-driven applications, and some of the new Windows Forms controls that are available in .NET 2.0. This appendix doesn't go into any detail on the data-bound controls because they have their own dedicated chapters in the book. If you are an experienced .NET Windows Forms programmer, you might want to skip over most of this appendix, with the exception of those sections that are noted as "new in 2.0." I've also marked the parts of other sections that use new features in .NET 2.0 or Visual Studio 2005 with a *(New in 2.0)* comment.

Your First Windows Forms Data Application

This first application will take you a small step beyond a "Hello World" application; you'll create a very simple application that loads some data and displays it in a grid. I explain the steps to create the application from a pure code perspective, and in the next section you will repeat the creation of the application using Visual Studio. This way you can get a sense of both what is going on behind the scenes and how to do things the quick and easy way with the Visual Studio designer. Then we will dig into what is going on under the covers so that you understand where all the functionality in the Windows Forms Framework comes from.

Okay, let's get started with the pure code approach.

1. Open a text file and name it **DataAppForm.cs**.

2. Declare a class that derives from `System.Windows.Forms.Form`:

```
using System;
using System.Windows.Forms;
public class DataAppForm : Form
{
}
```

This code includes the `using` statement for the `System.Windows.Forms` namespace, which is where the `Form` and `Application` classes are defined, as well as the controls that you will be adding shortly.

3. You also need a class that will contain the start-up code for the program. For this simple example, you can place this code in the same file:

```
static class Program
{
    [STAThread]
    static void Main()
    {
        Application.EnableVisualStyles();
        Application.Run(new DataAppForm());
    }
}
```

The `Main` method is the entry point for any .NET application. In Visual Studio.NET 2003, this was always placed in the first `Form` class added to a project. In Visual Studio 2005, the `Program` class is added to the project as a separate code file so that the `Main` method doesn't get lost if the first form is deleted from the project. We will mirror that approach here, but just put it in the same file for simplicity.

The STAThread attribute is needed if the application will use any ActiveX controls, the Clipboard, or any single-threaded apartment COM objects, so it is added by default to any Visual Studio Windows application projects, and in general, you always need it there. You need to bring in the System namespace with a using statement to make that attribute type available.

4. To compile this file using the C# command line compiler, open a Visual Studio command prompt (located in the Start menu under the Microsoft Visual Studio grouping, Visual Studio Tools submenu), switch to the folder where the file resides, and type the command:

```
csc DataAppForm.cs
```

Note that you need to have the environment variables set so that Windows can find the command line compiler (csc.exe) if you don't use the Visual Studio command prompt. You should now have an executable named **DataAppForm.exe** that you can run. If you do so, you will get a blank, square window.

5. That's a little boring, so let's add a grid and a button to the form. Listing C.1 shows the changes (in bold) to the class that you need to add the button and grid and to position them reasonably.

LISTING C.1: Adding a Button and Grid to the Form

```
using System;
using System.Windows.Forms;
using System.Drawing;

public class DataAppForm : Form
{
    Button m_LoadButton;
    DataGridView m_CustomersGrid;

    public DataAppForm()
    {
        // Change the form size
        Size = new Size(500,400);

        // Set the button properties
        m_LoadButton = new Button();
        m_LoadButton.Location = new Point(10,10);
```

```
        m_LoadButton.Text = "Load";

        // Set the grid properties
        m_CustomersGrid = new DataGridView();
        m_CustomersGrid.Location = new Point(10,50);
        m_CustomersGrid.Size = new Size(480,250);

        // Add the controls to the child controls collection
        this.Controls.Add(m_LoadButton);
        this.Controls.Add(m_CustomersGrid);
    }
}
```

The code in Listing C.1 is a little more involved, so let's walk through it. First you need an additional namespace, `System.Drawing`, for the `Size` and `Point` classes you use to specify the size and location of the controls. You then need to declare class members for each control that you are going to add to the form as a child control. In this case, you add a `Button` and a `DataGridView` member, which are defined as control classes in the `System.Windows.Forms` namespace. Then, in the constructor for the class, you create the instances of those controls, set the appropriate properties for them, and then add them to the child controls collection that form maintains.

For the form, you change its size by accessing the `Size` property of the base `Form` class and setting it to 500 x 400 pixels. Next you create an instance of the `Button` class and set its location and text. The location you specify is relative to the upper left portion of the form's client area, with positive x-axis values increasing to the right and positive y-axis values increasing down toward the bottom of the screen. The client area starts just under the title bar and inside the border that is drawn around the window. The text is what will be presented on the button's face when rendered on the form. The default size will be fine for this button because the text length is short. If you need to specify longer strings for the button text, you will need to adjust the size of the button to an appropriate width to fit the text, or better yet, set the `AutoSize` property to `true`.

For the grid, you create an instance of it and specify both the size and location to get it positioned underneath the button but within the bounds of the form. There are actually a lot of different options for laying out controls on a form (they will be covered later in this appendix), and the grid itself is a very complex type. But it is well designed so that for simple usage, you only need a few lines of code.

Once you have all the controls created and their properties set, you add them to the form's `Controls` collection using the `Add` method from the collection class. This makes them child controls on the form. When the form is rendered, it will walk through the list of child controls, asking each to paint itself on the form using its properties and built-in painting behavior. Each control encapsulates its own state and behavior, both in the form in the way it paints itself, and in terms of what events it will fire based on user or system interaction.

When you compile and run this application again from the command line, you will now get a larger form with a button and empty grid on the form's surface. For the final modification of this sample, you need to add an event handler for the button `Click` event and load some data in that handler and bind it to the grid.

In the constructor, add the following line of code to wire up a method named `OnLoadData` as an event handler for the `Click` event of the `m_LoadButton` button:

```
m_LoadButton.Click += new EventHandler(OnLoadData);
```

Then add the corresponding handler method to the class:

```
public void OnLoadData(object sender, EventArgs e)
{
    DataSet ds = new DataSet();
    ds.ReadXml("CustomersDataSet.xml");
    m_CustomersGrid.DataSource = ds.Tables[0];
}
```

Finally, you will need to add one more `using` statement at the top to bring in the `System.Data` namespace:

```
using System.Data;
```

The `OnLoadData` handler method has a signature (parameter and return types) defined by the `EventHandler` delegate that is used by many Windows Forms control events. In this example you can ignore the arguments that are passed to the method, but the method still must declare those arguments to match the event's delegate type definition.

You can use whatever method name you like for the event handler, but I suggest you have a consistent, easy-to-read convention for what you name your event handlers. I usually name them with an `On<action>` convention as in this example. You will often create these handlers through the designer, and it applies a slightly different naming convention, as shown in the next section, so I usually set my event handler names using the Properties window to get the method names I want.

The code in the event handler creates a data set object and loads some data into it using the `ReadXml` method as shown in Appendix D. The source XML can be any valid XML that is suitable for loading into a data set with at least one table of data in it. This case uses the same simplified version of the Customers data set XML that is shown in the Loading Data Sets from a File section in Appendix D.

Once the data set has been populated, you bind the first table (index zero) in the data set to the grid using the grid's `DataSource` property. The chapters in this book go into more detail on the mechanics of the data-binding process, but for the purposes of this appendix, suffice it to say that when you set the grid's `DataSource` property to a data table, the grid will extract the schema information and create a column for each column in the table, and then will iterate through each row in the table and add a corresponding row to the grid containing the data.

To get the sample running, place the XML file in the same directory as the DataAppForm.cs file and compile at the command line as described before. Then run the resulting DataAppForm.exe file and click the *Load* button, and presto, you have your first running data-bound Windows Forms application.

There are a couple of key things to notice about the code you have written so far. The first is that it is just code. There is no magic being done on your behalf by an integrated development environment. You just need a text file containing a few lines of source, an XML file containing some data, and a command line compiler to have a fairly rich presentation of bound data. Another thing to notice is that if you had a bunch of controls on a form, the code for initializing the properties could become very tedious very quickly. Luckily the Windows Forms designer of Visual Studio will write all this code for you, and Visual Studio gives a much more intuitive environment for visually laying out the controls on a form rather than try-ing to figure out what code to write yourself. So you will rarely hand-code that initialization code for the controls as you have done here. Finally, the complexity of data binding and rendering the data in the form is com-pletely encapsulated for you in the grid control, and happens just from set-ting the `DataSource` property on the control to a valid source of data.

Creating Windows Forms Applications with Visual Studio

Writing a form by hand is instructive for understanding the simplicity of the model, but you will rarely write Windows Forms code completely by hand. Usually you will use the Visual Studio IDE to design your forms the Rapid Application Development (RAD) way. Let's step through an example.

Creating an Empty Windows Forms Project

1. Open Visual Studio 2005 and create a new project by selecting File > New > Project. This displays the New Project dialog.

2. Select *Windows Application* as the project type.

3. Specify the name **VSDataApp** for the project. This will become the name of the solution and the project file, and a folder will be created for the solution, with a project folder created under that.

   If you want to override the default behavior of creating a separate solution folder, or change the name of that folder, you can do so with the options at the bottom of the dialog (see Figure C.1).

   Once the project is created, Visual Studio will create the main form for your application and will display it in the designer window within the main work area.

4. Grab the bottom right corner of the form, and drag it down and to the right to resize the default size for the form to be more rectangular and about the same size as the form you created with code in the last sec-tion (500 x 400). You can monitor the resizing of the form by looking in the bottom right of the status bar in the Visual Studio designer, which shows the current size of the form.

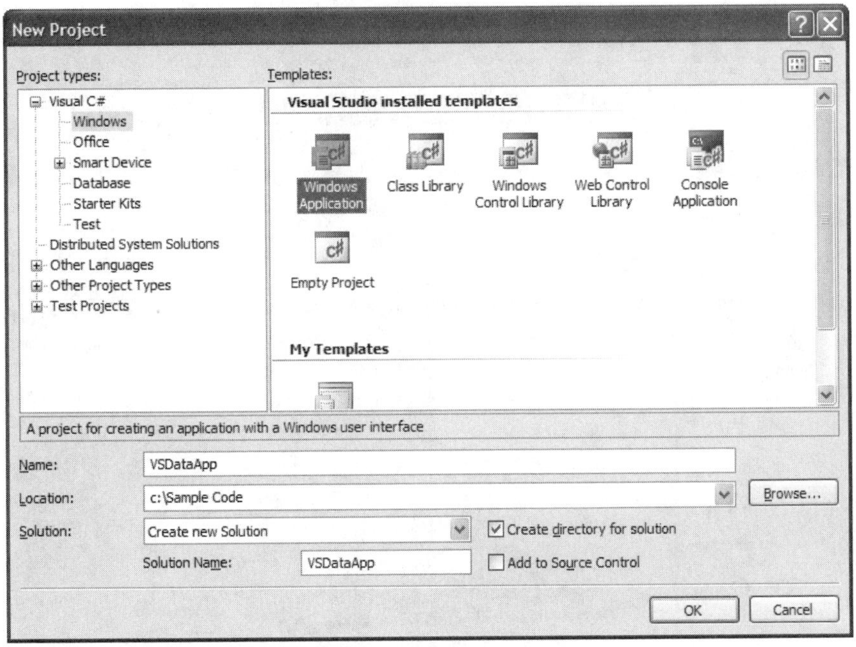

FIGURE C.1: New Project Dialog

Working with the Toolbox

1. If the Toolbox isn't visible, do one of the following (see Figure C.2):

   - Display it by choosing View > Toolbox.

   - If there is a *Toolbox* tab on the left side of the Visual Studio window, click on that and it will slide out.

   You can then dock the window by clicking on the pushpin icon at the top right.

2. If the *All Windows Forms* group tab isn't expanded at the top of the Toolbox (indicated by a plus sign next to it), expand it by clicking on the plus sign icon.

   The Toolbox displays a graphical palette of controls and components that you can drag and drop onto a form or designer surface to create instances of the control. The controls and components in the Toolbox are grouped into categories to help organize them into logical groups.

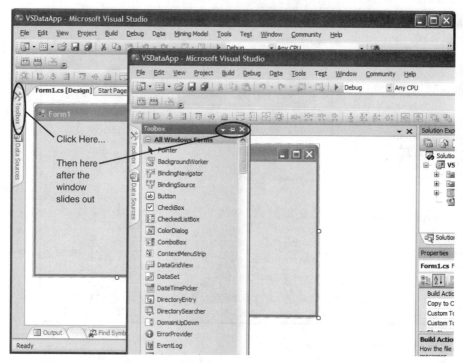

FIGURE C.2: Docking the Toolbox Window

You can customize the Toolbox to add your own or third-party controls to it or you can add additional group tabs. The *All Windows Forms* group at the top includes all the built-in controls in alphabetical order, so if you cannot remember what group a particular control belongs to, you can always find it there.

3. From the Toolbox, drag and drop a `Button` control from the Toolbox palette onto the form, and do the same for the `DataGridView` control *(new in 2.0)*.

When you first drag the `DataGridView` control onto the form, a little window will pop up (see Figure C.3) called a **smart tag** *(new in 2.0)*. This is an in-place control panel for some of the most common properties and actions you may need to manipulate on a control when you are working with it in the designer. You can dismiss the tag by clicking somewhere else in the form or on another control, or by pressing the Esc key.

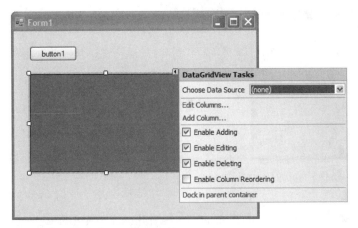

FIGURE C.3: Data Control Smart Tags

Once you have the controls on the form, you can click and drag on them to reposition them on the form. You can also click and drag on the corners or edges of the controls to resize them as desired. Note that as you drag the controls around the form, **snap-lines** will appear to help you align the control you are dragging with the other controls on the form. These subtle blue and magenta lines appear between the control being dragged and other controls or a dashed gray line between the control and the edges of the form. These help you precisely align the tops, bottoms, and sides of controls, as well as the baseline of the text in a control (the line that runs from under label2 through the text box shown in Figure C.4). When you drag and drop controls or components on a form like this, you are actually declaring and initializing member variables in the form class using a visual drag-and-drop metaphor. You will get to the generated code shortly, but the net result is very similar to what you coded by hand in the last section.

Adding Members to the Form

1. Select the *Data* grouping in the Toolbox to display the palette of data components.

2. Drag and drop a DataSet component onto the form, and a dialog will pop up letting you customize the kind of data set that will be added.

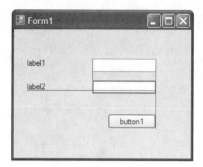

FIGURE C.4: Snap Lines Simplify Control Layout

For this example, select *Untyped dataset*, and a data set member will be added to the form.

It is displayed at the bottom of the designer in the components tray, and it is named dataSet1 by default. The components tray is where any components that are added through the designer and that don't have a runtime graphical rendering are displayed. This allows you to still select them and access any design-time features that they have, and set their properties through the Properties window.

3. Set the properties on the member controls that you created by dropping them on the form. Some of the properties are set automatically by the designer based on you moving and resizing the controls on the form, for example, the Size and Location properties.

4. If the Properties window is not displayed in the IDE, show it by selecting *Properties Window* from the *View* menu or press the F4 key.

5. Select the button on the form by single clicking on it, and then find the (Name) property in the Properties window.

By default, the Properties window displays a categorized list of properties, where the categories correspond to related behavior or presentation aspects of the control.

If you are trying to locate a control by name, you can sort the list alphabetically by clicking the button at the top of the Properties window with an *AZ* and down arrow on it (see Figure C.5). The (Name) property will appear at the top of the list with parentheses around it when sorted alphabetically in the Properties window. This is because the name is really just the variable name, which is a code artifact and doesn't present itself as a runtime accessible property value.

6. With the `(Name)` property selected, change the name of the control member to `m_LoadButton`.

7. Find the `Text` property of the button, and set its value to `Load`.

8. Select the grid in the form by single clicking on it, and set its `(Name)` property to `m_CustomersGrid`.

9. Select the data set in the components tray at the bottom and set its name to `m_CustomersDataSet`.

10. Select the form itself by single clicking in a blank area of the form or on the title bar, and set the `Text` property in the Properties window to **My First VS 2005 Windows Forms Data App**. Note that the text in the title bar of the form changes to this value.

Your IDE should now look something like Figure C.6.

At this point, you haven't written a single line of code, but Visual Studio has in fact written a bunch of lines of code for you. For starters, when it created the default form for the project, it declared a class named `Form1` derived from the `Form` base class for you. It also added a `Program` class with the `Main` method in it to start up the application (*new in 2.0*).

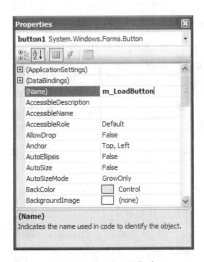

FIGURE C.5: Properties Window

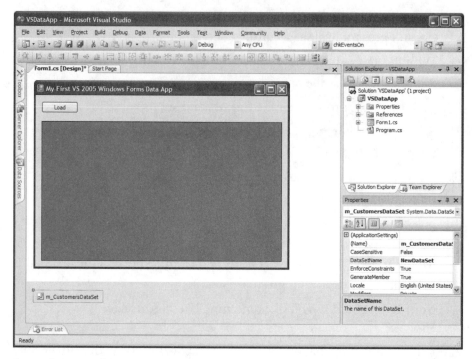

Figure C.6: A Work in Progress in the IDE

Next, when you dropped each control on the form, a member field was declared in the `Form1` class for that control, and properties were set for it based on your interactions in the designer and Properties windows. So at this point you effectively have the same code as you had just before declaring and coding the button click event handler in the previous section.

To create the event handler for the button, the simplest (although not the best) approach is to double-click on the button in the designer. This will add an event handler with the method name based on the name of the control instance and the event that you are subscribing to. This follows the naming convention `<control name>_<event name>`. In the case of your `m_LoadButton` button and the `Click` event, this translates to `m_LoadButton_Click`.

A better way, in my opinion, is to use the Events view of the Properties window to explicitly specify a method name for the handler, which lets you use whatever naming convention makes sense to you. To do this, click on the little lightening bolt icon at the top of the Properties window, find the name of the event you want to add a handler for, and then type in the name you want the handler method to have. When you press Enter, a handler method will be added to the class with the name you specified, the appropriate method signature based on the event delegate type, and the method will be hooked up so that it is called when the event occurs. The Code view of the form will also be brought up with the input focus in the new event handler method, allowing you to start typing your handling code immediately.

Hooking Up an Event Handler and Data Binding

Let's hook up the event handler using the Properties window to get a different naming convention.

1. Make sure the button is selected in the designer, and then go to the Properties window and click on the lightening bolt to get the events listing for the button.

2. Click in the input field next to the `Click` event, and type the handler name `OnLoadData`.

3. Press Enter. You will be dropped in Code view into the method body of the handler that was created (see Figure C.7), so you can start writing the event handling code.

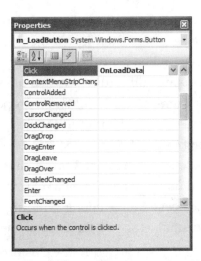

FIGURE C.7: Adding an Event Handler Through the Properties Window

Even though you are working with two different views of the `Form1` class, a Designer view and a Code view, the Designer view is really just rendered dynamically based on the code by Visual Studio. What happens is that when you open a source file containing a form class definition by double-clicking on it, the IDE sees that the class defined within the source file is derived from the `Form` base class. The `Form` base class (and some of its base classes) provides specific support for being used in the designer, so the IDE presents a Designer view of the class by default when you open the file.

You can switch to the Code view by either right-clicking anywhere within the designer and selecting *View Code* from the context menu, or by selecting the *View Code* button in the middle of the small toolbar at the top of the Solution Explorer window, as long as the form's class file is selected in the Solution Explorer tree. You can also use the F7 key to toggle between a form's Code view and Designer view.

To read in the data from the XML file and data bind the results to the grid, add the following lines of code to the `OnLoadData` method:

```
private void OnLoadData(object sender, System.EventArgs e)
{
    m_CustomersDataSet.ReadXml("CustomersDataSet.xml");
    m_CustomersGrid.DataSource = m_CustomersDataSet.Tables[0];
}
```

You will notice that you don't have to create an instance of the data set like you did in the first example, because you created it as a member by dropping it in the form in the designer. When you did that, code was added to create the instance as well. You are still setting the data binding between the grid and the data source by setting the `DataSource` property on the grid. Depending on how you create your data set in the designer, you may be able to set this data binding in the designer. (Setting up data binding with the designer is covered in detail in Chapter 5.) In this case, the structure of the data set isn't determined until it loads the data set from the XML file at runtime, thus the designer doesn't have enough information available at design time to bind to the first table, so you do it in code here.

In order for this code to work, you need to add the CustomersDataSet.xml file into the project files.

1. Right-click on the project in Solution Explorer, and select Add > Existing Item.

2. Find the XML file in the Appendix D sample code folder. You will need to download the sample code from the book's Web site, or type it into a new XML file from Listing D-1. Don't forget to change the file filter at the bottom of the dialog, because it defaults to only showing source code file types.

3. Click the *Open* button to complete the action. This copies the file to your project folder and displays it as part of the project in Solution Explorer.

4. Select that file in Solution Explorer, and change the *Copy To Output Directory* property to *Copy Always (new in 2.0)*. When you run a program in the Visual Studio debugger, it will run from the build output directory, which is under the \bin\Debug subdirectory of the project folder for a C# application. In order for the executable, which is running in that subdirectory, to locate the XML file in the `ReadXml` method call, it will need the file to be in that output folder, or it will need a relative or absolute path to that file wherever it resides.

You should now be able to run the application by selecting *Start Debugging* from the *Debug* menu. Pressing the F5 key with the default key mappings in Visual Studio will also start a debug run, as will the VCR-like start button shaped like a triangle pointing to the right in the toolbar. If you click the *Load* button while running, you should get the bound data displayed in the grid, just like you did in the first section when you wrote all the code by hand (see Figure C.8).

Windows Forms Designer-Generated Code *(New in 2.0)*

In the previous section, I mentioned that all your designer interactions were really just generating code for you. But when you went into Code view for the Form1.cs file, you didn't see much there besides the constructor for the form calling some method called `InitializeComponent` and

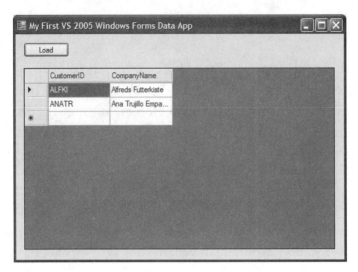

FIGURE C.8: Running the Application

the event handler method that you created through the Properties window. So where is all the code going that declares the member variables for the controls, sets their properties, hooks up the event, and so on? The answer to this question is one of the new and improved features of Visual Studio 2005.

In previous versions of Visual Studio, the designer-generated code was embedded in a region in the form code file itself. The problem with this was twofold. First, it often got deleted by mistake, killing the form. Second, the code that is generated by the designer should in general never be modified by hand, because any changes you make can be overwritten by the designer the next time you make changes from the Design view. Having the code inline in the main source file made it all too tempting to go in there and make changes (despite a comment that was generated with the code telling you to leave it alone), resulting in lost code and confusion for beginners.

A new language feature in .NET 2.0 is the ability to define partial classes. This lets you split the definition of a single class over multiple source files. Visual Studio 2005 leverages this capability to separate the designer-generated form code into a separate source file that is nested under the main form source file in the project in the Solution Explorer tree. If you want to view the contents of this file, expand the tree by clicking on the plus sign next to Form1.cs in the Solution Explorer window. Under Form1.cs you will see a Form1.Designer.cs file. If you open that file, you will find the designer-generated code in all its glory.

The first things you see at the bottom of the file are member variable declarations for all the controls that you added through the designer. You will also see a `Dispose` method and a collapsed region labeled *Windows Form Designer generated code*, just like you used to get inside the Form1.cs file in earlier versions of Visual Studio. If you expand that region, you will see the definition of the `InitializeComponent` method that was called by the constructor in your main `Form1` class file. This method is the single place that the designer injects all of the code it writes when you perform drag-and-drop operations or set properties in the designer. You can see that the code creates the instances of the member controls and components, then sets properties for them, and finally adds them to the `Controls` collection of the form, much like the constructor code you wrote by hand earlier in this appendix. You will see that the designer has set more properties than you did, and it does a few other little things in the `Initialize-Component` method to begin and end initialization and to suspend and resume layout. I won't go into detail about these things at this point because they are just some of the magic that the designer needs to do to give you a smooth design and runtime experience. See Chapter 8 for a discussion about initialization methods.

Controls have default values for all of the properties they expose, and those defaults are what will be used if no other value is set explicitly. The designer-generated code will only include code for setting properties to values that differ from the default values. For example, when you coded the form class by hand earlier in this appendix and ran the application, the title bar was blank because you hadn't set the `Text` property of the form itself. When you create a form in the designer, it automatically sets the `Text` property to the name of the form initially, so that is what is displayed in the title bar for the window at runtime and in the designer. You can change this property just like any other property through either the Properties window or in the code. Property values that have been set to something different from their default value will be displayed in a bold font within the Properties window in the designer.

As the comments for the `InitializeComponent` method indicate, you should avoid modifying the code in this method directly. A lot of the code in that method gets rewritten each time you modify something on your form in the designer. So depending on the kind of code you might add or modify in the method, your changes could be lost the next time you tweak something in the designer. Go ahead and close that file if you have it open; I just wanted to give you a sneak peek into what was going on behind the scenes.

As mentioned before, the first thing the constructor does is call `InitializeComponent` to get all the controls initialized to whatever you specified through the designer. You can insert any custom initialization code you need into the constructor after the call to `InitializeComponent` if you want to programmatically set the properties differently or initialize other members that haven't been declared through drag-and-drop operations in the designer.

If you are brand new to Windows Forms programming and Visual Studio, this example may have seemed a lot more complicated than just writing the code by hand, because of the descriptions of the different windows and designer features and the code that gets generated as a result of designer actions. But the fact is that for many things you will need to do in Windows Forms programming, you will be able to get these done significantly faster in the designer than you can by writing all the code by hand, especially the more familiar and comfortable you become with the designer and the IDE.

If you come from a Visual Basic 6 or prior background, or certain other RAD design environments like FoxPro or Delphi, you may not be all that impressed—yet. After all, VB6 had an outstanding design-time experience for laying out and programming simple forms, which is where a lot of the ideas for the Visual Studio design-time experience came from. The key thing to realize about the .NET experience is that you don't lose any insight or flexibility in overriding what the designer has done for you. Designer interactions just generate .NET code, and you can both view and modify that code as needed to make your application do exactly what you want it to do at runtime. Or you can stay in the designer and get almost everything you need done there.

A Brief Tour of the Windows Forms Architecture

A key thing to realize is that a form is simply another kind of .NET type. Specifically, a **form** is a class that you define that derives from the `System.Windows.Forms.Form` base class. In your derived class, you can include member variables, properties, methods, and events like any other .NET class. You will commonly define **member controls**, which are essentially variables that have types derived from the `Control` base class and that represent the UI elements that will be presented within your form. These members are referred to as **child controls** and will be contained within a collection of controls that is inherited from a base class, `ContainerControl`. In fact, there is a deep inheritance hierarchy in the Windows Forms Framework, and a lot of the functionality that many people think of as provided by a form or control is actually obtained from one of the many base classes in the hierarchy. A portion of the Windows Forms hierarchy is shown in Figure C.9.

As you can see from Figure C.9, Windows Forms classes derive from `Object` just like every .NET class. The next step in the parental lineage of forms and controls is `MarshalByRefObject`. Next up the chain is the `Component` base class. The `Component` class is used for classes that will be used in containment scenarios, either to reside in a parent container themselves or to contain other components. The `Component` base class also enables Visual Studio to present a design surface for the class, onto which other components and controls can be dropped. Those objects can be selected and configured through their properties in the Properties window, like you have already seen with Windows Forms and controls.

The next and probably one of the most important base classes is the `Control` base class. This is the class where most of the common UI behavior and properties exist. The `Control` class provides support for things like keyboard and mouse input, specifying foreground and background colors, and specifying size and location information. In fact, the `Control` class encapsulates a Windows handle and implements events corresponding to all the common Windows messages that a window can receive through the

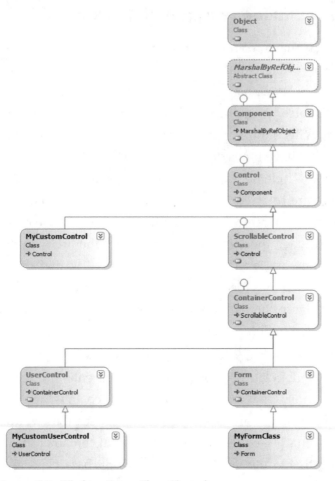

FIGURE C.9: Windows Forms Class Hierarchy

operating system. The `Control` class implements its own message handling loop and exposes the Windows operating system message-based events as .NET events to your controls and their containers, so that you don't have to worry about all the low-level operating system goo.

If you wanted to create your own custom control from scratch, and make that control responsible for drawing its own user interface, the `Control` class is the base class that you would want to derive from, as shown with the `MyCustomControl` class in Figure C.9. By deriving from `Control`, you would inherit the interface that forms and controls expect out of other controls, and then you could extend the behavior and rendering of that control as needed.

After `Control` in the hierarchy, there are the `ScrollableControl` and `ContainerControl` classes, whose names are fairly self-explanatory. `ScrollableControl` provides support for controls whose contents are larger than the area that they will be rendered into, providing derived classes with the ability to scroll the contents within a constrained area on the screen without having to write a bunch of custom painting code to accomplish that. `ContainerControl` provides the support for maintaining a collection of child controls and ensures that all of those child controls are called to render themselves whenever the parent control is redrawn.

Finally, there is the `Form` class, which will often be the direct base class for any forms you create in your Windows applications. The `Form` class provides a default rendering that includes a title bar, frame, and a dialog-like background surface onto which you can add child controls. There is a great deal of flexibility programmed into the `Form` class to let you customize almost any aspect of its presentation as needed.

A sibling of the `Form` class is a class called `UserControl`. This is the class you will want to derive custom controls from if you want them to start with a default drawing surface and have built-in support for child controls. A common example of this is if you wanted to design a login control that contained inputs for the username and password, and you wanted those controls to be contained on multiple forms in your application. You would probably want those controls to have the same layout and appearance wherever they were presented, but you wouldn't want to have to repeat code in multiple forms to declare and use those controls. This is the kind of scenario where a composite control derived from the `UserControl` class makes a lot of sense. You can encapsulate the layout and event handling from a set of controls within your custom composite control, and then add your composite control to one or many forms as needed. You would have one set of code to maintain, and you would get rich designer support for creating the control and adding it to other forms. See the section "Creating a Custom User Control" later in this appendix for an example of implementing a custom user control.

Forms have a specific lifecycle with which you should become familiar. Just like all classes in .NET, forms and controls have a constructor, which is where you will do the majority of your initialization of members and child controls. Forms and controls follow the .NET pattern of implementing the `IDisposable` interface, which provides a pattern-based way for clients to tell a class when they are done using the class, thus allowing it to clean up any unmanaged resources it contains. In forms and controls, there is a base class implementation of the `Dispose` method that you can override to provide any custom cleanup code for unmanaged resources that your form may encapsulate. If you override the `Dispose` method, that code will be called by the Framework when the form is closing. You should always remember to call your base class' implementation of `Dispose` to give it a chance to clean up any resources it is encapsulating. The Windows Form designer code file (<form_name>.Designer.cs) in Visual Studio 2005 contains an override of the `Dispose` method, and if you need to ensure that your own member variables are disposed, you will have to add code to that method in the designer code file to do so.

The rest of the lifecycle of a form is dictated by events fired by the base `Form` class, as well as events fired by controls contained by the form. One of the most important events you will often need to handle is the `Load` event of the form itself. This event is fired when the form is in the final stages of creation and is about to be rendered on the screen. This makes the form's `Load` event a good place to do final initialization of any controls on the form, especially if the parameters used for that initialization cannot be determined until runtime. If you want to do your initialization of some variable or control in your form as late as possible, but before the form is shown on the screen, putting that code in an event handler for the `Form.Load` event is the way to go.

The Dawn of .NET Execution—The Main Method

Every .NET executable has to have an entry point—the place where execution first enters your code. In .NET, that entry point is the `Main` method. The `Main` method has a couple of allowable signatures for it to be treated as the entry point for your application. First off, it needs to be a static method on one of the classes in the application, typically the static `Program` class in a Windows Forms application in Visual Studio 2005. It can return either void or an integer value. Typically you will return void unless you expect your application to be launched by another application that will be checking the returned value when the process exits. The other variation on the Main method is that it can either take no parameters or a single string array as a parameter. The following examples are all valid Main methods for an application:

```
static void Main(string[] args)
{
}
static void Main()
{
}
static int Main(string[] args)
{
}
static int Main()
{
}
```

If the Main method you use takes a string array as a parameter, it will be passed any command line arguments used when launching the application in that array. Unlike legacy C++ and C applications, the first argument isn't the name of the program itself. In .NET, the first argument passed to the Main method in the argument array will be the first argument after the name of the executable from the command line, if any. If no arguments were present on the command line, the argument array passed to the Main method will still be a live instance of a .NET string array, and it will have zero elements in the array, which can be determined by checking the Length property on the array.

You can have more than one Main method in your application, but you can only have one Main method defined in a given class. If you do have more than one class with a Main method in your application, you will have to specify which class is your startup object in the project properties in Visual Studio, or using the /main command line compiler argument.

For a lot of your Windows Forms applications, you won't need to make any modifications of the Main method that Visual Studio creates for you in the `Program` class. When Visual Studio creates a new Windows Forms project, the `Main` method has just a couple lines of code:

```
[STAThread]
static void Main()
{
     Application.EnableVisualStyles();
     Application.Run(new Form1());
}
```

The call to the `EnableVisualStyles` method allows your form to present themed control appearances when running on Windows XP or later. Finally and most important, the last line of code creates an instance of your form class and passes it to the `Application` class' `Run` method. The `Application` class provides a number of static methods and properties that allow you to code against the context of the executing application. The `Run` method basically sets up a Windows message processing loop on the current thread and starts your application running. If you aren't familiar with Windows programming from the days of old and don't know what a Windows message is, don't worry. Except for very advanced situations in .NET, you don't even have to know they exist. They are just the low-level way that window objects in the operating system communicate with each other, and as mentioned before, many .NET controls are just wrappers around operating system window objects.

Execution of your application will continue until the main window is closed, which kills the application's message pump and ends the main thread of execution. If you have spun off other threads in the running of your application, those threads may continue to run if they were started as foreground threads, which is the default threading model in .NET.

The `STAThread` attribute, mentioned earlier, is placed on the `Main` method by the Windows Forms Project wizard. This attribute is placed there to allow for easy integration of single-threaded apartment model ActiveX controls or COM components. .NET sets up a multithreaded apartment for COM interoperability by default, and that could cause problems for ActiveX controls and many COM components, particularly those developed with Visual Basic 6 or earlier. So for the maximum safety and compatibility for migration scenarios, you should always include this attribute in Windows Forms applications on the Main method that starts the application thread running.

For some applications, you may want to modify the Main method to do other forms of application initialization before the application starts. For example, say that the application was designed to take a single command line parameter that corresponded to the mode of operation for the application. The main form class could be modified to take that mode as a parameter to its constructor, so that it could initialize a member variable with the value. In that case, you might modify your Main method to do something like this:

```
[STAThread]
static void Main(string[] args)
{
    if (args.Length != 1)
    {
        throw new ArgumentException(
            "You must give the mode as a command line argument.");
    }
    Application.Run(new Form1(args[0]));
}
```

In this example, you check the arguments passed to the application to make sure you got what you expected. You then pass the first string in the array to the constructor of your form class. You would naturally also have to change or overload your form constructor to take a string argument to complete the scenario, and that constructor would then probably set a member field's value based on that parameter.

Another common thing to modify in your Main method is to set up a global exception handler for your Windows Forms application, so that uncaught exceptions don't bubble out to the runtime and cause your application to die with an ugly dialog presented to the user by the runtime. If you add a handler for the ThreadException event on the Application class in the Main method before calling the Run method, that event handler will be called any time an exception bubbles to the top of the stack without being caught. In your handler you can do any logging of the error you deem necessary and can then present the user with a little more user-friendly dialog that you can design. It is then up to you to decide whether to close the application or not, as shown in the following code:

```
using System.Threading;

[STAThread]
static void Main()
{
   Application.ThreadException += new
      ThreadExceptionEventHandler(OnUnhandledException);
   Application.EnableVisualStyles();
   Application.Run(new Form1());
}


private static void OnUncaughtException(object sender,
   ThreadExceptionEventArgs e)
{
   string msg = "I'm terribly sorry, but an unsolvable problem has"
      + " occurred. The programmers will be flogged at dawn.";
   MessageBox.Show(msg);
   // Log exception using e.Exception on event arguments
   Application.Exit();
}
```

Handling Control Events

As mentioned earlier, most of the lifecycle of a Windows Forms application is determined by handling control events. All controls inherit a large set of events from the `Control` base class. These events correspond to the common Windows messages that can get passed to any window by the operating system. This includes events like mouse clicks, keyboard events, Windows timer events, and repainting events. Many of these events are of the same delegate type—the `EventHandler` delegate type introduced earlier. If you need to know more about delegates and events, I would suggest picking up a good book on general .NET programming. (*Programming .NET Components*, second edition, by Juval Löwy includes great coverage of .NET events and delegates.)

Some events are defined using more specialized delegate types that include specialized event arguments. These arguments carry additional information about the event that can be used by subscribers to perform processing based on that event in their event handlers. For example, the

`Control` class defines events for `MouseDown`, `MouseUp`, `MouseMove`, and `MouseWheel` to name a few. These events are declared to be of type `MouseEventHandler`. The `MouseEventHandler` delegate type takes a `MouseEventArgs` object as the second parameter in its signature. The `MouseEventArgs` class defines several properties that can be used to perform conditional processing based on the specifics of the event. These properties include the X and Y locations in screen-based coordinates of where the mouse event occurred, which button was pressed and how many times if the event was a mouse click, and how many detents (notches) a mouse wheel was rotated if the event was caused by moving the mouse wheel.

The way you handle control events is no different than how you handle any .NET event. You need to subscribe to the event using the built-in mechanisms for your .NET language of choice. For C#, you subscribe to an event using the += operator, passing an instance of the appropriate delegate type initialized to point to the event handler method:

```
eventPublisher.MyEvent +=
    new EventHandler(mySubscriber.HandlerMethod);
```

Another notation to be aware of (and which I use a lot in this book) is the new C# 2.0 syntax for *delegate inference (new in 2.0)*. In this code, I explicitly created a new instance of the delegate type for the event, `EventHandler`, and passed that to the += operator. In C# 2.0, the compiler is smart enough to infer what the appropriate delegate type is based on the type of the event you are setting up a subscription on. So in C#, you can compact the notation to just the name of the handler method as follows:

```
eventPublisher.MyEvent += mySubscriber.HandlerMethod;
```

Even though I don't include any samples in Visual Basic in the text, all the sample code is available in Visual Basic for download. Because event handling syntax is one of the few places that Visual Basic code looks distinctly different than the C# equivalent, here's a Visual Basic example. In Visual Basic you can use the `AddHandler` keyword, passing the event and the handler method:

```
AddHandler publisher.MyEvent, _
    AddressOf subscriber.HandlerMethod
```

In Visual Basic, you also have the option of declaring the instance of the control using the `WithEvents` keyword, then using the `Handles` keyword modifier on the end of a method declaration to hook it up as an event handler:

```
Public Class MyForm
    Inherits Form
    Private WithEvents m_LoadButton As Button

    Private Sub MyButtonHandler(ByVal sender As Object, _
        ByVal e As EventArgs) Handles m_LoadButton.Click

    End Sub
End Class
```

Displaying Other Forms

You will frequently need to create additional windows or forms as part of your Windows Forms application. You might need to pop up a dialog to prompt the user for preference settings, or you might need to launch a separate viewing window to display the results of a particular query. The way you do these things with Windows Forms is very straightforward.

If you simply want to launch a new window to present some additional data, you create an instance of the form class for that window and call the `Show` method to display it:

```
private void ShowResults()
{
    DataForm df = new DataForm();
    df.Show();
}
```

This will bring up the new window in a nonmodal way—the form will be presented as a top-level window and you will be able to interact with it independently of the main form that launched it. However, the new form will still be executing on the same thread as the main form. You can interact with the forms at the same time because they are being serviced by the Windows message pump that was set up in the `Main` method when the application started. If you close the main form that hosts the message pump, the other forms will be closed and the application will shut down, because the main form message pump determines the lifetime of the main application thread. So you can think of forms launched in this way as child windows, or nonmodal dialogs.

If you want to present a form as a modal dialog, you do so by calling the ShowDialog method instead of the Show method. Doing so will block the interaction with the launching form until the form that was launched with ShowDialog is closed.

Containing Forms Within a Parent Form

The previous section showed how to launch a new form that can be moved around the screen independently of the form from which it was launched, even though the lifetime of that window is tied to the one that created it. What if you want to create a form that will be fully contained within the client area of its parent window? This style of user interface is called a **multiple-document interface (MDI)**, even though what you contain in the child forms may not be document-oriented at all. The terminology is a holdover from the days when earlier versions of programs like Microsoft Word and Excel opened each document in a child window that was contained within the outer window, or frame, which represented the application itself. Most of those programs have migrated to being more document-centric instead of application-centric and now present a separate top-level window for each document that is open. However, the application style that they introduced is still around and may make sense for many situations.

Creating MDI applications in Windows Forms is much easier than it was in C++ or VB6. First you will need to design your main form just like you would for any application. Because you are designing an MDI application, you will want to leave the client area of the main form blank since this is where the child forms will be presented. Typically you will just have a menu, toolbar, and status bar in the main form of an MDI application. You will also need to design any forms that you want to be contained within the main form's client area as child forms.

Once you have designed the forms, there are only two steps required to launch the child forms so they will reside within the parent form's client area. First you need to set the IsMdiContainer property on the parent

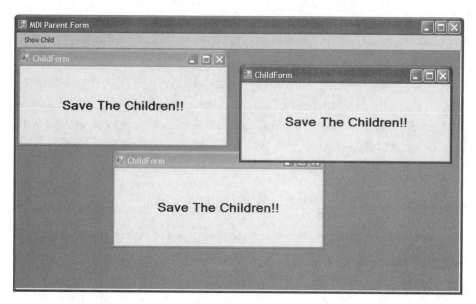

FIGURE C.10: An MDI Application

form to `true`. Then when you construct the child forms, but before you call their `Show` method, you need to set the `MdiParent` property of the child form to a reference to the parent form:

```
// Method in parent form
private void ShowChildForm()
{
   ChildForm child = new ChildForm();
   child.MdiParent = this;
   child.Show();
}
```

The result is an application that presents its child windows, as shown in Figure C.10.

Common Data Display Controls

Visual Studio ships with over 65 controls and components in the Toolbox that you can add to your Windows forms simply by dragging and dropping them onto the design surface. The chapters in this book focus on the use of controls for presenting data that is bound to data sources of various types. This section covers some of the most common controls you will use to present data, with or without data binding. A later section of this appendix covers some of the cool new controls in .NET 2.0 that are used for purposes other than data binding in your data applications. The main chapters of this book drill down into all the gory details of the data-bound controls, both those that existed in .NET 1.X and still remain viable today, and those that are new in .NET 2.0.

Because all of the Windows Forms controls derive from the base `Control` class, they share a common set of properties that can be used on any control. These include properties such as `Font`, `BackColor`, `Fore-Color`, and `BorderStyle` that affect the presentation of the control; `Position`, `Anchor`, and `Dock` that affect the layout of the control; and `Locked`, `Visible`, and `Enabled` that affect the user's ability to see or use the control. Later sections cover how you lay out controls and set their tab order so that users can use the Tab key to move from control to control in the expected order.

All of the controls described here can be used by writing code against their properties, methods, and events. You can also do almost everything you need with these controls through designer and property window interactions. Finally, all of these controls, except the `ListView` and `Tree-View` controls, also support some form of data binding through their properties and the inherent data-binding capabilities of Windows Forms.

Label Controls

Labels are a simple but important control for your forms. Many controls provide information about their purpose as part of their presentation, but others need a helping hand to tell the user what to do with them. Labels are exactly what they sound like: a simple control that can contain a label to indicate some piece of information to the user. The piece of information is most often text that indicates the name, content, or purpose of another control on a form. However, a label can also contain an image. If your primary purpose is to present an image to a user, though, you should use a `PictureBox` control, because it includes much better functionality for displaying an image.

You usually just drag and drop a label on a form, then set its `Text` property to whatever you want the label to display using the Properties window or in code. You should set the name of the label control as well, to make it clear which label is which, when you are working in the Code view. You should set the label's tab order to immediately precede the control it refers to. This will help users with disabilities who use the accessibility features of Windows to access functionality in your application.

Button Controls

A button control is certainly one of the most common controls for interactive applications. The `Button` class presents a standard Windows button on your form that can be used to trigger actions or invoke processing logic in your application. To use a button, you again typically drag and drop it on a form, set the `Text` property to whatever you want to display on the face of the button, and create an event handler for the `Click` event, so that you can perform whatever processing is appropriate in the event handler. Windows Forms buttons can also have an image set to display on the face of the button, in addition to or in place of the text.

Check Box Controls

The `CheckBox` control lets users select values that can be either true or false, yes or no, or on or off. The `CheckBox` control supports a three-state mode, where its value can be `Checked`, `Unchecked`, or `Indeterminate`, as determined by the control's `CheckState` property. To use this mode, you have to set the `ThreeState` property to `true`. The indeterminate state is rendered as a shaded square inside the check box.

A check box doesn't imply any relation between the value of the `CheckBox` control and the state or value of another control. The `CheckBox` control includes both the actual check box itself and the text caption that accompanies it. You will typically use a `CheckBox` control by dragging it onto a form, setting its `Text` property to indicate the meaning of the check box, and setting the `Checked` property to either `true` or `false` to indicate the default state of the control. You can wire up an event handler for the `CheckChanged` event to monitor when the checked state of the control changes, or you can simply check the value of the `Checked` property when needed to make decisions on other processing in your code. Or, if you want a three-state check box, you can set the `ThreeState` property to `true` and set the `CheckState` property to one of the three enumerated values: `Checked`, `Unchecked`, or `Indeterminate`.

Radio Button Controls

The `RadioButton` control is intended to be used in conjunction with other radio buttons. Radio buttons have an implicit intent of indicating mutually exclusive value selections among a set of values. For example, if you were implementing a control to set the current color of a traffic light, you would have three radio buttons—one red, one yellow, and one green—and only one of those buttons could be selected at one time. Otherwise, you could be the cause of some serious traffic accidents, and you wouldn't want that.

Like the `CheckBox` control, you can handle the `CheckChanged` event to monitor changes to the selection of radio buttons, or you can just check the value of the `Checked` property whenever needed for processing. The `RadioButton` class derives from `CheckBox`, which is where it gets the definition of these properties.

Please don't commit the cardinal sin of using a radio button where a check box is appropriate, or vice versa. Radio buttons are for mutually exclusive selections; check boxes are for independent selections. This is an often-abused user interface design point that you should keep in mind.

Text Box Controls

The `TextBox` control in .NET lets you create single and multi-line text boxes for user input and display. Like many controls, the `Text` property is the one that determines the string that is displayed within the text box. When you first place a text box on a form, the default mode is single line. If you want multi-line, you change the `Multiline` property to `true`. You also have control through the `Scrollbars` property over whether you have scroll bars when you are in multi-line mode. You don't have to use a different control for different kinds of text boxes in .NET like you needed to do in some previous development tools and languages. You are limited to plain text content within the text box control, but if you need to allow the user to format the text they input, you can provide a `RichTextBox` control.

RichTextBox Controls

The RichTextBox control lets the user enter and format text using formatting that is supported by the Rich Text Format (RTF) specification. Like the TextBox control, the string contents of the control are accessible through the Text property. The Rtf property exposes the contents with all of the embedded formatting codes. If the user pastes formatted text into the control from some other program that supports formatted text, such as Word or a Web page, the formatting will be preserved within the text in the control. If you want the user to be able to format text that they type into the control, you will have to provide other controls or hot keys that let them execute formatting commands on the selected text in the control.

DateTimePicker Controls

The DateTimePicker is a fairly complex control that allows the display and editing of formatted date and time information. It looks like a Combo-Box with the date and time information displayed in text form within it. The formatting of that display can be set based on a number of predefined formats or by using a custom formatting string. When the drop-down arrow is selected, a calendar control appears, allowing an intuitive and rich date selection mechanism. The ValueChanged event is the default event that can be handled to know when a date, time change, or date selection has occurred in the control.

List Box Controls

You use the ListBox control to present a list of items to users, typically allowing them to select one or more items in the list as part of a data input task. A list box is usually used when you want more than one item in a selection list to be visible to users at the same time, often in conjunction with allowing them to select multiple items.

List boxes maintain the items presented in the list as a set of object references held in a collection of type ListBox.ObjectCollection, a nested type inside the ListBox class. When the list box goes to render the items it holds, it will call the ToString method on each object reference that it holds, and the results of that method call are what will be presented to users. You can place any kind of object into this collection, so you can keep all the data associated with the displayed value in one place, and just the string representation of that object will be rendered into the items in the list.

For example, say you want to present a list of customers for selection in some task to users. However, when the form is processed, you will need the customer ID and perhaps other information associated with the customer to perform processing based on the user selection. To support this scenario, you could create a `Customer` class that overrides the `ToString` method inherited from the `System.Object` base class. In that method, you could return the customer name for presentation in the list box or other controls, but the `Customer` class definition could include members for the ID and any other associated data that you need to process a customer selection. At the point where you need to do that processing (typically a button click in the form or perhaps just a changing of the focus in the form), you can determine the current selection from the `SelectedItem` property, getting back a reference to the corresponding `Customer` object. Because `SelectedItem` is of type `Object`, you will have to cast the returned reference to the expected type to access the actual contents of that object. The following code shows this in action for a `ListBox` member control in a form named `m_CustomersListBox`.

```
private void OnProcessCustomer(object sender, EventArgs e)
{
    Customer customer = (Customer)m_CustomersListBox.SelectedItem;
}
```

You can monitor changes to the selection of the items in the list through the `SelectedIndexChanged` event. When you handle that event, you can use the `SelectedIndex` property to get the zero-based index in the list for single selections, or the `SelectedItem` or `SelectedItems` properties to get the object reference back for selected items in the list. `SelectedItems` applies if you allow multiple selections in the list box by setting the `SelectionMode` property to `MultiSimple` or `MultiExtended`. The difference between these two values is that with `MultiSimple`, selections in the list can be toggled as selected or not by clicking on them more than once. With `MultiExtended`, you can use the Shift and Ctrl keys in combination with mouse clicks to select multiple items or ranges of items. You should favor using `MultiExtended` for most list boxes, since that is the most common interaction model for list boxes and therefore will be most intuitive for your users. You can also set this mode to `None` if you are using a `ListBox` for display purposes only and don't want to let users be able to select any of the items.

Combo Box Controls

The `ComboBox` control presents a list of data as a drop-down list with a text box that can either be used to present the current selection or to let the user input a new value. Other than the way it presents the list and the fact that you can choose to make the current selection editable, it works a lot like a list box that only allows a single selection, but it takes up a lot less screen real estate. Like the list box, it maintains a list of items of type `Combo-Box.ObjectCollection` in the `Items` property, which it uses to render the list and that you can use to store more complex objects than just strings if desired. You set whether the current selection is editable by setting the `DropDownStyle` of the combo box. And like the list box, you can handle the `SelectedIndexChanged` event if needed.

List View Controls

The `ListView` control is a fairly complex control that lets you present a collection of information using a number of different views. This class wraps the underlying operating system control that is used by Windows Explorer, which you can use to switch between small icon, large icon, details, and list views of the items it contains. To populate the control with items for display, you have to construct instances of the `ListViewItem` class. This class provides a data container for each item, allowing you to specify the item text and an image that will be used for large and small icon displays. You can also associate a collection of subitems with an item, and those subitems will be used for display when showing the Details view of a list view. The `ListView` control doesn't support any direct data binding, because the need to properly construct these `ListViewItem` objects doesn't map in a clean, generic way to a relational set of data.

Tree View Controls

The `TreeView` control lets you display a hierarchical, navigable view of data within your application. The tree view presents a collection of nodes in a fashion similar to the Folder view in Windows Explorer. Each node in the tree is an object of type `TreeNode`, which has `Image` and `Text` properties that control what is displayed for the node. You can set whether lines are displayed between nodes, whether the plus/minus image is displayed at each node for tree expansion, and whether check boxes are shown at each node to select multiple nodes. Like the `ListView` control, the tree view doesn't directly support data binding, because there isn't a clean mapping of relational data onto a tree structure.

Picture Box Controls

The `PictureBox` is a powerful and convenient little control to use whenever you need to display an image within a form. All that is required to display an image in the `PictureBox` control is to construct a `Bitmap` object from the `System.Drawing` namespace and assign it to the `Image` property. The `PictureBox` control also has a `SizeMode` property that you can set to `Normal`, `AutoSize`, `CenterImage`, `StretchImage`, or `Zoom`. Based on the value you set for `SizeMode`, the `PictureBox` will automatically handle resizing the image when the form it is contained on is repainted or resized.

Data Grid Controls

The `DataGrid` control was the mainstay of tabular data presentation in .NET 1.X. It lets you bind data sets, tables, and collections of data to the grid for presentation in a tabular display. The control can discover the relations between multiple tables in a data set and provides a navigation scheme between parent and child rows of data. It allows easy sorting of rows based on a column selection, and lets you customize the appearance of columns and the table through style classes.

However, because the `DataGrid` had a lot of problems in terms of both usability and customization, the `DataGridView` control was added in .NET 2.0. The `DataGridView` control supersedes the `DataGrid` as the primary control for tabular presentation of data for new applications. If you are migrating existing applications that use the `DataGrid` control, you don't necessarily need to switch over to the `DataGridView`. Your existing `Data-Grid` code will continue to work as it did before, but I don't recommend using the `DataGrid` control for any new code in .NET 2.0 applications.

DataGridView Controls *(New in 2.0)*

This new control is the focus of Chapter 6. It is the control of choice for presenting tabular data of many forms in Windows Forms applications. It provides easy to use data-binding mechanisms and the ability to customize the appearance, handle large data sets, include unbound columns, as well as many other advanced features.

Creating a Custom User Control

Sometimes when you are designing an application, your forms will get a little complex, consisting of a large number of controls. In general you should avoid this, because too many controls on a single form means you better have a pretty sophisticated user. Often there will be clusters of controls on those forms that are functionally related, and the code that supports them is mostly separable from the rest of the controls on the form. You also may find situations where you have a common grouping of controls that need to be repeated on more than one form.

These situations cry out for encapsulation, and Windows Forms provides a nice design mechanism to address encapsulation of groups of controls—specifically **user controls**, which are controls that you design that derive from the `UserControl` base class. As you saw in Figure C.9, the `UserControl` class derives from the same base class hierarchy as the `Form` class. As such, it provides both control containment for child controls and a design surface that lets you easily add those child controls in a visual way.

Using custom user controls, you can encapsulate a set of controls into a parent control, including both their layout and all the code that initializes the controls and services events from them. By doing so, you can simply add the custom user control to other forms or even other user controls as an atomic unit, treating it as a single control from the perspective of its parent. You can even expose a data-binding experience around the custom control that models that exposed by other built-in .NET controls. This can lead to much easier-to-maintain code because of the encapsulation of code that results and the ease of use from the consuming code perspective. It also leads to more consistent user interface design, because you can present the same group of controls in exactly the same way in multiple places because they are actually running from the same code.

Let's take a look at a simple example: implementing a search user control that can be embedded on multiple forms that present tables of data. The control will be designed to encapsulate the process of gathering the search criteria from the user based on the fields presented in the table on the form, and it will create the search command that can be executed directly to return the matching rows ready to data bind. Follow these steps to create a project with a single user control.

1. Create a new project in Visual Studio with a project type of Windows Control Library, and name it **SearchControlLibrary**.

2. Select the *UserControl1* file in Solution Explorer, and then click on it again after a pause to edit the file name.

3. Change the file name to **SearchControl.cs**. When you press the Enter key, Visual Studio will detect that you have changed the file name (which is expected to match the name of the contained class), and it will prompt you, asking if you would like it to perform a rename throughout the project.

4. Click on the *Yes* button. This uses the Refactor-Rename capability in C# to find all the places that `UserControl1` was used as a class name and replaces them with `SearchControl`.

5. Grab the bottom right corner of the control and drag it to make the control a little wider.

6. Add two labels, a combo box, a text box, a check box, and two buttons. Set the `Text` properties on the controls so you end up with something like Figure C.11, and use control names that make sense to you. I named the controls `m_FieldSelect`, `m_SearchTextBox`, `m_ClearButton`, `m_SearchButton`, and `m_ExactMatch` going clockwise from the combo box, according to the naming convention for member variables and controls on a form.

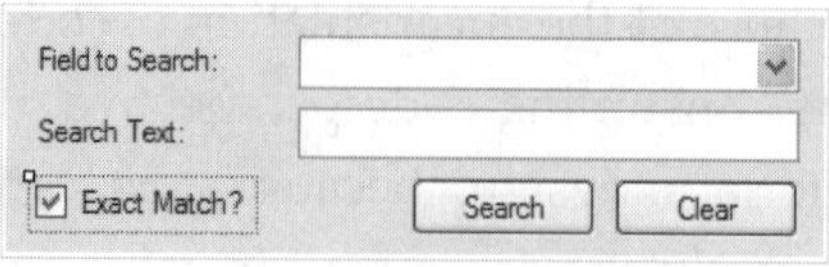

FIGURE C.11: The SearchControl User Control

You can find the full code for this control in the download code for this book. To try out the process, you don't actually need any functional code behind the controls. You could just do the layout, compile the project, and then investigate adding the custom user control to a form in another project. If you open your control library project in the same Visual Studio solution as another Windows Forms project, the control should show up automatically in the SearchControlLibrary Components grouping in the Toolbox, ready to drag and drop onto the form (see Figure C.12). Or, you can use the *Choose Items* context menu option from the Toolbox to add the control manually to the Toolbox by navigating to the compiled assembly. If you do that, you will see the control with any custom icon assigned, which the sample code includes.

If you add some search command creation functionality to the control like the download code sample does, you could then drag and drop this control on other forms, like those shown in Figure C.13. In this sample application that uses the `SearchControl`, by using just a few lines of code in each form that includes the control, it is easy to search the table on the form because the `SearchControl` encapsulates the creation of an appropriate search command. Then it is up to the form to execute the command and data bind the results.

FIGURE C.12: Custom User Controls in the My User Controls Toolbox Group

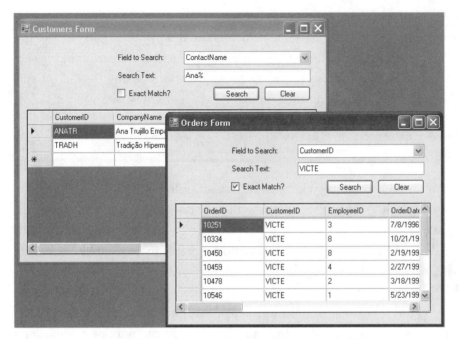

FIGURE C.13: A Data Application That Uses the Search Control in Multiple Forms

Laying Out Controls on a Form

Windows Forms includes several different approaches you can choose from for laying out the controls on your forms. You can mix and match the approaches, using whichever approach is appropriate for a given control. The three modes of positioning and sizing a control on a form include absolute positioning and sizing, anchoring, and docking controls. In addition to these layout modes for individual controls, you can achieve more complex layouts using some of the new container controls available for Windows Forms 2.0, including the `FlowLayoutPanel`, `TableLayout-Panel`, and `SplitContainer`.

Absolute Positioning and Sizing of Controls

When you drag and drop a control onto a form, place it in the position that you want it to appear, and possibly resize it by dragging the edges or corners of the control, you are using absolute positioning and sizing. What is happening behind the scenes when you do these things is that the designer is adjusting the `Location` and `Size` properties of the control to explicit values in pixels. Whatever values are set for these properties will be used if the `Dock` property is set to `None`, which is the default. You can also set the `Location` and `Size` values programmatically, as you did earlier in the section "Your First Windows Forms Data Application," using the `Point` and `Size` structures defined in the `System.Drawing` namespace:

```
myControl.Location = new Point(50,50);
myControl.Size = new Size(200,150);
```

One of the problems with absolute positioning is that if you allow the user to resize the form, the controls will just stay where they are. However, if you are going to let the user resize the form, you usually want the controls that are on the form to do something sensible to adapt to the new size of the form, either by repositioning themselves, resizing themselves, or both. You could handle this in Windows Forms applications in the same way you did in most legacy Windows applications: you could intercept the events associated with the form resizing, perform manual calculations based on the new size of the form, and then explicitly set the position and size of the controls to some appropriate value based on the new size of the form. However, this kind of coding is very tedious and error prone, and in most cases there are some common behaviors you want the controls to adopt for positioning and sizing themselves. Those common behaviors have been encapsulated as built-in capabilities of Windows Forms through the `Anchor` and `Dock` properties.

Anchoring Controls

For many kinds of controls and form layouts, you will want controls to stay in a constant position relative to one or more of the sides of a form. You may want the control to maintain its size, but only reposition itself to stay in the same location relative to two adjacent sides of a form, such as the top-left or bottom-right corner of the form. Or you may want the control's outer edges to stay in the same location relative to two opposite sides of the form, meaning that it will stretch or shrink as the form expands or contracts.

For example, take a look Figure C.14—this is the same form, but this shows it in different sizes. For a form like this, you would probably want the data grid to fill all the real estate of the form not being used by the buttons as it is resized. You would also probably want the button in the bottom left corner to stay in a fixed position relative to that corner, and likewise for the button in the bottom right. Finally, you would probably want the middle button to stay centered in the form and in a fixed location relative to the bottom edge of the form. As you can see by looking at the size of the grid and the location and size of the buttons in the two forms in Figure C.14, you can get exactly that behavior without writing a single line of code by hand by setting the `Anchor` property appropriately for each control through the Properties window.

The `Anchor` property takes an enumeration of type `AnchorStyles`, which has flag values `Top`, `Bottom`, `Left`, `Right`, and `None`. Because it is a flags enumeration type, you can combine the values using the Boolean "or" operator (|). The Windows Forms designer gives you a nice graphical

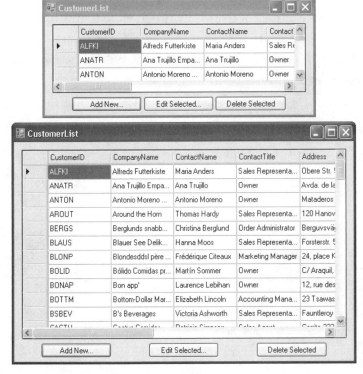

FIGURE C.14: Data Form Before and After Resizing

property editor, shown in Figure C.15, that lets you visually select the sides that you want the control to be anchored to. The resulting code is equivalent to the following for anchoring the data grid to all four sides so that it will resize to keep each of its four sides in the same relative position to the form's corresponding sides:

```
m_CustomersGrid.Anchor = AnchorStyles.Top | AnchorStyles.Bottom
    | AnchorStyles.Right | AnchorStyles.Left;
```

Docking Controls

Anchoring controls solve a lot of common layout requirements, but there is another form of layout that is very handy for certain situations as well. Windows Forms includes a docking feature through the `Dock` property of the `Control` base class. The `Dock` property is a `DockStyle` enumeration that works similarly to the `Anchor` enumeration just described. You can dock a control to one of five locations: `Top`, `Bottom`, `Left`, `Right`, and `Fill`. You can also choose to set `Dock` to `None`, which is the default.

When you dock a control to a given side, it will change its location so that the corresponding side of the control is always glued to that side of the form. Additionally, it will resize itself to fill out to the adjacent sides, filling the entire side of the form selected. The remaining side will be fixed based on the position you set, and the `Anchor` settings will be ignored.

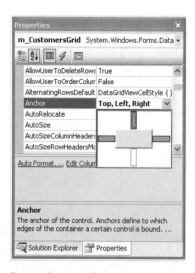

FIGURE C.15: Anchor Property Editor

For example, in Figure C.16, a `TreeView` control was added to the form and its `Dock` property set to `Left`. This made it automatically resize and relocate so that the left side of the control is always attached to the left side of the form, and the top and bottom edges of the control expanded until they filled out to the top and bottom of the form. The right edge of the control stays wherever it is placed.

A `ListView` control was also added to the form and its `Dock` property was set to `Fill`. This means that it will fill out the rest of the center of the form. In this case, since there are no other controls that are docked top, bottom, or right, it fills out the rest of the form. On the left side, it will fill to the border of the tree control that was docked left. If there were other docked controls on the form, they arrange themselves to their respective borders and then try to fill out to the adjacent borders. If you laid out your form this way, the two portions of the form wouldn't be resizable, so for this kind of layout you will usually want to use a `SplitContainer` (described later). In that case, the `TreeView` and `ListView` each become a child of the containers in the `SplitContainer` and can be set to `Dock.Fill` to fill their portions on either side of the split.

When you select a control on the form and select the `Dock` property in the Properties window, you get the graphical Properties editor shown in Figure C.17.

The order that you place controls on the form and set their `Dock` properties matters. If there is already another docked control in the way when a control tries to fill out to the adjacent sides of the one it is docked to, it will fill out to the edges of the other docked control that is in its way. So if you

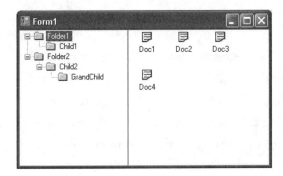

FIGURE C.16: Docked Tree and List Views

FIGURE C.17: Dock Property Editor

place one control on a form and set its `Dock` property to `Top`, then place another control on the form and set its `Dock` property to `Top`, the second control will dock to the bottom of the first control, and the first control will be docked to the top of the form. In this way, you can achieve pretty sophisticated layouts with `Docking`. However, it can be challenging to get the controls all on the form in the right order and set their `Dock` properties accordingly. The sequence is based on the order that they are added to the `Controls` collection of the container (z-order), which corresponds to the sequence you added them to the form through the designer.

Probably one of the most useful scenarios for using the `Dock` property is to get a child control to dock-fill the client area of a parent container control. For example, if you place a `TabControl` on a form and want to put a grid on each tab in that control, the best way is to select each tab in turn, drag and drop a grid onto its child control area (the center of the displayed tab control), and then set the grid's `Dock` property to fill. The drag-and-drop operation makes the grid a child control to the tab control, which is a container control itself. When you set the `Dock` property to `Fill`, the docking is relative to a control's container client area, which isn't necessarily the form.

Using Layout Container Controls *(New in 2.0)*

The `FlowLayoutPanel`, `TableLayoutPanel`, and `SplitContainer` controls can be extremely useful for achieving sophisticated layouts of controls on your forms with minimal effort. These three controls are new in .NET 2.0.

The `FlowLayoutPanel` control lets you achieve an effect similar to what the default layout behavior is for Web pages. Specifically, any controls in a `FlowLayoutPanel` container will rearrange themselves to fill the area of the container in the order that they were added to the parent container, flowing from left to right, and wrapping to a new line when they run out of room to the right. That is the default behavior, but you can also modify the `FlowDirection` property, setting it to one of the enumerated values `LeftToRight` (the default), `TopDown`, `RightToLeft`, or `BottomUp`.

The `TableLayoutPanel` control allows you to achieve tabular layouts of controls, where the controls maintain relative positions to one another and are laid out as a table or grid of controls on the form. You can use this control to achieve many of the same layout affects that advanced Web page designers use tables for in HTML. You can nest table layout controls within the cells of other table layout controls to get sophisticated but well-organized layout of controls that do sensible things when the form is resized. This is particularly useful for localization scenarios, where the labels or text in controls will be dynamically determined from resource files or the database, and the respective control will `AutoSize` itself based on its content width or height.

Finally, the `SplitContainer` control replaces the notorious `Splitter` control that was part of .NET 1.0 and 1.1. The `Splitter` control was very unintuitive to use, being based on the z-order of controls within a collection (basically the order that they were added to the parent container). The `Splitter` control is still around for backward compatibility, but the `SplitContainer` is much easier and more intuitive to use. It provides a splitter bar and a panel on each side of it that can act as container controls for anything you want to add to the respective sides of the splitter bar. This gives a better design-time and runtime experience in creating a split-window appearance.

Figures C.18 and C.19 show a simple sample application that demonstrates the effects of these three layout controls. In this application, a `SplitContainer` control was added to the form, a `TableLayoutPanel` container was added to the left pane of the `SplitContainer` and dock-filled, and a `FlowLayoutPanel` container was added to the right pane of the `SplitContainer` and dock-filled. Two labels, two text boxes, and two radio buttons were added to the six cells of the table layout panel. Four `PictureBox` controls were added to the flow layout panel. When the radio buttons for English or German are selected, the label prompts for the text boxes in the table layout panel are switched to that language.

Figure C.18 shows the application running with the thumbnail images initially, with just the fourth picture box scrolled around to a second row. The labels in the table on the left are flush against their text box, and they fill most of the available space. When I resize the form to make it a little narrower and switch the language to German, you can see the effects in the two layout panels in Figure C.19. The longer text of the German prompts automatically resizes the labels. The table layout panel is a fixed width and its parent split container has the left panel set to a fixed width, so the table layout panel resizes the column containing the text boxes, shrinking them slightly to make room for the expanded labels. You could also set the table layout panel to `AutoSize = true` and change the split container to not be a fixed width for the left column, and it would expand without shrinking the text boxes. On the right you can see that the reduced width of the form caused the flow layout panel to become narrower, which caused the third picture box control to flow down onto the second row of controls, which then forced the fourth picture box to flow to the third row. You can play with the LayoutContainers sample in the download code to get a better idea of this dynamic behavior than still figures can give you.

Setting Tab Order

An important thing to remember when laying out a form is to set the tab order of the controls properly. Windows Forms controls follow the standard Windows convention of letting a user move the input focus from one control to another using the Tab key. The order that the focus will transition

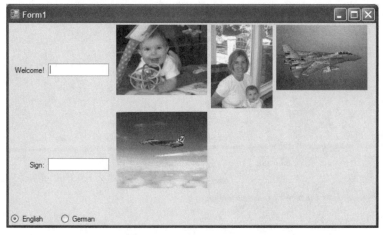

FIGURE C.18: SplitContainer, FlowLayoutPanel, and TableLayoutPanel Example (First View)

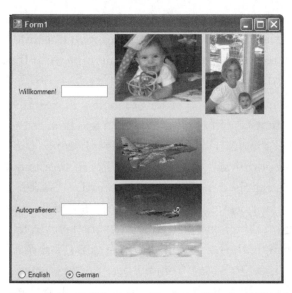

FIGURE C.19: SplitContainer, FlowLayoutPanel, and TableLayoutPanel Example (Second View)

from control to control is determined by the tab order. The tab order is set by a `TabIndex` property on each control. You can set these values manually and try to get them all straight, but it is much easier using the Tab Order view in the Visual Studio designer. If you select *Tab Order* from the *View* menu in Visual Studio when the form is displayed in the designer, the Form view will be modified to show the tab index of each control in a little box next to it, as shown in Figure C.20.

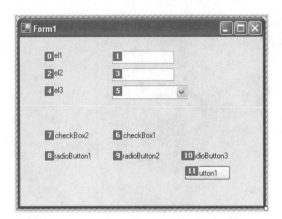

FIGURE C.20: Tab Order View

You can set the tab order while in Tab Order view by clicking on each control in the order you want the tabs set, starting with the first control. When you click through to the last control, the new tab order will be automatically set. Pressing Esc or reselecting the *Tab Order* menu item in the *View* menu will exit the Tab Order view.

Keep in mind that you should set the tab order of labels that describe other controls, such as a label that describes what goes in a text box, as the control immediately preceding the described control. This is because people with disabilities often use additional tools to help discern inputs on the screen, and many of those tools depend on the tab order. So for a vision-impaired user of your application, their screen reader tool may read the label text as they tab into the text box that follows the label in tab order. When the user tabs through, the focus will skip over `Label` controls because its `TabStop` property is set to `false` from the base `Control` class. Input controls such as `TextBox` override that property and set it to `true` by default, so they will accept the focus when the user tabs through the controls.

Command and Control of Your Windows Forms Applications *(New in 2.0)*

Three new controls that you will probably want to use in almost every Windows Forms application you write are the `MenuStrip`, `ToolStrip`, and `StatusStrip` controls. These controls are new in .NET 2.0 and replace their predecessors (`MainMenu`, `ToolBar`, and `StatusBar`) from .NET 1.X. Like the `Splitter` mentioned earlier, the old controls are still part of the Framework for backward compatibility. However, for any new applications you design, you should start using the three strip controls as your primary controls for these types of functionality.

As the names imply, the `MenuStrip` and `StatusStrip` are really just specialized versions of the `ToolStrip`. The `ToolStrip` itself is a sophisticated container control that lets you add other controls to the strip (labels, buttons, combo boxes, progress bars, etc.) that will be laid out in a row. The tool strip supports docking to any of the four sides of its container. You can also embed the `ToolStrip` into a `ToolStripContainer`. This allows multiple tool strips to be arranged in whatever order the user wants, just like most people are used to from the toolbars in Microsoft Office. Additionally, the tool strips support an overflow area, which allows controls to disappear off the right or bottom of the strip if there isn't enough room for the controls, but still be accessible through a drop-down arrow that appears on the end of the strip.

The `MenuStrip` defaults to docking to the top of the form, and lets you easily add menus and menu items, with text, images, and submenus as you would expect. Because the menu strip is a specialization of the tool strip, you can add all the same kinds of controls to a menu strip that you can to a tool strip. The `StatusStrip` is conceptually very similar, but it defaults to docking to the bottom of the form and provides `StatusStrip-Panels` that you add information to within the Status bar, as well as other controls, such as buttons and progress bars.

Each of the strip controls have smart tags (described earlier in this appendix) associated with them to let you quickly customize the control, including populating it with standard items such as the ones shown in Figure C.21 in the menu and a second tool strip. You also get some rich in-place editing capabilities with each control in the designer, with smart tags available for each item in the strip. You can also work with the items in the strip or the strip itself through the Properties window and the property editors presented from there.

FIGURE C.21: Strip Controls in Action

In addition to supporting most of the behavior of the toolbars and menus in Microsoft Office, the strip controls also support a themed look and feel. The default look and feel is almost identical to the look and feel of Microsoft Office 2003. The look and feel is managed through a **renderer**. There are several renderers that come with .NET 2.0, and you can create your own to customize the look and feel to a great extent.

Where Are We?

In this appendix, I have given you a quick but comprehensive overview of the things you need to understand to develop Windows Forms applications. You learned how to code Windows Forms by hand, and saw how the designer can save you a lot of coding with a much more intuitive and productive design-time experience for laying out your forms and controls and customizing the properties that drive their behavior and appearance at runtime. You got exposure to the event model and underlying infrastructure provided by the Windows Forms base classes, and learned about the many options for laying out your controls on a form. You learned to encapsulate functionality and related controls in user controls, and got exposure to some of the most common controls you will be dealing with in Windows Forms applications. Finally, you got a brief glimpse into the capabilities and features of some of the new Windows Forms 2.0 controls that were designed to make it easier to create rich functionality with well laid out and presented form controls in minimal time.

▪D▪

Accessing Data with ADO.NET

A N IMPORTANT PART of any real-world application is obtaining and managing the data that drives the application. The application could be something as simple as a game that is retrieving and storing user preferences and scoring data. At the other end of the spectrum, it could be a complex business application that retrieves, manipulates, and updates data from multiple data sources over a network or the Web and within the scope of a distributed transaction using asynchronous message-based communications. The spectrum of what constitutes data access is extremely broad and complicated, and is the topic of many other books.

This book, on the other hand, is focused on the presentation of data using Windows Forms, and this appendix isn't intended to teach you everything there is to know about data access. What I do want to accomplish is to give you a solid foundation in how to get data into and out of your Windows Forms application architecture. I also want to ensure that you understand enough about ADO.NET data access to follow the samples in the chapters of the book and, more importantly, how the different forms of data affect the presentation of that data.

So basically I am going to show you just enough to make you dangerous. You should be able to develop data-bound UI prototypes without needing a data access expert to come in and build you a data layer before you can get started designing and coding the presentation tier. On the other hand, you shouldn't build a client application that is tightly bound to the data tier. When it comes to data access, there are a lot of different ways to accomplish the same thing. This appendix covers data access at the lower levels—the basics of data access with ADO.NET. Chapter 2 describes how to work with typed data sets and how to do the kind of data access that you will want to use most often in your data applications.

If you have a solid foundation in ADO.NET, you can feel free to skip this appendix or just use it as a quick review of core concepts. If you will be coding up a data access layer, I'd suggest you pick up some data access books to learn all the various options and best practices for designing a data layer and handling more complex scenarios. (*Pragmatic ADO.NET* by Shawn Wildermuth [Addison-Wesley, 2003] is an outstanding place to start.)

Data can take on many forms and come from many sources when coding with ADO.NET. This appendix only focuses on two sources of data: relational data coming from a database like Microsoft SQL Server, and XML coming from a file or stream. The two worlds are certainly not mutually exclusive. SQL Server includes a lot of functionality for generating and consuming XML, and SQL Server 2005 includes a native data type for storing XML. You can load XML into a `DataSet` and work with it as relational data, and you can transfer relational data into an `XmlDataDocument` and work with it as an XML document. You might also load XML and iterate through the nodes in a document to extract data that you put into business objects that you then use for data binding.

How you code against relational and XML data is very different, as is how you might use them for data binding. This appendix focuses on the various ways to get data into business entities and data sets that you can use in your Windows Forms applications to present that data, and how to take any updates made to the data and push them back to the underlying data store.

Because this is such a dense topic, I am going to have to make a few assumptions about your knowledge. First, I assume that you understand the basic concepts behind storing data in a database and executing queries to retrieve and update it. Second, I will assume you have some basic knowledge of XML storage, the structure of a document, and the kinds of nodes that a document can contain. You certainly don't need to be an expert in these things, but you should at least have enough background to understand the terminology and what the basic processes and capabilities of those technologies are.

Relational Data Access

When dealing with relational data access, you generally follow the same process each time you need to touch the underlying data store to retrieve data or update it. You need

1. A connection to the data store.
2. A way to express the query that you are going to perform.
3. Something to contain any returned results from the query.

The classes defined in ADO.NET are used to encapsulate the state and behavior associated with each of these steps.

A key concept with relational data access in .NET is that it is based on a disconnected data model. Obviously you can't execute a query if you aren't really connected to the database. **Disconnected data access** means that you are expected to open a connection, use that connection to issue a query or a set of queries, and then close the connection. You may continue to work with the data resulting from the query for some time on the client. At some point in the future, you may reconnect to the database to either issue update queries or to refresh the data you have, but you don't keep a connection open to the database the entire time you are working with the data. This makes it a very different data model to work with than legacy database APIs, which typically favored a connected model. This is also different from the concept of offline operations of a smart client application. **Offline capabilities** are focused on being able to cache the operational data on the client to allow it to continue to support certain use cases even when not connected to a network. Disconnected data access generally assumes you have a network connection available, but that you just aren't keeping database connections open throughout the functioning of your application.

When dealing with data types in ADO.NET, there are two kinds of types that you come across: generic data classes and provider-specific classes The generic relational data classes and interfaces implement abstract constructs in the relational model—tables, rows, relations, constraints—and can be used to contain data coming from a variety of data sources. These generic data classes are all part of the `System.Data` namespace, which is the root namespace for ADO.NET class library constructs.

For the generic classes to be useful, though, you usually need to be able to connect to a data store and perform the queries that populate the generic data containers or update the underlying data store based on changes in them. The classes you use to make that connection and execute queries are the provider-specific classes that reside in child namespaces of `System.Data` and are specific to each provider. Table D.1 lists the providers that ship with the .NET Framework.

TABLE D.1: Managed Data Providers in the .NET Framework

Data Source	Provider Namespace	Description
Microsoft SQL Server	`System.Data.SqlClient`	Contains classes to use for all access to SQL Server. These include provider-specific features such as built-in data types, XML query and update capabilities, notifications, managed types as user-defined types, and other features. The classes in this namespace support SQL Server versions 7 and later.
OLE DB	`System.Data.OleDb`	Contains classes to use for access to any data source that exposes an OLE DB provider driver. Use this provider for Microsoft Access connectivity. One OLE DB provider you cannot use through this is the OLE DB to ODBC bridge. Use the ODBC-managed provider directly instead.
ODBC	`System.Data.Odbc`	Contains classes to use for access to any data provider that exposes an ODBC driver for data access.

TABLE D.1: Managed Data Providers in the .NET Framework (Continued)

Data Source	Provider Namespace	Description
Oracle	`System.Data.Oracle`	Contains classes that target the specific capabilities of an Oracle database. These classes support Oracle database versions 9i and later. However, this is a data provider for Oracle created by Microsoft and isn't intended to be a full-featured provider. Oracle has its own full-featured provider that is called the Oracle Data Provider, and this provider should be obtained for any production development against Oracle databases.

The managed provider classes are expected to implement a common set of interfaces that are defined in the `System.Data` namespace. These interfaces define the basic methods and properties for a set of classes that every managed provider is expected to implement. These include classes for establishing data source connections, creating commands to execute queries, creating data adapters used to fill data sets, and creating parameters that you associate with a command to pass to a query. In ADO.NET 2.0, there is also a set of abstract base classes for data providers in the `System.Data.ProviderBase` namespace that lets you program against different data sources in a provider-agnostic way. This allows you to switch out the underlying data source without needing to change any of your application code. This topic is a little beyond the scope of what I cover here, but you should be aware of the capability.

However, if you need to tap into provider-specific features such as XML handling in SQL Server, then you will need to program against the specific provider classes instead of the interfaces or generic classes for those capabilities. In general, you should pick a consistent approach in coding against the provider objects instead of switching back and forth between sometimes using the interface and sometimes using the provider-specific classes. You will have to figure out what the best approach is based on your application needs and the degree to which you want your code to be portable across multiple providers.

As a simple example of working with a specific provider, the following code shows how to open a connection to a SQL Server database and execute a command to fill a `DataSet` with a `SqlDataAdapter`:

```
private DataSet GetCustomersFromDb()
{
   // Create the disconnected data store
   DataSet ds = new DataSet();

   // Create the connection object
   SqlConnection conn = new SqlConnection(
   "server=localhost;database=Northwind;trusted_connection=true");

   // Create the command that wraps the query
   SqlCommand cmd = new SqlCommand(
      "SELECT CustomerID, CompanyName FROM Customers", conn);

   //Create the DataAdapter that bridges the provider-
   // agnostic DataSet and the provider-specific connection
   // and command
   SqlDataAdapter adapter = new SqlDataAdapter(cmd);

   // Opens the connection, executes the query,
   // puts the result in the DataSet, closes the connection
   adapter.Fill(ds, "Customers");

   // Return the result
   return ds;
}
```

I'll get into more details on data sets and data adapters shortly, but the intent here is to start with the basics. The process is:

1. Create a data set object that you are going to populate.

2. Create a connection object for the data store that you are going to operate against. Note that creating an instance of a connection object doesn't open the connection.

3. Create a command object that encapsulates the query that you are going to execute and associate it with the connection in its constructor.

4. Create a data adapter and associate it with the command that will be used to populate it.

5. Call the `Fill` method to populate the data set and return the results.

I'll get into more detail on all the magic that is happening in that `Fill` method later in this appendix. At this point I just want you to get an overview.

When you need to get an entire set of data into memory, use a data set so you can deal with it as a whole on the client or in the middle tier. Each managed provider also implements another way to retrieve the data from a query, called a **data reader**. For example, the SQL Server managed provider implements a class called `SqlDataReader`. You can think of a data reader as a fast, forward-only, fire hose-like cursor that you can use to iterate through the results of a query. There are ways to bind a data reader to Windows Forms controls through a `BindingSource` component, but it isn't a practice I would encourage, so I won't go into a lot of detail on it. Binding a data reader to Windows Forms controls tightly couples your presentation tier with your data tier. If it is a very small-scale application, and you are looking for the fastest way to get data presented to the user, that may be okay. However, for enterprise-scale business applications, that is something you should avoid. Using data readers in the presentation tier potentially keeps the connection open longer than necessary, limiting scalability, and also tightly couples the client to the data schema of the data tier. However, data readers are the fastest way to iterate through the rows returned from a query, so you may want to use them if you are going to push the results of a query into a collection of business object classes instead of using data sets. I'll show an example of this later in this appendix.

The Ubiquitous DataSet

The most common data type you will deal with in Windows Forms data binding is the `DataSet`, or a derived typed data set class. Data binding to custom objects and collections is also very easy in .NET 2.0, so that will be a very common approach as well and is covered in more detail in several places in the book. But data sets are specifically designed for data binding in .NET, and this appendix is focused on relational data access, so let's get our hands dirty there first.

A **data set** basically provides you with an in-memory data collection that can be used for everything from containing a single row of data to a complex schema of many tables with relations and constraints between them. Some would even go so far as to call it an in-memory database, but there are hazards in thinking of it that way if you start bringing too much data into memory. Figure D.1 shows the structure of a data set and the objects that are contained within it.

For simple tabular access to data returned from a query, you will usually only deal with a single data table in a data set, and that will be the target of your data binding. When you do so, the data set just becomes a fancy wrapper around a set of rows. You can actually just create a data table and populate it, and .NET 2.0 lets you create `DataTable` objects on their own, without a containing data set.

There are also many scenarios where you may want to retrieve rows from a table that have a parent-child relationship with rows from another table. In those cases, you will start to deal with data sets containing

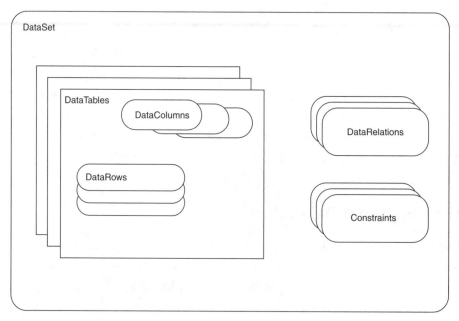

FIGURE D.1: DataSet Structure

multiple data table objects, one or more data relation objects that maintain the parent-child relationship between the tables, and constraint objects that enforce the integrity of the contained data. A **data table object** contains a collection of data columns that describe the name and type of each column in a table (the metadata of the column), and it also contains a collection of data row objects that contain the actual data itself.

You can populate a data set in one of three primary ways: by loading it from a file, programmatically, or through a query to a database. In .NET 2.0, you can also work with `DataTable` objects in isolation from a data set, and you can also load a data table using a data reader with the `Load` method. Let's go from the simplest to the most complex by starting with loading and saving data sets from files, specifically XML files.

Loading Data Sets from a File

The `DataSet` class supports two methods for saving to and loading from a file: `WriteXml` and `ReadXml`. If you have data in a data set and you want to save it to disk or a stream, you call `WriteXml`. When you want to read it back in, you call `ReadXml`. Because the underlying file format is XML, you could create an XML document some other way that is readable by a data set. It actually doesn't have to come from a file at all; the `ReadXml` method will accept a stream, which could represent a file, network stream, or memory stream. For example, you might receive an XML document over a Web service that you could read into a data set and then display it in a `Data-GridView` control. There is also a `GetXml` method that lets you get back the contents of a data set as an XML string.

The `ReadXml` method is fairly adept at inferring an appropriate schema from a simple XML file and being able to transform that XML into a data set. It will treat the root element as the container for the data set. It will then treat each element type that contains other elements as a row from a table, and each element that contains only text as a column in that row. It can also handle schemas where the elements represent rows from a table, but the column values are encoded as attributes on that element instead of child elements. For example, the straightforward XML in Listing D.1 will be loaded into a data set that contains a table of Customers and a table of

Orders, and will have foreign key constraints and relationships between the two tables representing the nested nature. The corresponding relational schema is shown in Figure D.2.

LISTING D.1: Customers Data in XML

```xml
<?xml version="1.0" standalone="yes"?>
<CustomersDataSet>
  <Customers>
    <CustomerID>ALFKI</CustomerID>
    <CompanyName>Alfreds Futterkiste</CompanyName>
    <Orders>
      <OrderID>10643</OrderID>
    </Orders>
    <Orders>
      <OrderID>10692</OrderID>
    </Orders>
  </Customers>
  <Customers>
    <CustomerID>ANATR</CustomerID>
    <CompanyName>Ana Trujillo Emparedados y helados</CompanyName>
    <Orders>
      <OrderID>10308</OrderID>
    </Orders>
    <Orders>
      <OrderID>10625</OrderID>
    </Orders>
  </Customers>
</CustomersDataSet>
```

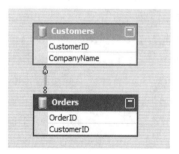

FIGURE D.2: Relational Schema for XML Customers and Orders Document

In the code in Listing D.1, if the XML contains an embedded XML schema, the data set will try to use it to establish the relational schema of the tables and relationships, and then will load the data into that schema. If the file was created by saving an existing data set, then things should work out fine when you read it back in. However, not every XML file is suitable for loading into a data set. If you have a schema where the same element type can exist at multiple levels in the hierarchy, you will get an `Argument-Exception` if you try to load it into a data set, because the data set will fail to coerce it into a relational schema. For example, if you added a Customers element as a child to an Orders element in the XML in Listing D.1 and tried to read it in with `ReadXml`, an `ArgumentException` would be thrown. Additionally, if you have malformed XML, an `XmlException` will be thrown when you call `ReadXml`, so you will definitely want to have the call to `ReadXml` wrapped in an exception handler.

To read a data set in from XML, the code is quite simple:

```
private void LoadXmlDataSet(string xmlFilePath)
{
    try
    {
        DataSet ds = new DataSet();
        ds.ReadXml(xmlFilePath);
    }
    catch (ArgumentException ex)
    {
        MessageBox.Show("Error reading XML into DataSet: " +
        ex.GetType().ToString() + " - " + ex.Message);
    }
}
```

The `ReadXml` method can take a path to a file, an open stream object, or an XML or text reader object. It also optionally takes an `XmlReadMode` enumeration that controls how the inference of the schema and XML operate.

Creating a Data Set Programmatically

To create and populate a data set programmatically, you need nothing more than to understand the object model and how to call methods and properties on those objects. Programmatically constructing data sets and populating them is fairly unusual, because it requires tedious and error-prone coding that will need to be updated any time the schema of your data changes. About the only time you will probably want to create data sets programmatically is if you have some hard-coded or nonstructured information in your program that you want to present in a tabular form; then you might stuff it into a data set so that you can bind the data set to a `DataGridView` control. But in that case it would be better to separate that structure into an XML file and load it from there so that you don't have to change your source code to change the structure or contents of the presented data. Another case where you might programmatically deal with a data set in this way is if you want to add a computed column to a table within a data set. The code in Listing D.2 shows how to create a simple data set, including a computed column, and load some data into it.

LISTING D.2: **Programmatic DataSet Creation and Population**

```
private DataSet CreateProgrammaticDataSet()
{
  // Create the DataSet
  DataSet ds = new DataSet();

  // Create a table with three columns
  DataTable dt = new DataTable("Customers");
  DataColumn col1 = new DataColumn("CustomerID",typeof(int));
  DataColumn col2 = new DataColumn("CompanyName", typeof(string));
  DataColumn col3 = new DataColumn("Computed Column",
      typeof(string), "CustomerID + ':' + CompanyName");
  dt.Columns.Add(col1);
  dt.Columns.Add(col2);
  dt.Columns.Add(col3);

  // Create a primary key constraint on the ID column
  UniqueConstraint pk = new UniqueConstraint("PK_Customers",col1,true);

  // Add the table to the DataSet
  ds.Tables.Add(dt);

  // Add a row to the DataSet
  DataRow row = dt.NewRow();
  row["CustomerID"] = 1;
  row["CompanyName"] = "Fred";
  dt.Rows.Add(row);

  // Return the results
  return ds;
}
```

The code in Listing D.2 constructs a data table and adds the desired columns to it, as well as a primary key constraint. Note that the computed column uses a third argument to the `DataColumn` constructor, which is the expression to use to compute the value of that column at runtime. It adds the new table to the data set and then creates a new row. Once the values of the columns in the new row are set, the row is added to the table's `Rows` collection. Note that you have to create the row from the table so that it will have the correct schema (columns) to be part of the table, but it doesn't actually become part of the table until it is added to the `Rows` collection.

If you care about maintainability, you will probably cringe at the code that sets the values of the two columns through the row indexer. This indexer exposes an object reference, into which you can attempt to stuff any object. The compiler won't be able to help you because it doesn't have enough type information to figure out what the actual type of the column is, so you won't know until runtime if you have tried to place an inappropriate value into the column. The other problem with this code is the hard-coded strings for the column names. Using column names in this case is more maintainable than the alternative, which is to pass the ordinal position of the column to the row indexer. However, if your schema changes, you are going to have to root out all the places in your code that you hard-coded column names, which is error prone at best. Typed data sets (described in Chapter 2) fix both of these problems, which is why you should favor them for most scenarios involving data sets.

Loading Data Sets from a Database

You may occasionally load data into a data set from an XML file that has been cached on the client machine, and you may even (more rarely) have occasion to programmatically create a data set as shown in the previous section. However, the vast majority of the time you will be using data sets in conjunction with some form of relational data store. When that is the case, you will be loading the data into a data set using one of the managed providers introduced earlier, or you will be using typed data sets, where the schema is built into the type instead of needing to be determined dynamically.

I am going to focus on the use of the SQL Server managed provider, as it is probably the most common database used in .NET applications. If you need to use the OLE DB, Oracle, or ODBC providers, the coding patterns are virtually identical, thanks to the fact that they are all based on the same interfaces. Keep in mind that the SQL Server managed provider can be used with either a full-up instance of SQL Server or with a SQL Server 2005 Express instance, which is just a scaled-down free version of the SQL Server engine.

I recommend that you use SQL Express for creating client-side or small application databases, rather than Microsoft Access databases. The SQL Express engine is much more robust for client-server applications, and you can use many features of the SQL Server engine that aren't available in Access, such as stored procedures and triggers. You can easily establish a connection to a SQL Express database just by specifying a file path to the MDF file that contains the database.

You have already seen one case of loading a data set from a SQL Server table earlier in the section Relational Data Access. You can also use a SQL Server 2005 Express database connection, as shown in Listing D.3.

LISTING D.3: Filling a DataSet Through a SQL 2005 Express Connection

```
private DataSet GetCustomersFromDb()
{
  // Create the DataSet
  DataSet ds = new DataSet();

  // Create the connection to the SQL Express DB
  SqlConnection conn = new SqlConnection(
    @"server=.\SQLEXPRESS;
    AttachDbFileName=|DataDirectory|\SimpleDatabase.mdf;
    trusted_connection=true");

  // Create the command and the adapter that uses it
  SqlCommand cmd = new SqlCommand("SELECT * FROM Customers", conn);
  SqlDataAdapter adapter = new SqlDataAdapter(cmd);

  // Opens the connection, executes the query,
  // puts the result in the DataSet, closes the connection
  adapter.Fill(ds, "Customers");

  // Return the result
  return ds;
}
```

Let's dissect the code in Listing D.3. First, to create a connection, you construct an instance of the `SqlConnection` class. The constructor for this class takes a connection string that can contain any number of parameters, as defined by the SQL Server managed provider. The set of allowable parameters in the connection string are determined by each managed provider and will be different for each. There are a number of different parameter names for some of the typical parameters; consult the documentation for the `ConnectionString` property of the `SqlConnection` class for a comprehensive list.

The most common parameters to use for a SQL Server database are the `server`, `database`, `trusted_connection`, `user id`, and `password` parameters. There are other parameter names that accomplish the same thing as these (such as `pwd` instead of `password` and `Integrated Security` instead of `trusted_connection`), so you can choose which ones you want to use for common connection scenarios. You can see from this example that with SQL Express 2005, you can use the `AttachDBFilename` parameter to specify the database based on a file path. The `|DataDirectory|` keyword is a special syntax that instructs the connection object to look in the working directory of the executing application. The connection string also specifies the server instance to be the default SQLEXPRESS instance, and `trusted_connection=true` uses integrated security, which will log you into the database using the credentials of the Windows account under which the application is running. You can also pass an explicit username and password in the connection string if you want to use a SQL Server login.

Normally, you wouldn't want to hard-code connection strings in your application code as shown in Listing D.3. A better way is to place them into your configuration file, and both Visual Studio 2005 and .NET 2.0 support a rich new model for placing connection strings and other custom user and application settings in your configuration file, while still allowing you to programmatically access those settings in a strongly typed way. These features are discussed in detail in Chapters 2 and 5.

Once you have a connection to work with, you create a `SqlCommand` object, passing the SQL text query to execute and the connection to use to the constructor. A command object can be provided with SQL statements or with the name of a stored procedure to use. For real data access layers, I recommend you wrap your data access at the database level in stored procedures and only consume those stored procedures from your data layer. Doing so decouples your application code from the specific schema of your tables, preventing small changes to the underlying schema from affecting application code. Stored procedures also let you use SQL Server's own security mechanisms to prevent direct access to the tables, and stored procedures sometimes have higher performance than dynamic SQL statements executed from the code in Listing D.3 (although the performance difference is insignificant for most queries in .NET). I have broken this guidance in many of the code samples in this book to be able to use the Northwind database with minimal modification, and so that you could clearly see what is being retrieved by the queries.

> **■ NOTE**
>
> When performing SQL text queries, you should specify the exact columns that you want returned from your query. Specifying * for the columns may return a lot more information than you need, affecting application performance. It also requires the command object to do more work to determine the exact schema of the result set that will be returned by the query.

Next, the code in Listing D.3 creates a `SqlDataAdapter` object, which is the bridge between the source-neutral data set and the specific data source that it will work with. In this case, I construct it by passing in the command object. Finally, I call `Fill` on the data adapter, which performs a number of steps. First, it sees if the connection in the underlying command object is already open. If not, the `Fill` method will open the connection. Next, it executes the query against the database. The adapter then takes the returned rows, determines if a `DataTable` with the required schema already exists in the data set, and if not creates one, and then places the returned rows into it. If the data adapter opened the connection, it will close it before returning from the method call. Unless you specify a table name when you fill the data set, the data table instance name will simply be *Table*, and as you add additional tables, they will be named *Table1*, *Table2*, and so on. Figure D.3 shows the entire stack typically used for working with data sets and relational data stores.

Typically a query or stored procedure will only return a single table of results, but you could return multiple tables with a single query or stored procedure as shown in Listing D.4.

LISTING D.4: Loading Multiple Tables in a Single Query

```
private DataSet LoadMultipleDatasets()
{
   // Create the DataSet and connection
   DataSet ds = new DataSet();
   SqlConnection conn = new SqlConnection();
   conn.ConnectionString =
     "server=localhost;database=Northwind;trusted_connection=true";

   // Create the command and the adapter
   SqlCommand cmd = new SqlCommand();
   cmd.Connection = conn;
   cmd.CommandText = "SELECT * FROM Customers; SELECT * FROM Orders";

   SqlDataAdapter adapter = new SqlDataAdapter();
   adapter.SelectCommand = cmd;

   // Opens the connection, executes the query,
   // puts the result in the DataSet, closes the connection
   adapter.Fill(ds);

   // Name the tables correctly
   ds.Tables[0].TableName = "Customers";
   ds.Tables[1].TableName = "Orders";

   // Return the result
   return ds;
}
```

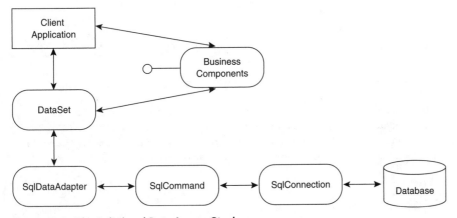

FIGURE D.3: The Relational Data Access Stack

In Listing D.4, two tables of results are returned in the `Fill` method, and the data set is populated with two tables, one for Customers and one for Orders. The `TableName` property of each of the resulting tables is then set to the appropriate string, because the default naming convention would just have them named *Table* and *Table1*. Note also the different syntax in creating the data objects in this method. Instead of specifying the various parameters for each object in their constructor, they are supplied through properties after construction instead.

Another way of getting the tables named correctly, as well as to handle the case when the name of a column in the database is different from the name of a column in the target data set, is to use the `TableMappings` property on the data adapter. The `TableMappings` property holds a collection of `DataTableMapping` objects, which is defined in the `System.Data.Common` namespace. Each `DataTableMapping` object lets you specify a mapping between the schema of a result set returned from the database and the schema of the data table into which the table adapter will place the results. The following code shows an example of using `TableMappings` to modify the table name and column names when the data adapter fills the data set.

```
public DataSet GetCustomersSchemaDiff()
{
    // Create the data set
    DataSet data = new DataSet();

    // Create the connection to the SQL Express DB
    SqlConnection conn = new SqlConnection(
      "server=localhost;database=Northwind;trusted_connection=true");

    // Create the command and the adapter that uses it
    SqlCommand cmd = new SqlCommand(
      "SELECT CustomerID, CompanyName FROM Customers", conn);
    SqlDataAdapter adapter = new SqlDataAdapter(cmd);

    // Set up the table mapping to name the table, and to
    // change CustomerID to ID, CompanyName column to Name
    DataColumnMapping[] columnMappings = new DataColumnMapping[2];
    columnMappings[0] = new DataColumnMapping("CustomerID", "ID");
    columnMappings[1] = new DataColumnMapping("CompanyName", "Name");
    DataTableMapping mapping = new DataTableMapping("Table",
```

```
        "Customers", columnMappings);
    adapter.TableMappings.Add(mapping);

    // Opens the connection, executes the query,
    // puts the result in the DataSet, closes the connection
    adapter.Fill(data);

    return data; // one table named Customers, with columns ID, Name
}
```

In this code, the data coming in from the SELECT statement would have been placed in a data table named Table with columns CustomerID and CompanyName. The `TableMapping` makes it so the table will be named Customers instead, and it will have columns ID and Name with the respective columns from the database mapped into them.

Most of the data classes in ADO.NET give you the option of using overloaded constructors and methods to specify all of the parameters for the object to do its work, or you can set them through properties. It is really just a matter of preference. The properties approach shown earlier requires more lines of code, but is a little easier to read for some, and is easier to debug because you can step through each line and inspect the property values as they are set. I have favored the constructor approach in this book to avoid killing too many trees in the production of this book. I'll leave it up to you to decide the best approach for your code.

Loading a DataTable with a DataReader

I'm going to show how to use a data reader to load a custom object model later on, but while we are on the subject of loading data sets, I thought I should highlight a new capability in .NET 2.0. If all you are dealing with is a single table at a time, the need to create a whole data set and index into the tables just to get to your data can be a lot of unnecessary overhead. In .NET 2.0, you can create, populate, and use a `DataTable` on its own without ever needing to deal with the complexities of a data set. You can also fill it in a quick and efficient way using a data reader instead of having to go through a data adapter or table adapter (table adapters are discussed in Chapter 2). The following code demonstrates this in action.

```
public DataTable GetCustomers ( )
{
    string connStr =
      "server=localhost;database=Northwind;trusted_connection=true";
    DataTable customersTable = new DataTable("Customers");
    using (SqlConnection conn = new SqlConnection(connStr))
    {
        SqlCommand selectCmd = new SqlCommand(
          "SELECT CustomerID, CompanyName FROM Customers", conn);
        conn.Open();
        SqlDataReader reader = selectCmd.ExecuteReader();
        customersTable.Load(reader);
    }
    return customersTable;
}
```

There are a number of new concepts in this one block of code, so let's step through them one at a time. The first thing the code does is to create an empty data table and name it Customers. Any time you need to execute a query, you need a connection object, so that is created next within a using statement. If you execute a command on your own (not through a data adapter), you will have to explicitly open the connection first. Any time you open a connection, you need to make sure you close it when you are done, and you need to make sure that happens even if an exception is thrown in the code that precedes the call to Close. One way to do that is to put the code that opens the connection and uses it in a try block, with the call to Close in a finally block. Another way that is used in this code is the using statement in C#.

In this code, the connection object is created in a using block, which causes the Dispose method to be called on the connection when the scope of the using block is left. The Dispose method on a connection object calls Close, and a using block will always set up a try-finally block for you, calling Dispose in the finally block. So the using block approach gives you a clean, readable, safe way to use your connection objects and make sure they are closed before the scope is left.

The next thing that is created is the command object that will execute the SELECT statement used to fill the data reader. That is created just like in the previous examples—by passing the SQL statement and the connection object. The connection is then opened, and the command is executed with the `ExecuteReader` method. This method returns a `SqlDataReader` object containing the results of the query. The data reader is then passed to the new `Load` method on the data table, which will iterate over the data reader to pull its contents into the data table.

Master-Details DataSets

As mentioned earlier, you can do a lot more with multiple tables in a single data set than just containing them as a collection of tables. You can also create parent-child relationships between them, and add primary, unique, and foreign key constraints. Data sets containing this kind of parent-child relationship are often called **master-details data sets**, because they are typically used in data-binding scenarios where the selection of a row in the parent table (the master) results in the display of all of the associated child rows (the details). The method in Listing D.5 again retrieves both the Customers and Orders tables, this time using two separate data adapters, and creates a master-details or parent-child relationship between them.

LISTING D.5: Creating a Master-Details DataSet

```
private DataSet GetCustomersAndOrders()
{
    DataSet ds = new DataSet();

    SqlConnection conn = new SqlConnection(
      "server=localhost;database=Northwind;trusted_connection=true");

    SqlCommand customersCmd = new SqlCommand("SELECT CustomerID,
      CompanyName, ContactName FROM Customers", conn);

    SqlDataAdapter customersAdapter = new SqlDataAdapter(customersCmd);

    // Set the adapter to add primary key information
    customersAdapter.MissingSchemaAction =
      MissingSchemaAction.AddWithKey;

    SqlCommand ordersCmd = new SqlCommand("SELECT OrderID, CustomerID,

      OrderDate FROM Orders", conn);
```

continues

```
SqlDataAdapter ordersAdapter = new SqlDataAdapter(ordersCmd);

// Set the adapter to add primary key information
ordersAdapter.MissingSchemaAction = MissingSchemaAction.AddWithKey;

// Add the customers to the DataSet
customersAdapter.Fill(ds,"Customers");

// Add the orders to the DataSet
ordersAdapter.Fill(ds, "Orders");

// Create the parent-child relation
DataColumn parentCol = ds.Tables["Customers"].Columns["CustomerID"];
DataColumn childCol = ds.Tables["Orders"].Columns["CustomerID"];
DataRelation dr = new DataRelation(
  "Customers_Orders",parentCol,childCol);

// Set the relation as nested for output XML
// (Orders are child elements of Customers)
dr.Nested = true;

// Add the relation to the DataSet's collection
// Adds a corresponding foreign key constraint as well
ds.Relations.Add(dr);

// Return the result
return ds;
}
```

Setting the data adapter's `MissingSchemaAction` property to `AddWithKey` before calling `Fill` will direct the data adapter to also determine the column(s) that comprise the primary key, if any, when the data adapter executes the query, and it will create corresponding unique constraints in the resulting table. To create the data relation, you need to specify what the primary key column in the parent table is, as well as the foreign key column in the child table. The easiest way to do this is using the `DataColumn` objects representing those columns. This will also implicitly specify which table is the parent table and which table is the child table, because columns can only belong to one table. Alternatively, you could specify the parent and child tables and columns by name. Adding the data relation also creates a corresponding foreign key constraint to enforce the rule that a corresponding row in the parent table must exist when a row in the child table refers to it. Notice that the code also sets the `Nested` property on the data relation to `true`. This only affects the XML that is output if you save the data set with `WriteXml` or get it as a string with `GetXml`. It would then show child rows as nested elements under the parent row elements.

Retrieving Data with Stored Procedures

When you work with stored procedures, you often need to provide parameters to them that affect their execution. The stored procedure might simply wrap a query that will return rows of data, or it might update, insert, or delete data in the database. In any of these cases, you usually have to tell the stored procedure which sets of data to operate on, and you do this through parameters.

Let's start with a simple example. In the Northwind database, there is a stored procedure defined named CustOrderHist. You provide it with a customer ID, and it will return a result set containing a summary of products and their quantity ordered by that customer. To call a stored procedure using ADO.NET, you use the `SqlCommand` class, as demonstrated earlier in this appendix. However, you need to tell the command object that you are calling a stored procedure instead of providing a textual query. You also need to provide the command object with any parameters that need to be passed to the stored procedure that it will execute. You do this as shown in Listing D.6.

LISTING D.6: Retrieving Data Through a Stored Procedure

```
private DataSet GetCustomerOrderHistory(string custId)
{
    // Validate the input
    if (custId.Length != 5)
        throw new ArgumentException(
            "The customer ID must be a 5 character string.","custId");

    DataSet ds = new DataSet("CustomerOrderHistoryDataSet");

    SqlConnection conn = new SqlConnection(
        "server=localhost;database=Northwind;trusted_connection=true");

    // Create the stored proc command to get customer history
    SqlCommand custHistCmd = new SqlCommand("CustOrderHist", conn);
    custHistCmd.CommandType = CommandType.StoredProcedure;
```

continues

```
            // Create the parameter for the customer ID
            SqlParameter custIdParam = new SqlParameter(
              "@CustomerID",SqlDbType.NChar,5);
            custIdParam.Value = custId;

            // Add the parameter to the command
            custHistCmd.Parameters.Add(custIdParam);

            SqlDataAdapter custHistAdapter = new SqlDataAdapter(custHistCmd);

            custHistAdapter.Fill(ds,"CustomerHistory");
            return ds;

}
```

In this case, you create the command object by specifying the name of the stored procedure you want to call instead of supplying a SQL query string, and you set the `CommandType` property on the command to `StoredProcedure` (the default is `CommandType.Text`). You then need to create a `SqlParameter` object (discussed later in this appendix) to encapsulate each of the parameters needed by the stored procedure and add them to the command's `Parameters` collection. Once everything is set up, you call the `Fill` method on the data adapter as before, and it will call the specified stored procedure, placing the result set returned into a table in the data set.

Updating the Database Using Data Sets

So far we have only been looking at retrieving data from a database. What happens when you have modified the data and want to save those changes back to the database? Well, another powerful capability of the `DataSet` class is the ability to keep track of changes made to the data contained in it. Changes come in three forms. You can

- Add new rows to a table
- Delete rows from a table
- Change the values in one or several of the columns of existing rows in a table

The data set handles this through a combination of holding two copies of each row, and through a `RowState` property on each row, which takes a value from the `DataRowState` enumeration. When you first retrieve a set of rows from the database, they are added to their table with a `RowState` value of `Unchanged`. When you modify a column value within an existing row, the state is set to `Modified`. When you add a new row or delete an existing one, that row's state will be marked `Added` or `Deleted`, respectively. And if you create a new row from a table, but have not yet added it to the `Rows` collection, the row's state will be `Detached`.

The row state lets a data adapter detect which rows should be used to perform inserts, updates, or deletes in the database table. When you change the values of an existing row, the current values for the columns are kept in one copy of the row, but the original values of that row from when the data was retrieved is also kept in a second copy of the row. This allows the original values to be used for optimistic concurrency detection (discussed the next section). The `RowState` values and their effects are described in Table D.2.

TABLE D.2: DataRowState Enumeration Values

Value	Description	Original Value	Current Value
Unchanged	The row has not been modified since the table was filled or since `AcceptChanges` has been called.	Row as filled	Row as filled
Modified	One of the column values has been changed since it was filled or since `AcceptChanges` was called.	Row as filled	Row with changes
Added	The row is a new row that has been added to the `Rows` collection since the table was filled or since `AcceptChanges` was called.	Empty	Row as created
Deleted	The row has had the `Delete` method called on it since the table was filled or since `AcceptChanges` was called.	Row as filled	Row as filled
Detached	The row was created through the table `NewRow` method, but has not yet been added to the `Rows` collection.	Empty	Row as created

You update the database with a data set by using a data adapter. Keep in mind that when I say "update" the database, I mean execute any update, insert, or delete queries needed. Try not to confuse this with the specific SQL UPDATE queries, which only affect modified rows and are only one of three forms of "updates."

So far, when constructing and using a data adapter to retrieve data, we have been setting its `SelectCommand` property to an instance of a `SqlCommand` that wraps a SQL text query or a stored procedure that returns the rows used to initially populate the table. To perform updates using a data adapter, you also need to provide command objects for the adapter's `InsertCommand`, `DeleteCommand`, and `UpdateCommand` properties, depending on which of those you expect to perform. As you might expect, the `InsertCommand` will be used for any rows marked as `Added`, the `DeleteCommand` for any rows marked as `Deleted`, and the `UpdateCommand` for any rows marked as `Modified`. If a data set doesn't contain any rows with a particular row state, the corresponding command doesn't have to be supplied since it won't be used. Generally speaking, you will want to provide all three because you cannot be sure that no rows will be in the modified, added, or deleted state when an update is performed.

Just like the select command used to fill a data set, the commands used for updating the database with a data set can use either SQL text queries or stored procedures, passing the columns of the updated rows as parameters. For simple applications that need to work directly against a single table in the database at a time, you can use parameterized SQL text queries. For larger scale applications, you may want to use stored procedures.

Either way, the commands you associate with the data adapter will be executed once for each row in the data set that needs to perform an update. This can result in a lot of network round-trips to the database for a large data set that has a lot of changes in it. To address this problem, in ADO.NET 2.0 the `SqlDataAdapter` class includes a batch updating feature that will group all of the queries and send them all to the database in one or several chunks. To use this feature, you set the `UpdateBatchSize` property on the `SqlDataAdapter` to some value other than 1 (the default). If you set the value to 0 (zero), then all of the updates will be batched into a single bunch. If you set some positive value greater than 1, the data adapter will batch sets of that many update queries and send them in chunks until all of the updates have completed. You do need to keep in mind, though, that when you send a batch of update queries using this approach, they will all execute as a single transaction in SQL Server. So if any one row in a batch fails to perform its update, the entire batch will fail.

To automatically formulate the update queries for working directly against the tables, the `SqlCommandBuilder` class can examine the select command that is in use by a data adapter and dynamically build insert, update, and delete commands for you. It will then populate the command properties of the data adapter with the generated queries. The command builder works well for simple data sets that contain tables generated from SELECT statements against a single table with a primary key constraint. This all happens by constructing a command builder object and passing in the data adapter that it is to create commands for. You won't actually call any of its methods or properties directly. The constructor for the command builder reaches into the data adapter and sets its `InsertCommand`, `UpdateCommand`, and `DeleteCommand` properties to suitable queries based on the columns that are populated with the `SelectCommand`. The following code demonstrates the use of a command builder to generate the update queries and use them to push the changes from a data set to the database. In this code, the data set and the data adapter are members on the enclosing class because they are used in a different method to populate the data set with a SELECT query.

```
private void btnSaveChanges_Click(object sender, System.EventArgs e)
{
    // Get the connection off the existing select command of the
adapter
    SqlConnection conn = m_Adapter.SelectCommand.Connection;

    // Create the insert, update, and delete commands
    // Simply constructing the command builder generates
    // and populates those commands on the adapter
    SqlCommandBuilder cmdBuilder = new SqlCommandBuilder(m_Adapter);

    // Call the update method on the adapter to save all changes
    // in the data set to the database
    m_Adapter.Update(m_CustomersDataSet,"Customers");

    // Refill the dataset to make sure any triggered changes
    // in the DB are reflected
    m_Adapter.Fill(m_CustomersDataSet,"Customers");
}
```

Using the `SqlCommandBuilder` is very handy for simple cases. However, it has a number of downsides, and you should avoid it in general for production code in favor of explicitly writing your own SQL statements or using stored procedures. The queries generated by the command builder always compare the values of all columns that were retrieved by the SELECT query to detect optimistic concurrency violations, as described in the next section. However, this is usually not the best approach. This also means the queries carry a lot more data along with them for each update than may be necessary. For larger scale systems, working with stored procedures is a better approach for reasons of security, maintainability, and performance. See the later section "Updating with Data Sets and Stored Procedures" for more details.

Handling Concurrency

One fundamental problem that almost always needs to be addressed when performing updates to a database is how to handle concurrent updates to the same data. Figure D.4 depicts a simple example of how concurrent updates can cause problems. In the figure, client 1 retrieves a row from the table. Client 2 comes along next and retrieves the same row. Client 2 is a little quicker in processing the row and commits its updates back to the database before client 1. The question that has to be addressed for concurrency is: What should happen when client 1 subsequently tries to write its changes to that same row?

You could allow a "last-in-wins" strategy, and always blindly write the values of an update to the row without considering its current contents. This is effectively no concurrency control. If you did this with the scenario in Figure D.4, the changes made by client 2 would be lost. If you are working with a connected data model, there are a number of ways to handle this situation with server-side locks on tables or rows that prevent concurrent access or updates depending on the level of isolation you want to provide. That is a very complex topic of its own that isn't really relevant in the disconnected data model employed by ADO.NET.

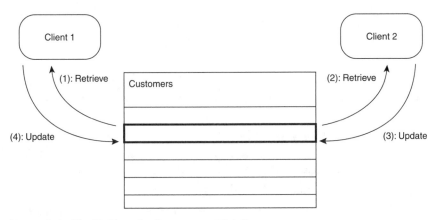

FIGURE D.4: The Making of a Concurrency Violation

To handle this in ADO.NET, the usual approach is to employ some-thing called **optimistic concurrency**, which basically means that you are going to assume that between the time you retrieve a row of data and the time you go back to the data source to update it, you don't expect any other query or client to come along and modify that row. If that assumption is violated, which could happen quite often in a highly concurrent system, your code needs to be able to deal with it in some way.

To deal with a concurrency violation, you first have to detect that it has occurred. This is done in ADO.NET by comparing the current contents of database columns (at the time an update is attempted) to those that were originally retrieved from the database. If the current contents of the data-base row are different from those that the ADO.NET client code has cached, then the optimistic concurrency assumption has been violated, and something needs to be done about it. As discussed earlier, the data set maintains the original values for any row that gets modified. This makes it very easy to use those original values to make optimistic concurrency deci-sions once a conflict has been detected.

Depending on the situation, you might want to compare the contents of every column in the row to the original values retrieved by ADO.NET. This is the approach used by the queries generated by the SqlCommand-Builder shown in the last section, as well as by the queries generated by Visual Studio .NET in a table adapter when you use the data set designer discussed in Chapter 2. For example, a parameterized update query for the Region table in Northwind might look like this:

```
UPDATE Region
SET RegionID = @RegionID, RegionDescription = @RegionDescription
WHERE (RegionID = @Original_RegionID) AND (
      RegionDescription = @Original_RegionDescription)
```

The `@RegionID` and `@RegionDescription` parameters would be populated by the current values in the row being updated, and the `@Original_RegionID` and `@Original_RegionDescription` would be populated with the original row values maintained by the data set.

However, for a large table, comparing the values of every column means carrying a lot of data back and forth across the connection to the database. A good compromise if you have control of the database schema is to include a timestamp, rowversion, or last-modified datetime column that gets updated every time any of the columns in the row gets updated. You can then just compare the value of this single column to detect concurrency violations (see Chapter 10 for an example of this approach). Another option is to use some subset of the columns in the row to determine whether a violation has occurred. For example, if the table storing the large images also contained their file name, size, and a hash of the image contents, you could compare those columns to decide whether the image had been updated concurrently or not.

The `SqlDataAdapter` class has built-in logic for detecting when optimistic concurrency has been violated, based on the `@@ROWCOUNT` SQL variable that indicates the number of affected rows when a query is executed. If the query that you execute to perform an update, insert, or delete indicates that the number of affected rows was zero, the data adapter will raise a `DBConcurrencyException`. You can tap into this detection logic both when you are using SQL text queries like the one in this code example and when you are doing your updates through a stored procedure. As long as whatever query gets executed by the command affects zero rows, the data adapter will throw the exception, which you can catch and handle appropriately. This happens because the rows affected should be equal to one, indicating that the update was successful.

However, throwing an exception may not always be the right thing to do. What if the data set contains 100 rows to update, and the violation happens on the 42nd row? The first 41 updates will have already been persisted to the database unless the update commands are associated with a single transaction (discussed later in this appendix), and the remaining 58 updates won't happen because the execution of the data adapter Update method is interrupted when the DBConcurrencyException is thrown. Instead, you may want to allow updating to continue even if an error occurs, and then decide what to do about any errors after all the rows have been processed.

The data set and data adapter support this scenario as well. Each DataRow in the tables of the data set contains a collection of errors exposed through the Errors property. If a problem occurs performing an update on a row, the errors collection will get populated with information about what happened by the exception that was thrown. That could include not only concurrency exceptions, but other built-in or custom SQL Server errors raised by the query or stored procedure execution. You can set the ContinueUpdateOnError property of the data adapter to true, and then if any exceptions are thrown in the processing of a row, the errors collection will still be populated for that row but processing will continue with the remaining rows. You are then expected to iterate through all the rows in the table being updated after completion of the Update method, and inspect the Errors property on each row and react accordingly. If you are doing batch updating in ADO.NET 2.0, the entire batch will be committed or aborted by the database within the scope of a transaction. If an exception is raised in the processing of a batch, all the rows of that batch will fail.

How you handle the presence of errors, or a thrown exception if you don't set ContinueUpdateOnError equal to true, is going to be application dependent. You may want to just log the problem, or prompt users with a list of failed updates and the current database values, and provide them with some kind of data merging user interface to resolve the conflict. If you are binding the data to a Windows Forms DataGridView or Data-Grid, the grid itself will detect the presence of errors and will depict the problem with an icon and tooltip help.

Updating with Data Sets and Stored Procedures

Not surprisingly, in order to talk about updates with stored procedures, we need some stored procedures that perform updates. If you run the script in Listing D.7 against the Northwind database, you will get simple SELECT, UPDATE, INSERT, and DELETE stored procedures for working with the Region table that are appropriate for working with a data set that will contain the Region table data.

LISTING D.7: Update Stored Procedures for Regions

```
CREATE PROCEDURE GetRegions
AS
SELECT RegionID, RegionDescription FROM Region
RETURN
GO

CREATE PROCEDURE UpdateRegion
@RegionID int,
@RegionDescription nchar(50)
AS
UPDATE Region
SET RegionDescription = @RegionDescription
WHERE RegionID = @RegionID
RETURN
GO

CREATE PROCEDURE InsertRegion
@RegionID int,
@RegionDescription nchar(50)
AS
INSERT INTO Region
(RegionID, RegionDescription)
VALUES (@RegionID, @RegionDescription)
RETURN
GO

CREATE PROCEDURE DeleteRegion
@RegionID int
AS
DELETE FROM Region WHERE RegionID = @RegionID
RETURN
GO
```

To keep things simple here and focused on the calling of stored procedures for updates, these stored procedures have no concurrency protection.

As mentioned earlier when discussing command builders, queries required to do optimistic concurrency checking based on every column in the row get messy and are very inefficient. A better way is to use a timestamp or rowversion column in your table, or have a column that gets updated with the current date and time every time a row is changed. You can then use that for concurrency violation detection, and you only need to check a single column and carry around one extra parameter to see if anyone has updated the row since one was retrieved.

Note that in this case, the RegionID column in the Regions table isn't an identity autonumbered column, so you have to pass in the ID as a parameter even for inserts. If you have an identity column that is going to be generated on the server side when the insert is performed, you will want to make the identity column an output parameter on the stored procedure, and then set that parameter within the stored procedure to the @@IDENTITY value. This way the new identity value gets passed back out of the stored procedure and will be placed in the row that originated the insert in the data table on the client side.

```
CREATE PROCEDURE InsertSimpleTable
    (
    @Val nvarchar(50),
    @ID int OUTPUT
    )

AS
    INSERT INTO SimpleTable (Val) Values (@Val)
    SET @ID = @@IDENTITY
```

Once you have the stored procedures to call, you need to write a little code to wire up all the commands needed to retrieve and update the data set using those stored procedures. The following code shows a simple method that calls the GetRegions stored procedure to populate a data set that is a member of the containing class.

```
private void GetRegions()
{
    // Clear the current contents
    m_RegionsDataSet.Clear();

    SqlConnection conn = new SqlConnection(
      "server=localhost;database=Northwind;trusted_connection=true");
```

```
SqlCommand selectCmd = new SqlCommand("GetRegions",conn);
selectCmd.CommandType = CommandType.StoredProcedure;

// Set the select command on the adapter
m_Adapter.MissingSchemaAction = MissingSchemaAction.AddWithKey;
m_Adapter.SelectCommand = selectCmd;

// Fill the member data set
m_Adapter.Fill(m_RegionsDataSet,"Regions");
}
```

The GetRegions method first clears the current contents of a data set that is held as a member variable of the class containing this method. It then sets up a connection object and passes that to a command object's constructor along with the name of the stored procedure that will be called. Any time you are going to call a stored procedure, you have to set the Command-Type property on the command object to the StoredProcedure enumerated value. The adapter is set up to retrieve the primary key information with the AddWithKey enumerated value on the MissingSchemaAction property, and its SelectCommand property is set to the command object just created. Finally, Fill is called, which will execute the stored procedure, placing the returned result set in a table named Regions within the data set.

The code in Listing D.8 shows an update method that uses a data set containing the Regions table of the Northwind database to make updates if any inserts, deletes, or modifications have been made to the table. The data set and the data adapter in this case are members of the containing class; this way, they can be accessed by both the method that populates the data set and by the method that performs updates and returns the number of rows updated.

LISTING D.8: Calling Update Stored Procedures

```
private int UpdateRegions()
{
    // Get the connection from the adapter's select command
    SqlConnection conn = m_Adapter.SelectCommand.Connection;

    // Create the insert command
    SqlCommand insertCmd = new SqlCommand("InsertRegion",conn);
    insertCmd.CommandType = CommandType.StoredProcedure;
    insertCmd.Parameters.Add(
        new SqlParameter("@RegionID",SqlDbType.Int,4,"RegionID"));
    insertCmd.Parameters.Add(
```

```
                new SqlParameter("@RegionDescription", SqlDbType.NChar, 50,
                            "RegionDescription"));

        // Create the update command
        SqlCommand updateCmd = new SqlCommand("UpdateRegion", conn);
        updateCmd.CommandType = CommandType.StoredProcedure;
        updateCmd.Parameters.Add(
            new SqlParameter("@RegionID",SqlDbType.Int,4,"RegionID"));
        updateCmd.Parameters.Add(
            new SqlParameter("@RegionDescription", SqlDbType.NChar, 50,
                            "RegionDescription"));

        // Create the delete command
        SqlCommand deleteCmd = new SqlCommand("DeleteRegion", conn);
        deleteCmd.CommandType = CommandType.StoredProcedure;
        deleteCmd.Parameters.Add(
            new SqlParameter("@RegionID",SqlDbType.Int,4,"RegionID"));

        // Associate each command with the adapter
        m_Adapter.InsertCommand = insertCmd;
        m_Adapter.UpdateCommand = updateCmd;
        m_Adapter.DeleteCommand = deleteCmd;

        // Perform the update
        int count = m_Adapter.Update(m_RegionsDataSet,"Regions");

        // Refill the dataset to reflect any concurrent changes
        m_Adapter.Fill(m_RegionsDataSet,"Regions");

        return count;
    }
```

This code is a little more verbose than the other examples in this appendix, because the update, insert, and delete stored procedures each take some parameters to decide what updates to perform. Let's step through it line by line.

The method first retrieves the connection to be used from the select command associated with the data adapter that is a member of the class. It then creates each of the stored procedure commands for the update, insert, and delete procedures. It creates SqlParameter objects to wrap each parameter to each of the commands and adds them to the Parameters collection on the command. The method then associates each of the commands with the data adapter and calls the Update method on the data adapter to execute the commands for each row in the data set that contains changes. The `Update` method on a data adapter returns the number of rows that were inserted, deleted, or updated using the data set. The method also calls `Fill` again on the data adapter before returning, so that any concurrent changes made in the database, or any columns that are computed by triggers, are refreshed in the data cached in the data set.

The `SqlParameter` class encapsulates the passing of parameters to stored procedures and parameterized queries. It is responsible for managing the translation of parameters between two different type systems: the type system of .NET and the type system of the database. The .NET type system contains primitives such as `Int32`, `Float`, `Double`, `DateTime`, and `String`, as well as every other class in the .NET Framework and every custom class and structure that you write. This type system stores values in a data set, because a data set is just another type in the .NET world that is capable of containing other .NET types through object references. SQL Server (or any other data source) has its own notion of a type system, and that system is used to store the data in the database.

So the `SqlParameter` class takes care of wrapping the values in the type system of .NET and passing them to the database in a form that is compatible with the type system in play there. You construct each `SqlParameter` object by specifying the name of the query parameter that it will provide, the database type of the query parameter, and the size of that parameter if it is variable length in the database (such as a `varchar` in SQL Server). There are different overloads of the `SqlParameter` constructor that let you skip specifying a size, and you can always set this information through properties as well. The name parameter passed to the constructor needs to match the name of the query parameter exactly, including the @ symbol for SQL parameters. This is specific to the SQL Server managed provider. If you use the OLE DB managed provider, you will use the `OleDbParameter` class. However, OLE DB parameters are always passed by position (order) in the statement, so the name is ignored.

When you are using a data set to perform updates through a data adapter, you also need to provide a column mapping between the column in the table and the parameter that it will be passed to. As mentioned before, these `SqlParameter` objects could be initialized using the properties exposed by the class, but this example instead uses one of the overloaded constructors that takes all of the values needed in one line of code. The column name that you specify for that last parameter allows the data adapter to automatically extract the current column value for each row and set it as the parameter value at the time the update occurs.

If there is any type mismatch between the value in the table and the type of the parameter, you won't know until runtime. Just as the query can throw exceptions, the setup code that precedes the query can throw exceptions as well. You will want to make sure that you have proper exception handling code wrapping any data access methods or the code that calls them to make sure your application doesn't blow up on you.

If you are working with stored procedures that have output parameters, such as the INSERT stored procedure shown earlier that returned the value of an identity column, you would need to specify the parameter's direction when you add it to the command object:

```
SqlParameter idParam = insertCmd.Parameters.Add(
        new SqlParameter("@ID",SqlDbType.Int,4,"ID"));
idParam.Direction = ParameterDirection.Output;
```

This would map the ID column in the data table to the output @ID parameter on the stored procedure. After the data adapter called the `InsertCommand` to perform the insert, it would take the value that was in the `idParam` after the command was complete and would put it into the respective column in the data table.

Searching Data Sets

Once you get data into a data set, you often need to be able to search and select data from within it, either to perform updates or processing on some subset of the data, or for display purposes. Keep in mind that the `DataSet` class and its related class aren't designed to be high-efficiency query engines. Although you can select and filter the data in a data table on the client, it may be faster in many cases to simply execute a new, more specialized query against the database to get the specific results you are looking for. This is especially true when working with a local database instance like with a SQL Express database.

However, if you already have the data in memory in a `DataSet` and want to select items without incurring a round-trip to the database, there are several approaches you can use. The simplest is to use the `Select` method of the `DataTable` class to perform SQL-like queries against the data contained within a table. You can also use data views to filter the data based on a selection criteria, or you can use the `XmlDataDocument` class to load a data set into an XML document container and perform XPath queries against it (data views and the `XmlDataDocument` are discussed in subsequent sections).

The `Select` method has a number of overloads, which let you search based on a string criteria that resembles a WHERE clause in SQL, and optionally provide a sort order or a `DataRowViewState` enumeration to search among records of a particular state or states. The `Select` method returns an array of `DataRow` objects containing references to the rows that matched the selection criteria. Once you have that array of rows, you can iterate over them and perform any processing you need on them. You are working against live references to the actual rows in the data set, so any changes made to them immediately affect the data in the data set. The following code shows a `Select` operation on a Customers data set using two of the overloads of the method.

```csharp
private DataRow[] SelectRows(string selString)
{
    DataRow[] rows = null;
    // Perform the selection
    if (selString == string.Empty || selString == "*")
    {
        // Select all
        rows = m_Customers.Tables["Customers"].Select();
    }
    else
    {
        // Select based on the criteria
        rows = m_Customers.Tables["Customers"].Select(selString);
    }
    return rows;
}
```

Merging Data from Multiple Data Sets

The `DataSet` class also supports a couple of ways of moving data between different data sets. Your first instinct might be to simply get a `DataRow` reference from one data set, perhaps from a `Select` operation or from iterating through, and then add that to the table in another data set. Unfortunately, this isn't allowed and will throw an exception. When a data row is added to a table, it becomes a part of that table, and it cannot belong to more than one table at a time. Only a row that has been created with the `DataTable.NewRow` method can be added to that table with the `Add` method on the table's `Rows` collection.

So how do you get a row or set of rows of data that belong to one data set into another? One way is to use the `Merge` method. The behavior of this method can get fairly complex because it has a number of overloads, and it depends on what the state of the rows (`Added`, `Modified`, `Deleted`) are in the data set they are coming from (the source), and whether there are corresponding rows in the data set they are being merged into (the target). For simple cases, though, things are pretty straightforward.

Consider a situation where you have the Customers table in one data set and the Orders table in another data set. You want to get them both into a single data set so that you can create a parent-child relationship between them based on the CustomerID foreign key that exists in the Orders table. To do this, you would simply call `Merge` on the data set containing the Customers table, passing in the Orders data set. The `Merge` method would create an Orders table in the Customers data set and copy over all the rows from the Orders data set. You could then construct the relation between the two tables in code as follows:

```
private DataSet MergeCustomersAndOrders()
{
    // Code to create and fill the two data sets...
    // customersDS contains just Customers,
    // ordersDS contains just Orders

    // Merge the orders into the customers
    customersDS.Merge(ordersDS);

    // Create the relation between the two tables
    DataColumn custIDParentCol =
```

```
    customersDS.Tables["Customers"].Columns["CustomerID"];
  DataColumn custIDChildCol =
    customersDS.Tables["Orders"].Columns["CustomerID"];
  DataRelation custOrders =
    new
  DataRelation("CustomersOrders",custIDParentCol,custIDChildCol);

  return customersDS; // Contains both tables and relation
}
```

If you want to add a row from a table in one data set into the same table in another data set with the row state of Added, you can pass the Item-Array property of the source row to an overload of the Add method on the Rows collection of the target table. This transfers the values of the cells as an array of objects into the target table, creating a new row to contain them. If you want to add a row from a source table into a target and preserve its state, you can use the ImportRow method on the DataTable class. The following shows both of these approaches.

```
private void AddAndImport(DataSet dsTarget, DataSet dsSource)
{
  // Add the values from a single row from the source
  // to the target with the row state set to Added
  dsTarget.Tables["Customers"].Rows.Add(
    dsSource.Tables["Customers"].Rows[0].ItemArray);
  // Import a single row preserving row state
  dsTarget.Tables["Customers"].ImportRow(
    dsSource.Tables["Customers"].Rows[0]);
}
```

A common use of Merge is in conjunction with the Select method to extract a set of rows and place them in another data set, either for display or transfer to another method or client.

```
private void OnSelect(object sender, EventArgs e)
{
  // Select the rows using helper method
  DataRow[] rows = SelectRows(m_SelectTextBox.Text);
  // Show the results
  if (rows.Length > 0)
  {
    // Create a new data set
    DataSet localDS = new DataSet();
    // Merge the selected rows into it
```

```
        localDS.Merge(rows);
        // Bind the grid to this
        m_ResultsGrid.DataSource = localDS.Tables["Customers"];
    }
}
```

Another way to get a row into a table as a new row is to use the Load-DataRow method on the table, passing in an array of objects that contain the column values. Typically you will get this object array from the ItemArray on the source row.

Because there isn't any way to directly set the row state of rows in a data table, if you want to get a row into a particular state, such as modified or deleted, there are some tricks you can play. For either of those states, you can first set the row state to unmodified by calling the AcceptChanges method on the row. To get the state set to modified, set the value of one of the columns to its current value by setting the column value against itself as shown next. To set the deleted state, just call Delete on the row:

```
DataSet data = new DataSet();
// Code to fill data set with Customers ...

DataRow modRow = data.Tables["Customers"].Rows[0];
modRow.AcceptChanges(); // Set state to unchanged
// Set state to modified:
modRow["CompanyName"] = modRow["CompanyName"];

DataRow delRow = data.Tables["Customers"].Rows[1];
delRow.AcceptChanges(); // Set state to unchanged
delRow.Delete(); // Set state to deleted
```

Working with Data Views

Another way to manipulate the data contained in a data set for processing or viewing is using a data view. A **data view** doesn't contain any data itself; as its name implies, it is just a view into the data in the table underneath it. You can think of it as a lens that you place over a table that makes it look different to the consumer of the view, even though the underlying data is still whatever data is stored in the table that the view represents.

You can modify the data exposed through a data view, and when you do, you are actually modifying the data in the underlying table directly.

Every instance of a `DataTable` already has a default `DataView` instance associated with it, and it is actually this view that is used when you bind a table to a grid. You can make modifications to the default data view, which will affect any controls that are bound to the underlying data table, or you can construct new instances of a `DataView` object to wrap a table for the purposes of sorting or filtering the data.

The `DataView` class implements `Sort`, `RowFilter`, and `RowState-Filter` properties that let you modify what data the view exposes. You set the `Sort` property to an expression that specifies what column(s) to sort on and in what order. You can set the `RowFilter` expression using the same syntax supported by the `DataTable.Select` method to restrict the rows presented by the view based on some criteria that is like a WHERE clause in a SQL statement. Finally, you can use the `RowStateFilter` to only look at rows in a particular state, such as all `Deleted` or `Added` rows. You can use all of these in combination with one another to specify fairly complex filtering and sorting criteria to expose data contained within a table in just about any way you need to:

```
private void OnView(object sender, EventArgs e)
{
    // Create the view wrapping the customers table
    DataView view = new DataView(m_Customers.Tables["Customers"]);

    // Sort by CompanyName ascending, ContactName descending
    view.Sort = "CompanyName ASC, ContactName DESC";

    // Only show German customers
    view.RowFilter = "Country = 'Germany'";

    // Only show inserted or edited rows
    view.RowStateFilter = DataViewRowState.Added |
        DataViewRowState.Modified;

    // Bind the view to a grid for viewing
    m_ResultsGrid.DataSource = view;
}
```

Working with Transactions

Sometimes you need to be able to execute multiple commands within the scope of a single database transaction, so that if any one of the commands fails, they all fail, and no changes are made to the database. You can do this inside of SQL Server and other databases by beginning a transaction within a stored procedure, and committing it or rolling it back based on the outcome of all the queries encapsulated within the stored procedure. However, sometimes you will want to control the transaction from within your ADO.NET code, wrapping the execution of multiple commands within a single transaction.

It is quite easy to do this. You can use the `SqlTransaction` class (or corresponding classes for other managed providers) in conjunction with the connection to manage a transaction from your data access code. For example, say you wanted to write code that first checked whether a row existed, and if it did, then make some modification to that row. Let's also say that you needed to do this with two explicit SQL text queries from within your managed code. You want to write bulletproof code, so you want to ensure that the row that will be affected by the update cannot be modified or deleted by another client or query between the time you check for its existence and when you update it. Using a transaction with an appropriate isolation level will work just fine for this scenario. Take a look at the code in Listing D.9.

LISTING D.9: Executing Multiple Queries Within a Transaction

```
private void OnTransactionalUpdate(object sender, System.EventArgs e)
{
    // Create the connection
    SqlConnection conn = new SqlConnection(m_ConnString);

    // Create the two commands you want to wrap in a transaction
    SqlCommand selectCmd = new SqlCommand(
        "SELECT CustomerID FROM Customers WHERE CustomerID = 'ALFKI'",
        conn);
    SqlCommand updateCmd = new SqlCommand(
    "UPDATE Customers SET CompanyName = 'FooBros' WHERE CustomerID =
    'ALFKI'", conn);

    // Declare the transaction
    SqlTransaction trans = null;
```

continues

```csharp
try
{
    // Open the connection
    conn.Open();

    // Start a transaction with the repeatable read isolation
    trans = conn.BeginTransaction(IsolationLevel.RepeatableRead);

    // Associate the transaction with the commands
    selectCmd.Transaction = trans;
    updateCmd.Transaction = trans;

    // Check for the existence of the customer
    string custID = (string)selectCmd.ExecuteScalar();
    if (custID == null)
    {
        throw new ApplicationException("Customer not found");
    }
    // Update the customer
    updateCmd.ExecuteNonQuery();
    // Commit the transaction if you got to here
    trans.Commit();
}
catch (SqlException ex)
{
    if (trans != null)
    {
        trans.Rollback();
    }
    MessageBox.Show(ex.Message);
}
finally
{
    conn.Close();
}
}
```

There are a number of things to discuss here. The first is how to create and employ the transaction. The code creates the connection and command objects the way you have seen before. The transaction is created by calling `BeginTransaction` on the connection, optionally specifying an isolation level (see Table D.3). The default isolation level is `ReadCommitted`, but to ensure that no one can modify the record once it has been read with a SELECT statement, you need `RepeatableRead`.

TABLE D.3: Transaction Isolation Levels

IsolationLevel	Description
Chaos	The pending changes from one transaction cannot be over-written by another, but they are visible and the rows aren't locked otherwise.
ReadUncommitted	Dirty reads are possible, meaning that changes made by other transactions that haven't been committed yet are visible.
ReadCommitted	Changes made by other transactions aren't visible, but locks aren't held, so changes committed by one transaction can result in nonrepeatable reads from others or the removal of records that were previously retrieved.
RepeatableRead	Locks are placed on all data used in a query, so no other transaction can modify a row until a transaction that reads the row commits.
Serializable	Provides the maximum protection possible. All data that meets the criteria for a query is locked as long as the trans-action for that query is uncommitted. This means that no other transaction can add, delete, or modify records that would affect the outcome of the original query if it was repeated from scratch after those changes were made.
Snapshot	Makes a copy of the data that a transaction will read and continues to use that copy to provide repeatable reads, even though the actual persisted data isn't locked for other updates. This level is only available for SQL Server 2005.

Once the transaction is created, you need to associate it with any commands you want to enlist within the transaction scope. After that, you can execute the commands. If everything turns out the way you want, you should call `Commit` on the transaction object to make all the changes done within the transaction permanent. If anything goes wrong or an exception gets thrown, you should `Rollback` the transaction to prevent any changes made by the commands enlisted within the command from becoming permanent. The best way to make sure this pattern is followed is with a `try-catch` block as shown in Listing D.9.

> **┗ TIP   Explicitly roll back transactions**
>
> If you close a connection on which you have begun a transaction and you haven't called `Commit` on that transaction yet, the transaction will be automatically rolled back. However, I recommend that you always make it explicit by calling `Rollback` yourself (typically in an exception-handling `catch` block) to make it clear when and where a `Rollback` is occurring.

In addition to the `try-catch`, you can see that because the connection was explicitly opened in Listing D.9, I made sure to close it in the `finally` block, so that no matter what, the connection gets closed before I leave the method. A couple of other new things you see here but that haven't been discussed yet are the `ExecuteScalar` and `ExecuteNonQuery` methods on the `SqlCommand` objects. `ExecuteScalar` is a convenience method for queries that are expected to return a single row with a single column as their result set. The method will extract the value in that column for you and pass it back as a return value from the method. It is returned as an object reference, so you will have to cast to the expected type, as shown in Listing D.9.

Closing Connections

If you explicitly open a connection in your code, always wrap the code that opens the connection and executes the queries in a `try` block. Follow this with a `finally` block, and close the connection in the `finally` block. This way, whether the method exits normally or because of an uncaught exception, the connection will be closed and freed up for other clients to use.

If you don't intend to use the connection object again, you can also enclose the use of the connection object in a `using` block, which will call `Dispose` on the connection when it leaves the block. The implementation of `Dispose` on a connection object calls `Close` for you, and the `using` statement automatically generates the `try-finally` block for you. This ensures that it is done safely in the face of exceptions.

The `ExecuteNonQuery` method is for executing commands for which you don't expect any returned rows, such as update, insert, and delete queries.

Scoping Transactions with System.Transactions

A whole new approach to writing transactional code was designed into .NET 2.0 in the `System.Transactions` namespace. Through the classes defined in that namespace, you can now easily start or join transactions in your code without being tied directly to the transactional capabilities of the database or other specific transactional resource managers. The transactions that are created through the `System.Transactions` classes can be either lightweight transactions against a single resource manager, such as a single SQL Server 2005 database, or they can be distributed transactions involving multiple resource managers, such as a SQL 2000 database, an Oracle database, and an MSMQ message queue. Another great feature of the new transaction capabilities is that a transaction will automatically promote itself from a lightweight transaction to a distributed transaction whenever it sees that a new resource manager is accessed within a transaction scope that requires a distributed transaction, so you don't have to worry about keeping straight the different models in your code.

To use `System.Transactions`, you first have to add a reference to your project to the System.Transactions.dll assembly from the .NET Framework. You then need to include the `System.Transactions` namespace in the code files where you will be using it. When you want to execute some code within a transaction, you set up a transactional scope by creating an instance of the `TransactionScope` class. You then execute the code that you want to be transactional, and if everything succeeds, you call `Complete` on the transaction scope object. The transaction won't actually be committed until you dispose of the scope object, and if `Dispose` is called without first calling `Complete` on the scope object, the transaction will be aborted.

The easiest way to do this is with a `using` block in C#. When you use the `using` statement in C#, you pass an object reference to the `using` clause that is a disposable object. When the `using` block is exited, `Dispose` will be called on that object automatically, even if an exception is propagating.

This is because the code that is generated by the compiler for a using block includes a try-finally block, and Dispose is called on the using clause argument in the finally block.

So if you create a TransactionScope object and pass it to a using block, when you exit that using block, the transaction that the scope represents will either commit or rollback, depending on if the Complete method was called.

Here is an example of this in action:

```
using System.Transactions;

public partial class Form1 : Form
{
    private void OnExecute(object sender, EventArgs e)
    {
        NorthwindDataAccess dac = new NorthwindDataAccess();
        using (TransactionScope scope = new TransactionScope())
        {
            DataSet data = dac.GetCustomerData();
            data.Tables["Customers"].Rows[0]["Phone"] = "030-0074321";
            dac.UpdateCustomers(data);
            scope.Complete();
        }
    }
}
```

In this code, a data access component named NorthwindDataAccess is used to retrieve some records from the database, make a modification to one of them, and then push the updates back to the database. If you want both the retrieval and the update to be part of a single transaction without having to worry about connection and transaction management yourself, you simply create a TransactionScope instance to bracket the data access component calls. You pass that instance to the using statement, and call Complete on the scope object at the very end of the using block after all of the query methods have been called. If you reach the call to Complete, the data access calls must have succeeded, because otherwise an exception would be propagating. When the point of execution hits the end of the using block, the scope object will be disposed of. If the Complete method was called, the transaction will be committed, and if not (such as when an error occurs in the update query), then the transaction will be rolled back.

You can use this approach to wrap multiple queries to one or more databases in a single transaction, ensuring that all of the queries either succeed or fail as one. The big benefit for using a `TransactionScope` to create and manage a transaction is that it requires very little code, and it is simple to declare and use. This code can also be several layers up the call stack from the actual data access code, so you don't need access to the database connection to set up the transaction. The code looks the same if the code uses one or many connections under the covers. There are a lot of other capabilities and ways to use a transaction using the classes in the `System.Transactions` namespace that are beyond the scope of this book. ("Introducing System.Transactions in the Microsoft .NET Framework, Version 2.0" by Juval Löwy, available on MSDN Downloads, provides comprehensive coverage of the capabilities of the `System.Transactions` namespace classes. See www.microsoft.com/downloads/details.aspx? familyid=AAC3D722-444C-4E27-8B2E-C6157ED16B15&displaylang=en.)

If the code that sets up a transaction scope as shown in this example is called from other code that already has a transaction in progress, the new transaction scope will become a nested transaction to the calling code's transaction and will only commit if the containing transaction commits. There are a number of complex combinations you can achieve using nested transaction scopes, cloning of transactions, and directly managing the underlying `Transaction` object yourself if you need to address more advanced scenarios.

The one downside to using a transaction scope as shown here is that unless you are working against a SQL 2005 database, the transaction that is created will be a distributed transaction even if you are simply accessing a single database, such as SQL Server 2000. This can have some negative performance impacts on your application, compared to managing a transaction yourself as shown earlier in Listing D.9. You will have to weigh the performance impact against the cleaner and easier to write code resulting from using the `System.Transactions` approach for your own applications. I would recommend starting with the `System.Transactions` approach and only reverting to low-level transaction management if you need to address a performance problem in a particular part of your application that is using transactions.

Client-Side Transactions

Sometimes you may need to work with data on the client side in a data set's form and have similar logic to that just presented for server transactions, so you can modify the data and back out changes if something goes wrong. You can simulate a transaction while working with client-side data by using the `AcceptChanges` and `RejectChanges` methods. As discussed earlier, any changes made to a data set are maintained through a combination of row state and the current and original values for each row.

If you have made any changes to the rows in your data set and call `AcceptChanges`, the original values for all modified rows will be replaced with the current values, and the state of all rows will be changed to `Unchanged`. If you call `RejectChanges`, the current values for any modified rows will be replaced with the original values, inserted rows will be discarded, and the state of all rows will also be set to `Unchanged`. The `AcceptChanges` and `RejectChanges` methods are defined on the `DataSet`, `DataTable`, and `DataRow` classes, so you can perform these transaction-like operations at any level of granularity within the data set that you need.

Using a combination of `AcceptChanges` and `RejectChanges`, you can code logic that accepts or rejects all changes to a table or data set based on some criteria. You should be aware when using these methods, however, that you generally want to avoid using them if the data in the data set will be used to update a database through a data adapter. As mentioned earlier, the data adapter figures out which commands to execute (update, insert, or delete) for which rows based on their row state. Rows with a row state of `Unchanged` don't get any command executed against them when performing an update. Because both `AcceptChanges` and `RejectChanges` set the state of rows to `Unchanged`, you will only want to use these methods with a data set to update the database when using them with the workaround discussed earlier to get a row into the `Modified` or `Deleted` state after first setting them to `Unchanged` with `AcceptChanges` or `RejectChanges`.

> **▪. NOTE**
>
> Do not call AcceptChanges on a data set if it contains changes and you need to update the database with those changes. Calling AcceptChanges sets the row state of every row in the data set to Unchanged and replaces the original values with the current values. Since all of the rows will have a state of Unchanged, no changes can be propagated to the database through a data adapter because it won't see any rows to perform updates with.

Data Set and Data Adapter Events

So far I have just discussed programming against the methods and properties of data sets and data adapters, and handling exceptions when something goes wrong. However, sometimes you need to be more in the loop as the processing is going on. There are a number of events that you can tap into from the DataSet, DataTable, and SqlDataAdapter classes that are useful for letting your code be notified when changes are occurring.

The DataSet class has two events:

- MergeFailed, which will be fired if you are performing a Merge operation and there is a primary key conflict between the target and source tables.

- Initialized, which will be fired when the DataSet has completed initialization of its contained objects and state.

The DataTable has the most useful events, which are described in Table D.4.

The events on the DataTable follow a common pattern for events that relate to modifications of some entity: there is a pair of events for each form of modification. One event fires before the change has occurred, and another event fires after the change is complete. This lets you code any pre- and post-processing of the change that you need to, including preventing the change from occurring.

TABLE D.4: DataTable Events

Event	Description
ColumnChanging	Fires before a column is changed and passes a Data-ColumnChangeEventArgs parameter that contains the column, row, and proposed value for the change. If you want to prevent the change, you will need to throw an exception and have a guard value, because it will be fired again as the value is changed back to its original after the exception is thrown.
ColumnChanged	Fires after a column is changed and passes a DataColumn-ChangeEventArgs parameter that contains the column, row, and proposed value for the change.
RowChanging	Fires before a row is changed, passing a DataRowChange-EventArgs parameter that contains the Action value of the DataRowAction enumeration, which indicates how the row has changed.
RowChanged	Fires after a row is changed, passing a DataRowChange-EventArgs parameter that contains the Action value of the DataRowAction enumeration, which indicates how the row has changed.
RowDeleting	Fires before a row is deleted, passing a DataRowChange-EventArgs parameter that contains the Action value of the DataRowAction enumeration set to Deleted.
RowDeleted	Fires after a row is deleted, passing a DataRowChange-EventArgs parameter that contains the Action value of the DataRowAction enumeration set to Deleted.

The ColumnChanging/ColumnChanged events pass a parameter of type DataColumnChangeEventArgs to your event handler. This parameter contains several useful values for controlling the update of a column. A read/write property named ProposedValue contains the value that the column will be changed to when the event handler completes. You can inspect this value in your ColumnChanging handler, and in combination with the Row and Column properties on the event arguments parameter, make validation decisions about changing that value.

If the value being proposed doesn't meet your validation constraints, you have two choices. First, you can change it to some acceptable value by assigning a different value of the appropriate type to the `ProposedValue` property on the event arguments parameter. If you do this, whatever value you assign to that parameter will be the one that is actually set for the column when the change is made. So you could also change the `Proposed` value to the original value by extracting the original value through the `Column` and `Row` property, as shown here, to effectively prevent the change:

```
private void OnCustomersColumnChanging(object sender,
                        DataColumnChangeEventArgs e)
{
    if (m_ConfirmChangesCheckBox.Checked)
    {
        DialogResult res = MessageBox.Show(
        "Column " + e.Column.ColumnName + " changing to value: " +
        e.ProposedValue.ToString() + ". Allow change?",
        "ColumnChanging Event",MessageBoxButtons.YesNo);
        if (res == DialogResult.No)
        {
            e.ProposedValue = e.Row[e.Column.ColumnName];
        }
    }
}
```

The one thing to be aware of with this code is that even though setting the `ProposedValue` back to the original value prevents the value from changing, the row will still be marked as modified, and the row will be updated in the database if you use it for an update with a data adapter. You could work around this by calling `AcceptChanges` on the row, but then if any other columns have been changed to new values in that row, their changes won't get sent to the database with a data adapter update. This is only usually a problem in a data-bound scenario, and in that case there are events on the data-bound control that you can usually handle to get into the loop sooner to cancel the change. However, this is something to keep in mind if you are trying to cancel a change through the `Data-Table` events.

You could also throw an exception from within the `ColumnChanging` event handler. This would effectively abort the event processing, and the value would get changed back to its original value. However, throwing an exception has a lot of overhead with it, and the code that is causing the change better have an exception handler to deal with that scenario. In the case of a `DataGrid` control, the `Changing` event handler will be called again as the value changes back to the original, so the original value better pass your validation logic or you could end up with your program blowing up from unhandled exceptions. In general, you should try to avoid the approach of throwing an exception.

There are three events on the `SqlDataAdapter` class to be aware of as well. The `FillError` event will be fired if an error occurs while filling a data set with the adapter, which gives you insight into what went wrong, and you can make programmatic decisions based on the error and the values that caused it. The `RowUpdating` and `RowUpdated` events work like those described for the `DataTable`, except these fire as each row is updated (UPDATE, INSERT, or DELETE query) in the database. The event arguments let you determine the cause of the error and tell the adapter whether to continue updating other rows or to stop update processing.

Reading Data into Business Objects

I have covered the use of data sets pretty extensively in this appendix because they are the richest and most often used relational data container in both Windows and Web client and middle-tier applications. There is one other important data access class that was briefly described earlier: the data reader. A **data reader** is a fast, forward-only, read-only cursor into a returned set of data from a database. Each managed provider is responsible for including a provider-specific data reader class. For SQL Server, it is named, not surprisingly, `SqlDataReader`.

A `SqlDataReader` lets you execute a query and quickly iterate through each row of the returned results to perform processing on those rows. Note that I didn't say the data reader is like a cursor into the database itself. You do need to maintain an open connection associated with the data reader as long as you are iterating through the results. But the data reader will buffer the results of the query on the client side, and you cannot modify the underlying data. All you can do is read the rows returned one at a time and act upon them.

When you are done using the reader, you need to make sure the connection gets closed as you do for any other query. It is not uncommon for a data access layer to pass a data reader back as the return value from some data access method.

```
public static SqlDataReader GetCustomers()
{
    SqlConnection conn = new SqlConnection(
      "server=localhost;database=Northwind;trusted_connection=true");
    SqlCommand cmd = new SqlCommand(
      "SELECT CustomerID, CompanyName, ContactName FROM Customers",
      conn);
    conn.Open();
    return cmd.ExecuteReader(CommandBehavior.CloseConnection);
}
```

This code allows a client to take that reader, iterate through the results quickly, and do with them what it will. But if you take a look at the code, you will notice that in order to do this, you need to open the connection to the database and leave it open so the client can iterate through the contents of the data reader. However, the connection is declared and opened down in the data access layer, and is not directly accessible to the client code to close the connection when it is done with the reader. So how can the client make sure the connection gets closed when it is done using the reader? You will see in this code that a CommandBehavior enumerated value of Close-Connection was passed to the ExecuteReader method on the command. Thus, if the client calls the Close method on the data reader itself, the underlying connection will be closed as well. Additionally, if the client simply iterates through all of the rows in the reader, the connection will be closed when the last row is read.

Returning a data reader is significantly faster than returning a data set, because you can't directly operate on the contents of a data reader; all you can do is use it to quickly pull data out of the reader and do something with it. Often the thing you want to do with the data is use it to construct and populate some object model, which is what the data set and data adapter have to do at the time you fill the data set. That is why the data set takes a lot longer to fill than a data reader does to return. With the data set, you have a full object model in memory that you have read/write and random access into. To achieve the same thing with a data reader, you will have to pull the data out of the rows from the data reader and stuff them into your own object model before you can do something meaningful with them.

In larger-scale, object-oriented systems, this may be exactly what you want to do in the first place. Typed data sets (covered in Chapter 2) make a great choice for fairly lightweight, easy to construct and maintain data transfer objects that you can pass around the middle tier for processing or pass to the client for presentation. However, often your middle-tier objects need to not only encapsulate data—they need to encapsulate behavior as well. In that case, you will probably be designing your own object model, where many of the objects might encapsulate state that is stored in persistent form in the database. The data reader works great in this case for quickly reading data into an object or set of objects resulting from a retrieval query against the database.

For example, let's say you have a `Customer` class defined in your business object model that encapsulates the state and behavior associated with customers. When you want to act on a collection of customers, you retrieve the data from the database like the previous code, getting back a data reader that lets you get the data associated with the customers. Now you need to pull that data into your customer objects.

The data reader exposes an interface similar to other reader classes in the .NET Framework. A reader acts like a cursor into a collection of items. The cursor is initially positioned just before the first item. To move the cursor to the next item, you call the `Read` method on the reader. The `Read` method will return `false` when there are no more items to be read. Once the cursor is positioned on an item, you can access the contents of that item through whatever access methods and properties the specific type of reader exposes. In the case of a `SqlDataReader`, the items are rows, and you can access the row contents through a combination of an indexer, the `Item` property, or Get*XXX* methods, where *XXX* is the type of the column you are requesting. The following code shows both the use of indexers and the `GetString` method.

```
private void OnGetCustomers(object sender, EventArgs e)
{
    // Create an empty collection of customer objects
    BindingList<Customer> custs = new BindingList<Customer>();
    // Call the data access method that returns a reader
    SqlDataReader reader = CustomersDataAccess.GetCustomers();
    // Loop through each row of data
    while (reader.Read())
```

```
    {
        // Create a new customer object
        Customer c = new Customer();
        // Extract the values from the columns
        c.Id = (string)reader["CustomerID"];
        c.Name = (string)reader["CompanyName"];
        c.Contact = reader.GetString(reader.GetOrdinal("ContactName"));
        // Add the object to the collection
        custs.Add(c);
    }
    //  Data bind the results to the grid
    m_CustomersGrid.DataSource = custs;
}
```

The indexer on the data reader returns an object reference, so you will need to cast the value to the expected type of the column you are retrieving. The indexer is overloaded so that you can pass it an integer index into the row representing the position of the column in the returned rows, or you can pass it the name of the column as shown here. Using column names is far easier to read and maintain, even though it is a tiny bit less efficient for retrieval.

The GetXXX methods are defined to extract the column value for each of the built-in .NET types. The GetXXX methods take a column index, or ordinal, for the position of the column to retrieve, and attempt to retrieve the column's value as the specified type, performing any conversion if necessary. For example, if you call the GetString method on a column that actually contains an integer, ToString will be called on the returned value to get it back as a string. If you try to use a GetXXX method that requests an incompatible type with the actual contents of the column, an exception will be thrown. To determine the position of a column based on the column name, this code uses the data reader's GetOrdinal method to look up the position of the column based on its name.

You can see that what the code does is to create an instance of your Customer business class for each row of data in the data reader. It stuffs the values from the reader that it cares about (I simplified the Customer class for brevity here) into the customer object, and then adds the object to a collection. In this case it just data binds the collection to a data grid, but if you were just data binding, you probably wouldn't go to this trouble. Presumably you would do this in a middle-tier business service where those

`Customer` objects were going to be used in the processing of the system and might include behavior, validation, and other capabilities that go beyond what a data set could do for you.

XML Data Access

XML data access in .NET is a huge topic unto itself and is mostly separable from relational data access. There are a number of things that make it a difficult topic to cover quickly. For starters, there is all the underlying standards knowledge that is a prerequisite for working with XML, such as the XML standard itself, XPath, XML schema, XSLT, and XQuery. For another thing, there are multiple models for dealing with XML in .NET. Finally, the XML capabilities in .NET Framework have been significantly enhanced in version 2.0.

There is no way to briefly cover all the ways you might program with XML in .NET, so I'll just focus on those things that will let you understand some of the ways that you might get XML data into your Windows application so you can display the data through Windows Forms controls. There is no way to directly data bind XML data to any of the Windows Forms controls that ship with the .NET Framework. To use XML data for data binding, you will need to either get the data into a data set, or you will need to read the data into custom business objects that are suitable for data binding.

The first thing to get your arms around with XML in .NET is all the different flavors of XML object models that exist. There is the `XmlDocument` class, which provides an implementation of the W3C XML Document Object Model (DOM) standard. This class lets you deal with XML in the form of documents that are read into memory in their entirety into a heavyweight object model. There is also the `XmlDataDocument` class, which is really just a derived class from `XmlDocument`. In addition to providing storage for XML using the DOM, this class encapsulates a data set that will let you deal with a document's contents as relational data. The `XmlDataDocument` will also let you place relational data into the object through a data set, and then you can manipulate the data as XML.

The `XmlReader` and `XmlWriter` classes provide a very lightweight stream-based approach to reading XML. These classes, and the classes derived from them, can be used with a number of other capabilities in .NET, such as XML serialization, XML data access from relational stores, and raw access to XML streams from disk or over a network. Finally, there is a new object model that was introduced in .NET 1.0 based on the `XPathDocument` and `XPathNavigator` classes. These classes form the basis for the preferred method of working with XML in .NET 2.0.

The following sections describe how to read XML data into an `XmlDataDocument` and access it in relational form through its encapsulated data set, and then discuss loading data into an `XPathDocument` and how to query and navigate data within that document. Then you'll have enough data access tools in your belt to understand all the data access that is done in support of the samples in this book, as well as enough background material to get data in many forms into your applications for prototyping and developing your Windows Forms applications.

Working with the XmlDataDocument Class

The `XmlDataDocument` class bridges the world of relational and hierarchical data. The class is derived from `XmlDocument`, so it "is an" `XmlDocument` in the purest sense of object-oriented inheritance (where "is an" is used to describe objects related through inheritance), and thus exposes all the capabilities of the `XmlDocument` class for storing and manipulating data as XML. It also encapsulates a `DataSet` as a property, which lets you access all or part of the contents of the `XmlDataDocument` as relational data.

There are two common ways to use an `XmlDataDocument`. The first is to load XML into the document, and then access its `DataSet` property for data binding, iterating through the contents with the `DataSet` object model, or synchronizing the contents with a database. The second is that you can take a `DataSet` that already contains data, construct an `XmlDataDocument` from it, and use XML processing or constructs to program against the data (that is, perform an XPath query against the data).

In order for loading XML into an `XmlDataDocument` and accessing it through its `DataSet` property to work, you have to set up the data set schema within the `XmlDataDocument` before you load the XML. The `Xml-DataDocument` won't infer a data set schema when reading in XML from a file or string the way that the `DataSet.ReadXml` method does. However, if you first supply its contained data set with a schema and then read in XML, the `XmlDataDocument` will then be able to associate XML elements and attributes that it reads in with the data set schema, and then that data can be accessed through the `DataSet` property on the `XmlDataDocument`.

Take a look at the XML in Listing D.10.

LISTING D.10: Customer XML Data

```
<?xml version="1.0" encoding="utf-8"?>
<Customers xmlns="urn:AW-Windows-Forms-Data-SimpleCustomers.xsd">
    <Customer>
        <Name>Fred Smith</Name>
        <Email>fred@foo.org</Email>
        <Address>
            <Street>123 Nowhere St.</Street>
            <City>Middletown</City>
            <State>OH</State>
            <Zip>54321</Zip>
        </Address>
    </Customer>
    <Customer>
        <Name>Edith Jones</Name>
        <Email>ej@rockon.com</Email>
        <Address>
            <Street>939 TakeMeBack Road</Street>
            <City>Fern</City>
            <State>TX</State>
            <Zip>86950</Zip>
        </Address>
    </Customer>
</Customers>
```

You can see that this data can be viewed as containing two kinds of data, Customers and Addresses, and that there is a parent-child relationship between the two. In a data set, this would be represented by two data tables and a data relation between the two. To load this data into an `Xml-DataDocument` and access it through the `DataSet` property, you first have to tell the `XmlDataDocument` what data set schema to use when reading in the XML. There are a few ways you could accomplish this. One would be to access the `DataSet` property and add tables and relations to it programmatically, as shown earlier in the "Creating a Data Set Programmatically" section. Alternatively, you could construct an empty `XmlDataDocument`, and then read the XML data in through the `DataSet` property using the `ReadXml` method. Another approach would be to construct an empty data set, initialize its schema, and provide that to the `XmlDataDocument` constructor to set up the schema of the encapsulated data set, as shown here:

```
private void OnLoadXmlDataDoc(object sender, EventArgs e)
{
    DataSet custData = new DataSet();
    custData.ReadXmlSchema(@"..\..\SimpleCustomers.xsd");
    XmlDataDocument dataDoc = new XmlDataDocument(custData);
    dataDoc.Load(@"..\..\SimpleCustomers.xml");
    DataRow row = custData.Tables["Customer"].NewRow();
    row["Name"] = "FooFooFoo";
    custData.Tables["Customer"].Rows.Add(row);
    m_ResultsGrid.DataSource = dataDoc.DataSet;
}
```

In this code, `custData` is a data set that is loaded with an XML schema that matches the XML shown earlier. The `custData` data set is passed into the constructor for the `XmlDataDocument`, and it will encapsulate the reference to this data set instead of creating its own. Once it has a data set with the appropriate schema, you can load the XML into the `XmlData-Document`, and the data set will be populated with the XML from the document loaded that matches the schema. The SimpleCustomers.xsd schema was created by loading the XML from Listing D.10 into the Visual Studio editor (minus the xmlns namespace declaration) and selecting *Generate Schema* from the XML menu.

An even simpler approach is to just read the XML in through the `DataSet` property:

```
private void OnLoadXmlDataDoc(object sender, System.EventArgs e)
{
    XmlDataDocument dataDoc = new XmlDataDocument();
    dataDoc.DataSet.ReadXml("..\\..\\SimpleCustomers.xml");
    m_dgResults.DataSource = dataDoc.DataSet;
}
```

This uses the default `XmlDataDocument` constructor, which doesn't take a data set as a parameter. It will create an empty data set internally, and then calls `ReadXml` on the contained data set, passing in the path to the XML data file. The contained data set will then infer the schema from the XML as it is read in as before. Once it is read into the `XmlDataDocument`, it can be treated as an XML node set and accessed through the `XmlDocument` base class methods as well as those of the contained data set.

Now let's tackle the angle of loading an existing data set containing data into an `XmlDataDocument` for the purposes of navigating the data as XML. You might want to do this if you have a complex data set and want to perform selections or queries across multiple tables in the data set, or if the data is hierarchical and navigating with the XML object model makes more sense for the situation. In this case, you again use the fact that the `XmlDataDocument` constructor can take a data set as a parameter, and it will hold a reference to that data set internally instead of constructing its own. The following code demonstrates creating a data set from a relational source, then constructing an `XmlDataDocument` and using the XML object model to perform operations on the data.

```
private void OnGetData(object sender, EventArgs e)
{
    string connStr =
      "server=localhost;database=Northwind;trusted_connection=true";
    SqlDataAdapter adapter = new SqlDataAdapter(
        "SELECT TOP 10 * FROM Customers",
        new SqlConnection(connStr));
    DataSet custData = new DataSet();
    adapter.Fill(custData, "Customers");
    XmlDataDocument dataDoc = new XmlDataDocument(custData);
    XmlNodeList custNames =
        dataDoc.SelectNodes("//Customers/CompanyName");
    string names = string.Empty;
    foreach (XmlNode node in custNames)
    {
        names += node.InnerText + "\n";
    }
    MessageBox.Show(names);
}
```

This code first retrieves the customer data into a data set, as shown earlier in the appendix. If you were really retrieving data solely for the purpose of manipulating it as XML, you would be better off using the XML query capability of SQL Server, returning the results as XML, and stuffing the results into an `XPathDocument`.

Once that data set is populated with the appropriate schema and the data, that is passed to the constructor of the `XmlDataDocument`. An XPath query is performed against the XML document using the `SelectNodes` method, and this method returns a list of XML nodes that then iterate through for constructing a simple display of the customer names.

An important feature to realize about an `XmlDataDocument` is that it can load and hold a lot of XML content that isn't exposed through the `DataSet` property, and that additional content can be accessed through the normal document object model of the base `XmlDocument` class. So you could load a document containing a set of data that matches a data set schema that you want to expose for data binding, and the document could also contain a bunch of other nodes that don't match the schema. The parts of the XML document that match the data set schema would be added to the data set, but the parts of the XML document that don't match would simply be contained within the `XmlDocument` base class' object model and could be accessed through normal XML navigation of the document. So if you need to jump back and forth between dealing with a set of data as relational and dealing with it as an XML object hierarchy, the `XmlData-Document` is one of the first places to look.

Working with the XPathDocument Class

As the name implies, an `XPathDocument` is an object model that is based on the hierarchical model exposed by the XPath specification. This is basically a new object model for storing XML content that was introduced in .NET 1.0 as a read-only store that is lighter weight and has higher performance than the `XmlDocument` DOM implementation. This class and its related classes all reside in the `System.Xml.XPath` namespace.

You generally don't work directly against the `XPathDocument` except for a few common operations. The first thing you will want to do is load data into the document. The data can come from a number of sources, including a file on disk, a network stream, a Web services call, or a database query. Once you have loaded the data into the document, the next step is to get an `XPathNavigator` for the document, which is the primary API for accessing the data within an XML document. You can also obtain `XPathNavigator` objects for `XmlDocuments` and `XmlDataDocuments` so that you can use a consistent programming model for XML across all three document types. Additionally, with `XmlDocument` and `XmlDataDocument` objects, you can edit the contained data directly through the `XPathNavigator`.

Other than those operations, most of what you will care about when working with an `XPathDocument` will involve programming against the `XPathNavigator` that you use to perform queries against the document and to navigate through sets of nodes.

Loading Data into an XPathDocument

There are two common ways of getting XML data into an `XPathDocument`. The first is from a file, which is a simple matter of passing the file path or URL to the constructor of the `XPathDocument` class:

```
XPathDocument doc = new XPathDocument("doc.xml");
```

The constructor can also take a stream, an `XmlReader`, or a `Text-Reader`. Whichever you use, the contents of the document will be loaded into memory and parsed into the underlying object model of the `XPath-Document`.

To get the data out of SQL Server, you can issue a FOR XML query, and load the `XPathDocument` with the `XmlReader` returned from a call to `ExecuteXmlReader` on the `SqlCommand` object.

```
private void OnLoadFromDB(object sender, System.EventArgs e)
{
    SqlConnection conn = new SqlConnection(
      "server=localhost;database=Northwind;trusted_connection=true");
    SqlCommand cmd = new SqlCommand(
      "SELECT * FROM Customers FOR XML AUTO, Elements", conn);
    try
    {
        conn.Open();
        XmlReader reader = cmd.ExecuteXmlReader();
        m_XPathDoc = new XPathDocument(reader);
```

```
    }
    finally
    {
        conn.Close();
    }
    DumpDocument();
}
```

Querying XML Data

Once you have data in memory in an XML document of some form (Xml-
Document, XmlDataDocument, or XPathDocument), you are likely to want
to query it to select some subset of the nodes contained in the document
based on some criteria you want to match against. For example, you may
want to select all Customers from the state of California, get all sales data
for the last six months, or look up the airspeed velocity of a laden swallow.
Whatever you need to look up, there are easy and powerful ways to perform queries against XML content in .NET.

To perform a query against XML data, you have to:

1. Load the data into a document object.

2. Select a set of nodes in that document by specifying the query
   (in XPath).

3. Iterate through the results.

Let's just focus on the one query method that all of the document types
support: XPathNavigator queries. The XPathNavigator class is the front
end to the underlying query engine for any of the XML document types in
.NET. In the last section you saw an example where the SelectNodes
method of the XmlDocument was called. That is a streamlined method for
node selection that really just uses an XPathNavigator under the covers.
The XPathNavigator uses a cursor-style navigation through a node set
that you can use to iterate through the document. It also exposes a number
of selection methods that let you execute queries against the contents of the
document or node it is pointing to. This section just focuses on querying;
the next goes into a little more about navigation.

To get an `XPathNavigator` for any of the XML document types, you call `CreateNavigator` against the document or one of its nodes. `Create-Navigator` passes back an instance of an `XPathNavigator` with the cursor positioned on the node from which it was created. Once you have the navigator, you call one of the query methods shown in Table D.5 to obtain an `XPathNodeIterator` containing the matching nodes.

The `XPathNodeIterator` class follows the pattern of other iterators in the .NET Framework. It starts out positioned just before the first item in the collection it contains. You repeatedly call the `MoveNext` method, usually in a `while` loop, and inspect the Boolean return value. If the value is `true`, then there was another node to move to and the iterator will be positioned on that node. If it returns `false`, there are no more nodes to iterate through.

TABLE D.5: XPathNavigator Query Methods

Method Name	Description
Select	Takes an XPath expression as a string or a compiled XPathExpression object and returns an XPath-NodeIterator containing the nodes that matched the query.
Evaluate	Takes a precompiled XPathExpression object and executes the query, returning an XPathNodeIterator containing the nodes that matched the query.
SelectChildren	Lets you select all child nodes of the current node with a particular node type or all child elements of a given name. This only selects matching nodes that are one level under the current node in the node hierarchy.
SelectDescendants	Lets you select all descendant nodes of the current node with a particular node type or all descendant elements of a given name. This selects all matching nodes, regardless of their level in the node hierarchy.
SelectAncestors	Lets you select all parent nodes of the current node with a particular node type or all parent elements of a given name. This selects all matching nodes, regardless of how far up the inheritance hierarchy they are.

The following code demonstrates the process of loading a document, performing a query, and iterating through the results.

```
private void NodeIteration()
{
    // Load the document
    XPathDocument doc = new XPathDocument("Customers.xml");

    // Get the navigator
    XPathNavigator nav = doc.CreateNavigator();

    // Perform the query
    XPathNodeIterator iter = nav.Select("//CompanyName");

    // Iterate through the results
    while (iter.MoveNext())
    {
        Console.WriteLine(iter.Current.Value);
    }
}
```

The `Current` property on the iterator returns a reference to an `XPath-Navigator` positioned on the current node, which you can then use to access the node contents or perform navigation or further queries based on that node. This example accesses the `Value` property of the current node, which in the case of an element or attribute is just the contained text content. There is also a `Name` property, which returns the name of the node.

The complexity of the results returned depends on the complexity of the query that you issue. For something simple like this query that just returns a set of elements that contain text nodes with the values you are after, the code is pretty straightforward. However, the results of an XPath query could return any type of node, so you will often need to have some conditional logic that checks the node type of each node, as it iterates through them, and modifies what it does based on the node type. The node type is exposed through the `NodeType` property on the `XPathNavigator`, and it returns an enumeration of type `XPathNodeType`.

Navigating an XML Document

Each of the different XML document types has a variety of specialized navigation methods that depend on the specific object model that they expose. However, all of the XML document types let you obtain an `XPathNavigator` for the document, which allows you to query and navigate those documents in a consistent way using the preferred object model for working with XML in .NET. In the previous section, you saw how to perform queries against a document, returning an iterator that you could use to step through each of the nodes that matched the query and perform processing on it. To work with the node, you obtained an `XPath-Navigator` reference to the node from the iterator's `Current` property.

Once you have an `XPathNavigator` to a particular node, you will often need to perform some navigation through the object model based on your current position within it. For example, if you have selected a set of Order elements, you may need to navigate through the attributes on that element to extract their values. Or perhaps you will perform a query to obtain an element representing a Customer, and then want to navigate all the child elements to extract their values without performing individual queries for each element.

The `XPathNavigator` exposes a set of `MoveToXXX` methods that let you navigate the object model it exposes, where the *XXX* portion of the method name indicates the node to which it moves the navigator's cursor (see Table D.6). Each of the `MoveToXXX` methods returns a Boolean indicating whether the move was successful, meaning there was a node in the intended location to move to. Note that attributes and namespaces are treated as special kinds of nodes because they can only be contained within the opening tag of an element node. To navigate attributes or namespaces, you use the separate set of `MoveToXXX` methods shown in Table D.7.

TABLE D.6: XPathNavigator Navigation Methods

Method Name	Description
MoveTo	Takes an `XPathNavigator` as a parameter and moves the current position of the navigator it is called on to the same node as the navigator that is passed as the parameter. You can achieve a similar result by calling the `Clone` method on an existing navigator to obtain a new navigator object positioned on the same node within the document.
MoveToNext	Moves to the next sibling node at the same level in the hierarchy. Does not apply to attributes or namespace nodes.

TABLE D.6: XPathNavigator Navigation Methods (Continued)

Method Name	Description
MoveToPrevious	Moves to the previous sibling node at the same level in the hierarchy. Does not apply to attributes or namespace nodes.
MoveToFirst	Moves to the first sibling node at the same level in the hierarchy. Does not apply to attributes or namespace nodes.
MoveToFirstChild	Moves to the first child node of the current node. Does not apply to attributes or namespace nodes.
MoveToParent	Moves to the parent node of the current node. Does not apply to attributes or namespace nodes.
MoveToRoot	Moves to the root of the document.

TABLE D.7: XPathNavigator Attribute and Namespace Navigation Methods

Method Name	Description
MoveToAttribute	Moves to the attribute with the specified name and namespace for the current element.
MoveToFirstAttribute	Moves to the first attribute for the current element.
MoveToNextAttribute	Moves to the next attribute for the current element. This method can be used to move to the first attribute as well, making it good for setting up a `while` loop to iterate through all the attributes.
MoveToNamespace	Moves to the namespace declaration with the specified name for the current element.
MoveToFirstNamespace	Moves to the first namespace declaration for the current element.
MoveToNextNamespace	Moves to the next namespace declaration for the current element. This method can be used to move to the first namespace as well, making it good for setting up a `while` loop to iterate through all the namespaces.

Where Are We?

In this appendix, I have given you a high-speed introduction to data access with ADO.NET, both for relational data and for XML data. You learned about the various capabilities of the `DataSet` class for containing relational data, which lets you retrieve data into the data set, make modifications to the data, and save that data back to a data source. The data set is the richest relational object for containing and manipulating data in the client, and it supports the widest range of data-binding scenarios. You saw how to get data into a custom object collection with which you could bind Windows Forms controls, and some of the different ways of interacting with both the client-side data and with the data sources from which you obtain data. The appendix stepped through some basics of dealing with data in XML form, and it showed how to load data into a document, work with that data as both hierarchical and relational data with an `XmlDataDocument`, and navigate and query the data using the `XPathNavigator` class.

Data access is a deep and important topic that is covered in much more detail by a number of other books. The intent of this appendix was simply to provide you enough information to be able to get data into your client applications for prototyping and to understand where the data was coming from for the chapters in this book dealing with manipulating and presenting that data in Windows Forms applications. By now your head is probably spinning if you haven't been exposed to data access in .NET before. If you have, then hopefully this provided a good refresher and reference for the basics while you are working with the rest of the book.

Index

Symbols

<%#...%> syntax, 508–509
? (question mark), 140
+ (plus sign), 202

A

Absolute positioning, controls, 589–590
AcceptChanges method
  client-side transactions, 650–651
  EndEdit method vs., 158
  setting row state in data tables, 641
accessDataSource control, 507
Add Column dialog, 264–265, 276–277
Add Connection dialog
  adding new data sources and connections, 7–8
  overview of, 182–183
  setting up typed data set connections, 45–46
Add method
  adding columns to TextBox cell, 223
  adding controls to Windows Forms, 552
  adding rows to grids, 224
  binding image columns to PictureBox, 142
  binding numeric columns to TextBox, 145–147
  IList interface, 300–301
  inserting items in BindingSource list, 124–126
  simple data binding, 91
Add Query Wizard, 75–77

add tag, connectionStrings, 58
Add Web Reference dialog, 185–186
AddBarChartControl method, 389–391
AddControlToGrid method, 531
AddCopies method
  adding rows in virtual mode, 234
  initializing grid, 238
  working with unbound columns, 231
AddCustomers method, 425
AddHandler keyword, 575
AddIndex method, IBindingList, 312
AddingNew event, 125–126, 131
AddNew method
  creating custom collection type, 427
  IBindingList, 312–313
  ICancelAddNew interface, 426
  using BindingSource as data storage container, 124–126
AddNewCore method, 427–428, 441
AddValueChanged method, 307
AddWithKey property, 622
ADO.NET, 601–670
  client-side transactions, 650–651
  creating data sets programmatically, 611–613
  data set and data adapter events, 651–654
  DataSet structure, 607–609
  handling concurrency, 628–631
  loading data into XPathDocument, 664–665
  loading data sets from database, 613–619
  loading data sets from files, 609–611

BOOKS ONLINE

ENABLED

THIS BOOK IS SAFARI ENABLED

INCLUDES FREE 45-DAY ACCESS TO THE ONLINE EDITION

The Safari® Enabled icon on the cover of your favorite technology book means the book is available through Safari Bookshelf. When you buy this book, you get free access to the online edition for 45 days.

Safari Bookshelf is an electronic reference library that lets you easily search thousands of technical books, find code samples, download chapters, and access technical information whenever and wherever you need it.

TO GAIN 45-DAY SAFARI ENABLED ACCESS TO THIS BOOK:

- Go to **http://www.awprofessional.com/safarienabled**

- Complete the brief registration form

- Enter the coupon code found in the front of this book on the "Copyright" page

If you have difficulty registering on Safari Bookshelf or accessing the online edition, please e-mail customer-service@safaribooksonline.com.